BRITAIN'S
FORGOTTEN WARS

To my family

BRITAIN'S FORGOTTEN WARS

COLONIAL CAMPAIGNS
OF THE *19th* CENTURY

IAN HERNON

This trilogy was first published as three separate editions by
Sutton Publishing Limited

Massacre and Retribution first published in 1998
The Savage Empire first published in 2000
Blood in the Sand first published in 2001

This edition first published in 2003 by
Sutton Publishing Limited

Reprinted in 2004 (twice), 2005, 2006, 2007

Reprinted in 2008 by
The History Press
The Mill, Brimscombe Port,
Stroud, Gloucestershire, GL5 2QG

Reprinted 2013

British Library Cataloguing in Publication Data
A catalogue record for this book is available from the British
Library.

ISBN 978 0 7509 3162 5

Typeset in 11/12.5pt Apollo.
Typesetting and origination by
Sutton Publishing Limited.
Printed and bound in England.

Contents

Part Two – The Savage Empire

Part Three – Blood in the Sand

Foreword

by

Sir Robert Rhodes James

There is a strange mythology that there was a golden age of peace between the ending of the Napoleonic wars in 1815 and the subsequent Congress of Vienna, where, as Duff Cooper eulogised, the participants danced and enjoyed themselves and 'created a hundred years of peace', and the opening of the Great War in 1914.

A century that included the Crimean War, the Indian Mutiny, the American Civil War, the Franco-Prussian War, the series of conflicts in Southern Africa, culminating in the 1899–1903 South African War, the Indian Wars in Northern America, the British conquest of Upper Burma, Egypt and the Sudan, almost incessant conflicts on the North-West Frontier of India, the gradual and bloody dismemberment of the Ottoman Empire and a succession of Balkan Wars, and the Russo-Japanese war, can hardly be described as notably pacific. Nor were Ceylon or New Zealand brought under the British Crown without bloodshed and hardship.

Ian Hernon's selection of some of the 'forgotten wars' of the nineteenth century adds further strength to the destruction of this mythology. What Kipling called 'the savage wars of peace' were often very savage indeed, including the brutal suppression of the Jamaica uprising by the British Governor Eyre, the Maori and Kandy wars, the extraordinary Magdala campaign in Ethiopia, the Riel rebellion in North-West Canada, the 1900 Ashanti campaign, and the terrible Modoc Indian War in the United States.

What is so sobering is that this list could have been much longer. As he states, 'there was not one month in which British forces were not engaged somewhere across the world', and not only British ones, either. It was a century of almost incessant conflict, culminating in the greatest one of all.

He describes these individually, with insight and shrewdness, and one of his most remarkable achievements is to bring them, and the people concerned, back to vivid life. I had certainly never heard of 'Shacknasty Jim', nor of many others who play varying roles, some honourable, many tragic, and others loathsome and deplorable. And he never loses sight of the fact that these were people; indeed, one of the great qualities of his accounts of these long-ago and too often bloody conflicts is the pervasive humanity with which he describes the sufferings of those involved, and of the guilty as well as the innocent.

There is in reality no such thing as 'a small war' for those involved. Whether the contestants are numbered in hundreds, thousands, or tens of thousands, the same grim rules apply. For some there may be glory, promotion, honours and fame; for the majority the end was an unknown grave far from home. Most died of disease rather than on the battlefield, but the result was the same.

These forgotten sagas have been sadly neglected by professional historians. I hope that Ian Hernon will continue to explore and relate others. There is, unhappily, no shortage of them.

Acknowledgements

The purpose of this book is not to ape, much less rival, the far more erudite and scholarly volumes already published about the military adventures which helped to create and sustain the British Empire. Rather it is to tell, I hope in the straightforward tone of a reporter, some of the astonishing stories largely forgotten outside academic, specialist and military circles.

Throughout I have used, whenever possible, the words of the participants themselves: semi-literate or beautifully scripted, bewildered or boastful, they are the authentic voices of their age.

The bulk of this book concerns British forces and their opponents. I could not resist, however, including one American colonial conflict. It shares many of the characteristics of the Empire wars, not least the unwillingness of the native defenders to act as expected. More importantly, it is a terrific if tragic story – and that has been the main criteria for choosing the sample of forgotten wars included here.

Many people have given me advice, practical help and encouragement, and I thank them all. In particular: the late Sir Robert Rhodes James, without whom the road to publication would have been much rockier; my agent Mike Shaw of Curtis Brown; Jonathan Falconer, commissioning editor at Sutton Publishing; and editor Sarah Fowle.

I must also thank my wife Pauline and my daughters Joann and Kim, not least for putting up with a lifetime partially spent trampling among 'piles of old bricks'.

Part One
Massacre and Retribution

Introduction

For Britain the nineteenth century began, in military terms, with the global upheavals of the Napoleonic Wars and ended with a 'modern' conflict in which machine-guns and a scorched-earth policy were deployed against the Boers. In between there was a supposed peace, marred only by glorious, if tragic, enterprises in the Crimea, Africa and Afghanistan, against the Zulus, the Boers, the Mahdi and Indian mutineers, providing the battles whose names remain proudly emblazoned on regimental banners: Balaclava, Sevastopol, Alma, Lucknow, Kabul, Khartoum, Omdurman. These are the campaigns, it seems, that forged an Empire unparalleled in size before or since, and built the careers of such military leaders as Garnet Wolseley and Lord Kitchener. They were the source of many *Boy's Own* stories and novels, as well as romantic cinema epics full of dramatic cavalry charges with sabres drawn against hordes of painted savages.

The long periods between such dashing conflicts have been dubbed the *Pax Britannica*, a time when the grip of the Empire was so strong and so benign that the simple presence of a few red tunics was enough to cow the natives. Yet this is misleading. In fact there was not one month in which British forces were not engaged somewhere across the world. Queen Victoria herself said that if Britain was to be truly 'Great' the nation had to be prepared for wars 'somewhere or other' at all times. They were what Rudyard Kipling called the 'savage wars of peace'. Some involved a handful of British officers and native levies, others were major expeditions, the Victorian equivalent of the Falklands campaign of 1982. Most are now forgotten outside regimental museums.

These small wars often came about by accident, or as a result of misunderstandings, incomprehension between races, an insult real or imagined. They were blatantly about race, trade, religion and, above all, land, the root causes of all wars since recorded history began. All were the inevitable result of Britain's 'Forward

Policy' which saw more and more of the world map coloured pink. Existing frontiers could be better protected by extending them. Trade routes and influence had to be safeguarded. British citizens had to be guaranteed safety and privilege wherever they were. And, as historian Byron Farwell wrote, 'Vigorous, self-confident, prideful, determined and opinionated people . . . will always provide themselves with armies and the temptation to use them to enforce national desires is seemingly irresistible.'

It is not the intention of this book to consider the rights and wrongs of colonial expansionism, but rather to celebrate the heroism, stamina and determination (and in some cases condemn the stupidity, cruelty and cowardice) of the participants in these forgotten wars. They came from all walks of life: gentlemen officers, foot soldiers from the Scottish Highlands, sappers from the Belfast docks, troopers from Northamptonshire estates, and brawny sergeant-majors born into the Army. Sent across the globe, they suffered dysentery, cholera, barbed arrows, gunshot, starvation, intense heat, freezing winds and the lash, all for a pittance during their service and, too often, the workhouse thereafter. They faced numerous adversaries: Maori warriors who swiftly overcame the terror of cannon and rocket attacks, the Riel rebels who fought for freedom and died on the gallows, the Ethiopian labourers who shifted mountains for their mad king.

The major wars of the era have remained in the collective folk memory. Most people know of Rorke's Drift, but not of another incident when five members of the same regiment won Victoria Crosses on the same day. The fate of General Gordon at Khartoum is remembered, but not another massive expedition to rescue European hostages from a remote African mountain-top. The Indian Mutiny is still taught in schools but not the massacre of a British column in the Highlands of Ceylon. Such amazing stories have been largely erased from the national conscience, partly because they often involved inglorious defeats, partly because their adversaries did not fit the domestic stereotype of howling, unsophisticated 'fuzzy-wuzzy' savages, slaughtered or cowed by British discipline and moral superiority. They were wars in which modern armies aimed to subdue the supposedly ignorant, wars in which well-disciplined and well-armed white men were meant to crush poorly equipped and ill-led heathens. It did not always go to plan.

* * *

The British Army saw superficial changes during that stormy century, such as the final transition from scarlet to khaki, but its regimental system remained essentially the same. It was based on class and caste distinctions. The staff officers were drawn from the aristocracy and squirearchy, the ruling classes and professions, from public schools and family estates. Farwell wrote: 'An army – that least democratic of social institutions – is dominated by its officers: it is they who establish its moral and social codes, the standard of discipline, and the degree of inhumanity to be tolerated; they determine its organisation, its tactics and strategies, its weapons and clothes, and, most importantly, its attitudes and opinions. As has often been proved, armies can be constructed from the most unpromising of human materials and be successful on the field of battle if they are provided with excellent officers, from subalterns to generals, who have time to mould their men.'

For much of the century commissions were bought and officers were too often drawn from a small pool of families whose sons might have been born on a different planet to the men who served under them. Such class distinctions were actively encouraged by the very idea of the 'officer-gentleman', the hostility of the generals towards any reform, the traditions of Wellington, the self-interest of the officers themselves, and the bureaucracy by which Army affairs were divided between the War Office, the Colonial Office, the Home Office, the Treasury, the Horse Guards and Royal Ordnance.

Even the abolition of purchased commissions did little to change the balance. Poor pay, which did not even cover the cost of lavish uniforms, never mind mess bills, meant that a private income was vital for any officer. Most came from public schools which did not teach military subjects, although half were subsequently trained at Sandhurst or Woolwich. The ordinary soldier came from a despised underclass – thieves, beggars, vagrants, drunkards, convicts, the destitute unemployed and starving – whom Lord Palmerston's biographer Jasper Ridley said joined the army 'to escape from the village constable or the irate father of a pregnant girl'.

The Army could never get enough men under the system of voluntary enlistment. Among the labouring classes the Army, with its poor pay, unsavoury conditions, long service requirements and traditions of suppressing domestic revolt, was simply not considered an honourable or worthwhile alternative to poverty at home. During the 1840s the natural wastage among infantrymen who served twenty-one years and cavalrymen who served twenty-four required 12,000 new recruits a year.

As a result recruitment depended on conning recruits with drink and fraudulent promises of pay, booty and women, at least until the late 1860s when attitudes changed and the Empire became inextricably linked with patriotism. The military authorities, who held their men in contempt, urged their recruiters to pursue 'the foolish, the drunken, the ungodly and the despairing'. The only requirements were a very basic physical fitness and a constantly fluctuating minimum height.

Such men were famously described by Wellington: 'The scum of the earth – the mere scum of the earth. It is only wonderful that we should be able to make so much of them afterwards. The English soldiers are fellows who have all enlisted for drink – that is the plain fact.' He continued: 'People talk of their enlisting from their fine military feeling – all stuff – no such thing. Some of our men enlist from having got bastard children – some for minor offences . . . you can hardly conceive such a set brought together.' Yet he could also say of them with justifiable pride: 'There are no men in Europe who can fight like my infantry . . . my army and I know one another exactly.' On an earlier occasion he said: 'Bravery is the characteristic of the British Army in all quarters of the world.' And those who have served in India 'cannot be ordered upon any Service, however dangerous or arduous, that they will not effect, not only with bravery, but with a degree of skill not often witnessed in persons of their description in other parts of the world.'

Such men, drawn from stinking gutters and gin houses, from gaols and poorhouses, from pit villages and dockyards, from behind ploughs and lowly desks, forged an Empire through their grit endurance and courage. Why? An escape from poverty or prison at home was one factor, certainly. So, too, was the lure of booty and a chance to exercise naked aggression. But the overriding reason lay with the nature of the regimental system itself. The Regiment was home, family, provider, past and future all wrapped in one. To let down your comrades, and through them your regiment, was unthinkable – more serious even than letting down Queen and Country. It was a narrow form of patriotism, and one that in its fully developed form saw men march slowly towards the guns across the bloody fields of Flanders and the Somme. The love of regiment united officers and men. Sons followed fathers into the same regiment, whatever their rank. Identity with regiment was strengthened by its original regional roots. Highland regiments are said to take Scotland with them wherever they go. They did not get on with the Welsh regiments. Regimental pride was strengthened with the roll of battle honours, and the nicknames they accrued. The Middlesex Regiment became known as the 'Diehards' because of the valour they displayed at Albuera in 1811; the men of the Northamptonshire Regiment, however, were known as the 'Steelbacks' as they never flinched at a flogging.

Throughout the century the pattern of recruitment shifted away from rural areas and towards the new, rootless and increasingly destitute unemployed in the mushrooming cities. In 1830 more than 42 per cent of NCOs and men were Irish, most of them Roman Catholics; a decade later that figure was 24.5 per cent. Even the famous Scottish regiments relied more and more on attracting men from the slums of Manchester, London, Leeds and Cardiff.

Soldiers and NCOs hardly ever moved from their company, much less their regiment, during their entire service careers. In *The Mask of Command* John Keegan wrote: 'The effect was to produce a high degree of what today is called "Small unit cohesion". The men knew each other well, their strengths and weaknesses were known by their leaders and vice versa, and all strove to avoid the taint of cowardice that would attach instantly to shirkers in such intimate societies. Motivation was reinforced by drill. Both infantry and cavalry fought in close order . . . under strict supervision and to the rhythm of endlessly rehearsed commands.' James Morris wrote:

'The Army lived ritualistically. Flags, guns and traditions were holy to it, and loyalty to one's regiment was the emotional keynote of the service.'

Such men would wade through malarial swamps, hack through jungles, clamber over mountain crags, to get at the enemy for the sake of their regiment. They would also beef and grumble and dodge duties, and drink and steal and pick fist-fights; they would abuse natives and women, they would loot and occasionally slaughter the defenceless. But the savage little wars of the nineteenth century bear witness to their courage. Without them no Empire would have been won, whatever the genius of generals and strategists, whatever the ambitions of monarchs and politicians.

'But for this a price must be paid,' wrote Sir Arthur Conan Doyle, 'and the price is a grievous one. As the beast of old must have one young human life as a tribute every year, so to our Empire we throw from day to day the pick and flower of our youth. The engine is worldwide and strong, but the only fuel that will drive it is the lives of British men. Thus it is that in the gray old cathedrals, as we look upon the brasses on the walls, we see strange names, such names as those who reared those walls had never heard, for it is in Peshawar, and Umballah, and Korti, and Fort Pearson that the youngsters die, leaving only a precedent and a brass behind them. But if every man had his obelisk, even where he lay, then no frontier line need be drawn, for a cordon of British graves would ever show how high the Anglo-Saxon tide had lapped.'

General Sir Garnet Wolseley, in his general orders for the 1873 Ashanti expedition wrote: 'English soldiers and sailors are accustomed to fight against immense odds in all parts of the world; it is scarcely necessary to remind them that when in our battles across the Pra (River) they find themselves surrounded on all sides by hordes of howling enemies, they must rely on their own British courage and discipline, and upon the courage of their comrades.'

The men themselves were rather more laconic, in an era which prided modesty, when describing their own acts. Sergeant Luke O'Connor of the Welch Fusiliers described a charge at the Russian guns at Alma: 'Getting near the Redoubt, about 30 yards, Lieutenant Anstruther was shot dead and I was badly wounded in the breast with two ribs broken. I jumped up and took the Colour from Corporal Luby, rushed to the Redoubt and planted it there.' O'Connor was awarded one of the first Victoria Crosses. Another old soldier, G. Bell, recorded the storming of the French defences at Badajoz: 'Hundreds fell, dropping at every discharge which maddened the living; the cheer was ever on, on, with screams of vengeance and a fury determined to win the town; the rear pushed the foremost into the sword-blades to make a bridge of their bodies rather than be frustrated. Slaughter, tumult and disorder continued; no command could be heard, the wounded struggling to free themselves from under the bleeding bodies of their dead comrades; the enemy's guns within a few yards at every fire opening a bloody lane amongst our people, who closed up and, with shouts of terror as the lava burned them up, pressed on to destruction. . . .'

By 1814 the British Army had been trained and tested against the might of Napoleon. Its men were hardened, disciplined and experienced in warfare anywhere from hot arid plains to steaming jungles. They were its muscle, sinews and blood. Its NCOs, risen from the ranks, were, in Kipling's words, its backbone. The officers had been blooded too and were beginning to display the talents of a professional elite; men who, as Wellington put it, 'have something more at stake than a reputation for military smartness'. At last, after years of bought commissions and talentless amateurism, they were beginning to provide some brains.

General Sir John Moore's reforms of the Light Brigade had an impact throughout the Army. There was less emphasis on ceremony and drill and more on training which reflected actual battle and campaign conditions. Riflemen were taught to support each other as they moved into the best positions to slay the enemy. As Arthur Bryant wrote: 'At the back of every rifleman's mind Moore instilled the principle that the enemy were always at hand ready to strike. Whether on reconnaissance or protective duty, he was taught to be wary and on guard . . . It was the pride of the light infantryman never to be caught napping . . . each one an alert and intelligent individual acting in close but invisible concert with his comrades.'

The ordinary soldier's firepower, however, was inadequate in an age of quickly changing technology. Too often British forces, as in the Maori Wars, found themselves facing 'savages' armed with more modern weapons than they carried themselves. From Waterloo until the 1850s the standard infantry weapon was the flintlock musket which weighed 10.5 lb and was accurate to 80 yards. It was cumbersome and slow to load. Lieutenant John Mitchell wrote: 'In nine cases out of ten the difficulty of pulling the trigger makes the soldier open the whole of the right hand in order to aid the action of the forefinger; this gives full scope to the recoil: the prospect of the blow makes him throw back his head and body at the very moment of giving fire; and as no aim is ever required he shuts his eyes, from the flash of the pan, at the same instant, so that the very direction of the shot becomes a matter of mere accident.' Small wonder that Charles Napier wrote: 'The short range and very uncertain flight of shot from the musket begets the necessity of closing with the enemy, which the British soldier's confidence in superior bodily strength, due to climate, pushes him to do.' He added: 'No troops in the world will stand the assault of British troops, if made with the bayonet and without firing. Firing is a weapon . . . of defence, not of attack.' The British soldier's affection for the bayonet as a trustworthy weapon outlived the century. Its reputation in retrospect seems misplaced: various types either bent or fell off, and they were all unwieldy. The bayonet was no match against pikes or the long Chinese spears at Canton. At Merthyr in 1888 the 93rd Highlanders with bayonets fixed confronted Welsh dissidents with staves – and were defeated. And bayonets had bent at the battle of Abu Klea in 1885, causing a public outcry over the quality of British weaponry.

Gradually firepower improved. In 1830 muskets were converted to percussion cap ignition, which reduced misfirings. From 1851 the foot soldiers were rearmed with the Minie rifle, although initially in an unrifled model so that massive stockpiles of musket balls would not go to waste. The Minie was sighted to 1,000 yards and was accurate to 800. At that range 77 out of 100 hits were registered on a target 8 ft square. At ranges between 300 and 600 yards the experts calculated that 150 men armed with Minies could equal the slaughter achieved by 525 equipped with the musket. It was a muzzle-loader, so still slow, but its effective range of more than ¼ mile dramatically changed the nature of ground engagements.

Colonel F.T. Maitland described the universal adoption of the rifle as 'a complete revolution in the art of warfare'. William Napier said it 'must paralyse the action of cavalry against infantry and artillery within that range'. In 1866 there was a long-overdue breakthrough. The Snider breech-loading rifle began to be issued. Although still a single-shot weapon, it allowed soldiers, for the first time, to fire lying down, from behind defensive positions. The Snider was replaced by the metal-cartridged Martini-Henry during the 1870s. By the 1890s the Army was using the bolt-action, magazine-fed Lee Metford .303 rifle which would remain the basic infantry weapon up to and beyond the Second World War. In 1891 smokeless powder was introduced, a vital improvement because soldiers firing from cover were not given away by a puff of white smoke.

The vast improvements in firepower slowly changed the nature of mounted warfare. It was the beginning of the end of the proud cavalry regiments. Tactician Captain L.E. Nolan concluded ruefully: 'The great improvements made in firearms, and the increased range of the infantry musket, leave but little chance for cavalry, unless the speed at which they can pounce upon the infantry lessens the number and the effect of the discharge to be received during their advance.' Earlier he had written: 'With the cavalry officer almost everything depends on . . . the felicity with which he seizes the happy moment of action. There is little time for thought, none for hesitation. . . .' Increasingly, however, the cavalrymen, armed with lance, sword and pistol, and, later, carbines, were used for reconnaissance, skirmishing and attacking convoys, and as advance guards. George Cathcart, commander of the King's Dragoon Guards in Canada in 1838, stressed in orders that cavalry should take up advance positions with 'great promptness', then dismount and hold their ground until they could be relieved by the slower-moving infantry. The charge could still be deployed (although it rarely was) in open country against natives; for this reason the long sword was developed for use against tribesmen who fired their weapons from prone positions. Mounted infantry proved to be well suited for the colonies, especially for police duties. A small number of mounted men could garrison and patrol much larger tracts of remote countryside than a greater number of foot soldiers.

The development of field artillery was steady throughout the century but for the colonies the mainstay was the six-pounder. It was light and manageable, with a range of 1,200 yards at 4 degrees elevation. The main types of ammunition used were round shot (which bounced off the ground causing carnage among a column of men), grapeshot, common shell and shrapnel. Common shell included a time fuse which exploded a hollow round, despatching fragments in all directions. Shrapnel incorporated round shot but technical problems delayed its introduction. Once these problems were ironed out it proved devastating against a massed foe. After shrapnel was deployed to halt a river-crossing during the Second Sikh War a witness wrote: 'Never was it more clearly demonstrated that shrapnel, when directed with precision, is one of the most formidable and effectual inventions of modern times.' Rockets were often used during the first half of the century but were deemed inaccurate, unreliable and useful only for frightening the horses.

Fighting, the ultimate task of any trained soldier, was generally only the culmination of any campaign. A teenage Lieutenant Samuel Thorpe wrote of the 1808 retreat to Corunna: 'When we reached Astorga . . . want of shoes and food and long marches had much altered the appearance of the Army; the number of sick and stragglers was immense, and the men generally bare-footed. The Welch Fusiliers' Official History, recording a South African campaign as the century closed, said: 'Averaging nearly 17 miles a day, over apparently endless prairies, in blazing sun and bitter cold swept now by hot and choking dust storms, now by rushes of icy hail, fording rivers and floundering through sand, with scanty food and shelterless bivouacs, their toil unenlightened by anything but hope. Marching is the true rigour of campaigning. Of fighting, the welcome relief, they had too little to lighten the dullness of their task.' Astonishingly it was not until 1843 that soldiers were issued with left and right fitting boots. Previously, identical footwear had been issued with instructions that they should be swapped over on alternate days to ensure even wear.

Unsuitable uniforms and heavy equipment added to the soldiers misery on the march, especially on other continents. By the start of the century powdered wigs had been phased out and heavy greycoats issued for winter wear. But most foot soldiers wore scarlet tunics, heavy felt shakos and the hated 'stock', a stiff leather support for a high collar. After Waterloo uniforms became more ornate. The infantry of the Line saw their sensible grey trousers replaced with white ones which were impossible to keep clean. Garnet Wolseley, writing of the 1853 Burmese expedition, said that the Queen's Army took an 'idiotic pride' in dressing for Asia as though it were an English parade ground. He wrote: 'We wore our ordinary cloth shell jackets buttoned up to the chin, and the usual white buckskin gloves. Could any costume short of steel armour be more absurd in such a latitude?' It was not until the 1870s, thanks to enlightened commanders like Wolseley, that scarlet could be put aside in hostile climates and replaced with grey serge jackets and Indian sun helmets.

Marching was, of course, rather different in peacetime, especially for the officers. General Sir Charles Dobell described a march across Northern India in 1887: 'Full Officer's Mess furniture accompanied us as we entertained in the usual way at all stations on the line of march. Transport consisted of camels or bullock carts . . . We were followed by 60 polo ponies, the property of the officers. We played wherever there was a ground and did a little mild pig-sticking as well. At each station cricket and football matches were arranged against the local regiments and there was frequently some shooting to be enjoyed.'

Food was a constant cause for complaint among the men. The standard daily ration was 1 lb bread eaten at breakfast with coffee, and 12 oz meat for dinner. The meat was boiled beef or mutton thickened into a broth in large copper vessels. Cash was deducted – 6d a day until 1854 – from the soldier's basic pay of one shilling a day for such rations. Extra vegetables were bought and paid for by the men themselves.

Incompetence and, it was often suspected, corruption caused appalling hardship and contributed to the epidemics that often devastated armies and expeditionary forces. In home barracks soldiers could expect to be hospitalized once every thirteen months but in overseas stations the numbers of cases swelled immeasurably. Between 1825 and 1836 the mortality rate among soldiers on the

Gold Coast was 668 per 1,000. Soldiers in Jamaica, Ceylon, South Africa and North America were sick enough to be hospitalized several times a year. Between 1839 and 1853 the British Army suffered 58,139 deaths at home and abroad, the vast majority of them through sickness. The mortality rate among officers was half that of NCOs and men.

Major Daniel Lysons wrote of his camp in the Crimea: 'The food is very bad and insufficient. A lump of bad beef without any fat, boiled in water, and a bit of sour bread are not sufficient to keep men in good condition. We can get no vegetables whatsoever, and the people in the village here will not sell us anything.' Cholera broke out and his unit lost thirty-seven dead in three months. Later, after the battles of Balaclava and Inkerman, Lysons wrote home: '12 December 1854. Unfortunately our commissariat transport has broken down and we only get short rations; sometimes a quarter of a pound of salt pork and half a pound of biscuit a day, very short commons for men at hard work . . .

14 December. We had 73 deaths last month. This month we have had an average of two a day, till the day before yesterday when there were five, yesterday eight . . .

24 January 1855. I have only 206 men now left fit for duty; there were seven deaths yesterday.'

The Welch Fusiliers lost 754 men during the Crimean War, 530 of whom died of disease. Such an attrition rate, not caused by enemy fire, caused a scandal at home and conditions gradually changed with improved regulations covering hygiene, medical care and resources. Wolseley was able to sanction seventy doctors for 2,400 men on the Ashanti expedition.

Earlier in his career, when stationed in the West Indies, Lysons found some light relief during a cholera epidemic: 'One poor fellow, who was given over by the doctors and supposed to be dead, was measured for his coffin, and the coffin was made. In those hot climates there is no time to be lost. The man, however, disappointed the doctors and recovered. Then came the question, who was to pay for the coffin? It was charged to the man, but he refused to sign his accounts with this charge against him, saying that he had not ordered the coffin and did not want it.' A compromise was reached

— the soldier paid for the casket, provided he could keep it in his barracks where, fitted with shelves, it held all his gear.

Drink could be a comfort or a curse. The young Lieutenant Thorpe described the destruction of supplies to prevent them falling into the hands of the enemy: 'As we marched through the town, the rum was running down the canals of the streets, and with much difficulty we prevented the men from remaining behind and getting intoxicated; those who had shoes slipped them off their feet, and filling them with rum and mud drank it off at a gulp before the officers could prevent them; others filled their caps for the same purpose.' After the same campaign a private of the 71st Foot wrote: 'The great fault of our soldiers at the time was an inordinate desire for spirits of any kind. They sacrificed their life and safety for drink, in many ways; for they lay down intoxicated upon the snow and slept the sleep of death; or, staggering behind, were overtaken and cut down by the merciless French soldiers.'

At the height of the Raj in Karachi Corporal Andrew Morton recalled: 'The canteen was open all day . . . and you could buy over three pints of spirits for one rupee or two shillings, and this arrack or rum was over-proof . . . There was men dying every day from the effects of drink which did more for death than fever . . . At the time the battle money was served out there were about thirty men in hospital from drink . . . Drink was the rage in India.' Corporal Alexander Morton described regular drunken fights in the bazaars: 'The native police, under the superintendence of a European Inspector, would make haste to the scene of the disturbance and endeavour to put a stop to it. If a row was continued the native police carried nets which they threw over the drunkards' heads, knocked them off their feet and rolled them up.'

During the Opium War British and Indian soldiers plundered the island of Chusan after looting vast stocks of the Chinese spirit Samsu. An officer reported: 'Its effect on them was of the most dreadful nature and very different from that of the spirits we are used to in England. A man no sooner took a small quantity than he was in a most dreadful state and committing the most horrible atrocities.'

Desertion was always a problem, averaging 4 per cent among troops serving in Australia and New Zealand during the 1850s. Such frontier lands offered safe havens in which a man could disappear and earn his fortune in goldfields or land grabs.

Discipline was harsh throughout the century. The penalty for desertion, cowardice, armed robbery, mutiny and murder was death throughout the nineteenth century and into the twentieth, and every expedition had its executioners. During the fourteen months up to February 1813 it is estimated that forty-one men were executed in an army of 100,000. However, it was the cat-o'-nine-tails which kept the rankers submissive. In 1814 more than 18,000 men were flogged. During a Commons debate that year Lord Palmerston, then Secretary for War, argued successfully that only the lash could instill fear in men who were used to settling their own arguments with fists, feet and cudgels. Wellington asked: 'Who would bear to be billed up [confined to barracks] but for the fear of a stronger punishment?'

Up to 1829 courts martial had powers to impose unlimited flogging, which often amounted to a death sentence. In that year the maximum was set at 500 lashes; in 1833 this was reduced to 300, in 1836 to 200 and in 1846 to 50. The issue was hugely political, linked as it was to the abolition of slavery and the introduction of proper policing and penal reform. During the mid-1840s military prisons were built as an alternative to execution or the lash, although military authorities were keen to retain flogging as a punishment for insubordination and the theft of Army property. Flogging in peacetime was abolished in 1869, but continued on active service until 1881 – a century after it had been scrapped in France, Austria and Prussia. Its final abolition marked an acceptance that soldiering was now an honourable profession.

More emphasis was placed on rewarding good soldiers through good conduct pay, badges and medals, and recreation. Proper canteens and messes were introduced for all ranks. Reading classes and regimental schools were established despite the splenetic rage of the Old Guard who preferred to keep their troops ignorant in all things but personal sacrifice. Sporting facilities were improved to ease the deadly boredom of barracks life. Fines and loss of good service pay were imposed for drunkenness in lieu of the lash.

Barracks, both at home and abroad, were generally miserable places. Overcrowding and poor or non-existent sanitation were universal, whether a soldier was stationed in Dublin Castle or in a stilted cabin in the Hondorus swamps. Army regulations said that each man was entitled to 300 cubic feet of air; in British gaols the minimum was 600. In the West Indies the sleeping space allocation was 23 inches width per man. Ablutions were conducted at standpipes in the yards while inside the piss-tub overflowed at night. Many barracks were built over or adjoining sewage ditches. The barrack rooms, draughty or poorly ventilated, were used for sleeping, eating and killing time.

Living in the same barracks were the wives and children of those men permitted to marry, their numbers swelled by unofficial wives and smuggled-in girlfriends, some of whom earned a few pence by cleaning laundry, cooking and cutting hair. Privacy was, at best, a blanket slung over a rope and behind such makeshift curtains women lived, loved, washed and even gave birth.

In many regiments, however, only 12 of 100 men were allowed official wives and marriage was frowned upon among the rank and file. The rest took their pleasures when and where they could. There were camp followers behind most regiments, and native girls along the way, although the incidence of reported rape appears low compared with that of other armies. In a letter home Trooper Charles Quevillart described a Karachi brothel: 'The sight of the older women was simply disgusting for they were one and all deplorably ugly and little was left for the imagination as a yard of calico would have furnished a dozen of them with a full dress. Some had breasts hanging as low as their waists and I noticed one party with appendages so long that she was enabled to suckle her child by throwing them over her shoulders.' But then, he might have been reassuring his mother. Other soldiers, less restrained, wrote glowingly of the dancing maidens of India and Arabia, the delicate Chinese women of Malaya, Nigerian princesses, the mixed-blood women of the West Indies. E. Sellon wrote that native women 'understand in perfection all the arts and wiles of love, are capable of gratifying any tastes, and in face and figure they are unsurpassed by any women in the world'. In hotter climes there were fewer sexual taboos than at home, and British soldiers could use their money, their power and position, and their novelty to rampage sexually across the world.

Prostitution grew immeasurably wherever the flag was planted, and venereal disease mushroomed. In India so many men were laid low that British authorities sanctioned regulated prostitution. From 1860 to the late 1880s seventy-five cantonments were designated brothel areas with regular medical inspection, registration and hospital treatment centres. Such methods worked and the rate of syphilis in the army in India was lower than in the barracks back home. But in 1888 the 'moral purity' lobby forced the Army to suspend the arrangements. The result was a dramatic upsurge in cases, peaking at more than 25 per cent of Indian Army rankers in 1895.

Among officers sex scandals, particularly those involving the wives of fellow officers, ruined promising careers. An indecent act in a railway carriage halted the upward rise of Army modernizer Valentine Baker. Allegations of homosexual activity often resulted in suicide, as in the case of 'Fighting Mac' MacDonald (see Appendix).

When Victoria took the throne in 1837 the British Army was around 100,000 strong and consisted mainly of infantry. By 1859 the total stood at 237,000, of whom well over half were overseas garrisoning the Empire. Of the 130 infantry battalions, around 50 were in India, 37 in the Colonies and 44 at home. Most soldiers came from rural communities and there was a high proportion of Scots, Irish and Welsh.

As the century grew older so too did the generals. Arrogance, out-dated methods, senile incompetence, laziness and corruption trickled down from the top. Politicians demanded glorious adventures to distract the unruly mob at home while cutting back on military spending. The result was unnecessary, bloody fiascos such as the First Afghan War and the Crimea, as well as the innumerable smaller wars that are the subject of this book.

During the middle part of the century the incompetence of commanders was endemic. Major-General Elphinstone, commander of the ill-fated Afghan expedition, was elderly, inexperienced and disinterested. One writer summed up a widely held view: 'I state unhesitatingly that for pure, vacillating stupidity, for superb incompetence to command, for ignorance combined with bad judgement – in short, for the true talent for catastrophe – Elph

Bey stood alone . . . Elphy outshines them all as the greatest military idiot of our own or any other day.' More famously William Howard Russell described the Crimean commander thus: 'I am convinced from what I see that Lord Raglan is utterly incompetent to lead an army through any arduous task.' But Elphinstone and Raglan were not alone, as we shall see.

In 1868 Edward Cardwell was appointed Secretary for War and began his long-awaited reforms. He introduced short-time enlistment which resulted in a younger and fitter Army. He built up the Reserves. Most importantly, he scrapped the long-established practice, endorsed by Wellington, allowing the privileged classes to purchase commissions and promotion regardless of ability.

To many British politicians the small wars of the frontier were despised as 'nigger-bashing'. Armchair strategists believed that the 'lower races' could not stand up to colonial superiority, in terms of morality, Christianity and firepower. The abolition of slavery had not been universally acclaimed and troublesome natives and released slaves had engendered racist attitudes which had transcended the patronizing traditional image of 'Sambo' on the world's stage. The ordinary British soldier, however, had ambivalent attitudes to native enemies. Racism and bigotry were prized attributes at home in those Empire-building days and the new recruits shared them. But seasoned campaigners, used to fighting alongside sepoys, native regiments and local levies, took a broader view. The 200,000-strong Indian Army, although British-officered, was made up of Sikhs, Mahrattas, Dogras, Rajputs, Muslims and Gurkhas, all of them volunteers. In many other parts of the Empire local levies were raised because they knew the territory, were more resistant to the climate and, most importantly, were cheaper and could be dismissed without pensions when no longer needed. Such forces, always officered by whites, were widely deployed in the Caribbean, Guiana, West and South Africa, Ceylon, Malaya, Java, Goa, Mauritius and Mozambique. Malay soldiers were reckoned to be efficient, cheerful and healthy. 'Hottentots' were valued for their tracking skills in the bush.

Furthermore, the British soldier respected a courageous and determined foe, whether he was African, American or Oriental. (In broad terms, that is; there were exceptions, of course, when vengeance or fear were involved: witness the incredible savagery of the British following the Indian Mutiny and the Jamaica 'revolt'.) Rudyard Kipling, who better than anyone understood the attitudes of the common soldier, wrote: 'So 'ere's to you, Fuzzy-Wuzzy, at your 'ome in the Soudan; You're a pore benighted 'eathen, but a first-class fighting man . . .'.

And the memoirs of British officers and men repeatedly record the acts of incredible bravery among their adversaries. The 18th (Royal Irish) Regiment, after an assault on a Chinese temple, found they had captured a butcher's-shop. Those Tartar defenders not killed in battle had slain themselves rather than be taken prisoner. William Napier described the charge of Sind troops at the battle of Miani in 1843: 'Guarding their heads with large dark shields they shook their sharp swords, gleaming in the sun, and their shouts rolled like peals of thunder as with frantic might and gestures they dashed against the front of the 22nd.' At Omdurman 50,000 natives 'streamed across the open to certain death'. At Ulundi, according to another participant, the Zulus 'fell in heaps' as they ran in waves through volley fire. In battle the Zulus sometimes threw their own dead before them to blunt the redcoats' bayonets. On the Aroji plateau Abyssinian warriors in scarlet shirts merely ducked when fired upon by rockets and then ran headlong into massed rifle and cannon fire.

A civilian witness at the battle of Tamai in 1884 saw Muslims attack General Buller's disciplined ranks: 'Not one man could get near enough to use his spear. It was an awful sight, and as an exhibition of pluck, or rather fanaticism, it could not be equalled. Poor deluded Arabs! thinking that they could do anything with their spears and swords out in the open against disciplined British troops armed with rifles.'

Courage was not just displayed in the heat of battle but also in its agonizing aftermath. Lieutenant Robarts of the Victoria Mounted Rifles described the Zulu wounded after Nyezane: 'They were very quiet, and seemed to bear pain well, no groaning or crying out. We could not do anything for them except give them water to drink . . .'. Captain William Molyneux described a visit to a Zulu kraal after the 1879 War where he met an old man 'who had lost half his right arm . . . the bone had been smashed by a bullet below the elbow; but he had cut the loose part off, and the wound had healed now. The many little mounds covered with stones, told how many of the poor fellows had crawled home simply to die.'

All ranks respected the concept – myth or real – of warrior peoples and their effectiveness at unconventional warfare. One regimental history written during the 1840s said of the Pathan: 'For centuries he has been on our frontier . . . subject to no man. He leads a wild, free, active life in the rugged fastness of his mountains; and there is an air of masculine independence about him which is refreshing in a country like India.' Sir Percival Marling recalled that 'the black Soudanese fought like blazes' at Tel-al-Kebiv. The Dervishes at El Teb, according to a sergeant of the 18th Hussars, were without doubt 'the most fierce, brave, daring, and unmerciful race of men in the world'.

In the 1890s Colonel C.E. Callwell praised the Pirah tribesmen for their grasp of partisan warfare – the ability to move quickly over hard ground, appear where they were least expected and disappear when faced with superior forces. He said: 'Such methods are bewildering to the commanders of disciplined troops opposed to them.'

It can be recognized now, and many soldiers knew it at the time, that such opponents were fighting for their freedom, their country, their faith: causes which they believed were worth dying for even when they themselves were ruled by bloodthirsty despots. It is for such men and women, whose stories are not recorded in regimental histories, that this book was principally written.

ONE

The First Kandy War, 1803–5

'The troops in Kandy are all dished, Your Honour'

'The Kandians had no sooner entered than they began to butcher indiscriminately everyone in the hospital, robbing them at the same time, cursing and reviling them, and spitting in their faces.' This description by one of the few survivors of the Kandy massacre reeks of horror. Yet Western travellers described the peoples of Ceylon as gentle and civilized. There is no contradiction. They were, and are, a peaceful people grown skilled in warfare. Scots wanderer Henry Marshall said they were 'hardy, brave and, like most mountaineers, passionately attached to their native hills'.

The British military disaster in the wild fastness of central Ceylon was a foretaste of many wars which dragged through the century. A modern Westernized force marched to the tunes of glory against a native population which was, to Western eyes, unsophisticated, ill-armed, medieval, craven, even corrupt. The invaders suffered hideously from that misjudgement. The campaign was ill-conceived and badly planned. Poorly equipped troops and raw recruits battled against the alien terrain and a people who well knew how to use it. The Kandyans used the landscape as a weapon of war. A people who would have been treated as exotic curiosities in the salons of London and Paris defended themselves against an army whose technology was more geared towards the battle plains of Napoleonic Europe than Ceylon's tropical rainforests, malarial swamps and saw-toothed mountains. It was a war like many others, marked by courage and cowardice, treachery and confusion, suffering and comradeship, brutality and nobility.

It was a small war but a costly one. For sheer savagery it has rarely been out-done.

* * *

Three thousand years ago King Solomon is said to have purchased elephants from Sri Lanka to woo the Queen of Sheba. Sri Lanka, 'the Blessed One', was the paradise designated by Buddha as the place where his religion would flourish. The Westernized history of the island was written in blood and fire. In 1505 the Portuguese discovered a treasure house of gold and spice on the prime trade routes: they found gems, king coconuts, a high grade cinnamon unique to the island, chillis, leopards, the white egret and beautiful women; they found excellent harbours, paddyfields, lofty mountains and a lushness that inspired awe even in eyes adjusted to the colours of the Orient. Inevitably it became a magnet for freebooters, explorers, soldiers, rogues and swindlers. The Sinhalese had suffered centuries of invasions from the Indian subcontinent but had created a civilization that the Romans had considered 'just and gentle'. Over 150 years the Portuguese created from the richness a ruin, a prize to be plundered and despoiled and fought over by the European nations.

The Sinhalese fought back against Portuguese armies made up largely of native allies and paroled convicts, perfecting guerrilla tactics from their mountain capital Kandy. They were years of carnage in which the invaders used every torture invented by the Inquisition. Finally the Sinhalese bottled up the Portuguese in Colombo and massacred columns loaded with booty from ransacked Buddhist temples. In one battle in 1638, 6,000 lives were lost. After another battle, fifty prisoners were returned to Colombo with only ten eyes between them and no testicles.

The Sinhalese then reached a deal with the Dutch to help them sweep the Portuguese into the sea in return for an overseas trade monopoly. That achieved, the Dutch simply renewed the plundering, corruption and land seizure under the guise of bureaucracy, and established a circle of coastal provinces protected by strong forts. In 1761 the Kandyans in the central mountains declared war on the coastal provinces, giving the Dutch an excuse to invade the highland kingdom. The first campaign saw the Dutch crushed by falling boulders, impaled by spears, trapped and slaughtered in ravines, lost in jungles. A second expedition captured Kandy City which the natives had abandoned, but monsoons forced

the Dutch to retreat and a peace treaty was made. These campaigns
were dress rehearsals for the British wars which followed. Western-
led forces were able to control the coastal plains and paddyfields
but the Kandyans were almost unbeatable in their mountain
strongholds.

History repeated itself and the Dutch became victims of a deal
between the Sinhalese and another foreign power. In 1795, 1,000
British infantry and four Indian battalions captured Trincomalee,
the second city of the coastal provinces. Colombo surrendered
bloodlessly and the Dutch withdrew ingloriously.

The British pact with the Kandyans proved an uneasy alliance
from the start, with accusations of treachery and deceit on both
sides. Partly to blame were the inevitable misconceptions which
arose when East met West. The Kandyans could be an enigma.
European chroniclers had described the islanders as a gentle and
generous race, but one capable of great barbarity. Executions by
trained elephants and by impaling did occur but their Buddhism
made them reluctant to take life. Kandyan peasants lived in a fruitful
land and could live comfortably without too much effort. Most
visitors agreed they were handsome, dignified and devout – yet
capable of irrational rage. Even the more affluent lived in simple
huts, although they built magnificent temples and palaces. Hardest
for Europeans to understand was their love of ritual and ceremony
for its own sake. This led to a delight in intrigue, bargaining and
labyrinthine plotting which gave them a reputation for deviousness.
Robert Knox, a seventeenth-century captive, wrote of them: 'In
their promises very unfaithful, approving lying in themselves but
misliking it in others.' It was a harsh verdict, and one based on
ignorance, but the British soon came to agree.

Under the terms of the Madras Treaty the British inherited the
coastal provinces but would allow the Kandyans access to the
ports for supplies of salt and fish and for limited trade with the
outside world. After two years the Treaty had not been ratified.
The Kandyans belatedly realized that it gave the British the same
coastal possessions and almost the same trade monopolies as the
Dutch had enjoyed before them. By 1797 poor administration and
British ignorance of local custom and land laws sparked a revolt in

the provinces around Colombo. The Kandyans gave the rebels moral backing but stayed clear of the fighting.

Whitehall appointed Frederick North, third son of the Prime Minister, as Governor-General of the Ceylon territories in 1798. His task was to run them as a Crown Colony, against the wishes of the East India Company which retained the responsibility for trade and revenue. North was initially successful. The revolt fizzled out as he reformed land laws, tackled corruption, set up a legal code seen to be fair, and improved education and health. However, he quickly concluded that the coastal provinces could never be fully secure while the Kandyan kingdom posed a threat from within. That kingdom was then in turmoil and gave North his most pressing diplomatic problem.

Three months earlier King Rajadhi Raja Sinha had died. Pilima Talauva, his *Adigar* (Prime Minister) wanted power for himself but was wary of seizing the throne directly. Instead he installed as puppet monarch the eighteen-year-old Kannasemy, who was the son of the dead king's sister-in-law and perhaps, according to persistent rumours, also the *Adigar*'s own child. The youth was invested with the sword of state as King Sri Wikrama Raja Sinha. In manhood he was described as 6 ft tall with Herculean limbs, his features handsome, his eyes intensely black and piercing. He was to prove no puppet.

North began talks with the new regime, meeting Pilima Talauva with great ceremony but reaching no conclusion. As the months dragged on North's conviction grew that the kingdom was a barrier to progress. Meanwhile the young king began to show his independence, much to the dismay of the 'king-maker' Pilima Talauva who began plotting his downfall. The full truth may never be known but North undoubtedly began playing off the chief minister against the monarch, a diplomatic double game, confident that he could pick up the pieces to the benefit of Empire.

At a second summit meeting, North was allegedly shocked by Pilima Talauva's discreet proposal to kill Sri Wikrama and refused to send a British force to help him do so. Pilima Talauva, sick with VD and fistulas, grew increasingly desperate as his power at court diminished. He proposed that North should send an ambassador to

Kandy City to negotiate a new treaty; he should be accompanied by a strong escort which would achieve a dual purpose: it would both intimidate the king and demonstrate British power and the benefits of living under its protection. North agreed and the ambassador chosen was the veteran Major-General Hay Macdowall. His orders were to offer support to whichever faction at court was most likely to reach a deal favourable to British interests.

In March 1800 Macdowall, with five companies of Madras foot, Malay infantry and Bengal artillerymen, was met just inside the Kandyan border by a reception force of 1,000 soldiers and seven elephants which was to escort them to Kandy itself. For 8 miles the men dragged the heavy guns through mud and fog, suffering blistering days and torrential nights. Progress was so slow that Macdowall left most of his column behind and continued with a few hundred Malays and Sepoys. Those he left behind at Ruwanwella were incapacitated by malaria, dysentery and other diseases known then by the catch-all 'jungle fever'. Of the men on the march with him one died from disease, another by drowning and another in the jaws of a crocodile. Officers described the track up to the Kandyan plateau as 'almost perpendicular' in stretches. It was crowded by the British column and their Kandyan escort. Baggage trains jostled with troopers cursing their ill-luck.

Four weeks after leaving Colombo Macdowall reached the royal palace at Kandy. He was graciously received with courtesy, sweet cakes, honey . . . and a maze of baffling protocol. The king's confidence and authority grew daily. Pilima Talauva demonstrated his wiles and cunning. The British ambassador could not penetrate the conflicting conspiracies. Neither could he perceive which faction to negotiate with. After several exasperating weeks his talks came to nothing.

Macdowall did achieve one thing. The £5,000 cost of the expedition had, in effect, financed a detailed reconnaissance of the hinterland, highlighting the need for proper transport and communication routes. It was a blueprint for future invasion. Valuable lessons were learnt, although most of them were subsequently forgotten.

The situation grew volatile. North, wearied by the endless negotiations, was moving towards a military solution. Kandy was also mobilizing for war. Troops were recruited from outlying villages and drilled in the defence of the city. The spark was provided by a seemingly trivial incident. Pilima Talauva, anxious to dispel rumours that he was a British agent and to promote his own authority, seized stocks of areca nuts from coastal traders and ignored British demands for compensation. There is much evidence that Pilima Talauva wanted to provoke an invasion. He may have hoped, after months of secret talks, that British action would destroy Sri Wikrama and leave him as a 'client king'. From that ambition a tragedy was born.

* * *

At the start of 1803 Macdowall was ordered to retrace his footsteps to Kandy, this time at the head of a full invasion force. Colonel Barbut led another force from Trincomalee, a longer route.

Marching with jaunty confidence from Colombo, Macdowall's force consisted of 1,900 fighting men: Britons of the 51st and 19th Foot, two companies of Bengal artillery, a company of Malays and 1,000 recruits to the Ceylon Native Infantry, plus many times that number of coolies, pioneers, drovers and ammunition carriers. Morale in the 51st was low after three years' garrison duty. Some, like Macdowall, were hardened veterans of the Corsican campaign but others were regarded as 'old men and boys'. The 19th was in better shape. Two of its companies had fought in the Mysore War a few years previously, while five more had seen action elsewhere and the rest had helped to suppress tax riots. They were relatively used to the climate, experienced and healthy. The Malay unit had a fearsome reputation for plunder and the swiftness of their krises. The Bengal gunners were battle-hardened. The Native Infantry, despite the name, consisted largely of recruits from India, Africa, Java and Malacca. Early attempts to recruit lowland Sinhalese had failed.

Macdowall chose a northerly route alongside the River Maha Oya, across level plains towards the massive escarpment that was their destination. The first stage was not arduous. The soldiers, hot and heavily laden, were greeted by friendly villagers anxious to sell them produce and cooling drinks. A supply depot was set up in the foothills and dubbed Fort Frederick. The next hilly stage proved more gruelling and the baggage train became an unwieldy burden. Even though most tents had been left at the depot the pack bullocks stumbled and the elephant handlers struggled to control their beasts. Macdowall was well aware of the need for a speedy and decisive campaign before the onset of the April rains, yet progress remained slow. Barbut suffered the same frustrations and setbacks as his column trundled slowly from the opposite direction.

First contact with the enemy came when troops surprised a Kandyan scouting party. A Malay was wounded but one prisoner was taken. He confirmed that the Kandyans were concentrating their forces around the capital, content to allow the mountains and jungle wear down the invaders. Macdowall met the first real resistance from a stone redoubt 50 ft above the track at Girihagama, close to the gateway to the plateau. Kandyans poured steady if inaccurate musket fire on a company of 19th Grenadiers before retreating through a rear door. They left a bloody trail as they dragged away their wounded. One Grenadier died, while another was lucky to survive a ball through a lung. The road to the capital was now open.

Barbut's smaller column, with five companies of the 19th, more Malays and one company of Madras artillery, saw no enemy at all until they reached the Balakaduwa Pass. A cursory shelling sent the defenders fleeing and Barbut reached the top with no casualties. He saw Kandy City burning.

The two columns met at the outskirts of the city. They found only ashes and half-burned buildings. All the inhabitants, the king and his court, had simply decamped for the mountains of Uva, taking with them their treasures, religious relics, arms and provisions. There was no one to fight, nothing to loot, no glory to be had.

Meanwhile North, in a calculated gamble, recognized an alternative candidate for the Kandyan throne A dignified Malabar called Muttusamy, who was brother-in-law to the old dead king, was despatched with an escort to the now British-occupied capital. Once there Muttusamy proved difficult and refused to cede land to the British. It hardly mattered. Few others recognized the pretender. He was ignored by the city garrison and neighbouring villagers. He sat alone, save for a few servants, holding pathetic court in the charred remains of the royal palace.

The acknowledged king, Sri Wikrama, was 18 miles away in another palace at Hunguranketa. The British learnt this from the double-dealing Pilima Talauva. Two columns of 500 and 300 men were sent across the steaming mountainsides to capture the king. Within a few miles they suffered heavy fire from native gingals or 'grasshopper' guns which were highly effective when aimed down the narrow tracks. Several troopers were mown down but the columns marched steadily through the high-altitude swamps and thickets, sweeping the areas ahead with light artillery in the text-book fashion. On the second day they reached their target . . . only to find the king and his entourage had once again decamped. The frustrated force returned to the capital under sporadic fire. This time the Kandyans concentrated on killing the baggage handlers, a classic tactic of mountain warfare. Many officers believed that the failed pursuit of the king had been a cunning trap laid by the wily Pilima Talauva.

Conditions for the garrison in Kandy deteriorated fast. Troops unused to the jungle, worn out by patrolling the sodden hills and harried by snipers, quickly lost their spirit. Stragglers and those who wandered too far foraging were butchered. Small parties of coolies, some Sepoys, the wives of several Malay soldiers and one unnamed European were found cut to pieces in gullies and underbrush. Sri Wikrama promised villagers a bounty of 10 rupees for the head of a European and 5 for that of a native soldier. Supply lines to both Colombo and Trincomalee were repeatedly severed. The worst enemy of all was disease. It spread through the insanitary ruins of Kandy as the rainy season began. Malarial fever and yellow-jack slew European and native alike. So did beri-beri, dysentery and infected wounds. One officer wrote: 'Nothing is so apt to bring on that plague, the berryberry, as low living and exposure to heavy dews.' Of his company he reported 48 hospitalized and 4 dead. A few weeks later the death list had grown to 28. He wrote again: 'If they keep us much longer in this hole you will see very few of these fine fellows.' He warmly praised Barbut's efforts to improve the conditions of the enlisted men. Macdowall's force, pitifully reduced by disease and warfare, half-starved and demoralized, was no longer an army of occupation: they were prisoners in the Kandy rubble.

The Kandyans, though also suffering from fever, were moving freely. Large groups of warriors were sent into the Western and Northern provinces and the supply depot at Fort Frederick came under threat. The fort was abandoned although no enemy attackers were ever seen. By then most of its defenders, including the commander, Bullock, were dead of the fever.

North was unaware of the full danger but the campaign was proving miserable and costly. He dared not ask his overlords for reinforcements because of the more pressing priorities in India and war-torn Europe. His judgement in supporting Muttusamy was being called into question. Macdowall's force was being whittled away in the mountains and the garrisons in the coastal provinces were fully stretched. North and Macdowall agreed to withdraw a large part of the Kandy force to the coast but the return routes were treacherous. Pilima Talauva offered an apparent solution: a truce in return for help in deposing the king. Or so the *Adigar* alleged. The ceasefire was eagerly accepted.

On 1 April Macdowall left Kandy with the bulk of his force, leaving Barbut in command of a garrison of 300 Green Howards, 700 Malays and a considerable number of hospital cases. The Kandyans kept to the truce and the returnees went unmolested. Some 400 survivors of the 51st were given a hero's welcome in Colombo, having left 100 of their comrades dead or hospitalized in the mountains. Almost every man who returned was himself hospitalized and three months later barely 100 were left alive.

North opened new peace talks at Dambadeniya and Barbut briefly joined the parley. He gave a strangely positive report on conditions at Kandy, saying the fever would soon burn itself out. Barbut then collapsed, was taken delirious to Colombo and died some weeks later. At the peace conference Pilima Talauva agreed that the king should be handed over to the British along with much of eastern Ceylon. In return the *Adigar* would, with British blessing and support, rule over the reduced kingdom with the title Grand Prince. No one will ever know whether Pilima Talauva was serious. Some rumours suggest that the peace talks involved an unrealized plot to capture North. The Governor certainly believed the talks offered hope.

Macdowall was sent back, while the truce lasted, to replace Barbut in command in Kandy. What he found was shocking: the death toll was rising every day, the filthy hospital wards were crowded to bursting, the sick were too weak to stagger to the latrines. The rains were by now continuous and temperatures plunged at night. Food was scarce and rotten. Officers reported that few Europeans were capable of walking a mile. The coolies had fled. There were just three artillerymen fit for duty. The Malays lost thirty men dead in a month while others had deserted because of a dispute over 10 weeks' missing back pay, and opium.

North suspected that the fragile truce would not last much longer. Spies reported that Pilima Talauva's loyalty was suspect at Sri Wikrama's court. Macdowall decided to return to Colombo to emphasize the growing peril and to stress the need to evacuate Kandy while the truce still held. The General was sick when he headed down the mountain track, leaving the charnel city in the charge of Major Adam Davie. Reluctant to take command, Davie fully admitted that he was an inexperienced officer who had seen no previous action during his year in Ceylon.

North finally agreed to bury his pride and issued orders for a full retreat from Kandy. Sadly, his orders came too late to halt the remorseless drift towards disaster.

* * *

The Kandyans were ready to strike. Levies had been raised by the king and his generals throughout the mountains. As the forces encircling the city grew in numbers and boldness, Pilima Talauva informed the hapless Davie that the truce had collapsed and an attack was imminent. The outlying posts were abandoned without a shot and Davie concentrated his dwindling command in the old royal palace, a rambling structure of interlocking compounds which included the makeshift hospital. He positioned four three-pounders to cover the main approaches. There were barely twenty

European troops fit enough to join the Sepoys and Malays manning the defences. The palace would have been virtually indefensible even if Davie had had large numbers of operational troops under his command. The building was flanked on three sides by an ornamental wall, on the fourth by a flimsy stockade overlooked by a sheer cliff. That weak spot was covered by a three-pounder, a mortar and ten native troops. They were the first victims of a pre-dawn swoop.

Before daybreak on 24 June the little battery was overrun in total silence and the men captured. Two officers of the 19th who were talking on a verandah immediately below the outpost were unaware of the attack until by dawn's early light they made out several hundred Kandyans swarming down the hillside. The attackers, led by the Malay mercenary chief Sanguaglo, stormed the stockade. They slashed Quartermaster Brown to death with their krises. His companion, Ensign Barry, parried several blows and stuck Sanguaglo with his bayonet. Major Davie appeared in the mêlée and finished off the chief with his sword. The subsequent confusion halted the attack, allowing hastily mustered gunners time to fire a round of grapeshot from a three-pounder. At point-blank range the effect was devastating. A ragged hole appeared in the Kandyan ranks; twenty-four of them dropped in bloody heaps and the rest retreated.

The Kandyans were alarmed at the firepower still at the disposal of the enfeebled garrison. They held back but maintained steady gunfire on all sides of the 800-yard perimeter. This caused few casualties but the covering fire allowed infiltrators to slip into the tangle of palace buildings. Native defenders saw several of their former comrades – deserters or captives – among the attackers, offering proof of good treatment if they surrendered. Four officers of the Malay regiments approached Davie to urge capitulation. When Davie refused, one officer bizarrely tried to blow his own brains out. Such madness had the desired effect. Davie, weakened by sickness and fear, decided the position was hopeless. Together with the Malay adjutant Captain Nouradin he left the stockade under a white flag.

Davie and Pilima Talauva agreed surrender terms which would allow the fit survivors to march freely to Trincomalee and safety. Those too sick to be moved would be tended where they lay until they either expired or could be evacuated. They were generous terms, unbelievably so given the circumstances.

In the late afternoon 34 Europeans, 250 Malays, Muttusamy and his entourage, a few Bengal gunners, native wives and children followed Davie out of the city. With them went the garrison's two doctors, a sure sign that they regarded the surrender terms as too good to be true. The sick were left behind as the column marched off in torrential rain. The weather covered the sounds that emerged from the capital minutes later.

Thousands of Kandyans swarmed into the palace complex from all sides. In one long narrow room converted to hospital use they found 149 Europeans crammed side by side in cots and crude panniers, on stretchers and on the bare floor. Sergeant Theon, one of only two Europeans to survive, later described the horror: 'They mostly knocked out the soldiers' brains with clubs then pulled them out by the heels, the dead and the dying, threw many of them into a well and numbers of the bodies were left in the streets and devoured by dogs, but none were buried.' Theon was knocked senseless. He awoke naked under a pile of bodies in the palace courtyard. As he struggled free a Kandyan soldier discovered him and hanged him from a beam. Astonishingly the rope broke before he strangled and he crawled to a hut to hide. A week later he was found again, taken captive and treated well. He lived in Kandy as a royal pensioner for twelve years, raising a son by his Muslim bride. The only officer left behind, Adjutant Plenderleath, was beaten to death with his men. There is no sure record of what happened to 23 Malays and 17 Moorish gunners left in a separate wing of the hospital. Some sources suggest they were victims of the general bloody frenzy, others that they were spared.

Unaware of the carnage behind him Major Davie and his column reached the swollen banks of the Mahaweli Ganga just before nightfall. After a night's soaking they received an official delegation from King Sri Wikrama, who demanded that the usurper Muttusamy be handed over. Twice Davie refused, ignoring assurances that no harm would befall his charge. But his resolve collapsed on the third demand when he was told that 50,000 Kandyans were poised to attack. Muttusamy and his kinsmen were led away. They were later given a swift trial before the king. Muttusamy and three relatives were condemned and beheaded. Two servants were hanged and the rest released minus their ears and noses.

At the riverbank Davie's men built bamboo rafts for a crossing. The next day they awoke to find themselves surrounded by Kandyans led by the ferocious Joseph Fernando. After tremendous difficulties a rope was secured across the river waters, only to be cut by natives on the other bank before any raft could be hauled across. Emissaries from the king issued new demands. Davie and his men must give up their arms and return to Kandy. Word had by then reached them of the massacre in the city and several old campaigners protested that only death awaited them there. Nevertheless Davie, exhausted and in despair, agreed to the new conditions.

The British and Asian troops were disarmed and separated. The Asians were sent back towards the city. The British troopers were in turn separated from the officers and taken a short distance away. They were robbed of any valuables and marched in pairs to a hollow hidden by thick vegetation. There they were cut down by swordsmen working in relays. Only one British soldier, Corporal George Barnsley, survived, feigning death after a neck blow had sliced his tendons.

The officers were dying too, some by their own hand. Three shot themselves, a fourth threw himself into the river. The majority were brained with clubs or put to the sword. Two officers, one of them Doctor Greeving who had deserted the hospital, slid down the tangled hillside unobserved and hid in a pit. They remained there for four days, covered by the bodies of dead comrades. The last two officers, Davie and his second-in-command Captain Rumley, were led out for execution but were saved by the timely arrival of Pilima Talauva who ordered them to be sent to the King.

The Asian troops were given the choice of death or service in the Kandyan army. Some, including Bengal gunners, protested that they had sworn an oath to the British king and could not bend their knee to Sri Wikrama. They were swiftly killed. The remainder joined the Kandyans.

A column was sent to take the small Fort Macdowall on the British supply line. En route they captured the wounded Corporal Barnsley, who had been heading in great pain in the same direction. The fort was held by Captain Madge with two officers, a surgeon, 22 Malays and 32 soldiers of the 19th, of whom 19 were too ill to move and the rest sick on their feet. The Kandyans sent Barnsley into the fort to relay terms. His first words to the astonished Madge were: 'The troops in Kandy are all dished, your honour.'

His description of the mass murder by the river left Madge in no doubt that surrender was pointless and that he must do his best for those men capable of flight. He decided to evacuate the fort, leaving the immovable sick behind to certain death. Those who could walk, including Barnsley, crept out in the night after lighting lamps in the fort to fool the surrounding natives. They had been gone for some time before the Kandyans realized the fort was no longer defended. They followed in maddened pursuit, after first slaying the sick in their cots. Madge and his ill, weary and tattered little force fled through the jungle hills, harassed by the enemy all the way. It was a hideous and terrifying flight, with death snapping at their heels, but the soldiers kept their nerve and their luck held.

On the fourth day they met, by sheer good fortune, a column of 150 Malays. Together they were too strong for the Kandyans to tackle and the last three days to Trincomalee were unopposed. Perhaps the luckiest man of all was Barnsley. He survived the march and recovered from his gruesome wounds. He was promoted sergeant but quickly reduced to the ranks for drunkenness. In 1805 he was invalided home.

Among the British, Davie, now a pathetic, sick captive in Kandy, was held responsible for the whole military disaster. He was the obvious scapegoat. North was especially vitriolic, and was also determined to avoid any blame himself. In official reports North greatly exaggerated the strength of the garrison's defences in Kandy. He made hardly any reference to the weakened condition of the troops under Davie's command, the spread of epidemics and the strength of enemy forces fighting on their own terrain. Davie was certainly a poor commander, inadequate and indecisive, but he was not alone in that. Moreover, he had not sought out the job, fully recognizing his own shortcomings. His decisions to parley when in a hopeless situation and then to abandon Kandy were understandable.

But his surrender on the riverbank, after hearing of the hospital massacre, was not.

There is still confusion over who ordered the massacre. Pilima Talauva could certainly be ruthless but he is an unlikely candidate. He was a crafty fox with his eye always on future negotiation, on keeping open avenues for intrigue. The evidence points at the hot-blooded young king, Sri Wikrama. According to some reports he was enraged at his chief minister's decision to allow the British to leave Kandy under truce, revoked the safe conduct and ordered the killing to assert his authority. Later each man blamed the other. Whatever the truth the savagery in the hospital and on the riverbank must have been in part due to the bloodlust which leaders can often harness but not control. The Kandyans were, after all, defending their mountain realm from an invader. So far they had been spectacularly successful.

Davie was at first badly treated, his illnesses and sores neglected. Later the king, perhaps with feelings of remorse over the spilt blood, gave him medical aid, cash, presents and household servants. Everything, indeed, but his freedom. Repeated British efforts to achieve his release failed. In one message passed to Colombo he said 'Let not my friends know I am alive as I expect not to survive for many days.' He became a familiar figure in the kingdom, ragged and depressed and possibly half mad. He never tried to escape. His body broken by illness, his will-power sapped by the shame of ignoble defeat, Davie died still a captive in either 1812 or 1813.

* * *

One small fort, Dambadeniya, was left in Kandyan territory. It was a simple staging post. Behind its rough earth banks and a flimsy barricade of stacked rice bags were thirty-six troopers and Malays under Ensign Grant. All the men had fever to varying degrees and Grant himself could barely walk. The fort soon came under strong attack. The besiegers under Migastenna kept up continuous sniping fire and each day emissaries were sent to demand surrender. Grant stubbornly – and sensibly – refused. After a two-week siege, rescue came with the arrival of Captain Robert Blackall at the head of a relief column. The Kandyans pulled back. Grant was ordered to return to Colombo after first destroying the fort's large store of provisions. In doing so several soldiers drank copiously from stocks of arak, a fiery native liquor. One drunken Briton and several Sepoys lagged behind as the column marched out of the fort. Their bodies were never found.

The British soldiers remaining in their coastal towns and garrisons were now seriously depleted by war and sickness. At the beginning of the year their forces had numbered more than 5,000 able-bodied men; just six months later 2,000 of them were dead or missing while most of the rest were ill. The hospitals in those pre-Nightingale days were full to choking and few men were fit for duty. Opposing them were tens of thousands of Kandyans who might at any time sweep down from the highlands and swamp the thinly spread garrisons. Fortunately the British were given a breathing space. The Kandyans suspended warfare to celebrate their Perahera, the biggest religious festival of the year. While the Kandyans rejoiced and caroused, Macdowall strengthened his defences. Convalescents dug ditches alongside the few fit men.

Their festivities over the Kandyans attacked and together with lowland Sinhalese swarmed around the British-held forts. The first strike was against Matara in the south. Its commander was paralysed with fear and North sent the remarkable Captain Beaver to replace him. Only just out of the fever-bed, the forty-year-old officer took sixty hours to cover 103 miles, some of that over sea. Within two days he had driven the enemy from the vicinity of the fort. A few days later he forced the Kandyans out of an outlying post previously abandoned to them. Within a few weeks, with only 60 European troops, 140 Sepoys and 170 Malays, Beaver had subdued the entire Southern province.

Colombo itself was threatened by a large force which halted 5 miles from the city. The beleaguered North had no effective troops, only a hastily raised militia of 500 men. From this, Macdowall put together a tiny strike force under Lieutenant Mercer and sent them out to meet the enemy head on. The Kandyans, taken by surprise, fled back across their border, leaving prisoners and dead.

Throughout the coastal provinces the pattern was repeated.

Instead of waiting passively behind their rough barricades, the British commanders sallied out and harried the Kandyan attack columns, creating dismay, confusion and panic. Attack did indeed prove the best form of defence. The tactic was so successful that the Kandyans only managed to lay proper siege to one fort, a tiny outpost at Chilaw close to the kingdom's border. As many as 3,000 attackers faced two young civil servants and sixty native troops. When their grapeshot ran out the defenders fired nothing but powder from their small cannon, hoping that the noise and smoke alone would dissuade the enemy from making an overwhelming frontal attack. The ploy worked and the Kandyans withdrew after four days.

Sri Wikrama now decided to lead a new attack on Colombo, marching in person at the head of an army of Malabar Guards, Malays and 12,000 Kandyans. In his path lay the ruined fort of Hanwella, commanded by the doughty Lieutenant Mercer. The king's men attacked on 3 September but were repulsed. A second attack the following day also failed, despite the ramshackle defences, but left most of the small garrison wounded. Mercer himself was extremely sick. Captain William Pollock rode from Colombo, dodged the encircling enemy, and took command of fewer than a hundred men in poor condition. The Kandyans bombarded the dilapidated stone walls with three- and six-pounders serviced by Bengal and Madras artillery lascars captured at Kandy. Those gunners deliberately loaded the cannon with grape instead of ball, which splattered harmlessly against the fort's walls. Others set the angle of fire too high so that the shot whizzed overhead. Unaware that the cannonade had been ineffectual, the Kandyans rushed to attack but halted 200 yards from the muzzles of the defenders crouched below the low parapets. The attackers were packed into the steel jaws of an ambush, caught in an open killing ground.

Mercer, with half the garrison, had crawled into the jungle bordering the clearing. Now they opened fire, tearing great holes in the Kandyan flank. Their volley was also the signal for the fort's cannon to open up with grapeshot, with brutal effect. Pollock and his infantry sallied out in orderly ranks, pouring volley after volley into the struggling, panicking, dying mass of humanity. The carnage continued for two hours. Only a handful of Malay mercenaries were able to return fire. At last the gunfire was stilled as the last survivors escaped. Eight Kandyan soldiers and much weaponry were captured. Much to their delight 176 gun lascars rejoined the British. The following day they helped bury 270 Kandyans where they had fallen in that awful field. The death toll was much higher. All paths leading away from the clearing were choked with the bodies of those who had fled mortally wounded. The garrison suffered just two casualties and both survived.

Sri Wikrama and his court followers took to their heels, leaving behind sharpened posts upon which he had intended to impale British captives. He blamed his general at Hanwella, Levuke Rala, for the disaster and had him beheaded. The leading troops, those who survived, were ordered to work on a 2,000-acre paddyfield as punishment. Three days later Pollock, reinforced by Europeans from Colombo, crossed the Kandy border in pursuit. Across the Kelani River the king's army was camped at Ruwanwella, protected by well-placed batteries. A British detachment forded the river under intense but ineffective fire, seized one of the gun emplacements and killed all twenty-six defenders. The Kandyans, hugely superior in numbers but dispirited and caught between military pincers, again fled in terror, narrowly escaping Pollock's attempt to entrap them in another killing ground. Pollock destroyed tons of stores at Ruwanwella and burnt over 1,000 huts, denying the enemy food and shelter. It was the start of a scorched-earth policy.

Pollock returned to Colombo a hero, the saviour of the city. His extraordinary verve, audacity and ruthlessness were matched in smaller episodes across the provinces. British officers led small forces deep into Kandyan-held territory using speed and surprise as their main weapon. They also savagely suppressed Sinhalese communities which showed any sign of rebelling and joining the enemy. Captain Robert Blackall boasted of burning ninety-three villages and extensive paddyfields without a single casualty among his men. Fishing fleets were burnt to the waterline and scuttled, crops were destroyed and several village leaders were flogged to death. No records exist to reveal how many died of famine or exposure but the numbers must have been high. The British were no doubt partly motivated by a desire to avenge the Kandy massacres. However, their brutal methods certainly worked in military terms. The Kandyans were denied the countryside and potential rebels were terrorized into submission. Much of the lowlands were laid waste but at least the coastal garrisons and trading ports were no longer under threat.

Reinforcements finally arrived from India and the Eastern Islands to defend Trincomalee, now virtually denuded of fighting men through sickness. To strengthen the other forts African slaves were bought at £37 a head, including purchase, 'freight', provisions and agents' fees, in the Mozambique markets to serve as mercenary soldiers. The purchase caused controversy. The negroes were regarded as a bargain: they were easy to administer and well suited to the tropics – and the natives of Sri Lanka viewed them with terror.

Macdowall's period of service now came to an end. He was often blamed for the Kandy disaster but his masterly conduct of the war in the provinces redeemed him in the eyes of his superiors. He was promoted commander-in-chief at Madras but quickly fell out with the civil authorities. He died in 1809, shipwrecked on his voyage home to Britain. His successor in Ceylon took command in March 1804. Major-General David Wemyss was, at forty-four, a veteran of campaigning in the Americas, Flanders and Italy. His military experience was never in doubt but he lacked the tact needed to deal with civilians. The delicate relationship between Governor and military overlord was shattered when Wemyss clashed with North over field allowances. He outraged Moslem Sepoys by ordering them to attend divine service. He quarrelled with judges over the use of a parade ground. He challenged civilian rivals to duels. Relations became so fraught that North drew up contingency plans to have Wemyss arrested if necessary. Such squabbling undermined the British counter-attacks. The raids continued with mixed success. Wemyss divided his forces into smaller units stretched around a 700-mile frontier. He maintained a blockade to deprive the Kandyans of salt and other commodities.

Pilima Talauva continued to play an apparent double-game. He kept up a regular correspondence with the British, at one stage proposing a peace conference at which his own most troublesome and war-hungry ministers could be snatched. North rejected all proposals which left Sri Wikrama on the throne. He was determined on a further offensive to depose the king and avenge the massacre. The coastal campaigns had shown how effective light mobile columns could be, even against an enemy fighting on home ground. North proposed a three-month campaign with British-led forces striking throughout the island in fast-moving columns up to 600 men strong. Preparations were made for September when the monsoon season ended. Until then warfare was suspended.

* * *

During a tour of the garrisons Wemyss met Captain Arthur Johnston, the commander at Fort Batticaloa. Johnston knew the country well and was experienced in jungle warfare. He had been one of the lucky ones evacuated from the hospital at Kandy before the slaughter. He must have made a good impression because soon afterwards he received secret papers ordering him to prepare a strong force to march on Kandy. Similar columns, he was told, would converge from other garrisons around the coast to meet on the heights above the city on 28 September. However, the wording of the instructions was ambiguous, the routes to be taken were vague and the timings imprecise. A second set of orders was even more confusing. It was the beginning of an almighty débâcle.

Putting aside any doubts Johnston set off on the 20th with two officers and 70 men of the 19th, a sergeant and 6 gunners of the Royal Artillery. They were joined upriver by 53 Malays and 175 Sepoys. In addition there were 550 pioneers and coolies with ponderous bullocks to carry the supplies. A fast-moving strike force it was not.

Johnston's column moved through a region devastated by smallpox and crossed the border into the wild uplands. The hills were desolate and empty. The Kandyans had learnt well from the British scorched-earth tactics. Every village on Johnston's route had been cleared, its stores and animals dispersed. The march was exhausting from the start and after a week some men were sent back with the fever. Ominously, a Kandyan sharpshooter, captured in a skirmish with snipers, told Johnston that there were no reports of other columns invading the kingdom from other directions. Puzzled, or perhaps dismissive, Johnston pressed on.

On the tenth day they reached the banks of the Mahaweli Ganga and crossed its turbulent waters by raft. Ahead lay a tortuous trail through jungle, jagged rocks and ravines to the royal city of Hanguranketa: it was a three-day slog, harassed by sniper fire which killed one soldier and uncounted coollies and bullocks. On the last day they traversed a narrow ridge, inching along artificial footways from which several pack animals crashed with their precious loads into the gorge below. That night Johnston camped in a state of almost total exhaustion. His men were roused by musket fire which was too high to do any harm. The attackers were beaten off by Sepoy pickets and suffered heavy casualties.

The column continued along the riverside, hemmed in between rock and stormy waters, and under continuous fire from the opposite bank. The noise maddened the bullocks and some broke free, adding to the confusion on the narrow pathways. After 3 painstaking miles their progress was blocked by a large house which had been turned into a fort, supported by a battery on the far bank. It seemed impregnable, but the defenders put up only token resistance before fleeing. After a night of intermittent cannon fire Johnston sent a small squad across the river to take the battery from the rear. The unexpected raid worked smoothly and the emplacement was abandoned. Within an hour Johnston captured a small palace nearby at Kundasale. The fine building was richly carved and gilded but its cellars were packed with munitions. Johnston reluctantly torched the lot.

Once again a British-led force found the road to Kandy City open. Apart from some long-range musket fire from the hills above it was undefended. Once again the city they found was deserted, save for a woman and a small boy. They marched into the eerie city streets on 6 October. There was no sign of any other British column. They encamped in the royal palace, long since cleansed of the blood of their forerunners. A Malay officer, captured by the Kandyans during an earlier expedition but now escaped, brought Johnston fearful news. Six British columns had indeed set out but the other five had either turned back or were beaten back. They were on their own.

Johnston was by now fully aware of his desperate predicament. He had succeeded only in taking an empty city. The Kandyans were gathering in the mountains around the city, waiting only for sickness and desertion to sap his strength before attacking. Already disease was cutting into his defences and the men were running low on ammunition and supplies. They were jittery and unnerved. Some raided arak stores and got dismally drunk. The native troops heard shouts from former comrades urging them to join them in the hills, to fight for riches rather than the Crown. A sensible and diligent officer, Johnston decided his first duty was to his men. Staying would be suicidal. So too would be a retreat along the route they had taken. Instead he decided to move his little army to the left bank of the Mahaweli Ganga where they could construct better defences. After just two days in the empty city they marched out at dawn and met a grisly scene: skeletons dangled brokenly from treetops. They were the remains of Davie's officers. The bones of his enlisted men lay where they had been butchered near the river ferry, a place known afterwards as the Shore of Blood.

Johnston's force crossed the river on two small rafts and established a bridgehead by dislodging enemy soldiers at bayonet point. The action caused him to think again. The difficult crossing, the increasing boldness of the Kandyans and the dwindling stocks of ammunition persuaded him it would be folly to stay. He set off in the opposite direction to his incoming route, towards Trincomalee. Each man was issued with six days' rations and the surviving bullocks were destroyed.

They fought their way up a hillside track, scrambling over tree trunks felled by the enemy, charging over a series of breastworks, and took the summit, with 13 soldiers and 30 coolies killed or wounded. Days of ferocity followed. They hacked and shot and clawed their way through the dense jungle of Matale. Kandyan raids became confused mêlées, with bayonet and musket butt matched against sword and spear. Powder was wet, the ammunition all but gone, and shooting was rare in the close-quarter fighting. A company of the 19th moved forward so fast it became separated from the rest of the column. Johnston and his men battled on through bloody encounters, sweltering days, rain-soaked dusks and cold nights, as sickness and wounds multiplied. Coolies deserted in terror, leaving behind wounded soldiers who were captured, trussed up like chickens and carried off to torture and eventual, welcome, death. More of the injured were abandoned when their comrades lacked the strength to carry them further. The march of death continued to Lake Minneriya where the column caught up with the missing vanguard and the Kandyan attacks diminished. By now Johnston was so ill with dysentery he had to be carried in a cloak, his body dangerously weakened, his spirits low, his mind troubled by fears that he faced a court martial for retreating from Kandy without orders.

Johnston's column marched into Trincomalee 'cold, wet, dirty and lousy,' according to one observer. 'Almost naked, many bare-footed and maimed, officers and all alike starved and shrivelled,' said another. Every soldier was admitted to hospital and there almost all of them died. Johnston's march had proved as deadly as the Kandy massacre. And it had all been for nothing. The epic and heroic adventure had been the result of a communications blunder. Johnston learnt that the second set of vague orders received from Wemyss weeks before should have cancelled the march on Kandy City. The British columns were merely intended to enter the kingdom, inflict the greatest possible devastation to avenge the massacre, and then retire. The other columns had done just that, suffering minimal casualties, and returned to the safety and comfort of their barracks.

Johnston was exonerated at a court of inquiry which praised his courage and skill. Indeed he was commended for the way he had held his disparate force together in seemingly impossible conditions and against massive odds. He survived his illness and served in Sri Lanka for another six years but the after-effects of his ordeal were blamed for his eventual death in 1824. In a bitter postscript to the march Sergeant Henry Craven was sentenced to transportation for life for abandoning four of his wounded men to certain death on the trail. He died of fever before he could be shipped to Botany Bay.

While Johnston had been fighting his way to and from Kandy other British forces had been busy on punitive raids. One column caused widespread destruction in the Western province to within one day's march of Kandy City. Another column made an unsuccessful bid to capture Pilima Talauva. The Kandyans in turn launched attacks on British regions but they were half-hearted and easily repulsed. A familiar pattern was repeated as the British counter-attacked across a lush countryside raped by war, starvation and smallpox. The war was dragging to an inconclusive end.

Governor North was exhausted by the effort. He wrote to London asking to be relieved because of his 'shattered and unstrung' nerves. He confessed uncertainty over whether he had acted 'like a good politician or a great nincompoop'. North had done his best and his achievements were fully recognized. He reformed the island's civil administration, improved revenue, abolished torture and established a modern system of public instruction. With hindsight he was often too impatient to see his changes through and it was his vision of ruling all Ceylon which had caused the war. On returning to England he came into the title Earl of Guildford and travelled extensively in Europe. He set up the Ionian University in Corfu. That experiment failed amid much ridicule and he died in 1827.

On 17 July 1805 he was replaced by Major-General Sir Thomas Maitland who, because of his extensive Army background and political contacts, took both full civil and military authority. Wemyss was ousted, much to his own disgust but to the relief of many others. Maitland was a Scots aristocrat, a veteran administrator and a realist. He set himself the task of ending the costly war, reducing all military spending and sorting out Ceylon's crippled economy. With warfare virtually at a standstill Maitland managed to both cut the armed forces and increase their efficiency. He tackled with gusto the corruption behind much of the discontent felt by lowland Sinhalese. He issued a statement rejecting any more 'foolish expeditions', adding: 'I shall not throw away the lives of His Majesty's subjects by disease in burning and destroying the defenceless huts of the innocent natives.'

Within two months he approached the Kandy priesthood seeking a peace treaty. Such a pact proved elusive, although 300 captured Malays and Sepoys were freed. Nothing was signed but tacitly the two warring neighbours agreed to leave each other alone. The disastrous war simply petered out and there was relative peace for ten years.

* * *

King Sri Wikrama grew in stature and power. He had begun his reign as the puppet of his chief minister but he became a self-confident autocrat as Pilima Talauva's influence waned. The two men quarrelled incessantly. The arch-plotter hatched a plan to assassinate the king and take the realm by force without the British assistance he had cultivated during years of war. The revolt was premature and easily crushed. Pilima Talauva and his son-in-law were captured and beheaded. Six minor chiefs were impaled in a circle around them.

Maitland grew sick of dealing directly with the Kandyan royal house. He and his envoys made deals with important chieftains and created a web of secret alliances which undermined the king. When war inevitably broke out again a British invasion force once more tramped the hilltop paths. This time it met little resistance and the campaign was over in forty days. The king was deposed and Kandy ceded to the Empire by a convention signed by the chiefs on 2 March 1815. It pledged the British to honour Kandyan customs, protect the power and privileges of the chiefs and guarantee as 'inviolable' the rites of Buddhism. Sri Wikrama himself was captured and in January 1816 he was sent with his wives to Madras. More than 2,000 years of Sinhalese independence was over. His kingdom was plundered. The king's personal treasure and royal regalia were dispersed among friend and foe. Part was later recovered by the authorities and sold by auction in Colombo. It raised £3,840 for the Prize Fund which, as was Army practice at the time, was to be shared out among the victors. Exquisitely crafted gold and jewelled artefacts were broken up for the worth of their base metal. Others simply vanished into the bags of officers and men. They can still be found in the dusty glass cases and vaults of British country houses and provincial museums.

Sri Wikrama lived in rich exile until 1832 when he died of dropsy.

He was fifty-two. He had been condemned during his lifetime as a butcher and a despot. He had also been exalted as a protector of his people and culture against British expansionism, a leader who had defied the mighty Empire and slaughtered its armies. Both were true.

In 1818 a full-scale rebellion was suppressed, the power of the chiefs reduced and heavier taxes imposed. Minor outbreaks occurred in the Highlands throughout the 1820s, followed by a bloodless revolt in 1834 and more bloodshed in 1848. But it can be argued that colonial rule delivered a century of peace until rioting between Tamils and Sinhalese began in 1958. That violence escalated during the following decades into a vicious civil war.

Sri Lanka is a paradise ruined by greed and hatred. It is bleeding again.

TWO

The Falklands, 1833

'Rejoice, rejoice'

The first clash of arms on the remote, wind-lashed Falklands (or Malvinas) occurred almost 150 years before a much larger conflict. It was not a war, rather a brief outburst of butchery involving just a handful of men, but the passions involved had vastly bloodier echoes many generations later. It too involved sea voyages across huge distances, diplomatic bungling and a power struggle over specks in the ocean once thought worthless.

It is as a precursor of the 1982 Falklands War – itself considered the last of British Empire-style small wars – that it is included here.

* * *

The Falklands, or the Malvinas, those desolate, remote, beautiful, storm-tossed islands in the South Atlantic, have always been dogged by controversy, including who it was that first set eyes on them. Argentinians claim it was Spain's Amerigo Vespucci in 1502 but there is precious little evidence to support this. England's John Davies claimed to have seen them in 1592 but that may have been wishful thinking. The best contender was neither Spanish nor British, but the Dutch adventurer Sebald de Weert, on 16 January 1600, and for many years the Falklands were called the Sebald Islands by Dutch cartographers. But there is no doubt that the first landfall was made in 1690 by John Strong, a Plymouth sea captain.

During much of the eighteenth century the islands were used as a staging post for British and French ships heading for the Horn. Both nations established small communities because of their trade and political interests in the South American continent. Spain paid

France to abandon all claims to the islands and the British withdrew their settlers in 1774.

The Spanish established a colony on the main western island and ships' captains registered the few babies born there as Spanish. But across the Falklands Sound on the eastern island the crews of British and American sealing and whaling ships put in regularly, establishing permanent encampments. They recognized no Spanish sovereignty, nor indeed any laws but self-preservation and the common good of their fellow seamen.

In 1820 the Argentinian Government in Buenos Aires sent an American, Colonel David Jewett, to take possession of the islands. He found fifty ships sheltering in the jagged coves, vessels registered from Liverpool to New York. His dictates were ignored by the tough, weather-forged seamen and, unable to exercise any control, he returned to Argentina.

In 1829 Buenos Aires contracted a Franco-German immigrant, Louis Vernet, to establish a settlement at Port Louis on the eastern island. He set off with several English families, Germans, blacks, gauchos, Indians and transported felons. He found seventy settlers, mainly English, ahead of him. He organized his workforce and rounded up the wild cattle, and paid an English seaman, Matthew Brisbane, to patrol the coast in his schooner *Elbe*, collecting taxes. The captain of the American vessel *Harriet* refused to pay the required levy and the ship was impounded pending a court hearing in the Argentine capital. In retaliation Captain Silas Duncan of the USS *Lexington* was despatched to the islands. He took a number of colonists prisoner and ordered his crew to destroy as much of Vernet's settlement as possible. He arrested Brisbane and took him to Buenos Aires where the legal ramifications of the whole affair were thrashed out.

Port Louis had not yet been properly rebuilt in 1832 when a sergeant, José Francisco Mestivier, was appointed Governor of what the Spanish now called the Malvinas. José María Pinedo, commander of the *Sarandi*, replaced Brisbane as guardian of the coastline. Mestivier found the small army of colonists in rebellious mood, demanding the back pay which Vernet had promised them. Numbers of felons mutinied and Mestivier was cut down and slain. Pinedo took command and captured the mutineers with a detachment of his crew. He had no sooner done so when on 2 January 1833 Captain John James Onslow of the newly arrived HMS *Clio* informed him that he was claiming the islands for the British Crown. Pinedo, his own force weakened and demoralized, did not resist. The Argentine flag was lowered at Port Louis. Argentina later described the 'invasion' as an act of colonial piracy, a view which continues to feature in its school books. Pinedo with his men, some settlers and his prisoners sailed for Buenos Aires. Seven mutineers accused of Mestivier's murder were swiftly executed.

Captain Onslow, thirty-six years old, had served off the coasts of Spain, Jamaica and South America. His ancestors included a former Speaker of the House of Commons. His father, Admiral Sir Richard Onslow, had been a doughty fighter in the Napoleonic Wars. After a period chasing smugglers as Commander of the Coast Guard at Great Yarmouth the younger Onslow had been put in charge of the 18-gun, 389-ton sloop *Clio* in 1830 as she was being fitted out for the South American station. After his success Onslow ordered storekeeper William Dickson, an Irishman not highly regarded by visiting British officers, to fly a Union Jack whenever a ship anchored off the colony. He called in the farmworkers and labourers employed by Vernet and offered them a deal: they would continue their work and if within five months no one returned to pay them they could take the equivalent of their wages in wild cattle. Onslow set sail, either unaware of or indifferent to the potential trouble he left behind him. His offer was effectively a licence to rustle.

The colonists tried to return to normal under the new flag, isolated from international power play. Brisbane returned as superintendent of Vernet's business projects. Charles Darwin called for a few days on board HMS *Beagle*. The workmen faced appalling weather and grumbled about their unpaid wages as their debts mounted in Dickson's store. After five months the men tried to claim the cattle they had been promised but Brisbane and Dickson prevented that happening.

The mood in Port Louis – by now reduced to 21 men and 3 women – turned ugly. Legitimate grievances spawned talk of violence. Eight men, led by 26-year-old Antonio Rivero from Buenos Aires, plotted to take forcibly what they considered their due. They were initially deterred by the presence of Captain William Low, a sealing sailor and businessman, and nine seamen who were awaiting repatriation after their vessel had been sold. But at dawn on 26 August 1833 Low and four of his men sailed out of Berkley Sound for a brief seal hunt. Rivero saw his opportunity and struck with his followers, two gauchos and five Indian convicts. Their targets were settlement leaders they believed had wronged them, and what followed was certainly premeditated murder. They armed themselves with muskets, pistols, swords and knives and headed for Brisbane's house.

Brisbane was shot and killed. The captain of the gauchos, an Argentine representative called Juan Simón, was hacked to death with swords, as was the storekeeper Dickson. A German named Anton Wagnar was also slain in the murderous spree. A witness to the killings, Ventura Pasos, tried to flee but was brought down by an Indian's bolas. He was stabbed to death by Rivero. The murdered men, all unarmed, were the principals of the settlement.

The other colonists, mainly Argentinians, escaped from Port Louis. A dozen men, the women and two children took shelter in a cave on Hog Island at the head of Berkley Sound a few miles away. The rebels rampaged through the settlement, looting every home, and then drove the disputed cattle inland.

It was another two months before relief came, on 23 October, in the shape of the British survey ship *Hopeful*. Its captain offered help to the settlers but was unable to chase the renegades inland. He found the settlement 'ravaged'. He sent a message, warning 'if an English ship of war does not arrive here soon, more murders will take place', to the British South Atlantic commander in Rio de Janeiro who despatched HMS *Challenger*. On 7 January 1834 Lieutenant Henry Smith, appointed Officer Commander of East Falkland Island, stepped ashore with six Marines.

Smith, who had volunteered for the Navy in 1810, had enjoyed a moderately distinguished war service. He had specific instructions to keep the British flag flying over the Falklands, for which he was given an allowance of seven shillings in addition to naval half-pay. He was just in time to save the colonists huddled on Hog Island, who had lived largely on seabirds' eggs, from further attack. The Union Jack was hoisted while *Challenger* provided a 21-gun salute.

Smith and his men set after the Rivero mutineers. They combed the Eastern islands on horse and foot, relying on informants and dogged pursuit. Rivero, meantime, was negotiating with the master of the US ship *Antarctic* the sale of a fat cow and six steers. Smith heard of the deal from a missionary but Rivero vanished. His escape did not last long: his hiding place was betrayed by friends seeking amnesty and he surrendered to Smith. There was no further violence.

Rivero and five fellow renegades were sent in chains to Rio de Janeiro and then on to London. A court there refused to accept a trial because of confusion over whose jurisdiction the crimes came under. The Argentinian Government had already lodged a strong protest over the British occupation of the Malvinas and Britain did not want to spark further complaints about abuse of Rivero's human and legal rights. To avoid further antagonism the Rivero party was quietly shipped back across the Atlantic and put ashore at Montevideo later that year. The murder and carnage they had inflicted on unarmed men was forgotten. The Commander-in-Chief in Rio, Rear-Admiral Sir Graham Eden Hamond, conceded, 'It is a very slovenly way of doing business.'

Smith, meanwhile, was left virtually unaided to make the islands both secure for Britain and self-sufficient so they would not be a drain on the Crown. That task he set about with gusto, raising potatoes and corn, taming cattle and horses, cultivating and improving soil, repairing shelters vandalized by American and British sealers. By the time he was recalled he had built up stockpiles of supplies and seeds, and 350 tame cattle for slaughter. He had also made the Crown 4,200 Spanish dollars by the sale of 850 hides.

The Falklands formally became a British overseas colony in 1841. Argentina offered to accept that provided a previous loan was cancelled. The offer was declined and the islands have been in dispute ever since, with tragic consequences in 1982. The British taxpayer has shouldered the burden.

THREE

The Flagstaff War, 1845–6

'Opening the doors of a monster furnace'

The Maori was arguably the Victorian soldier's most formidable foe, and one he never properly beat. Yet the story of campaigns in the stinking mud and dense jungles of New Zealand, as fierce as any, is now an almost forgotten chapter in the forging of an Empire.

The first Maori War on North Island erupted four years after New Zealand became a colony. It was, absurdly, sparked by the destruction of a flagpole but there was nothing comical about the way the natives fought. The British forces expected to subdue a band of naked, undisciplined savages. Instead they faced a sophisticated warrior class, as disciplined as any Empire troops and often better equipped with more modern firearms. Instead of hit and run skirmishes and mopping up operations against defenceless villages the British repeatedly found themselves laying siege to strong, intricate fortresses complete with gun emplacements, rifle pits and bomb shelters. It was in part a throwback to medieval siege warfare, in part a foretaste of the trenches in a later, bigger war.

The British fighting men quickly recognized an equal adversary and their journals lack the sneering contempt for natives found in other colonial wars. Despite instances of cruel torture and possible cannibalism the historian Sir John Fortescue could later write: 'The British soldier held him in the deepest respect, not resenting his own little defeats, but recognising the noble side of the Maori and forgetting his savagery.'

*　*　*

It was 800 years since the Maoris, a Polynesian people, had discovered *Aotearoa*, the land of the long, white cloud. In that time they had developed, through tribal disputes over land and honour, a fast and furious form of warfare. Fleet-footed warriors, armed with spears or clubs edged with razor coral, would charge straight through the enemy, striking only one blow and running on to another. The crippled enemy would be finished off by those coming behind. In a rout one man, if he were fast enough, could stab or club ten or more. To counter such raiding tactics the tribes built complex fortifications on hilltops, surrounded by ditches, palisades and banks. Over 4,000 such sites have been found in modern times, each providing evidence of communal defence and organized labour among forty tribes whose total population was somewhere between 100,000 and 300,000. The French explorer Marian du Fresne who sailed into the Bay of Islands in 1772 wrote: 'At the extremity of every village and on the point which jutted furthest into the sea, there was a public place of accommodation for all the inhabitants.'

Captain James Cook's 1777 journals described a fertile land of spectacular beauty inhabited by natives who, while aggressive, were intelligent and willing to trade. By the turn of the century European and American traders and whalers were using the Bay of Islands on the northern peninsula as a base. The settlement of Kororareka became a rowdy frontier town, a place of grog-shops, gambling dens and at least one brothel where pretty native girls exchanged their charms for liquor. It was known as the hell-hole of the Pacific. The Maori tribes traded extensively with the incomers and grew rich in the twin benefits of civilization – alcohol and modern firearms. The Colonial Office in London finally shook itself out of torpor and in 1840 the Union Flag was hoisted above the town, shortly before the rest of New Zealand came under the Crown.

The Maoris were – and remain – a tribal people with a strong sense of honour, of respect for the family, of a mystical sense of oneness with their land. Children were taught that the land was sacred and that an insult must always be avenged. One proverb ran: 'The blood of man is land.' They were happy to trade with the white man but trouble flared when the Europeans began, slowly at first, to buy up, settle and fence off the ancient Maori homelands. More settlers flooded in. Land sharks from Sydney persuaded some chiefs to sell at rock bottom prices, creating a norm. It is a sickeningly familiar story of avaricious newcomers playing on the naive greed of individual chiefs at the expense of all.

The Colony's new Lieutenant-Governor Captain William Hobson set out in 1840 to defuse an explosive situation. He decreed that no land could be bought from the Maoris except through the Crown. He called a meeting of the chiefs at Waitangi and proposed a treaty in which they would cede their sovereignty to the British Queen in return for guarantees that they would retain undisputed possession of their remaining lands. Among the chiefs to speak in favour was Hone Heke Pokai of the Ngaphui. He argued that the only alternative was to see their strength sapped by 'rum sellers'. Five hundred chiefs signed the treaty.

A band of adventurers calling themselves the New Zealand Company had meanwhile established themselves near Wellington and declared that the treaty was not binding on them. After disputes over who owned what Hobson set up a land commission to investigate competing claims between the Company and the tribes. In July 1843 the Company clashed with two major chiefs, Te Rauparaha and his nephew Te Rangihaeata, over a slab of land just across the Cook Strait on South Island. Warriors harassed a survey team led by Captain Arthur Wakefield. The officer foolishly tried to arrest the two chiefs but in a confused mêlée succeeded only in shooting dead Te Rangihaeata's wife. The enraged warriors took a terrible revenge and when the skirmish was over nineteen Englishmen and four Maoris were dead.

In the Colony's new capital of Auckland the Governor believed that the massacre had been provoked. The settlers, however, demanded military protection and Hobson sent 150 men from the North and further reinforcements from New South Wales. The tension quickly faded and there was no more bloodshed around Wellington. The reinforcements were sent back to Australia after missionaries complained about their drunkenness and fornication.

In the Bay of Islands the slaughter of the Englishmen had a profound impact on the mind of Hone Heke. He was a renowned warrior by birth and experience, in his mid-thirties, described by one officer as 'a fine looking man with a commanding countenance and a haughty manner'. He was not as heavily tattooed as other chiefs and had a prominent nose and a long chin. Like many of his people he was a Christian convert, having renounced youthful slaughter to train at Henry Williamson's mission station. Although he had backed British rule at Waitangi he had since become disillusioned. The new government encouraged the whalers to find new ports and trade with the Maoris subsequently declined. Customs duties on those ships calling into port replaced the native tolls. The living standards of his people suffered. American and French traders, jealous of British annexation, told Heke that the Union Flag represented slavery for natives and he began to see the flagstaff above Kororakeke township as a sign that the British intended stealing all tribal lands. It became an obsession with him. When Heke heard of the massacre in the south he asked: 'Is Te Rauparaha to have the honour of killing all the *pakehas* (white men)?'

In July 1844 he raided Kororareka to take home a Maori maiden living shamefully with a white butcher. The woman had previously been one of Heke's servants and at a bathing party on the beach she referred to him as a 'pig's head'. Almost as an afterthought a sub-chief cut down the flagstaff. His bloodless action triggered a bizarre charade. A new pole was erected by the garrison, now reinforced by 170 men of the 99th Lanarkshire Regiment sent from Australia. Heke cut it down. Another replaced it, only to be chopped down a third time. The matter became a test of wills when Governor Hobson died and he was replaced by Captain Robert Fitzroy, better known now as the captain of the *Beagle* during the voyage of Charles Darwin. He ordered a taller and stronger pole to be erected – an old ship's mizzen mast – defended by a stout blockhouse.

Fitzroy was particularly angered when Heke called on the United States Consul for support and later flew an American ensign from the stern of his war canoe. Between the toppling of the various poles the dangerous idiocy on both sides was almost ended several times. Heke guaranteed to replace the poles and protect British settlers. Fitzroy agreed to abolish the unpopular Customs charges which had hit Maori trade. But on the other side of the globe a House of Commons select committee chaired by Lord Howick, the future Earl Grey, decided to reinterpret the Treaty of Waitangi. They argued that the Maoris had no rights at all to the vast hinterland of unoccupied lands and urged that they should automatically fall to the Crown. The committee's report also criticized the 'want of vigour and decisions in the proceedings adopted towards the natives'. The implicit threat of a breached treaty was passed to the Maoris by helpful missionaries.

At dawn on 11 March 1845 Heke struck with unprecedented savagery. An officer and five men digging trenches around the blockhouse were swallowed by a flood of slashing, stabbing natives. As the troopers died the flagstaff was toppled. At the same time two columns of Maoris attacked the township below to create a diversion. Sailors and Marines guarding a naval gun on the outskirts fought hand to hand with cutlass and bayonet, pushing the attackers back into a gully before themselves being forced back with their officer severely wounded and their NCO and four men dead. Troops in another blockhouse overlooking the main road exchanged fire with the attackers, as did civilians and old soldiers manning three ship's guns. Around 100 soldiers held the Maoris back as women and children were ferried out to the sloop *Hazard* and other ships anchored in the bay, including the US warship *St Louis*, an English whaler and Bishop Selwyn's schooner. Heke remained on Flagstaff Hill, satisfied with his day's work and not too anxious to press home the attack on the settlement if it meant too many casualties among his own men. Uncoordinated and half-hearted fighting continued throughout the morning, periods of eerie silence being shattered by bursts of gunfire and screams and the crackle of wooden buildings put to the torch. At 1 p.m. the garrison's reserve magazine exploded and fire spread from house to house. The cause of the conflagration was later attributed to a spark from a workman's pipe. Although Heke had shown no sign of attacking the township, save as diversionary tactics, the senior officer present, Naval Lieutenant Philpotts, and the local magistrate decided on a full evacuation of all able-bodied men. The remaining defenders scuttled for the ships and the safety offered by *Hazard*'s 100 guns.

The Maoris rampaged through the burning buildings, sparing two churches and the house of the Catholic Bishop Pompallier. When looters carried off some of the Bishop's household goods Heke threatened to have the thieves executed. Only a 3-mile hike by the Bishop to Heke's camp, after which he urged a pardon as enough blood had been shed, saved them. The Anglican Bishop Selwyn protested when Maoris calmly and soberly began to roll away casks of captured spirits. He said: 'They listened patiently to my remonstrances and in one instance they allowed me to turn the cock and allow the liquor to run upon the ground.' Other clergymen who later went ashore were well treated. Six settlers who returned to rescue valued possessions were not. They were butchered on the spot. In all 19 Europeans were killed and 29 wounded. The ships took the survivors to Auckland. To the Maoris, despite the reported loss of thirty-four of their own men, the white men had been humbled and the flagstaff, symbol of their pride and greed, lay in the mud.

* * *

Lieutenant-Colonel William Hulme, a sensible, no-nonsense veteran of the Pindari campaigns in India, was ordered to put down Heke's rebellion and avenge the deaths. He had under his command a small force of the 96th Regiment reinforced by a detachment of the 58th Rutlandshires, newly arrived from New South Wales: 8 officers and 204 men under Major Cyprian Bridge. Bridge was thirty-six, a literate and able commander whose journals contain a straightforward account of the frustrations and setbacks of the ensuing campaign. When they anchored in the Bay of Islands the regimental band played 'Rule Britannia' and 'The King of the Cannibal Islands'.

They were met by 400 friendly Maoris under Tamati Waaka Nene, a devoted ally of the British who saw Heke's revolt as a shameful breach of the oaths sworn at Waitangi. Hulme took great pains to ensure his troops knew the difference between hostile and friendly natives and promised severe punishment for any soldier who harmed a Maori ally. Many of the soldiers were uneducated country lads who were astonished at the natives' appearance: tall, fine-looking men, their bodies heavily tattooed, their cloaks richly decorated with feathers and pelts, their ears pierced with bone, ivory and brass. They were even more astonished to be joined by a few *pakeha* Maoris, white men who had 'gone native'. These included the colourful ex-convict Jackey Marmon from Sydney who boasted about the tribal enemies he had slaughtered in battle and eaten at cannibal feasts.

The flagstaff was quickly re-erected over the smoking and deserted settlement and Hulme's main force set off for the mouth of the Kawakawa river to deal first with Pomare, a local chieftain who had sided with Heke. The ships anchored off Pomare's *pa*, or fortress, which stood on an imposing headland. Pomare was arrested under a white flag. The chief was taken aboard the *White Star* and persuaded to order his men to surrender their arms. The soldiers looted the empty *pa*, found a few rifles, and burnt it to the foundations. It was an inglorious start to the campaign but those thirsty for blood soon found it.

Hulme's next target was Heke's own *pa* at Puketutu near Lake Omapere 15 miles inland and close to the friendly Waaka's stronghold. The infantry were augmented by seamen, Royal Marines and a three-pounder battery under Lieutenant Egerton RN. They were ferried up the Kerikeri river and then marched in good order through increasingly foul weather. Fierce and sudden downpours added to the misery.

Hulme sent some men ahead with local guides to report on Heke's position. They found a strong fortress with three rings of palisades made musket-proof with flax leaves. The outer barricades were angled to pour crossfire on any assailant. Between each line of defence were ditches and low stone walls which offered shelter from bombardments. Maori riflemen manned ditches behind the outer palisade, their guns pointing through loopholes level with the ground.

Despite a lack of adequate artillery Hulme decided to attack the next morning and his force advanced to within 200 yards of the *pa*. Three storming parties were prepared. Hulme's plan depended on a terrifying bombardment by Lieutenant Egerton's rocket battery. The Maoris believed the rockets would chase a man until he was killed. The truth soon proved rather more laughable. Egerton's first two rockets sailed hopelessly over the *pa*, carving crazy patterns in the still air. The third hit the palisades with a thunderous noise but when the smoke cleared there was virtually no damage. The remaining nine proved to be just as useless.

British troops and Waaka's Maoris were closing with the enemy when 300 hostile natives, led by Heke's ally Kawiti, dashed from concealment behind them, brandishing axes and double-barrelled guns. The men of the 58th turned around, fired and counter-charged with fixed bayonets. Kawiti's men later complained bitterly that the soldiers came at them with teeth gritted and yelling unseemly and unnecessary curses. The counter-charge shattered the enemy but the rest of the British force was then hit by a sally from the *pa* itself. Vicious hand-to-hand fighting around the Maori breastworks eventually drove the defenders back behind their palisades.

It was stalemate. British musket fire was ineffective against the strong defences, the rockets were used up, and Hulme realized that without heavier artillery he had no hope of a breakthrough. There was more inconclusive fighting amid nearby swamps but the first real battle of the war was over, a low-score draw. The British pulled back with 14 killed and 38 wounded. Their enemy, by British accounts later disputed, lost 47 killed and 80 wounded, including Kawiti's two sons. The Maori's own flagstaff, carrying the Union Jack as an act of ironic derision, remained aloft above Heke's *pa*. The British returned, in low spirits, to their ships.

Hulme returned to Auckland leaving Major Bridge in command. Bridge decided to attack a *pa* up the Waikare river rather than allow his men's morale to sink even lower, kicking their heels in the Bay of Islands. His men barely rested, he set off with three companies of the 58th. At the river's mouth they switched to small boats, manned by sailors, with Auckland Volunteers and friendly Maoris as guides. Bridge intended to make a surprise attack and the raid was well planned at the start. The outcome was a messy if largely bloodless shambles.

Several miles upstream the boats stuck fast on mudflats. Small bands of soldiers were disembarked among scenes of noisy confusion. Some became bogged down in the mire, while Maori allies engaged in a running fight with natives who sallied from the forewarned *pa*. Waaka's men got the best of the skirmish but the enemy simply disappeared into the thick brush. The soldiers entered an empty *pa* and found only 'pigs, potatoes and onions.'

The *pa* was destroyed and, with the river's tidal waters high enough to float the boats off the mud, Bridge withdrew his tired and grimy force. There had been no British casualties but two of Waaka's men were dead and seven wounded. In less careful hands Bridge's expedition could have been a disaster. Misled by dubious guides and faulty intelligence Bridge had nevertheless behaved with calmness and common sense. Such qualities were not noticeable in the new commander of the British forces.

* * *

The forging of the British Empire saw its share of bone-headed bunglers. Colonel Henry Despard of the 99th is widely regarded as a prime example of that species. Despard received his first commission in 1799. His military thinking was stuck fast in the conventions of the Napoleonic era. He saw considerable action in India before taking up peacetime duties as Inspecting Officer of the Bristol recruiting district. In 1842 he took command of the 99th Lancashires, which had recently arrived in Australia. In New South Wales he outraged local civilians by snubbing a ball held in his honour, by blocking public roads around the barracks, and by having his buglers practise close to their homes. Despard insisted that his new command abandon its modern drill manuals and return to those of his younger days. The result was parade ground chaos which did not augur well for an active campaign. He was prone to apoplectic rages and rarely, if ever, listened to either advice or complaints. He had no doubts about his own abilities. Now aged sixty, it was thirty years since he had seen active service. He arrived in Auckland aboard the *British Sovereign* on 2 June with two companies of his regiment. Major Bridge's journal describes his mounting frustration at the arrogance and short-sighted stubbornness of his new CO.

Despard gathered his disparate force to move on the Bay of Islands. It was the biggest display of Western armed might yet seen by fledgling New Zealand: 270 men of the 58th under Bridge, 100 of the 99th under Major E. Macpherson, 70 of Hulme's 96th, a naval contingent of seamen and marines, 80 Auckland Volunteers led by Lieutenant Figg, to be used as pioneers and guides, all supported by four cannon – two ancient six-pounders and two twelve-pound carronades.

At Kororareka Despard was told Heke had attacked Waaka's *pa* with 600 men but Waaka had beaten them off with his 150 followers. Heke had suffered a severe thigh wound. Despard decided to launch an immediate assault on Heke's new *pa* at Ohaeawai, a few miles from Puketutu, despite foul winter weather which was turning tracks into quagmires.

During a miserable 12-mile march the cannon became stuck fast in the mud and the little army took shelter at the Waimate mission station. Despard was reduced to ranting fury. Waaka arrived with 250 warriors but Despard said sourly that when he wanted the help of savages he would ask for it. Luckily for him his Maori allies did not hear of the insult, and Despard must have changed his mind and the Maoris joined the British.

Most of the force stayed at the station for several days until fresh supplies were brought up. On 23 June, at 6 p.m., an advance detachment came within sight of Heke's *pa*. Alert Maoris swiftly opened fire but the scrub was up to 10 feet high and the skirmish line escaped slaughter, carrying back eight wounded comrades. The enemy marksmen retired to the safety of their stockade. The main British force caught up and encamped in a native village 400 yards from the *pa*. Waaka and his men occupied a conical hill nearby to protect the British from a flanking attack. A breastwork and battery for the guns was swiftly erected.

Heke's new *pa* was twice as strong as that at Puketutu. It was built on rising ground with ravines and dense forest on three sides, giving the defenders an easy route for supplies, reinforcements or withdrawal. There were three rows of palisades with 5-foot ditches between them. The outer stockade was 90 yards wide with projecting corners to allow concentric fire. The defenders, standing in the first inner ditch, aimed through loopholes level with the ground. The ditch was connected by tunnels to bomb shelters and the innermost defences. It was a sophisticated citadel and was well stocked. The Maoris had a plentiful supply of firearms and ammunition, some of it looted, the rest bought or bartered before the uprising. Four ship's guns were built into the stockade.

Officers, *pakeha* Maoris and native allies warned Despard of the fort's great strength. So too did Waaka. All such doubts were rebuffed. After one angry exchange Waaka was heard to mutter in his own language. Despard insisted on a translation. He was told: 'The chief says you are a very stupid person.'

The British battery opened fire at 10 a.m. on the 24th but 'did no execution'. The Maoris returned fire and until nightfall there was no let-up in the fusillades of shell, ball and grape. Bridge wrote that much shot burst within the *pa* and 'I fancy they must have lost many men.' The following day the bombardment continued but the flax-woven palisades made it impossible to see how much damage was done to the defences. The shot was simply absorbed by the flexible material.

Despard decided that only a night attack would breach the stockade. He prepared storming parties with ladders ready for 2 a.m. He ordered the construction of flax shields, each 12 feet by 6, to be carried by advanced parties. That night Sergeant-Major William Moir said: 'The chances are against us coming out of this action. I look upon it as downright madness.' Luckily for everyone concerned a storm in the early hours prevented the night attack. The following morning the flax shields were tested and to the surprise of few the shot passed clean through. After that demonstration few soldiers trusted Despard's ability and some doubted his sanity. Another of his bright ideas involved firing 'stench balls' at the enemy. That also flopped.

The physical condition of the British deteriorated as rain poured incessantly on their crude shelters. Their clothing was reduced to rags, in some cases barely recognizable as uniforms. There was no meat and little flour but a gill of rum was given to each man every morning and evening. Taken on an empty stomach and supplemented by local native liquor the result could be devastating. Drunkenness, a problem throughout the New Zealand campaign, increased. There were fights over the firm-limbed and cheerful native women.

A new battery was built closer to the *pa*'s right flank and quickly came under hot fire which wounded several soldiers and killed a sailor. An enemy raid was beaten off but the guns were withdrawn. Despard demanded that HMS *Hazard*'s 32-pounder be dragged from the mouth of the Kerikeri. After a brutal and agonizing haul it was manhandled into position halfway up the conical hill by twenty-five sailors. Despard planned to attack as soon as the big gun had softened up the outer defences. He told Bridge: 'God grant we may be successful but it is a very hazardous step and must be attended with great loss of life.'

On the morning of 1 July the enemy launched a surprise attack on Waaka's camp on the conical hill, aimed at killing Waaka himself. A number of Heke's men moved undetected through the forest and emerged behind the camp. Caught off guard, the native allies streamed down the hill with their women and children. Despard, who had been inspecting the cannon, was engulfed in the panic-stricken human tide. He ran into the British camp and ordered a bayonet charge up the hill. The soldiers came under crossfire from hill and *pa* but by then only a few of the enemy were left on the summit and it was quickly retaken. The attackers withdrew when they realized that Waaka had escaped.

Despard was driven to characteristic fury by his ignominious sprint into his own camp. His temper must have deepened with ill-concealed sniggers from the ranks of his tattered army. He decided to attack that same afternoon. The bombardment had clearly failed to leave gaping holes in the outer stockade and the enemy appeared unscathed. His troops and their Maori allies regarded a frontal assault as suicidal. But no appeals to caution would persuade him otherwise. The scene was set for tragedy.

His plan, such as it was, was to focus the attack on a narrow front at the *pa*'s north-west corner, which Despard believed had been damaged by the cannonfire. Twenty Volunteers under Lieutenant Jack Beatty were to creep silently to the outer stockade to test the defenders' alertness. They were to be quickly followed by 80 grenadiers, some seamen and pioneers under Major Macpherson, equipped with axes, ropes and ladders to pull down sections of the wood and flax perimeter. Behind these were to be 100 men under

Major Bridge who were expected to storm through the gaps into the *pa*. They in turn were to be backed by another wave of 100 men under Colonel Hulme. Despard planned to lead the remainder of his force into the stockade to mop up and accept the enemy surrender.

The Maori plan of defence was less elaborate. One unknown chief called out: 'Stand every man firm and you will see the soldiers walk into the ovens.'

At 3 p.m. precisely on a bright and sunny afternoon the storming parties fell in. There was no surprise. They charged in four closely packed ranks, according to regulations, with just twenty-three inches between each rank. Fifty yards from the *pa* the men cheered. Corporal William Free later wrote: 'The whole front of the *pa* flashed fire and in a moment we were in a one-sided fight – gun flashes from the foot of the stockade and from loopholes higher up, smoke half hiding the *pa* from us, yells and cheers and men falling all around. A man was shot in front of me and another was hit behind me. Not a single Maori could we see. They were all safely hidden in their trenches and pits, poking the muzzles of their guns under the fronts of the outer palisades. What could we do? We tore at the fence, firing through it, thrusting our bayonets in, or trying to pull a part of it down, but it was a hopeless business.'

The Maoris allowed Macpherson's men to come within yards of the stockade before opening up with every gun they had. Their blistering fire was later described as like 'the opening of the doors of a monster furnace'. Only a handful of men with axes and ladders reached the barrier. Despard, supported by Bridge, later claimed that the Auckland Volunteers had dropped flat at the first fusillade and would not budge thereafter. The surviving men at the foot of the stockade scrabbled hopelessly at the interwoven flax, firing at the occasional glimpse of a tattooed face within.

Bridge was no slacker and he and his men were soon caught in the same murderous fire. He wrote: 'When I got up close to the fence and saw the way it resisted the united efforts of our brave fellows to pull it down and saw them falling thickly all around, my heart sank within me lest we should be defeated. Militia and Volunteers who carried the hatchets and ladders would not advance but laid down on their faces in the fern. Only one ladder was placed against the fence and this by an old man of the Militia.'

Despard watched the bloody shambles from the rear earthworks. Even he realized that such slaughter was worthless. A bugle call to withdraw was ignored in the heat of battle. A second call finally penetrated the brains of men conditioned to believe that retreat in the face of half-naked savages was unthinkable. The survivors dragged as many of their wounded comrades back with them as was feasible. Some soldiers returned two or three times through a hell of musket smoke and shot to rescue their mates. One wounded man was shot dead as he was carried on the back of Corporal Free, who dropped the corpse and carried another soldier to safety. Hulme's supporting party covered the retreat well with substantial fire which kept enemy heads down. But the casualties suffered in just seven minutes of fighting were fearful. At least one-third of the British attackers had been killed or wounded. Three officers, including Beatty, were dead and three injured. Some 33 NCOs and privates were killed and 62 wounded, four of whom later died. The Maori lost ten at most. Bridge wrote: 'It was a heartrending sight to see the number of gallant fellows left dead on the field and to hear the groans and cries of the wounded for us not to leave them behind.'

The jubilant Maori defenders rejected a missionary's flag of truce and during that long night held a noisy war dance. The dispirited troops huddled in their camp and mourned their dead and tended their casualties and wondered who would be next. They were tormented by the 'most frightful screams' from within the *pa* screams which haunted all who heard them.

Two more days passed before Heke allowed the British to collect their dead from the charnel field in front of his stockade. Several corpses had been scalped, beheaded and otherwise horribly mutilated. One, that of a soldier of the 99th, bore the marks of being bound, alive, by flax. His thighs had been burnt and hacked about. A hot iron had been thrust up his anus. The soldiers knew then the source of those terrible nocturnal screams.

Despard prepared to break camp and return, beaten, to Waimate. Waaka and his chiefs, hungry for loot, persuaded him to stay a few more days at least. More shot and shell for the cannon were brought up and the bombardment of the *pa* resumed. It continued ceaselessly for another day. That night dogs began howling within the *pa*. It was a sign, according to Maori allies, that the enemy were withdrawing. The following morning, while the British slept, Waaka's warriors slipped into the fort and found it empty. They looted everything, including weapons taken off the dead. They condescended to sell the outraged British the odd sack of potatoes. Everything else they kept for future trade. One officer missing in action, Captain Grant, was found in a shallow grave near the palisade. Flesh had been cut off his thighs, apparently for eating.

After inspecting the *pa*'s defences from the inside Bridge wrote: 'This will be a lesson to us not to make too light of our enemies, and show us the folly of attempting to carry such a fortification by assault, without first making a practicable breach.' The *pa* was burnt but there was no sense of victory. Heke had simply moved to build a new stronghold elsewhere, no great inconvenience. Too many lives had ended for no good reason.

* * *

Despard reported back to Auckland, anxious to pin blame for the carnage on anyone but himself, and taking with him the men of the 99th and 96th. Major Bridge was left in command of the 58th at Waimate. Back pay for all ranks was sent up to the mission station. Much of it was spent immediately on drinking and gambling by men anxious to blot out the horror and shame of Ohaeawai. Inevitably discipline grew lax. One private, a veteran who had been wounded at Puketutu, was accidentally shot dead on guard duty. The dead man, 22-year-old Private Ingate had been a Norfolk farm labourer before enlisting. His comrade Sergeant Robert Hattaway wrote: 'He allways told us he would never Be shot by a Maorie. It was true for him. . . .' One man was caught in the act of stealing rum from a barrel. But he was a family man and Hattaway, a newly promoted NCO, spared him a court martial. Another offender was not so lucky: an American Volunteer with a record for insubordination, he was found guilty at a drumhead court martial of cursing the British flag and immediately suffered fifty lashes.

Bridge tried to keep his men occupied by building stout earthworks and other defences around the camp as protection against an enemy elated by victory. These were almost complete when Despard returned, bubbling with his now familiar petulance. He said it was demeaning to build ramparts to defend a well-armed European force against a 'barbarian enemy'. He ordered the earthworks flattened. Bridge held his tongue but clearly believed that the slaughter in front of Heke's *pa* had taught his commander nothing.

Governor Fitzroy, anxious to get Heke to make peace, ordered the 58th withdrawn to camp among the ruins of the Kororareka settlement. His willingness to talk, and his careful conduct in the run-up to the Flagstaff War, were severely criticized in Auckland and London. He was accused of being over-protective of the interests of the aborigines and 'losing sight of the fundamental principles, that indulgence may be abused and forebearance misconstrued'. In his own defence he later wrote: 'Had I not treated them with consideration, and had not the public authorities been very forebearing, the destruction of Auckland and Wellington would have been matters of history before this period. An overpowering multitude have been restrained hitherto by moral influence.' He added: 'My object always was to avoid bringing on a trial of physical strength with those who, in that respect, were overwhelmingly our superiors; but gradually to gain the necessary influence and authority by a course of scrupulous justice, truth and benevolence.' Such sentiments did not match the thirst for revenge and Fitzroy was recalled.

His replacement was 34-year-old Captain George Grey whose early service in Ireland had convinced him that the frontiers of the civilized world must be widened to provide fresh opportunities for the poor, landless and hungry. He had served in Australia, and on the *Beagle*, and had impressed his superiors with his efficiency, diligence and courage. His remit was to punish the natives, end an increasingly costly conflict and bring 'financial and commercial prosperity' to the settlements. He told the Legislative Council: 'You may rely that my sole aim and object shall be to settle upon a sure and lasting basis the interests of yourselves and of your children, and to give effect to her Majesty's wise and benevolent desire for the peace and happiness of all her Majesty's subjects in this interesting portion of her empire, and upon which the regards of so large a portion of the civilized world are now anxiously fixed.' He also warned the settlers that he would, if necessary, use his full powers under martial law and aim to secure in any peace the 'freedom and safety' to which the aborigines were also entitled.

Grey decided he must see the troubles in the North at first hand. On reaching the Bay of Islands he made some attempts to parley with Heke and Kawiti. But becoming impatient, he demanded an immediate reply to Fitzroy's earlier peace moves. Further delays gave him the excuse to mobilize his forces. Those forces were now impressive as Grey had brought with him considerable reinforcements from Auckland. They included 563 officers and men of the 58th, 157 of the 99th, 42 Volunteers, 84 Royal Marines, a 313-strong Naval Brigade, 450 friendly Maoris – a total of just over 1,600 men plus six cannon including two 32-pounders, four mortars and two rocket tubes.

Between 7 and 11 December the British decamped and moved up the Kawakawa river to attack the 'Bat's Nest' – Kawiti's *pa* at Ruapekapeka, strongly built on a densely wooded hillside. Again drunkenness impeded the expedition. A few 'old troopers' were over-ready to blast away at anything that moved in the woods . . . wild pigs, birds and shadows. The advance faltered as bullocks, heavy carts and cannon stuck fast in the liquid mud. Christmas was celebrated by the men in teeming misery relieved only by rum. Officers noted in the diaries that the Christian natives showed great devotion in observing the day and attending mass.

By the 27th several cannon were in position overlooking the Bat's Nest and opened fire. Despard heard worrying reports that Heke had left his own refuge and was marching with 200 men to join Kawiti at Ruapekapeka. After exasperating delays which drove Despard into deeper rages, the big 32-pounders were dragged up to join the first cannon in a formidable battery 1,200 yards from the enemy *pa*. The Maoris, however, were well entrenched and their defences included solid underground bunkers which resisted every shot. After each bombardment they simply emerged to repair the little damage done to the stockades. Despard later wrote:

'The extraordinary strength of this place, particularly in its interior defences, far exceeded any idea I could have formed of it. Every hut was a complete fortress in itself, being strongly stockaded all round with heavy timbers sunk deep in the ground . . . besides having a strong embankment thrown up behind them. Each hut had also a deep excavation close to it, making it completely bomb-proof, and sufficiently large to contain several people where at night they were sheltered from both shot and shell.'

Most of the British column, including several cannon and mortars, were still on the trail. Bridge complained that the bombardment was pointless until all men and guns were in place and deployed to concentrate intensive fire on the *pa*'s weakest points. Instead Despard, bizarrely and to conserve ammunition, would not allow more than one cannon to be fired at any one time. Bridge wrote: 'How deplorable it is to see such ignorance, indecision and obstinacy in a Commander who will consult no one . . . and has neither the respect nor the confidence of the troops under his command.' He added: 'Our shot and shell are being frittered away in this absurd manner instead of keeping up constant fire.'

The lacklustre bombardment continued until another battery was built closer to the *pa*, protected by 200 men. This was swiftly attacked in a sortie from the stockade and the enemy were beaten back with only light casualties on either side. The fiercest fighting was between Kawiti's men and friendly Maoris on 2 January. In a confused and fragmented fight in thick brushland the enemy were driven back into the *pa*. From its barricades they taunted the white men, daring them to charge as they had done at Ohaeawai.

The siege dragged on through wet days and nights. Conditions in the British lines grew appalling. Disease and exposure put many men out of action. Reinforcements and fresh supplies were lost or abandoned on forest trails. Drunkenness continued and could not be curbed. Ammunition was wasted not just by Despard's tactics but by jittery soldiers who saw a foe behind every bush. Men and officers who had proved themselves ready to be heroes if given the chance sank into despair at their shabby leadership.

On 8 January eighty of the enemy were spotted leaving the safety of the *pa* and disappearing into the forest. Governor Grey urged

Kawiti by message to send away the Maori women and children as he did not want them hurt in the bombardment. The British received more reports of small bands of warriors melting away with their families. The determination of those who stayed within the *pa* was stiffened, however, by the arrival of Heke, although he had with him only sixty men and not the reported 200.

At last, on 10 January, the entire British arsenal was in position – the 32-pounders, smaller cannon, mortars, rockets and small arms. They opened up a ferocious crossfire on the *pa*'s outer defences. Despard wrote: 'The fire was kept up with little intermission during the greater part of the day; and towards evening it was evident that the outer works . . . were nearly all giving way.' The stockade was breached in three places. Despard was almost delirious with excitement and prepared for a frontal assault. A Maori ally, guessing his intent, shouted at him: 'How many soldiers do you want to kill?' Other chiefs told Grey that an attack now would result in the same waste of life as at Ohaeawai, but if they waited until the following day the enemy would have fled. Grey listened, agreed and overruled Despard, much to the colonel's irritation.

On the following morning Waaka's brother William and a European interpreter crept up to the stockade. They heard nothing from inside except for dogs barking. The *pa* seemed deserted and a signal was given to the nearest battery. A hundred men under Captain Denny advanced cautiously with native allies. Some men pushed over a section of fencing and entered the *pa*.

It had not been deserted. The explanation for the eerie silence was rather more strange, and rich with irony. It was a Sunday and the Christian Maoris, the majority of the defenders including Heke, had assumed that Christian soldiers would never attack on the Sabbath. Heke and the other believers had retired to a clearing just outside the far stockade to hold a prayer meeting. Only Kawiti and a handful of non-Christian warriors were left inside when the British stepped through the breach.

Too late Kawiti realized what was happening. He alerted the Maoris outside and threw up hasty barricades within the *pa*. He and his men managed spasmodic fire against the incoming troops. Heke and the rest of the garrison made a determined effort to re-enter the *pa*, firing through holes in its walls created earlier by the British cannon. Several British troops were killed and wounded but more troopers and native allies swarmed into the *pa*. In a topsy-turvy engagement the defenders became the attackers and vice versa within moments. Heke and the rest were pressed back to the tree-line of the surrounding forest and sheltered behind a natural barrier of fallen tree trunks.

A party of sailors, seeing action for the first time, charged this position and were shot down one by one. Three sergeants – Speight, Stevenson and Munro – and a motley band of soldiers, seamen and natives emerged from the *pa* and threw themselves at the makeshift barricade with such fury that the enemy withdrew deeper into the forest. The sergeants were each commended in orders and when, in 1856, the Victoria Cross was instituted Speight's name was put forward for a retrospective citation. The award was vetoed on the grounds that no VCs could be awarded for action prior to the Crimean War.

Kawiti and his stragglers fought their way clear of the *pa* and joined Heke and the other fleeing warriors in the forest. The battle was over. The British had succeeded because the Christian Maoris were more scrupulous in observing the faith than the Christian Europeans. It may have been farcical but it was not a bloodless victory. Friendly Maori casualties were not recorded but the British lost 12 men killed, including 7 sailors from HMS *Castor*, and 30 wounded, two of whom later died. Despard claimed that the enemy's losses were severe, including the deaths of several chiefs, but he was keen to add to the scale of the victory. He explained that a body count was not possible as the Maoris 'invariably carry off both killed and wounded when possible'. Ruapekapeka was burnt. The First Maori War, an unconventional campaign, had ended in a suitably offbeat way.

* * *

Despard did not enjoy popular acclaim for the victory. He exaggerated the scale and ferocity of the final battle in his despatches, although his reference to 'the capture of a fortress of extraordinary strength by assault, and nobly defended by a brave and determined enemy' contains some truths. His bravado cut no ice with the colonial press who lambasted him mercilessly. An editorial in *The New Zealander* condemned his 'lengthened, pompous, commendatory despatch'. Puzzled, angered and saddened by such barbs Despard left for Sydney on 21 January. Bridge noted caustically that his departure was 'much to the satisfaction of the troops'. Despard retained command of the 99th until he was seventy but, happily for the men under him, never saw active service again. He died, a major-general, in 1858. He never, according to contemporaries, understood the ill gratitude he received. Many of his men, grieving for fallen comrades, would quite happily have hanged him.

Heke and Kawiti first tried to join up with their former ally Pomare but that wily old brigand knew which way the wind was now blowing and refused them aid. The rebel chiefs knew that the time to talk peace had now come. They opened negotiations with Governor Grey using their enemy Waaka as a go-between. Kawiti was prepared to agree peace for ever more. Heke, however, insisted that a Maori flagstaff should be erected alongside the Union Jack. Grey for his part rescinded all threats to seize Maori lands and granted free pardons to both chiefs and their men. He promised that all concerned in the rebellion 'may now return in peace and safety to their houses; where, so long as they conduct themselves properly, they shall remain unmolested in their persons and properties'. Her Majesty, he said, had an 'earnest desire for the happiness and welfare of her native subjects in New Zealand'.

The clemency shown by the Governor was not due to humanitarian feelings. Grey needed to bring the Northern troubles to a swift conclusion because his troops were desperately required in the South to deal with violence which had flared up around Wellington. The causes were familiar: a new clash between the land-hungry New Zealand Company and the chief Te Rangihaeata, whose earlier massacre of white men had so encouraged Heke.

The murders, sieges and inconclusive campaigning that followed in the South cannot properly be regarded as part of the Flagstaff War. Rather it was a foretaste of the bloodshed that was to follow with little let-up for another two decades. But in the North, around Auckland, the peace treaties were honoured by both sides and the occasional violent clash was small in scale.

Most of the 58th, which had done the lion's share of the fighting, left for Australia after a riotous ball organized by the grateful ladies of Auckland. Bridge and almost every other officer in the regiment were mentioned in despatches for their bravery, although these were the days before medals for courage were awarded. Bridge, after a long wait, took command of the regiment, at the age of fifty-one. His military career after New Zealand was uneventful. He retired in 1860, broken-hearted by the death of his second wife and of all but one of his many children. He died in Cheltenham in 1885, aged seventy-eight.

Corporal Free, who had written such a vivid account of the attack and tragedy at Ohaeawai, stayed in New Zealand and served with the Rifle Volunteers. He died, aged ninety-three, in 1919. Sergeant William Speight, the hero of Ruapekapeka, may not have been awarded a Victoria Cross but years later he was granted a Meritorious Service Medal and a £10 annuity for that action; he was the only veteran of the first Maori War to receive the medal. He stayed with the 58th and retired, a staff sergeant-major, in 1858 to settle permanently in New Zealand.

In 1848 Heke, who never fully accepted British rule, caught consumption which left him defenceless against other illnesses. He died two years later at Kaikohe, aged only forty. His one consolation was that the hated British flagstaff was not re-erected in his lifetime. Kawiti was converted to Christianity. He too died young, in 1853. It is likely, although impossible to prove, that had they lived longer both chiefs would have been leaders in the uprisings that devastated New Zealand through the 1850s and 1860s. The pattern set in their initial war was repeated with rising casualties and greater atrocity on either side.

The Maoris were never truly beaten but neither could they win against the tide of colonists who flooded to their green land. By 1858 there were 60,000 incomers, a decade later 220,000. The British Government decided they now sufficiently outnumbered the natives to be able to take care of themselves and the last troops were withdrawn in 1870. The wars were over but random butchery continued in isolated glades. Overwhelming numbers and disease crippled and contained the daring Maori. But the spark of resistance did not die out. In 1928 an anonymous Maori wrote: 'We have been beaten because the *pakeha* outnumber us in men. But we are not conquered or rubbed out, and not one of these *pakeha* can name the day we sued for peace. The most that can be said is that on such and such a date we left off fighting.'

FOUR

The Jamaica Rebellion, 1865

'Skin for skin, the iron bars is now broken . . .'

On 7 October 1865 at Morant Bay in Jamaica a black boy was convicted of assaulting a woman of his own impoverished village; the magistrate fined him two shillings with twelve shillings and sixpence costs. Over the next few days almost twenty officials and policemen, half of them white, were butchered and another thirty-five wounded. Within five weeks 439 blacks were killed in a merciless campaign of revenge. No fewer than 354, including seven women, were shot or hanged after summary courts martial, often on the flimsiest evidence. Fifty prisoners were killed without trial by soldiers and sailors, 25 by Maroons and 10 in other ways. Around 600 more were viciously whipped, some – including women – with cat-o'-nine-tails 'enhanced' with twisted wire. Fifty lashes were the norm but some received 100. Over a thousand homes were destroyed by fire.

It is one of the worst stains on the history of the British Empire. Military might, religious fervour and blind fear combined together in a campaign of racist vengeance rare even by the cruel standards of the age. For many the possession of a black face in the wrong place was punishable by death. The origins lay in slavery, land rights and injustice. White arrogance and perceived black ignorance played their part in fanning a little local difficulty into such obscene over-reaction.

As insurrections go it was a small affair but it sparked a heated debate at a time when the queen and her privileged subjects prided themselves on the benevolent and paternal nature of British rule. A *Times* editorial said: 'Though a flea bite compared with the Indian Mutiny, it touches our pride more and more in the nature of a disappointment.' And the horrific aftermath divided public opinion bitterly. The *Annual Register*, not noted for its liberal interpretation of events, recorded: 'On the one side it is alleged that the severest measures were imperatively necessary to save the colony from destruction, and on the other it is clamorously asserted that a riot was mistaken for a revolt, and that the course pursued by the authorities implicates them in the crime of murder.'

* * *

Jamaica is another island paradise whose history has been shaped by the cutlass and the musket, in blood, anguish and greed. Lush and temperate, with mangrove, 200 species of orchids and a plateau of grey limestone, its central position in the Caribbean has always attracted adventurers.

It is alleged, but hotly contested, that the West 'discovered' the island when Columbus landed in 1494. During the Spanish conquest and settlement the native Arawak Indians were completely exterminated and Negro slaves were imported to replace them in the fields. Oliver Cromwell's commanders expelled the Spanish in 1660 after a five-year campaign and the slaves, whose blood had mixed with the Spaniards' and who were now called Maroons, took to the mountains. They fought to the end of the eighteenth century in fruitless attempts to gain their independence.

Under nominal English rule Jamaica became a haven for buccaneers, with planters and merchants supplementing their incomes with a bit of piracy. After a decade of mayhem the buccaneers were suppressed and in 1672 the Royal Africa Company, with its monopoly of the English slave trade, turned Jamaica into a huge market in human beings. In 1692 an earthquake destroyed much of the capital Port Royal and Kingston was built to replace it. French and Spanish invasions were beaten off in 1782 and 1806. During this period Jamaica was, for the white planters, at the peak of its prosperity. The sugar and coffee trade was booming and there were more than 300,000 slaves at work. But the abolition of the slave trade in 1807, together with a drop in sugar prices when the war ended, ended the boom days.

The 1833 Emancipation Act was a further blow although planters were paid £19 per slave compensation. Many of the freed slaves left the plantations to become hill farmers, leaving behind a chronic shortage of cheap labour. Sugar prices dropped further with the scrapping of tariff protection. White farmers faced an uncertain and impoverished future. Many went bust and between 1804 and 1854 the number of sugar estates fell from 859 to 330 and sugar production dropped by a half. Although their real grievance was with the British the planters, and therefore the Jamaican authorities, blamed the alleged laziness of the black labourers who had chosen to stay behind. Resentment against the blacks rose.

So, too, did the whites' terror of a black insurrection. A 1760 uprising resulted in the execution of one rebel by slow burning, starting with his feet, while two more were starved to death in a public hanging cage. The 1831 Baptist rebellion, encouraged by preachers, left hundreds of slaves dead.

After emancipation, renewed fears had been stoked by the creation of the black-ruled Republic of Haiti during the Napoleonic Wars. An abhorrence of blacks, possibly explained psychologically by fear of the unknown coupled with guilt at their exploitation, was reflected in the literature of the day. Sir Richard Burton compared Africans with animals; the explorer Sir Samuel Baker said they were 'not to be compared with the noble character of the dog'. The horrors of the Indian Mutiny remained fresh in British minds, as will be seen later. And Jamaica's Governor, Edward John Eyre, writing later to justify his actions, blamed the Press and rabble-rousers for leading an 'ignorant, excitable and uncivilised population' into 'rebellion, arson, murder'.

In 1860 Jamaica saw the 'Great Revival' centred on the local Baptist and Methodist Churches. Religious revivalists and political agitators made natural allies. White pastors and nonconformists had long supported their poor black congregations but the discontent expressed in church services developed overtly political overtones. One commentator reported 'fanaticism, disorder, delusion'. Foremost among the agitators was a self-ordained Baptist minister, George William Gordon, the illegitimate son of a rich white planter and a black mother. He was born about 1820 and his father, Joseph Gordon, was an attorney who represented absentee-owned sugar plantations, earning enough to be able to buy several estates in the foothills north of Kingston. He eventually rose to be an Assemblyman and Custos of St Andrews but offered little care, support or even acknowledgement to either his son or the mother. The young George taught himself to read and at eighteen he was well regarded as a bright, popular charmer with a gift for public speaking. He was also deeply religious but became dissatisfied with the structures of existing churches. He established a store selling local produce and was praised as a 'man of ready business habits'. The business prospered and by 1842 Gordon was reckoned to be worth £10,000. He sent his twin sisters to be educated at his expense in England and France, and married Lucy Shannon, the white daughter of an Irishman. Meanwhile his father's fortunes declined badly. Although his father had ignored him since infancy – George was never allowed into the family home – Gordon sorted out the elder man's tangled financial affairs. He paid off debts on his father's estates and helped support him and his 'legitimate' white family. Gordon was described as 'a man of princely generosity and unbounded benevolence'. He also never forgot his mother. On one occasion, with tears in his eyes, he pointed to a grassy mound in a copse and said: 'My mother is buried there. She was a Negro and a slave, but she was a kind mother to me and I loved her dearly.'

During the 1850s Gordon, by now the owner of several estates, was elected to the House of Assembly where he championed the cause of peasant farmers and newly emancipated slaves. He was for a period the owner of the *Watchman* newspaper, became a magistrate and helped found the Jamaica Mutual Life Assurance Society. He set up an independent Baptist Church and preached from his own chapel in Kingston. In both religion and politics he was renowned as a gifted orator. Never an advocate of armed rebellion or the overthrow of white rule, he did, however, get involved in petty disputes within his parish of Morant Bay. One, over the conduct of a fellow-magistrate, led to his removal from the bench. Another, involving his application to be a churchwarden, would have devastating personal consequences. He was rejected by the local Custos, Baron von Ketelhodt, on the grounds that he was not a member of the Church of England. Gordon challenged the Custos twice through the courts. He lost both times and costs were awarded against him. A third trial was pending in October. The Jamaica Commission later reported: 'All these proceedings had produced considerable irritation in the western part of the parish, and especially among the members of the Native Baptist Communion to which Mr Gordon belonged.'

It was hardly surprising that he clashed, often and vehemently, with the new Governor, Edward John Eyre. Eyre arrived in 1862 as stand-in for Captain Charles Darling, who was on leave in England. After two years Darling was dispatched to Australia and Eyre was confirmed as his successor.

Prior to his arrival in Jamaica, Eyre had a decent record as a colonial administrator among native people. As a young man he was a noted explorer of Australia. He was appointed Protector of Aborigines and was later promoted Lieutenant-Governor of New Zealand. In the West Indies he was Protector of Indian labourer immigrants in Trinidad and was again promoted Lieutenant-Governor, this time of the Leeward Islands. But he was also stubborn to the point of blindness and a fervent Anglican who hated dissenters, particularly Baptists, which perhaps makes it easier to understand his antipathy towards Gordon and his followers. Clinton Black wrote: 'He associated only with the white ruling class to whose interests he was sympathetic. He was incapable of mixing with and understanding the black population, nor did he understand the multi-racial future that was the only possible one for Jamaica.'

Eyre regarded Gordon as a dissenter and a rabble-rouser. He had Gordon removed from his post as a member of the St Thomas Vestry because he dared to complain about the filthy conditions in the local gaol, where a vagrant was found dying, unattended, in a latrine. In January 1864 Gordon berated the Governor in the Assembly, declaring: 'If we are to be governed by such a Governor much longer, the people will have to fly to arms and become self-governing.' This was the typical rhetoric of the Assembly: outside Gordon advocated peaceful protest only.

The general grievances of the blacks were simple. The planters' pay was too little. The labourers felt that little had been gained from their emancipation save the right to live in poverty wherever they chose. They resented the different treatment afforded the Indian immigrants brought in to fill labouring shortages. The slightly more affluent black 'free settlers', who farmed the 'backlands' unwanted by the whites, demanded they should be allowed to do so rent-free. And the judicial system was designed to keep blacks poor and whites in power. Hardship and misery had been increased by cholera and smallpox epidemics during the 1850s which had killed 40,000. A severe drought ruined many plantations, unemployment rose and the outbreak of the American Civil War in 1861 raised the price of food previously imported in large quantities. By 1865 the position of the black population was desperate and they submitted a petition to the queen, begging for assistance, relief from poverty and permission to cultivate some Crown lands.

Governor Eyre would have none of it. He spoke for the planters when he later insisted: 'I know of no general grievance or wrong under which the Negroes of this colony labour. Individual cases of hardship or injustice must arise in every community, but, as a whole, the peasantry of Jamaica have nothing to complain of. They are less taxed, can live more easily and cheaply, and are less under an obligation to work for subsistence than any peasantry in the world . . . They ought to be better off, more comfortable, and more independent than the labourers of any other country. If it is not so, it is due to their own indolence, improvidence and vice, acted upon by the absence of good example and of civilising influences in many districts, and by the evil teaching and evil agencies to which I have already referred.' He said earlier: 'There is scarcely a district or a parish in the island where disloyalty, sedition and murderous intentions are not wholly disseminated, and in many instances openly expressed.'

Acting on Eyre's reports the Secretary of State replied to the blacks' petition, saying that the solution to their problems lay with themselves. He urged them to work 'not uncertainly or capriciously, but steadily and continuously at the times when their labour is wanted, and for so long as it is wanted'. It was in their own 'industry and prudence' that their salvation lay. There was no word of sympathy. It amounted to a victory for Governor Eyre and he had 50,000 copies of the document, known as the Queen's Letter or the

Queen's Advice, pasted up across the island in July. The blacks, who revered Her Majesty as 'Missis Queen', were astounded. Many did not believe that she would write such a thing and regarded it as a forgery by the Governor. Gordon said she was 'too noble-hearted to say anything unkind even to her most humble subjects'. Others saw it as the death of their last hope of fair treatment. Some even feared it would be followed by a return to slavery.

Secret black militias were formed under the guise of Church activities, weapons were stolen, night exercises were organized and inflammatory sermons spoken from pulpits. Three weeks before the inevitable tragedy secret oaths were sworn at various meeting houses. The free farmers were the most vociferous. In the summer of 1865 one rent collector was told: 'Soon we shall have the lands free and then we shall have to pay no rent.' Most especially in the parish of St Thomas-in-the-East, Morant Bay, grew the 'vague expectation' that in future their rents would be lifted.

And it was a dispute over land rent which sparked the conflagration. A black farmer called Miller refused to pay rent on an estate near Stony Gut, not far from Morant Bay. He, like other occupiers, argued that the land belonged to the queen and should therefore be rent-free. He lost the case but stayed on the estate. He was summoned to appear before magistrates at Morant Bay on a charge of trespass. Local tempers were running high.

* * *

Paul Bogle, a prominent black agitator, was uneducated but driven by a belief that he had been chosen by God to bring justice to his people. Gordon had made him a deacon and he had raised enough cash in his district to build a large native Baptist church. In August he had walked 50 miles to Spanish Town at the head of a deputation to lay complaints to the Governor. Eyre refused to see him and Bogle, much embittered, walked all the way back. He was an admirer and political supporter of Gordon and advocated that blacks should set up their own system of courts, constables and justice.

On market day, 7 October 1865, Bogle led a group of up to 150 men, armed with sticks and preceded by a musical band, who marched to the court-house square at Morant Bay. They were determined that Miller should not be sentenced by the chief magistrate. That official was Baron von Ketelhodt, who was still in dispute with Gordon, and who was regarded by the free settlers as one of Eyre's toadies in the pocket of the white plantocracy. The touchpaper was lit even before Miller's case was heard. When the young boy was fined for assault a man called Geoghegan shouted that he should pay the fine but not the costs. Uproar ensued, the court was suspended and constables were ordered to seize the heckler. In a dispatch sent to Kingston the following Monday von Ketelhodt reported: 'A man having been ordered into custody on account of the noise he was making in the court-house, a rush was made by a body of men . . . and the man rescued from the hands of the police, one of whom was left with his finger broken, and several others beaten and ill-treated. In consequence of this outrage, warrants were issued yesterday against 28 individuals who had been identified, and the warrants placed today in the hands of six policemen and three rural constables for execution.'

The police officers set out on the morning of Tuesday, 10 October, to arrest Paul Bogle who, like Miller, lived at Stony Gut, a Negro settlement 5 miles away. They found Bogle in his yard but, having first insisted that the warrant be read out, he refused to be arrested. A confederate known as Captain Grant yelled 'Turn out, men.' At this signal more than 300 men armed with cutlasses, sticks and pikes rushed from a chapel where Bogle regularly preached and from an adjoining cane field. The police were swiftly and easily over-powered. Some were severely beaten. Three were held prisoners, two of them in handcuffs, but were released several hours later when they swore on a Bible produced by Bogle that they would join their captors. The oath said they must 'join their colour' and 'cleave to the black'.

According to one of the freed policemen Bogle said that he planned to attend a vestry in Morant Bay the following day. It was said, allegedly by others, that they intended to 'kill all the white men and all the black men that would not join them'. The threat was reported that night to von Ketelhodt and the Inspector of Police at Morant

Bay. The Custos summoned the Volunteers of the parish to assemble and wrote to the Governor asking for military aid.

A document signed by Bogle and others was later used as proof that the original rioters were planning armed insurrection from the start. It read: 'Skin for skin, the iron bars is now broken in this parish, the white people send a proclamation to the Governor to make war against us, which we all must put our shoulder to the wheels and pull together . . . Every one of you must leave your house, takes your guns, who don't have guns take your cutlasses down at once . . . blow your shells, roal your drums, house to house take out every man, march them down to Stony Gut, any that you find in the way takes them down, with their arms; war is at us, my black skin war is at hand from to-day to to-morrow. Every black man must turn at once, for the oppression is too great, the white people are now cleaning up they guns for us, which we must prepare to meet them too. Chear men, chear, in heart we looking for you a part of the night or before daybreak.'

On Wednesday 11 October the Vestry, consisting of elected members and *ex officio* magistrates, assembled in the courthouse at noon and conducted their normal business. The Clerk of the Peace wrote: 'About three o'clock in the evening, and while the vestry was still sitting, a band of music was heard, and shortly after, from about 400 to 500 men appeared, armed with sticks, cutlasses, spears, guns and other deadly weapons.' They first ransacked the police station in search of firearms, taking some old muskets with fixed bayonets. By the time they reached the main square a guard of Volunteers had been hastily called and faced them uneasily across the dusty square. Baron von Ketelhodt stood on the courthouse steps and appealed to them to go home peacefully. When the crowd cried 'War' he read the Riot Act. While he was doing so, stones began to fly and one struck Captain Hitchins, commander of the Volunteers, on the temple. The Captain, having been given authority by the Custos, ordered his men to open fire. A volley rang out and several in the crowd fell dead or dying. There was later a dispute over whether the firing began *before* the stones were thrown but black civilian witnesses later attested that some women had sparked the bloodshed by throwing stones they had collected in their baskets.

The crowd reacted with fury to their casualties. They leapt on the Volunteers, some of who surrendered their weapons, before they could reload. Some of the Volunteers were swiftly battered or hacked to death, while others fled. A bugler guarding a bag of ammunition was harpooned with a fish spear. Most were forced back into the courthouse. Some escaped immediately through the rear windows but the majority were trapped inside. The building was pelted with stones and hit by musket fire, which the defenders returned. Cries were heard from outside: 'Go and fetch fire,' and 'Burn the brutes out.' The adjoining schoolhouse was set ablaze and the fire rapidly spread to the court-house roof. As the timbers began to cave in the defenders were compelled to leave the burning building under cover of darkness. Some were quickly butchered. Baron von Ketelhodt was 'murdered in the most brutal and savage way', according to the Clerk. The eyes and hearts of some men were torn out and 'the women showed themselves to be even more cruel than the men'.

Eyre's subsequent self-justifying dispatch to London claimed that the rebels cut out the tongue of the Island curate of Bath, the Revd V. Herschell, while he was still alive and 'an attempt is said to have been made to skin him'. Lieutenant Hall of the Volunteers 'is said to have been pushed into an outbuilding, which was then set on fire, and kept there until he was literally roasted alive'. Eyre added: 'Many are said to have had their eyes scooped out; heads were cleft open and the brains taken out. The Baron's fingers were cut off and carried away as trophies by the murderers. Indeed the whole outrage could only be paralleled by the atrocities of the Indian Mutiny. The only redeeming trait being that, so far as we could learn, no ladies or children had as yet been injured.'

During the night more people were dragged out of hiding places and slaughtered. Charles Price, a Negro and former Assembly minister, who 'had by his abilities raised himself to a position in life superior to that of most of his race', was among the victims. Some rioters argued that he should be spared because he was black and 'we have orders to kill no black, only white'. Another voice said: 'He has a black skin but a white heart.' He was beaten to death. According to Eyre's official report he was 'ripped open and his entrails taken out'. Others were beaten and left for dead.

A few escaped. Four men were released unharmed: a Maroon, two doctors and another man who pretended to be a doctor and swore to Bogle he would never again dress a white man's wound. There were now 18 dead and 21 wounded, and the town was held by the rioters overnight. The town gaolers were forced to open the cells and fifty-one prisoners were released to join Bogle's 'army'. Stores were ransacked and a large quantity of gunpowder taken. An attempt was made to force the door of the magazine where over 300 stands of arms were stored, but the door stood firm. Bogle returned to Stony Gut and held a service in his chapel during which he gave thanks to God that 'he went to this work, and that God had succeeded him in this work'.

* * *

For three days Bogle's insurgents, numbering up to 2,000, rampaged around the countryside up to 30 miles from Morant Bay. A party of 200 armed men with bayonets mounted on sticks went first to Coley, a few miles from Stony Gut, and threatened fellow blacks with instant death if they did not join them. Estates in the Plantain Garden District were attacked. The small town of Bath was taken bloodlessly, most of the inhabitants, white and black, having fled to the bush. The insurgents themselves fled on hearing the horn of the Maroons who, at the request of the resident magistrate, relieved the town. (Bogle and his lieutenants made several attempts to recruit the Maroon communities to their cause, without success.) At one estate in Blue Mountain Valley, a few miles from Bath, about fifty men attacked the book-keeper who died of his wounds shortly afterwards. Only the intervention of the black overseer prevented the book-keeper's son being murdered also.

The Amity Hall estate, also near Bath, was attacked by 400 men. Mr Hire was killed and his son left for dead. Two more white men, including the stipendiary magistrate Mr Jackson, were severely wounded. When Jackson told the attackers he was a friend of Gordon's they 'rubbed him up and brought him back to life'. They set fire to Dr Crowley's bed, but on hearing he was a doctor they put it out. In most of the attacks the chief targets appear to have been judicial men and officials. Nevertheless the general cry heard across the parish was 'Colour for Colour'. The widow of one victim heard one of his killers say: 'We must humble the white man before us. We are going to take the lives of the white men, but not to hurt the ladies.'

More estates were plundered but in each case the whites had escaped well in advance, in some cases aided by their black labourers. At Hordley estate more than twenty women and children hid in woods for a day and two nights. The proprietor of Whitehall estate, Mr Smith, died of exposure after fleeing into the bush. Most of the houses were ransacked and fine furniture smashed. An exception, the subsequent inquiry was told, was the Great House at Golden-grove, one of the most valuable estates in the east of the island. One black leader said: 'That is to be saved for Paul Bogle – those are the orders of the general.' Throughout the short-lived insurgency many of the blacks were convinced that they would retain possession of the estates. The crops were left untouched and one of Hire's killers said: 'We are going down river to take up the crops.'

Bogle himself remained at Stony Gut the day after the massacre, giving sermons to his men in the little chapel and later drilling them. His followers were told that 'this country would belong to them, and that they were about getting it, to take possession, that they had long been trodden under sandals'. The following day Bogle was seen at the head of 200 men marching up the valley from Chigoe Foot Market. On the 15th he was at Mount Labanus Chapel with 100 men when the alarm was given that soldiers were coming.

Governor Eyre had not been idle. As soon as he received the initial plea for martial aid at Spanish Town he sent off expresses to Major-General O'Connor at Kingston urging 100 men be made ready for embarkation, and to the senior naval officer at Port Royal requesting that a man-o'-war should be made available to convey them to Morant Bay. This was done and the troops arrived at Morant Bay in time to prevent a second attack. News of the courthouse massacre was sent back to Eyre together with intelligence that insurgents were marching up the valley along the Yallahs River. More troops of the West India Regiment were sent to Morant Bay and Port Antonio where military posts were established. A party of the 6th Regiment was ordered to march from Newcastle towards Blue Mountain Valley to block the insurgents. Seamen and marines were landed at Morant Bay from the warship *Wolverine* to back up the regular troops. Maroons were deputized to protect Port Antonio as well as Bath.

Eyre called an emergency meeting of the Privy Council which unanimously agreed to declare martial law. Under law this required a Council of War which duly met on the morning of the 13th. It decided that martial law should cover the whole of the county of Surrey, which included the parish of St Thomas-in-the-East, but should not cover Kingston town. The proclamation referred to 'grievous trespasses and felonies' and declared that: 'Our military forces shall have all power of exercising the rights of belligerence against such of the inhabitants of the said county . . . as our military forces may consider opposed to Our Government, and the well-being of Our loving subjects.'

Meanwhile the swift deployment of troops by sea successfully contained the insurgents within the neighbourhood of St Thomas-in-the-East, preventing the spread of disturbances to other parts of the island. Troops were sent also to Linstead, 14 miles from Spanish Town, and Volunteers, pensioners and special constables enrolled to protect Kingston.

On the 13th Captain Luke left Morant Bay with 120 men of the 1st West India Regiment and marched overnight to Bath. At the Rhine estate they found nearly 100 women and children who had taken refuge from nearby estates. Many of them had suffered 'severe privations' and some were severely wounded. They were escorted back to Port Morant en route to Kingston. That same day, near the burnt-out courthouse, a black man, said to have been a rebel who had allegedly threatened the life of the Collector of Customs, was tried by court martial and immediately executed. The revenge had begun.

Also on the same day a party of fifty marines and sailors under naval Lieutenant Oxley advanced from Morant Bay westwards to Easington. Two Negroes seen running ahead on the road were shot dead after ignoring a command to stop. A prisoner was shot dead while trying to escape. A fourth man was tried and executed at Easington.

Ninety men were sent from Morant Bay to Bogle's village at Stony Gut. Shots were fired from within one of the huts. The culprit was fired on but escaped, although he was wounded. The troops held prisoner a black woman to act as a cook, tethering her with a cord tied around her wrist. The next day they burnt the chapel and eight cottages.

More parties were sent out by Brigadier-General Nelson, commander at Morant Bay. His orders were 'to make excursions in any direction supposed to be advantageous, care being taken that any firing of huts and buildings be not carried to excess'. At Leith Hall a prisoner accused of firing on Volunteers was tried and executed. Near Harbour Head a black, Charles Mitchell, was tied to be flogged for minor offences. Before the lash descended evidence was given that he had attacked a white man. He was tried on the new charge and executed in his own back yard.

Governor Eyre was himself busy, touring the military posts on the *Wolverine* and another ship, the *Onyx*. Although George Gordon was in Kingston throughout the disturbances Eyre reported that everywhere he found 'unmistakable evidence' that the member of the House of Assembly 'had not only been mixed up in the matter, but was himself, through his own misrepresentation and seditious language, addressed to the ignorant black people, the chief cause of the whole rebellion'. He told Edward Jordan, the Island Secretary, 'All of this has come of Mr Gordon's agitation.' Eyre obtained, under oath, a deposition that Gordon had sent seditious material to the rebel leaders through the Kingston post office – an unlikely way to foment revolt. The deposition contradicted itself, saying that the material was printed, and later that it was in Gordon's handwriting. Eyre ordered the Kingston Custos to issue a warrant for his arrest but Gordon, after a short time in hiding, surrendered himself to General O'Connor. He was placed on the *Wolverine* and sent to Morant Bay for trial. Eyre followed shortly afterwards with supplies of arms and ammunitions for the loyal Maroons.

Eyre received legal advice that Gordon should face a civilian court, but the Governor was determined he should be tried under martial law, a conviction and harsh sentence being certain. Eyre said in his report to London: 'Great difference of opinion prevailed in Kingston as to the policy of taking Mr Gordon. Nearly all coincided in believing him to be the occasion of the rebellion, and that he ought to be taken; but many of the inhabitants were under considerable misapprehension that his capture might lead to an immediate outbreak in Kingston itself. I did not share this feeling. Moreover, considering it right in the abstract, and desirable as a matter of policy, that whilst the poor black men who had been misled were undergoing condign punishment, the chief instigator of all the evils should not go unpunished, I at once took upon myself the responsibility of his capture.'

There was then, and remains, a question mark over the legality of his arrest in Kingston, where martial law did not apply, and his trial at Morant Bay, where it did. Eyre got around that by arguing that if it could be proved he took an active part in the insurrection such niceties were irrelevant. Moreover his house was within the parish where the blood was spilt. But most importantly the white planters feared his eloquence on behalf of the black peasantry, and any black victim was now reckoned fair game in their bloody thirst for vengeance. They accused him of calling for an end to white rule and the setting up of a New West India Republic. Gordon denied both charges, pointing to his record as a magistrate and Assemblyman and to his support for constitutional reform rather than armed revolt. It didn't do him any good. On 20 October Gordon was hastily tried before a military court consisting of two naval lieutenants and an ensign. He was found guilty of high treason and sedition, and inciting murder and rebellion. The court martial refused, however, to impose the death penalty. Their decision was overruled by Eyre who ordered that execution should follow almost immediately.

While awaiting his death Gordon wrote a letter to his wife which, when published in newspapers, aroused great sympathy. He said: 'I do not deserve this sentence, for I never advised or took part in any insurrection. All I ever did was to recommend the people who complained to seek redress in a legitimate way; and if in this I erred or have been misrepresented I do not think I deserve the extreme sentence. It is, however, the will of my Heavenly Father that I should thus suffer in obeying His command, to relieve the poor and needy, and to protect, as far as I was able, the oppressed . . . I certainly little expected this.' He told his wife: 'You must do the best you can, and the Lord will help you, and do not be ashamed of the death your poor husband will have suffered. The judge seemed against me; and from the rigid manner of the court, I could not get in all the explanation I intended. The man Anderson made an unfounded statement . . . but this testimony was different from the deposition. The judges took the former and erased the latter. It seemed that I was to be sacrificed. I know nothing of the man Bogle. I never advised him to the act or acts which have brought me to this end.'

Less than an hour after his trial finished, Gordon was hanged, with eighteen others, from a beam in front of the burnt-out courthouse. Their bodies were thrown into a trench behind the building.

* * *

Soldiers, militia and Maroons were meanwhile fully engaged in suppressing the insurrection. All searched for Paul Bogle, who had not been seen since the 15th when he had been dissuaded by one of his most active associates from attacking a body of soldiers coming over a grassy brow at Fonthill. On his failure to attack his followers became panic-stricken and fled. The fighting, what there had been of it, was over and the butchery just begun.

More troops were sent from Barbados and the Bahamas to reinforce the local troops. Another detachment was dispatched from Halifax but returned without landing. Two Spanish warships were sent from Cuba, but they were not required.

In the Blue Mountain Valley district 120 men of the 6th Regiment under Colonel Hobbs occupied the Monklands coffee estate and used it as a base to make incursions to small villages up and down the valley. Hobbs reported that 'numbers of the rebels had come in, having thrown away their arms, seeking protection; and though worthy of death [I have] shrunk from the responsibility of executing them, without first receiving the General's or Governor's wishes respecting them.' Major-General O'Connor's aide replied that he 'can give you no instruction, and leaves all to your own judgement'. A few days later, however, Hobbs received new instructions in which the Major-General, according to the Commission, 'expressed a hope that the Colonel would deal in a more summary manner with the rebels, and on no account to forward prisoners to Kingston.'

Hobbs did not need to be told twice. During the march to Chigoe Foot Market eleven prisoners were tried and executed. At the market were twenty-seven prisoners who were named as known rebels by a man who claimed he had been pressed into their company by Bogle. They were all sentenced to death. Sixteen were taken to their home village of Coley a few miles away where 14 were shot and 2 escaped. Nine others were shot and their bodies hung up in a chapel at nearby Fonthill. Hobbs also ordered a local 'Obeah' man, or witch-doctor, Arthur Wellington, be taken back to Monklands for trial. Following Wellington's inevitable sentencing, Hobbs decided to demonstrate the nonsense of the widespread belief that an Obeah's supernatural powers made him invulnerable. Wellington was marched up the valley side overlooking the estate to a spot visible from the surrounding heights. He was killed by volley and a constable, acting without authority, sliced his head off. Body and head were buried in a trench at the bottom of the hill but during the night heavy rain washed the head out of the grave and carried it along a stream, after which it was stuck on a pole. Hobbs released several prisoners, charged with minor offences, who told him they would never believe in an Obeah again. He was not lenient with suspected rebels. At Monklands nine men were made to kneel in a line above the trench that was to be their mass grave and then shot dead. One prisoner, showing signs of life, was allegedly hit on the skull with a pickaxe.

More than thirty were shot at the estate before the soldiers left and Major-General O'Connor informed the initially reluctant Hobbs 'I am much pleased by your adopting a decided course with regard to captured rebels.' The Commission later reported: 'During the operations along the Valley about eight casual deaths were inflicted without authority, on inhabitants in some of the villages. Some of these persons were shot in their houses, others while passing in the road, and two of the number were infirm persons, incapable of resistance. One of the two latter, however, suffered through a mistake. About 493 dwellings, situate in the various settlements of this district, were destroyed by fire during the same time.'

Hobbs went in hot pursuit of Paul Bogle, burning and killing as he went. In a dispatch to Major-General O'Connor he said: 'I found a number of special constables, who had captured a number of prisoners from the rebel camp. Finding their guilt clear, and being unable to either take or leave them, I had them all shot. The constables then hung them up on trees – eleven in number. Their countenances were all diabolical, and they never flinched in the very slightest.' He moved on to Stony Gut and utterly destroyed Bogle's 'vile and rebellious settlement'. Guiding him reluctantly was Bogle's unnamed valet: 'a little fellow of extraordinary intelligence; a light rope tied to the stirrups, and a revolver now and then to his head, causes us thoroughly to understand each other . . .'. The valet, Hobbs reported, 'knows every single rebel in the Island by name and face, and has just been selecting the captains, colonels and secretaries out of an immense gang of prisoners just come in here, whom I shall have to shoot tomorrow morning.'

On the 23rd Paul Bogle was caught by a party of Maroons and sent to Morant Bay for court martial. He chatted calmly to his captors and denied that Gordon had in any way incited violence. After the briefest of trials, he was hanged from the arch of the ruined courthouse. The slaughter of his followers, congregation and neighbours continued.

On the north side of the island at Port Antonio 54 prisoners were tried under martial law and executed. In the neighbouring villages 217 cottages were burnt. At Morant Bay and the Plantain Garden River district 194 were so executed, 68 at Monklands and 3 at Up-Park Camp. This 'reign of terror' was overseen by Captain Ramsay the Provost Marshall, a Crimean War veteran who had survived the Charge of the Light Brigade. Samuel Clarke was hanged simply for saying at a public meeting that the 'Queen's Letter' was a lie and Eyre should be recalled. Another black man, while being flogged, had the effrontery to glare at Ramsay full in the eye. The brave captain ordered the flogging to end and had the man hanged instead. Ramsay, almost certainly mad, later committed suicide.

On 17 October Captain Hole reported to HQ: 'On arriving yesterday at Long Bay I found the huts full of plunder. I had every house within a quarter of a mile of the road in which the plunder was found fired, and in doing so upwards of 20 of the rebels were killed.'

Captain Hole marched with 40 men of the 6th Regiment and 60 men of the 1st West India Regiment under Ensign Cullen the 20 miles from Port Antonio to Manchioneal. Their orders from Brigadier-General Nelson were 'not to leave the line of march in search of rebels, nor to allow prisoners to be brought in except leaders of rebels; and that those who were found with arms were to be shot'. Twenty-five blacks were killed along the line of march by 'casual shooting'. At his destination Hole immediately organized the execution of a man called Donaldson who was found with the horse and saddle of the murdered Mr Hire. A prisoner who had been released from Morant Bay gaol by the insurgents was shot for possession of a cutlass and another for carrying a flask of powder. During eleven days of courts martial at Manchioneal 33 people were sentenced and shot. Many more were flogged for trivial offences, twenty of them women. Hole argued that there were no prison cells for women who were often described as the 'principal plunderers'.

Three soldiers of the 1st West Indians were separated from their unit guarding a plantation. They returned with two wagon-loads of stolen property taken from Mr Hire and reported to Hole that they had shot ten implicated men. A black soldier of the same regiment who had deserted stopped three constables escorting four prisoners on the road near Long Bay. He took them off the policemen and shot them one by one. Later in the day, on the same road, a man presumed to be the same deserter shot six prisoners as a head constable looked on. Of this incident the Commission noted: 'These ten deaths were attended with such barbarity on the part of the soldier, and such cowardice on the part of the constables and other persons who witnessed what was done without interfering to prevent it, as to call for special notice and condemnation.'

Hole did his utmost to enforce military discipline in his own ranks. Two corporals were demoted for being absent. One soldier was sentenced to seven years' penal servitude for burning homes without orders.

Meanwhile Maroons under the command of Colonel Fyfe had received different orders from Brigadier-General Nelson: 'You are never to molest a woman or child, and you are not to shoot any man who surrenders.' During the operations Maroon detachments killed no more than twenty-five men, the majority in action. Seven were killed in an attack on a rebel makeshift fort at Torrington, and more at a barricade of felled tree trunks on the Stony Gut road.

By contrast the killings of blacks by British troops while on the march was later judged to be indiscriminate and in the face of 'no active resistance'. Blacks were executed on the flimsiest evidence – in one case the accused man had been seen beating a drum – while in some cases condemned men named others in the misplaced hope of a reprieve. One man was executed because, while in Kingston gaol, he had said: 'I have seen too much gun. If it had been in Africa we would have known what to do immediately.'

The Commission put the total number of blacks killed at 439 with more than 1,000 homes burnt, 100 men imprisoned for terms ranging from 6 months to 12 years, and no fewer than 600 flogged. One man was sentenced to fifty lashes and three years' imprisonment for travelling without a pass. Nearly fifty men suffered floggings in one day at Bath alone, and between thirty and forty on other days, until it was stopped by Colonel Fyfe on his return from leading the Maroons. The Commission reported: 'The mode of inflicting the punishment at Bath calls for special notice. It was ordered by a special magistrate, after a very slight investigation, and frequently at the instigations of book-keepers and others smarting under the sense of recent injury. At first an ordinary cat was used, but afterwards, for the punishment of men, wires were twisted around the cords, and the different tails so constructed were knotted.'

At the opening of the Jamaica Chambers, Governor Eyre spoke of a 'most diabolical conspiracy to murder the white and coloured inhabitants of this colony'. He said: 'The valuable lives of many noble and gallant men, who were ornaments to the land, have been sacrificed (while peaceably meeting in the discharge of their duties to the State) by a most savage and cruel butchery, only to be paralleled by the atrocities of the Indian Mutiny.' The rebellion had been 'fairly crushed' within the first week and the district had been scoured to capture and punish those of the guilty 'who had not yet met their just doom'. He went on: 'So widespread a rebellion so rapidly and so effectually put down is not, I believe, to be met with in history, and speaks volumes for the zeal, courage and energy of those engaged in suppressing it . . . One moment's hesitation, one single reverse, might have lit the torch which would have blazed in rebellion from one end of the island to the other, and who may say how many of us would have lived to see it extinguished.' He said that the colony remained 'on the brink of a volcano'. His words were largely for consumption in Westminster and Whitehall, although if he thought they could quell the rising anger and shock at home over the brutality employed in suppression, he was wrong, but they worked well enough in the Jamaica Chambers.

The following day the Legislative Council thanked Eyre for the 'energy, firmness and wisdom with which you have carried the island through this momentous crisis'. The House of Assembly was even more fulsome and passed an address which said, in part, 'We desire to express our entire concurrence in your Excellency's statement that to the misapprehension and misrepresentation of pseudo philanthropists in England and in this country, to the inflammatory harangues and seditious meetings of political demagogues, to the personal, scurrilous, vindictive, and disloyal writings of a licentious and unscrupulous Press, and to the misdirected efforts and misguided counsel of certain miscalled ministers of religion, is to be attributed the present disorganisation of the colony, resulting in rebellion, arson, and murder.' A bill was introduced for abolishing the Constitution and substituting a new one with just one Chamber in which dissent would be discouraged.

In his first dispatch to Edward Cardwell, Secretary of State for the Colonies, Eyre placed great stress on the perceived danger of the insurrection infecting the whole island, thereby justifying his harsh measures. He said: 'We have been singularly fortunate in capturing or shooting a large number of the principal ringleaders in the rebellion, and many of whom were personally concerned in the atrocious butcheries on the 12th of October, at the Morant Bay

Courthouse, or in the subsequent destruction of life and property further to the eastward, as the rebellion extended in that direction. Very many acknowledged their guilt before the execution.' He added: 'It is a remarkable fact that, so far as we can ascertain, the rebels at Morant Bay did not proceed in any considerable numbers to the adjacent districts, but the people of each district rose and committed the deeds of violence and destruction that were done within it. This fact shows how widespread the feeling of disaffection is, and how prepared the people of each parish were to catch the spirit and follow the example of their neighbours. It shows, too, the extreme insecurity which yet exists in nearly all the other parishes of Jamaica, where the same bad spirit prevails. In the lately disturbed districts the rebellion is crushed; in the others, it is only kept under for the present, but might at any time burst into fury.'

Cardwell's initial reaction was to heartily endorse the Governor's actions. In a letter sent from Downing Street on 17 November Cardwell conveyed to Eyre 'my high approval of the spirit, energy, and judgement with which you have acted in your measures for repressing and preventing the spread of insurrection'. Later in the letter he said: 'I entirely agree with you that measures of severity, when dictated by necessity and justice, are in reality measures of mercy, and do not doubt it will appear that you have arrested the course of punishment as soon as you were able to do so. . . .'

A week later, however, Cardwell had received reports of the scale of reprisals and, in particular, Gordon's execution and its doubtful legality. He wrote twice on 23 November demanding from Eyre a fuller explanation of the evidence against the slain insurgents, without which explanation 'the severity would not appear to have been justified'. Of Gordon's case he said: 'I desire also to see it clearly established that he was not executed until crimes had been proved in evidence against him which deserved death; and that the prompt infliction of capital punishment was necessary to rescue the colony from imminent danger . . .'.

* * *

Indignation at the ferocity of the suppression, and in particular the judicial murder of Gordon, led to a heated political debate in England. The statesman John Bright said that the nation 'has never received a deeper wound or darker stain' on its reputation. John Stuart Mill wrote: 'The question was whether the British dependencies, and eventually, perhaps, Great Britain itself, were to be under the government of law or of military licence.'

Eyre had his defenders, including Charles Kingsley, Lord Tennyson and Charles Dickens, who argued that the Governor had acted by the rules of circumstance rather than malice, but the furore grew. Eyre was suspended and recalled to London. A temporary replacement, Lieutenant-General Sir Henry Storks, was sent hastily to Jamaica from Malta, and arrived there before the end of the year. The Government set up a Commission of Inquiry made up of Russell Gurney, MP, QC and Recorder of London, and J.B. Maule who were also dispatched to Jamaica to work together with Storks.

The Commission spent fifty-one days examining 730 witnesses, most of them 'uneducated peasants, speaking in accents strange to the ear, often in a phraseology of their own, with vague conceptions of number and time, unaccustomed to definiteness or accuracy of speech, and . . . still smarting under a sense of injuries sustained'. The Commission concluded that martial law had continued too long after the threat had passed, that the courts martial should have ceased, and the punishments were too severe in cases where the evidence of rebellion was flimsy. The death sentence was 'unnecessarily frequent' and the burning of 1,000 homes was 'wanton and cruel'. They recommended compensation to be paid to those families innocent of crimes whose homes had been burnt. They also expressed distaste at the method of flogging with wire: '. . . it was painful to think that any man should have used such an instrument for the torturing of his fellow creatures'. In general the floggings were 'reckless, and at Bath positively barbarous'.

Their report focused strongly on the trial and execution of Gordon. They found that although Gordon's writings and speeches might have influenced Bogle and other insurgents this was a long way from treason: 'We cannot see any sufficient proof either of his complicity in the outbreak at Morant Bay or of his having been a party to a general conspiracy against the Government.' In other words, Gordon had been wrongly executed.

But overall the Commission praised Eyre for his prompt action and accepted that there had been a planned resistance to lawful authority with roots in disputes over land and rent. Although the rebellion had been initially confined to a small portion of one parish the disorder quickly spread over a large tract. The report said: 'Such was the state of excitement prevailing in other parts of the Island that had more than a momentary success been obtained by the insurgents, their ultimate overthrow would have been attended with a still more fearful loss of life.'

As a result of the Commission's report the Government thanked Eyre for his prompt action in suppressing a revolt that could have consumed Jamaica and spread to other islands. (The Lieutenant-Governor of St Vincent stated that there had been much excitement on his island when reports were received and 'the sympathies of the lower orders were almost universally enlisted in favour of the malcontents'.) But ministers also blamed him for the savage reprisals. The Colonial Secretary, the Earl of Carnarvon, told the Lords: 'Promptitude, courage, fearlessness of responsibility, if not accompanied by a sound judgement on the part of the person who possesses them, become faults rather than virtues . . . The first attribute demanded of a Governor is not only justice but perfect impartiality and the power of rising above panic and the apprehensions of the moment. It is to the fatal want of this quality in Mr Eyre that we may trace at least half of the mischief which arose after the outbreak . . . Much has been said respecting the case of Mr Gordon. It is a most terrible case and one that is indefensible.'

Eyre was charged with murder at the instigation of the Jamaica Committee chaired by John Stuart Mill, but the case was dismissed by local magistrates in Shropshire, where Eyre was living. Lieutenant Brand, the naval officer at Gordon's trial, and Colonel Sir Alexander Nelson who confirmed his sentence, were also charged and committed for trial at Bow Street. The Chief Justice, Lord Cockburn, pressed the prosecution case strongly but a Grand Jury refused to find a true bill against them. In 1868 the case against Eyre was revived and he too was charged at Bow Street, but again a Grand Jury threw it out. The following year a Jamaican called Phillips took out a civil action against Eyre, charging him with false imprisonment, but Eyre took refuge behind an Act of Indemnity passed by the Jamaica Legislature.

Eyre was awarded a state pension by the Disraeli Government in 1874. During his long retirement he kept his silence, refusing either to defend or to justify himself outside a court of law. He died in 1901 and his *Times* obituary said that 'he did many good and brave things and atoned for one error in his life by a silence so dignified and so prolonged'.

The old, terrified Jamaica Assembly had voted for its own extinction after 200 years in existence and London duly complied. An 1866 Act created a Crown Colony. The new permanent Governor, Sir John Peter Grant, swiftly set to work reorganizing the entire island. He sacked the local planter-justices and replaced them with stipendiary magistrates, created a proper police force, introduced a public medical service, irrigation schemes for infertile areas and a public works department, and reformed land tenure laws. Education was improved and by 1867 there were 379 schools on the island, of which 226 received financial aid from the Government. Grant encouraged the trade in bananas which quickly became the colony's biggest export trade and principal crop. There were no more revolts, although poverty and discontent continued.

The Jamaican Rebellion, its suppression and subsequent controversy, gave the British an excuse to abolish the old and fundamentally corrupt administration which had become dominated by white planter power. More Crown colonies were established throughout the West Indies, with only a handful of exceptions. In the short term this meant direct rule from London but it reduced the power of an arrogant white minority and paved the way for more responsible Government and, much later, independence.

In 1962, however, when Jamaica finally won full independence George William Gordon and so many other innocents had been long cold in their graves.

FIVE

The *Arracan* Expedition, Andaman Islands, 1867

'No ordinary exertion'

They may have been the 'Good Spirit' islands mentioned by Ptolemy; they were certainly referred to by the fifth-century Chinese Buddhist I'Tsing, while Marco Polo, passing within sight in 1292, called them the 'Angamans' and said that the natives were cannibals with the heads of dogs. Nicolo dei Conti translated their name as 'Islands of Gold', although it probably derives from the monkeys which populated the forests. The Andaman Islands were the epitome of tropical paradise: the tips of a range of submarine mountains scattered like a necklace with 204 jewels across almost 2,500 square miles of the Bay of Bengal. Their countless natural harbours and rugged inlets were laced in turn with dazzling coral, while dugong and turtles swam the crystal waters. There were mangrove swamps, hills gashed by narrow valleys, forests of valuable redwood. At the start of the nineteenth century the islands lay on the main trade routes and offered shelter from the cyclones which lashed the Bay but never seemed to touch the islands.

The native people were largely untouched by the civilizations with which they came into contact. They had a policy of killing all foreigners. The people traced their blood lines to the pygmies of the Philippines and the Semang of Malaysia. They were hunters and gatherers, never farmers, on rocky outcrops where irrigation was unheard of. They fished from canoes with nets and four-pronged arrows. Their weapons were made of shell and broken shards of iron collected from shipwrecks. Sailors, merchants and explorers noted their ferocious hostility: hostility that was created, not inherent.

Conti and Cesare Federici, who visited the islands in 1440 and 1569 respectively, wrote of peaceful natives in canoes. But hideous raids by Arab slave traders changed all that. The coastal tribes, who greeted strangers with simple gifts, were virtually wiped out. The inland Jarawa tribes were also friendly at first but clashed with foreign sailors who accused them of theft, a concept alien to tribes who regarded property as communal. A later British ambassador, M.V. Portman, said: 'It was our fault if the Jarawas became hostile.' An early incident on Tilanchong illustrates this point. In 1708 a vessel commanded by Captain Owen was shipwrecked and the crew ferried to nearby islands by courteous and kindly natives. Captain Owen put down a four-inch knife he had saved and it was picked up by an islander. Owen snatched it back, kicking and punching the native. Hamilton's *Voyages* records: 'The shipwrecked men could observe contention arising among those who were their benefactors in bringing them to the island . . . next day, as the captain was sitting under a tree at dinner, there came about a dozen of the natives towards him and saluted him with a shower of darts made of heavy wood, with their points hardened in the fire, and so he expired in a moment.' His crew, however, were protected and given two canoes with water and food. They were told not to return. One canoe, with three men on board, survived the journey.

In 1789 Captain Archibald Blair had established a penal colony for prisoners from Bengal at Port Blair on Chatham Island. Two years later, under Admiral Sir William Cornwallis, it was transferred with a naval arsenal to Great Andaman. This proved too costly in both cash and lives – most prisoners and many guards died quickly of tropical diseases – and it was scrapped in 1796. The local population did not welcome strangers any more. In 1844 they killed the stragglers from the troopships *Briton* and *Runnymede*, which were driven ashore in a gale. Attacks on shipwrecked crews and the huge numbers of prisoners taken during the Indian Mutiny of 1857 pushed the British into establishing a settlement and another convict colony close to the original site at Port Blair. Ravaged by sickness, many died before swamp reclamation created healthier conditions. During the early years deportation to the Andamans was considered a death sentence.

The English tried to deal with the war-like Jarawas by arming the remnants of the coastal tribes, the Arioto, with firearms. Given such unique power they began to slaughter every Jarawa they could find. Portman wrote: 'On our arrival the Jarawas were quiet and inoffensive towards us, nor did they even disturb us, until we took to constantly molesting them by inciting the coastal Andamanese against them.'

In 1867 some of the crew of the vessel *Assam Valley* were reported missing and captured by natives on Little Andaman Island. A detachment of the 2nd Battalion, 24th Regiment, South Wales Borderers, was dispatched on board the *Arracan* to find them.

* * *

The 24th Battalion had spent nearly six years in Mauritius, enjoying bathing, boating, cricket and local hospitality under balmy skies, before being sent to Rangoon. Three officers and 100 men were sent from there to the Andaman Island. Among them was a 26-year-old Canadian medical officer and four privates who were to join the most distinguished roll call in military history – the company of VC-holders.

Assistant-Surgeon Campbell Mellis Douglas, himself the son of a doctor, was born at Grosse Île, Quebec, and had been attached to the 24th in Mauritius. The privates, three of them Irish, were also in their twenties. David Bell, from County Down, had enlisted at Lisburn seven years before; William Griffiths, a County Roscommon man, had previously been a collier; and Dubliner Thomas Murphy had worked as a cloth dresser before enlisting. The fourth private, James Cooper from Birmingham, was illiterate when he signed up; he was the son of a jeweller and a stay-maker.

Shortly before the Andaman expedition Douglas, an accomplished boatman, had prepared a boat for entry into a regatta at Burma. The crew he trained for the event proved so strong that after winning the first race their boat was excluded from the competition to give others a chance. The names of his crew are not recorded but, given the later events, it is likely they included the Irishmen and the Brummie.

On 17 May 1867 the steamer *Arracan* reached Little Andaman, buzzing with rumours that the missing crew had been butchered by cannibals. On arriving at the scene of the alleged massacre, two boats were filled with armed soldiers and rowed inshore under the command of Lieutenant Much.

The *Regimental History* records: 'A heavy surf was beating but one boat's crew waded ashore through deep water and began moving towards a rock where the massacre was believed to have occurred, the other boat moving parallel to cover their movements. As they advanced natives began to show themselves and let fly their arrows freely but could not prevent the party from reaching the rock and finding the skull of a European, when, as they had nearly exhausted their ammunition, the signal for recall was made. In trying to embark those ashore near the rock the shore party's boat was upset, so the men started back towards the original landing place, en route discovering the partially buried bodies of four more Europeans.' As the plight of the men on the beach became all too obvious, increasingly desperate efforts were made to reach them through the surf, first by boats and then by rafts from the *Arracan*. As more boats were battered to pieces Assistant-Surgeon Douglas and the four privates volunteered to man a gig to renew the attempt. Their first bid to get through the roaring surf failed when their little boat was half-filled with water. During another attempt Lieutenant Much and others were swept off a makeshift raft. A correspondent wrote: 'While in this critical and very dangerous predicament Dr Campbell Douglas showed all the qualities of a real hero. Being an excellent swimmer, and possessing great boldness and courage, he swam after the drowning men. Twice was Lt Much . . . washed off the raft, and, while struggling in the rolling waves, Dr Douglas flew to his rescue, and brought him back safe to the raft.' Chief Officer Dunn of the *Arracan*, confused and sinking, was also plucked to safety by Douglas, but Lieutenant Glassford was less lucky. The correspondent, writing for the *Liverpool Gazette*, added: 'Dr Douglas, having struck his head against the rocks in diving after one and another of those he saved, felt himself confused and bruised, and his strength giving out. He could not follow Mr Glassford, who was carried some sixty or seventy yards away, and he was drowned. As night was rapidly approaching, the whole party had to make the most herculean efforts to save themselves from the risks and dangers which now beset them on every hand.'

On two occasions Douglas and his crew got through the surf and brought back seventeen men, 'the whole shore party being thus rescued from the virtual certainty of being massacred and eaten by savages'. The *Regimental History* added: 'The surf was running high and the boat was in constant danger of being swamped, but Assistant-Surgeon Douglas handled it with extraordinary coolness and skill and, being splendidly supported by the four men, who showed no signs of hesitation or uncertainty, keeping cool and collected. . . .'

The expedition, having discovered the fate of the missing Europeans, steamed away but the exploits of Douglas and his gallant crew reached the ears of the Commander-in-Chief in India, Sir William Mansfield. Hostile natives, though a threat during the early part of the incident, had not been evident when Douglas arrived on the scene but officers who were present, not least those who had been saved, wanted the rescuers awarded the highest honour. The newly created Victoria Cross was intended only for heroism in the face of the enemy, but the officers, and some newspapers, argued that the courage displayed in a boiling surf on a hostile shore was more than enough. A large factor was that very few Victorian Britons could swim and the sea was thus held in some terror. Luckily, an amendment in 1858 had made it possible for the Victoria Cross to be awarded for exceptional heroism far from the front line – Private Timothy O'Hea had previously won it for putting out a fire in an ammunition wagon in Canada.

On 17 December 1867 the War Office confirmed the queen's decision to reward all five men with the Victoria Cross. The citation for each was identical: 'For the very gallant and daring manner in which they risked their lives in manning a boat and proceeding through a dangerous surf to rescue some of their comrades who formed part of an expedition which had been sent to the island of Andaman, by order of the Chief Commissioner of British Burmah, with the view of ascertaining the fate of the commander and seven of the crew of the ship *Assam Valley*, who had landed there, and who were supposed to have been murdered by the natives.

'The officer who commanded the troops on the occasion reports: "About an hour later in the day Dr Douglas and the four privates referred to, gallantly manning the second gig, made their way through the surf almost to the shore, but finding their boat was half-filled with water, they retired. A second attempt was made by Dr Douglas and party and proved successful, five of us being passed through the surf to the boats outside. A third and last trip got the whole party left on shore safe to the boats."

'It is stated that Dr Douglas accomplished these trips through the surf to the shore by no ordinary exertion. He stood in the bows of the boat, and worked her in an intrepid and seamanlike manner, cool to a degree, as if what he was doing then was an ordinary act of everyday life. The four privates behaved in an equally cool and collected manner, rowing through the roughest surf when the slightest hesitation or want of pluck on the part of any of them would have been attended with the gravest results. It is reported that seventeen officers and men were thus saved from what must otherwise have been a fearful risk, if not certainty, of death.'

The five were the first of the 'Old Green Howards' to receive the Victoria Cross and the last to win it anywhere away from battle. By 1904 the regiment had sixteen VCs to its credit, of which seven were famously won at Rorke's Drift.

Assistant-Surgeon Douglas enjoyed a long and illustrious career. The Royal Humane Society awarded him a silver medal for the same act of heroism. He was Medical Office in Charge of the field hospital during the second Riel Expedition in 1885, during which he made an epic 200-mile canoe trip carrying dispatches. He wrote papers on nervous degeneration among recruits, and on military doctoring. His favourite recreation was, naturally, sailing. He reached the rank of Brigade Surgeon and married the niece of Sir Edward Belcher. In 1895 he made a single-handed crossing of the English Channel in a 12-ft Canadian canoe. He also patented a modification to a folding boat which was later put into general use. He died, aged sixty-nine, at his daughter's home near Wells, Somerset, on 31 Decem-ber 1906. A painting displayed in the RAMC Headquarters on London's Millbank shows him standing bravely on the bows of the rescue boat.

Less is known of the four privates. Thomas Murphy emigrated to Philadelphia and died in March 1900 aged sixty. James Cooper left the Army, although he continued in the Reserves, and followed his father's trade as a jeweller. He died in Birmingham in August 1882. David Bell became a sergeant but was discharged in 1873. He was employed as a skilled labourer at no. 8 machine shop, Chatham Dockyard. He died, aged seventy-eight, in 1920 at Gillingham.

William Griffiths, still a private, was killed by Zulus at Isandhlwana on 22 January 1879. He was buried in a mass grave on the battlefield, far from the sound of pounding surf.

SIX

The Magdala Campaign, 1867–8

'The ruthless hand of war'

On a plateau below a great ruined fortress atop a mountain in modern-day Ethiopia a massive cannon lies on its side in the dust. In the royal palace of Windsor a brass plaque set in the Chapel Royal wall commemorates a young African prince. The story that binds them together covers one of the most remarkable military campaigns of the last century.

It is remarkable because its commander spared no monetary expense to ensure that none of his men died unnecessarily. His success did much to counter the shameful memory of the cruel shambles in the Crimea. It is remarkable because it mobilized armies from three continents and crossed some of the most savage terrain on earth for one purpose – to free a handful of unappreciative hostages. And it is remarkable for the main protagonist, Kassa – an African Emperor who was fanatically Christian, brave, educated, patriotic . . . cruel, barbaric and, certainly by the end probably raving mad.

At the heart of the story is a seemingly impregnable citadel perched on a mountain in the Abyssinian highlands and called Magdala.

* * *

Kassa, known to Europeans as Theodorus and to his people as Tewodros, Elect of God, the slave of Christ, Emperor of All Abyssinia, was born in 1818. It was a time of chaos and bloody carnage: the power of the hereditary emperors had declined while the barons or *rases* were out of control and divided the land. Kassa was the son of a local prefect and a peasant woman. When his father died he was sent to a monastery to train as a deacon in the Abyssinian Church which practised an ancient form of Christianity. Surrounded on all sides by Islam, the Abyssinian Church was forgotten or ignored by the rest of the Christian world. His training left Kassa with a profound love of the Abyssinian faith and a sense of his own mystic heritage which were to stay with him for the rest of his life.

When his monastery was destroyed in a raid Kassa was one of the few survivors. Aged around twenty, he took to the hills as a guerrilla, already well blooded in tribal warfare. He was by then a notable scholar, a theologian, a fine horseman, marksman and spear-thrower. His wild followers respected his courage and strength and loved his unusual habit of dividing plunder equally with his men. His band caused so much mayhem that in 1845 the region's governor, Ras Ali, offered terms including the hand of Tewabach, the beautiful daughter of a northern nobleman. They married and Kassa remained devoted to her.

Two years later he led a rebellion, snatching control of the imperial city of Gondar. Ali, armed with British guns, tried to wipe out his younger adversary. Both men were by now rival claimants to the vacant imperial throne. After eighteen months of hard campaigning Kassa slaughtered Ali's army at the battle of Gojjam. Kassa won the support of the Established Church by promising to expel Catholic missionaries. The civil wars continued but Kassa defeated his last rival at Deresye in February 1855. He was crowned King of Kings in a small village church. He chose his new imperial name from the legend of a Messiah called Tewodros who would rescue the country from years of rule by idiots and women. Within a decade he had united Ethiopia under his overlordship, although he still faced encroachments from Egypt and the constant threat of rebellion by the warlike Galla tribe.

Europeans who came into contact with the new Emperor were impressed by the strong magnetism of his eyes. The British Consul William Plowden, a colourful adventurer who had been appointed in 1848, told London: 'He is generous to excess and free from all cupidity. He salutes his meanest subject with courtesy; is sincerely though often mistakenly religious . . . When roused his wrath is terrible and all tremble.'

The first years of his reign were busy and fruitful. He abolished the slave trade and polygamy, with mixed success. He mobilized an army of 60,000 and subdued the troublesome Gallas, snatching their mighty fortress at Magdala. He subjugated the Tigrai province. After one battle he reportedly cut off the hands of 787 prisoners. He was far gentler with those he did not consider rebels, traitors or enemies. He dressed simply and lived in a tent of scarlet and yellow silk among his soldiers. When he was in residence at the palace of Gondar, the tent was pitched in the gardens. He identified with the common people rather than with the *rases*, whose power he reduced by dividing each province into small administrative areas with his own trusted men in key positions. He scrapped some of the more horrific criminal punishments, such as flaying alive, and simplified the penal code. He was merciless with corrupt judges.

His popularity among his troops and the poorer people grew swiftly. So too did the hatred of the *rases* and judiciary. During his first two years on the throne he was wounded six times in seventeen assassination attempts. He was never seen without a sword and revolver and he walked with a lance in his hand. As he grew older such plots, revolts and insurrections were crushed with increasing ferocity. The Emperor began to believe in his own Divinity. Only three people could with sweet reason calm his rages and curb his excesses: his wife Tewabach; Consul Plowden; and his friend John Bell. Within a few short years all three had died, and their benign influence removed.

During these turbulent times tensions grew between the Abyssinian Church, which had followed its own separate path for centuries, and Catholic and Protestant missionaries from Europe. Tewodros tolerated the missionaries as long as their missions included artisans who could bring with them such skills as mending firearms, making gunpowder and building roads. In 1858, when his beloved wife was stricken with illness, he viewed with gratitude the sadly unsuccessful efforts of mission doctors to save her. He rewarded them with land to build more homes and a school. The missionaries he liked and trusted the most were Swiss and German craftsmen. He promised they would never be 'molested or tormented' but at the same time warned them not to try to convert his Christian subjects.

Early in 1860 Consul Plowden was speared to death, reportedly by a runaway nephew of the Emperor who had joined Tigrai rebels. In a long apologetic letter to Queen Victoria, Tewodros told how he had pursued his young relative and his supporters and killed them all, '. . . not leaving one alive although they were of my own family, so that, by the power of God, I may get your friendship.' Plowden's death plunged Tewodros into a black despair which must have accelerated his decline towards insanity. His second wife, Terunesh, was comely but haughty and treated him like a peasant unworthy of her royal pedigree. The slide was mental, emotional and physical. He caught an unspecified disease of a 'peculiar and formidable nature'. He even suffered a broken leg. Excessive drinking and debauchery exposed the darker side of his nature.

Plowden's successor was Charles Duncan Cameron, a veteran of the Zulu campaign and a former diplomat to the Russias. He arrived with a goodwill letter from the British Government and a gift from Queen Victoria – a matched pair of engraved revolvers. After some delays Cameron was granted an audience with Tewodros in 1862. The Emperor received him 'in a reclining posture, with a double-barrelled gun and two loaded pistols by his side'. Despite his threatening appearance Tewodros treated the consul with kindness, although he also made it quite clear from the start that he could never replace Plowden in the royal esteem and affection.

Later that year Tewodros wrote a round-robin letter to the British Queen, the French Emperor and the Russian Tsar. It included an attack on Islam in general and especially on the Turks occupying much of coastal Ethiopia. He suggested a Christian alliance against his Moslem neighbours. In the version sent to London he specifically asked permission to send his own envoys to explain at first hand how the Turks were oppressing good Christians. Cameron was given precise orders to deliver the letter to the queen but instead relied on a string of messengers and it arrived in London early in 1863. By then the Foreign Office was incensed by its belief that Cameron was meddling in internal Abyssinian affairs. A combination of bureaucracy and bloody-mindedness left the Emperor's letter gathering dust in some Whitehall pigeon-hole. After eight months Cameron had no reply to convey. The French were a little more diplomatic – but only just. Tewodros found a convenient excuse to imprison the French consul, Lejean, until he received a reply. When it came it was signed not by Napoleon III but by his foreign minister. Tewodros stormed: 'Who is that Napoleon? Are not my ancestors greater than his?' Nevertheless he released the French consul, who, once safely across the border, let loose a flood of abuse against Tewodros, with little thought for those Europeans who remained within reach of the Emperor's wrath.

Into this explosive situation bumbled Henry Aaron Stern, a German missionary from the London Society for Promoting Christianity Among the Jews. A volatile and self-important character, he was unpopular among the other missionaries. During an audience with a heavily drunk Tewodros one of Stern's interpreters committed a blunder. Tewodros ordered that unfortunate man and another servant to be flogged so wickedly that they died. When the horrified Stern objected he was beaten unconscious and imprisoned. His baggage was searched and letters were found in which Stern and his colleague Rosenthal were critical of the Emperor. A book of travel writing by Stern included the insulting claim that Tewodros' mother had sold medicine for tapeworm. The two missionaries were chained up and their servants shackled to wooden yokes.

Meanwhile Cameron, embarrassed by London's tardiness, tried to steer clear of further trouble. It did him no good. Tewodros came to believe inaccurate reports that Britain and France were moving to support Turkish and Egyptian claims to Abyssinia's northern territories. The British consul and some of his staff joined the missionaries in chains.

London finally awoke to the urgency of the situation. Over a year after the Emperor's letter had been received a reply was drafted. It flattered Tewodros but insisted he could best demonstrate his affection for the queen by freeing the hostages. The task of delivering it was given to a Turkish Assyriologist called Hormuzd Rassam, a member of the British agency in Aden. The choice may seem strange, but no doubt the Foreign Office considered him expendable. After yet more delays he arrived at Massawa with Dr Henry Blanc of the Indian Army Medical Service and a regular soldier, Lieutenant Prideaux. They took with them 500 out-dated muskets as goodwill gifts. For weeks they were kept sweltering at the hot and humid coastal port while Tewodros played cat and mouse. It was not until January 1866 that they were permitted into the Emperor's silk tent to hand over the queen's reply – three years and three months after the original letter had been sent. Tewodros was pleased to see it had been signed and sealed by Victoria herself. Honour satisfied, he agreed to pardon the prisoners, by then being held in the Magdala stronghold. Blanc later wrote: 'The expression in his dark eyes was strange. If he was in good humour they were soft with a kind of gazelle-like timidity which made one love him; but when angry the fierce and bloodshot eyes seemed to shed fire.'

Rassam and company spent a pleasant month enjoying lavish court hospitality until the hostages were brought to them on the shore of Lake Tana. There were eighteen prisoners: Cameron and four of his European servants; five German missionaries: Stern, Rosenthal, Martin Flad, Staiger and Brandeis; the French messenger Bartel; two natural history collectors; the European wives of Flad and Rosenthal and three Flad children. Stern and Cameron, whom Tewodros had grown to detest, were in very poor physical condition.

Rassam, who realized his task was not complete until they were across the border, was determined that the captives should not come face to face with their imperial gaoler for fear of infuriating him again. He sent them on a roundabout route towards the border while he and his party crossed the lake waters by boat to pay their respectful farewells. They were ushered into the royal tent, only to find the throne empty. While Tewodros watched from behind a curtain the emissaries were seized. On the other side of the lake Cameron and the rest were again taken captive.

Tewodros claimed that Rassam had tried to spirit away the Europeans before they had formally made their peace. He also suspected that they would follow the Frenchman's example and shower him with abuse once safely out of range. But the chief reason for his action must have been the Europeans' continuing value to him as hard currency. In another letter to London he held them openly to ransom in return for the skills, arms and equipment he needed to bring his divided, feudal country into the modern age. He specifically asked for 'a man who can make cannons . . . and an instructor of artillery'. The letter was delivered by Flad, who was forced to leave his wife and children behind as surety.

The Earl of Derby's new Conservative Government agreed to many of the Emperor's demands. A list of willing artisans was drawn up, including a gunnery sergeant. Six-pounders from Aden and arms worth £500 were collected as ransom, together with telescopes, field glasses and ornamental tumblers. A civil engineer and six technicians were sent towards Massawa before they were halted by disturbing reports.

At first the hostages had been treated well, especially the women. But then Tewodros set off on a series of marches to re-establish control over troublesome tribes. Cameron, Rassam, the original captives and some more were sent to Magdala where conditions were primitive and harsh. Three days later they were placed in chains. Blanc described their physical mistreatment as a great torture. Both he and Cameron were later accused of exaggerating their hardships. Rassam, who was proving himself to be a cool and courageous man, later wrote: 'Not one of the captives can justly complain that his imprisonment . . . was aggravated by privation. Nevertheless the chains were a great indignity for the Europeans even though their hands were free and their movements not seriously curtailed. They must have suffered considerable mental anguish when they considered that they were at the mercy of an unstable and unpredictable host.' Britain's Resident in Aden called for a rescue expedition. For a while the Cabinet resisted such pressure, despite growing public opinion and letters from the hostages themselves which suggested the Emperor was becoming madder by the day because of 'hot baths and concubines'. Finally Tewodros was given a three-month deadline to free the prisoners.

The ultimatum went unanswered. Tewodros was being threatened on all sides by internal revolt, desertions from his army and disputes with the Church. He seems to have convinced himself that the surest way of uniting his kingdom was to provoke a British attack which he could then claim was backed by Abyssinia's old Islamic foes. The Cabinet suspected such motives but agreed that Britain and her subjects could not be so abused. They were anxious, too, for a demonstration of British military power to dissuade the Russians from any encroachments on India. Chancellor Benjamin Disraeli proposed an extra penny on income tax to raise the £2 million thought necessary for a punitive expedition. All that was left was to find the right commander.

* * *

Lieutenant-General Sir Robert Cornelis Napier had been born a soldier. His middle name commemorated the 1810 storming of a fort in Java in which his artilleryman father had died. He was born that same year in Ceylon and after an English education sailed to India as an eighteen-year-old lieutenant in the Bengal Engineers. For the first seventeen years of his service he saw no action but built roads and bridges, painted, wrote poetry and collected rock and plant specimens. His devotion to art never left him and he was still taking lessons at the age of seventy-eight. That relatively peaceful life was shattered by the First Sikh War in 1845. Twice, in the battles of Mudki and Ferozeshah, horses were shot from under him. In the second engagement he continued his charge on foot until badly wounded, although his injuries did not stop him fighting at Sobraon. He saw more action in the Second Sikh War and in 1852 led a column in the Black Mountain expedition on the North-west Frontier. In the Indian Mutiny he saw both the first relief of Lucknow and its final capture. There was more fighting against rebels in Oudh and Gwalior and in 1860 he commanded a division in the China War. He had fifteen children by two wives. He excelled, too, at innovation and administration, bothering himself with such unglamorous but vital matters as camp latrines and the good health of his men. He was fifty-seven and the Commander-in-Chief of Bombay when he received orders to lead the Abyssinian expedition.

Napier realized from the start the enormous scale of the task facing him. The Foreign Office had envisaged a speedy dash into the wild Ethiopian heartlands, the snatching of the prisoners from an ignorant barbarian, and an equally swift withdrawal. The Duke of Cambridge suggested 'a flying column should be pushed forward . . .

and finish the business before the rains set in'. The Cabinet certainly did not want an extensive, and therefore expensive, campaign. Napier knew better the logistical problems of fighting in hostile, rugged and largely unknown terrain. He believed that a flying column would simply be swallowed up and its men would perish in unnamed ravines. Instead he made detailed plans for a steady march with all supply lines defended. Given his glittering and successful campaigning career it would have taken a foolish man, even in the Cabinet, to contradict him. He got what he wanted.

His force was made up of 13,000 British and Indian soldiers – cavalry, infantry and sappers. The troopers included the 23rd Regiment of Foot, better known as the Duke of Wellington's. Its commander was Alexander Dunn who had won the Victoria Cross in the Charge of the Light Brigade. His men were largely Irish with a reputation for hard drinking and harder fighting although they included a good number of Germans who had signed on for the Crimea and never went home. The British troops and some Indian cavalrymen were armed with the latest breech-loading Snider rifles which had proved their worth in the American Civil War. The rest of the Indians, in line with Army policy since the Mutiny, carried the less efficient Enfield muzzle-loaders or the even older smooth-bores. In addition to the active soldiers there were over 8,000 auxiliaries: cooks, teamsters, grass-cutters, animal handlers and camp-followers. There were also eleven journalists, one of whom was Henry M. Stanley, yet to become famous for finding Livingstone, as well as a metallurgist, a geologist and a zoologist. The livestock amounted to 36,000 beasts, horses, mules, bullocks, beef cattle, camels and 44 elephants. Supplies included 70,000 lb of salt beef, 30,000 gallons of rum, 3,000 tins of condensed milk, 250 dozen bottles of port wine, 800 leeches in the medical carts and, especially for the Sikhs, a 'certain quantity of opium'.

It took 291 ships of every description to ferry them all from India, Aden and Europe to the Abyssinian coast. Napier travelled on the steam-powered naval frigate HMS *Octavia* and arrived at Annesley Bay to the south of Massawa on 3 June 1867. For three months the army had taken shape on the sandy shore. A constant supply of fresh water was ensured by the latest condensers and pumps from the United States. A photographic unit was established to copy maps. Two 300-yard piers were constructed to reach ships anchored in deeper waters. Stanley described his own disembarkation: 'It was as if a whole nation had immigrated here and were about to plant a great city on the fervid beach.'

The traditional reds and blues of the British uniforms mingled with the new and much more suitable khaki. The gaudy tunics of the Indians contrasted with the drab workclothes of Arabs, Africans, Turks. All struggled in the dust and the heat to bring that mobile city ashore. A score of languages competed with the braying of mules, the whinnying of horses, the trumpeting of elephants. In charge of all this organized mayhem was Major Frederick Roberts, a veteran of the Umbeyla expedition. It is a measure of the efficient job he did that, although he was to see no action in the campaign, Napier recommended him for a brevet lieutenant-colonelcy. It was another illustration of the prudent and methodical way Napier was determined to conduct this African adventure. Memories of the tragic waste of the Crimea were still vivid. Napier was determined that such cruel inefficiency would not be repeated.

He pestered London for more food and clothing before he would move out of his bridgehead. He busied himself with every detail, from the holes in his men's socks to camp sanitation which, one of his officers sniffed, was 'one of his pet hobbies'. He saw that dead mules were quickly replaced with fresh shipments, that sappers improved the roads, that a 10-mile military railway was built across a nasty stretch of coastal desert. Napier was criticized for his lengthy and detailed preparations. He brushed that aside and dismissed more talk of flying columns as dangerous, romantic nonsense. He had seen a lot of blood during his career. He was determined that not a single man would die because of his neglect. Christmas dinner that year was guinea fowl shot in carefully placed rows to conserve ammunition.

Meanwhile the hostages at Magdala were kept in two crude huts within the imperial compound at the heart of the mountain stronghold. After a few months they had turned these hovels into substantial homes with bedsteads, furniture and carpets given to them by Tewodros. Food was supplied by friends and relatives on the outside, augmented by tomatoes, potatoes and greenstuff from a garden and vegetable patch they planted themselves within the walls. They were weakened by the poor quality of some of their food, bored by the lack of variety, but they were far from starving as some of their champions had claimed in the British Press. Indeed they may even have fared better than their guards.

Those on the outside kept them informed through posted letters and clandestine messages. The first news they heard of a rescue expedition came shortly before Christmas. Any joy they might have felt must have been dissipated by news of Tewodros who had been away campaigning for a year. He and his army were on the move again, and heading towards Magdala. The war was to be a race to see which commander would reach them first.

Tewodros had failed to suppress the rebel tribes and his power was fading. He now gambled everything on beating the British in a glorious war. He told Martin Flad, who had risked the royal wrath by rejoining his family in captivity, 'I asked them for a sign of friendship which is refused to me. If they wish to come and fight let them come. By the power of God I will meet them and call me a woman if I do not beat them.' His Swiss and German artisans manufactured cannon and artillery pieces including a great mortar capable of propelling a 1,000-lb ball. He named this 7 ton monster 'Sebastopol'. It was the most cumbersome part of the army Tewodros led from Gondar towards Magdala. After desertions he was left with 5,000 fighting men, over 40,000 baggage-handlers, drivers and camp followers, the European craftsmen who still served him for pay, and several hundred native prisoners captured in his domestic wars. They made painstakingly slow progress through some of Abyssinia's wildest terrain. On the approaches to the high plateau of Zebrite thousands of men hacked and blasted a zigzag road for the new, prized artillery in which the Emperor placed so much faith. A contemporary engraving shows hundreds of men hauling Sebastopol with ropes while others placed logs and stones behind its wheels. Tewodros worked passionately alongside his workmen, lifting rocks with his bare hands. While this road was being constructed he heard the first firm news that the British were on the move. He said ironically: 'We must be on the watch as I hear that some are come to steal my slaves.' His toughest task was the crossing of the Jidda gorge, a deep gash which bisected the central highlands. It took eighteen days to cut a route to the floor of the ravine and another three weeks to scale the other side but by 20 February 1868 his entire army, including Sebastopol, was on the fertile plain of Delanta.

* * *

Napier had decided to divide his force into two separate parts. The larger division was to garrison and protect the long lines of supply and communications between their coastal bridgehead and their target. The smaller division, consisting of 5,000 fighting men, was to be the main striking force.

Advance parties set up a base 70 miles into the country at Senafay. As fresh troops reached it the first group, now rested, went forward to the next stepping stone at Guna Guna. In this methodical fashion the unwieldy army advanced in good order until the whole column was on the move. Napier aimed to take full advantage of the widespread discontent with Tewodros' rule and to win allies among the local barons, the *rases* who had their own reasons for hating the Emperor. These included Ras Kassai of Tigrai, a thirty-year-old warlord. In delicate negotiations Napier enlisted the aid of Captain Charles Speedy, who had first gone to Ethiopia to shoot elephants and who had once been part of Tewodros' entourage. He was 6 foot 6 inches tall, wore a bushy red beard and impressed the tribesmen with his ability to split a sheep along its backbone with one sweep of his sword. He spoke fluent Amharic and always wore native robes. Speedy used his inside knowledge of Ethiopian politics to steer the British commander through a minefield of tribal allegiances and vendettas to secure promises of safe passage through Tigrai, supplies and intelligence. By the end of January the British force was spread over 100 miles, the strike 'head' to the front, its long 'tail' guarding the supply lines back to the coast. Ras Kassai and the other barons could only be trusted so far.

The Europeans found the march easier than had been anticipated. They followed the crest of a watershed – rough going but not brutal for troops hardened in the boiling cauldrons of Afghanistan, India and Aden. They marvelled at pyramid rocks, fantastic stone columns, castles for giants with which nature mocked the puny efforts of mankind. Professional reportage and personal journals describe sheer precipices, gurgling crystal-clear torrents, the flowering of roses, violets, jasmine, the blurred wings of hummingbirds. The weather was clement but that would not last. Napier, who reached Adigrat on 6 February, knew he had to speed the march up if he was to complete his mission and bring his men back before the unbearable heat of July. At roughly the halfway mark the main strike force of 5,000 men had with it 1,356 horses, 518 regimental mules, 33 elephants, 1,969 camp followers, more than 5,000 baggage mules and 1,800 muleteers. Napier sent servants and many camp followers back to base with much of the baggage he deemed luxuries. There was much grumbling when he reduced the baggage allowance, even for officers. But the army's pace stepped up noticeably and began to average 10 miles a day. Two days ahead of the main force was a reconnaissance and pioneering party under Colonel Phayre. Napier led the vanguard of around 1,000 men, equally split between British and Indian. Then came the main strike force while the steady reliable elephants brought up the rear.

The land itself now began to fight for the Emperor. The route ahead was slashed by deep gorges and high ridges. Nevertheless Napier was confident he would reach Magdala by the end of the month. His intelligence reports told him Tewodros would reach the fortress at roughly the same time. It was going to be a close-run thing. An error by Colonel Phayre swung the race in the enemy's favour. He and his advance party had been striking far ahead. He was directed by a rascally local chieftain called Wolde Jesus along some of the worst tracks they had yet seen. Finally even those petered out in the 1,600-ft pass of Fulluk Eimuk Oonzool. They turned back and the main column then took the obvious and direct route over the Amba Alajl Pass, but Phayre's mistake cost them six precious days.

They marched on through the spectacular mountains of Wojerat Province. The *Times* man reported: 'The country heaved with mountains in every direction, like a rough sea.' The pace of the elephants and other animals fell below 8 miles a day. Again Napier ordered officers and men to shed more of their baggage, especially tents. Combined with fatigue and the prospect of ever more saw-toothed mountains to cross, this led to more restlessness in the ranks. One officer reported an increase in 'swearing, grumbling and discontent . . . obscene and violent language'. Napier paraded the Duke of Wellington's Regiment, gave the tough Irishmen a severe tongue-lashing and switched them from their coveted place at the head of the column to the inglorious rear.

Weather and terrain worsened. Steep tracks, swollen rivers and hair-pin bends tested the ingenuity of the Sapper trail-blazers until Napier's column reached the relative ease of the Wadela plateau. On this high plain the tribesmen were reputed to be the best and fiercest horsemen in Africa. Aware of the danger Napier halted to allow stragglers to catch up. After a much-needed rest they marched the 40 miles across the plateau until they reached the Jidda gorge, 3,500 ft deep and 8 miles across. Napier was startled to see clear evidence that Tewodros was ahead of him: the mammoth new roadway that the Abyssinians had cut in the sides of the precipice. He was astonished also to discover that it was not blocked by the Imperial army or even by a rearguard. If it had been, Napier wrote home, he would not have had a chance of getting across. Instead the British column enjoyed a route made easy by the enemy.

Some 12 miles from Magdala Napier saw the outlying spurs which hid the fortress itself. He realized at once the 'formidable character of the whole position'. He wrote that he might need every man, on foot or steed, to scale its dizzy heights. Napier decided that the first flat-topped ridge at Fala should be his first objective. He aimed to muster his men on the level ground at Aroji, below a hill where, unknown to him, Tewodros had already positioned many of his heavy guns.

Tewodros had decisively won the race to Magdala. He entered the fortress on 27 March and carefully positioned his artillery on the ledge of Salamji and the twin peaks of Fala and Salassie which together overlooked the only viable approaches to the stronghold. For weeks while his army was on the move Tewodros had behaved like a general, a fine soldier, skilled tactician, a true leader of men. Once within the brooding, sinister Magdala fortress his unpredictable moods returned.

In a fit of belated generosity he ordered the prisoners freed of their shackles and given compensation of 2,000 silver thalers, 100 sheep and 50 cows. That order was quickly rescinded and Rassam was the only hostage unchained. Rassam used all his wiles to persuade the Emperor to unchain first Blanc and Prideaux, then Cameron and the other hostages. They were invited to stand with Tewodros to watch the heavy guns being dragged up the heights. He was in good humour even when the first British forces came within range of his telescope. He told one captive to take the glass and directed him: 'There thou will see thy brethren who had come from England to kill me. I am pleased to see those red jackets.' He was distressed only at the tattered appearance of his own men. He asked Rassam: 'How can I show these ragged soldiers to your well-dressed troops?'

In another generous fit he began to release some of the hundreds of native prisoners, a good number of whom were crippled and starving, who had also been held at Magdala. On the first day 186 women and children and 37 minor chiefs were freed. Seven men were executed. The next day Tewodros decreed that all the rest should be released, apart from a handful of political prisoners. The removal of several hundred sets of shackles inevitably took time and some Galla prisoners unwisely demanded food and water. Tewodros went berserk. He screamed: 'I will teach them to ask for food when my faithful soldiers are starving.' He speared several prisoners on the ground. His soldiers, fearful and infected by the same bloodlust, carried on the grisly work with swords and guns until between 200 and 300 lay dead or dying. Both corpses and wounded were thrown off the high cliff at Salamji.

The following day, 10 April, was Good Friday. Tewodros joined a concentration of gunners and troops on Fala. Below them were coats of red and khaki. He exhorted his men to smite the English as David smote the Philistines.

* * *

The British expedition had so far been almost faultless in its care, preparation and execution. Napier made his first major error when he allowed the unguarded baggage train to pass onto the Aroji plateau, under the false impression that Phayre's advance column would protect it. In fact Phayre was deep in a neighbouring ravine in search of a more suitable route for the pack animals and the heavy guns. The Abyssinians on the heights above saw the chance of easy prey. Napier quickly recognized his error and despatched the 23rd Punjab Pioneers and the King's Own Regiment to save the baggage. By this time Tewodros' tribesmen were swarming down the mountainside. The cannons on Fala, Selassie and Salamji opened fire at maximum range. They were too far away to do much damage but one heavy ball landed yards from Napier as he sat on horseback directing his hastily assembled troops.

The Sikhs were first in position at the head of a ravine between the attackers and the train. The King's Own, with some engineers and members of the Naval Brigade, formed a line across the plateau just as the Abyssinians reached the level ground. The attackers, dressed in medieval armour and colourful cloaks, formed a solid mass of horsemen and foot soldiers 1,500 yards wide and seven men deep. The most reliable witnesses suggest they were 3,500 strong. They advanced not at some unruly ramble but at a steady, purposeful pace and with a cool courage that surprised the toughest British trooper. Facing them in the front line were perhaps 300 men of the King's Own, strung out across a shooting gallery as flat as a billiard table. Their firepower, including double-barrelled rifles, was awesome. The new Snider rifles were effective at 500 yards and their breech-loading mechanism made them capable of firing seven rounds a minute. What followed was not battle. It was butchery.

The first shots fired were the rockets of the Naval Brigade. They passed narrowly over the heads of the King's Own, causing more discomfort to the British than to the enemy. The British line opened fire at 250 yards. The first rank of Abyssinians fell. Among those initial casualties was the elderly General Babri, dressed in a red tunic laced with gold, whom some of the British mistook for the Emperor. Neither the shock of the rockets nor the withering volley caused the attackers to slow their pace. They were battle-hardened troops and their tactics had always been to soak up heavy casualties in the first volley and then rush forward while their enemy was reloading. They had no experience of the Sniders, the first metal-cartridge breech-loaders generally issued by the British Army. There was no time between volleys for them to dash to the front line: no respite from the non-stop fusillade. Hundreds fell before the attackers took cover behind scattered rocks and returned fire with their elderly and inefficient muzzle-loaders. A group of sixty warriors scorned their comrades' good sense and marched to within 100 yards of the British lines until they too broke. The British counter-attacked as the day's light faded but Napier ordered a halt. He did not want this first proper engagement to deteriorate into a series of night skirmishes over unknown territory from which his own men could all too easily emerge as the losers.

In the meantime a smaller Abyssinian force launched a flanking attack on what they thought was the baggage train. In fact it was a light mountain battery whose guns were already limbered up. They opened fire at 500 yards but shot and shell failed to stem the onrush of warriors. Neither did two volleys from the out-of-date muskets carried by the Sikh Pioneers. The tough, hugely built Indians met the charge of savage but smaller Amhari warriors head on, with bayonets fixed. It was basic, brutal killing. The bloody hand-to-hand fighting all but massacred the attackers. A splinter group managed to get around the Sikh defences but were met by searing volleys from a detachment of the King's Own firing from behind the baggage. The survivors turned and fled, only to find themselves in a killing ground between the Sikhs and the mountain battery. Most died.

The night on the plateau was punctuated by the wails of women searching for their dead, the last death-throes of the dying and the snuffling of wild beasts. Stanley wrote: 'In ravenous packs the jackals and the hyenas had come to devour the abundant feast spread out by the ruthless hand of war.' British and Indian burial parties found that few Abyssinians had discarded their weapons as they attempted to flee the hail of shot. To the Victorian mind they had died like the very best kind of soldier. There was little rejoicing, much less gloating, in Napier's camp that night. They buried 560

Abyssinians. The true death toll was estimated at 700 minimum with 1,500 wounded, many of whom must have perished later. Napier lost 2 dead and 18 wounded.

Tewodros watched the slaughter from the Fala hilltop. He was furious at the ineffectiveness of the heavy cannon he had dragged, sometimes with his own blistered hands, over the mountains. One of the largest guns, his namesake Theodorus, splintered on its first firing. Tewodros was driven to despair at the defeat of his army by what he knew could only be the vanguard of the main British force. He returned to Alamji and told Rassam to compose a letter of conciliation to Napier. Prideaux and Flad were sent to the British camp in the early hours of the following morning. Napier showed both European and native emissaries his cannon, his elephants and the rest of his forces which had doubled overnight, with more men streaming in by the hour. Napier's letter of reply said: 'It is my desire that no more blood may be shed.' But his demands were tough. The prisoners must be released. Magdala must be given up. Tewodros must surrender unconditionally although Napier pledged 'honourable treatment' for the Emperor and his family. Tewodros was outraged. He scornfully described Napier as 'that servant of a woman'. The two Europeans were sent back to the British camp with a threat that all hostages might be executed and with the message: 'A warrior who has dandled strong men in his arms like infants will never suffer himself to be dandled in the arms of others.' Tewodros then fell back into one of his commonplace moods of black despondency. He put a pistol in his mouth and pulled the trigger. His retainers wrestled the gun from his hand but the bullet grazed his head. His few trusted advisers persuaded him to make a gesture of peace.

Hardly believing their luck Rassam, Cameron and forty-seven other prisoners were allowed to pick their way down the mountain slopes to the British camp. Mr and Mrs Martin Flad stayed behind, along with European artisans who worked under contract to the Emperor and who had never considered themselves hostages. The British soldiers were surprised at the captives' sleek, well-fed appearance. It had been assumed they had suffered horribly at the hands of the mad Emperor but there was precious little evidence of that. One of Napier's staff officers wrote: 'I must say I think they are a queer lot, taken as a whole. The rag-tag and bob-tail they have with them in the shape of followers etc., are wonderful to behold. They have about 20 servants of each sort, and the idea of being able to move with less than three mules for baggage seems to Mr Rassam as utterly impracticable.' Overnight the number of freed hostages swelled to fifty with the birth of a baby to one of the wives. The captives found that after years of living, albeit as prisoners, in some considerable luxury they were now expected to sleep on the ground under canvas, like any common trooper, and eat tough soldier's beef and chapatis. It was not a joyful reunion. Napier sent them grumbling to the rear where their dissatisfaction would not infect his troops.

Tewodros, by now desperate to appease, sent down the traditional Abyssinian gesture of peace: 100 cows and 500 sheep. They were rejected. Close to panic the Emperor ordered the remaining Europeans to descend to the British lines. They did so with 187 native servants, 323 domestic animals and large quantities of baggage, including more tents than were possessed by the British advance column.

Every European was now free and Napier had achieved everything, except the surrender of the Emperor. He wrote to his wife: 'It is not easy to express my gratitude to God for the complete success as regards the prisoners.' However, his strict military sense dictated that the war must end with the surrender, capture or death of Tewodros. His army had been unmolested, indeed fed, by various tribes on the understanding that the British would rid them of the despot. If he failed to do so he would probably have to fight for every foot of the road back to the coast. He reassured one of the rebel barons: 'We have come this far with an army to punish Theodorus for his ill-treatment of British and European servants.'

Tewodros gathered 2,000 followers within Magdala and planned to escape by a steep southern path to regroup elsewhere. Those of his supporters who elected not to fight with him 'to the end' he gave permission to flee or surrender. Many warriors did just that, including the commanders of the batteries on Fala and Selassie who agreed to surrender their positions in return for safe conduct. Thus Magdala's outer defences, for which Napier had planned tough and bloody frontal assaults, fell without a shot. The way was clear for a direct attack on Salamji and the mighty Magdala fortress beyond.

* * *

The attack began at 9 a.m. on 13 April 1868. The Duke of Wellington's Regiment led in fine drill formation, the band playing 'Yankee Doodle Dandy' as they marched. They were met not by a hail of fire but by a disorganized flood of refugees and warriors who threw down their weapons as they fled down the track. One British trooper likened the scene to the flight of the Israelites. Napier's men found the Salamji plateau abandoned. Peering over the far edge they saw heaps of naked bodies, piled brokenly several corpses deep, the prisoners who had fallen victim to the Emperor's earlier rage. The stench was horrible. The gruesome sight stiffened resolve among the horrified onlookers and did much to counter the stories of Tewodros' civilized grace and courage which had circulated among the troops. The 300 twisted corpses were an eloquent vindication of the entire expedition. In the middle of the small plateau lay the giant gun Sebastopol. It had proved too heavy to drag the last stretch to the fortress. It, too, was a silent witness to the Emperor's grandiose dreams, now lying in the dust.

As the British and Indian troops were assembling on the level ground ten or twelve horsemen burst from the fortress in a wild dash aimed at carrying off some small, abandoned brass cannon. Leading them, clad in a white tunic and lionskins, and carrying rifle, spear and sword, was Tewodros himself. It was typical of the man: gallant, medieval, hopeless. He shouted a challenge of single combat, preferably with Napier. The British commander was not present and the most senior officer on the plateau answered the challenge with a salvo of artillery fire. Tewodros, his robes swirling, his steed's hooves raising a cloud of dust, screamed abuse at the British ranks. He and his wild warriors used their swords to make the sort of rude gestures that are universally understood, fired their rifles in the air, wheeled around and galloped back to the ancient fortress.

At 3 p.m. Napier ordered the final assault. A steep track flanked by sheer rock and thorn hedges climbed the final 300 feet to the twin gateways of Kokit Bir. After surveying the defences by telescope he assumed that defenders were concealed behind rock slabs overlooking the narrow approach and hidden within the craftily designed hedges. Napier's artillery, 4 twelve-pounders, 12 seven-pounders, two 8-inch mortars and 16 rockets, bombarded those positions for an hour with little clear evidence of success. Napier recognized it could be a risky business which would mean heavy casualties if the fortress was heavily defended. He later wrote: 'If simply old women had been at the top and, hiding behind the brow, had thrown down stones, they would have caused any force a serious loss.' Colours flying, the attack was led by the scarlet-jacketed Royal Engineers and a detachment of Madras Sappers, followed by ten companies of the Duke of Wellington's in their khaki. Two further regiments and two more companies of Indian Sappers – the Baluchi and Punjabi Pioneers – were lined up in support. Napier's plan was for the Wellingtons (33rd) to give covering fire while the engineers blew the main gate.

A heavy downpour turned the path into a slippery mudbath. The attackers came under lacklustre musket fire which suggested that the morale of the defenders was broken. There were not even old women hurling rocks. The Irishmen of the 33rd were 'firing and shouting like madmen'. So enthusiastic were they that some of the Sappers ahead were grazed by British bullets. The defenders on the gate were more spirited and inflicted nine casualties, none of them fatal, on the engineers milling in confusion below them. The Sappers were unable to force the gate because the Abyssinians had piled heavy stones to a distance of 15 feet behind it. They could not blast their way through because, through an incredible oversight, no one had brought gunpowder, axes or even ladders.

The commander of the 33rd, Major Cooper, sent his men around the right side of the ramparts to find a weak spot. One massive Irishman, Private James Bergin, got a handhold on the wall and used his bayonet to hack an opening in the wicked thorns that surmounted it. He asked drummer boy Michael Magner to give him a heave up but he was too heavy for the lad. Instead he hauled the boy on to his shoulders and then pushed him up the final few feet with his rifle butt. Sitting astride the wall in clear view of the Abyssinians Magner coolly pulled up his comrade and then more of the 33rd while Bergin poured shot after shot into a knot of defenders behind the outer gate. Ensign Walter Wynter, who carried the regimental colours, later wrote: 'It was a tough pull up, but I was hardly ever on my feet as the men took me and the colours and passed us on to the front. I shall never forget the exhilaration of that moment.' As more troopers added their rifle power to Bergin's, the warriors at the gate broke and retreated across the outer bailey, taking casualties all the way. They ran through the inner gateway without bothering to lock it behind them.

Unknown to the Irish on the wall the warriors had included Tewodros. It was the final humiliation. It later emerged that only 250 men had stayed with him inside the huge fortress. He had been further disheartened by seeing his chief minister, Ras Engada, blown to pieces in the opening bombardment. The Emperor of All Abyssinia, Elect of God, King of Kings, sat down behind a hayrick and again put a pistol barrel in his mouth. This time there were no loyal retainers to deter him. With the last shot of the siege he blew an enormous hole in the back of his head. The pistol was silver-plated with an inscription on the butt declaring it had been presented to him by Queen Victoria 'as a slight token of her gratitude for his kindness to her servant Plowden'.

When the British reached the inner fortress, passing through the unlocked gateway, they met no further resistance. The remaining warriors had laid down their weapons, with the Emperor's permission, during his last moments of life. The burial parties got busy. The artillery bombardment killed 20 Abyssinians and wounded a further 120. Another 45 had been slain by British rifles, most of them in the turkey shoot between the two gateways. Napier's forces suffered 10 wounded and 5 scratched by rock splinters. Most British reports admitted it had not been the most glorious or hard-fought battle in the history of the Empire. No one, however, begrudged Bergin and Magner the Victoria Crosses they were awarded on their return home. The citation read: 'For their conspicuous gallantry on the 13th April last. Lieut.-General Lord Napier reports that, whilst the head of the column attack was checked by the obstacles at the gate, a small stream of officers and men of the 33rd Regiment, and an officer of Engineers, breaking away from the main approach to Magdala and climbing up a cliff, reached the defences, and forced their way over the wall and through the strong and thorny fence, thus turning the defences at the gateway. The first two men to enter, and the first in Magdala, were Drummer Magner and Private Bergin.'

* * *

The British and Indian troops plundered Magdala, guzzling many gallons of captured honey beer. Their loot included brand-new English rifles, silver-mounted spears, toy soldiers, photographic equipment, state umbrellas and Persian carpets. All such items were auctioned within the fortress and the £5,000 raised was divided among the troops, who each received 25 shillings or 15 rupees. A representative of the British Museum, one of the scholars who had gone with the expedition, spent £1,000 on 350 beautifully illustrated religious books, lovingly and piously collected by the dead Emperor. All but two remain in the Museum. The imperial crown of gold was sent back to London and presented to Victoria. Many years later George V returned it to Ethiopia as a goodwill gesture to Haile Selassie.

The Emperor's wife Terunesh was discovered – a 'pretty, fair girl of about 25 with large eyes and long hair', according to an officer. She remained haughty in manner and treated the soldiers as servants. As a result she suffered the indignity of having her bottom smacked by coarse British hands until Napier took her under his protection. Tewodros' eight-year-old son Alamayu was treated well. Napier respected his father's wishes that he be given an English upbringing and education.

Tewodros' body was cleaned and laid out briefly in state, then buried alongside a ramshackle church known as the Madhane Alam or Saviour of the World. His shallow grave was in unconsecrated ground as he had died by suicide, a poor end for a man who, however fatally flawed, had shown himself a devout and zealous patriot.

Napier ordered the destruction of fifteen smooth-bore cannon on Magdala's ramparts and the dismantlement of the fortress walls. They were never rebuilt. Sebastopol was too heavy to move and lies there still. Everything else not looted by the victorious army was put to the torch. Napier recorded: 'Magdala, on which so many victims have been slaughtered, has been committed to the flames, and remains only a scorched rock.'

Napier's force retraced their steps, dragging a huge tail of refugees. Terunesh sickened and died on the march, despite the efforts of British doctors. She was buried with full honours. The column was hit by storms and by marauding bands of their recent allies, the war-like Gallas. Provisions ran low, although there were always daily issues of rum for the men, port and brandy for the officers and Press. Mules died in their hundreds and five of the elephants had to be shot. Other tribes were less friendly now that the tyrant was dead. Some even forgot past hatred and regarded Tewodros as a fallen hero, a martyr. Finally the exhausted and tattered force reached the coast and by 10 June the entire army was embarked on the waiting fleet. The drifting sands covered most signs of their passing. The *Illustrated London News* reported: 'The military expedition to Abyssinia . . . so reluctantly determined upon, so carefully organised, so wonderfully successful, has come to a close.'

Napier returned home in triumph. Disraeli praised the campaign's 'completeness and precision'. He told the Queen: 'So well planned, so quietly and thoroughly executed, the political part so judiciously managed, the troops so admirably handled during the long, trying march, the strength of Anglo-Indian organisation so strikingly demonstrated in the eyes of Europe, wiping out all the stories of Crimean blundering – the Abyssinian expedition stands apart.'

Napier's casualty rate had been astonishingly light. Just thirty-five Europeans had died, mainly through illness and exhaustion on the long marches. Three hundred were ill or wounded. Losses among the Indian troops, although not precisely recorded, were much the same. Such a carefully planned and well-provisioned campaign did not come cheap and there was some political disquiet in London about the financial cost. Parliament had voted £2 million but the final bill came to £8,600,000. A Commons select committee found that some profiteers had made a fortune from the supply of mules. Almost 28,000 animals, most of them mules, had been lost, stolen or destroyed. The P & O Steamship Company was also criticized for its excessive transport charges. Disraeli replied: 'Money is not to be considered in such matters – success alone is to be thought of.'

In his address to his troops Napier wrote: 'You have traversed, often under a tropical sun, or amidst storms of rain and sleet, 400 miles of mountainous and difficult country. You have crossed many steep and precipitous ranges of mountains, more than 10,000 feet in altitude, where your supplies could not keep up with you . . . A host of many thousands have laid down their arms at your feet . . . Indian soldiers have forgotten the prejudices of race and creed to keep pace with their European comrades . . . You have been only eager for the moment when you could close with your enemy. The remembrance of your privations will pass away quickly but your gallant exploit will live in history.'

In a dispatch from Suez he summed up his late adversary: 'Theodorous had acquired by conquest a Sovereignty which he knew only how to abuse. He was not strong enough to protect his people from other oppressors, while yet able to carry plunder and cruelty into every district he himself might visit. I fail to discover a single point of view from which it is possible to regard his removal with regret.'

Napier asked for and was given a peerage, becoming Lord Napier of Magdala. He was given a pension of £2,000 a year and the Freedom of the City of London. He was made an honorary citizen of Edinburgh and honorary colonel of the 3rd London Rifles. He received the thanks of Parliament, an honorary degree from Oxford and fellowship of the Royal Society. He was made a Knight Grand Commander of the Star of India. Although he saw no more action he served for several more years as Commander-in-Chief in India, becoming a field-marshal, before being appointed Governor of Gibralta. He died, aged eighty, of influenza in 1890. The German Emperor praised his 'noble character, fine gentlemanly bearing, his simplicity and his splendid soldiering'. R.H. Vetch wrote: 'Napier was a man of singular modesty and simplicity of character. No one who knew him could forget the magic of his voice and his courteous bearing. He had a great love of children . . . He never obtruded his knowledge or attainments and only those who knew him intimately had any idea of their extent and depth.' He was buried in St Paul's. No state military funeral since that of the Duke of Wellington in 1852 had been so imposing a spectacle.

Cameron received no honours on his return. His behaviour up to and including his ordeal as a hostage fell well short of what London expected of its overseas emissaries. He was pensioned off as consul and died shortly afterwards, complaining bitterly of his treatment to the end. By contrast Rassam, the expendable Turk, was given much well-deserved praise. He was awarded a special payment of £45,000 for services rendered. (Blanc and Prideaux received £2,000 each.) Rassam married an Englishwoman and died peacefully in Brighton. Magner and Killbricken-born Bergin continued their service with the West Riding Regiment although the latter eventually joined the 78th Highlanders. He died at Poona in 1880. Magner died in 1897.

With the British gone from Abyssinia the Egyptians occupied the coastal regions while bloody anarchy and civil war reigned inland. Various overlords fought to fill the throne left vacant by the death of Tewodros. It culminated in the savage battle of Adowa in 1872, won by Kassai of Tigrai who was aided by modern arms bought from the British. He was crowned Emperor Vohannes IV. His seventeen-year reign was not peaceful and the country was carved up between himself and Menelik, King of the Shoa, who by common consent succeeded Vohannes on his death. Both men inflicted crushing defeats on the Egyptians, subdued the Gallas, and reinstated the conditions for religious tolerance. For a time tensions faded and mass slaughter ceased until the Italians appeared on the scene – but that is a twentieth-century tragedy.

Alamayu was treated as an honoured guest and was brought up as a young English gentleman. He was schooled on the Isle of Wight, in India, in Cheltenham and finally at Rugby. He was thoroughly unhappy with the rigours of public school life and his mood did not improve when he was sent to Sandhurst to train as an officer.

He took ill and became convinced he was being poisoned. He refused all food and medical aid and on 14 November 1879 he died, a sad and lost nineteen-year-old.

The queen was 'grieved and shocked'. A brass plaque was set in the wall of the Chapel Royal at Windsor. It reads: 'Near this spot lies buried Alamayu, the son of Theodore, King of Abyssinia . . . He was a stranger and ye took him in.'

SEVEN

The Modoc Indian War, 1872–3

'All must suffer'

The Modoc War was a bloody shambles that has some claim as America's most inglorious conflict. The US Government engaged more than 1,000 Regular soldiers, over 100 California and Oregon militiamen, and around 80 Indian scouts yet still failed to humble a band of 'degenerate' Modoc tribesmen never numbering more than seventy-five warriors and their families. In skirmishes, raids and open battle numerically inferior natives repeatedly thrashed well-trained soldiers, veterans of the Civil War, and enthusiastic Volunteers. In the end it was internal dissent and betrayal which beat the Modocs, not force of arms. By then the US had lost 65 killed, including 2 scouts and 16 Volunteers, 67 wounded and £500,000, making it proportionately the nation's costliest war. Among the army dead was Edward Richard Sprigg Canby, the only Regular army general to be slain in the history of Indian wars. The Modocs lost 11 men, including their chief Captain Jack and three confederates executed after hostilities had ceased, at least 11 women and an unknown number of children. It is hardly the stuff of regimental honour, to be toasted at military academies. But the ironies and the individual tragedies involved make this war rather more than a ferocious footnote in the development of the American West. It echoes the wider brutalities, misunderstandings and mutual suspicion which soured every stage of the settlers' dealings with the native population and it has a resonance with the conflicts which erupted during the forging of the British Empire. Its two chief protagonists, more victims than heroes, were both decent men who tried to avoid bloodshed. General Canby and Captain Jack were fine men by the standards of their respective tribes. Their words retain dignity across more than a century. If matters had been left in their hands alone the war could never have happened, but both lost control and allowed themselves to be swept along to a bloody finale. Both died by treachery, ill-served by lesser men.

* * *

The Indian wars of the Pacific North-west have never received the attention given to the more glamorous sweep of the Plains or the dust-dry ferocity of Apache country, but they were every bit as savage. The native inhabitants of this, the last frontier, were unaware of the encroachment of the white man's civilization until relatively late. They enjoyed a bountiful land, teeming with game. When the first settlers came they were welcomed, as there was more than enough for all. Then the miners came northwards from California, bringing with them the soldiers. The Pacific seaboard gave the Indians nowhere to go in their search for new lands. The newcomers had crossed a vast continent and were in little mood for compromise or accommodation. Their demands for land and access turned Northern California and Oregon into a place of bitter grudges, prejudice and occasional violence. It was likened to a kettle constantly coming to the boil. There was the Cayuse War of 1848, the Rogue River Wars of the 1850s, the Yakima War of 1853–6 and its successor the Coeur d'Alene War of 1857. General Cook's victory over the Paiutes in 1868 ended war in the rough lakelands until settlers began to complain about the 'apparently hostile dispositions' of a sizeable splinter of the Modoc tribe led by Kintpaush, known by the whites as Captain Jack.

The Modocs were a division of the once-powerful Lalacas who split from their brothers the Klamaths after a dispute over fish from the Lost River at around the time of the American War of Independence. The Modocs won their own independence but remained at odds with the Klamaths. Their land straddled the present Oregon–California boundary around Tule Lake and the Lost River basin. When white settlers began to squeeze on to their territory the Modocs numbered around 600 under the head chief, Old Schonchin.

During the 1850s the Modocs regained the warlike reputation of their forefathers with a series of attacks against white and Indian interlopers. But they were on good terms with some of the miners at Yreka, 50 miles to the west, with whom they traded. Old Schonchin (who should not be confused with his brother John) displayed great courage in early skirmishes with the whites but grew tired of conflict and remained neutral in the final war. A series of murders and small-scale massacres near the shore of Tule Lake, at a place thereafter called Bloody Point, claimed many lives but the local tradition that more than sixty settlers died in a single attack is a myth. After one raid two white girls were taken captive and adopted the dress and customs of the tribe until they were killed by jealous Modoc women. The citizens of Yreka decided to punish the tribe for the deaths of the girls, and Ben Wright was put in charge of a Volunteer company. On reaching Modoc land Wright claimed he had found the bodies of twenty-two white people. He invited the Indians to a parley under a flag of truce and a feast was prepared. Witnesses later testified that Wright had brought strychnine with which to poison his guests. (Later Wright's men admitted that they had planned a massacre, but not by poison which would have been 'unsportsman-like'.) Fearing treachery the Modocs refused to eat before the whites had themselves tucked in. Wright and his men then opened fire, killing around forty unarmed Indians. Only a handful escaped. This treacherous act was not forgotten by the Modocs and greatly influenced their behaviour twenty years later. Their own subsequent acts of treachery must be weighed against this white precedent.

Purple-prose writers later claimed that Captain Jack's own father died in the Ben Wright affair. In fact he was the son of a Lost River chieftain who died in battle with Warm Springs and Tenino Indians when Kintpaush was an infant. This gave him a claim to royal blood. He was born at Wa'Chamshwash village on Lower Lost River around 1837. His Indian name means literally 'He has water brash' (pyrosis). Little is known of him until he was twenty-five, when he appears as an advocate of peace, a cool-headed realist who believed that further warfare would destroy his people. He befriended some prominent citizens at Yreka and carried documents from them attesting to his good character. He became known as Captain Jack either because of the brass-buttoned coat he wore, a gift from an officer, or because of his resemblance to an earlier 'character' of the little mining town.

In 1864 North California's Acting Superintendent of Indian Affairs, Elisha Steele, concluded an informal treaty with the Modocs in which the tribe relinquished their lands and agreed to settle on an ill-defined reservation on Klamath territory. At a council the two tribes, feuding for so long, agreed to keep the peace between themselves as well as with the whites. It was at this peace meeting that Jack was first recognized as a sub-chief.

Almost immediately Jack regretted signing the treaty and told Old Schonchin so. However, the Modocs did their best to settle on the new ground, struggling with homesickness and trying to ignore the resentment and hostility of the Klamaths who, despite the treaty agreement, bullied the newcomers. Indian Affairs Commissioner Edward P. Smith, in his later report, made it clear that at this stage the Modocs were the victims, not the perpetrators, of antagonism: 'There is evidence that Captain Jack and his band were prepared at this time to remain upon the reservation and settle down in the way of civilisation, if there had been ordinary encouragement and assistance, and if the Klamaths, who largely outnumbered Captain Jack's band, and who were their hereditary enemies, had allowed them to do so. This band began to split rails for their farms, and in other ways to adopt civilised habits; but the Klamaths demanded tribute from them for the land they were occupying which the Modocs were obliged to render. Captain Jack then removed to another part of the reservation, and began again to try to live by cultivating the ground. But he was followed by the same spirit of hostility by the Klamaths, from whom he does not seem to have been protected by the agent. The issue of rations also seems to have been suspended for want of funds, and for these reasons Captain Jack and his band returned to their old home on Lost River, where they became a serious annoyance to the whites who had in the meantime settled on their ceded lands.'

Old Schonchin and most of the tribe remained on the reservation near Fort Klamath while Jack and his followers found themselves hemmed in on their old lands. There they stayed for almost four years as pressure for their removal was put on the military and the Indian Bureau.

Contemporary reports differ greatly as to the band's behaviour and the attitudes of their white neighbours. Considerable commerce was done with respectable white citizens and a farmer called Miller voluntarily paid the Modocs grazing rent for his livestock. Jack made some distinguished white friends whose affection outlasted the subsequent bloodshed. But inevitably on both sides there was deep-seated suspicion and prejudice. The encampment was described as a 'degenerate band', prone to getting drunk and 'selling children'. Another commentator wrote: 'They were a degenerate tribe, by common standards, whose men forfeited all claim to local esteem by profiting in the immoralities of their women, while affecting to be affronted by the proposal that they themselves be put to work.' Such is the language of bigotry, though doubtless it was substantiated by a dissolute and unruly minority of the Modocs. Among the whites old fears and the memory of Bloody Point and other raids must have been vivid, while they were determined to hold on to the Modoc lands given to them by the Government.

In 1865 Fort Klamath's commander Captain MacGregor made an unsuccessful and bloodless bid to return the Modoc band to the reservation. Two years later Jack and his men threatened to fire upon Superintendent Huntingdon who was on the same mission. Jack consolidated his leadership of the band by showing such resolution while curbing the bloodlust of his most warlike followers.

In December 1869 Superintendent Alfred Meacham again urged Jack to return to the reservation. During the negotiations Jack dubbed all white men 'liars and swindlers' and refused to touch Meacham's proffered food for fear of poison. Nevertheless the parley continued, aided by the white trapper Frank Riddle and his Modoc wife Winemah, a cousin of Jack also known as Tobey. At one point in the delicate negotiations Meacham feared that Jack was planning murder. He said: 'I am your friend but I am not afraid of you. Be careful what you do. We mean peace but we are ready for war. We will not begin, but if you do it shall be the end of your people.'

Among the Modocs Schonchin John, the old chief's brother, urged the deaths of Meacham and his party. Jack once more insisted on peace and honour. Their wrangling was ended by the arrival of 200 soldiers, summoned by Meacham, who encircled the camp. The Modocs, disarmed but granted face-saving gestures by Meacham and the Army officers, agreed to return to the despised reservation.

It was a short-lived solution. The Modocs met the Klamaths for another peace ceremony. Meacham told them: 'This country belongs to you all alike. Your interests are one. You can shake hands and be friends.' Within three months such hopes had been shattered. Impetuous young Klamath warriors repeated their taunts and insults, and the bigger band tried to exploit the outnumbered and dispirited Modocs. The two tribes simply could not live together. Jack called a council and led the majority of his followers, around seventy families, back to Lost River. He remained convinced of the justice and common sense of his decision and won verbal support from some of his white friends.

Meacham, by most accounts – particularly his own – a reasonable man, now believed that the band should be forcibly returned to the reservation. The new Commander of the Department of the Columbia, General Canby, disagreed. Canby would not commit his troops to such dangerous and disruptive action while the Government dithered over the site of a permanent home for the Indians. Even the informal treaty of 1864 had remained unratified for two years and waited a further six before it was proclaimed by the President. Canby believed it would be 'impolitic if not cruel' to force the Modocs back. In the winter of 1870–1 Canby, a humane man, authorized a limited issue of food from Camp Warner to Jack's band.

Such an uneasy peace could not endure. The flashpoint, unusually, did not involve a clash with the white settlers. In June 1871 Jack was the arbiter in a matter of Indian justice. A shaman, paid in advance, failed to save the life of a sick child. Thus his own life was forfeit and, urged on by the child's relatives, Jack either killed the medicine man himself or authorized his execution. Friends of the dead man invoked the white man's law. An attempt to arrest Jack for murder failed, and Meacham knew that the territory was close to war. In a last bid to prevent the kettle exploding Meacham forwarded to Canby a scheme from a noted surveyor to create a small new reservation on Lost River for Jack's band. Canby saw it as a possible route towards permanent peace and revoked the order for Jack's arrest. Two Commissioners and two guards met Jack's force on his home ground. Again the militant faction among the Modocs – led by Schonchin John, Hooker Jim and another shaman, Curly-Haired Doctor – urged assassination. They were overruled by Jack with the aid of his lieutenant Scarface Charley.

Tragically the plan came to nothing. Jack agreed to the proposed new reservation, as did the Commissioners, and Canby himself. The proposal was sent to Washington. It was filed in some dusty cubbyhole of the Indian Department and there it remained. The failure of the faceless bureaucrats in Washington to grasp this sensible opportunity can now be seen as a major cause of the now inevitable war.

Jack authorized a raid on a cattle train to underline the urgency of the situation. The leader of that raid, Jack's half-brother Black Jim, was to be one of the victims of the final tragedy. Antagonistic whites continued to agitate for the removal of the Modoc band. The Modocs gave them little cause but every theft in the neighbourhood was laid at their door. One petition from Jackson County, Oregon, called on the 'strong arm of the Government' to be used against this 'petty Indian chief with 20 desperadoes and a squallid [sic] band of miserable savages.'

In spring 1872 the sympathetic, if cynical, Meacham was replaced as Superintendent of Indian Affairs by Thomas Odenal, a stubborn and self-satisfied official who understood little of Modoc grievances and appeared to care less. Odenal saw himself as a new broom, determined to sweep away such Modoc nonsense, and strongly recommended a forced return to the reservation without further delay. In July the Indian Bureau agreed with him. Canby had his orders and forwarded them to Fort Klamath and Camp Warner. The stage was set for conflict. Two Yreka judges advised Jack not to resist further and even offered their services as attorneys. Jack refused but clearly felt that such friends would help him if it came to a head-on collision with US authority.

Canby, always a stickler for obeying both the spirit and the letter of his orders, cautioned Lieutenant-Colonel Frank Wheaton of the

21st Infantry and Major 'Uncle Johnny' Green of the 1st Cavalry that if troops had to be used 'the force employed should be so large as to secure the result at once and beyond peradventure'. Odenal waited until November before moving. Jack refused to talk to him, claiming the protection of natural justice and his influential white friends. Odenal clearly underestimated the strength of Modoc resolve not to be shifted again. On 27 November he asked the Army to carry out the July order 'at once'. Both Canby and Major Green, the senior officer closest to the scene, accepted Odenal's judgements uncritically. But the Army's obligation to follow Odenal's directive was questionable then and seems even more so now.

Green ordered Captain James Jackson and forty-three officers and men of B Troop, 1st Cavalry, to take charge of Jack's band. The detachment approached the west bank of Lost River, where Jack and fourteen Modoc families were camped, while a force of around twenty-five Linkville citizen Volunteers aimed for the east bank portion of the Indian village, where Hooker Jim was sub-chief and Curly-Haired Doctor the shaman. The troopers reached their target at dawn on 29 November and would have taken the Modocs completely by surprise if it had not been for a solitary gunshot from an early morning hunter. The two sides agreed to parley, the Modocs wiping the sleep from their eyes under the barrels of Army guns. Jackson's demand for the surrender of weapons began to be obeyed and an Indian Department messenger, One-Armed Brown, was despatched to Linkville to report the success of the mission. On the far shore the militiamen had met with similar success, their charges sheepishly acquiescent.

All that changed when Scarface Charley, on Jack's side of the river, refused to give up his rifle, swearing and waving his weapon in Jack's face. A lieutenant was instructed to disarm him and advanced on Charley 'calling him vile names'. Charley then fired the first shot of the war, missing the foul-mouthed officer but setting off a mutual fusillade. The ensuing sage brush battle lasted three hours. Jackson claimed sixteen Indians slain but in fact only one, Watchman, died. The Army lost two dead and six wounded. Jack directed his force, firing for the first time an ineffectual shot at an Army messenger. Jackson withdrew, burning the Indian encampment as he left. Meanwhile on the far river bank the militiamen tried to stop the Modocs running to their canoes to go to the aid of their brothers. In the fight that followed several citizens died, while the Modocs lost one woman, her dead infant cradled in her arms. The Volunteers broke and ran.

The Modocs gathered to survey their short-term victory and hopeless prospects. Jack took the majority of his band to the natural fortress of the lava beds to the south of Tule Lake. Scarface Charley, whose shot had sparked the battle, insisted on staying behind to warn friendly white farmers, including the noted rancher John Fairchild, of the danger. But the militants, once again led by Hooker Jim and including Curly-Haired Doctor, Steamboat Frank and others, wanted a vengeance raid. Their war party took a longer route to the lava beds, around the east side of the lake, attacking every homestead along the way. They did not touch the women or children but dragged out the men, most of whom Odenal had neglected to warn of the impending action, and butchered them. At least fourteen died, including the farmer Miller who had been on such friendly terms with the band. His supposed friend Hooker Jim shot him dead, later claiming that he had not recognized him. The killers, laden with plunder, scalps and stolen ponies, reached Jack's stronghold with blood on their hands and a taint of dishonour that was to remain with the tribe forever.

Jack bitterly denounced the murderers, perhaps sensing the scale of white vindictiveness about to be unleashed. Jack wished to hand over Hooker Jim and the others to the white authorities but he was overruled by a large majority vote after Curly-Haired Doctor vowed to 'take medicine' to protect them. Jack settled back to await the onslaught. His band was joined by fourteen more families from Hot Creek, led by Shacknasty Jim, who were fleeing from the violence of outraged Linkville citizens. In one of the many ironies of a messy war this group had been saved from lynch mob fury by the timely intervention of John Fairchild: the same rancher who had been warned of danger by Scarface Charley.

* * *

Jack's refuge was a superb natural stronghold, a portion of the lava beds rippling to the southern shore of Tule Lake, likened by Army officers to 'an ocean surf frozen into black rock'. Formed of the roughest type of lava, its ridges and escarpments, up to 50 feet high, provided battlements while its pitted surfaces provided natural rifle pits and trenches. Countless caves and tunnels provided shelter and lines of escape. Crevices, gorges and sinuous canyons made it impossible to traverse in good military formation, the broken landscape perfectly designed for absorbing cannon blast. Circular soil mounds and grass patches provided pasture for the Modoc cattle. Sagebrush gave them fuel. Water could be obtained, for a time, from winter ice in the darkest caverns, and more could be sneaked from the lake shallows. The rough terrain was ideal for the sort of fighting that the Modocs excelled in. They also knew every square yard of it.

Major Green tracked the band to what became known as Jack's Stronghold. He was joined on 21 December by Colonel Wheaton from Camp Warner, who assumed command. They waited for more reinforcements, including troopers from as far away as Vancouver, and three companies of Volunteers from both sides of the Oregon–California line. Wheaton's force grew to more than 325 men. He seriously overestimated the number of warriors facing him, putting it at 150, more than double the actual number.

On the night of 16 January 1873 the Government force split into two, commanded by Major Green and Captain Reuben Bernard, and approached the Stronghold from north and south. These officers and other seasoned Regulars knew what to expect. The callow recruits and over-enthusiastic Volunteers expected an easy, exhilarating victory. Most did not even bother to take blankets and bedrolls, expecting to be tucked up safely in camp the following night.

A dense fog fell around them and at 4 a.m. on the 17th the bugles sounded the attack. Two 12-pound mountain howitzers dropped shells ahead of the skirmish lines. Cavalrymen dismounted and joined the infantry and Volunteers, tramping over ground that grew increasingly hard and treacherous to the foot. Men crashed into each other in the murkiness, their yells destroying any sense of surprise, their positions pinpointed by the clatter. From the fog ahead there was only silence; there was no sign of the Modocs and it was assumed that the enemy had fled. Then, without warning, the fog was sliced by yellow streaks of rifle fire. The first soldier to fall was hit in the neck. A second dropped and the soldiers responded with indiscriminate firing, fog and rocks their only targets. Army howitzer shells began to fall too close for comfort to the advancing bluecoats and the cannon were silenced. Green called a charge but after several hundred yards in which more men fell the Modocs remained invisible. The accuracy and intensity of their sniping continued throughout the day as the two US columns floundered about ineffectually. Both columns came upon chasms wide open to Indian fire which the officers thought suicidal to cross. An attempt to unite the two Army groups almost succeeded but the fog lifted and the sunshine exposed even further the vulnerable troopers to enemy fire. Colonel Wheaton called a council of his senior officers as bullets whined overhead. Everywhere soldiers were in retreat or pinned down by murderous fire. The dead and wounded lay scattered among the rocks, lost to their comrades. Two troopers turned back for a wounded friend, but one was shot as they reached him. After further attempts to rescue them, both wounded men were left for the scalping knives. Trapped pockets of frightened men waited until nightfall before slipping away in the dark.

It was a humiliating rout. Some of the soldiers did not stop running. Many Volunteers drifted home shame-faced. The men they left at the Army camp were disheartened. They faced the prospect of cold, miserable winter billets and a long campaign with little glory. The confusion in the camp makes a true assessment of the US casualties difficult. Some reports put it at up to forty dead but that figure includes some missing men who may have deserted. More reliable reports put it at 11 dead and 26 wounded. Not one Modoc was hurt in the battle. Few troopers claimed to have even seen a single warrior. One brave who took part was suffering from wounds inflicted in an earlier skirmish.

That night the soldiers' bodies were stripped and scalped. The sound of the victory dance was carried on the night breeze to the ears of the chastened soldiers. Jack did not dance. Curly-Haired Doctor, supported by Schonchin John, boasted of the protection his medicine had given the Indians and Jack knew that he could soon face a challenge to his authority. He told his men that only the first battle was won and the white man would come again in greater numbers. But he pledged to fight on himself and would not make peace until 'the Modoc heart says peace'.

* * *

General Canby, who commanded the Department of the Columbia from his headquarters in Portland, was neither an Indian-hating martinet nor a self-seeking careerist thirsty for personal glory, unlike so many of his contemporaries. The testaments of fellow officers and men who served with him throughout his career describe a compassionate, devout man, zealous in his sense of duty, brave but not foolhardy, a born administrator although lacking in imagination and handicapped by an awe of greater authority.

He was born in 1817 and graduated from West Point in 1839. His promotion, though steady, was not meteoric. He did not enjoy the privilege of an influential family but relied instead on a gruelling series of tough campaigns and thankless tasks in some of North America's most inhospitable corners. As a lieutenant he waded through Florida swamps, fever-ridden and deadly, to the battle of Palaklakaha Hammock. As a captain in the Mexican War he was pinned down in the sandhills around Vera Cruz, witnessed the taking of Mexico City and fought in the battles of El Telégrafo, Cerro Gordo, Contreras and Churabusco, being twice breveted for gallantry. In various frontier postings he hunted deserters heading for the California goldfields, and took part in the expedition sent to subdue rebellious Mormons. He advocated that troublesome Shawnee and Kickapoos should be treated 'with kindness and compassion'. Colonel Riley reported that he was 'at all times active and zealous in the performance of his duties'. As Colonel of the 19th Infantry in 1861 he opposed General Sibley's Confederate invasion of New Mexico. He fought and lost the battle of Valverde and from then on avoided combat, drawing the invaders deeper into the desert and letting hunger, heat and thirst whittle down the enemy. His tactics were wholly successful. Sibley lost half his force and the survivors staggered back into Texas. In 1864 as Major-General commanding the Division of the Mississippi he was shot by a Confederate sniper while sailing the White River on the gunboat *Cricket*. He was reported killed in Washington and obituary notices were printed, but he recovered quickly enough to assemble his forces to attack Mobile. The city fell on 12 April 1865 and the finest moment of his Army career came when he took the surrender of the armies of Taylor and Kirby Smith, the last Confederate forces on the field.

For five years Canby was switched around the South, smoothing the path of Reconstruction following the war between the States, unblocking administrative bottlenecks. He fed freed Negro slaves and protected them from assault, while trying to stop unscrupulous northern firms stealing southern cattle markets. 'Wherever he went order, good feeling and tranquillity followed his footsteps,' enthused soldier-author General George Washington Callum.

A Colorado Volunteer in an earlier campaign described him: 'Canby is usually seen near the head of the column, attended by his staff and a few mounted troopers as an escort. Tall and straight, coarsely dressed in citizen's clothes, his countenance hard and weather-beaten, his chin covered with a heavy grizzly beard of two weeks' growth, a cigar in his mouth which he never lights – using a pipe when he wishes to smoke – he certainly has an air of superiority, largely the gift of nature, though undoubtedly strengthened by long habits of command. His person is portly and commanding, his manner dignified and self-possessed, his whole appearance such as to inspire confidence and respect . . . I think of him as a man of foresight and judgement – patient, prudent and cautious – of great courage, both moral and physical, and as true to the Government as any man in existence.' There were some too who considered him a prig and a cold fish, dull and pedantic, smug. Yet the variety and diligence of the career which took him to the desolate lava beds of Modoc County tend to belie such views and only highlight the tragedy that was to end it.

Captain Jack told the friendly rancher John Fairchild, one of the few men trusted by both sides, that despite the brave words uttered at the scalp dance he wanted no more war. Former Superintendent Meacham agreed and others argued in Washington that a peace commission had a better chance of bringing the Modocs to heel than further force. The Secretary of the Interior, Columbus Delano, agreed also and in turn persuaded President Ulysses S. Grant, whose own wider-ranging peace policy was now largely discredited. Canby was told that the President 'seems disposed to let the peace men try their hands on Captain Jack'. Meacham was appointed head of the peace commission and in late March Canby was put in overall charge, his orders giving him 'the entire management of the Modoc question'. Other commission members were a Methodist minister, the Reverend Ezekiel Thomas, and the Indian Agent of the Klamath Falls Agency, LeRoy Dyer. The interpreters were Frank and Tobey Riddle.

Canby set up his field headquarters at Fairchild's ranch and the Commissioners made contact with the Modocs, initially through the Indian women Mathilda Whittle and One-Eyed Dixie, then again through Fairchild. For weeks second-hand negotiations proved frustrating and inconclusive. An apparent willingness by the Modocs one day was reversed the next. The cause was not any deceit by Jack, as was then supposed, but increasingly damaging dissent in the Indian ranks. Jack's leadership was under constant challenge from Curly-Haired Doctor and Hooker Jim and he could not afford to bend too far towards peace and an honourable surrender. He demanded an amnesty for all his people and a reservation on Lost River. Canby and his civilian colleagues demanded that Jack should hand over those who had committed the Lost River massacres. In a freelance bout of negotiations authorized by Canby the sympathetic Judge Steele mistakenly believed that the Modocs had agreed to unconditional surrender. He waved his hat in the air and shouted: 'They accept peace.' He was lucky to escape with his life when he returned to the lava beds the following day and Hooker Jim and his cronies discovered that under the Judge's proposals they were to be handed over to white man's justice. But they need not have worried – Jack had no intention of handing them in.

Fairchild, one of the few men to emerge with credit from the next sad chapter, explained to Jack the terms of an armistice while negotiations continued. Jack agreed, pledging that the white men would be safe if they met him on neutral ground, scrubland at the foot of a bluff just outside the lava beds. He insisted that there should be no soldiers with the commission and promised in return that his warriors would keep their distance and 'we will not fire the first shot'.

Two Modocs, Boston Charley and Bogus Charley, returned with Fairchild to Canby's headquarters. The commissioners agreed to Jack's proposals for talks but sent the two Charleys back to Jack with the proviso that the delegations must be either both armed or both unarmed. The Charleys added their own observations. They told the rest of the band about gossip in the Army camp of a Grand Jury indictment against the Lost River killers, of the lynch-mob temper of Linkville citizens, of the white man's desire for revenge. Such talk fostered among the Modocs the belief that the commissioners were plotting treachery. That belief was strengthened by the very visible build-up of Canby's forces as reinforcements arrived almost daily. The troops facing the Stronghold had moved to bivouacs closer to the lava beds and were now under the command of Colonel Alvin Gillem, 1st Cavalry. The Modoc militants advocated the assassination of the commissioners as a pre-emptive strike. Canby for his part wrote to his wife that the only hope of permanent peace was to remove the tribe as far as possible so that they could never again come home to Lost River.

Frank and Tobey Riddle, in constant touch with Modoc friends and relatives, were keenly aware of the intentions of Hooker Jim and the war-mongers. They repeatedly warned the commissioners to be on their guard. On 4 March the Modocs invited Meacham and several unarmed companions to a meeting inside the lava beds. Meacham believed the proposal 'undoubtedly means treachery' and refused. By April, however, hopes of a settlement had blossomed again. Modocs wandered freely about the Army camp. The commissioners' tent was erected on the spot Jack had suggested below the bluff, a mile from the Stronghold and roughly the same distance from the Army lines. On 4 April it was used for the first time, in the middle of a fierce snowstorm. Jack talked for seven hours with Canby, Meacham, Fairchild and Judge Roseborough, who had been added to the commission on a temporary basis. A further week of talking left all concerned pretty well exhausted. Canby refused a new Modoc request that they should be allowed to set up a new reservation in the lava beds but expressed his desire that a permanent settlement must include 'liberal and just treatment of the Indians'. Writing again to his wife Canby described his adversaries: 'They are the strangest mixture of insolence and arrogance, ignorance and superstition . . . They have no faith in themselves and have no confidence in anyone else. Treacherous themselves, they suspect treachery in everything.'

At a tribal council on 10 April the Riddles' worst fears were realized when the bloodlust of the militants overruled Jack's restraining authority. Despite their own misgivings about Canby's intentions, Jack and Scarface Charley bitterly opposed a scheme to murder the commissioners. Hooker Jim and others placed a bonnet on Jack's head, a shawl around his shoulders and called him a woman. They told him: 'The white man has stolen your soul. Your heart is no longer Modoc.' Shamed by the taunts, Jack threw the garments to the ground and declared: 'I am a Modoc. I am a chief. It shall be done if it costs every drop of blood in my heart. But hear me all my people – this day's work will cost the life of every Modoc brave. We will not live to see it ended.'

The decision made, Jack set about the planning of the crime with ruthless determination, as if to show his people that he was worthy to lead them to destruction. As chief he claimed the right to kill Canby himself. Schonchin John and Hooker Jim were to kill Meacham. Boston Charley and Bogus Charley were to kill the Reverend Mr Thomas. Shacknasty Jim and Barncho were to kill Dyer. But Scarface Charley vowed that he would kill any Modoc who touched his friends Frank and Tobey Riddle. Tobey, in one of her many visits to the Modoc camp as messenger, was told as she left: 'Tell old man Meacham and all the men not to come to the council tent again – they get killed.'

The following morning, Good Friday, 11 April, Jack and his co-conspirators waited at the tent, guns hidden inside their clothing. More warriors with rifles were hidden among rocks a short distance away. Canby emerged from his tent in the camp wearing full uniform but without his customary sidearms. Frank Riddle urged him and the other commissioners not to go. Most people appeared to share his disquiet. The scent of treachery was almost tangible but Canby seemed impervious to it. The Reverend Mr Thomas insisted that they at least should honour the terms of the peace conference and go unarmed. Meacham refused the offer of a pistol and wrote to his wife that she might be a widow by morning. Tobey, weeping, said: 'You no go, you no go, you get kill.' A small Derringer was dropped in Meacham's pocket where he allowed it to remain. Dyer permitted himself the same precaution. Canby meantime had ridden on ahead, unarmed, alongside Bogus Charley who carried his rifle in plain sight. The subsequent trial ensured that what followed is well recorded.

Shortly after 11 a.m. the commissioners, together with the Riddles who had come along to interpret despite their strong fears, reached the council tent. Here the smell of treachery was even stronger. The council fire around which peace terms were to be discussed had been set out of sight of the troops, there were eight Modocs instead of the agreed six, and Jack himself was clearly troubled. He told them that in his dealings with other tribes he had been given the name 'Indian's Friend'. Jack demanded the withdrawal of all US troops and when this was refused he fell into a moody silence. Schonchin John closed his speech with the words, 'I talk no more.'

There was a pause, then a war whoop which brought every man to his feet. Two youths, Barncho and Slolux, emerged from the rocks with rifles held ready. Jack took a revolver from the folds of his coat and shouted 'Ot we kau tux', the Modoc for 'All ready.' He pointed his gun at Canby's head but the first shot misfired. He turned the cylinder and fired again as the other Modocs opened up on their own targets. Jack's bullet entered Canby's head below the left eye and sliced downward, breaking his jaw. He stumbled away but Jack held him down while Ellen's Man cut his throat and shot him again in the head. They both stripped the body.

Boston Charley shot Thomas above the heart and Bogus Charley shot him in the head as he lay on the ground. The Reverend's corpse was also stripped. Commissioner Dyer and Frank Riddle turned and ran. Hooker Jim fired repeatedly at Dyer, missing each time. Then Dyer stopped and turned to face him, drawing his own Derringer. Hooker Jim dropped to the ground to avoid the shot, giving Dyer extra time to escape. Jack's half-brother Black Jim, who had been prominent at the peace talks, pursued Dyer further but turned back to help strip the bodies. Mindful of Scarface Charley's warning, no attempt was made to harm Riddle.

Meacham, who had known these Modocs personally for several years and who had done his best to both curb and aid them, refused to play the easy victim. At Jack's first signal he outdrew Schonchin John and pressed his Derringer against the Indian's chest. Twice it misfired. Schonchin John fired point-blank at Meacham's face but missed. Meacham retreated backwards uncertainly. Schonchin John emptied his revolver, missing every time. He took another gun but twice his aim was spoiled by Tobey Riddle who grappled with his arm despite several blows to her head. Shacknasty Jim took aim but Tobey turned on him and knocked the gun from his hand. Schonchin John sat on a rock and took more careful aim. He scored a direct hit in Meacham's face but by some freak combination of ballistics and bone it merely gouged out a slice of eyebrow. Meacham fired back and struck Schonchin John, who fell wounded off his rock. Other Indians fired, hitting Meacham twice more and bringing him down. He lay twitching as Shacknasty Jim began to strip him, turning away Slolux who was about to shoot him in the head, saying 'He is dead.' Tobey was left wailing beside the body but Boston Charley returned to take his scalp. The knife had begun its work before Tobey chased him off, hurling rocks and telling him that soldiers were coming. Incredibly, Meacham was still alive although the troopers found him muttering in delirium, 'I am dead, I am dead.' Brandy was forced down his throat and Surgeon Cabanis operated and saved his life.

On the far side of the Stronghold Curly-Haired Doctor tried to lure Colonel Mason into a similar trap. Mason, an experienced Indian campaigner, was suspicious and refused to talk. The Modocs attacked two officers, wounding Major Boyle in the thigh. Gillem, left in command of all the US forces, was dazed. His troops turned out in battle order but by then the damage had been done.

* * *

Newspaper reporters in the Army camp dispatched the story of Canby's murder to a shocked world. It sparked fury, shame and disgust. In Yreka and Jacksonville Secretary Delano's effigy was hanged because of his efforts at conciliation. In Washington the news was greeted with 'horror-stricken surprise'. The *Times* of London labelled it 'an outrage'. The *New York Times* reported: 'Seldom has an event created so deep a feeling of horror and indignation.' Other newspapers demanded the immediate extermination of the renegade band. One of the few dissenting voices came from the *Athens Northeast Georgian*. Canby's Civil War successes were bitterly remembered in that part of the South and the newspaper's headlines gloated: 'Capt Jack and Warriors Revenge the South By Murdering General Canby. Three Cheers for the Gallant Modocs.' The Army was appalled and enraged by the only casualty of such high rank in the Indian wars to that date. (George Armstrong Custer, a later victim, was merely a brevet general and not entitled to the rank at the time of his death.) General Sherman telegraphed: 'Any measure of severity to the savages will be sustained.' In another message to officers he added: 'You will be fully justified in their utter extermination.'

The murders did grave damage to President Grant's peace policy, but that strategy was almost certainly dying in any case. For five years Grant, a hardened professional soldier, had counselled mercy, understanding and humanity in dealing with the Indians; that his policy had survived so long is in itself surprising.

Canby's troopers in the field took the salute over his body in a simple ceremony. His remains were taken to Yreka and from there by special train to Portland where he lay in state. The tributes paid were almost equal to those paid to Lincoln. After four services across the continent Canby was at last buried in Crown Hill Cemetery, Indianapolis.

On 14 April the War Department named Canby's successor. He was the tough Jefferson Davis, Colonel of the 23rd Infantry and a brevet Major-General, but the man on the spot was still Colonel Gillem. He was joined at his camp on the south shore of Tule Lake by Donald McKay and seventy-two Warm Springs Indian Scouts, all clad in US Army uniforms. An escaped Modoc prisoner told Jack of their arrival, of Gillem's planned attack with 1,000 men, and of Meacham's survival. Jack sent the children and the elderly to well-protected caves and placed his men behind natural and artificial barricades. The women stayed to carry water and ammunition to their men.

Reinforced by the Scouts, Gillem's assault plan was very similar to Wheaton's. This time, however, there were enough men to give it a good chance of success despite the lava maze, there was no fog to add to the confusion, and there were fewer raw recruits and over-confident Volunteers. On the other hand the Modocs were now better armed, having stripped Wheaton's fallen men of their more modern rifles and ammunition. For three days Gillem's forces advanced slowly and methodically from two sides into the lava beds. At night howitzers and four mortars softened up the Indian positions. On the first day the Army lost five men dead and a large number wounded, the latter taken away by mule litters and by boats across the lake. The advance was temporarily halted, but Gillem and his men wore down their enemy with fatigue and force of numbers. The soldiers advanced, then rested while others took their place. The Modocs in their rifle pits and entrenchments, their nerves stretched by the night-time bombardments, enjoyed no such relief. To the immediate west of Jack's Stronghold one Lieutenant Egan tried to cross an exposed wasteland. He soon fell wounded but he and his men had dug into a crucial position within range of the Indian defenders. The young officer was tended at his post by the tireless Surgeon Cabanis. Even now the onslaught might have failed to dislodge the Modocs save for the desperate shortage of water. The band's supply, never great, had dwindled to nothing. Jack sent warriors crawling through the sagebrush to bring back water from the lake. Clashing with Army pickets, they failed to break through, but neither were they beaten back and a temporary stalemate ensued. The Army did let several old Indian women cross their lines to the shore. Among them was discovered a young warrior in disguise. He was killed and scalped by soldiers, who managed to take five scalps from his head as trophies of their daring. Hooker Jim led a raid on the Army teamsters, killing a man called Hovey. The raiders tried to encircle the baggage camp but withdrew after a few shots. This was the last action of a gruelling three-day battle that had consisted mainly of sniping and the occasional burst of individual initiative.

On the morning of the fourth day the soldiers found the Indian positions eerily deserted. Jack and his band had slipped away, leaving the bodies of two warriors and a woman, and a sick old man who was too infirm to move. The soldiers decided, incorrectly, that he was Schonchin John and shot him to pieces. Once again an Indian scalp was divided into many ugly trophies. The fusillade that killed the unknown geriatric was faintly heard by Jack's band hiding a few miles to the south. Far from being defeated they had merely retreated deeper into the lava beds where there was a little more precious water. They concealed themselves so well that the Army had little idea of their whereabouts. For several days there was an uneasy lull as the Modocs rested, creeping out from time to time to pick off the odd sentry.

Fourteen Modocs under Scarface Charley were spotted returning to the lake for more water. They beat off a company of troopers who returned to camp with three dead. The Modocs fired into the lines of Army tents. Artillery was swung around to bear on them. As each round curved through the air the Indians simply sheltered behind rocks, emerging after each shellburst to taunt the gunners. They fired bunched volleys into the camp while several hundred soldiers stood by and made no effort to stop them. All fourteen braves returned unscathed to the Modoc hide-out.

By 26 April the Warm Springs Scouts had found the Modoc camp but Gillem was determined to proceed cautiously as he did not want another tragedy. Sadly, that is exactly what he got. Captain Evan Thomas and at least sixty-four officers and men were sent ahead to reconnoitre the Modoc positions. Their chief task was to discover whether artillery could be placed to bombard the camp. Gillem expressly ordered Thomas to avoid engaging the enemy. The detachment stopped for lunch under a butte and Thomas called in his skirmishers to eat. Lieutenant Arthur Cranston and five men volunteered to explore the rugged ground and were soon out of sight of the main party. They were ambushed by twenty-four Modocs hidden in rocks on either side. Every man died in the brief slaughter. Thomas, hearing the gunshots, sent two more lieutenants, Wright and Harris, with men to dig in at the side of the butte. When they reached it the Modocs, firing from above, simply continued the massacre. Thomas's command was thrown into fatal confusion as the two dozen soldiers panicked and ran. The rest stayed for what they were sure would be a doomed last stand. Donald McKay and fourteen of his Scouts arrived on the scene to prevent their total annihilation, but not in time to save Thomas himself. All five field officers were dead, alongside twenty enlisted men. Sixteen were wounded, including the only officer to survive the engagement, Assistant-Surgeon B. Semig. Not one Modoc was reported even hurt. Indians later claimed that Scarface Charley had permitted some soldiers out of the trap, calling on his fellows to stop shooting and crying: 'My heart is sick seeing so much blood and so many men lying dead.'

Army morale plunged while its shame soared. For three hours the battle had raged within sight and sound of an Army signal station. More than twenty survivors limped back to base camp before any reinforcements were sent. A superior force had been routed and half wiped out by a small band of savages. The Army was humiliated and 'despondency pervaded the entire command'. The shock waves that this new fiasco sent through the War Department were heightened by the family connections of the dead officers: Thomas was the son of Lorenzo Thomas, a former Adjutant-General; Thomas Wright was the son of the famous Indian fighter General Wright who had drowned at sea eight years earlier; Lieutenant Albion Howe was the son of Major-General Albion P. Howe of the 4th Artillery.

On 2 May Davis arrived to take command, deeply contemptuous of much of his command. In his eyes the Thomas massacre proved that many were 'only cowardly beefeaters'. His first move was to send out McKay's Scouts to locate the enemy and protect local settlers. He waited for further reinforcements and, with the force of his personality, raised camp morale. On 6 May the bodies of Cranston and his men were found. The following day a score of Modocs attacked a supply train escort of equal numbers, sending the white men fleeing with three wounded. Davis sent two companies, under Captain Henry Hasbrouck, to sweep the region outside the lava beds. They were issued with five days' rations. On 10 May, at Dry Lake, they were attacked at dawn. Determined perhaps to atone for the shame of the previous engagements the soldiers stood their ground and coolly returned fire. Ellen's Man, who with Jack had butchered Canby, was killed in the skirmish. Jack was seen amid the fighting, wearing Canby's plundered jacket. Once again the Scouts proved invaluable. They helped push the Modocs back 3 miles towards the lava beds. It was the Army's first real, if modest, victory in the whole campaign.

The Modocs returned to their encampment with just a few casualties. But the death of Ellen's Man caused Jack more trouble. He was accused of keeping his own relatives out of danger while better men risked their lives in the forefront of battle. The band began to split in two, this time permanently. Hooker Jim, Curly-Haired Doctor and others who had been the first to urge the killing of the commissioners were losing heart. The lack of water remained a desperate problem. The setback at Dry Lake had exposed as a fraud the medicine man's supposed protection. The Modocs' winning streak was over. The band broke into two groups and both left the lava beds for the last time.

* * *

Fourteen families under Hooker Jim went west. On 18 May they blundered into a mounted squadron commanded by Hasbrouck and scattered south of Lower Klamath Lake after a running fight. Four days later most had surrendered. Hooker Jim and his fellows offered Davis their help in tracking down Jack, with or without the promise of an amnesty. It was a remarkable act of double treachery as all had earlier voted for war and several were involved in the killing of Canby and Thomas. Some had been on the brutal Lost River raid. Davis himself regarded Hooker Jim as 'an unmitigated cut-throat'. He accepted the offer.

Hooker Jim, Bogus Charley, Shacknasty Jim and Steamboat Frank were set free and pursued their task with diligence. They guessed correctly that Jack and their former comrades would head for Willow Creek, an offshoot of Lost River. They found them after three days. The four urged Jack's followers — thirty-seven warriors and their families — to surrender, saying they could not fight and run for ever. Jack's men were war-weary, tired, cold and hungry, and many were wounded. Yet the renegades were called squaws and Jack told Hooker Jim: 'You intend to buy your liberty and freedom by running me to earth . . . You realise life is sweet but you did not think so when you forced me to promise that I would kill that man Canby.' Jack sent them away to 'live like white men.'

The four men reported to Davis on 28 May that Jack intended to attack a nearby ranch. A cavalry detachment under Major John Green was the first to reach the ranch while two squadrons under Hasbrouck and Jackson followed. The following afternoon the troopers surprised Jack's band on Willow Creek, just across the Oregon state boundary. The Modocs fled to Langell Valley. The various US units now in the field vied with each other to be the first to kill or capture Captain Jack. The Modoc war ended as 'more of a chase after wild beasts'. The Indians scattered as warriors sought to save their women and children. In ones, pairs or family groups they surrendered to the soldiers.

On 3 June Jack and his family were cornered in a cave by cavalrymen under Captain David Perry. The chief was utterly dejected and only two or three braves remained with him. He agreed to give up without a struggle, explaining simply: 'My legs have given out.' He was taken in manacles to join the rest of his dispirited band at the Tule Lake Army camp. General Sherman was not best pleased with the sordid, inglorious round-up which had closed the war. He wrote: 'Davis should have killed every Modoc before taking him if possible. Then there would have been no complications.' The tribe, he said, should be dispersed throughout the reservations 'so that the name of Modoc should cease'. But Davis, not a noted humanitarian, had good reason to show restraint. He was aware of the acrimony heaped upon officers involved in the massacre of Indians elsewhere and Grant's peace policy was still not quite dead. Davis had decided that instead of taking general vengeance on the entire band, Jack and eight other supposed ringleaders should face a drumhead trial followed by swift execution. A scaffold was built. Ironically new orders from Sherman stopped it being used.

The general had decided that Jack and the others involved in Canby's murder should be tried by military court while Hooker Jim and the Lost River murderers should be handed over to state courts. Six men were charged by Davis's military court. None of the four renegades joined them in the dock.

After the round-up of the last scattered Modocs Fairchild's brother James took charge of fifteen men, women and children to take them by mule wagon to the Army camp. They met a group of Oregon Volunteers who threatened the families but Fairchild persuaded them that his prisoners were unimportant Indians. A few miles on he was stopped by two horsemen who held a pistol to his head. They killed four unarmed braves in the wagon and wounded a woman before fleeing as an Army patrol approached. The murderers, although well known locally, were never pursued or charged, never mind brought to trial.

Meanwhile there was still the matter of the Lost River killers and Sherman's orders that they be handed over to civilian justice. Davis invited the families of the dead settlers to the camp to pick out the murderers. Two widows identified Hooker Jim and Steamboat Frank. The two women pulled out a knife and a pistol but were disarmed by soldiers. Neither man ever faced trial. The Modoc renegades had helped the Army restore its pride and so were rewarded. Curly-Haired Doctor, perhaps the greatest villain of the whole affair, conveniently blew out his own brains.

At Fort Klamath on 5 July the military trial opened in a bare hall dominated by a rough wooden table. Beside Jack stood his half-brother Black Jim, Schonchin John and Boston Charley. On the floor sat Barncho and Slolux, the two youths who had supplied the rifles for the *coup de grâce* on Canby and the attempt on Meacham. The Judge Advocate was Major H.P. Curtis and the panel included Captain Hasbrouck. The Riddles were present throughout, acting as both witnesses and interpreters. An Army unit with fixed bayonets stood to one side. Among the unruly crowd of spectators, widows and reporters stood Hooker Jim, Bogus Charley, Shacknasty Jim and Steamboat Frank, who watched the proceedings with interest, occasional amusement and not the slightest sign of guilt. The defendants were charged with the murders of Canby and Thomas 'in violation of the laws of war' and the attempted slayings of Meacham and Dyer.

On the third day the Modoc renegades gave their damning evidence. That afternoon Meacham, still suffering from his terrible wounds, limped into the courtroom to give his testimony. Later he offered his services as counsel for the Modoc defendants but was persuaded by friends to withdraw the gesture. Only three witnesses were called for the defence: Scarface Charley and two Modocs whose words carried precious little weight, Dave and One-Eyed Mose. Jack's own speech was defeated and dismal. The following day all six were sentenced to death. The judge ruled that no others should be brought to trial, an instruction which greatly helped Hooker Jim and his confederates avoid the civilian courts. An Oregon sheriff later arrived with warrants for their arrest but was turned away.

On 2 October, as six nooses dangled from the scaffold, the fort chaplains explained the sentences to the condemned men. Jack said, without any obvious bitterness, that he had believed his surrender would be rewarded with a pardon. The four renegades, he claimed, had beaten both himself and the US Government. Asked who should be chief when he was gone he said that he could no longer trust any Modoc to do the job. Black Jim said he should be allowed to live to lead the tribe but Jack snorted in derision. The youngsters Barncho and Slolux simply denied that there was any blood on their hands, which was strictly true. Boston Charley confessed his involvement in the murders but declared he had believed that Canby and the commissioners were themselves plotting treachery. Schonchin John said: 'War is a terrible thing. All must suffer – the best horses, the best cattle and the best men.'

As dawn broke on 3 October 1873 the roads to Fort Klamath were packed with sightseers. There was a carnival atmosphere. At 9.30 a military detail drew up outside the guardhouse. Six figures stumbled into the morning sunshine. A wagon held just four coffins. The prisoners sat beside the boxes while a blacksmith cut their shackles. Then the wagon trundled to the scaffold where Barncho and Slolux were left on board – President Grant had commuted their sentences to life imprisonment.

Jack stood on the extreme right. Beside him, in order, were

Schonchin John, Boston Charley and Black Jim. Corporal Ross put the halter around Jack's neck while fellow infantrymen did the same for the rest. One stroke of an axe cut the rope securing the trap door beneath all four men. From within a nearby stockade Modoc prisoners screamed their anguish. When the men were dead, their bodies were cut down and placed in their rude coffins. Colonel Wheaton, in charge of the arrangements, was offered £10,000 for Jack's body by a showman. He indignantly refused the offer. Instead the heads of all four were hacked off and sent to the Army Medical Museum in Washington.

Jack left two widows, Lizzie and another woman whose name was not recorded. The survivors of his band were again split in two. The larger band, 155 strong, was sent to a malarial patch of earth in the south-west corner of Indian Territory, next to the Quapaws reservation. By 1905 they had declined to just fifty-six souls. The second group rejoined their fellow Modocs on the Klamath reservation. There they held their own and thirty years later numbered 223. The Modoc name did not vanish but never again did it pose a threat to the white man.

In the 1940s the executors of a dead Army officer in Portland found three skulls in a box in a basement. One was labelled 'Captain Jack'.

EIGHT

The Riel Rebellion, 1885

'I am sure that my mother will not kill me'

At Fort Benton Louis Riel said farewell to a Jesuit priest. He pointed to a nearby crest and called, 'Father, I see a gallows on top of that hill, and I am swinging from it.' A year later, after leading his second uprising of Metis half-breeds in the swiftly growing nation of Canada, his hand-written message from death row said: 'I have devoted my life to my country. If it is necessary for the happiness of my country that I should now soon cease to live, I leave it to the Providence of my God.' He believed he was a Prophet. Some, friends and enemies alike, believed him mad.

The year was 1885. Canada was about to be joined from coast to coast by the last spike of the continental railway. Riel's rebellion came at the beginning of the modern age and was much more than a revolt that flickered briefly and faded after a few skirmishes. His influence was pivotal in the making of modern Canada. And the passions he inspired, among natives and Europeans, British and French, Protestant and Catholic, continue to divide Canada to this day.

* * *

The Metis were people of mixed blood who grew out of Canada's pioneer infancy. Most were the offspring of French and native Indians, although many of their cousins had English and Scots parents and grandparents. They were devout Catholics who had been trapping and settling Canada since the 1650s, the descendants of Champlain's men, the founders of Quebec. The different blood that flowed in their veins gave them a powerful sense of identity. These were no ragtag of illegitimate drifters but a proud people who had carved their own lives out of the wilderness.

They were farmers and landsmen but also hunters. By 1840 there were 5,000 of them, far outnumbering the white settlers. On one occasion more than 400 hunters, backed by 200 stockmen and 1,000 women and children, took part in a great buffalo hunt, their caravan of home-built carts stretching for miles. They left with the blessing of the Bishop of St Boniface. That evening 1,375 buffalo tongues were brought into camp and more than a million tons of meat was dried, loaded and divided democratically among all.

The Metis were described by English aristocrats as 'tall, straight, well-proportioned, lightly formed and enduring'. They were dark-skinned and sometimes called 'bois brûlé', or scorched wood. They were as tough as hardwood, brave and honest, proud and independent. They wore buckskin, blue velvet, red sashes and fur, and rode horses as fierce as the plains and hills they traversed in raging sun and storm-lashed snow.

But their individualistic domination of the empty lands was not to last. In 1811 the Earl of Selkirk, a stockholder in the Hudson's Bay Company, bought 116,000 square miles of Rupert's Land, the area between Lake Superior and the Rockies, for a token ten shillings. His aim was to create a new land for Scottish Highlanders who were the victims of the Clearances. The first white settlers of the land abutting Red River quickly clashed with their Metis neighbours, with disputes over the rights to sell pemmican from buffalo hunts, and tensions over farming and hunting rights encouraged by the rival North West Company.

The first blood was shed in 1816 when a party of Metis was confronted by the colony's governor, Robert Semple, and twenty-six armed men. Insults were exchanged, and then musket balls. Only three white settlers survived. It was an act of butchery almost unique in Metis history.

The elder Louis Riel was a miller and businessman who argued incessantly with the Hudson's Bay Company over Metis rights. The Company was increasing its control over the region, quietly shutting the Selkirk colony after several failed crops, and concentrating entirely on fur. Farms fell into ruin and European colonists drifted across the American border. The Metis reclaimed lands lost earlier and asked to be left alone. The Company imposed their own definition of fair trade and in 1849 prosecuted a Metis trapper for trading across the 49th Parallel. Riel led 300 armed men to surround the courthouse. The accused man was released without violence after a new jury acceptable to both Company placemen and Metis free-traders was convened. It was an emotive victory and showed the benefit of coupling a just cause with force.

An uneasy peace held for two decades with the Red River Metis trading freely with St Paul to the south, ignoring Company edicts. But Canada was becoming a nation with the federation of four British provinces into a Dominion. The Government in Ottawa began to take notice of the settlements in Metis hands and the vast tracts controlled by the Company. There was a real threat too from the south. Thousands of American soldiers were left jobless by the end of the Civil War and many wanted a slice of the unclaimed territories north of the Parallel. Fenian sympathizers even mounted a short-lived invasion. The Government in Ottawa decided to act to expand the Dominion and extend their own ambitions as leaders of an emerging nation.

On 9 March 1869 the Government bought Rupert's Land from the Hudson's Bay Company for £300,000 although the Company would retain six million acres of the Fertile Belt, which stretched from Fort Garry to the British Columbia border, and 50,000 acres around Company posts. The deal completely ignored the wishes of the settlers – 6,000 French-speaking Metis, 4,000 English-speaking cousins, and 1,600 whites – and, unsurprisingly, the vastly larger Indian population. The people who lived there and worked and hunted on the land felt they were being bought and sold by faceless men in the Company headquarters in Ottawa and London.

The Metis had good reason to fear the annexation of their land. Protestant Orangemen from Ontario moved steadily into the Red River region. They used whisky to buy from the Indians land to which there was no title. They regarded the Metis as contemptible half-breeds and bragged openly that this land was theirs for the taking. Their newspaper urged that the 'indolent and careless' native peoples should make way for a 'superior intelligence'. Its editor and their unelected leader, Dr John Christian Schultz, was a bigot and a bully.

The spark of conflict was provided when Prime Minister John Macdonald sent a team of surveyors to section off the Red River region into townships based on 800-acre squares. The Metis farmed their land in long strips so that everyone shared equally river bank, forests, fields and prairie. The proposed new boundaries cut through these long-established lines, leaving some with fertile fields, others with desert. In October 1869 Captain Adam Clark Webb and his team of surveyors began to lay a chain across a hayfield farmed by the Metis André Nault. The farmer knew no English, the officer no French, so an interpreter was sent for. The man who appeared, leading fifteen more Metis horsemen, was the younger Louis Riel.

Louis was born in 1845. He was only just a Metis, being one-eighth Chippewa Indian. His father, a lifelong militant and leader of the court-house revolt, encouraged a passionate belief in the Metis' right to continue their traditions. His mother taught him arithmetic, grammar, history and an equally passionate Catholic faith. Aged seven he went to study under the Grey Sisters of St Boniface and later under lay brothers in the parish library. He was still only thirteen when Bishop Tache picked him as one of the four brightest pupils sent to finish their education in Montreal. Louis won a scholarship to the seminary of St Sulpice where he gained plaudits for the sciences, Latin, Greek, French and maths. By the age of nineteen he was well briefed in the great philosophers and considered becoming a priest. But the following year he was thrown into a depression by the death of his father. 'Papa always acted with wisdom,' he tearfully wrote home. His faith was shaken and he rambled angrily about politics. Then he had a doomed love affair with a girl whose parents refused to let her marry a Metis. He walked out of the seminary in March 1865. A disturbed young man, he spent three years in Montreal, Chicago and St Paul before arriving back at his Red River homeland.

In the hayfield the would-be interpreter told Webb: 'You go no further.' The surveying party wisely withdrew. The small incident turned Riel into a leader. 'The Canadian Government had no right to make surveys in the Territory without the express permission of the people of the settlement,' he said.

Meanwhile a new Governor was en route to Red River via

Minnesota. William McDougall was a well-known annexationist and no friend of the Metis. Riel, with forty armed followers, barricaded the border road and warned him not to cross the line without consent. To reinforce the point 400 more followers took over the Hudson's Bay Company's central post, Fort Garry, with no bloodshed. The Company supplies in the fort included a large amount of pemmican, enough to feed a modest army for the winter. After some bluster McDougall and his party retreated back into the United States.

Riel and his followers established themselves in Fort Garry and drew up a list of demands to be ratified by Ottawa and London. They covered eighteen points by which the Metis' rights to land and trade were guaranteed. Prime Minister Macdonald had been warned that the fearless Metis buffalo hunters were a 'very formidable enemy', and was happy to wait until things cooled down. But McDougall was seething with humiliation and ordered aides to raise a military force armed with 300 rifles.

Predictably Dr Schultz and his Canada First bigots were the first to join but McDougall could only muster sixty men. English-speaking Metis who had refused to join the rebellion also refused to play any part in crushing it. Only a few Saulteaux Indians took up the offer of free rifles – and then promptly vanished. Schultz and his force gathered at his storehouse in Winnipeg, then a nearby hamlet. Riel quickly surrounded it with 200 men and trained a small cannon on the gate. After a brief skirmish the Canadians surrendered and were taken prisoner to Fort Garry. McDougall returned to the capital.

The Comité des Métis within the fort proclaimed itself a provisional government. Macdonald was willing to conciliate because he believed that the Metis problem would eventually be solved when they were 'swamped by the influx of settlers'. A delegation of half-breeds was told, apparently with the prime minister's authority, 'Form a government for God's sake and restore peace and order in the settlement.' On 9 February 1870 a convention of all settlers, whites as well as Metis, elected the 25-year-old Riel as President.

Riel proposed to give his prisoners formal amnesties but around a dozen of them escaped beforehand, including Schultz, who had made a rope out of shredded buffalo hide, and a rough-hewn Irishman from Ontario called Thomas Scott. They began to plot their counter-revolution. They marched through snowdrifts towards Fort Garry, only to be recaptured by the renowned buffalo hunter Ambroise Lepine. Scott swore to kill Riel and may or may not have attacked the new President when Riel visited him in his cell; the evidence is unclear. Either way Scott was charged with bearing arms against the state. Lepine headed a jury of seven men which sentenced him to death. Scott was executed by firing squad on 4 March. In life he was regarded as a braggart, a bully and a drunk but in death he became a martyr. The firing squad sparked an outcry among white Canadians. Every possible prejudice against the half-breeds was whipped up by Schultz and his legions.

Riel sent a delegation to Macdonald setting out conditions for the Red River lands to join Canada as a full self-governing province, not a colony. The Prime Minister agreed to almost all the demands – except for an unconditional amnesty for all who took part in the insurrection – and the Manitoba Act was passed on 18 July. It appeared that Riel had won a stunning and almost bloodless victory and he said: 'I only wish to retain power until I can resign it to a proper Government.'

But the Manitoba Act included a clause designed to appease the vengeful Ontarians. The governor of the new province was to be accompanied by 1,200 troops to keep the peace and protect settlers from Indians. Their real task was to tame the Metis and exact punishment for Scott's death. Colonel Garnet Wolseley, the future victor of the 1873 Ashanti War, the 1879 Zulu War, the 1881 Boer War, the 1882 Egyptian War and the Sudan campaign of 1884–5, was to lead the military force. He told his wife privately: 'Hope Riel will have bolted, for although I would like to hang him to [sic] the highest tree in the place, I have such a horror of rebels and vermin of his kidney, that my treatment of him might not be approved by the civil powers.'

At thirty-seven years old, Wolseley was the Deputy Quartermaster-General of the Armed Forces in Ottawa, and the recent author of the *Soldiers' Pocket Book for Field Service*. Intelligence Officer Lieutenant W.F. Butler, later to become one of

Wolseley's 'Ashanti Ring' of officers who snatched command in some of Queen Victoria's more glamorous wars, described him: 'Somewhat under middle height, of well-knit, well-proportioned figure; handsome, clean-cut features; a broad and lofty forehead over which brown chestnut hair closely curled; exceedingly sharp, penetrating blue eyes from one of which the bursting of a shell in the trenches of Sevastopol had extinguished sight without in the least lessening the fire that shot through it from what was the best and most brilliant brain in the British Army. He was possessed of a courage equal to his brain power. He could neither be daunted nor subdued. His body had been mauled and smashed many times. In Burma a gingall bullet fired within thirty yards of him had torn his thigh into shreds; in the Crimea a shell had smashed his face and blinded an eye. No one ever realised that he had only half the strength and the sight which he had been born with.'

The Red River expedition has been described as 'one of the most gruelling military movements in history'. The rebellion had touched a jingoistic nerve across the rest of Canada and volunteers flocked to join it. The expedition left Toronto on 31 May 1870. It took ninety-six days to cross the 600-mile wilderness, mainly by boat and canoe, north-west of Lake Superior. The army of 400 British Army regulars and 800 inexperienced Canadian militiamen, helped hugely by skilled Iroquois boatmen, endured forty-seven portages along the rivers – places where rapids forced them to manhandle baggage and boats over rocky trails several miles long. Sam Steele, later to become the most famous Mountie, carried a 200-lb barrel plus his own kit over one such obstacle. Redvers Buller, who became renowned as a Boer War general, was said to have managed 300 lb. And the future Duke of Somerset is alleged to have carried two barrels of pork weighing 400 lb in total. It rained for forty-five days of the journey and the men were plagued with blackflies and mosquitoes but no one signed off ill. No alcohol was allowed and there was no crime. Captain Redvers told his men of the 60th King's Royal Rifle Corps that he would not overwork them provided they overtook the other boats. They did so with a mixture of muscle power and a cunning ability to find the best routes across lake, river and rapids. On the last leg the trusting

Riel sent four boatloads of experienced river Metis to guide the soldiers.

The troops arrived at Fort Garry on 24 August. Minutes before the mud-splattered army waded the Red River shallows Riel, who had intended to welcome them personally, was told by a friendly white of their real intention. He fled for his life, leaving his breakfast unfinished, and became a fugitive, saying to one supporter: 'Tell the people that he who ruled in Fort Garry only yesterday is now a homeless wanderer with nothing to eat but two dried fish.' Buller found Riel's breakfast and ate it – it was still warm. Wolseley could have pursued the rebels but he had not been given powers of civil authority and, despite the instincts he had expressed to his wife, he let them go. Riel went south to exile in the United States.

The entire military operation cost only £400,000, barely a quarter of which was paid for by London. The British Regular infantrymen were home before Christmas, not having lost a single man. The rebellion had been crushed and a Dominion Governor installed. It was an overwhelming success – but it failed to solve the real problem.

Four members of the jury that had convicted Scott were murdered. Another was savagely beaten and left for dead on American soil. Riel's own house was ransacked. One by one the promises made to the Metis in the Manitoba Act were abandoned. Security of tenure was not delivered and the Metis received only a tiny fraction of a pledged 1.4 million-acre land grant. Metis land was snatched by incoming Ontarians. The unrest led directly to the formation of the North West Mounted Police.

But the uprising had also established Manitoba as a Canadian Province, helping to ensure that Canada would eventually stretch from ocean to ocean. And Riel had given the Metis a voice and a taste for resistance.

* * *

Riel settled in the Metis town of St Joseph, now called Valhalla, on US territory. The Ontario Government offered a $5,000 reward for the capture of him or any others involved in Scott's death. Prime

Minister Macdonald, however, arranged to pay Riel and Lepine £1,000 to stay quietly on the American side of the border. Despite the threat and the bribe Riel frequently slipped back into Manitoba, moving from settlement to settlement consolidating support. In 1873 he won *in absentia* the federal seat of Provencher. His arrival in the House of Commons in Ottawa to take the oath of office caused violent uproar but he was spirited safely out of the city that night.

In 1875 Macdonald granted pardons for both Riel and Lepine, provided they remained banished for a further five years. Riel began again to have mystic visions and his grip on reality weakened. He is alleged to have been a patient in several Quebec mental hospitals between 1876 and 1878. On his release he wandered the northern United States, dreaming frequently that he was divinely inspired to save his people. Although he remained in the Catholic Church he considered it soiled and corrupt, and urged that the papacy should be transferred from Rome to the Americas and a new Pope be anointed. He believed that the Metis were the chosen people destined to purify the human race. He was their 'David', picked directly by the Almighty. He described one vision: 'The same spirit who showed himself to Moses in the midst of fire and cloud appeared to me in the same manner. I was stupefied; I was confused. He said to me: "Rise up Louis David Riel. You have a mission to fulfill."' Many agreed with his opinion. One Jesuit priest said that to his followers Riel was 'a Joshua, a prophet, even a saint'. He married and became an American citizen, putting David as his Christian name on both certificates. After years of relying on hand-outs from sympathizers he settled in St Peter's, Montana, where he taught in the mission school. The flame of destiny still burned.

Meanwhile other leaders were emerging among the Metis and the Indians to the north. Gabriel Dumont, known as 'the prince of the prairies', had long led the annual buffalo hunt. Sam Steele wrote of him: 'He would kill bison by the score and give them to those who were either unable to kill or had no buffalo.' He was a renowned horseman and sharpshooter. He gradually became the leader of the Metis hunters and trappers who moved north to Saskatchewan to follow the increasingly scarce buffalo herds. The Metis set up new encampments in the St Laurent area on the South Saskatchewan, and these quickly became settled townships. Dumont built a substantial log house, with a stable, root cellar and 20 acres of cultivated land. When not leading the hunt he operated a ferry service and a small store with a billiard table. In 1875 at Batoche he and his friends organized an informal provisional government. The Metis forwarded land claims to the Canadian Government from across the north-west.

The Metis of Manitoba were overwhelmed by incomers but those who followed the buffalo to the Saskatchewan Valley were determined to beat off the white land speculators and homesteaders. They regarded the land as theirs by right, handed down to them by their Indian forefathers. The Canadian Government, having bought the wilderness from the Hudson's Bay Company, believed that any land not held by title belonged to the Crown. A new homestead law decreed the Metis had to register their holdings like new settlers, even if the land had been held in the family for generations, and then had to wait three years for the deeds. Ottawa finally agreed that the Metis were not mere squatters but had a natural right to the land they occupied. But bureaucratic bunglings stirred up a hornets' nest of affronted Metis farmers. Worse still the Government repeated its earlier mistake in Manitoba and insisted on surveying the Metis holdings in squares rather than in the traditional strips which guaranteed access to water for all. A priest complained that Government-set boundaries would divide houses, cut off farmsteads from fields and create hardship.

Dumont and other leaders repeatedly sent petitions to Ottawa. They demanded sensible surveys, an end to delays in ownership patents, and a say in their own affairs. It was not just the Metis who felt aggrieved. White farmers and businessmen around Prince Albert, Battleford and Edmonton attacked Ottawa's incompetence and the *Edmonton Bulletin* argued that only a rebellion would force the Government to recognize their territorial rights.

But the whole issue might have remained bogged down in administrative wrangles if another factor had not come into play: the plight of the Prairies' full-blooded Indians. In the winter of 1869–70 the native Indians – Piegans, Sarcees, Bloods and Blackfeet – were massacred by smallpox caught from infected blankets handed over by white men. Stoney Indians traded pelts for whisky and guns with

Americans operating on Canadian soil. In 1873 a band of drunken American wolfers slaughtered thirty Assiniboines in the Cypress Hills, in revenge for some stolen horses. The deployment of the Mounties in 1874 kept the lid on the potential powderkeg, even with the influx of Sioux following the Battle of Little Big Horn, but in 1878 a drought on the Canadian plains forced the buffalo south, and the Indians north of the Parallel faced starvation. By the following year they were eating carrion and their own dogs and horses. The Mounties did their best to distribute food but in 1883 the cash-strapped Government cut back on emergency food supplies. An agent reported that many tribes were reduced to 'mere skeletons'. Indian anger over the loss of traditional hunting lands grew in tandem with the Metis'. A band of Crees uprooted 40 miles of railroad survey stakes. Other bands refused to stay on their allotted reservations where they were supposed to learn how to plough.

Among the plains Cree, dissent over various treaties was focused by the chiefs Big Bear, Piapot and Poundmaker. They demanded their own hunting territories which they would govern themselves. In 1884 Big Bear convened the biggest assembly of plains chiefs in North American history at Battleford on Poundmaker's reserve. There one chief said they had been blind in ceding their land to the white man. During another assembly at Duck Lake the chiefs were addressed by Louis Riel. The chiefs agreed to send the Government a petition listing broken treaty promises and demanding greater autonomy. Big Bear united the plains people. His strategy was to seek a political solution rather than an armed revolt. But their growing militancy, especially among the splinter faction led by Poundmaker, heightened the Government's fears of uniting the Metis with 90,000 Indians.

Dumont realized the potential for using such fears to force Ottawa to agree to the Metis' terms. However, he spoke no English and even in his own language was no great orator. Someone else was needed to negotiate. With three companions he rode 700 miles to the Church of St Peter's mission. He told the forty-year-old Riel, now pale-skinned and gaunt, that French, English and Indian were ready to join the old cause. Louis Riel had his divine mission at last.

Riel gathered his wife Marguerite, two young children and a few possessions into a Red River cart and headed north. Outside Fort Benton he had his vision of the gallows. He ignored it and in early July the little band reached Batoche, by now the chief Metis township in the Saskatchewan Valley. At first Riel was treated as a valuable friend but not as a ruler and he failed to incorporate native soil rights in the declaration sent to Ottawa that winter. But Riel was listened to carefully by English-speaking Metis who had never followed him before, and he retained the support of the Catholic Church whose priests saw him as a hunted soul. Riel's influence grew as the Government dithered over a proposed bill of rights which demanded deeds to existing riverfront lands, a fairer deal for Indians, extra land for the Metis, reduced taxes, representation at the Dominion Parliament and a rail link to Hudson's Bay. Macdonald neither agreed nor disagreed but made secret arrangements to set up a Mounties post at Fort Carlton, 20 miles from Batoche. He also prepared to establish an investigatory commission into Metis' land claims and sent flour, bacon, tea and tobacco to the Indians. His concessions came too late.

Riel was by now convinced that a constitutional solution was impossible. He roared for armed resistance. On 5 March 1885 he declared: 'We are going to take up arms for the glory of God, the honour of religion and for the salvation of our souls.' He used an almanac to persuade his less educated followers that a partial eclipse of the sun was a sign from God. He and Dumont seized an arms cache in a Batoche store and took several white hostages. On 19 March Riel formed the Provisional Government of Saskatchewan with himself as God's Prophet. Dumont was the Adjutant-General charged with organizing 400 Metis into a cavalry squadron. Dumont's nominees were to form the council to manage the new state.

Riel demanded the surrender of Fort Carlton, manned by Major Leif Crozier and a force of Mounties. He offered them safe conduct if they surrendered, and a 'war of extermination' against those who refused. Crozier cautiously sent out a small scouting party to investigate but they were turned back by armed horsemen. Crozier then blundered, deciding on immediate action rather than waiting for reinforcements. On 26 March he led a column of 100 men – fifty-five Mounties, the remainder volunteers – with a small cannon and twenty horse-drawn sleighs to Duck Lake to deny the Metis arms and food held in the village store. Gabriel Dumont with Metis and Indian allies were waiting for them.

The column approached the small town in single file, struggling through deep, soft snow. Metis riflemen could be glimpsed through the trees, slowly encircling them. Crozier formed the sleds into a makeshift barricade and advanced to parley under a white flag along with his interpreter John McKay. Dumont's brother Isidore and an Indian met them but a scuffle broke out which resulted in Crozier giving the order to fire. Isidore was hit and later died of his wounds. The white men took cover behind their sleds and blazed away at caps and feathered bonnets visible above the snow, only to realize they were wasting their ammunition on headgear stuck on poles. The Metis fire grew steadily stronger as up to 150 fighters joined the fray. Crozier and his men were in a desperately exposed position. The seven-pounder was brought to bear but after three harmless shots a panicky gunner ruined it by ramming home a shell before its powder. Metis sharpshooters fired from the tree line, from a vacant log cabin, from dugouts in the snow. Riel appeared on a hill crest, riding a horse and holding aloft a large crucifix. Troopers fired at him but all missed, spurring Riel's men into more ferocious volleys.

After twenty minutes Crozier had lost a quarter of his force, 12 dead and 14 wounded, while the Metis had lost 5 men. When Crozier called the retreat Dumont, bleeding from a scalp wound, yelled for their total annihilation. Riel called a stop to that, saying: 'For the love of God kill no more of them.' The Metis collected arms and ammunition from the dead and then carried their bodies to the little cabin which had held snipers during the battle. The surviving Mounties were given safe passage to collect the corpses and Metis rebels helped them load the bodies on to wagons.

The Mounties' reputation for invincibility had been shattered. Their defeat sparked panic across Canada and encouraged Cree hotheads to launch their own attacks. Most crucially it marked the real beginning of an armed uprising. For the Metis there could be no going back.

Crozier's force staggered back to Fort Carlton, to be joined by 108 more Mounties from Regina under Commissioner A.G. Irvine. The new commander saw no point in trying to defend the flimsy fort which had been designed as a trading post, not a stronghold. Irvine decided to concentrate the entire force at Prince Albert. Over 350 Mounties, volunteers and traders were evacuated. They left a blazing fort, accidentally set aflame by a straw mattress left too close to a stove. Dumont planned to ambush the demoralized column but he was again restrained by Riel.

Irvine had a wooden palisade erected around Prince Albert's Presbyterian Church and within days 1,800 defenders, townspeople and terrified refugees from the countryside were packed within it. Corporal Donkin wrote: 'The enclosure was filled with sleighs and a restless, surging throng. The interior [of the church] was simply a vast nursery of noisy children and screaming females.' Women tended frostbitten feet and served food from two long tables. The perimeter was defended by 200 policemen and 300 volunteers. They were not attacked.

Back in Ottawa Macdonald ordered the immediate raising of a Canadian militia army. It was to be Canada's first national army. Young recruits raced to enlist, thirsty for adventure out west. Militia regiments were mustered in Winnipeg, Quebec (including the French-speaking 65th rifles), and Nova Scotia. Ontario supplied 2,000 troops. Within two months 8,000 soldiers were mobilized to subdue an estimated 1,000 fighting men among the Metis.

As exaggerated tales of slaughter spread throughout the Provinces the whites feared most that the rebellion would shift to the reservations, leading to a full-blown Indian war across Western Canada. After Duck Lake Riel did send messages to several chiefs, urging them to capture all policemen they could find. In reality few tribes saw any future in battling against the redcoats. There was no co-ordinated Cree or Blackfoot movement to reinforce the Metis in a joint revolt, as some historians have suggested. But there were some young warriors of the Cree and Assiniboine bands who saw the Duck Lake fiasco as a signal to cause some mayhem of their own.

Two days after Duck Lake Poundmaker led a breakaway band of 200 Crees on Battleford, 100 miles to the west. Over 500 people were sheltered in the NWMP barracks just outside town, alongside its garrison of just forty-three Mounties. Poundmaker's force demanded supplies and ammunition and some braves began looting Company stores and ransacking the town. Neighbouring farmsteads were burnt and one white settler who had stubbornly stayed put was killed. The Indians kept out of range of the barracks cannon and laid siege to the barracks for three weeks, but gave up and left once it became clear the defenders had plenty of food, water and ammunition.

Further north, near Fort Pitt on the North Saskatchewan, a much worse tragedy was enacted. Big Bear and his followers had wintered on a reservation at Frog Lake. On 2 April a war party of Crees from a warrior society known as the Rattlers halted a Mass at the mission church and then seized the Hudson's Bay store. They rounded up thirteen white settlers and ordered them to their camp, but the Indian agent, Thomas Trueman Quinn, refused to go. Wandering Spirit, a white-hating war chief with eagle feathers in his bonnet denoting his five previous kills, screamed at Quinn to move or die. Quinn, a burly Minnesotan, was adamant. Big Bear was too late to stop the white man taking a bullet in the chest from Wandering Spirit's rifle. The war chief started yelling 'Kill, Kill,' and other Crees took up the chant. The white captives were shoved out of the church and fell before Indian fire. Two priests were among the dead, one of them shot in the neck by Wandering Spirit. Only four of the thirteen whites survived: two widows and a young clerk were dragged off as captives and Quinn's nephew escaped to take news of the murders to Fort Pitt. Big Bear then regained control of his Crees and when the Indians surrounded the Fort he promised its defenders safe passage. The fort was handed over without a shot being fired.

So far only around 400 of an Indian population over 20,000 strong had taken up the gun and hatchet. Macdonald sent more supplies to the Blackfoot, Stoney and Saulteaux tribes to keep them loyal to the Crown. Macdonald's main priority was to get his new army into place. He reached a deal with the Canadian Pacific Railway to transport the fledging army in return for loans to meet payroll debts. The problem lay with a section of line along the north of Lake Superior which contained 86 miles of gaps where engineers were still cutting rock and building escarpments through swamp. The railroad promised to transport the troops on to the prairie in eleven days via a shuttle system of horse-drawn sleighs and wagons. For the new recruits the trip proved a nightmare as temperatures dropped to -35 degrees Fahrenheit. After one trek across the ice of the lake one trooper wrote home: 'We dared not stop an instant as we were in great danger of being frozen, although the sun was taking the skin off our faces.' He reported that one of his comrades was blinded by snow-glare and another went mad.

By mid-April the North-West Field Force had reached its dispersal point beyond Winnipeg. The first column of 800 men under Major-General Frederick Dobson Middleton was already marching north from Qu'Appelle towards Metis territory. A second column of 550 men marched out of Swift Current under Lieutenant-Colonel William Otter to relieve Battleford. And a third under the well-named Major-General Thomas Bland Strange set off from Calgary. The strategy was for Middleton to subdue the hard core of Riel's ragged army, estimated at 350 strong, of whom only 200 carried firearms. Middleton and Strange would then form a pincer to pacify the Cree Indians near Fort Pitt.

Middleton advanced slowly and cautiously. A Sandhurst graduate who had fought policing actions in New Zealand and India, the fat and be-whiskered Middleton had little faith in his green troops. He believed that a long march would teach them something of soldiering. He had absolute faith in the old-style tactics of a slow, steady advance in force and in the British square which had served so well at Waterloo. He left most of his cavalry to guard rail line and supply posts. But Canada's wild wilderness with its tough, mobile peoples was not the Waterloo plain. Dumont, who had fought the Sioux along the Missouri, believed in swift guerrilla campaigns with night raids and hit and run tactics. He was again restrained by Riel who was afraid of losing his general, but Dumont was finally allowed to plan an ambush.

On 24 April Dumont hid with 130 Metis and Indians in a coulee or small ravine on Fish Creek, a few miles ahead of Middleton's force. They dug rifle pits among the trees and thick brush, their weapons pointing uphill to catch the troopers exposed as they crossed the brow of a hill. The ambush should have been ruined when some young rebels revealed themselves by chasing stray cattle, and others fired too early. But Middleton doggedly ordered his column over the hill's crest in parade-ground ranks. They were greeted by deadly volleys from the concealed sharpshooters. Middleton's artillery men could not sufficiently depress the barrels of the two cannon and their shot shattered tree-top twigs but hit no ambushers. The Metis sang rebel songs as they blazed away; one played a flute; Dumont drank medicinal brandy from kit abandoned by a Canadian doctor. At dusk Middleton withdrew. He was so shaken that he stopped for two weeks to regroup, bury the dead, tend the wounded and call for reinforcements. He lost fifty men dead or wounded. Dumont, well dug in but still outnumbered five to one, lost four dead and two wounded.

On the same day Otter and his column received a rapturous welcome as they marched into Battleford. After a few days' rest Otter went in pursuit of Poundmaker and his braves, aiming to surprise the Indians sleeping in their camp at Cut Knife Creek. But the Cree were too wily for that and as Otter unlimbered his artillery they melted into the bush. Otter bombarded empty tepees but after a few minutes was suddenly thrown on the defensive as Indians appeared on all sides. Although Poundmaker's 300 men were armed with old muskets and bows they kept Otter's 350 well-armed men pinned down for seven hours. The Canadians eventually fought their way back to Battleford, losing 8 dead and 15 wounded. Their survival was partly due to Poundmaker who ordered his braves to let the white men return to the fort in peace.

Middleton's stalled column was now reinforced by two fresh companies and an American manufacturer with the latest war technology, a rapid-fire Gatling gun. He was also given his own navy – the flat-bottomed *Northcote* which had previously delivered mail along the territory's waterways and which the Government had rented for fifty-eight days at a cost of $14,500. Middleton armed it with the Gatling, a seven-pound cannon and thirty-five riflemen, intending to use it to bombard Batoche while his main force attacked. This plan proved to be a farce.

Dumont, now in Batoche, had been alerted by scouts who witnessed the transformation of the steamer. As the vessel approached the town it came under a furious crossfire from both banks. The skipper ordered more steam to speed through the ambush. Across the river ahead the Metis had rigged two ferry cables spaced well apart. The *Northcote* steamed under the first and its crew watched helplessly as it dropped behind them, cutting off their retreat. The second cable began to lower to catch the ship like a rat in a trap. The Metis were fractionally too slow and the steel rope scraped over the superstructure, cutting masts and rigging and severing the smokestacks which set alight the debris-strewn deck. The crew doused the flames with buckets as they dodged Metis bullets until finally their ship rounded the bend out of rebel range.

That same day, 9 May, Middleton's vanguard reached the outlying parts of Batoche. The small town appeared deserted as cannon opened fire on the houses and tepees. As Middleton ordered his first wave forward down a long grassy hillside all hell broke loose. Dumont was repeating the tactics he used at Fish Creek. His men were concealed in an intricate network of trenches and rifle pits to catch the troopers as they crossed the skyline. As troopers fell the dry brush was fired to prevent the defenders being outflanked. The soldiers fired volleys blind into dense smoke. When dusk fell Middleton ordered his men back to spend a miserable night in the shelter of a wagon stockade, their sleep broken by sporadic gunfire and a rocket which Dumont detonated at midnight.

The following day Middleton held his men back from the Metis trenches. For two more days both sides faced each other, sniping and goading, but refusing to close. Louis Riel crept back and forth along the trenches, praying with his men and urging them to trust in God. Ever more practical Dumont told them not to waste their ammunition, which was running out fast. The stalemate might have continued for much longer were it not for the frustration of Middleton's officers and men. They urged a bayonet charge, arguing that their 900 men should easily swamp barely 200 buffalo hunters. Middleton, whose nerve must have been shaken at Fish Creek, did not want to risk many more casualties.

Finally the Ontarian Colonel A.T.H. Williams took action while Middleton was eating lunch on the fourth day of the siege. Williams led his Midland Battalion pell-mell down the hillside.

Their enthusiastic charge was infectious and they were joined by riflemen from Winnipeg and Grenadiers from Toronto. Middleton ordered a bugle recall but it was ignored and he was forced to move up his main body in support. Luckily for the attackers the Metis had virtually run out of bullets and were reduced to firing pebbles, buttons and scrap metal. The troopers overran the first line of trenches before they could reload. The rebels manned a second line but that too quickly fell to the roaring soldiers. One Metis who would not run was 93-year-old Joseph Quellette. Dumont urged him to retreat but the old man refused, saying he wanted to slay another Englishman.

Some Metis continued fighting right to the riverbank while others took shelter in the ruins of the town. By nightfall further resistance was useless. Men surrendered to safeguard their women and children from further bombardment. Riel and Dumont were among those who slipped away. Quellette's body was found riddled with bullet or bayonet wounds. The Metis lost 16 dead, including 75-year-old Joseph Vandal, while Middleton suffered 8 dead and 46 wounded. One in ten of all those who took part were casualties.

Riel hid and prayed in the woods for three days before giving himself up to scouts. Middleton was surprised to find him a 'mild-spoken and mild-looking man'. He appeared famished and freezing and the general gave him a greatcoat to wear over his narrow shoulders. Under heavy guard he was sent by river to Saskatoon and from there by wagon to the territorial capital, Regina, and a Mountie blockhouse. Middleton then marched to relieve Prince Albert, its inhabitants still cramped within their stockade. After being greeted as a hero he travelled on the repaired *Northcote* to receive the unconditional surrender of Poundmaker and his Crees outside Battleford.

Meanwhile General Strange and his column of 3,375 infantry, 25 Mounties and 100 volunteers completed their 250-mile march from Edmonton to Fort Pitt. The Mounties were headed by the now legendary Sam Steele in all his scarlet splendour. The force tracked Big Bear and his 200 warriors and the two sides skirmished at Frenchmen's Butte. Strange, a canny if eccentric soldier, pulled back from encircling horsemen because he knew the dangers of 'committing Custer'. Middleton with 200 more troops joined Strange's column on 6 May and took command. The fighting was almost over. Big Bear retreated into impenetrable swamps but the Indians were starving. A squad of Mounties surprised a band of Crees at Loon Lake and an inconclusive firefight ensued. Sergeant Billy Fury was wounded and several Indians killed. They were the last battle casualties of the war.

Big Bear released some white prisoners and pleaded for the shooting to stop. As his men limped in small bands to surrender at Fort Pitt, Big Bear and his twelve-year-old son walked 100 miles eastward as police, militia and soldiers turned the country upside-down looking for him. He walked unannounced into Fort Carlton and gave himself up to a Mountie sergeant. It was a brave final gesture from a chief now half-starved and ragged.

Eighteen Metis were convicted of treason at Regina and jailed for up to seven years. Eleven Crees implicated in the Frog Lake massacre were sentenced to death at Battleford. Three were reprieved but Wandering Spirit and seven others were hanged. Big Bear and Poundmaker were sentenced to three years' imprisonment, a generous gesture in white eyes but a cruel punishment to Indians. They were freed after two years but, weakened physically and spiritually, they both died within six months. Most of the seventy-three Metis prisoners were discharged and others acquitted. Riel's secretary, Jackson of Prince Albert, was found insane and sent to the Selkirk Asylum, from which he escaped and was last seen in America.

Dumont, the best general on both sides, used all his famed frontier skills to evade capture. Once convinced the war was lost he fled to Montana and plotted a daring rescue mission. He set up a secret network of relay stations along the 450 miles from Regina to Montana, each stocked with fresh horses to speed Riel to safety. But the scheme came to nothing. The guard around Riel was increased and the breakout plan abandoned. Several years later Dumont was the star of Buffalo Bill's Wild West Show.

* * *

On 28 July 1885 the trial of Louis Riel began in a hastily erected courtroom in Regina. In the opening submissions the prosecutor said it was possibly the most serious trial ever to take place in Canada. Riel faced a part-time magistrate and a jury of six white settlers. Reporters from a dozen newspapers were at the Press table. Ladies, including Middleton's wife, sat in a separate section. Riel sat in a wooden box, with two Mounties on either side. His four-man defence team, hired by Quebec sympathizers and including Chief Justice Sir Charles Fitzpatrick, wore robes and wigs. The crowded room was oppressively hot.

The Government had faced severe criticism for its leniency fifteen years before, for the failure to punish Scott's murderers, and for its amnesty for Riel. Equally many French Canadians, Catholics and some white Westerners saw Riel as a patriot heading for martyrdom. Prime Minister Macdonald appears to have been genuine in his determination that there should be a fair trial under the law, rigorous justice and no more clemency if guilt were proved. There was never any real doubt about that:

Riel's indictment claimed that in committing high treason he had been 'moved and seduced by the instigation of the devil'. Standing erect and with a firm voice Riel declared himself 'Not Guilty'. The prosecution read a letter Riel had written threatening to exterminate the whites. Witnesses quoted Riel as demanding 'blood, blood . . . everybody that is against us must be driven from the country'. The facts of the uprising were not in dispute.

On his arrest Riel had claimed that captured papers would show he had never intended to make war, only to convince the Government of the need to concede a fair land deal to his people. Riel's defence team knew that such excuses would not be acceptable in court. Whatever the motives Riel had incited revolt. They gambled on saving his life with a plea of insanity. Riel protested loudly, interrupting his own lawyers several times and saying: 'Here I have to defend myself against the accusation of high treason or I have to consent to the animal life of the asylum.' Two doctors gave evidence that Riel suffered from 'megalomania', but they could not agree on the causes of his alleged madness.

Riel defeated his own lawyers in his final statement at the end of the trial. He spoke lucidly and passionately for an hour. Everyone in the hushed courtroom listened spellbound to an electrifying defence of the Metis. His less than perfect English did not detract from its eloquence. He said: 'It would be an easy matter for me today to play the role of lunatic. The excitement which my trial causes me is enough to justify me acting in the manner of a demented man. When I came here from Montana I found the Indians starving. The half-breeds were subsisting on the rotten pork of the Hudson's Bay Company. This was the condition, this was the pride, of responsible government! I directed my attention, to assist all classes, irrespective of creed, colour or nationality . . . No one can say the North-West was not suffering last year . . . but what I have done, and risked, and to which I have exposed myself, rested certainly on the conviction I had to do, was called upon to do, something for my country.' If anyone was mad, he argued, it was 'a monster of irresponsible, insane Government'. He added: 'The North-West is also my mother and I am sure that my mother will not kill me. She will be indulgent and will forget . . . I say humbly through the grace of God, I believe I am the prophet of the new world.' A newspaper report said that Riel spoke with terrible earnestness and the force of a trumpet blast, adding: 'That every soul in court was impressed is not untrue, and many ladies were moved to tears.'

The trial lasted five days. The jury found him guilty but his speech moved them to ask for clemency. This was denied and Riel heard Mr Justice Richardson's words: 'It is now my painful duty to pass the sentence of the court upon you, and that is . . . that on the 18th of September next you will be taken to the place appointed for your execution, and there be hanged by the neck till you are dead, and God have mercy on your soul.'

Petitions for mercy were sent to Ottawa and the political backlash from the sentence threatened to tear Quebec apart. Reprieves were granted three times to hear appeals and Macdonald ordered a new investigation into Riel's mental state. Two medical men and a North-West Mounted Police surgeon were sent to Regina. They found that Riel suffered hallucinations and held many 'eccentric and foolish' views on religion but, crucially, concluded that he was entirely capable of judging right from wrong and was therefore responsible for his actions. The police surgeon Dr Jukes said: 'I cannot escape the conviction that except on purely religious questions relating to what may be called divine mysteries he was, when entrusted to my care, and still continues to be, sane and accountable for his actions.'

During the trial and its aftermath evidence was submitted that Riel had spent nineteenth months in 1877–78 at the Beauport Asylum and other institutions in Washington and Longue Pointe. In a letter published later by the *Toronto Globe* Dr Daniel Clark of that city's Asylum for the Insane said: 'I spoke to some of the half-breeds who were in all his fights, and they said positively that Riel was apparently rational enough until the Duck Lake fight, and that after the excitement of that fight he seemed to have changed entirely and become a religious fanatic; he organised no opposition, did no fighting, but was looked upon as inspired – running about with a crucifix and calling upon the Trinity for aid.' He added: '. . . had he been an obscure man there is not an asylum in Christendom but would have committed him on the evidence, and legally so; but because he had been the indirect cause of a deplorable outbreak, his mental condition became of secondary importance, as political exigencies arose paramount.'

Appeals of mercy were swamped by others demanding that sentence be swiftly carried out. Many predictably came from Old Ontarian enemies, Protestant leaders and white businessmen. But the French-speaking and Catholic communities were also divided. Catholic missionaries in the battle area around Batoche and Duck Lake denounced Riel for the misery he had caused. And the venerable Bishop of St Albert had no pity for Riel, only for his followers. The bishop wrote to Macdonald: 'These poor halfbreeds would never have taken up arms against the Government had not a miscreant of their own nation, profiting by their discontent, excited them thereto. He gained their confidence by a false and hypocritical piety, and having drawn them from the beneficent influence of their clergy, he brought them to look upon himself as a prophet, a man inspired by God . . . and forced them to take up arms.'

Riel spent most of his time in the condemned cell praying and writing a last memoir in which he celebrated the Metis way of life. His mother and brother Alexandre visited him. His wife Marguerite did not. She suffered a breakdown when her third child died in premature childbirth while her husband was imprisoned. She was slowly starving herself to death.

Riel smuggled out several messages to friends, family and reporters. In one he scribbled: 'I have devoted my life to my country. If it is necessary for the happiness of my country that I should now cease to live, I leave it to the Providence of my God.'

On 16 November Riel walked into the crisp morning sunlight of Regina alongside a deputy sheriff and two priests, and on to the jailhouse gallows platform. He carried a crucifix and held himself with grave dignity, although onlookers detected a film of perspiration on his pale face despite the cold. One priest stumbled and Riel whispered: 'Courage, mon père.' Riel asked the crowd for forgiveness on behalf of himself and others, then knelt to pray. He stood to say the Lord's Prayer with Father McWilliams as a white hood was placed over his head. On the words 'lead us not into temptation but deliver us . . .' the trap was sprung.

* * *

The Federal Government spent over $5 million to subdue a few hundred ill-armed Metis and fewer Indian allies. The cost included $15 spent on rye whisky for Middleton's victory party. Around eighty whites and a similar number of rebels had been killed. Towns were devastated. The Government's victory helped to boost Canadian nationalism and pride at a crucial point. That sense of nationhood was further cemented nine days after Riel's death when the final spike was hammered in to complete the 2,900 miles of the Canadian Pacific Railway. The troops and Mounties stayed to further tame the wild North-West. As a direct result of the rebellion the territory finally won parliamentary representation, four seats in the Commons and two in the Senate. Land reforms were introduced. The federal grant to the territories was doubled to over $65,000. In 1888 the North-West was granted a full legislative assembly. All of these changes benefited the white population.

The Indians, especially the Cree, suffered more broken treaties and ceased to be an autonomous people. Their tragedy applied on both sides of the 49th Parallel. For the Metis the dream of a sovereign nation was over. Their townships, including Batoche, were pillaged and burnt by soldiers. Some who could prove they had played no part in the revolt received compensation. Others abandoned land claims in return for a quick cash settlement. Others struggled on even though the hostilities meant that few crops were harvested in 1886. Jobs were scarce and living was harsh until the boom years at the turn of the century. By then a great many Metis had simply uprooted their families and moved on. Metis communities sprang up in Montana and Dakota, while others spread further north and west, in places like Battle River, Green Lake and Lac La Biche.

Riel's body was cut down and given a simple burial at Regina. Three weeks later, with official approval, the corpse was sent secretly by rail in a rough pine coffin to St Boniface. He lay in his mother's house overnight and on 12 December was carried to the cathedral. The casket was placed on a platform surrounded by candles. Villagers from the region came by horse, sleigh and carriage to the requiem Mass said by Archbishop Tache, the man who had sent Riel to school in Montreal twenty-seven years earlier. Everyone was wearing black. Whole families, the tough menfolk included, shed tears. Riel lies in the cathedral yard at St Boniface, under a granite slab inscribed: 'RIEL, 16 NOVEMBRE 1885.' He was a flawed prophet who caused much suffering for a noble cause. He remains an enigma still. But his great last speech carries a resonance, a simplicity and a beauty that a century has not reduced. It included the prophecy: 'Though it may take 200 years my children's children will shake hands with the Protestants of the new world in a friendly manner.'

NINE

The Ashanti War of the Golden Stool, 1900

'A coffin'

In 1663 Nana Obiri Yeboa negotiated with an old lady under a Kum tree. The land he acquired became Kumasi, seat of the kings of the mighty Ashanti empire. On a Friday in 1700 within the precincts of the royal palace a golden stool, it is said, descended from the heavens to give the king a symbol of his authority. The Ashanti regalia in use until then was buried in a place marked by a sword buried to the hilt into the ground. The stool became a symbol of spiritual unity between the living and the dead, between a king and his people, between clan and state. It was sacred, political, practical and priceless.

On 25 March 1900 His Excellency Sir Frederick Mitchell Hodgson, Governor of the Gold Coast, demanded the stool for Queen Victoria. He ordered that it be brought to him, so that he might sit upon it himself. Within hours he, his wife and entourage were forced to take refuge in Kumasi's small British fort, garrisoned by a handful of British soldiers and loyal Hussans, while Ashanti snipers peppered the walls. It was the start of a strange and unnecessary small war at a time when the British Empire was preoccupied with a vastly bigger one in South Africa. A great deal of blood was shed in Britain's search for what was, for them at least, merely a political and military trophy.

* * *

The Portuguese were the first to establish trading posts and then forts on the Gold Coast, quickly followed by the Dutch and the British. They bought gold and ivory from the Fanti tribes and fought each other for domination. The Portuguese built the substantial

Elmina Castle, started in 1482, but were bombarded out by the Dutch in 1637. For two centuries control of the coastal forts swung between the Dutch and the English, with encroachments by the Spanish, French, Swedes, Danes and Brandenburgers.

The source of wealth so bitterly contested switched from ivory, wood and produce, to human cargo. The plantations of the West Indies and the American cotton states depended on slave labour. Millions of men, women and children were chained in the fetid slave dungeons before being packed into stinking ships bound west. No one knows for sure how many West Africans were enslaved, but at the slave trade's peak the British alone were shipping out 40,000 captives a year, enriching merchants in Bristol, London and Liverpool.

One of their main suppliers was the Ashanti empire which controlled the high forests 150 miles to the north. Their warriors took numerous prisoners in countless wars, sacrificed some to their fetishes and sold the surplus. It was a profitable trade for European and Ashanti slavemasters alike.

The Ashanti were a union of small states established in the early seventeenth century by Akan immigrants from the West. Before the appearance of the Golden Stool these states paid tribute to the Denkera, a more powerful regime to the south-west. The Stool was used to create spiritual unity among the states enabling them to defeat the Denkera. According to tradition the wooden stool embellished with gold was summoned from the sky by the priest Anokye before a great assembly. It descended gently on to the lap of the new king, Osei Tutu. The priest declared that the stool contained the spirits of the Ashanti ancestors and the strength of the nation depended on its preservation. From then on every Ashanti had allegiance to the Golden Stool and its guardian the King, and to his state stool and tribal chief. The Denkera were indeed defeated and the unified Ashanti nation embarked on decades of conquests, extending their empire to the northern Akim states of Sefwi, Tekyiman, Gyaman, Banda, Wassaw and Akwapim. Each conquest, each war and skirmish, brought more slaves for the ships that called to the coast. The Ashantis needed to subjugate the coastal people to control trade and profits and ensure a steady supply of Western munitions for war inland. This was what brought them into conflict with the British.

In 1807 the slave trade was banned in all British dependencies. Later that year the Ashanti crossed the sacred River Prah, attacked the Fanti federations and reached the sea. The British and Dutch commanders in their forts were forced to accept Ashanti control of the coastal region and had to pay rent for their trading establishments. With the end of the slave trade the Dutch gradually retired from the region while British merchants switched to palm oil. Cask roads were built to the ports but these were vulnerable to Ashanti raids. Tensions increased and the Ashanti refused to bear responsibility for the behaviour of their Fanti under-lords. In 1821 the British Government took over administration of the coastal forts and refused to pay any more rent to the Ashanti. The first Crown Governor, Sir Charles McCarthy, a strong abolitionist, refused to accept Ashanti authority over the Fanti chiefs. He launched a brave but doomed expedition against a new Ashanti incursion, was deserted by his native allies, and ran out of ammunition. In honour of his courage the Ashanti cut off his head and took it back to Kumasi. His skull was turned into a ceremonial drinking cup for state occasions.

Almost forty years of peace followed during which the British set up a Protectorate in the coastal regions. The Ashanti were content to maintain their power in the North and the central uplands, trading in palm oil, gold, and hardwood, farm maize, manioc, plantain, bananas and yams. But their war-like nature, built out of necessity and commercial realities, erupted when King Kofi Karikari sent an army of 12,000 warriors once again across the Prah. The Protectorate tribes were reduced to 'a heap of scattered fugitives at the mercy of a pitiless and bloody foe, whose delight is to torture and who will drive them by thousands into slavery, and slaughter all the weak and sick'.

British sailors and marines garrisoning the coastal forts held back the invaders as an expedition force was dispatched from Liverpool. Its commander was Major-General Sir Garnet Wolseley, chosen out of 400 generals to lead the campaign. After fierce fighting Wolseley and his army took Kumasi at dawn on 4 February 1874.

The famous journalist and explorer Henry Stanley wrote: 'We were anxious and curious to see Kumasi, the capital of the Ashantis, with its most remarkable objects – the King's palace, the place of execution, the great market, the town square. The streets were numerous; some half a dozen of them were broad and uniform. The main avenue on which the British and local troops bivouacked during the night was about 70 yards wide; here and there were great shade trees. The houses in the principal streets were wattled structures, with alcoves and stuccoed facades, embellished with Arabic patterns. Behind each of the big buildings were groups of huts for the women, children and slaves, enclosing small courtyards. By the general order and neatness . . . I was compelled to the conclusion that they were a very clean people.'

Winwoode Reade of the London *Times* wrote: 'The King's palace consists of many courtyards, each surrounded with alcoves and verandahs having two gates or doors secured by padlocks. The rooms upstairs reminded me of Wardour Street in London.' He found books in many languages, the 17 October issue of his own newspaper, Persian rugs, Kidderminster carpets, Bohemian glass, a sword inscribed from Queen Victoria, gold-studded sandals with Arabic on the soles, caps of beaten gold covered with leopard skin, velvet umbrellas and other treasures 'too numerous to describe or even catalogue'.

The British forces looted and then dynamited the deserted King's palace. Sappers burned most of the city. The captured booty was taken by thirty porters to Cape Coast.

Wolseley, who had directed his forces from a hammock carried by four soldier-porters, puffing on a cigar while bullets whistled past in best *Boy's Own* fashion, left after two days. Karikari's envoys agreed at the Treaty of Fomena to keep the road from Kumasi to Cape Coast Castle clear and open for trade and peaceful travel. The British agreed to withdraw in return for 50,000 ounces of pure gold in reparations for the £200,000 that Wolseley had budgeted for the war. There was peace for another twenty years.

In 1895 the British asked permission to station a garrison at Kumasi because they were fearful of German and French empire-building to the north. The request was repeatedly turned down by King

Prempeh I, whom British propagandists painted − probably rightly − as a bloodthirsty tyrant. A British column marched into Kumasi the following year without firing a shot. They found numerous skulls and traces of human sacrifice, adding to the Ashanti's fearsome reputation in Britain. King Prempeh and thirty of his close royal relatives and state officials were arrested and detained at Elmina Castle. Their alleged crime was failure to pay the 1874 reparations in gold. They were exiled, first to Sierra Leone and then to the Seychelles. The British stationed seven military or administration officers in Ashanti. A small British fort was built in Kumasi and garrisoned with a few British officers and Hausa troops brought over from Nigeria. A British President was installed.

The Ashanti and northern territories remained nominally independent of the British colony to the south, but resentment simmered on both sides. It was a decapitated kingdom. The British authorities believed that with Prempeh an ocean away on another continent there was nothing to stop them winning ultimate authority over a surly, mutinous and troublesome people. The key to that authority was the Golden Stool.

The symbolic important of an Ashanti stool cannot be over stressed. Since ancient times ancestor worship had been central to the Akan peoples who became the Ashanti. Clans and states were believed to be composed of both the living and the spirits of the dead. A chief was the earthly representative of his clan's most important ancestors while his own spirit was left in his ceremonial stool, which became the symbol of a clan's spiritual unity. The blackened stools of dead chiefs were kept in stool houses which on important occasions ran red with the blood of human sacrifices. The stool represented power, unity and communion with sacred ancestors at a local level. The Golden Stool represented the same, only more so, on the national stage. The British recognized that and wanted it for their own, and none more so than the Chief Commissioner of Ashanti, Captain Cecil Armitage, who was later knighted and became Governor of Gambia. He persuaded Governor Hodgson to leave the British seat of government at Christiansborg Castle at Accra and endure the 140-mile trek to the Ashanti capital.

The Governor, with Lady Hodgson and a mixed bag of British

troops and local levies, reached Kumasi on 25 March 1900. Hodgson was typical of his era: bombastic, brave, loyal, cunning as far as his intellect would allow. Above all he had an unshakeable belief in his own superiority and that of the Empire he represented. He was a product of that rigid structure. Now aged forty-eight, he was a bureaucrat rather than a soldier. The son of a Wareham rector he had previously worked in the Post Office, rising to the post of Postmaster-General of British Guinea. His military experience was confined to Volunteer forces, including the Gold Coast levies he had raised in 1892. His wife Mary was the daughter of a former Gold Coast Governor.

Despite their king's absence the Ashanti were determined to honour Queen Victoria's representative. Important chiefs and their officials were summoned to welcome the Governor and his wife at a colourful grand durbar. Royal personages, state drummers, court criers, musicians, merchants and warriors in their finery packed the city's central square.

Buglers called a military fanfare as Hodgson, resplendent in full colonial uniform with medals sparkling at his chest, climbed on to a platform decorated with flags and garlands. His crass and insensitive remarks soured the mood of celebrations and sparked a war.

He boomed: 'Your King Prempeh I is in exile and will not return to Ashanti. His power and authority will be taken over by the Representative of the Queen of Britain. The terms of the 1874 Peace Treaty of Fomena which required you to pay for the cost of the 1874 war have not been forgotten. You have to pay with interest the sum of £160,000 a year. Then there is the matter of the Golden Stool of Ashanti. The Queen is entitled to the stool; she must receive it.' According to African translators he then went on: 'Where is the Golden Stool? I am the representative of the Paramount Power. Why have you relegated me to this ordinary chair? Why did you not take the opportunity of my coming to Kumasi to bring the Golden Stool for me to sit upon? However, you may be quite sure that though the Government has not yet received the Golden Stool at his [sic] hands it will rule over you with the same impartiality and with the same firmness as if you had produced it.'

Hodgson spoke with arrogance and with ignorance, having been improperly briefed by Armitage. The arrogance alone may have worked, or at least been ignored. The ignorance, to Ashanti eyes, was unforgivable. Hodgson did not initially recognize the deep offence he had caused. The Ashanti were sophisticated power-brokers and fully understood the Englishman's desire for the symbolic stool. They had expected nothing less. What they could not stomach was Hodgson's desire to sit himself upon the Golden Stool. It demonstrated that Hodgson had entirely missed the point. To try to use the stool for political purposes was reasonable and forgivable. But to demand to sit upon it as a representative of the English Queen's fat bottom was sacrilege. No Ashanti King had sat upon the Golden Stool as a matter of respect for long-gone ancestors. It was incomprehensible that a foreigner should wish to do so, no matter what power he represented. It was the 'height of sacrilege and an affront to the Ashantis'.

The Ashanti chiefs were too polite to reveal their feelings. The durbar required that their guests were treated with full kindness and they simply expressed their thanks to the Governor and their loyalty and friendship to the British Empire. They stuck to their prepared speeches which took no account of the mood of the audience. The crowd was muttering ominously and melted away in the back alleys of Kumasi to 'cook' war against the British. The Queen Mother of Edweso, Nana Yaa Asantewa – whose name is often used as the title of the subsequent war – urged her men to fight the British. She said: 'Why should they deport the King Prempeh and then come and take the Golden Stool of Asante? We must fight them.'

Governor Hodgson was still blissfully unaware of the trouble he had caused. He sent troops and officials under Captain Armitage to search for the Golden Stool in the bush. They were quickly surrounded and outnumbered by well-armed Ashanti. Armitage decided that a display of stiff upper lip was called for. He called for afternoon tea and troopers set up their officer's field kit of folding table, chairs, stove, cups, spoons, condensed milk, tin openers and sugar. It was a bad mistake. After five minutes Ashanti snipers let rip, shattering the cosy affair. Biscuits and bone were pierced, marmalade spilt along with blood. Luckily a sudden downpour dampened the native guns, giving the British time to drag their wounded back to Kumasi.

Hodgson realized that he had insufficient troops available to back his authority. With great dignity he retreated to the fragile safety of Kumasi's small fort. With him went his wife, sixteen Europeans of whom six were missionaries, plus the mixed-race workers of the type who made the British Empire work: trading clerks, letter-writers, pastors, teachers and minor civil servants. The garrison was made up of 300 Hausas from Nigeria with 6 seven-pounders and 4 Maxim guns.

The Ashantis made one serious assault on the fort on 29 April but the Maxims spattered carnage and they were repulsed with heavy losses. Both sides settled down for a long siege. For a month the defenders remained crammed in the fort, playing and singing patriotic songs. They were hot and hungry. They were hopelessly outnumbered and the Ashanti snipers kept up a continuous bee-sting barrage, pot-shots rather than lethal attacks. The telephone wires between Kumasi and the coast had, not surprisingly, been cut. The director of Posts and Telegraphs in Accra was sent to investigate the breach in communication. He was picked up by friendly Ashanti who lashed his feet to bloody ribbons with a section of the cut wire. His life was spared and he limped to a nearby village, his shirt wrapped around his feet. The Ashanti also knew how to organize a blockade. Roads and tracks to the coast were severed. Messengers were intercepted and detained in great discomfort, but rarely killed. The Kumasi refugees were running low on food, ammunition and morale.

A relief column was sent from the coast but it was a poorly organized feeble affair. Around 250 men arrived but half were either wounded from Ashanti ambushes or ill. They brought no extra food or ammunition. They were simply more mouths to feed. Only the well-oiled machine-guns and cannon pointing from the fort's ugly and claustrophobic parapets prevented a massacre at the fort. The Ashanti generals had no intention of attacking the fort and spilling unnecessary blood. They intended to starve them out. As the weeks dragged on their strategy seemed to be working. Over 600 people, military and civilian, European, half-caste and African, were packed into an area designed to take a tenth of that number. Dozens died daily and their deaths went mostly unrecorded. Two exceptions were Basel Mission School teachers Frederick Okanta and Helena Sakyiama. Their bodies, and the other victims of malnutrition and disease, were rolled or thrown outside the fort's walls. No one – for obvious reasons – was buried within. Rats and mice were consumed. The normal colonial niceties broke down. Black and white fought, cheated and stole for food. Troops on the parapets fired rockets and guns at the stars in the hope that a proper relief column was on its way.

Early in June a second column with 700 native troops under Major Morris arrived, the men already suffering from malnutrition. A council of war within the fort decided that positive action was needed to break the stalemate. It was agreed that the Governor and Lady Hodgson, together with several hundred Hausa troops and a large number of baggage handlers, should break out and make a dash for the coast. By now refugees had swelled the numbers within the fort to around 1,000. They were to be left in the charge of Captain Bishop, the medical officer Dr Hay, two clerks, 25 fit soldiers and around 90 semi-invalid troops. Their orders were to hold out with three weeks' starvation rations. If they were overrun they were told to die fighting and where possible to destroy their weapons before they perished.

At dawn on 23 June Hodgson's party moved out, treading softly as Ashanti pickets slept.

* * *

The break-out had been planned with great secrecy and caught the surrounding Ashanti off guard. An advance party under Captains Armitage and Leggett attacked an Ashanti stockade guarding the main escape route. In a short and fierce fight the Ashantis were driven off – at a cost. Leggett and another officer died of their gunshot wounds five days into the march. It took the Ashantis two days to organize an effective pursuit with a force up to 15,000 strong. Villages on the route to Accra had by then set up crude barricades while small groups of warriors harried Hodgson's rearguard.

Hodgson's party included the four loyal Kings of Mampon, Juabin, Aguna and Insuta, who had shared the hardships of the siege. Sir Frederick and Lady Hodgson were carried in a hammock, although the lady later recorded several times when she had been forced by urgency to walk like everyone else.

There is no question about the bravery of such colonial figures, no matter how comic they appear almost a century later. Kumasi was, and is, carved out of Africa's densest forest among hills rising to 1,000 feet. The escape column moved down primeval tracks darkened by mammoth mahoganies and wawa trees, their lower canopies clothed in lichens and orchids, the ground a swampy tangle of bamboos and broad-leafed herbs. Their enemies, well armed and numerous, were heathens with a proven record of mass human sacrifice if not cannibalism. Food and water was scarce. One officer had kept ground meat in a Bovril bottle which he shared with Lady Hodgson to keep up her energy and spirits. It was the rainy season and torrents battered escaper and pursuer alike. One Basel missionary died and was buried by the roadside. Others died of fatigue or eating poisonous roots.

An officer had earlier described the ordeal faced by another expedition on the same route: 'Some of them were worn to skeletons, all had drawn, haggard features; down with fever one day, staggering on the next; eating wretched food, fighting, urging, wrestling with recalcitrant carriers; streaming with perspiration all the time. They worked their way through great, gloomy forest, endless arches of colossal cotton trees under which flourished two other growths of forests. The lower a mass of twisted and tangled evergreens, the middle one hung with spiral creepers like huge serpents hundreds of feet in length. Below all there was the hot, wet earth emitting foul odours from its black mudholes, and many pools of slime-covered water.'

Reuters later reported: 'Eventually the carriers became so weakened by hunger that everything they carried was thrown away. The Governor and the whole party lived on plantains and endured great hardship. Fortunately the rains were not that heavy, otherwise Sir Frederick Hodgson thinks that all would have succumbed.' After crossing the Ofin the force was divided into two detachments to reduced the difficulty of finding food. Fever kept the Governor an extra day at the hamlet of Mampon.

They finally crossed the Prah River into the colony. During the break-out and march the column had lost 2 officers and 39 loyal Hausa troops dead and twice that number wounded or missing. The troops formed a square with Hodgson and his wife in the centre. Buglers sounded a royal salute. Hodgson responded and then fell in a dead faint. The Governor and his wife finally arrived at Cape Coast Castle and boarded the gunboat *Dwarf* for the final leg to Accra. He told reporters that he regarded his escape as 'one of the most marvellous on record'. He attributed its success to 'the secrecy maintained concerning the route chosen and the rapidity of the movements of the force during the journey from Kumasi to the coast'. The column arrived back in Accra after a march of sixteen days. The official report notes: 'The Governor and his whole party had been nearly starved on a diet of plantain. The carriers were too weak from hunger to carry the baggage and so left it behind, and in crossing a swamp near the Ofin River the party were wading shoulder high in water for two hours, finally securing a canoe and a raft by which they saved themselves.'

Hodgson reported that the Ashanti rebels had arms and ammunition 'but not in any quantity'. He said that when he left Kumasi 'the garrison was provisioned for 24 days at the end of which nothing but famine awaits them unless they are relieved'.

A full relief column under Major James Willcocks was by then approaching Kumasi. The column included 1,000 men, six pieces of artillery and 6 Maxims. The troops included men from local forces organized along the coast: the constabulary, the West African Frontier force, the Central Africa, West Africa and Nigeria Regiments, the Sierra Leone Frontier Police and detachments of the 1st and 2nd West India Regiment. Their dashing and confident commanding officer had given a personal pledge to relieve the remaining garrison on 15 July, the day the last stocks of food were due to run out. Willcocks was a 43-year-old veteran soldier whose chest bore a glittering array of medals bravely won in Afghanistan, on the Waziri Expedition, in Sudan, Burma and Chin Lushai. Tough, honest and experienced, he had taken command of the West Africa

Frontier Force two years earlier. He attacked swiftly and not always prudently. Four days before Hodgson's return he threw his men at heavily defended stockades protecting Kokofu, whose local king had joined the rebels. They were repulsed bloodily. Lieutenant Brownlie of the West African Regiment and several native soldiers were killed in action; 6 white officers and 70 native soldiers were wounded. Willcocks pressed on regardless, although with more caution.

Their advance was well organized, properly supplied and disciplined against a largely unseen enemy and the ever-present dangers of the forest. Wolseley had concluded in his previous expedition that military operations in West Africa could only be conducted with safety between December and February. Pestilence had given the Gold Coast a reputation as 'the white man's grave'. One officer asked an experienced fellow what kit he should take. 'A coffin,' was the response. Advances in military hygiene and medical resources were, however, catching up with the new century.

The enemy, while not a 'regular' army in the accepted sense, were no disorganized rabble. Under the Ashanti social system virtually the entire male population could be swiftly mobilized in tribal and clan groups. Most carried firearms, some flintlocks of dubious quality but others of British manufacture, bought in trade. Although the ammunition was poor and barrels had a tendency to explode, the Ashanti impressed the British with their understanding of marksmanship, their discipline and their musket-drill. The limited range of their weapons was no handicap in forest and bush fighting where the enemy were generally only a few yards away in dense cover. They carried swords as badges of office and knives to dispatch the fallen and to take heads as trophies or religious offerings.

Willcocks and his officers were following the path of previous expeditions whose lessons had been well learnt. An Army handbook written after the 1874 war and recently published warned: 'The topographical character of the country was such to illustrate in every engagement the difficulties and uncertainty that beset disciplined troops when fighting in woods and copses. The normal tactical formations of the Ashantis was a loose skirmishing order, which permitted them to display their aptitude for concealment and for rapid movements through thickets apparently impenetrable, to great advantage.' Wolseley's own dispatch after an early skirmish was quoted: 'One point stands forward prominently from the experience of this day – viz., that for fighting in the African bush a very exceptionally large proportion of officers is required. Owing to the dense cover an officer can only exercise control over the men close to him, and for this kind of work there should be at least one officer to every twenty men.'

After a smart march Willcocks relieved a small British outpost and mining station at Beckwai. Bounties of up to £100 were offered to any native prepared to take a message to the besieged garrison, but no takers were found. A runner from the fort, however, reported that the garrison was almost without food 'while a final parade for the inspection of the troops has been held'.

Those remaining inside the little fort prayed for rescue and anxiously scanned the sky above the surrounding treetops for signal flares. Captain Bishop of the Gold Coast Constabulary and Mr Ralph of the Lagos police kept the native soldiers hard at drill and watch duties. According to a later tribute: 'They held their ground unflinchingly, knowing that the end must come in a short space of time if relief failed to reach them. They were assured, of course, that whatever was humanly possible would be done by Colonel Willcocks to relieve them before the last ration was eaten and the last cartridge was fired. But they could not be sure that there would not be some fatal error in the reckoning of time.'

For Willcocks the route ahead was cleared by loyal levies raised around Beckwai. They told him that many thousands of the enemy were waiting for him behind strong stockades. Sure enough he found four stockades guarding the approaches to the city on perfectly selected high land hidden by almost impenetrable bush. Mindful of his self-imposed deadline Willcocks ordered an immediate attack. Repeated bayonet charges by Yorubas of the Frontier Force 'absolutely paralysed the enemy'. After two days' fighting and sporadic sniping Willcocks entered Kumasi on 15 July to enfeebled cheers from the garrison and native soldiers 'too weak to stand upright'. British officers told him they could not have held out for more than another two or three days. Skeletal survivors were given food and medicine. Captain Bishop and Dr Hay, whose endurance and cheerfulness had saved many lives, were later awarded the Distinguished Service Order and the Companion of the Order of St Michael and St George respectively.

Two days later Mr Chamberlain announced the relief of Kumasi to loud cheers in a House of Commons otherwise preoccupied by the Boer War, the Boxer Rebellion in China and the Irish Question. A *Times* editorial said: 'In these dark days the escape of the gallant little band who were left to hold the Ashanti capital after the Governor had made his bold and successful dash to the coast is a thing of which to be proud . . . We rejoice most heartily that the gallant little band which Sir Frederick Hodgson left behind him have joined hands with the British troops under Colonel Willcock's command.' The leader writer insisted that Sir Frederick's decision to evacuate the fort and abandon wounded and civilians was justified: 'Being closely invested by vast and increasing hordes of Ashantis for several weeks he was running short of both ammunition and food. The withdrawal of the greater part of the garrison was a bold and well-managed move which, although it involved very considerable losses, averted a disaster the moral effect of which might have shaken the power of all civilised nations in West Africa.' The 'Thunderer' went on: 'But while the skilful manner in which the retreat to the coast was effected is worthy of all praise, the country should not forget the heroism of the men who remained behind to keep the Imperial flag flying in the face of savage and ruthless rebels.' It concluded: 'The honour of the British name has been upheld in West Africa and the native races will not fail to appreciate the consequences!'

After caring for the sick and wounded, and securing the Kumasi perimeter Willcocks sent out flying columns to destroy nearby stockades. He beat a large Ashanti force at Obassa on 30 September. And he had the grim satisfaction of reversing his earlier costly setback at Kokofu. A column under Lieutenant-Colonel Morland, with 800 men and three 75-millimetre guns, swooped on the large Ashanti encampment. Willcocks sent a telegram to the Colonial Office: 'Rebel force taken entirely by surprise and, as they rushed from their war camp to occupy stockade, Major Melliss, with the

F Company, Hausas, in the face of their hurried fire, charged with bayonet and dashed over the stockade, forcing rebel forces back.' The stockade was taken before the Ashanti could occupy it and those who tried were met with cruel volleys from British guns now balanced on the ramparts. The Hausas, aided by Yoruba and Nupos troops, pressed on, taking a second stockade and not stopping until they entered the town 'on the heels of the enemy'. The suddenness of the charge and the element of surprise ensured no casualties among Morland's men. The Ashanti defenders lost thirty warriors, a large quantity of guns, carbines, Sniders and powder. Their most important war camp, a rallying point for rebellious tribes, was utterly destroyed. In his telegram Willcocks praised Morland's 'able disposition' and Melliss's gallantry which in his opinion saved many lives. He added: 'There can be little doubt that Ashantis will not await arrival of bayonet charge.'

Charles John Melliss was awarded the Victoria Cross for leading the bayonet charge against the stockades. Then aged thirty-eight, he was later knighted and rose to the rank of major-general. He served in the First World War and died, aged seventy-three, in 1936.

Many other actions followed but none as dramatic. Sixty chiefs were taken prisoner before December, the rest surrendered by the end of the month, and the Ashanti warrior kingdom ended with a whimper. The Ashanti Queen, Yaa Asantewa, was captured and exiled. Total casualties, including deaths from disease among the British-led forces, were 1,007. The casualties on the Ashanti side are not known. Several Europeans allegedly saw the Golden Stool as it was taken into hiding. They described it as 'very massive, with two heavy gold chains and solid balls the size of oranges, and adorned with two symbolic figures.'

* * *

In Accra Sir Frederick Hodgson, fully recovered from an ordeal of his own making, celebrated the escape with a garden party on the well-manicured lawns of Christiansborg Castle. The guests included Gold Coast kings, Fanti chiefs, elders, European soldiers, missionaries, civil servants, African pastors, all dressed in a dazzling array of costumes from a dozen cultures. Black boys in livery passed imported drinks and small chops as an orchestra played and Lady Hodgson glowed as she described 'terrible privations'. It was her husband's swansong. He was transferred from the Gold Coast to Barbados as Governor and Commander-in-Chief. Whitehall could not openly blame him for the fiasco but was determined not to overly reward him either. He stayed in the Caribbean for four years before governing British Guinea between 1904 and 1911. He retired to his home in South Kensington, enjoying his gentlemen's clubs (Conservative, Ranleigh and West Indian) while Lady Mary published her own account *The Siege of Kumasi* to some acclaim. Frederick died in 1925, aged seventy-three.

Willcocks won immediate promotion to a brevet colonelcy on the relief of Kumasi. He was one of the last of the flamboyant Victorian adventurers and his subsequent career continued much as before. He was given the Freedom of the City of London and a sword of honour for the exploit and won a mention in King Edward VII's first speech at the state opening of Parliament. He commanded a field force in South Africa at the tail-end of the Boer War, served in India and on the 1906 Zakka Khel expedition, gaining both a knighthood and his general's pips. Although by then in his sixties, he was mentioned in dispatches twice on the Western Front in 1915 before peacefully cruising into retirement as Governor of Bermuda until 1922. He wrote several memoirs, including the splendidly titled *Romance of Soldiering and Sport*. He died in 1926.

Hodgson was succeeded as Gold Coast Governor by Sir Matthew Nathan who imported the first motor vehicle in 1903. The Ashanti kingdom was placed under martial law but there was very little more fighting. On 26 September 1901 it was formally declared a Crown Colony. Many chiefs were de-stooled and thirty more joined King Prempeh in distant exile. He was not allowed to return until 1924, after almost thirty years. He died six years later, aged fifty-nine, a sad and broken figure. Two airy, sun-swept rooms in which the king and his household spent their first period of imprisonment can now be visited on top of the seaward bastions of Elmina Castle.

Ashanti was ruled by the Gold Coast Governors through a chief commissioner in Kumasi. Tennis courts and croquet fields were created as that town was developed into one of the most modern and tranquil in West Africa. Christian missions helped with education as roads and railways were built. The power of the chiefs was undermined. A cannon was fired in Kumasi at noon every day until 1935 to remind its people of British control. A war memorial was built outside the post office. If it was colonial tyranny it was relatively benign. The fort which had seen so much suffering from battle wounds, disease and starvation was well preserved and is now a military museum.

The Gold Coast was the first in West Africa to achieve freedom from colonization in 1957. It was called Ghana after a sixth-century Sudanese empire which had flourished a thousand miles away. The country has seen its share of turmoil, *coups* and revolutions but it has escaped the worst horrors of the continent. The Ashanti people, two million or more, continue to flourish.

The Golden Stool was hidden in a hole in the buttress of a tree outside Kumasi. Responsibility for keeping it safe and out of British hands was handed down through the generations. In 1920 a Government anthropologist, Captain R.S. Rattray of Oxford University, convinced the administration of the Stool's religious symbolism and the British gave up their search. At around the same time some tribesmen found the hiding place and stole its golden ornaments. That was sacrilege, a crime punishable only by death under tribal law. A council of Ashanti chiefs was called but the British ruled that the criminals should be deported rather than executed. The power of the Golden Stool never recovered.

Appendix

The fifth son of a poor Scots crofter, Hector worked as a draper's assistant before running off at the age of eighteen to enlist in the Army. He rose through the ranks to become a colour sergeant of the 92nd Gordon Highlanders by the age of twenty-one. In 1879 during the Second Afghan War a column of the Kabul Field Force was attacked by 2,000 tribesmen. General Frederick Roberts was struck by the courage and leadership shown by MacDonald in the short but vicious fight and offered him the choice between the Victoria Cross and a battlefield commission, an extremely rare promotion for an enlisted man. MacDonald chose the latter.

In 1881 Macdonald, now a 28-year-old subaltern, was among those who climbed Majuba Hill and suffered the devastating Boer attack which resulted in a bloody British retreat. MacDonald tried to hold one flank of the mountain with twenty men but within an hour he had only one private left alive and he was captured by the Boers. Three years later he was among twenty-five British officers seconded to the Egyptian Army during the failed attempt to rescue Gordon in Khartoum. He fought in battles such as Gemalzah, Toski, Tokar, Firket and Hafir, and there earned his nickname.

When in 1898 Kitchener ordered a new invasion of Sudan Macdonald was put in charge of a brigade of Egyptian and Sudanese infantry. It was Macdonald who averted disaster at the crucial battle of Omdurman. Kitchener believed that the slaughter of 10,000 Dervish infantry had concluded the battle and unwittingly ordered his army into a line of march across the front of the main Dervish army which had not yet attacked. The column was hit by a charge of 20,000 enemy. Kitchener panicked but Macdonald swung his 2,000 black troops in an arc to meet the onslaught, a technique that was later taught at Staff College. He and his men coolly held their ground and cut down the attackers.

They saved Kitchener's army from destruction and ensured victory. When the battle finished Macdonald's men had on average just two rounds left per man. 'Fighting Mac' was a national hero.

Macdonald again distinguished himself in the Boer War, rising to the rank of major-general and commanding the Highland Brigade with successes at Magersfontein and Modder River. He later commanded British forces in Ceylon. In 1903 a group of schoolboys, one of them an aristocrat, alleged he had sexually assaulted them on a train. They were supported by an alleged witness, a British tea planter with a grievance against Macdonald. Charges were laid before Ceylon's Governor, Sir Joseph West Ridgeway, who became convinced that Macdonald was a practising homosexual who had used relaxed Sinhalese sexuality to take his pleasure with a large number of young men and boys. Macdonald returned to London to try to clear his name but his fall from national hero to ignominy was quickly apparent. Field-Marshall Lord Roberts told him he must prove his innocence or quit the Army.

He was ordered back to Ceylon for a court of inquiry. En route and facing public disgrace he stopped at Paris. In a room of the Hotel Regina he shot himself.

The charge against him was never substantiated and there was a widespread suspicion that he was the victim of a smear campaign motivated by class. Aristocrats and less talented officers resented the rapid promotion of a crofter's son. There was even speculation that the fat and sexually rapacious King Edward VII told him that the only honourable thing to do was commit suicide. Six commissioners appointed in Ceylon published their report in June 1903. They acquitted 'Fighting Mac' on all counts and deplored the sad circumstances which led to his suicide.

The controversy has continued ever since. In January 1995 a correspondent wrote in the *Daily Mail*: 'The disgrace of Hector Macdonald was particularly embarrassing to the British Army because almost everyone in military circles knew that General Kitchener was living with his military secretary. Court martialling Macdonald over unfounded accusations was most unfair.'

Valentine Baker (1827–89)

Valentine was the son of an Enfield merchant with rich estates in Jamaica and Mauritius. At twenty-one he went with two brothers – one of whom, Samuel, was to become a famous African explorer – to establish a farming colony in the highlands of Ceylon. He did not like hill farming and joined the Ceylon Rifles as an ensign, transferring to the 13th Lancers to fight with valour in the 1855–7 Kaffir War. In the Crimea he saw more action at the battle of Tchernaya and at the siege of Sevastopol.

By thirty-three he was in command of the 10th Hussars and reorganized the cavalry to modern efficiency. He was a distinguished author of books, pamphlets and manuals on military science and national defence. He was a spectator at the Austro-Prussian and Franco-Prussian wars, explored wild parts of Persia and Russia, and in 1874 was appointed assistant quarter-master-general at Aldershot.

The following year the 48-year-old Baker was convicted of 'indecently assaulting a young lady in a railway carriage'. He was sentenced to a year's imprisonment, fined £50 and dismissed from the Army. After his release from gaol Baker offered his services to the Turkish Army and was made a major-general. British feeling then was intensely anti-Turkish but Baker felt that the greatest threat to Europe came from Russia. The Turks were in retreat from the Russian forces but Baker commanded superb rearguard actions which averted total defeat and he was made lieutenant-general.

In 1883, after the invasion of Egypt, the British were intent on rebuilding the shattered Egyptian army along British lines. Baker was offered its command but that was withdrawn after some officers protested over his previous shameful conviction. Instead he was given command of the gendarmerie and he and his semi-military but ill-trained force were sent to the Red Sea port of Suakin in Sudan to defend it against the Mahdi's hordes. He was ordered to act with prudence and caution and to avoid any fighting. Baker took no notice.

Five weeks after landing he gathered a 3,500-strong force of gendarmerie, black Sudanese troops and a few Europeans and set out to relieve a besieged garrison 20 miles away at Tokar. At El Teb they were attacked by a much smaller force of Dervishes. Although armed with rifles, cannon and two Gatling machine-guns against Dervish clubs and spears, the Egyptian gendarmes panicked and their fighting square collapsed. They ran back and forth to avoid the slashing spears. Some knelt and begged while their throats were slit. It was total confusion and the handful of resolute Sudanese troops and British officers could do little. In total 96 officers and 2,225 men were killed. No prisoners were taken.

It was a disaster, coming shortly after the massacre of Hicks Pasha's army, and a fresh force of British regulars was dispatched to relieve Tokar. Lieutenant-General Gerald Graham routed 6,000 Dervishes at El Teb, the site of Baker's débâcle. This time disciplined fire left 2,000 Dervishes dead. Valentine Baker, seriously wounded in the face, was one of 189 British casualties.

Baker never fulfilled his hopes of reinstating himself, through battle, in the British Army. His *Times* obituary said that if it had not been for an isolated incident in a railway carriage 'his career might have been among the most brilliant in our military service'.

Bibliography and Sources

Introduction

Burroughs, Peter, 'An Unreformed Army?' included in *The Oxford History of the British Army* [general editor, David Chandler] (Oxford University Press, 1996)

Callwell, Col. C.E., *Small Wars* (London, 1906)

Farwell, Byron, *Queen Victoria's Little Wars* (Allen Lane, London, 1973)

Glover, Michael, *That Astonishing Infantry – The History of the Royal Welch Fusiliers,* (London, 1989)

Haythornthwaite, Philip J., *The Colonial Wars Source Book* (Arms and Armour Press, London, 1995)

Hibbert, Christopher, *The Great Mutiny* (London, 1978)

James, Lawrence, *The Savage Wars – British Campaigns in Africa, 1870–1920*

Judd, Denis, *Empire – The British Imperial Experience from 1765 to the Present* (HarperCollins, 1996)

Keegan, John, *The Mask of Command* (London, 1987)

Lysons, Daniel, *Early Reminiscences* (London, 1896)

Morris, James, *The Pax Britannica Trilogy* (Faber & Faber, London, 1968)

Spiers, Edward M., *The Late Victorian Army* (Manchester University Press, 1992)

Strachan, Hew, *From Waterloo to Balaclava: Tactics, Technology, and the British Army, 1815–1854* (Cambridge University Press, 1985)

Strawson, John, *Beggars in Red – The British Army 1789–1889* (Hutchinson, London, 1991)

——, *Gentlemen In Khaki – The British Army 1890–1990* (Secker and Warburg, London, 1989)

The First Kandy War, 1803–5

de Silva, Chandra Richard, *Sri Lanka, A History* (1987)

de Silva, K.M., *A History of Sri Lanka* (1981)

Knighton, William, *The History of Ceylon* (1845)
Ludowyk, Evelyn F.C., *The Modern History of Ceylon* (1966)
Miles, Lennox A., *Ceylon Under British Rule* (1964)
Pearson, Joseph, *The Throne of the Kings of Kandy* (1929)
Pieris, P.E., *Tri Sinhala, The Last Phase* (1939)
Powell, Geoffrey, *The Kandyan Wars – The British Army in Ceylon* (1984)

The Falklands, 1833

Ferns, Henry S., *Britain and Argentina in the Nineteenth Century* (Clarendon Press, Oxford, 1960)
Gough, Barry, *The Falkland Islands/Malvinas – The Contest for Empire in the South Atlantic* (Athlone Press, London, 1992)
Graham-Yooll, Andrew, *Small Wars You May Have Missed* (London, 1983)
Rock, David, *Argentina 1516–1982: From Spanish Colonization to the Falklands War* (University of California Press, 1985)

The Flagstaff War, 1845–6

Barthorp, Michael, *To Face the Daring Maoris* (Hodder & Stoughton, 1979)
Buick, T. Lindsay, *New Zealand's First War* (Wellington, 1926)
Cowan, J., *The New Zealand Wars* (Wellington, 1922–3)
Gibson, Tom, *The Maori Wars* (London, 1974)
Harrop, A.J., *England and the Maori Wars* (London, 1937)
Holt, Edgar, *The Strangest War* (London, 1962)
Knox, R., *The Maori–European Wars* (Wellington, 1937)
Ryan, T., and Parham, W.T., *The Colonial New Zealand Wars* (Wellington, 1986)
Sinclair, Keith, *The British Empire – New Zealand* (Time Life/BBC Publications, 1972)
——, *A History of New Zealand* (Allen Lane, London, 1959)

The Jamaica Rebellion, 1865

Annual Registers, 1865–6
Black, Clinton V., *History of Jamaica* (Longman Caribbean, 1958)
Burns, Sir Alan, *History of the British West Indies* (George Allen & Unwin, 1954)

Jamaica Royal Commission: *Report, 1866*
Judd, Denis, *Empire* (HarperCollins, 1996)

The Arracan Expedition, Andaman Islands, 1867

Cipriani, Lidio, *The Andaman Islanders* (London, 1966)
Kloss, C. Boden, *In the Andamans and Nicobars* (London, 1903)
Portman, M.V., *A History of my Relations with the Andamese* (Calcutta, 1899)
Radcliffe-Brown, A.R., *The Andaman Islanders* (1948)
Regimental History: The South Wales Borderers and Monmouthshire Regiment

The Magdala Campaign, 1867–8

Acton, Roger, *The Abyssinian Expedition and the Life and Reign of King Theodore* (London, 1870)
Annual Register, 1868
Bates, Darrell, *The Abyssinian Difficulty* (Oxford, 1979)
Blanc, Dr Henry, *A Narrative of Captivity in Abyssinia* (London, 1868)
Bond, B., *Victorian Military Campaigns* (London, 1967)
Markham, Clement R., *The History of the Abyssinian Expedition* (London, 1869)
Myatt, F., *The March to Magdala* (London, 1970)
Ullendorff, Edward, *The Ethiopians* (London, 1969)

The Modoc Indian War, 1872–3

Cook, Sherbourne F., *The Conflict Between the California Indians and White Civilisation* (1976)
Dockstader, Frederick J., *Great North American Indians*
Dunn, J.P., *Massacres of the Mountains*
Glassley, Ray H., *Pacific North-West Indian Wars* (1953)
Heyman, Max L., *Prudent soldier, A Biography of Maj-Gen E.R.S. Canby* (1959)
Meacham, Alfred B., *Wigwam and Warpath* (1875)
Murray, Keith A., *The Modocs and their War* (University of Oklahoma Press, 1959)
Smith, Edward P., *Report of the Commissioner of Indian Affairs, November 1 1873* (pp. 380–2)

The Riel Rebellion, 1885

Charlebois, Dr Peter, *The Life of Louis Riel* (NC Press, 1975)
Friesen, Gerald, *The Canadian Prairies* (University of Toronto Press, 1984)
Hill, Douglas, *The Opening of the Canadian West* (Longman Press, 1967)
Maxwell, Leigh, *The Ashanti Ring – Sir Garnet Wolseley's Campaigns 1870–1882* (Leo Cooper, 1985)
Pope, Sir Joseph, *The Day of Sir John Macdonald* (Glasgow, Brook and Company, Toronto, 1915)
Ross, Alexander, *The Red River Settlement* (London, 1856)
Tanner, Ogden, *The Canadians* (Time-Life, Virginia, 1977)
Williams, Sir John, *Sir Wilfred Laurier* (Oxford University Press, 1928)

The Ashanti War of the Golden Stool, 1900

Agyermang, Fred, *Accused in the Gold Coast* (Presbyterian Press, Accra, 1972)
Allison, Philip, *Life in the White Man's Grave* (Viking, 1988)
Annual Register, 1900
Hall, Major W.M., *The Great Drama of Kumasi* (London, 1939)
Maxwell, Leigh, *The Ashanti Ring* (Leo Cooper, 1985)
McFarland, Daniel Miles, *Historical Dictionary of Ghana* (Scarecrow Press, 1985)
Myatt, Major F., *The Golden Stool: An Account of the Ashanti War of 1900* (London, 1966)
Pakenham, Thomas, *The Scramble for Africa* (Weidenfeld & Nicolson, 1991)
The Times Archives

Part Two
The Savage Empire

Introduction

The Roman Empire was never at peace, from the beginning of its history to the rule of Augustus and, as Victoria foresaw, war became part of the everyday British experience, too; war of a small and distant kind, it is true, but none the less real for that – none the less noble for those who saw it as an instrument of greater ends, none the less exhilarating for those who loved the smell of the gunsmoke, nor the less tragic for those, friend or foe, who had not yet learnt to ask the reason why.

James Morris

In his *Inquiry into the Nature and Causes of the Wealth of Nations*, published prophetically in 1776, Adam Smith wrote:

The discovery of America, and that of a passage to the East Indies by the Cape of Good Hope, are the two greatest and most important events recorded in the history of mankind. Their consequences already have been very great, but in the short period of between two and three centuries which have elapsed since these discoveries were made, it is impossible that the whole extent of their consequences can have been seen. What benefits, or what misfortunes to mankind may hereafter result from these great events, no human wisdom can foresee. But uniting, in some measure, the most distant parts of the world, by enabling them to relieve one another's wants, to increase one another's enjoyments, and to encourage one another's industry, their general tendency would seem to be beneficial. To the natives, however . . .

It was a big however. During the subsequent century the various empires of the west subjugated, conquered, exploited, evicted and even wiped out entire races. By the standards of the time the motives were often 'pure' – the propagation of Christianity, trade, remorseless imperial conquest, glory, riches, social advancement – but the results were still fire-blackened villages, scorched hunting grounds empty of game, the destruction of civilisations older than our own, mass slaughter, epidemic, social inferiority and poverty.

It is not the intention of this book to judge or condemn the part the British Empire played in such worldwide suffering. To do so, in any case, would be irrelevant. It is unfair to impose today's standards on a century which preceded ours. And bigger books by better historians have already covered the social and political forces involved in creating a global empire. My purpose is simply to tell some more stories of martial glory and disgrace which have been broadly forgotten by several generations of writers, readers and teachers. Taken together they form a patchwork which, I hope, can help to explain the broader sweep of perhaps the most dynamic century in history.

Smith's work was published in the same year as Britain lost America, with the result that British ambitions turned away from the New World. Traders, explorers and soldiers looked instead to the south and to the east. The century began with Britain fighting the Napoleonic Wars which, on land at least, were largely confined to Europe; it ended with the imperial pink scattered across the globe, in Asia, Africa and Australasia. Of course Britain had settled those continents before, but generally only as trade centres, ports and islands on the main sea routes. As the century progressed vast territories were opened up. For much of that time the British public were only vaguely aware of such imperial expansion. Unlike the conquest of the North American continent, in which the drive west was remorseless and unstoppable, there was no grand plan, no Manifest Destiny. In *The Climax of Empire* James Morris wrote: 'The acquisition of it all had been a jerky process. Absence of mind it never was, but it happened so obscurely that to the ordinary Briton the rise of the Empire must have seemed like some organic movement rather than the conscious result of national policies. One thing simply led to another.'

Successive British governments, preoccupied by expensive wars against France and Russia and by social turmoil at home, tried to rein in the expansion when it involved costly administration. Time and again they were thwarted by officials on the spot, trade moguls with an eye to a quick profit, and military men hungry for glory. Gradually the empire seeped into the consciousness of the British nation and became part of its national identity. Denis Judd noted: 'It also provided manifold opportunities for personal, financial and sexual aggrandisement. It introduced strange and exotic foods, foreign flora and fauna, useful words, outlandish philosophies, new sports, other cultures, and a whole host of unfamiliar experiences into the British way of life.'

What it did to the rest of the world was equally profound. The most beneficial aspect, in terms of humanity, was the part Britain's armies and navies played in the abolition of slavery and the policing of that veto. It can be argued that it too often replaced chains and whips with economic slavery, destabilised ancient societies and was spurred on by profit rather than by genuine humanitarianism. That may have been true in some cases, but not in others. British power was actively engaged in stamping out an evil trade many decades before it was outlawed in America.

The empire also freed many people from petty princelings and brutal local dictators. Much of the empire was carved out by collaboration with the local populace rather than by outright conquest. Britain may have plundered the world, but it built much that has lasted on great continents and in far-flung corners. Nevertheless the technological advances which led to bridge-building and an industrial society hungry for materials also created weapons of mass destruction. As the century continued they were used with sanctimonious ferocity by the civilised against foes who became increasingly defenceless.

The courage of British soldiers fighting far from home, in malarial swamps and dense jungle, against enemies who refused to play according to the white man's rules of the game of warfare, should never be despised. The terrors they faced in alien landscapes were very real. Ensign Thomas Lucas, writing about a Xhosa massacre in South Africa in 1851, recalled the terror of butchery and torture committed by 'primitive' people:

Stretched out in fantastic positions across the path, lay the bodies of thirteen infantry soldiers in hideous array, horribly mutilated, the agony expressed in their glassy upturned eyes showing that they had met with a lingering death by the sharp assegais of the Kaffirs. Painful experience has since taught me that this peculiar horror of expression always attends death when produced by sharp weapons.

But it is difficult to see how such terror can compare, as the century progressed, with that imposed on native people by the western technology of war. Steamships and railways were used whenever possible to transport well-armed troops and artillery as close as possible to the startled enemy. Repeating rifles, machine-guns and shell-firing cannon became the weapons of choice against enemies armed with spears, single-shot muskets and raw, naked courage. Lawrence James noted:

In pitched battles, native warriors still relied on such traditional close-combat weapons as thrusting spears, swords, clubs and bows, arms which had rarely been seen on European battlefields since the end of the Middle Ages. Fighting with these weapons, the native had either to wait in ambush for his adversary so as to take him unawares or else rely on his own courage or religious faith and charge him in the open. His success depended upon his physical strength, fitness and skill at arms and on his being in a countryside he knew better than his enemies.

British blood-lust was evident in conflicts where well-educated officers and ignorant men faced races they considered inferior; the slaughter of such peoples was often likened to sport. At Ulundi in 1879 an NCO described a cavalry charge against fleeing Zulus: 'We had a glorious go in, old boy, pig-sticking was a fool to it.' Officers who prized their sharpshooting skills described their personal body-counts as 'bags'. A civilian observer during the 1885 Sawakin campaign wrote: 'It was a pretty sight seeing a good shot at work, and what awe the Arabs stand in of a first-class rifle shot.'

The use of firepower to murderous effect was a deliberate

strategy, a way of bringing troublesome peoples to the imperial heel. An outrage, real or manufactured, against the British Crown and its representatives was inevitably followed by a lesson in brute power. A senior officer told defeated chiefs in Sierra Leone in 1887: 'The Queen has shown you her power by sending her force and taking the country which now belongs to me and the governor. When people make war, those who have been conquered have to suffer for their misdeeds.'

During that remarkable century it was not just aboriginal natives who faced Britain's technological superiority, but also older civilisations in Spain, Persia, Burma and China. All fell before the shell splinters, high explosive and massed firepower concentrated with ruthless effect. Too often these were not isolated skirmishes but the harnessing of technology for mass murder. In that sense Britain's was a 'savage empire'. And that, too, should not be forgotten in the tumult of imperial flag-waving.

TEN

The Capture and Loss of Buenos Aires, 1806–7

'Success to grey hairs but bad luck to white locks.'

Lieutenant-Colonel Lancelot Holland wrote painfully in his diary:

> We were ordered to march out without arms. It was a bitter task, everyone felt it, the men were all in tears. We were marched through the town to the Fort. Nothing could be more mortifying than our passage through the streets amidst the rabble who had conquered us. They were very dark-skinned people, short and ill-made, covered with rags, armed with long muskets and some a sword. There was neither order nor uniformity among them.

Their ordeal marked the humiliation in South America of British arms, not once but twice, at the hands of a ragbag army of soldiers, civilians and gauchos quite different to the disciplined armies of Europe currently embroiled in global conflict. That shame resulted in the court martial of the senior officer involved but British pride quickly recovered on the glorious battlefields against Napoleon, and a bizarre adventure in South America was just as quickly forgotten. But on the southern continent it marked the beginning of the end of Spain's greedy grasp and the pride felt at the humbling of Britain led eventually to revolution and the making of Argentina.

*   *   *

In 1493 Pope Alexander VI decreed that the New World between California and Buenos Aires belonged to Spain, to be plundered and settled for the benefit of the kings of Castile. English mariners and freebooters challenged that decree from the start and the vast continent of South America became the bloody focus of global power politics.

The settlement of present-day Argentina began after Amerigo Vespucci discovered the Rio de la Plata in 1501. He was followed by such renowned explorers as Ferdinand Magellan and Sebastian Cabot. The land was disputed between Spain and Portugal but a 1535 expedition led by the Spaniard Pedro de Mendoza founded a new town: Nuestra Senora Santa Maria del Buen Aire, or Buenos Aires. Mendoza died on the journey home but his lieutenants pushed the boundaries of the new territory a thousand miles up the Plata and Paraguay rivers. Buenos Aires was neglected in favour of a settlement at Ascuncion which became the main centre for Spanish expansion for fifty years.

Buenos Aires, re-established in 1580, was isolated from the more settled northern part of the country, and in 1725 had a population of only 2,000. It relied on Indians working the corn and potato fields, and on cattle and horses imported from Spain. The whole of Argentina, less prosperous than other neighbouring Spanish colonies, was a subordinate part of the viceroyalty of Peru until 1776. By then Buenos Aires was fast coming into supremacy thanks to a shift in trade eastwards as the silver mines of Peru declined. It was becoming a bustling cosmopolitan city in which Europeans mingled with gauchos and Spanish merchants, traders with freebooters, priests with intellectuals. It was made the capital of the new Spanish viceroyalty of La Plata which incorporated present-day Argentina, Uruguay, Paraguay and southern Bolivia. The port of Buenos Aires was opened to transatlantic trade which increased its wealth immensely. It also increased the smuggling trade with Spain's traditional enemies, Portugal and Britain, and with France. The city boasted teachers of dancing and music and a French-built organ for its cathedral. By 1800 the population had swelled to 45,000. The spirit of independence grew with it, boosted by the imported ideas of European Enlightenment, the example of the French Revolution and the increasing numbers of fiercely self-reliant gauchos known as the 'centaurs of the pampa'. Encouragement came from Britain, Spain's old foe.

In 1790 a plan was put to Prime Minister William Pitt to overthrow the Spanish yoke by force and gain independence using British support. The architect of the plan was Francisco de Miranda, a Venezuelan who had gone to Spain at the age of seventeen to become an army officer. When Spain and France decided to help the American colonists in their war of independence against Britain, Miranda's unit was sent to cooperate with the French. His experiences gradually inspired him with the enthusiastic desire to emancipate his own country. At the close of the American war he resigned his commission and travelled through a Europe aflame with revolutionary thinking. In Russia he became a favourite of Prince Potemkin and the empress, who circulated letters to her ambassadors putting him under imperial protection. She threw in a gratuity of £4,000, presumably for services rendered. Miranda had to flee revolutionary France after a tribunal acquitted him of spying but left him dangerously under suspicion.

In London he produced his plan to free his country. An army of 10,000 troops would be raised in North America while Britain furnished money and ships for the expedition to oust the Spanish authorities. Pitt was keen on the idea. In return for Britain's assistance, the colonists that Miranda represented pledged £30 million, and Florida would be ceded to North America. They wanted a defensive alliance between themselves, Britain and the USA, and a treaty of commerce with Britain; in return they promised the opening up of the Panama isthmus via Lake Nicaragua, and a link between the Bank of England and those of Lima and Mexico, giving Britain command of the precious metals in those regions. But the American President Adams was tardy in agreeing terms and the plan was postponed indefinitely. However, Spain's hold on its South American possessions weakened year after year. Blockades, famine and the falling silver output all contributed to the dissent. In an effort to control the spread of nationalism, Spain eased its veto on trade with America and Portugal and even permitted the supply of jerk-beef to British colonies in the Caribbean.

In 1895 war broke out between Britain and Spain, now allied to Napoleon's France. Six years later the Miranda plan was revived, only to be halted by the peace of Amiens. Renewed hostilities in

1804 gave Miranda his best chance yet. Lord Melville and Sir Home Riggs Popham acted as liaison between Miranda and the British Government, but once again he failed to reach an agreement and the operation was again suspended under pressure from the Tsar of Russia, who hoped to win Spain over to the coalition against Napoleon.

Miranda tried once more in the United States, taking with him letters of credit from Mr Pitt and the good wishes of the British Cabinet. At New York in February 1806 he embarked upon the hired warship *Leader* with 200 volunteers, mainly young South American exiles of good reputation. The expedition did not get off to a good start. Another ship supposed to bring reinforcements was seized by American officials under pressure from the Spanish and French ambassadors. The Spanish were ready and waiting for his little force when it arrived off Caracas in a heavy gale. Some 500 soldiers and 700 Indian levies poured a heavy but ineffectual fire on Miranda's troops as they landed at dawn. However, a few determined volleys from the landing parties threw the defenders into panicked retreat. Miranda marched on the town of Coro and took it without bloodshed, but failed to win over the citizenry to his cause. Sympathetic British naval officers promised him support and a ship of the line and two frigates were actually sent to give every assistance to Miranda's 'little army' which by now numbered 500 men. But the expedition then came to a standstill. When rumours reached Miranda of a peace deal between Britain and France he was thrown into despair and returned with his followers to Trinidad. Sadly for him, the rumours were false. The affair may have ended in shambles but it cemented in the minds of senior British officers the possibility of breaking Spain's stranglehold on a rich continent. Foremost among them was Admiral Sir Hope Popham, Miranda's former intermediary.

Popham had been born forty-four years earlier at Tetuan in Morocco where his father was consul. He was his mother's twenty-first child and she died giving him life. As a young naval officer he saw action off Cape St Vincent but it was as an entrepreneur, commercial adventurer and technician that he thrived. He made important friends while serving in Calcutta but his fortunes almost foundered when a trading mission to China was stopped by the British because some of the cargo was believed to be French-owned. Popham lost £40,000 and was only partially recompensed after a lengthy lawsuit which finally cleared him of illegal embargo-breaking. Returning to naval service he soon made important royal connections while attached to the army serving in Flanders under the Duke of York. The duke praised his 'unremitting zeal and active talents' and ensured his protégé's promotion. Popham won friends at court and in the government and Pitt selected him to command the abortive missions in support of Miranda's dreams of an independent South America. Popham met Miranda many times and was fired both by his enthusiasm and by the promise of riches and glory.

During the last years of the eighteenth century Popham revamped Britain's sea defences from Deal to Beachy Head, commanded the naval part of an expedition to destroy the sluices of the Bruge Canal, arranged the embarkation of Russian troops for service against the Dutch, was made a Knight of Malta by a grateful Tsar, and provided efficient naval support for an ill-fated army assault on the Alkmaar Canal. In 1800 he was appointed commander of a small squadron ferrying troops from India and the Cape of Good Hope to Egypt. During that service he was accused of running up 'enormous and profligate' refitting expenses, a charge he was not cleared of until 1805. On his exoneration he was appointed commodore to an expedition against the Dutch in the Cape in cooperation with a land force under Sir David Baird.

Popham's squadron arrived near Robben Island on 4 January 1806 and the troops were fully disembarked by lunchtime on the 7th. The landing was not easy because of a violent swell, and a capsized boat cost the lives of thirty-five Highlanders. Enemy sharpshooters on nearby heights caused only a few casualties. The British force of about 4,000 men, with two howitzers and six light field guns, crossed the Blue Mountain and made contact with the main Dutch body of 5,000 men, most of them cavalry. The Dutch at first held their position with obstinacy but broke and ran from a charge by the Highland Brigade. Dutch losses were put at 700 men killed or wounded while British losses were 'very inconsiderable but consisting chiefly of officers'. The march on Cape Town was hampered by thorn scrub, the burning sun and a lack of water, but on the 10th the Dutch garrison surrendered and Baird took possession of the town. The brief campaign was over. Brigadier-General William Beresford was detached to occupy the countryside and secure the passes. In recognition of a gallant defence the Batavian troops were not treated as prisoners of war but were instead sent back to Holland under oath that they would not take any action against Britain or her allies until they arrived home. The whole of the settlement of the Cape, with all its South African dependencies, was given up to the British.

In April Popham was told by Captain T. Wayne of the American slave-ship *Elizabeth* that the people of Buenos Aires and Montevideo were 'groaning under the tyranny' of their Spanish masters and would welcome a British expedition to free them. Popham, long an advocate of British intervention in the region and still smarting over the failure of successive attempts to support Miranda's aspirations, was all too ready to believe such unsubstantiated reports. He had also just learnt of the setbacks the allies had suffered at the hands of Napoleon's armies, culminating in the battle of Austerlitz. He persuaded himself that the reason for Pitt's failure to embark on a South American adventure – the hope that Spain might switch sides and join the confederacy against France – no longer applied. He also heard that the French Admiral Villaumez was sailing his squadron to the West Indies rather than the Cape and no longer seemed a threat to Britain's new South African possessions. Popham convinced Baird that here was a golden opportunity to counter European setbacks with a glorious, and easy, victory across the Southern Atlantic. With no authorisation whatsoever he proposed a British invasion, launched from the Cape of Good Hope, to liberate the people of La Plata from Spanish rule. He signalled his intentions to the Board of Admiralty who remained happily unaware of his maverick enterprise until long after it was too late.

Popham persuaded Baird to lend him 1,200 men under Beresford and sailed westwards, leaving the newly acquired South African settlement with no naval force for its defence. One verdict on his actions, published a year later in the *Annual Register*, said:

In every point of view his conduct was unwarrantable. If an officer is to permit himself, either through desire for fame or cupidity, to undertake remote expeditions not within the bound prescribed in his orders, the most able minister may be perpetually counteracted by the mistaken zeal of the persons whom he employs. The best combined system of policy may be frustrated by the mischievous activity of a general or an admiral, who thus presumes to deviate from his line of duty, and arrogates to himself the functions which belong only to the united deliberations of a Cabinet.

It is most completely evident that he was invested with no discretionary powers; but his imagination was so much fired with the ideas of conquest, wealth and rewards, that he resolved to risk every danger to realise the splendid reveries that dazzled his understanding; to overleap every obstacle, and vault into the possession of imaginary consequence. The benefit of his country might unquestionably be amongst the most powerful motives that influenced him in this resolution; yet it is the duty of subordinate characters, when they have no express latitude of action allowed them, to reflect that their best merit is to perform the services required at their hands. It is also possible that Sir Home thought that success would atone for his deviating from the strict import of his orders. Success may captivate popular applause, and popularity screen an individual from reprehension; but success cannot alter the nature of right and wrong, nor make amends for the destruction of a single link of that chain of combined duty which is so material to the welfare of the state.

*　*　*

Popham arrived off Cape Santa Maria on 8 June 1806 on board the 32-gun frigate HMS *Narcissus*. After calling at St Helena for some infantry reinforcements, his fleet arrived in the Rio de la Plata a week later with 1,460 rank and file on board under Beresford's command. The soldiers were mainly from the 1st Battalion, 71st Highland Light Infantry, under 34-year-old Lieutenant-Colonel Dennis Pack. There were also 300 marines, a dragoon squadron and an artillery company with eight field guns. The fleet consisted of the 64-gun frigate *Diadem*, the smaller frigates *Raisonable* and *Diomede*, the brig *Leda* and four transport ships, as well as *Narcissus*.

Major-General William Carr Beresford, the illegitimate son of the Earl of Tyrone and the younger brother of a vice-admiral, was thirty-eight and had one empty eye socket as the result of a shooting accident in Nova Scotia. He saw action against Napoleon in the Mediterranean, won a battlefield promotion after leading the storming party against the tower of Martello in 1794 and was present at the captures of Bastia, Calvi and San Fiorenzo. The following year he took command of the 88th, or Connaught Rangers. He had served alongside Baird and Murray in India and Egypt before the Cape expedition.

Popham and Beresford agreed that their first target should be Buenos Aires itself, the capital of the province, rather than Montevideo. Troops, marines and some seamen were transferred from the line-of-battle ships into the transports and *Narcissus*. Adverse winds and currents, thick fog and the treacherous shoals at the mouth of the great river delayed the landing for eight days. During that time Popham's flagship *Diadem* blockaded the port of Montevideo while the *Raisonable* and the *Diomede* cruised before Maldonado as a diversion.

The main force disembarked near the point of Quilmes on the 25th, watched by around 2,000 Spanish soldiers lining the brow of a hill, who did nothing to oppose them until reinforcements arrived the following morning. Then an ill-directed fire was opened up which did little damage to the invaders. The British marched in cool formation to well within musket range and sent the Spanish into retreat with just one volley. Popham reported: 'We had the satisfaction of seeing from the ships near 4,000 Spanish cavalry flying in every direction, leaving their artillery behind them, while our troops were ascending the hill with that coolness and courage which has on every occasion marked the character of the British soldier.' The Spanish soldiers, mainly poorly trained militia led by confused and incompetent officers, burnt behind them a wooden bridge over the smaller River Chuela and formed up behind hedges and houses on the opposite bank of the river.

Beresford ordered his men to cross over by raft and pillaged boats at dawn the following morning. Again, they met little effective challenge. Beresford reported: 'The opposition was very feeble and the only difficulty was the crossing of the river to get at them.' The British quickly discovered that the Spanish troops had abandoned Buenos Aires. Beresford's entire casualties in the landing and subsequent skirmishes and in the capture of a great South American city totalled one man dead and thirteen wounded, including Captain Le Blanc whose leg was amputated above the knee.

The Viceroy of the Province, Rafael, Marques de Sombremonte, had been among the first to flee, much to the disgust of his subjects. With him went the city's leading merchant, Manuel Belgrano, who later became a military commander and national hero. Brigadier-General Jose Ignacio de la Quintana was left to agree surrender terms. These were rather more generous than was customary at the time, as the British commanders regarded their action as a liberation rather than a conquest. Beresford pledged that all private property would be unmolested by his soldiers, all private citizens protected, local magistrates would continue to raise taxes as usual, the Catholic religion would be honoured, and captured vessels in the harbour should be restored to their owners along with their cargoes (valued at one and a half million Spanish dollars). Official reports described Beresford's conduct as 'exemplary'. The British, however, did seize public property belonging to the Spanish Crown. The huge sum of 1,086,000 dollars was sent back to London on the *Narcissus*. Munitions captured included 45 cannon, 41 mortars and howitzers, 550 whole barrels of powder, 2,064 muskets with bayonets, 616 carbines, 4,019 pistols, 31 musketoons and 1,208 swords. Merchandise snatched consisted mainly of stores of Jesuit bark and quicksilver. Beresford proclaimed that Britain intended to open up free trade with South America and to reduce duties bearing too heavily on traders. In a letter to Lord Castlereagh he said: 'I trust the conduct adopted towards the people here has had its full effect, in impressing upon their minds the honour, generosity and humanity of the British character.'

Popham sent dispatches to London stressing the importance of the colony and the immense profits which it could offer to English corporate traders. Long before his enthusiastic and self-serving narrative reached London the situation had changed dramatically.

Beresford's terms may have been generous but they did not amount to the declaration of freedom that had been expected by at least some of the region's people, most especially the poor, the gauchos and 'people of colour'. Sorely disappointed, they listened eagerly as Pueridon, a municipal member and agitator, secretly preached insurrection. Weapons were stockpiled and hidden in various parts of the city. Meanwhile Santiago de Liniers y Bremond, a Knight of the Order of Malta in the service of Spain, collected men from the countryside around Colonia. Spaniards and gauchos from the outlying districts realised the numerical weakness of the British and began mustering outside Buenos Aires. On 1 August 550 soldiers under Pack, with six field guns, sallied out and defeated an irregular force. The following day Pueridon, having 'thrown off the mask', advanced on Buenos Aires with 1,500 men. They were halted by Beresford's cannon.

Offshore Popham tried unsuccessfully to prevent Liniers' force of 2,500 men crossing the Plata to link up with the 'insurgents' on its right bank. Popham's squadron was buffeted by stormy weather and Liniers made good use of the thick fog to blanket his crossing of the river. He and his men crossed unobserved by the British warships. Torrential rain fell for three days making the roads impassable for the British foot soldiers and cannon but not for the local cavalry and gauchos.

Liniers marched through the cold driving rain to the outskirts of Buenos Aires, installed siege artillery and threw a cavalry screen around the city. In a tough two-hour fight on 5 August the British were pushed back from their outside encampments, suffering 157 casualties compared with 205 on the Spanish side. The British troops found themselves besieged within the city they had captured so easily just weeks before.

On 12 August the enemy's forward posts began a smart fire which was returned by British cannon placed in the main avenues radiating from the central square. The firefight prompted large numbers of city dwellers armed with muskets to crowd the flat roofs of surrounding houses, which were protected by parapets.

They opened up a murderous fire on the British troops and gunners below. Those without firearms poured down torrents of scalding water and boiling fat, and hurled stones and bricks at soldiers huddled in doorways or sheltering under what little protection they could find in the blood-spattered streets and alleys. A dispatch recounted: 'Reinforcements crowded the tops of all the houses commanding the Great Square, and our troops were considerably annoyed by people they could not get at.'

Heavily outnumbered, and having lost nearly 180 men in the desperate action, Beresford decided to capitulate. He and his small army were taken prisoner. At first, Beresford and his officers were interned near the city but later they were dispersed to remote provinces for greater security. Many of the ordinary troops were disarmed and, under oath not to flee or to cause trouble, were given the freedom of the city. Many lodged with local families favourably disposed towards Britain.

Popham and his ships were powerless to help except by mounting a blockade. A small reinforcement arrived from the Cape in October under Lieutenant-Colonel Backhouse who, together with Popham, tried to take Montevideo by assault. They found the waters too shallow to allow the ships close enough to the town for an effective cannonade and the plan was abandoned.

More successful was an attack on 29 October when 400 men under Lieutenant-Colonel Vassal assaulted the coastal village of Maldonado. Backhouse reported: 'To the cool intrepidity of our little column much praise is due, as it advanced with the utmost steadiness and alacrity, and without firing a shot, until sufficiently near to make a certainty of carrying both the guns and the town, which was principally done by the bayonet, notwithstanding the advance was made under heavy discharges of grape and musketry.' The 240 defenders, both regulars and militia, fled leaving behind 50 dead and wounded and two field guns. At a cost of two dead and four wounded Backhouse's force then overwhelmed a 12-gun battery at Punta del Este while Popham seized without bloodshed the fortified island of Gorriti with its 20-gun battery. The British at least now had a convenient winter station for the troops and ships, but Popham was faced with the problem of feeding both his own men and the

Spanish prisoners taken from captured vessels. Rather than simply putting them ashore, where they might join the Spanish forces, he stranded 200 of them on the small uninhabited island of Lobos in the mouth of the Plata. In what was later described at home as an act of 'inhumanity scarcely credible' he left them without shelter, water or food. Forty of the castaways managed to swim ashore with the help of inflated sealskins and a Spanish vessel was sent to rescue those left behind.

Popham's callous action aroused fury in the province and two British officers being held as prisoners were murdered. Beresford protested to Colonel Liniers, who had assumed chief command of La Plata, and the Frenchman agreed to guarantee the security of all British prisoners of war. In his correspondence Liniers stressed the respect that he and the people of the province had for Beresford, and also the disgust with which Popham was regarded.

*   *   *

Back in London, because news took long months to cross the Atlantic, everyone was blissfully unaware of the disaster which had overtaken Popham's dangerous enterprise. *The Times* of 15 September proudly reported the capture of Buenos Aires:

> The circumstances which attended this success are in the highest degree honourable to the British name, and to the character of our brave army . . . By our success in La Plata, where a small British detachment has taken one of the greatest and richest of the Spanish colonies, Buonaparte must be convinced that nothing but a speedy peace can prevent the whole of Spanish America from being wrested from this influence, and placed forever under the protection of the British Empire.

When *Narcissus* arrived at Portsmouth a few days later and disgorged six wagon-loads of booty, the newspaper reported: 'The procession was followed by vast numbers of seafaring persons in this port; the population of the town turned out to witness it, rending the air with their patriotic acclamations in honour of the bravery of their countrymen and of the triumph and treasure they have gained from the foe.'

Popham's dispatch stressing the value of his prize sparked a frenzy among the mercantile community, speculators and adventurers. Ships were quickly fitted out for the four-month journey and loaded with cargoes expected to appeal to the South Americans. The *Annual Register* reported: 'Enthusiasm revelled in imaginary wealth. The fortunate individual who could command a vessel, and the no less happy trader who was admitted as a sharer in joint concerns, equally expected to see their warehouses filled with the produce of Spanish opulence, or crowded with the ingots of Potosi and Peru.' The speculators did not trouble to consider that most British manufactured goods, with which they were filling their ships, had long been available to the South Americans, either through official Spanish merchants or through the extensive contraband trade. The British Government did not deter the commercial armada and the Treasury relished the prospect of fixed duties of $12^{1/2}$ per cent on exports sold.

Government ministers were initially furious at hearing of Popham's unauthorised expedition, and regarded his actions as contemptuous of their authority. But he had, they still believed, delivered them an unexpected victory. They decided to send out reinforcements to support Beresford and hold the province. On 9 October an advance force of 4,800 men under General Sir Samuel Auchmuty set sail while preparations were made for a bigger expedition to follow.

Auchmuty was a fifty-year-old warhorse, the son of a New York lawyer. Barely out of his teens, he had fought with the loyalists at the battles of Brooklyn and Whiteplains, for which he was given a lieutenancy without purchase. In England he found it impossible to live on his pay and exchanged into the 52nd Regiment then under orders for India. He saw much action, serving in the war against Hyder Ali, the 1790 and 1791 campaigns against Tippoo Sultan and at the siege of Seringapatam. Having left England a penniless lieutenant, he returned fourteen years later a lieutenant-colonel with powerful patrons. After being sent to Egypt to help subdue the French there, he and Baird became popular heroes following their heroic, if over-romanticised, march across the desert and passage down the Nile. He was knighted, made a general and for three years commanded the garrisons on the Isle of Thanet.

Auchmuty's force, comprising men of the 40th Regiment of Foot and the 95th Rifles, embarked in ships commanded by Rear-Admiral Charles Stirling. Delayed by leaky transport vessels, they were forced to put into Rio de Janeiro for water; there they learnt of the recapture of Buenos Aires and the imprisonment of Beresford and his army. Undeterred, the fleet arrived in the Rio Plata in early January and found Popham's garrison in Maldonado close to starving and without artillery or supplies: some 400 enemy horsemen blocked all their attempts to forage. Auchmuty decided to abandon Maldonado, judging it indefensible, but left a small garrison on Gorriti. Stirling meanwhile superseded Popham and ordered him home to England to face a court martial.

Auchmuty determined to attack Montevideo and on 13 January landed in a small bay 9 miles from the town. Although the enemy were present in large numbers on the heights they did not contest the landing and the British were able to form a bridgehead a mile deep. After a few days they moved out under a heavy fire of round and grapeshot and established advance parties in the town's suburbs which were hastily evacuated by the Spaniards.

Inside the city were 10,000 inhabitants and 3,500 troops under Governor Pascual Ruiz Huidobro. Outside another 2,500 riders mustered under Sombremonte. Around 1,300 Spanish soldiers and levies, supported by cavalry and two field guns, attacked the British vanguard in two columns. They were defeated with heavy losses after a spirited fight and a devastating flanking manoeuvre led by Lieutenant-Colonel Brownrigg. Auchmuty reported that one British charge 'was as gallantly received and great numbers fell on both sides'. The general had a horse shot from under him in the action but the Spanish retreated within the city ramparts with 100 casualties. Many of the area's armed inhabitants, serving as cavalry, now dispersed, allowing the British forces to encircle the town walls.

Huidobro sent out 2,300 troops to attack again, supported by 1,700 riders under Sombremonte. Their aim was to cut off Auchmuty's force from the sea. On 20 January the Spanish infantry collided with the British left flank at Cristo del Cordon. Auchmuty deployed his light brigade and the 95th Rifles in cornfields along the line of march, catching the Spanish in a lethal cross-fire. The Spanish fled after suffering heavy losses: 200 dead, 400 wounded and 200 captured; the British casualties totalled 149. Sombremonte's cavalry watched the slaughter from a safe distance but did nothing.

The British did not have enough trenching tools to make a direct approach and after several days of bombarding the town with cannon on shore batteries and from ships offshore their supplies of powder ran low. The town's southern rampart was breached, however, and Auchmuty ordered an assault at 3 a.m. the following day, 3 February. Before dawn his troops came under destructive cannon and musket fire before discovering that during the night the defenders had barricaded the 11-ft breach with cow-hides. In the darkness the head of the column missed the gap and blundered around under constant fire for fifteen minutes. Eventually the disguised breach was spotted by Captain Renny of the 40th Light Infantry, who was shot dead trying to scale it. His men rushed to the breach and forced their way into the town. At the top of the main streets the enemy had positioned cannon which for a short time did great execution. But the British troops streamed in from all directions, some clambering over the town walls rather than searching for the breach, cleared a passage with their bayonets and overturned the guns. By daylight the British had possession of all key points except the main citadel where the defenders made a show of resistance until the sun's rays revealed their hopeless position, and they surrendered. Auchmuty noted in dispatches:

The gallantry displayed by the troops during the assault, and their forbearance and orderly behaviour in the town, speak so fully in their praise that it is unnecessary for me to say how highly I am pleased with their conduct. The service they have been engaged in since we landed has been uncommonly severe and laborious, but not a murmur has escaped them; everything I wished has been effected with order and cheerfulness.

The victory was costly. During the brief but savage action Auchmuty lost 134 rank and file, several sergeants and drummers, and eight officers killed. Lieutenant-Colonels Vassal and Brownrigg, who had displayed great courage on several occasions, died of their wounds. A further 335 men, 20 sergeants, 6 drummers and 28 officers were wounded. Auchmuty had effectively lost one-eighth of his army. According to British accounts, the Spanish lost around 800 dead, 500 wounded and 2,000 taken prisoner. Another 1,500 escaped in boats or hid themselves in the cellars and attics of the town. Stirling seized 57 ships in the harbour plus 15 sloop-rigged gunboats and 6 row-boats armed with guns. Despite such booty an observer noted: 'The vigour and resolution with which Montevideo was defended proved the error of the persuasion that any port belonging to the Spanish in South America would be an easy target.'

The stout Spanish resistance had not included the Marques of Sombremonte who, having fled Buenos Aires when Beresford approached, similarly deserted Montevideo before Auchmuty attacked. He remained in the area, however, and Auchmuty wrote to him demanding that the British prisoners in the capital be released. After some confusion it was finally reported back that the Marques was himself barred from the city he had deserted and had no authority to make any bargains. Liniers, who now commanded Buenos Aires, sent out a detachment which arrested Sombremonte and took him prisoner.

Auchmuty dispatched Pack to take Colonia, which he did without opposition. A surprise but half-hearted assault on his garrison a few weeks later by 1,500 men was repelled with single-figure casualties on both sides.

Meanwhile, hearing of the fall of Montevideo, Liniers sent General Beresford under guard 300 leagues inland. Beresford, aided by two Spanish officers of noble birth who wanted to negotiate with the British, escaped with difficulty and, after hiding for three days, reached a British vessel. He, like Popham before him, was sent home.

Auchmuty, through correspondence with the capital, considered that there were two parties in Buenos Aires:

The party in power were mostly natives of Spain, in the principal offices of church and state, and devoted to the Spanish Government. It had been their policy to inflame the minds of the lower orders against the English, by every species of exaggeration and falsehood, and to lead them to such acts of cruelty as might preclude the possibility of any communication with them . . . The second party consisted of natives of the country, with some Spaniards who were settled in it. The oppression of the parent state had made them most anxious to shake off the yoke of the mother country; and though from their ignorance, their want of morals, and the barbarity of their disposition, they were totally unfitted to govern themselves, they aimed at following the steps of the North Americans and erecting an independent republic.

Auchmuty believed, however, that he would need 15,000 men to retake even such a divided city. His own force was depleted by battle and disease, his supplies were running low, and the countryside was hostile to his foraging parties. He sensibly decided to keep his army in Montevideo and await reinforcements.

*   *   *

Before Auchmuty's dispatches reached London the British Cabinet had agreed another expedition to capitalise on Popham's supposed success. Consequently, four thousand men, including two companies of artillery, under 43-year-old Brigadier-General Robert Crauford, embarked in a fleet under Admiral George Murray. Their orders were to gain a British foothold on the Pacific coast of South America in Chile. They were to limit their operation to securing the peace and goodwill of the local inhabitants, improving the lot of Negroes, halting the importation of slaves and establishing a line of posts across the Andes to enable communications with Buenos Aires. As soon as Auchmuty's news of Beresford's surrender reached London the sloop *Fly* was sent to overtake Murray with orders for the fleet to wait at anchor off the Cape of Good Hope. A further force of 1,630 men, including a company of horse artillery, was sent to join them.

General John Whitelocke was appointed overall commander with the mission to recapture Buenos Aires, free the British prisoners and send into exile those officials responsible for the city's 'insurrection'. Whitelocke arrived at Montevideo on 10 May with an army composed mainly of the 88th Regiment and the Light Brigade, with 350 horses and 16 field guns. He immediately took command from the battle-scarred Auchmuty whose successes in such difficult circumstances were hard to follow. Whitelocke could not match them.

Now aged fifty, Whitelocke had obtained his first commission through well-connected friends of his family. His brother-in-law, Matthew Lewis, was deputy secretary of war while Whitelocke advanced his military and diplomatic career in Jamaica. In 1793 he suppressed San Domingo but saw many of his men die of yellow fever. Major Sir Brent Spencer described him as an officer 'who carries with him such universal approbation and so well earned applause'. He was made colonel of the 6th West India Regiment in 1795, Brigadier-General in Guernsey in 1798 and Lieutenant-Governor of Portsmouth in 1805. He had not seen any action in the main theatres of war. He began to make preparations for an attack on Buenos Aires. Sloops of war and other light vessels were sent to reconnoitre the southern bank of the river Plata. They discovered that the water was too shallow to allow a landing under cover of warships anywhere to the west of the city. The closest place to the east was the bay of Barragon, almost 30 miles from the capital.

Crauford now arrived with his diverted expedition, bringing Whitelocke's total force to 9,400 men. Meanwhile, on 7 June, Pack and fewer than 1,000 men marched quietly out of Colonia to surprise Colonel Elio's encampment at San Pedro. After a four-hour march they confronted 2,000 forewarned Spanish in battle array with sixteen guns deployed. But Pack and his men drove through the line without pause and scattered Elio's army; they lost 5 dead and 40 wounded. Spanish losses were much greater: 120 dead, hundreds wounded and 105 taken prisoner, while 8 cannon and 250 muskets were also captured.

Whitelocke, aware that heavy rains made July and August the most unfavourable months for campaigning, decided to press on without delay rather than wait for more reinforcements. Leaving a garrison of 1,300 men at Montevideo he sent his forces up-river in small divisions because navigation was notoriously intricate. The troops suffered many delays because of foul winds but the landing at Barragon on 28 June was unopposed.

His army in the field now consisted of 7,822 rank and file, including 150 mounted dragoons. It was supported by eighteen artillery pieces with ammunition conveyed by 206 horses and mules. In the ships was the reserve artillery of heavy pieces, mortars and howitzers, together with entrenching tools for 1,000 men, six pontoons with their carriages, and provisions for two months. Great difficulty was encountered in getting the guns and supplies across a morass which ran parallel to the shore and it was a very fatigued army that reached the Chuelo. On the river's left bank the enemy had constructed batteries and a formidable line of defence. Whitelocke decided to split his men into two columns which would by-pass the Spanish defences, cross the river higher up, and reunite in the suburbs of Buenos Aires.

General Crauford, with the light infantry and the 95th Regiment, made contact at the Corral de Miserie ranch with Spanish forces under Liniers strongly positioned behind hedges and embankments. A bayonet charge dislodged the enemy in five minutes and Liniers fled to the city leaving behind 60 dead, 70 prisoners, 9 guns and a howitzer. It now became clear that Whitelocke had blundered by splitting his force. If the main body had been present the city could have been taken that evening, according to some witnesses. Instead Crauford's force made camp to await the rest of the army, giving Liniers precious time to organise resistance in the city's barricaded streets.

On 3 July an ultimatum was sent to Liniers: all British citizens detained should be given up and 'all persons holding civil offices dependent on the government of Buenos Aires' and all military officers should become prisoners of war. All arms, ammunition and public property should be surrendered but protection would be given to religious and private possessions. Not surprisingly, Liniers rejected the demands.

Whitelocke and his main force, further delayed by an incompetent guide, did not arrive until that afternoon. He quickly formed his line. Auchmuty's brigade was on the left, extending towards the convent of the Reciketas 2 miles away, with the 36th and 88th Regiments on their right, Crauford's brigade in the centre, and the dragoons and the 45th Regiment on the right of the whole, towards the Residencia. The rains had already begun, making any further delays unwise. Whitelocke decided against a general bombardment, partly because of the difficulty in getting his artillery into place in the sodden conditions, and partly to avoid unnecessary civilian loss of life which would set the entire populace against him. At 6.30 a.m. on 5 July Whitelocke sent eight battalions, totalling 5,800 men, into the city streets in thirteen columns.

The town and suburbs of Buenos Aires, with a Spanish garrison of 7,000 and a civilian population of 42,000, was divided into sections which formed enclosed squares of about 140 yards on each side. The houses had flat roofs, making each square a potential death-trap. Auchmuty's objective was the Plaza de Toros. Other columns were to fight their way through the barricades in the main streets and take the Residencia. Two corporals, equipped with tools for breaking down the doors of the houses, were placed at the head of each column. All the troops were ordered to rush on with unloaded muskets, and no firing was permitted until they had reached their appointed targets. A cannon shot down the central avenue was the signal for the army to advance.

Whitelocke had previously remarked on the defensive suitability of Spanish towns, with their flat roofs and narrow alleys, which were ideal for ambush – but he appears to have ignored his own advice with his plan of attack. The *Annual Register* noted: 'The indecision of General Whitelocke upon several occasions, in the march from the heights of Barragon, had been remarkable; but it is singular, notwithstanding his apprehensions regarding the weather, that he should have adopted a plan which seemed to militate against all his own ideas on the subject of the attack.'

Inevitably the British troops quickly found themselves exposed to fire of the most destructive kind. An official report noted:

The streets were intersected by deep ditches, behind which were planted cannon that poured showers of grape-shot on the advancing forces. Independently of the enemy's troops, a great proportion of whom acted on the roofs of the houses, all the inhabitants, with their negroes, defended their dwellings which were, in fact, so many fortresses, the doors of them being so strongly barricaded that it was almost impossible to force them. Discharges of musketry, hand grenades, bricks and stones saluted the British soldiers, who were also torn to pieces by grape-shot at the corners of streets.

Auchmuty's column took the strong-points of the Retiro and the Plaza de Toros, along with 32 cannon and 600 prisoners after a vigorous fight which saw heavy casualties on both sides. The 5th Regiment met comparatively little opposition and captured the convent and church of Santa Catalina. The 36th and 88th Regiments, commanded by Brigadier-General Lumley, reached their targets after beating back stiff resistance. But the 88th, being closest to the Spanish fort, suffered so many casualties that they were overpowered and captured. This disaster exposed the flank of the 36th and that regiment, together with the 5th, retired to Auchmuty's post at the Plaza de Toros. During the retreat the grenadier company distinguished themselves by attacking 500 of the enemy and spiking two of their guns. The two British six-pounders deployed down the central streets met with superior fire and four troops of carabineers supporting them failed to capture the Spanish battery despite several charges.

The left division of Brigadier-General Crauford's brigade, under the gallant Pack, fought through almost to the river and then turned to seize the Jesuit college. But that stout building proved impregnable and, after suffering heavy losses, one part of the brigade took refuge in a house; this proved untenable and they were forced to surrender. The other part retired on the right division commanded by Crauford himself. His men had reached the river and turned towards the great central square and fort 400 yards away. Learning of the fate of his flank Crauford took refuge in the convent of San Domingo. There he and his men mounted a 'most gallant resistance against superior numbers'. The enemy surrounded the convent on all sides and attempted to seize a British three-pounder in the street outside.

Part of a company of light infantry under Major Trotter – described as an officer of great merit – charged out. Most, including Trotter, were killed 'in an instant'. The official dispatch noted: 'The brigadier-general was now obliged to confine himself to the defence of the convent, from which the riflemen kept up a well directed fire upon such of the enemy as approached the post; but the quantity of round shot, grape and musketry to which they were exposed at last obliged them to quit the top of the building.' The enemy brought up cannon to force the wooden gates of the convent and Crauford, cut off and persuaded by the absence of gunfire close by that the other columns had also failed, capitulated at 4 p.m. The 45th Regiment, the furthest from the enemy centre, took and held the Residencia without too many problems. The shooting dwindled as night approached. The day had cost the British 311 killed, 679 wounded, 208 missing and 1,600 taken prisoner.

Throughout the day's fighting Whitelocke had waited with the 1,000-strong reserve in the suburbs at the Corral de Miserie ranch. After remaining passive all day he returned to his headquarters to dine and sleep. He did not realise the scale of the disaster until he received a dispatch from Auchmuty the following morning. He joined his battle-weary subordinate at the Plaza de Toros which the British still held along with the Residencia and much of the city centre.

Liniers proposed a mutual exchange of all prisoners, including Beresford's defeated army, provided that the British agreed to evacuate the Rio Plata and Montevideo within two months. He hinted that, given the mood of the civilian population, he could not guarantee the safety of the prisoners if hostilities did not cease. Whitelocke could have ignored the offer. His forces commanded a sizeable part of the city and he still had 5,400 effective fighting men. Captain Fraser of the artillery pledged to have thirty cannon aimed at the city by the following morning. But Whitelocke agreed to Liniers' terms, much to the disgust of many of his men. The British left the city in the circumstances described by Lieutenant-Colonel Holland.

Alongside Spanish and Creole graffiti celebrating victory, British soldiers scrawled obscene messages directed at Whitelocke. A favourite toast among officers became 'Success to grey hairs but bad luck to white locks.'

In his dispatch to London Whitelocke robustly defended his decision. He claimed that the whole male population of Buenos Aires was actively employed in its defence. He played up the danger to the British prisoners taken in the two battles for the city and added: 'Influenced by these considerations and reflecting on how little advantage would be the possession of a country, the inhabitants of which were so absolutely hostile, I resolved to forgo the advantage which the bravery of the troops had obtained, and acceded to the annexed treaty.' He was supported by Rear-Admiral George Murray who reported back that the treaty had achieved the prime objective of releasing British captives. He added that Whitelocke 'saw no prospect whatever of establishing ourselves in this country as there was not a friend to the English in it'.

On 24 July General Ackland, with more than 1,800 troops, arrived at Montevideo but in the light of the British débâcle and the demeaning treaty signed by Whitelocke they moved on to India a week later, along with the 47th and 87th Regiments. On 9 September Whitelocke left Montevideo for the last time, arriving in England with his dispirited men on 7 November. It was not a glorious home-coming.

*   *   *

The shameful news had preceded Whitelocke. *The Times*, which a year earlier had so joyfully reported the capture of Buenos Aires, said that the disaster was 'perhaps the greatest which has been felt by this country since the commencement of the revolutionary war [with France and her allies]'. A thorough official investigation was promised into the 'apparent mismanagement' of the commanders. Whitelocke was lampooned in cartoons while Popham's claim for a share of the spoils taken early in the first campaign was ridiculed.

On 28 January 1808 Whitelocke faced an array of charges at a general court martial at Chelsea. He was accused of measures ill-calculated to effect the conquest of Buenos Aires, of enraging the population by declaring that civilian officials would be taken prisoner, of splitting his force at a crucial time, of sending his troops into heavily defended streets without proper support, of failing to show leadership by holding himself back in reserve, and of shamefully surrendering his army's position by agreeing to Liniers' terms. Such conduct was 'tending to the dishonour of his majesty's arms, and being contrary to his duty as an officer, prejudicial to good order and military discipline, and contrary to the articles of war'.

There was much to say in Whitelocke's defence. His expedition had been conceived by others under the profoundly wrong assumption that much of the local population would be friendly. He faced huge problems from the swampy terrain and the onset of the rainy season. And it was argued that if Crauford had fallen back on the Residencia, as Pack had advised, Buenos Aires might have surrendered the following day. But such a defence could not disguise Whitelocke's incompetence throughout the campaign. He too easily listened to conflicting advice. He was prone to dithering, but always determined when it came to asserting his own authority. And his behaviour in wining, dining and sleeping without bothering to discover what had happened to his men was indefensible.

After a seven-week trial the court of nineteen officers, all of them lieutenant-generals, found him guilty on all counts save for the part of one charge which related to his order that the columns should not begin firing until they reached their allotted targets. The court agreed that precautions had been needed to prevent the unnecessary discharge of weapons. But that did not take the sting out of the overall verdict. The court decreed that Whitelocke be cashiered 'and declared totally unfit and unworthy to serve his majesty in any military capacity whatever'. The king confirmed the sentence and ordered that it be read at the head of every regiment and inserted in every orderly book 'with a view of its becoming a lasting memorial to the fatal consequences, to which officers expose themselves, who, in discharge of the important duties confided in them, are deficient in that zeal, judgement and personal exertion which their sovereign and their country have a right to expect from officers entrusted with high commands'.

Whitelocke spent the rest of his life in retirement and died in 1833 at Hall Barn Park, Buckinghamshire, the seat of his son-in-law. He is buried in the west aisle of Bristol Cathedral.

Popham, the architect of the original ill-judged adventure, escaped similar ignominy. The previous year he had been arrested on his return to England and suffered a three-day court martial on board *Gladiator* in Portsmouth Harbour. He was charged with withdrawing his squadron from the Cape of Good Hope without orders to pursue his maverick plan, leaving that newly won colony in great danger from French attack. He argued forcefully that Cape Town was not threatened and that it was his duty to seize any opportunity to distress the enemy, as he had tried to do in South America. He claimed that his command was, by its nature, discretionary. He pointed out that Admiral Rooke had no direct orders when he took Gibraltar. Neither did Lord St Vincent when he attacked Tenerife. And neither did the illustrious Lord Nelson when he pursued the French fleet to the West Indies and back. Popham also claimed that his assault on Buenos Aires had been approved in private interviews with the late Mr Pitt. The court found him guilty of highly censurable conduct and issued a severe reprimand but decided against any further action.

The City of London regarded Popham's adventure as a gallant attempt to open up new trade markets to enrich its coffers, and presented him with a sword of honour. Even in the Royal Navy the reprimand did little to impede the wily admiral's career. The following year, to the horror of many senior officers, he was appointed captain of the fleet in the expedition against Copenhagen and helped to settle the terms by which all Danish men-of-war were surrendered. In 1812 he had command of a small squadron on the north coast of Spain, co-operating with the guerrillas ashore. In 1814 he was made rear-admiral and from 1817 was commander-in-chief of the Jamaica station. His health broke and he died at Cheltenham shortly after returning to England in 1820. In naval circles he is best remembered as the adaptor of a code of signals used for many years. Popham was a greedy, unscrupulous adventurer. He was also a superb navigator, a cautious surveyor and a commander who preferred to use guile than to risk unnecessary bloodshed. According to some naval experts, the best-selling novelist C.S. Forester used Popham, at least in part, as the inspiration for his fictional sea-dog Horatio Hornblower. In 1999 the historian John Grainger, after researching the *Naval Chronicle*, wrote: 'The parallels between their careers are clear, becoming in the end almost identical.'

Beresford was also untarnished by the South American shambles, and enjoyed a long and distinguished military and political career. After being wounded in Portugal, he reorganised the Portuguese army and was knighted for his services at the battle of Busaco. He showed poor leadership at the battle of Albuera, however, and was best regarded as an organiser. He commanded with greater distinction during the invasion of France. Back home he enjoyed rich rewards, sitting in the House of Lords. He was governor of Jersey from 1820 until his death, aged eighty-five, in 1854. Wellington said that he would have once recommended Beresford to succeed him in command of the entire British Army, not because he was a great general, which he was not, but because he alone could feed an army.

Auchmuty, whose abilities in South America had put Whitelocke to shame, became commander-in-chief at Madras. In 1811 he captured Java despite stubborn resistance from the Dutch defenders. For the second time he received the thanks of Parliament, and he was made a Knight of the Bath and colonel of the 78th Regiment. In 1821 he was appointed commander-in-chief in Ireland but did not enjoy that high command for long. The following year he was killed when he fell from his horse in Phoenix Park and he was buried in Christchurch Cathedral. The *Dictionary of National Biography* noted: 'His great merit is shown by the high rank which he, the son of a loyal and therefore ruined American colonist, without money or political influence, had managed to attain.'

The sense of dishonour felt in Britain was profound, not least among those merchants who had been told about a profitable new market, only to see it closed to them. A third British expedition under the Duke of Wellington was proposed to salvage some national pride but had to be abandoned when developments on the Iberian peninsula demanded that he stay in Europe.

The main impact of the two failed British invasions was to weaken Spain's authority in the province of La Plata and breed a new, proud spirit of independence among the Argentine people. It was they, not Spain, who had defeated the British and united the previously squabbling factions. The regular Spanish army had been defeated by Beresford. Sombremonte and Belgrano, the leading citizen, had both fled Buenos Aires at the first whiff of danger, leaving the people to look after themselves. That the people had successfully united to capture, repel or otherwise defeat the invaders was a matter of great and lasting pride. A poem written to celebrate the British defeat gave wide currency to the name Argentina.

To the local populace the real heroes were Liniers, who had created an 8,000-strong militia, and Martin de Alzaga, a Basque from a poor family, who had been one of the leaders of the uprising against the British. Liniers became interim viceroy and, to help bankroll his militia of largely common folk, opened up trade with the British merchants who had followed Whitelocke and whose ships were still waiting with their cargoes off Montevideo.

The position changed in 1808 when Napoleon installed his brother on the throne of Spain and the Spanish patriotic *junta* opposed him, aided by the British. Old enemies became allies and *vice versa*. Liniers came under suspicion because of his French background and Alzaga attempted a *coup d'état* on 1 January 1809. Among the militia his rebellion was supported only by Spanish units but these were quickly disarmed by the large native section made up of Argentine-born artisans, farmers, gauchos, creoles and blacks. Spanish rule nevertheless continued, in name at least, until 1810 when the *cabildo*, or city forum, in Buenos Aires set up an autonomous government to administer the region until the restoration of King Ferdinand VII. In the event, Ferdinand proved to be a terrible monarch and an assembly on 9 July 1816 declared an independent nation, the United Provinces of Rio de la Plata.

Years of hard fighting continued, with Spanish armies threatening the borders, and one by one the outlying regions of Paraguay, Bolivia and Uruguay were lost. But the regions which had successfully beaten off the British, despite the weakness of their Spanish masters, became the core of modern Argentina. Thus an adventure conceived by a pompous British admiral indirectly gave birth to a nation.

ELEVEN

The First Burma War, 1824–6

'The invading army of rebellious strangers.'

The conflict which first robbed Burma of large chunks of its territory has been called the worst managed war in British military history, but that judgement may be too harsh when compared, for example, with the later horrors of the Crimea. For the British statesmen, generals and administrators it was an almost total victory which greatly extended the empire. But for the men who fought an exotic and underrated foe, it was a nightmare of malarial swamp, dense jungle, blistering heat, hunger and thirst. For too many of them a sweat-drenched and sordid hospital cot was their place of dying, rather then the field of battle.

*   *   *

Ptolemy mentioned Burma in the second century AD, but the country and its people remained largely unknown to the outside world for a millennium. Civilisation came from India, although the Burmese shunned many aspects of Indian culture, most notably the caste system. The kingdom of Pagan, which included what became Lower Burma, was overrun by the Mongol hordes and then for several centuries remained divided into states under Shan princes. The sixteenth century saw the rise of the Toungoo dynasty which until 1752 was occupied largely with internal conflict, beating off encroachments by China, and with unsuccessful attempts to invade Siam. The kingdom of Ava was also conquered and its chief city on the Irrawaddy became the seat of power.

The first European known to have visited Burma was the Venetian merchant Cesar Fredericke in 1455, but the country's physical position adjoining Bengal and Assam made contact with Britain inevitable. In 1586 the English prospector Ralph Fitch sailed up the Irrawaddy River, which bisects Burma longitudinally. In his memoirs he described great gilded pagodas, royal white elephants fed from silver dishes, and Buddhist monks in yellow robes. The women were 'white, round-faced with little eyes'. The missionary Father Sangermano also reported the celestial white elephants which were an important part of Burmese court and ceremonial life. When such a beast was caught in the forest of Pegu, he said, it was bound with scarlet cords and waited on by the highest mandarins. A silken net was draped over it as protection from mosquitoes and, once aboard the specially constructed boat designed to ferry it to the royal palace, gold-embroidered silk protected it from the sun.

The East India Company made contact in 1617 and both it and its Dutch counterpart opened depots. Trade was initially not good, as the westerners failed to fully comprehend Burma's natural riches. They used their footholds largely to repair and build teak ships. Visitors were nevertheless entranced by the lush tropical forests, the exotic buildings, the tinkle of the temple bells, the smells of spice and strange fruit, and, above all, by the colours. Much later Rudyard Kipling wrote of 'lilac, pink, vermilion, lapis lazuli, and blistering blood-red under fierce sunlight that mellows and modifies all'. The American traveller Frank Vincent described the Burmese as 'a simple-minded, indolent people, frank and courteous, fond of amusement and gay-coloured apparel, friendly amongst themselves and hospitable to strangers. They appreciate a quiet life, smoking, and gossiping, and sleeping throughout the day, and listening to wild music and singing throughout half the night. Stern ambition is among them, indeed, a very rare trait of character.' He remarked on the red and yellow fabrics worn by both sexes, loosely wrapped so that one of a woman's legs was always immodestly exposed; on the tattoos sported by the men from hips to knees; and on the enormous cigars wrapped in green leaves incessantly smoked by men, women and children. 'Burmese boys take to smoking even earlier than do the youth of this country,' he wrote. 'I have frequently seen babes at the mother's breasts alternating the nourishment of Nature's Nile with pulls and puffs at their cheroots.' Legend suggested that the bare legs of the women and the tattoos of the men was a ruse dreamt up by an ancient queen disgusted by male infidelity so that 'by disfiguring the men and setting off the beauty of the women, the latter may regain the affections of their husbands'. Vincent added: 'Burmese laws on the whole seem wise, and evidently are calculated to advance the interests of justice and morality; but they very often prove futile, owing to the tyranny and rapacity of the king and the venality of many of his officers.'

The kings of Ava were generally despotic tyrants and each succession was marked by the massacre of hundreds or thousands of potential rivals, their families and followers. Western powers, including Britain, wrongly assumed that the Burmese people would welcome the overthrow of such rulers, but they did not appreciate the populace's devout belief in kingly divinity. The Burmese rulers, in turn, misunderstood western attitudes. One snorted in disgust, 'These hat-wearing people cannot bear to see or hear of women being beaten or maltreated.'

In 1755 the Peguan rulers of Burma were overthrown by a chieftain of military genius who assumed the royal title *Alaungpaya*, or 'Embryo Buddha'. He suspected the British of aiding the Peguans and promptly burnt the Company trading post at Negrai. He slaughtered thousands of Burmese whose loyalty he distrusted and deported thousands more. His invasion of Thailand was ended when he died of an accidental wound during the siege of a city.

His successor, King Bodawpaya, continued his policy of aggressive military expansion. Thailand was again invaded, the kingdom of Mon was savagely destroyed and rebellions bloodily suppressed. Territorial conquests, however, were largely lost as armies had to be pulled back to beat off Chinese attacks in the north. The constant blood-letting led to a regular trickle of refugees to neighbouring states, but the trickle became a flood after the conquest of the coast region of Arracan. Many refugees headed for British-held Chittagong, and used it as a base for counter-invasion sorties. Burma now had a common frontier with British India and border incidents were inevitable. Dispatches to London referred to the 'violent and haughty character' of the Burmese people. Anglo-Burmese relations were further soured in 1795 when a small Burmese force entered Chittagong in pursuit of robbers. The friction sparked flames in 1820 when the Burmese generalissimo Maha Bandula conquered Assam and neighbouring Manipur, sending even more refugees fleeing into Bengal.

Britain strongly suspected that Bandula planned to strike at Calcutta, and their fears were strengthened when the Burmese seized the island of Shapuri. A small guard of sepoys was driven off with the loss of several lives. In 1824 Lord Amherst, Governor-General of the East India Company, sent a note to the new Burmese king, Bagyidaw, with a stern reprimand, and demanded the removal of his forces from the island. In fact, this had already occurred and it was reoccupied by British naval soldiers, but they found the island so unhealthy that they withdrew shortly afterwards. Bagyidaw regarded the note as an act of weakness and became even more pugnacious. Two British naval officers from the Company schooner *Sophia*, who had been sent to help define the Burmese border in a British bid to avert war, were kidnapped and sent to the interior for imprisonment, although they were later freed unharmed. Amherst felt he had no option but to declare war formally on 5 March 1824.

Justifying his decision, Amherst said:

The Burmese Government, actuated by an extravagant spirit of pride and ambition, and elated by its conquest over the petty tribes by which it is surrounded, has ventured to violate the British territories, to attack and slay a party of British sepoys, to seize and imprison British subjects, to avow extensive schemes of mischievous aggression, and to make hostile preparations on our frontier.

The war had already started before the formal Declaration. Burmese troops moved into the small state of Cachar, a British protectorate, and threatened the frontier of Sylhet. The Burmese excused their action by claiming to be in pursuit of bandits and criminals. They demanded that the rajah of Sylhet acknowledge submission and allegiance to the king of Ava. Their planned invasion was, however, halted by the advance of British troops.

In Cachar they constructed stockades on the principal mountain passes and high roads, palisades of teak beams and bamboo, behind which were earth entrenchments with cannon batteries, further protected by deep ditches. Early in February a detachment under Colonel Brown marched on strongly defended stockades at Doodpatlee. The Burmese occupied a narrow slip of flat land flanked by steep hills and the River Soorma, with a ditch about 14 feet wide in front of a cannon-proof fortified wall. Solid redoubts and spiked bamboo strengthened the defences while the road approaching it was so steep that 'a few determined men might bid defiance to hundreds'. Several spirited attacks were made under cover of heavy fire from three six-pounders, but each failed in turn. At the end of a long, gruelling day the British gave up and retired to Juttrapore. Captain Johnson of the 23rd and four other officers were hurt, while around 150 sepoys had been killed or wounded in the inglorious action. One officer reported that the Burmese, estimated at 2,000 strong, 'defended themselves with great bravery and their losses must have been considerable'.

This early defeat convinced some British officers that the enemy was not to be despised, but their commanders in India continued to underestimate the calibre of the Burmese and the strength of their defences, often with fatal consequences. Early reports confirmed the dismissive attitude of the Calcutta generals: the Burmese forces were a loose concoction of tribal fighters, numbering just 15,000 men, of whom barely two-thirds had firearms, the rest making do with spears and swords. Nevertheless Calcutta speedily sent reinforcements into the provinces of Sylhet and Assam, which they reoccupied with little trouble. The main British effort was, however, to be directed in the south. The first target was the important seaport of Rangoon. From there naval power would be harnessed to take troops up the mighty Irrawaddy to deliver a knockout blow aimed at Ava itself.

A joint army and naval force assembled in May 1824 at Port Cornwallis in the Andaman Islands. There were 63 ships and 11,500 British and Indian troops, including a royal regiment of cavalry and two of infantry. The ships included *Diana*, a 60 horsepower paddle-steamer with a funnel almost as tall as the masts of more conventional vessels. She was the first steamer to be employed in the British forces and her appearance provoked wonder among the natives. The whole force was under the command of Lieutenant-Colonel Sir Archibald Campbell of the 38th Regiment.

Campbell came from a prosperous but not wealthy Perth family; now aged fifty-five, he had been a serving soldier since he was eighteen. He saw extensive action in India, Mysore, Cochin and Ceylon. His gallantry at the first siege of Seringapatam ensured rapid promotion. Despite faltering health he served with distinction during the Peninsular War and commanded Portuguese regiments at the battles of Albuera, Vittoria, the Pyrenees and the Nivelle, when he was mentioned in dispatches. Further battle honours followed until the end of the Napoleonic Wars saw him knighted and serving as aide-de-camp to the Prince Regent before being posted to India as colonel of the 38th.

As the main expedition set sail from Port Cornwallis, a force of Bengal Marines on board the warships *Slancy* and *Mercury* took the island of Cheduba off the Arracan coast with only 'trifling' losses. The rajah, who paid allegiance to Ava, was imprisoned and seven companies of sepoy infantry garrisoned the island, which they described as of 'uncommon fertility'. At the same time another detachment, consisting of the 17th Madras light infantry, sailed against the island of Negrai at the mouth of the Irrawaddy, which they intended to use as a stepping stone for an attack on the town of Bassein further up the river. The Burmese were dug in behind a strong stockade on the island. The Indians took it by frontal assault, but their officers considered it too precarious to hold against counter-attack, and it was abandoned.

The main expedition reached the Rangoon River on 10 May and the following morning took the town itself with ease. Barely a hundred inhabitants were found: the rest had fled, leaving stockpiles of ammunition. Several artillery pieces were also captured, although they were poorly regarded by the invaders. Some soldiers found large stocks of brandy in a merchant's house and quickly became drunk. According to one officer 'they went rambling from house to house with lighted torches, and as may be fully anticipated, the town was set on fire and a great portion of it consumed in consequence'. Despite such poor discipline, the first stage of the operation had gone smoothly, but the British were about to suffer a major setback in the north.

A detachment of British troops had been posted at Ramoo, in advance of Chittagong, with the intention of preventing any further Burmese encroachments into Bengal. On 13 May, after several days of skirmishing, a 5,000-strong Burmese force advanced on the British positions and entrenched on the south side of a nearby river. The following day a party under Captain Trueman, with two six-pounders, bombarded them out of their positions and drove them into the surrounding hills. The day after that the Burmese reformed within 300 yards of the British ranks. On 17 May they captured several outposts, deserted by panicked provincial troops. All hopes of reinforcements had by this time been dashed, the British flanks were exposed, and the defenders were demoralised by thirst, hunger and fatigue. The commanding officer, Captain Noton, ordered a retreat which was conducted in good style for the first mile, but then became disorganised flight. The enemy cavalry pressed them hard while sharpshooters harried the column, and stragglers were cut down. Most of the British officers, including Noton, were killed. The Burmese were seen to be using mainly European muskets. They also deployed *jinjal* guns tied to tree trunks. A dispatch recorded: 'The event of this encounter, though obviously accountable by the great numerical superiority of the enemy, considerably shook the courage of our provincial allies in this quarter, and it was not for some time that they could be induced to face the enemy.'

A freed Bengali soldier later delivered a letter from the Burmese commanders to the British commandant at Chittagong. It said: 'Our master of the Lord of the White Elephant, the Great Chief, the Protector of the Poor and Oppressed, wishes that the people of both countries should remain in peace and quiet.' It claimed that the British were the aggressors, that sepoys had fired on a delegation bearing a flag of truce and that they had taken pains not to assault the local population. 'Our soldiers injured none of the poor inhabitants, and committed no oppression, and destroyed no habitations, yet the English gentlemen, with the Bengalee Sepoys, began firing on us from muskets and cannon,' the letter continued, '. . . a battle ensued, many were wounded, and many put to flight. The people of Ramoo set fire to their own village, and burned it.'

Meanwhile, the British in Rangoon were threatened by large Burmese forces assembling behind stockades encircling the town. On 10 June Campbell sent out a column of 3,000 men to attack the enemy's fortified camp at Kemmendine with four eighteen-pounders, four mortars and several light field guns. Two divisions of ships were sent up-river to block the Burmese escape route. Two miles from the town the column bombarded a strongly built stockade and within half an hour breached its walls. Men of the Madras European Regiments, supported by the 41st, poured into the breach, while on the other side companies of the 13th and 38th Regiments scaled the 10 foot high defences. Every one of the 150 men found inside the stockade was killed. The column moved on for another mile and then, linking up with the naval flotilla, hacked their way through the riverside jungle to assail the main Burmese stockade. During that night the British forces were occupied erecting batteries, while the defenders inside were heard exhorting one another to resist to the death. At daybreak the cannon and mortars opened fire. The bombardment lasted two hours. When a breach was observed a detachment was sent forward, only to find that the enemy had fled, taking their dead and wounded with them.

The king of Ava, irritated rather than alarmed at this setback, ordered a general attack on Rangoon towards the end of June. Spies forewarned Campbell and their intelligence reports were confirmed by sentries who observed large bodies of Burmese troops crossing the river above Kemmendine. On 1 July three columns, each about 1,000 strong, crossed the front of the British positions and moved towards their right. They came into contact with the piquets of the Madras Native Infantry which held steady under attack but were unable to stop the enemy advancing between their posts. The Burmese occupied an old pagoda and several houses on a hill, from which they commenced a 'feeble and harmless' fire. Campbell instantly moved to the point of attack. Supported by a gun and howitzer from the Bengal artillery, three companies charged the hill and drove the Burmese out at the point of the bayonet. The enemy fled into the comparative safety of the jungle, leaving about 100 dead.

The war now became one of attrition, with the British constantly frustrated by the elusiveness of their enemy. Most seasoned officers still held to the textbooks of the Napoleonic Wars and expected their foes to stand and fight. The Burmese could not see the point in defending positions once they became untenable. Their mode of warfare in many ways appears to have a twentieth-century flavour. Each infantryman, armed with a musket, long spear and short sword, carried entrenching tools. Once they took up a position they dug neat foxholes, each capable of holding two men with their supplies of food, water and firewood, which protected the occupants from both enemy fire and the elements. Above their trenches they built observation platforms in the treetops, with guns lashed to the trunks. Their stockades were so well-built they could withstand light cannon.

Campbell went on the offensive. On 8 July he launched a general attack on the enemy lines and his men took ten stockades by assault. The artillery was bloodily effective and estimates of enemy losses, although perhaps inflated, were of over 800 dead. In all, 38 pieces of Burmese artillery, 40 swivel-guns and 300 muskets were captured. Campbell lost 4 men dead, and an officer and 38 rank and file wounded. The Burmese withdrew a greater distance from the British lines but lack of provisions and the onset of the rainy season prevented Campbell from following up his successes. His army settled down in Rangoon until the end of the year. In the meantime they launched sporadic attacks on enemy stockades, while warships burnt Burmese river-craft. On 4 August a successful attack took the town and temple of Syriam. Troops dug holes under the pagoda, searching, with little result, for the valuable offerings presented annually by devotees at the shrine of divinity.

One expedition did, however, see the British checked. A detachment moved against the pagoda of Keykloo but had to stop to deal with entrenchments intersecting the road. The troops took each with charges but were exhausted by the time they reached the main Burmese stockade, which was more formidable than any of the others encountered so far, and even boasted a cannon behind a strong parapet. The Burmese held their fire until the British were within 50 yards and then opened a steady and well-directed fusillade. The sepoys were forced to throw themselves flat on the ground. Their commanding officer waited in vain for a supporting column which had been misdirected by disloyal guides. A retreat was ordered but the sepoys, herded together from all sides, became a confused mass. A second expedition was mounted a few days later and the pagoda was taken with some loss of life.

At around the same time expeditions were fitted out against several Burmese sea-ports. A force commanded by Colonel Miles took Tavoy and Mergul, two of the most important stations on the Tenasserim coast. Another under Colonel Sir Henry Godwin had a harder fight at Martyaban. His seaborne expedition set off on 14 October but was delayed by calms and contrary currents, and by the ignorance of the pilots, and it did not reach its target until 29 October. The town was guarded by rocky cliffs and a 2-gun battery behind masonry walls up to 20 feet thick. The stockade ran along the shore for more than three-quarters of a mile and joined a large pagoda which projected into the water to form a bastion. It was a strong position garrisoned by over 3,000 troops but it was stormed by 220 men of European and native regiments with the loss of 7 killed and 40 wounded. The booty included many cannons, 150 wall-pieces, 500 muskets, 7,000 round iron shot, 1,500 grapeshot, saltpetre and sulphur. Most of the munitions were destroyed when Godwin ordered the magazine to be blown up. The remainder of the long, narrow Tenasserim territory submitted to British protection, and British garrisons occupied the whole coast from Rangoon eastwards.

The court of Ava ordered a general conscription of men to drive the invaders into the sea. A grand army consisting of almost 60,000 of the best Burmese troops, including the Imperial Guard, moved towards Rangoon under the command of General Bandula and accompanied by two royal princes. In the height of the rainy season Bandula led his cumbersome army down the Arracan coast, over a mountain range and through dense jungle. As a military feat it was comparable to Hannibal's crossing of the Alps. He arrived outside Rangoon at the end of November, along with a train of artillery and Cassay cavalry, and drew his lines in front of the great pagoda of Dagon. For five days his men busily erected stockades and batteries, and suffered losses in continual skirmishing. Before their lines were fully fortified Campbell directed an attack on the left wing. In the early morning light two columns, one of 1,100 men, the other of 600, supported by cavalry of the Governor-General's guard who had arrived from Calcutta only the night before, broke through the enemy lines and drove them from the field with 'great slaughter'. The victory was not followed through, and Bandula was able to spend the night and the following day rallying his men and reinforcing his right and centre lines. He pushed forward towards the great pagoda and closed on the British trenches and breastworks. He prepared a general attack but at 4 a.m. on 8 December all the British batteries opened up with a 'most murderous' fire of grape and rockets, while a column sallied out to attack the Burmese left flank again. Bandula's men initially held their ground but soon broke and fled in every direction, leaving behind almost all their artillery, stores and ammunition. Burmese casualties were reckoned by the victors to have been 5,000 dead and wounded. Total British losses were said to have not exceeded 200 and Campbell jubilantly reported the 'total defeat' of Bandula.

Despite the severity of his losses, Bandula, an inspiring commander, largely succeeded in rallying his army and five days later took up positions near the village of Kokine, roughly 3 miles from the British advance posts. He had constructed the usual defensive stockade with such judgement as to the best position as, Campbell himself noted, 'would do credit to the best instructed engineers of the most civilised and warlike nations'. The 20,000 men behind the stockades were still panicky, however, and a column of 1,300 British infantry took the position at the first assault. The defenders fled, offering no resistance, and leaving their baggage and ammunition behind. Marines destroyed 200 Burmese fireboats. It was the last major action of the year.

The *Annual Register* reported: 'The result of the campaign was to give us the command of some of the most important maritime stations of the Burmese; and, what was perhaps of more moment, to impress upon them a salutary sense of our military superiority.'

In the north the preceding months had been much quieter. The Burmese were forced to evacuate most of their occupied territories but remained in Ramoo for several weeks and took the stockade of Tek-Naaf owing to the timidity of the 150 provincial troops garrisoning it. In August Colonel Innes took command of the Sylhet frontier and, slowly but steadily, cleared the province of Cachar of Burmese invaders by the end of October. Over the same period Assam province was also liberated, although the British commander there, Brigadier MacMorine, died of cholera along with many of his troops. His campaign was completed under the command of Sir Edward Paget. But Britain's military top brass were then shaken by an event potentially more shattering than any battlefield defeat.

Three native regiments, the 26th, 47th and 62nd, stationed at Barrackpore, were ordered to march to reinforce troops employed in driving the Burmese out of Assam and Cachar. Discontent grew within the ranks over several days. On 31 October they were ordered to draw up in marching order for an inspection of their knapsacks. A large number refused to put on their knapsacks, claiming that the carrying of baggage was degrading to their caste. The commanding officer, Colonel Cartwright, addressed each company in succession, pointing out the draconian penalties for mutiny. Some finally obeyed the order, but most left their knapsacks on the ground. Another parade was ordered for the following morning in front of General Dalzell. Fewer than 400 men, including all the native officers and NCOs, lined up. The remainder held back, their muskets loaded. Dalzell rode up to remonstrate with them but they drove him off and compelled most of the obedient soldiers, apart from the officers, to rejoin them.

Some shots were fired and that evening 130 men of the 62nd and 20 of the 26th seized their colours. Paget arrived with the Royals, the King's 47th and the artillery and the next morning his troops were drawn up in position. The mutineers did likewise and were solidly determined not to give in. They said that they had taken an oath not to surrender, and intended keeping it. Two signal guns were fired and artillery opened up from the rear on the mutineers, lined up in dense ranks. A volley from the Royals sent them running for cover in every direction. Around 100 were either killed on the parade ground or drowned attempting to cross the adjoining river. Most of the rest were captured. Twelve of the supposed ringleaders were executed but the sentences of the rest were commuted to fourteen years' hard labour in irons.

News of the mutiny, a foretaste of a much greater affair, caused alarm in England where it was seen as evidence of wider discontent in the entire Indian army. The price of East India Company stock nose-dived but then recovered.

*   *   *

The British forces in Rangoon did not enjoy the occupation and illness began to reduce their numbers dramatically. From the start their billets were far from ideal and the lack of supplies was a constant problem. One officer wrote:

> Deserted as we found ourselves by the people of the country, from whom alone we could expect supplies, unprovided by the means to move either by land or water, and the rainy monsoon setting in – no prospect remained to us but that of a long residence in the miserable and dirty hovels of Rangoon, trusting to the transports for provisions, with such partial supplies as our foraging parties might procure from time to time by distant and fatiguing marches into the interior of the country.

Campbell's army had few pack animals to help them forage, and a march further into the interior would have been impossible even without the rains. After barely a month two-thirds of Campbell's garrison was unfit for anything but the lightest of duties and of the incapacitated an alarming number of both Europeans and sepoys were seriously ill.

One of the transports ran down *Diana*, throwing the steam engine out of level and badly injuring the only engineer. She was repaired only through the efforts of 32-year-old naval officer Frederick Marryat, who had previously served on St Helena until the death of Napoleon. It was Marryat who had first suggested the deployment of *Diana* and who had overcome intense hostility to the idea of bringing along such a new-fangled vessel. Later in the operations, when the naval commander, Commodore Grant, became ill, Marryat took responsibility for the entire squadron, most notably organising the drinking water for the fleet.

In January 1825 Campbell urged the local inhabitants to return to Rangoon. He could not help boasting of his victories: 'The ancient kingdom of Pegu has become a desert from the rage of war. The most powerful armies possible for your court to get together have been sent against us; we have dispersed them like chaff.' He said that Britain only wanted peace, that Burmese property would not be looted and the townspeople would not be abused in any way, provided they behaved themselves. He added: 'It only remains for me to carry the victorious English arms, not only to your capital, but to the remotest parts of your kingdom, till your court is brought to a proper sense of that justice, honour and policy, due from one neighbouring state to another.' His appeal was partially successful and large numbers of the inhabitants did return to Rangoon. Campbell hoped that the people of Pegu would become allies to throw off the yoke of Ava.

Early in February Lieutenant-Colonel Godwin dislodged Bandula's advance division at Tantabain. That allowed Campbell, now supplied with mules and oxen to haul the field pieces and supplies, to move with a large force towards Prome. His column met no opposition for 50 miles and a strong Burmese division under Maha Silwah, which had been occupying an old Talian fort, melted away before the British advance. The local population appeared grateful at the expulsion of the Burmese troops and brought the British column supplies of rice and buffaloes, and even helped with road-building.

A substantial Burmese force remained at Danubyu, a fortress commanding both the water route to the north and Ava, and the vital road from Rangoon, from which Bandula sent out sorties to harry the British. Campbell described one such attack by Burmese using elephants as fighting vehicles:

. . . a scene at once novel and interesting . . . Seventeen large elephants, each carrying a complement of armed men, and supported by a column of infantry, were observed moving towards our right flank. I directed the [Governor-General's] bodyguard, under Captain Sneyd, to charge them, and they acquitted themselves most handsomely, mixing boldly with the elephants; they shot their riders off their backs, and finally drove the whole back into the fort.

Campbell directed 42-year-old General Willoughby Cotton, a commander with a growing reputation for mediocrity, to take a river-borne force up the Irrawaddy to attack the Danubyu stronghold. The river could be both placid and turbulent, spiked with hidden obstacles, mudflats and rapids. The soldiers looked on a changing scenery of gigantic elephant grass, sandy beaches, villages constructed of bamboo and palm mats, brightly dressed Burmese gazing silently at the 'barbarians', ornate pagodas and the crumbling ruins of more ancient civilisations, banana plantations, and dense jungle foliage with tendrils trailing in the water.

At Teesit they destroyed three abandoned stockades. Two men of the naval light division were killed when fired upon from the bank. Their comrades stormed an enemy breastwork to take revenge. The flotilla anchored out of gunshot range of the stockades of Panlang and during the night the Burmese floated fire-rafts among the British ships, but to no effect. The following morning a strip of land was occupied close to the extensive stockades and a battery of four mortars and two six-pounders erected within an hour of landing. Shortly before dusk the steam-vessel *Diana* arrived and anchored between two stockades while columns of infantry advanced along both sides of the river. But as the attacks were launched each stockade in turn was found to be deserted.

The enemy was protected by a succession of formidable stockades, beginning at the pagoda and increasing in strength until reaching the main work surrounded by a deep *abatis*. Their guns seemed to be numerous and the garrison crowded the walls. A prisoner was sent in under a flag of truce with a demand to surrender the place. The Burmese refusal was 'civil but decided'. Bandula replied: 'We are each fighting for his country, and you will find me as steady in defending mine, as you in maintaining the honour of yours. If you wish to see Danubyu come as friends, and I will shew it to you. If you come as enemies, land.'

Covered by a light division and some sharpshooters in rowboats,

160 men of the 89th beat back an enemy outpost dug into a bank of the river. The British boats advanced under incessant fire from about thirty heavy Burmese cannon. Their accuracy gave substance to reports that Bandula had been practising his artillery crews for some time. Cotton's force had only 600 infantry available to assail a fortress which held perhaps 12,000 Burmese, well-furnished with artillery and muskets. Rather than attempting a suicidal frontal attack on the main positions, Cotton decided to knock out the successive stockades one by one, while the flotilla kept up a strong fire from the river.

At dawn the following day he landed 500 men with two six-pounders and a small rocket battery to attack the white pagoda. All were exposed to a heavy fire which was kept up to the last 'with perseverance and spirit'. The pagoda stood in a narrow gorge and the Burmese had no way of escape except over their own defences. They stood their ground until overwhelmed. The cost to the British of taking this first line of defence was 20 men killed or wounded; the Burmese lost 400.

The second stockade, about 500 yards away, proved a tougher nut to crack. Two more six-pounders, four more mortars and a fresh supply of rockets were brought up and placed in position at a bamboo and teak house. After an apparently devastating bombardment, 200 men of the 89th under Captain Rose advanced in two storming parties. They were greeted by a destructive fire from the stockade which forced the two columns to diverge and take refuge in a ditch. This was found, too late in many cases, to be laced with sharp spikes. Those who managed to find cover between the lethal spikes discovered the ditch was cunningly scarped to expose it to fire from the stockade. Every man who tried to get out was knocked down. Rose, already wounded, was felled by a second shot while struggling to maintain the attack. Other officers were killed or wounded while the losses among the men were 'extremely heavy'. They were ordered to retire if they could. More cannon and mortars were brought up to increase the battery, but the enemy strengthened their works and towards evening brought their own heavy guns to bear. Cotton reckoned that taking the stockade would cost so many lives that it would threaten his ability to storm the main defences. He decided to retire and await reinforcements. Captured enemy cannon were spiked and the British artillery reshipped. British losses were 129 killed, wounded or missing.

Campbell and his main army, who had been moving northwards towards Ava, spent three weeks marching to join Cotton. On 1 April his bombardment of the stubborn stockade began and continued to the following morning. As the British advanced, the enemy's small rearguard was found in full retreat towards the jungle. The main fortifications had been evacuated during the night after Bandula, Burma's greatest general, had been killed by a rocket while he was engaged on his daily round of inspection. Other chiefs who wished to carry on the fight could not stem the panic-stricken flight of the garrison troops towards Lamina. Within the defences the British found sufficient stocks of grain to feed themselves for several months.

Elsewhere British operations met with less costly success. In the north the Burmese capitulated at the siege of Rangpoore, their last foothold in Assam. In Cachar progress was slower because of the savage terrain and because heavier than usual rains made road construction almost impossible. A series of brilliant operations in March gave General Morrison full possession of the coastal province of Arracan. General Macbean occupied without resistance the islands of Ramiree and Sandowey.

Campbell made his headquarters at Prome where his army was trapped until November by the rainy season. Here, Campbell was faced with the greatest problem of the campaign – his men began to die at an alarming rate. The army had been poorly equipped by a Calcutta administration almost entirely ignorant of the climate and terrain of inland Burma. Sanitary conditions were appalling, and the men had few means to keep dry. Cholera, malaria, dysentery and jungle rot all took their toll, although precise numbers appear to have been covered up by the authorities, afraid of both mutiny and public scandal. The captured grain supplies ran out, while the Burmese employed a precocious scorched-earth policy to deny the British supplies from the surrounding country. Scarce provisions were moved laboriously up-river from Rangoon, about 150 miles away, by a flotilla of small boats under Captain Alexander of the

Alligator. Despite his efforts, the supply was erratic and insufficient. The rains continued to fall with mounting ferocity and much of the nearby farmland was flooded, increasing the epidemic. The Burmese constantly made small-scale raids which whittled down the numbers of fit men, and swiftly disappeared into the jungle when they were counter-attacked. Those British and Indian troops who dared follow them faced not just ambush, but swamps infested with leeches and the *Anopheles* mosquito.

In the meantime peace negotiations were held at Meeady between senior British officers and envoys authorised by Saha Menjee Maha Mengom, the king's first minister at Ava. A ceasefire was agreed for 17 October along with articles providing for a demarcation line between the two armies. As a result Campbell met the Burmese Commissioners Kee Woongee and Lay Mayn Woon for a parley at Nemben-zick. Compliments and courteous speeches were passed on both sides. The Burmese envoys politely asked after the health of the British king. The following day more chiefs came from Ava; having failed to persuade Campbell to withdraw all his forces and territorial claims, they asked for an extension of the armistice to 2 November so that they could consult with King Bagyidaw. Campbell agreed, and invited twelve chiefs to dine with him. Toasts were drunk to the royal house of Ava and one chief, referring to the differences between their two nations, said, 'the sun and moon are now eclipsed, but when peace is restored they will dazzle the world with increased splendour'.

The war, however, was not over.

*　　*　　*

The extended armistice allowed Campbell time to see his depleted army through the rainy season and for the less seriously ill to recover. The Burmese authorities used the time to collect and prepare new military forces. Neither side was prepared to give in.

King Bagyidaw, on hearing of the British demands to annexe much of the southern part of his realm, flew into 'the most intemperate bursts of impotent passion'. Thanks to the vigorous preparations a new army of over 50,000 men had been gathered. To lead them the King sent Maha Nemiow, a general of great experience, though previously overshadowed by Bandula. Nemiow attached to his army 8,000 Shans, men of 'high character' and an envious reputation for gallantry, who had yet to meet the British in battle. Along with them were three high-born women believed to be endowed with the gifts of prophecy and the miraculous ability to turn aside musket balls and bullets. The agreed demarcation line was swiftly crossed and the Burmese laid waste the countryside almost to the walls of Prome, broke British supply lines and threatened communications between Campbell's military HQ and Rangoon. The king's envoys rejected the peace proposals and sent Campbell a laconic ultimatum: 'If you wish for peace, you may go away; but if you wish either money or territory, no friendship can exist between us. This is the Burmese custom.'

The army of Ava moved along the banks of the Irrawaddy against Prome, then held by fewer than 6,000 British and sepoy troops. Nemiow split his army into three columns, each marching along parallel routes. His tactics were seriously flawed. Hills, ridges and dense jungle separated the columns and prevented them from supporting one another. Nemiow took personal command of the left division, 15,000 strong including the Shan horsemen, marching inland from the eastern bank. The central column, over 25,000 men headed by the royal minister of state, marched along the river bank supported by a large number of war-boats. The third column, 15,000 men under Sudda Woon, moved up the opposite bank of the Irrawaddy. The three divisions moved slowly, risking no general engagement and encircling Prome at a distance.

Colonel McDowgal with two brigades of native infantry was sent to dislodge Nemiow's advance guard at the village of Watti-goon, 16 miles to the north-east of the town. One division approached the enemy, while two more circled around the flank and rear. The British plan for a simultaneous attack from three directions was thrown awry by the Burmese who moved forward to meet the frontal assault head on, bringing up large numbers of Cafray cavalry. The British force beat them back but McDowgal was killed in the action. The central division, seeing no sign of the other two, was then forced to retreat with heavy casualties. Three more British officers and 61 men had been killed, 40 were missing in the dense jungle and 120 were wounded.

Nemiow was emboldened by this victory to move closer to Prome, but at a snail's pace, building earthworks and barricades at every stop. By the end of November his central column was visible, stockaded on the Heights of Napadee, which ran along the river bank 5 miles above Prome, with another column dug in on the opposite bank. Nemiow's column moved up to the stockade at Simbike and Kyalaz on the Narwine River, where they threatened the British river traffic. Despite his initial success, Nemiow was proving himself an unskilled tactician. His army was still divided into three, each separated from the others by wide or fast-flowing river waters or by thick forest. Campbell decided to go on the offensive by attacking each component in turn with his much smaller force.

At daybreak on 1 December Campbell left four sepoy regiments to defend Prome and marched the rest out to attack Nemiow's corps on the Narwine River, while his river flotilla and some extra sepoys mounted a diversionary assault on the Napadee Heights. Campbell split his force into two columns. One, under General Cotton, advanced along the left bank of the river while the other, under Campbell himself, forded the river and moved up the far bank. The idea was that whichever column reached the enemy first would instantly attack, while the other would block the Burmese retreat. Despite difficult and unfamiliar terrain, the tactic worked, with Cotton engaging first. One report noted:

In less than ten minutes every stockade was carried, the enemy completely routed, and the second column had only an opportunity of cannonading his panic-struck masses as they rushed fast through the openings of the jungle in front. Everything had been confusion within the stockades from the moment that General Cotton's column entered them; the very numbers of the enemy, crowded within their works, disabled them for effective resistance. The Shans alone maintained their character, and fought bravely. Animated by their young prophetesses, and the example of their *chobwahs*, or chiefs, they maintained the contest until the greater part of them were cut down. One of the prophetesses received a mortal wound, and old Maha Nemiow himself fell, encouraging his men in the hottest of conflict, to desperate resistance.

The Burmese left column was completely dispersed and Campbell now turned his attention to the centre column on the Napadee Heights. He gave his men just two hours' rest before marching them back to the hamlet of Zeouke to bivouac for the night. During that day they had performed a harassing march of 29 miles and fought and won a battle. At daylight on the 2nd they were again on the move. Dense jungle forced them to take a road leading to the front of the fortified ridge which was inaccessible on three sides. The British artillery opened up on the lofty stockades, backed by cannon fire from the flotillas under Commodore Sir John Brisbane on the river below. Brigadier Elrington was directed to advance through the jungle to the right where 'the enemy opposed him with great gallantry and resolution, defending every tree and breast-work with determined obstinacy'. Six companies of the 87th drove the Burmese outlying posts to the bottom of the ridge, clearing the valley floor. The main hilltop complex of stockades and earthworks, all filled with musketmen, extended for 3 miles and there was only one narrow road up to them. Once the artillery and rockets had silenced several enemy guns, the 1st Bengal Brigade was sent in to make the frontal assault, while the 38th hacked their way through the jungle to the right. An officer recorded:

Nothing could surpass the steadiness and resolute courage displayed in this attack. Scarcely a shot was fired in return to the enemy's continued volleys. The 38th, which led, first entered the enemy's entrenchments of the heights, driving him from hill to hill, over precipices which could only be ascended by a narrow stair, until the whole of the formidable position was carried.

During the attack Brisbane's flotilla pushed past to capture all the Burmese army's boats and stores.

Both the Burmese divisions which had advanced on the eastern side of the Irrawaddy were now scattered, leaving only the right column under Sudda Woon, stockaded on the western bank. That general had kept his men so quiet and well concealed that Campbell at first thought he had retreated silently. A rocket brigade and mortar battery was set up during the night on a small island in the river, opposite the enemy works. They opened fire early on the 5th as troops under General Cotton were ferried across the water. The Burmese retreated from their riverside positions to much stronger stockades half a mile into the interior, the walls mounted with heavy guns. Cotton, supported by reinforcements, plunged ahead and the position was swiftly taken. The enemy fled in all directions, leaving behind 300 dead and 350 muskets.

The *Annual Register* reported: 'Thus, in the course of four days, the immense army of Ava, which had threatened to envelope Prome and swallow up the British army troops, had melted away like vapour, and Sir A. Campbell was at liberty to march upon the capital, still distant about three hundred miles.'

After a day's rest, Campbell began that march in two divisions. The first, under his personal command, advanced in a curve to sweep up the remaining enemy river defences and to prevent a rally by the Burmese. The second, under Cotton, marched parallel to the river to act in cooperation with the flotilla. The early stages were through thick and tangled jungle which ruined provisions and drenched the men. Cholera again broke out on the route and several men died before healthier, higher ground was reached. The two columns reached Meeady, the supposed Burmese rallying point, after thirteen days' hard slog but found it just evacuated. The remainder of the Burmese army retreated to Melloone, a town on the right bank of the Irrawaddy, and regrouped. Some 12,000 strong, once again they constructed strong stockades on fortified heights with 600 yards of fast-moving river in front of them. The two armies sat watching each other from opposite sides of the stream. On the 26th the Burmese sent across a messenger under a flag of truce, bearing letters from the chiefs stating their desire to end hostilities. A minister had arrived from Ava with full authority to negotiate and ratify a peace.

After several false starts a truce was agreed and the Burmese provided two war-boats to act as pilots for Brisbane's flotilla which was having difficulty negotiating the river channels. A peace conference opened on 1 January 1826 with a new Burmese negotiator, Kolein Menghi. To the first British demand for war indemnity, he said that they did not grow rupees but might be able to pay a million baskets of rice within a year. Alternatively, the British might cut down and take away fine teak timber in lieu of cash. The Burmese would not give up Arracan, 'not on account of its value, for it was rather a burden to Ava than a source of profit, but because the nation was proud of the conquest which had been achieved by the valour of their ancestors, and the national honour was engaged not to yield it'. Campbell stuck rigidly to his demands and, faced with British cannon ranged upon the Burmese positions, Menghi agreed after three days' palaver and a treaty was signed by both sides. Under its terms the four provinces of Arracan, Mergui, Tavoy and Zea were to be ceded to the East India Company; the kingdoms of Assam, Cachar, Zeating and Munnipore were to be placed under princes named by the British Government; British ships would be allowed entry to Burmese ports and could land their cargoes free of duty; and Ava was to pay the Company a crore of rupees (ten million rupees) by instalments to cover some of the costs of the war. The treaty document had to be ratified by King Bagyidaw and returned to Campbell within fifteen days.

During that period the British observed the Burmese in Melloone, under Prince Memiaboo, strengthening their defences in violation of the truce. On the fourteenth day three Burmese officers claimed there had been unexplained delays in getting the treaty to the king and begged for an extension. They offered to pay a cash instalment and present hostages if the British army would retire to Prome. Campbell regarded that 'a proposal too extravagant and absurd for any court but that of Ava to make'. He stuck to the agreed deadline and said that if the treaty were not ratified and returned by midnight on the 18th, hostilities would recommence.

When that hour passed work immediately began on constructing batteries and landing heavy ordnance from the flotilla. The operation was so zealously performed that by 10 a.m. the following morning twenty-eight heavy cannon were in positions threatening the full mile's length of the enemy works across the river. An hour later the batteries and rockets opened up while troops were embarked in boats to cross the torrent. The current and a strong breeze carried the first brigade under Lieutenant-Colonel Sale to the attack point well ahead of the rest of the force. Sale was wounded in his boat, but the men of the 38th rushed on and swiftly took the earthworks facing them. The second brigade landed in time to cut off the escape route of the Burmese troops. In spite of the initial confused landing, the British lost only 9 men killed and 34 wounded in the assault.

In Prince Memiaboo's house they found 30,000 rupees in specie and both the English and Burmese copies of the treaty which, having been signed, had never been sent to Ava. When Campbell later sent a note to the chief minister suggesting sarcastically that he supposed it had been left behind in the hurried departure from Melloone, the minister coolly replied that, 'in the same hurry he had left behind him a large sum of money, which also he was confident the British general only waited an opportunity of returning'.

On 25 January Campbell resumed the march on Ava. Six days later his army was met by an American missionary, Dr Price, and Assistant-Surgeon Sandford, who had been taken prisoner some months before and who had been released by the king to act as messengers of peace. Bagyidaw was asking for terms and Campbell stuck to those agreed at Melloone. He refused to halt his onward march but agreed as a gesture to pause for two days at Pagahm-Mew, ten days' march ahead and halfway to the capital. When the British approached that neighbourhood they found 16,000 Burmese troops, including refugees from Melloone and fresh levies from Ava. Their commanders were pledged to defeat the 'Invading Army of Rebellious Strangers'.

Campbell decided to assault their positions both in the Logoh-Nunda pagoda and within the old walls of the city. On the morning of 9 February the British troops, including Cotton's men who had marched all night to catch up, left camp for the assault. For the first time in the entire war they found the Burmese forces outside their defences, ready to meet them on open ground. The Burmese commanders, Ta-Yea-Soogean, Woon-dock and Ne-Woon-Breen, had chosen their ground well. It was overgrown with prickly jungle which made it difficult for regular troops to manoeuvre while concealing large numbers of irregular troops. The Burmese were lined up in a crescent, hoping to engulf the British in its 'horns'. The British, however, were in larger numbers than expected, thanks to Cotton's forced march, and the Burmese tactics failed. Campbell led the 13th light infantry and four guns on the right attack; the 38th attacked on the left; and the 43rd Madras advanced on the banks of the Irrawaddy. The Burmese held their ground for some time but were forced back under the rapid fire of their more disciplined adversaries. A large number took refuge in a well-constructed field-work but the sepoys were so close on their heels that they did not have time to form themselves into defensive lines. Between 300 and 400 Burmese died, either on the point of the bayonet or by plunging into the river in a desperate effort to escape.

The main Burmese force was still intact; believing that the British centre was unoccupied, they pushed forward along the main road until checked by the sight of the 39th in reserve. Throughout the day the Burmese cavalry charged in fruitless bids to turn the British right, but they were repulsed every time. Gradually they were beaten on all sides and left Pagahm-Mew, with all its arms, stores and personal possessions, in British hands. The Burmese commander Nee-Woon-Breen, who had persuaded the king to launch this last, ill-fated attack on the invaders, carried the news of the disaster back to Ava. He was executed on the spot.

There was no effective force left between Campbell's army and the capital. Their onward march was, for the first time, through country not devastated by the enemy's scorched-earth policy. The soldiers passed through rich and well-cultivated fields, thick with copses and pretty villages. Temples and pagodas glittered along the river banks.

The army had reached Yandaboo, within four days' march of Ava, when on 24 February Dr Price again appeared with more freed British prisoners, the stipulated first instalment of war compensation and the treaty ratified by King Bagyidaw. The war was over. Campbell and some officers visited Ava where they were met with every honour by the humbled monarch. The army retraced its steps to Rangoon. They no longer faced Burmese ambush but a much more hostile enemy – disease – continued to reduce their numbers.

* * *

The financial cost of the war to Britain was £13 million, of which £1 million was recovered from the Burmese in indemnity. The human cost was far, far greater. Accurate figures of the death toll from disease and exposure are difficult to obtain. One estimate suggests that of the 40,000 British and Indian troops engaged in total, including those on the northern frontiers, around 15,000 died. Of the 3,586 British and European troops who first occupied Rangoon, 3,115 perished in Burma – but only 150 of them were killed in battle.

There was no great public outcry in England. The largest numbers deployed, and therefore those with the highest casualties, were sepoys whose deaths were not even counted in the British press. The death rate had shocked the Calcutta administration, but Amherst and his pen-pushers were not eager to expose the incompetence and bad planning which left troops without adequate food, medicine and other supplies. And, after all, Campbell had delivered a significant victory which enriched and extended British rule. Under the treaty Arracan, Assam and Tenasserim were ceded to the British, while King Bagyidaw undertook not to interfere in Manipur, Cachar and Jainta. Trade with Burmese ports was opened to fill the coffers of the Company and other English merchants. The outcome of the war, rather than the cost, was greeted with great public enthusiasm in London.

Campbell was voted a gold medal and an income of £1,000 a year by the Company board of directors and he received Lord Amherst's official thanks. For three years he governed the ceded provinces of Burma and Siam, but ill-health took him home in 1829. He was treated like a hero when he arrived and was later created a baronet, with a special coat of arms bearing the title 'Ava'. From 1831 to 1837 he was Lieutenant-Governor of New Brunswick and was nominated commander-in-chief in Canada. In 1839 he was offered the command of India but turned it down owing to his failing health. He died in 1843.

Frederick Marryat and *Diana* had proved the worth of steamships in military campaigns and the little craft had many successors in the waters of the Irrawaddy. Marryat retired from the navy in 1830, at the age of thirty-eight. For the next eighteen years, until his death, he devoted himself to writing stirring adventure novels, mostly set at sea. His most famous are still read: *Mr Midshipman Easy*, *Peter Simple* and *The Children of the New Forest*.

General Sir Willoughby Cotton served in Bengal, Jamaica and Afghanistan. In the latter arena, after thirty years' service, he had still not learned to send out reconnaissance patrols while leading his troops through country crawling with hostile Sikhs. At the outbreak of the Crimean War, Cotton, despite his self-confessed 'advancing years and unwieldy figure', unsuccessfully applied for a fighting command. He died in 1860, aged seventy-seven. Lord Amherst was made an earl and subsequently served as Governor-General of Canada. He was eighty-four when he died in 1857.

After the Treaty of Yandaboo British forces remained in Rangoon until all its terms were fulfilled, finally leaving in November. The former governor of Syriam, Gun-lat, seized the surrounding territory for the Talien tribe and bottled up a Burmese garrison in Rangoon. King Bagyidaw assembled another army 'to catch, murder and squeeze the beggarly Taliens'. His army succeeded in driving out the usurper the following February. Bagyidaw, known as the 'Golden Foot', never forgot nor forgave the British for the humiliations they heaped on him. He continued to use intrigue and subterfuge to water down the terms he had agreed to, but was outwitted by a succession of envoys who knew that, if needs must, they could always use gunboat diplomacy. His frustrations were cited as the cause of his mental breakdown after March 1831. Four years later his brother, Tharrawaddy, seized the throne in a palace coup and renounced the 1826 treaty.

Tharrawaddy, too, became insane and was succeeded in 1846 by his eldest son, Pagan Min, who cautiously executed most of his relatives and then less cautiously arrested the captains of two British merchant ships. The Second Burma War ensued in 1852. The British commander was Sir Henry Godwin, now elevated to the rank of general. He wanted to repeat the operations of the earlier war, notwithstanding the terrible cost, saying 'nothing that was not done then can be done now – everything that was done then must be done now.' Fortunately for the men under his command he was tactfully overruled by the new Governor-General of India, Lord Dalhousie. Rangoon, Martaban and Bassein were taken easily before the rainy season and then the province of Pegu was annexed. The British now ruled the whole of Lower Burma.

Pagan Min was deposed and replaced by the greatly esteemed Mindon Min who built the great city of Mandalay as his capital, established a fleet of British-run steam vessels, introduced European technology to factories and constructed a telegraph system. When he died his younger son Thibaw resurrected many of the old despotic ways. His attempts to negotiate with France and to impose cash penalties on British timber firms led to the Third Burma War of 1885–6. A British force under General Sir Harry Prendergast took Mandalay. Thibaw and his surviving family were deported to India. The kingdom of Ava had fallen and Britain annexed the entire country. Burma's wealth in precious metals, teak, petroleum and food were fully exploited by Britain.

During the Second World War Burma suffered a brutal Japanese invasion before gaining independence on 4 January 1948. Now it trembles under another type of dictatorship.

In Britain Burma retained a vivid hold on the popular imagination for many years, not least for the poems of Rudyard Kipling. One summed up the feelings of those soldiers who did come home from its wars:

By the old Moulmein Pagoda, lookin' lazy at the sea,
There's a Burma girl a-setting, and I know she thinks o' me;
For the wind is in the palm trees, and the temple bells they say:
Come you back, you British soldier; come you back to Mandalay!

TWELVE

The Black War – Tasmania, 1824–30

'For every man they murder, hunt them down, and drop ten of them.'

Princess Lalla Rookh, known to her own people as Truganina, was born in the first decade of the nineteenth century. At that time there were at least 8,000 and possibly as many as 20,000 native aborigines living on the island of Tasmania. They were nomads, hunters, gatherers, a naked people ill-prepared for the coming of European settlers, sealers and hardened convicts. By the time Lalla Rookh was twenty there were 320 of her people left.

She was a beauty who was not shy about giving sexual favours freely. One settler wrote: 'She sadly tried the patience of several husbands. Her features, despite her bridgeless nose, were decidedly pleasing . . . when lighting up her sparkling black eyes in animated conversation.' As the young wife of a chief of the Bruni tribe she witnessed the most one-sided war in the history of British colonialism. She was repeatedly raped and saw her first intended husband shot before her eyes. Her mother was also shot by a British soldier and her sister was kidnapped by sealers for use as a sex slave. She died in May 1876, aged something over seventy. She was the last of the Tasmanians.

*   *   *

The history of the Tasmanians as a separate aboriginal people began twelve thousand years ago when their mountainous peninsula was cut off from mainland Australia by rising seas. A Stone Age people without the ability to build craft able to sail the dangerous 200-mile wide straits, they were cut off from the rest of humanity. And from predators.

The first European known to have landed on the large island to the south of Australia was an employee of the Dutch East India Company named Abel Jans Tasman. While on a voyage of exploration he made landfall in November 1642 and marked the unknown territory on his maps as Van Diemen's Land, in deference to one of his Company bosses. No contact with the natives was made. The aborigines were left in peace for over 150 years, although various expeditions followed Tasman's to fill in the blank spaces on their seafaring maps.

However, in 1802 the British administration at Port Jackson on the mainland become suspicious of a French scientific expedition, and decided to encourage settlement of an island nominally under the British flag. The new territory was scouted by men such as Matthew Flinders who founded the harbour in the north of the island. It was an island of rugged mountains, dense eucalyptus forests, scrubby bush, fertile valleys and impenetrable rainforests. One early visitor described 'innumerable flights of parrots, cockatoos . . . legions of black swans . . . we were disturbed by two savages who ran towards the beach, both of them shewing the most extraordinary gestures of surprise and admiration'.

Contact between the early settlers and explorers and the aboriginal inhabitants were brief, rare and largely friendly. Captain Collins, who later founded Hobart Town, recorded one meeting: 'His face was blackened, and the top of his head was plastered with red earth. His hair was either naturally short and close, or had been made so by burning . . . He was armed with two spears, very badly made and of solid wood only.' The native took no interest in the landing party's firearms, but was fascinated by the red silk handkerchiefs which the sailors wore around their necks.

The Frenchman François Peron described a woman in her mid-twenties with a kind and benevolent appearance:

She was entirely naked, with the exception of a kangaroo skin, in which she carried a little girl, which she continued to suckle. Her breasts, a little withered already, appeared otherwise to be pretty well-formed and of the pendulous type, and were sufficiently furnished with milk. Her eyes were the most expressive part [of her face], and there seemed to be even something spiritual, which surprised us.

Another early visitor remarked that Tasmanian eyes were 'dark, wild, and strongly expressive of the passions'.

The aborigines were a loose-knit confederation of tribes with up to ten distinct languages. A typical clan consisted of several extended families, with around eighty people in all. Men and women coupled for life and looked after their children and ageing relatives. The most populous regions were coastal, but there is evidence that some tribes inhabited the most inhospitable areas. Europeans described them as of average height and dark-skinned, but with facial features quite different from those of mainland Australia. The women, as described above, wore kangaroos skins around their shoulders, mainly to carry children and equipment, and little or nothing else. The men went completely naked save for decorative strips of skins and shells. Both sexes adorned themselves with charcoal and ochre.

They were a healthy people and early visitors saw no signs of starvation. The men hunted kangaroo and wallaby while the women gathered berries and roots, dived for shellfish and scooped up cockles from the beach. The eating of scaled fish was taboo. A low-alcohol cider was made from gum trees but the main drink was water. The aborigines had not learnt to use metal and all implements and weapons were made from wood, bone and stone. Canoes were made from bark and rushes and were used to hunt seal. Women served the men who, in turn, jealously guarded them from marauders. They believed in spirits, good and bad, and superstitions, and the breach of taboos led to internal conflict, retold by generations of storytellers. But there is no evidence of any sort of large-scale war between the tribes or clans.

After one peaceful encounter Peron wrote: 'The general union of the several individuals of the family, the kind of patriarchal life which we had witnessed, had strongly affected our feelings: I saw realised with inexpressible pleasure those charming descriptions of the happiness and simplicity of a state of nature, of which I had so often read, and enjoyed in idea.'

Peron was clearly influenced by Rousseau's concept of the 'Noble Savage' but, while it is easy to overstate the simplicity and harmony of such unspoilt people, European observers agreed that the natives appeared to live in peace, at one with their environment. As nomads they saw no need for permanent encampments, far less buildings. They sheltered under crude windbreaks and in caves and hollow tree trunks. The white men who landed on their shores were alien and incomprehensible to the native Tasmanians. They soon learnt to be fearful.

Settlers began to stake out their claims around the mouth of the River Derwent in the south, and the Esk in the north. Clashes with the aborigines over food supplies occurred when the early settlers faced bouts of famine. European sealers in the north kidnapped women and children for sex and servitude. But the real violence began when the London and Australian authorities realised that the remoteness of Van Diemen's Land made it ideal for convict colonies. Prisoners were steadily imported to what swiftly became one large open gaol. Other settlers were twice-convicted prisoners from Port Jackson. Many convicts simply walked out of the penal settlements and roamed the island's rugged interior, becoming bushrangers. Others were allowed to roam freely as stockmen and herders for their masters. As writer Lloyd Robson pointed out, the result was a 'bandit society' in which the roaming convicts were joined by refugees from labour gangs. They learnt the bush skills of tracking and survival and roving bands became such a threat to the settlements that Lieutenant-Governor Thomas Davey declared martial law, although that was quickly suspended by the Sydney authorities. The bushrangers were a much greater threat to the aborigine whom they considered, quite literally in many cases, to be fair game.

The bushrangers killed Tasmanian men and children for sport and raped the women (called *gins* by the whites). Males were tied to trees and used for target practice. One former bushranger recalled: 'I would as leave shoot them as so many sparrows. At the same time, I derive much amusement from this form of sport.' The murder of a husband was usually followed by the rape of his wife. A correspondent wrote of one incident: 'The Bushranger Carrots killed a black fellow, and seized his gin; then cutting off the man's head, the brute fastened it round the gin's neck, then drove the weeping victim to his den.' In an incident that shocked even some of the most hardened murderers an aborigine baby was buried up to its neck in sand in front of its mother and its head kicked off. A sealer confessed to an officer that he 'kept a poor young creature nude and chained up like a wild beast, and whenever he wanted her for anything, applied a burning stick, a firebrand from the hearth, to her skin'.

There are many explanations for such conduct, such as the scarcity of women and the absence of all moral and social constraints which is found on any frontier. The convicts had themselves been brutalised. Many were outcasts from the Industrial Revolution who had survived journeys that killed their friends and families. Others were ruthless criminals and known murderers. All had been the victims of severe judicial cruelty including repeated floggings, starvation, routine buggery and the shadow of the rope. They thought nothing of inflicting similar cruelty on black beings whom their rough society did not recognise as humans. But nothing can excuse the sadistic delight with which they pursued and tormented their quarry.

But it was not just the lowly criminal classes who engaged in such sport. In some areas hunting aborigines was regarded as a family entertainment among gentlemen and their ladies. The white women would prepare picnics while the gentlemen and their convict servants hunted the blacks with dogs or shot them from a distance. If none were found in the bush, occasionally a previously captured woman would be paraded before the marksmen. One settler had a pickle tub in which he kept the ears of all the blacks he had shot. In that harsh frontier society it was all considered great fun. Captain Holman recorded a stockman who approached a native with a pair of pistols, only one of which was loaded. He fired the empty one at his own head and invited the aborigine to do the same with the other weapon. The black man innocently complied and blew his brains out against a tree trunk.

The aborigines fought back, often to rescue stolen womenfolk or avenge a rape. A convict stockman who flogged a black girl with a bullock whip to prepare her for the 'marriage bed' was speared to death while carrying water. Stock-keepers at Salt Pan Plains raped two black women who later escaped while the men were drunk.

The women told their husbands and the tribe surrounded the hut and killed two of the three men inside. Another band, unable to kill the heavily armed rapist and bushranger Dunn in his den became so frustrated they instead murdered several of his inoffensive white neighbours. The outrages continued and all suffered. A typical Tasmanian tactic was to wound or kill isolated stock-keepers and shepherds by setting fire to the roofs of their huts and then spearing them as they emerged choking and blinded by smoke. The killing of outlaws was one thing, but the murder of settlers pushing back the frontiers of civilisation was something quite different. Bands of militia, vigilantes and soldiers struck deep into the bush in search of black miscreants. The real slaughter began.

The first organised conflict occurred in 1804, at Risdon, 5 miles from Hobart. A settler called Burke complained that large numbers of aborigines were menacing him because he had built his hut on sacred hunting grounds. A detachment of troops was sent out under Lieutenant Moore, a notorious drunkard. In the late morning a mass of aborigines was seen swarming down from the heights, driving a herd of kangaroos towards a hollow where they were slaughtered for a feast. The aborigines were unarmed except for the waddies or clubs used for killing kangaroos, and with them were their families. The soldiers of the New South Wales Corps, most of whom were as drunk as their officer, opened fire either in panic or for sport. At least fifty men, women and children were killed. A witness of the massacre, Edward White, gave evidence to the subsequent inquiry, saying that he was hoeing turnips when he saw several hundred aborigines come down the hillside in a half circle, driving the kangaroos before them. 'They looked at me with their eyes,' he said. 'I went down the creek and reported them to some soldiers, and then went back to my work. The Natives did not threaten me in any way, and I was not afraid of them. The Natives did not attack the soldiers. They could not have molested them. The firing commenced about eleven o'clock. There were many Natives slaughtered and wounded. I don't know how many. But some of their bones were sent in two casks to Port Jackson in New South Wales to be studied.' A later chronicler, Captain Holman, wrote of the incident: 'From this moment on, a deep-rooted hatred sprang up among the aborigines for any strangers, and since that time all endeavours at friendship have proved ineffective.'

For twenty years the skirmishes and bloody raids continued, dying down in one part of the island, only to flare up in another. Sometimes the disputes arose over the herding of cattle across aboriginal lands; at other times they resulted from brutal outrages committed by convicts and settlers. Every time the aborigines retaliated, retribution followed. Soldiers and vigilantes, pursuing supposed murderers, fired indiscriminately into any aboriginal encampment they encountered. One witness to such a night attack wrote: 'It was interesting to see how they fell after they were shot. One man, being shot while bending over the fire, sprang up, turned round and round and round like a whipping toy, before he fell dead.' The Wesleyan builder G.A. Robinson reported:

A party of military and constables got a number of natives cornered between two perpendicular rocks, on a sort of shelf, and in the end killed 70 of them. The women and children had pressed themselves into the crevices of the rocks, but were dragged out and their brains dashed out on the convenient rocks.

Another incident was described to Brough Smith:

A number of blacks with women and children were congregated in a gully near Hobart and the men had formed themselves into a ring around a large fire, while the women were cooking the evening meal of opossums and bandicoots. They were thus surprised by a party of soldiers, who without warning fired into them as they sat, and then rushing up to the panic-stricken natives started to go in at them with rifle butts. A little child being near its dying mother, the soldier drove his bayonet through the body of the child and pitchforked it into the flames.

Such savagery was applauded on the wild frontier but there was a growing backlash in the newspaper offices, courtrooms and pulpits of the mushrooming towns. One clergyman wrote: 'The wounded were brained; the infants cast into the flames; the musket driven into quivering flesh; and the social fire, around which the Natives gathered to slumber, became, before morning, their funeral pyre.'

The first Bishop of Tasmania, Dr Nixon, said:

There are many such on record, which make us blush for humanity when we read about them, and forbid us to wonder that the maddened savage's indiscriminate fury should not only have refused to recognise the distinction between friend and foe, but have taught him to regard each white man as an intruding enemy, who must be got rid of at any cost.

An 1818 editorial in the *Hobart Gazette* said:

The aborigines demand our protection. They are the most helpless members, and being such, have a peculiar claim upon us all, to extend every aid in our power, as well in relation to their necessities as to those enlightening means which shall at last introduce them from the chilling rigours of the forest into the same delightful temperature which we enjoy.

But the aborigines would not, could not, be civilised as servants and gardeners and for every smugly enlightened white dove there was a hawk who wanted nothing less than the extermination of the 'niggers'. A writer to the *Courier* said: 'Let them have enough of Redcoats and bullet fire. For every man they murder, hunt them down, and drop ten of them. This is our specific – try it.' That proved to be a conservative ratio of retribution as the scattered bush wars continued.

* * *

By 1820 the aborigines of Tasmania were facing extinction. Epidemics of diseases introduced by the white men swept through the tribes, killing more than marauding parties of bushrangers and soldiers could ever do. The once-plentiful game dwindled as civilisation encroached, causing starvation and further illness. Tree-felling and new cultivation squeezed them into smaller and smaller pockets of terrain, ending their nomadic way of life. And they stopped having children. No one knows the full reason. Constant pursuit and despair made the women barren, according to some sources. When tribes were being remorselessly chased, infants were an encumbrance they could not afford; according to other sources, infants were slain at birth because their parents couldn't feed them. Crude forms of contraception were employed, according to yet others. Historian David Davies reckoned there were 7,000 aborigines left in 1817; seven years later there were just 340. Whatever the reason, the remaining population aged and dwindled, with little fresh blood invigorating the tribes. Where once there were thousands, now there were hundreds. And still the carnage continued.

The whites' fear and contempt of the blacks was heightened by the activities of Mosquito, an Australian aborigine who was transported to Tasmania for the murder of a black woman. He quickly became the leader of a gang of desperate Tasmanians who hung around the townships to drink and steal. Many settlers regarded his rampage in 1824 as the start of the Black War. He was an unlikely, and unworthy, hero. His men were blacks who had lost all fear of the white man; according to his white prosecutors he dispatched them to raid and murder. The Oyster Bay region on the east coast was terrorised for a while and Mosquito's cunning helped him to elude all forces sent against him. His outrages were compounded by his henchman Black Jack, who delighted in torturing to death white captives and whose catchphrase was 'I'll kill all the white bastards.' They were finally captured by Tegg, a seventeen-year-old aborigine tracker who was hired by the constabulary with the promise of a boat as reward. Mosquito and Black Jack were tried for murder in Hobart and hanged in public. Tegg never got his boat. The writer Gilbert Robertson remarked: 'Although Mosquito has been removed, yet the lessons he afforded the aborigines of this island have not been forgotten by them; experience has taught them craft, cunning, activity and watchfulness, and at this moment they have found the means to spread terror among the Colonists residing in the interior.'

It was into this climate of fear and ferocity that a new Governor stepped in 1824. Colonel Sir George Arthur was forty and a hardened veteran of the Napoleonic Wars. He had served in Italy, was severely wounded in the attack on Rosetta during the Egypt campaign, and was again wounded in the attack on Flushing. During the latter battle he and his single company took prisoner 5 officers and 300 men. On his return to London he was awarded a sword and the Freedom of the City. After further service in Jersey and Jamaica he was made Governor of British Honduras, where he suppressed a slave revolt. But his dispatches condemning the institution of slavery influenced and aided the emancipation crusade of William Wilberforce, and by the standards of the time he was regarded as a humane man. His task in Van Diemen's Land was principally to reform and improve the system of transportation and penal servitude. His biographer wrote:

> His strong good sense and humanity indicated the possibility of a middle course between the extreme severity of the system which would make transportation simply deterrent, and the over-indulgence of the system which aimed at reforming the convict by gentle treatment. He held that it was possible to make transportation a punishment much dreaded by criminals, while offering every facility for reform to those who were not hardened by crime; but he entertained no quixotic expectations of frequent reformation. His plans were never allowed a fair trial.

His main opponents were colonists who wanted Tasmania to grow into something more than a penal settlement. That meant fewer convicts and a solution to the aboriginal problem.

Arthur's first dealings with the aborigines was benevolent. He was shocked, on his arrival, to see and hear evidence of the barbarity inflicted on the blacks by the white race. One tribe asked him for his personal protection, which he readily gave and helped them settle on a tongue of land at Kangaroo Point. Arthur's efforts to protect other tribes, however, proved ineffectual and hostility against them intensified as they grew bolder in their sporadic attacks on outlying farms and settlements. During a period of six years 121 attacks were recorded in the Oatlands district alone. In a typical incident Mr Miller, a farmer on the River North Esk, was returning home when he saw a number of aborigines on his property. He ran to a neighbouring farm for help but found the owner dead in his yard and his foreman dead with eleven spears in his body. He ran back to his own silent homestead where there was by now no sign of the raiders. Inside he found his wife lying on their bed, her brains bashed out by waddy blows. The aborigines had taken his meagre stocks of sugar, flour and clothing. In another attack near the town of Jerico, aborigines lay in ambush for three days before catching the farmer, Mr Hooper, unarmed. They speared him to death and went on to butcher his unprotected wife and seven children. Another band, the 'Ouse Mob', burnt down the hut of a shepherd and killed him as he emerged. His small daughter begged for mercy on her knees and was spared. The colonists and soldiers responded with their now customary ferocity. Clans were hunted down and massacred with little regard as to whether they included the guilty men.

Towards the end of 1828 the increasingly frustrated Governor Arthur issued a new proclamation placing a bounty on aborigines who would not stay within strict boundaries. Authorised hunters were employed to bring them in alive. Captured adults were worth £5 each and children £2. In addition, successful hunters were promised grants of land. Clerics and supposed champions of the aborigines persuaded many blacks to come in of their own accord, and pocketed the reward money. The policy worked for a time and there seemed to be a real prospect of peace. But the few hundred remaining blacks were outraged by the idea that they could be sold. Simmering resentment boiled over and once again panic spread throughout the white settlements as out-stations, travellers and isolated farmhouses came under attack. Arthur declared martial law in every part of the island.

Sturdy, fortified farmhouses offered some protection from marauding natives but not from a determined raid. There were several instances of aborigines clambering down chimneys to murder the families inside. White men taken alive suffered agonising deaths. They were tortured with fire and spear points until the warriors were tired of them. Those captives who were still alive were handed over to the aborigine women, who smashed their genitals to mush with sharp flints. The aborigines also became superb guerrilla fighters. They knew the terrain and could move with astonishing speed – there were some recorded instances in which raiders travelled 50 miles a day on foot. The very scarcity of the aborigines, their mobility and their cruel experiences at the hands of the whites meant that the old military tactics of surprise, night ambushes and massacre were no longer effective against them. Something drastic had to be done to solve the problem once and for all. The result was 'The Line'.

Arthur was persuaded to authorise an audacious plan to form a line of soldiers, militia and civilian volunteers right across the island, to drive the aborigines before them – like 'beating' game in a country estate shoot – towards the narrow-necked Forester's Peninsula in the south. There they could be easily rounded up. Government order 166 was issued on 27 August 1830 to 'repel and drive from the settled country those Natives who seize every occasion to perpetrate murders, and to plunder and destroy the property of the inhabitants'. Arthur asked that consignments of convicts should be of useful classes – 'not Irish' – so that they might aid the enterprise. Volunteers were offered no special reward, only the thrill of the chase.

The Australian press was sceptical from the start. One editorial said: 'It is little better than idiocy to talk of surrounding and catching a group of active, nimble-minded, naked men and women, divested of burdens of all sorts.' Another said:

> We call the present warfare against a handful of poor, naked, despicable savages, a humbug in every sense of the word. Every man in the isle is in motion, from the Governor down to the meanest convict. The farmer's scythe and reaping hook are transmuted to the coat of mail and bayonet! The blacksmith, from forging shoes for the settler's nag, now forges the chains to enslave, and whets the instruments of death.

Sir George Murray wrote: 'the adoption of any line of conduct, having for its avowed or secret object the extinction of the native race, could not fail to leave an indelible stain upon the British Government'.

The Line operation started on 7 October with the Oyster Bay and Big River tribes as the principal targets. A chain of rallying posts was thrown across the island from St Patrick's Head on the east coast to Campbell Town on the west. In all, 3,000 armed men were deployed, comprising units of the 63rd, 57th and 17th Regiments, several hundred constables, volunteers and 738 convicts. The non-military parties were organised into groups of ten, each with a guide. The daily ration for each party was one and a half pounds of meat, three ounces of sugar, half an ounce of tea and two pounds of flour. Alcohol was brought by the men themselves. Supplies were organised by General Browne, who efficiently provided drays and pack-horses, although boots suitable for the rough terrain were in short supply, as were heavy duty trousers and jackets. Most units, however, were well armed. A central depot was established at Oatlands, containing 1,000 spare muskets, 30,000 cartridges and 300 handcuffs.

In fits and starts the various components of the Line began to push south. They quickly found that it would be no easy country shoot. The broken nature of the rough terrain made it impossible to maintain good order. Captain Donaldson's Launceston Corps scaled a high bluff but spent a miserable night without shelter, battered by icy wind and rain. Other units found their inadequate clothing slashed to rags by sharp-thorned bushes. A soldier gathering firewood was pierced in the leg and shoulder by spears thrown by an unseen enemy. Progress was slow and arduous and the thrill of the chase soon wore off. Free tobacco was issued to ease the discomfort of the cold, black nights.

Despite the repeated issue of new regulations which decreed the correct distance between men, campsites and fires, the Line was impossible to secure through the day and night. In the darkness shadows were glimpsed crossing the Line, evading sentries who, in the flickering light of the campfires, were uncertain as to whether they were natives, animals or ghosts. One sentry tripped over a log, only to see it stand up and melt away into the trees. Thousands of rounds were expended shooting at genuine shadows, or at branches shaken by the night breezes.

The Line plodded on, and occasionally there was some limited success. Mr Walpole recorded that on 26 October he spotted the rough camp of a small group of foraging aborigines. 'I returned for the rest of my party, and in the evening placed them within 300 yards of the Natives,' he wrote, 'where we waited until dawn of day and crept to one of the Natives, without being perceived by any of the others in the windbreak and there I caught him by the leg. The other four rushed away. One, however, was caught after he had fallen into the creek, and two others were shot.' The rest of the forty-strong tribe were alerted and rushed through the Line in a body, spearing one settler in the leg as they passed.

At the beginning of November some of the most experienced soldiers were ordered to clear aborigines out of the Three Thumbs, a chain of tree-covered hills about 300 yards apart, near Prosser's Bay. It was believed that this natural citadel held the largest remaining body of blacks. The ashes of camp fires, wood chippings and aboriginal artefacts were found but the soldiers were unable to cut their way through the dense scrub and undergrowth. They fired volley after volley into the trees while beaters created a storm of noise to drive away the game. Half-starved blacks, deprived of their food supplies, smothered the cries of their few remaining infants whenever the soldiers got too close. Governor Arthur personally led several sorties in the hope of a triumphal return to Hobart with chained captives. Finally, after criss-crossing the area he had to concede defeat – the aborigines had melted away, slipping through the Line while the soldiers blasted empty glades.

They and other clans, by now enraged, attacked farms behind the Line. Newspapers, critical of the Line from the start, questioned why the northern part of the island had been left defenceless. After four white men were speared near Launceston, a northern magistrate wrote: 'I have no person I can send after these Blacks. I have no-one that I can spare, nearly all the constables being out of the country, catching the Blacks in Buckingham.' Such reports of endangered homes caused an upsurge in desertions along the Line.

Arthur, however, was determined to press on, heartened by reports that blacks had been seen on Forester's Peninsula. He issued an address to his scattered commanders:

A few days must now terminate this great work in the most satisfactory manner, and His Excellency earnestly hopes that the leaders will, for the remaining short period, continue to show the excellent spirit which has all along been so conspicuous in their parties, for they will perceive that the advance of the scouting parties will render redoubled vigilance necessary on the part of those who guard the Line, as the Natives, when disturbed in the interior, will undoubtedly increase their efforts to break through the positions.

He gave his men four days to advance, driving the blacks before them, to East Bay Neck, a narrow sliver of ground which connected the peninsula to the mainland. Everything went to plan and each unit met its strict timetable. The shorelines were watched to prevent aborigines escaping by canoe. At last Arthur's forces crossed the Neck and entered the peninsula. Not a single aborigine was there.

The Line operation had cost the Government £30,000 and the Colony as a whole over £70,000. It had involved, including back-up forces, reinforcements, suppliers and transporters, upward of 6,000 Europeans. And the net result was two aborigines captured by Walpole's party. The Revd John West wrote: 'The settler-soldiers returned to their homes, their shoes worn out, their garments tattered, their hair long and shaggy, with beards unshaven, their arms tarnished, but neither blood-stained, nor disgraced.'

Governor Arthur believed that, disappointments aside, the Line had achieved an important objective. In his parting order of 26 November he said that the remaining aborigines, having seen at first hand the military and numerical power of the white man, would be persuaded to surrender without more bloodshed. Events proved him partially right. The aborigines were dispersed, hungry, cut off from their traditional hunting grounds. Constant pursuit and harrying had taken their toll. A small northern tribe, about thirty souls, did indeed surrender. Individual aborigines were lured out of the bush and forests by relatives who told them that the white man's life offered comfort and glittering presents.

The Line may have been a farce in strictly military terms, but it demonstrated that the nomadic way of life which had sustained the native population for centuries was over.

*   *   *

George Augustus Robinson was a classic nineteenth-century mixture of humbug, high-minded Christianity, personal greed and ambition mixed with compassion and an unbreakable certainty in his own infallibility. It was a lethal concoction, and it resulted in the destruction of an entire race. An Englishman with few family connections, he was Hobart Town's chief bricklayer and preacher. His Wesleyan zeal was focused on the protection of a 'lesser race' from the ungodly excesses of a white society which he considered equally barbaric. He became the self-styled 'Defender of the Aborigine'. He believed that God had commanded him to save the aborigine and that meant 'civilising' him.

Before, during and after the Line operation Robinson embarked on a series of epic journeys into the hinterland, trying to gain the trust of the tribes and to persuade them to come in. He was greatly helped by 'semi-civilised' natives, women spies and go-betweens including Truganina, and by aboriginal trackers whom he converted by bribery and the promise of eternal salvation. His treks were a success and, of course, Robinson saw no reason to spurn the bounties in cash and land which were his reward on earth for his Christian endeavours. He became a very rich man. His success in bringing out of the bush small groups of half-starved natives brought him to the attention of Governor Arthur and the Hobart Aborigine Committee. There was certainly a need for new tactics. The Line operation had spurred on the few warriors left to acts of increasing, almost suicidal, savagery. John Batman, a farmer near Ben Lomond and Robinson's chief rival as a humane native-catcher, wrote:

> The Natives last Thursday week murdered two more men at Oyster Bay, and the next day they beat a sawyer to death. On the Sunday after they murdered a soldier. On last Wednesday, they attacked the house of Mr Boultby, when he was absent;

and if it had not been for a soldier who happened to be there, they would have murdered Mrs Boultby and all the children. On Friday last they murdered three men at a hut belonging to Major Gray, and left a fourth for dead.

Robinson, Batman and others traversed the island to persuade the aborigines that their only hope was to trust the white man, give up their lands and move to a wondrous new land teeming with game. The result was the Flinders Island Reservation, an early example of a concentration camp. The man placed in charge, at an annual salary of £100, was G.A. Robinson. In 1832 the first group of 220 aborigines were sent to their new home. They were horrified by what they found. Flinders Island is 40 miles long and 12 to 18 miles wide. As promised, it had a small population of kangaroos for hunting. It had wild and beautiful mountains. But generally it was exposed to storms and lashing rain, cold, barren and desolate. Some aborigines tried to leap overboard, others moaned and twitched convulsively in dismay. Weakened already by famine, rheumatism, consumption and sea travel, many aborigines felt they were looking at the place of their own death. They were proved right. Almost immediately scores died of the common cold – against which they had no antibodies – tuberculosis, pneumonia and cultural shock.

Robinson chose a bay on the island's south-western side for the building of his new model settlement, to be called Wybalenna. Exposed to the western winds, neither forest nor high ground offered the bay any protection, but nevertheless it was here that he decided to try out his theories on moral and social reform. Soldiers built long huts of wattle and daub to provide shelter before more permanent buildings could be erected. Sympathetic settlers donated a small flock of sheep. Conflict broke out almost immediately. Quarrels between feuding clans were daily occurrences. Soldiers clashed with white sealers over the favours of the naked black women. The black men resented the whites' attitude to their wives and daughters, who were themselves becoming uncontrollable. The men became dissipated and listless. Food was continually in short supply. A number of blacks protested and the soldiers' commander, the tough old convict-flogger Sergeant White, called it a rebellion. As a punishment he marooned fifteen aborigine men on a granite rock out to sea without food, shelter or water, save for whatever they could scoop up from rainwater puddles. They were rescued after five days by Batman, although several later died from their treatment.

The subsequent scandal led to White's replacement by the more humane Lieutenant Darling, who swiftly ordered all sealers off the island, and moved the main encampment to a more hospitable site. Robinson moved to the island two years later and claimed the credit for Darling's initial humanitarian work. The island was supplied with cows, shoes and crude furniture. Well-meaning souls sent the aborigine women petticoats and checked aprons. But still the aborigines died in alarming numbers. They died of dysentery, cholera, venereal diseases, influenza and occasional violence. Some seemed simply to give up on life and wandered into the rocky hinterland, never to return. Their spirits withered as they came to terms with what was effectively imprisonment without conviction; they were convicts with no foreseeable end to their sentences. The Revd Dr Lang of Sydney wrote to one newspaper that the blacks had been given 'the security of death . . . the happiness of leaving their unburied bones to be bleached by the sun and rain in every nook and dell of that island'. In July 1837 a single epidemic claimed twenty-nine lives. By January 1838 the 220 original captives had been reduced to 93 – 39 women, 38 men, 5 adolescents and 11 children under ten.

Despite the high death rate, Robinson pressed on with the creation of a model settlement in which the surviving aborigines would embrace Christianity and the white man's ways. Robinson renamed all his charges with names of classical, literary and religious significance. Truganina, who was growing old disgracefully, was named Lalla Rookh after an Arabian princess in a popular poem. Other women were renamed Cleopatra, Queen Adelaide, Juliet, Andromache and Semiramis. Decrepit warriors he called Napoleon, Ajax, Achilles, Columbus, Nimrod and Romeo. Robinson may have been amused by his own inventiveness, but he also claimed a higher purpose: a new name allowed sinful blacks to embrace the Christian virtues of decency and chastity.

By the beginning of 1838 the forty-three whites on the island, including the garrison, were well housed. Robinson and his family lived in a fine brick mansion, while officers, storemen and others lived in cosy cottages with gardens. There was a small hospital, a store, barracks and decent accommodation for the sixteen convict labourers and their families. A brick chapel towered over the settlement. The aborigines lived in a 'terrace', also made of brick. Robinson established a school for all aborigines who could be bullied or bribed into attendance. The adults were paid four pence a week to attend night schools twice a week and Sunday attendance at chapel was compulsory. A visiting party of Quakers was very impressed. One wrote: 'A large party of aborigine women took tea with us at the Commandant's. They conducted themselves in a very orderly manner; and, after washing up the tea things, put them in their places.' In one progress report Robinson wrote: 'Some of the native youths were able to answer questions in regard to the leading events of the Scripture History, Christian Doctrine and Duty, Arithmetic, the principal facts of Geography, also on several facts of useful information. Some very fair specimens of handwriting were exhibited on such occasions.' Robinson praised an essay by a fifteen-year-old youth: 'It was expressed in simple and tolerably correct language, and breathed a warm spirit of gratitude to myself.'

But Robinson was deluding himself and few others. Between January and July 1838 another nine blacks died. It finally dawned on him that all would perish if he continued with his experiment. In any case, he had now been appointed Chief Protector of Aborigines at Port Philip on the Australian mainland. Robinson did try to persuade the authorities to allow him to take his remaining Flinders Island charges with him but was unsuccessful and, ultimately, he abandoned them in his pursuit of further fortune and spiritual enlightenment. He was a man of God – but the aborigines would have been much better off if he had never touched their lives.

The Tasmanians left behind fell into a lethargic depression which saw their numbers cut down even further. The simple cause, according to some medical opinion, was homesickness. One authority wrote:

They have been treated with uniform kindness; nevertheless the births have been few, and the deaths numerous. This may have been due in great measure to their change of living and food; but more so to their banishment from the mainland of Tasmania, which is visible from Flinders Island, and the aborigines have often pointed it out to me with the expressions of the deepest sorrow depicted on their countenances.

Eventually the new governor, Sir John Franklin, whose wife had adopted a pretty black girl as her servant and then dumped her when she found other amusements, took pity on the survivors. By now the aborigines were such a pathetic bunch that they posed no threat to the settlers. In 1847 the remaining forty-four aborigines were removed from Flinders Island to Oyster Cove. Only ten men were left.

For a time their new home revived their spirits. They were given provisions to stock their gardens with peas, beans and potatoes. The women learnt to sew their own clothes and to boil or roast their food. An official wrote: 'Their houses are comfortable and clean. They are as contented as possible.'

However, all attempts at 'improving' the sullen natives resulted in frustration. Their temperaments were not suited to a settled life and, although conditions were much better than on Flinders, the men had lost the will to live. By the end of 1854 only 3 men, 11 women and 2 boys were left. Most had died, although some children had been removed to a notorious orphanage which was a virtual death sentence, and some of the girls and women moved in with rough whites and half-castes. The writer James Bonwick described a visit to the settlement: 'I saw a miserable collection of huts and outbuildings, the ruins of the old penal establishment, profoundly dirty, and fleas were swarming everywhere, as I found to my cost.' The sleeping huts were bare and filthy. Government-issue blankets had either been stolen by white men, or sold by the blacks for liquor. Dogs shared the 'bed and board' of the natives.

Governor Arthur, who had returned to England in March 1837, was festooned with honours. His reforms of the convict system were judged a great success and the fate of the aborigines under his stewardship was rarely commented upon. He became lieutenant-governor of Upper Canada and later of Bombay where he took a great interest in the education of the natives. He died in 1854, a baronet, a knight, a lieutenant-general, a privy counsellor with an honorary doctorate from Oxford University. His biographer noted: 'He was an eminently unselfish man, imbued with a deep sense of religion, and as much respected for his unswerving integrity in private as in public life.' He left a grieving widow and ten children.

Meanwhile, the blacks of Oyster Cove made no more children and died one by one during the 1860s. The last man was William Lanney, also known as King Billy, who had been one of the few aborigines born on Flinders Island. He died of alcohol poisoning in 1869, aged thirty-four. At his burial it was discovered that his head had been removed and sent, surreptitiously, to the Royal College of Surgeons for study. A surgeon had secretly skinned his head in the mortuary and replaced it with another skull. Others cut off his hands and feet. After burial the rest of his body disappeared.

The reason for such grave-robbing was simple. The destruction of a race coincided with an upsurge of medical, scientific and amateur interest in anthropology and the origins of man. The Tasmanians had by custom cremated the bodies of their relatives. Consequently high prices were paid for Tasmanian skulls. Body-snatchers went to work in the graveyards of Flinders Island and Oyster Cove. The Royal Society obtained over twenty skulls. This collection was bombed during the London Blitz and the pathetic, charred remnants were swept out with the debris.

The last surviving true Tasmanian was Truganina, who was haunted by fears that her body would suffer the same fate as Lanney's. She had survived venereal disease contracted from a white man, a trial in which she was acquitted of the murder of two Europeans (two co-defendants were hanged) and the privations of Flinders Island. For several years she had been in the care of a white woman, Mrs Dandridge, who was paid a government allowance for her trouble. After Truganina's death on 6 May 1876 Mrs Dandridge successfully petitioned the Hobart administration to continue her payments.

Truganina's body was buried for security in the grounds of Hobart's women's penitentiary. Two years later, under the terms of a special Act of Parliament, she was dug up and her bones put on display in Hobart Museum.

In barely seventy years an entire race had been driven to extinction. It is a stain which has never been removed from the banners of the British Empire.

The Opium War, 1839–42

'I am sick at heart of war.'

On 3 March 1843 five massive wagons, each hauled by four horses, arrived at the Mint in London escorted by a detachment of the 60th Regiment. The wagons were filled with wooden boxes, one of which had been broken on the journey, spilling out strange silver coins. Troopers held back a curious and avaricious crowd which gave a 'lusty cheer' when the word went around that the money was an instalment of the 'China Ransom' – payment on account of the war indemnity imposed on that far-away Celestial Empire. The Chinese war had been a popular one in Britain and the victory pumped back to the Exchequer almost £5.75 million in 'China money'. Other spoils of war included the Crown colony of Hong Kong.

At Westminster the Duke of Wellington and the high-spirited Lord Stanley moved a vote of thanks to the officers and men involved in the China operation, by whose valour and skill 'a series of brilliant and unvaried successes' was given to England. In May the young Queen Victoria received presents from the defeated Emperor of China. They included a golden bedstead, ear-drops worth a staggering £1,000 apiece; a shawl decorated finely with portraits of 'every kind of beast known to them', rare silks and a box full of exquisite jewellery.

The Chinese Emperor was humbled, thousands of men, women and children had been lost in one-sided battles, and the defeat at the hands of western military technology resulted in the forcible opening up of China after centuries of voluntary isolation. But the British lost something too . . . the respect of civilised people at home and abroad. The war had been fought to protect the opium trade. Even by the standards of the day this was seen as a despicable ambition. MP Justin McCarthy said: 'The principle for which we fought the China

War was the right of Great Britain to force a peculiar trade upon a foreign people.' Thomas Arnold, the headmaster at Rugby, called it a national sin of the greatest possible magnitude. The American missionary Howard Malcolm thundered: 'The proud escutcheon of the nation which declaims against the slave trade is made to bear a blot broader than any other in the Christian world.' Lord Ashley, on hearing that the war was won, rejoiced that 'this cruel and debasing war is terminated'. He added: 'I cannot rejoice in our successes; we have triumphed in one of the most lawless, unnecessary and unfair struggles in the records of history.' In 1843 Balzac said that while before they had been regarded as noble-hearted, the China War had demonstrated how 'the English flaunt their perfidiousness in the face of the whole world'. Britain lost its good name and, in the Far East at least, would never fully regain it.

*　*　*

The Quing dynasty ruled the most extensive Chinese empire in history, with boundaries encompassing the Ili Valley and Kashgar, Tibet and Nepal, with Korea and Annam as vassal states. The population had almost doubled from 200 million in the seventeenth century and food shortages and famine sparked unrest. But despite recent revolts in Formosa and Kweichow which were suppressed ruthlessly, it was an empire largely at peace. The Emperor sat at the apex of a strong central administration which controlled the judiciary, education and the arts. He was patron to a classic period of painting, literature and the production of superb porcelain. His Summer Palace and the Forbidden City in Peking, while not quite so grand as in previous generations, were warrens of sumptuous halls, audience rooms and private chambers, beautifully carved, tiled and painted. Lord Macartney, on an abortive mission to the Summer Residence in 1793, marvelled at the ornamental buildings: 'They have not the air of being crowded or disproportionate; they never intrude upon the eye but wherever they appear they always show themselves to advantage, and aid, improve and enliven the prospect.' The people largely practised differing blends of Confucianism, Taoism and Buddhism under

THIRTEEN

the broad umbrella of ancestor worship. The cornerstone of every community was the sanctity of the family.

It was a cultured world but one that was closed to virtually all foreigners. Trade with the outside world was permitted and thrived as the west craved tea, but from 1757 foreign ships were confined to the single port of Canton to keep at arm's length the pernicious influence of the 'Ocean Devils'. British, French, Dutch and American ships would sail from Macao harbour up the Hsi Chiang river to sell opium from India for silver which would then be used to buy tea and silk. Western traders had to deal solely with the Co-hong, a designated group of merchants.

To undiscerning westerners China was a strange land, so populous that 'multitudes are compelled to live in boats, floating about to pick up dead dogs for food'. It was tyrannised by a Tartar government which regarded all Europeans as 'barbarians', and believed that 'their sole endeavour in regard of foreigners is to insult and mock them'. In fact, Harriet Martineau reported, merchants of any nation who had lived long enough in the neighbourhood gave a very different account: 'They declare that the government is on the whole favourable to the industry and comfort of the people; that the rights of property are respected; that the Chinese possess a greater body of literature than Europe can show.' It was difficult to assess the importance of that literature, she admitted, because 'nothing is known among us of its quality'.

Despite Martineau's over-rosy portrait of commerce, the balance of trade was heavily in China's favour in opium-for-tea transactions, and disputes often flared up. They were exacerbated by the absence of fixed tariff charges, the corruption of some officials and the refusal of the Chinese authorities to treat foreigners as equals. But the real problem was the nature of the trade itself. Opium had been used as a pain-killer in China for at least a thousand years and initially the British felt little sense of guilt in stepping up its export to feed a growing addiction among the Chinese people. In India and Britain it was drunk as a stimulant and was used both to alleviate dysentery and as a vital aid to surgery. It was generally regarded as a more exotic form of alcoholic spirit. The East India Company had, however, long understood its dangers when taken by the rich for relaxation. Warren Hastings said it was 'pernicious'. The Chinese had banned its importation in 1729 and again in 1796, by which time annual imports had risen from a thousand chests, each weighing 140 lb, to four thousand. The trade remained stable until 1830, when it doubled, and by 1836 it stood at 30,000 chests. Uniquely, the Chinese smoked opium by mixing it with tobacco, which greatly increased the risks of addiction and overdose.

The East India Company, which had limited opium production, was forced into a price war by private growers. Prices fell to a level where mass consumption became possible in the huge Chinese market. By the 1820s one-seventh of the Company's revenues in India were derived from opium. Its exchequer in Canton received eighteen million Mexican dollars a year from opium sales. One-twelfth of British revenues at home came from duties on tea, which could only be purchased through the opium trade. Opium was crucial to British trade in the East, and therefore vital to an economy free to expand after the ravages of the Napoleonic Wars.

The opium was bought by British and Parsee merchants and shipped to China, commission agents in Canton handling the next transaction. As the trade was nominally illegal the cargo was taken ashore by Chinese boats crewed by outcast Tanka sailors. An 'unofficial' tax was levied by the controller of customs in Canton, who in turn paid up to a million dollars annually into the emperor's private coffers. The Chinese opium merchants were backed by the huge Shanxi banks who also acted on behalf of the Chinese Government. Distribution inland was generally handled by the Triad secret societies. Official duplicity could not, however, hide the increasing cost of addiction suffered by the ordinary Chinese populace and in 1821 the Chinese Government tried for the first time to enforce their anti-opium legislation.

The edict came from the very top, the Emperor Daoguang (or Ch'ing Tao-kuang), who had taken the Dragon Throne the year before. He was a well-meaning but ineffectual man who wanted to boost the imperial prestige which had been weakened by westerners who had ignored earlier crackdowns with impudence and impunity. The emperor, whose name meant 'Glorious Rectitude', was politically naive but later historians agreed that he really tried to help his people. Morality was not his only concern. Economic instability was being caused by the quantity of silver draining into the foreign pockets of opium importers. Opium ships were ordered out of the river and the traders were forced to use Lintin Island as their distribution centre.

By then the East India Company's monopoly on the opium trade had been broken and private traders were less willing to put up with the restrictions and bureaucracy imposed by the Chinese. The opium ban did not halt the trade, but only increased the bribes necessary to do business. The Hongs prospered in Canton through smuggling not just opium but also saltpetre and salt. Trading expeditions along the coast broke Chinese laws which were impossible to enforce. The British traders, crammed into their 'factories' on Lintin, complained bitterly that the Hongs were cheating them and welshing on debts.

Canton Governor-General Lu Kun, anxious to avoid more tension, and aware of the dwindling influence of the Company whose Charter was due to end shortly, urged the British to appoint an official to represent the British merchants. The merchants in turn wanted just such an emissary to break the stranglehold enjoyed by the Hongs. In 1834 Lord Napier was appointed 'Superintendent of Trade' and dispatched to Canton on a misguided mission which would only heighten the tension, increase the misunderstandings between two cultures, and eventually spark bloody warfare.

William John, the eighth Baron Napier, was a 47-year-old sea captain who had seen action at Trafalgar. He had also fought bravely in the attack on the French fleet in Aix Roads. With that war over he settled comfortably in Selkirkshire to a life of sheep-farming and road building. His 1822 book *A Treatise on Practical Store-farming as applicable to the Mountainous Region of Etterick Forest and the Pastoral District of Scotland in general* was well received. On succeeding to his peerage he commanded the frigate *Diamond* on the South American station for two years from 1824. None of his experiences or his diverse talents qualified him for his new post.

Napier's instructions were clear. He was to aid the lawful pursuits of British merchants, ensure they conformed to Chinese laws 'so long as these were fairly and equally administered', and investigate the possibility of extending trade. He was not to enter negotiations on behalf of the Crown, nor use menacing language, nor appeal for help to British warships forbidden to enter the Canton River at Bocca Tigris, 'the Tiger's Mouth'. He was, in short, to raise as little fuss as possible and employ diplomatic skills not usually associated with Scottish sheep-farmers and sea captains. He broke just about every instruction.

Napier arrived at Macao on July 15 and was outraged to discover he was expected to stay there until the necessary permits had been arranged for him to travel up to Canton. Governor-General Lu had asked for a simple merchant to act on behalf of the British traders, yet he had been sent a government representative. He argued, quite reasonably, that permission should have been asked in advance. Napier was also not carrying any credentials from the Palmerston Government which Lu could forward to Peking. Napier simply ignored all the protocol and, dodging the Chinese officials sent to intercept him, arrived in Canton on 25 July. He announced his arrival in a letter which did not conform to any of the Chinese diplomatic niceties, and Lu promptly returned it. An interview between Napier and Canton officials broke down because the seating arrangements would have put the proud Scot in a position lower than the Chinese. Napier also took offence when he discovered that the Chinese interpretation of his name, when written down, was 'laboriously vile'. No offence was intended by this, but Napier failed to understand that the Chinese expressed names new to them by the words in their language which came closest phonetically. Mr Morrison, for example, was written as 'a polite horse'. Napier, like many westerners after him, bitterly resented being called a 'barbarian' or 'barbarian eyes' by the Chinese. Again, no insult was intended. The literal translation is 'head of the southern people' or 'foreigners from the south' – the direction from which the ships came. Westerners often complained about the 'childish arrogance' of the language used by Chinese officials. Again this was not intended to be insulting, only to underline the importance of the emperor. Historian Brian Inglis pointed out:

The Emperor had to rule over a vast population, with the additional handicap that his dynasty were usurpers; and this had led to an exaggerated insistence upon respect and reverence for the Dragon Throne. His subjects, it was felt, must perpetually be reminded that their country was the centre of the civilised world, the Middle Kingdom, to which all others were tributary; and that their emperor was *the* Emperor, the representative on earth of the divinity.

Such considerations did not occur to Napier who lost both his composure and any chance of promoting a peaceful mission. He described Lu as a 'presumptious savage' and told London that trade could be extended to the whole of China by the use of a force smaller than that needed to take a 'paltry West Indian island'. Lu ordered Napier back to Macao. Napier refused to go and summoned two men-of-war into the river. Alarmed and perplexed, the Chinese authorities suspended all trade. Napier's household servants were withdrawn and he was forced to suffer 'many petty annoyances'. He sent orders to the British frigates to attack. The ships fired on shore installations and lost three men when batteries fired back. The stress and climate made Napier seriously ill and his surgeon told him he must leave Canton. He arrived back at Macao at the end of September and died two weeks later. He left two sons, five daughters and a legacy of distrust and disdain which irretrievably soured relations between two mutually incomprehending empires.

Lu expressed sympathy for his death but proclaimed:

The Chinese nation has its laws. It is so everywhere. England has its laws; and how much more so the Celestial Empire. The said foreign minister having crossed a sea of many thousand miles to inquire into, and take the superintendence of commercial affairs, ought to be a person acquainted with the principles of government, and with the forms essential to its dignity.

Napier's death, and Lu's good sense, had prevented a clash of etiquette escalating into war, and tensions eased for two years.

Charles Elliot, a 35-year-old naval captain who had impressed Lord Palmerston with his ideas on China, was appointed the new Superintendent of Trade in Canton in June 1836, having already spent two years there as secretary to the trade commissioners. As a junior naval officer he had served in the East Indies, off the African coast and Jamaica, where he was commander of the hospital ship at Port Royal. This was the peak of his naval career. Since 1828 he had held diplomatic or colonial posts, including working as the protector of slaves in Guyana. A nephew of former Governor-General Lord Minto, he had good contacts in the Colonial Office and boasted of friends in high places. A political rival complained he 'has now in his writing desk a copious expression of their sentiments, views, decisions and plans for the future' which he kept secret. Elliot believed that Chinese protocol should be accepted and wrote: 'Practically speaking, the aggregate of our trade with China is less burdened than it is in any country with which we have commerce.' British dignity, however, was affronted by the requirement to negotiate with the Chinese through petition, and Palmerston ordered Elliot to halt that practice, offending Chinese sensibilities. The Hongs were instructed to open and read all letters from foreigners.

Meanwhile the volume of opium trade increased and the Chinese authorities began seriously to consider bringing it under control by legalisation. Lu and several powerful friends at the Imperial Court advocated it, as did many smaller British traders. For several months legalisation seemed inevitable, but opponents fought back. They were led by the bigger opium-runners who could afford the risks and reaped the rewards of prices kept high by illegality. Officials from inland regions pointed to the 'moral degradation' that opium had inflicted on the soldier classes – an 1832 campaign against Yao aborigines had been aborted because the fighting men were weakened by addiction. One estimate suggested that by the mid-1830s between ten and twelve million Chinese were incurably addicted. The emperor, also aware of the drain on silver which threatened his economy, agreed that urgent action was vital and a serious effort to suppress the opium trade was launched late in 1836.

In Canton the new Governor-General Deng Tingzhen ordered all foreign opium ships out of the river. The trade was brought to a standstill and even the biggest trader, Jardine & Matheson, warned shareholders that this time the Chinese meant business. In London the government officially backed the crackdown and Palmerston acknowledged China's right to halt imports, saying that any losses would have to be suffered by the traders themselves. Captain Elliot described the opium trade as 'a traffic which every friend to humanity must deplore'. The opium merchants took violent action to evade the ban. British ships crewed by lascars landed their cargoes on to the Canton wharves from where heavily armed vessels spread their poison along the Chinese coast. There were one-sided clashes with unwieldy Chinese junks. The violent anarchy outraged both Chinese and British officials. The American firm Russell & Co. withdrew from the opium trade in February 1839. Deng and Elliot were both prepared to cooperate to stamp out the smuggling, but were hampered by the diplomatic stand-off which prevented proper communication. Their efforts to prevent disaster effectively ended when a hard-liner from Peking arrived on 10 March 1839.

Imperial Commissioner Lin Zexu was one of the richest men in China, a renowned scholar and a leading member of the reform party. He was born in Foochow, had studied Manchu at the Hanlin Academy and had risen rapidly through the ranks of the civil service where he was regarded as a highly able administrator. Then in his mid-fifties, he was a large man, running to fat, with a heavy black moustache and a long beard. He walked with dignity and a 'rather harsh or firm expression', according to one English witness. His own journal suggests that he was a humane and learned, if calculating, man. His scholarship was tempered with ruthlessness. As Governor-General of Hunan and Hubei he had suppressed home-grown opium addiction by executing all known dealers. Addicts were given eighteen months, with medical help, to break their habit. If they failed they, too, were executed. Such draconian actions had worked, but the 54-year-old commissioner knew that the immediate execution of foreign importers was not an option. He was convinced, however, that the opium merchants had no support at home and believed, wrongly, that the import of opium to Britain was illegal. He also mistakenly believed that British ships involved in the trade must be unlicensed pirates. But his biggest mistake was to regard Elliot, a potential ally in ending the trade, as a renegade opium merchant rather than as a British official. Lin ignored Elliot's assurances, despite the captain's stated view that 'the Chinese government had just grounds for harsh measures'. As a signal of intent, just before Lin's arrival a native opium smuggler was publicly strangled with military pomp.

Lin issued proclamations to the Chinese population ordering all smokers to hand over their opium and pipes within two months. Students were organised into five-man teams pledged to ensure that none of their number smoked. In a special assembly 600 students of the Confucian classics were asked to name opium dealers as part of their examinations. Within a few months over 1,600 Chinese had been arrested and about 50,000 pounds of opium and over 70,000 pipes had been confiscated.

Lin turned his attention to the British, urging them to stick to their legitimate trade in tea, silk and, bizarrely, rhubarb which he believed was essential to the good health of all foreigners. In a letter to Queen Victoria Lin appealed to her personal morality to end the opium trade at source, in the poppy fields of India. He wrote:

> It appears that this form of poison is illegally prepared by scoundrels in the tributary tribes of your honourable country and the devil-regions under your jurisdiction, but of course is neither prepared nor sold by your sovereign orders. . . . Not to smoke yourselves, but yet to dare to prepare and sell to and beguile the foolish masses of the Inner Land – this is to protect one's own life while leading others to death, to gather profits for oneself while bringing injury upon others. Such behaviour is repugnant to the feelings of human beings, and is not tolerated by the ways of God.

It is doubtful whether Queen Victoria even saw that appeal. There was, in any case, no reply.

Lin ordered the surrender of all foreign opium supplies stored at Lintin, so that it could be burnt. His edict also required a bond that ships should land no more opium and those crews that did so would forfeit their cargoes and their lives. Lin had already demanded the surrender of opium in the hands of Chinese dealers, saying he would spare them the death penalty if they complied within an agreed time. The British merchants argued that the opium in their stores did not belong to them, as they were merely agents of companies in India, and they had no legal mandate to give it up. Lin responded by demanding that the senior British merchant in Lintin, Mr Dent, be handed over to a Chinese court. When the traders refused Lin moved troops to surround the island factories. The British community as a whole, rather than one man, had been taken hostage.

The blockade lasted six weeks. Any Chinese who worked in the factories, as servants, dockers or labourers, were ordered to stay away. Heavily armed soldiers manned barricades blocking the entrances. A mixed fleet of junks and other craft patrolled the river. Lin warned that if any attempts were made to breach it he would obtain imperial permission to close the harbour forever. Moreover he would enforce Chines law, including the death penalty for opium smuggling, on all foreigners.

Eventually Elliot persuaded the traders to hand over the drugs, even though he had no legal powers to insist, by promising that the British Government would compensate them. He had no authority to make such a promise, either, although the traders did not know that. For them, ironically, it promised an end to their worries. If the opium had remained in their Chinese depots the price would plummet when the next year's shipment arrived from India. Instead they had the promise of indemnity at market prices backed, they believed, by the British Government. They did, however, fear that Lin or other, perhaps corrupt, officials would not destroy the confiscated opium, but sell it on, drastically affecting the prices of subsequent crops. Such fears were groundless.

A total of 20,283 chests were surrendered, close to three million pounds of raw opium. Lin ordered the digging of three trenches, each 7 feet deep and 150 feet long, into which the balls of opium were hurled. Five hundred labourers broke up the balls and mixed their contents with water, salt and lime until dissolved. The resulting sludge was flushed into the Pearl River. The British were free to leave. Sixteen traders were detained at the factories but permitted to leave later, under injunction never to return. For the Chinese the action had been a success. But Lin's tactics changed the entire nature of the tussle. Most British officials and ministers had previously sympathised with the suppression of the trade, but the confinement of British subjects, many of them unconnected with the opium trade, and the destruction of British property, however disreputable, was quite another matter. In a dispatch to Palmerston Elliot said that for 'the first time, in our intercourse with this Empire, its government has taken the unprovoked initiative in aggressive measures against British life, liberty and property, and against the dignity of the Crown'. From now on there could be no peace.

*   *   *

Reports of the imprisonment of the British in their factories reached London on 21 September 1839; they were soon followed by news of the surrender of the opium. There was widespread outrage, especially among businessmen, those involved in the China trade and chambers of commerce. Canton's wealthiest trader, Dr William Jardine, who had returned to Britain earlier that year, headed a merchant delegation with a $20,000 war chest. Through pamphlets they portrayed the siege of the factories as another Black Hole of Calcutta, although the Lintin hostages had suffered little deprivation. The confinement of the traders, officials and families was a deadly insult to Her Majesty's flag. Jardine had been given enough money to 'secure, at a high price, the services of some leading newspaper to advocate the cause'. The public, which before then had barely known of the opium trade, were told that Englishmen were in danger in a foreign country and that they were being harshly treated and recklessly imprisoned. Jardine avoided the issue of morality, arguing that the government owed the merchants a responsibility for permitting the growing of opium in India for the China market. One observer unconnected to the trade said that while the crisis may have begun with opium, the issue now was how to restore trade without 'the most cringing and humiliating concessions'. Captain Elliott had written urgently to Lord Auckland, the Governor-General of India, asking for as many warships and armed vessels as could be spared 'for the defence of life and property'.

Meanwhile Lin withdrew Chinese servants from the British factories following the death of a peasant, Lin Weihi, in a drunken brawl. He demanded that the murderer should face Chinese justice but the British refused, saying they did not know which of a gang of sailors was responsible for the crime. Elliot held an official inquiry, which was inconclusive, and refused to hand over a symbolic culprit to the Chinese executioner. The British, fearing a repeat imprisonment, left Canton and sailed to the island of Hong Kong, which already had a rapidly growing British community. The opium ships which Elliot had ordered out of the Canton River provided them with some defence. Local Chinese poisoned wells on the rocky outcrop and refused to sell food to the foreigners.

On 3 November Chinese war junks approached the 28-gun British frigate *Volage* and the sloop *Hyacinth* in the Kowloon estuary and again demanded the execution of the sailor who had murdered the peasant. At noon Captain Smith of *Volage* gave the signal to engage the imposing force of twenty-eight war junks and fire-ships. The *Annual Register* reported:

> The ships then lying hove to at the extreme end of the Chinese line, bore away ahead in close order, having the wind on the starboard beam. In this way, and under easy sail, they ran down the Chinese line, pouring in a destructive fire. The lateral direction of the wind enabled the ships to perform the same evolution from the other extreme of the line, running up again with their larboard broadsides bearing.

The Chinese 'answered with much spirit' but the impact of a British broadside was devastating. One war junk blew up after a pistol shot from *Volage*, three were sunk, and several others became water-logged. In his dispatches Captain Smith paid tribute 'to the gallantry of the Chinese admiral, who in a junk mounting 12 guns bore down upon the ships, and sustained for some time a very heavy fire; he was at last compelled to turn, his vessel evidently being in a sinking state'. The remaining vessels limped back to their anchorage and

Captain Smith let them go. His clemency, and the fact that he soon rejoined the main fleet at Hong Kong, allowed the Chinese Admiral Kwan to claim victory in the sea battle. One man on *Hyacinth* was slightly wounded and that ship, the captain reported, which 'was for some time surrounded by junks, has got her main-yard so much damaged that I fear it will be necessary to get a new one'.

Palmerston, urged on by Jardine, sent Elliot word that an expeditionary force would reach China by the following March to blockade Canton and the River Peiho below Peking. The decision to declare war was reached at a Cabinet meeting in which the only issue raised was the question of compensation. It was agreed that with the Melbourne administration already in deficit, Parliament would never accept extra taxes to compensate the merchants. Therefore the Chinese would have to pay, not only for the destroyed opium but also to cover the costs of the expedition to be mounted to chastise them. Palmerston acceded to Jardine's demands that to the reparations would be added a commercial treaty, the opening of four new China ports, and the formal occupation of several islands, including Hong Kong.

In February 1840 Elliot and his cousin, Admiral George Elliot, who had sailed from the Cape, were appointed heads of the expeditionary force. Their orders were to blockade China's major ports and capture the island of Chusan, which was to be held as surety for reparations.

In Britain the impending war was broadly, but not universally, popular. During a Commons debate on a Tory motion of censure the young minister Thomas Macaulay said that the Canton merchants 'belonged to a country unaccustomed to defeat, to submission or to shame; to a country which had exacted such reparation for the wrongs of her children as had made the ears of all who heard it to tingle; to a country which had made the Bey of Algeria humble himself in the dust before her insulted consul; to a country which had avenged the victims of the Black Hole on the field of Plassey. . . . They knew that, surrounded as they were by enemies, and separated by great oceans and continents from all help, not a hair of their heads would be harmed with impunity.' But the young William Ewart Gladstone replied:

A war more unjust in its origin, a war more calculated to cover this country with permanent disgrace, I do not know. The right honourable gentleman opposite spoke of the British flag waving in glory at Canton. That flag is hoisted to protect an infamous contraband traffic; and if it were never hoisted except as it is now hoisted on the coast of China, we should recoil from its sight with horror.

The Tory anti-war motion was narrowly defeated after Palmerston declared that the paramount point was that Great Britain and her citizens had been insulted. The war was on.

*   *   *

By June 1840, 16 British warships carrying 540 guns, 4 armed steamers and 28 transport ships carrying 4,000 soldiers had assembled off Macao. Their cargo included 3,000 tons of coal for the steamers and 16,000 gallons of rum for the men. Already in the Canton River were the frigates *Volage*, *Druid* and *Hyacinth*.

The Chinese army numbered about a million men. Its nucleus was the Bannermen, mainly cavalrymen, a hereditary army of Manchu Tartars organised in eight divisions known as the 'Eight Banners'. Their weapons were obsolete matchlocks and bows, but they were adroit at using them from horseback. These were the troops the British were generally to face in the open field. The defenders of forts and cities were largely Chinese levies who had acquired the knack of gunnery. Most ordinary infantrymen carried spears, poleaxes and swords. Some still wore chain armour. Captain Granville Loch wrote:

If drilled under English officers, they would prove equal, if not superior, to the Sepoys. The matchlock man carries the charges for his piece in bamboo tubes, contained in a cotton belt fastened about his waist. He loads without a ramrod, by striking the butt against the ground after inserting the ball; the consequence is that he can charge and fire faster than one of us with a common musket. The best marksmen are stationed in front and supplied by people whose only duty is to load [for] them.

The British accused the Cantonese of sending a boatload of poisoned tea to be sold to the English sailors. In fact, the consignment was stolen by pirates and sold to Chinese civilians, many of whom died. A Chinese proclamation was issued offering rewards to those who destroyed the English. Anyone who captured a man-of-war carrying eighty great guns and delivered it to the mandarins would receive 20,000 Spanish dollars. The bounty for taking alive a foreigner peaked at 5,000 dollars for a warship's chief officer, sliding down a scale linked to other ranks. The reward for killing officers was one-third that for capture, on the production of evidence that the dead man held the alleged rank.

As more British ships assembled the Chinese let loose eighteen fire-rafts 'constructed of old fishing-boats and some cargo boats chained together two and two, and filled with combustible matter of all descriptions'; the alarm was raised among the British as their flames lit up the darkness. The *Canton Register* reported:

> The appearance was very beautiful. The wind and the tide were then favourable for their course. As they approached they blew up like some (fire) works, what in English pyrotechnical science would be called a flower pot. The beauties of the sight, however, did not dissipate the alarm felt on board the ships, who were also fearful there might be other crafty schemes in progress, and that they might be attacked from other quarters; consequently, most of the ships slipped their cables and moved out of danger, each more anxious than his neighbour to get into the rear. The scene and danger caused great excitement; the night was very dark.

Some British ships collided, but escaped serious damage. When light came some of the wreckage of the fire-rafts was collected: enough to supply the fleet with firewood for a month.

Unaware of this action, Palmerston hoped that the minimum use of force would be enough to force the Chinese to seek peace with suitable reparations and the legalisation of the opium trade. He issued orders to Elliot to bypass Canton, sail to the mouth of the Peiho and present a note to the Chinese Emperor dictating terms. Captain Elliot disagreed, knowing that a mere blockade would be ineffectual, but he dared not disobey such direct orders. A small force was left to blockade Canton, while the rest of the fleet headed north.

Admiral Elliot had meanwhile fallen ill – he was invalided out of the navy later that year – and was effectively replaced as an interim measure by 54-year-old Commodore Sir James John Gordon Bremer who had served assiduously but without special distinction during the later Napoleonic Wars. During a chequered career he had been shipwrecked on Newfoundland, founded a colony on Australia's Melville Island and took part in the first Burma War. A series of timely deaths of superior officers had seen him briefly hold the senior officership in India.

The Cantonese believed that the English had been frightened off by their shore batteries but on 5 July the fleet launched an attack on Chusan Island in Hangzhou Bay, intending to use it as a temporary base. Chusan officials at first thought they had come to trade but naval commander Bremer quickly demanded the surrender of the city-port Ting-hai. The Chinese officials prevaricated and Bremer gave them notice that hostilities were about to begin. His look-outs reported that the hills, shores and walls of the town were packed with large numbers of troops. Twenty-four small-calibre cannon were positioned along the town's wharf and on a nearby round tower. War-junks were also preparing for battle. Two divisions of British troops under Major-General George Burrell landed about a mile from the town on 5 July, and Bremer's ships bombarded the town for exactly nine minutes. Casualties in the city were severe, although Bremer used round shot instead of grape or canisters to minimise the carnage. Burrell, commanding men of the 14th Royal Irish Regiment, Royal Marines and Madras Sappers reported: 'I pushed forward advanced posts to within 500 yards of the city [walls] which, although in a dilapidated state, are extremely formidable and difficult of access, being surrounded on three sides with a deep canal of about twenty-five feet wide, and a continued flat of inundated patty land.' Musket fire from troops stationed on a nearby hill poured fire into the city's disorganised defenders all through the day and evening.

Early next morning the town was silent. A couple of unarmed Chinese hung a placard from the shot-scarred walls which read 'Save us for the sake of our wives and children.' A company of the 49th took the main gate and hoisted the British flag. Those defenders who survived the bombardment had fled during the night. Troops looted shattered buildings, picking their way among numerous bodies. The army commander, however, declined to billet his men in the town, to avoid causing more resentment within the civilian population. Instead they camped under canvas in a malarial swamp where fever and dysentery soon kept the burial parties busy. The troops drank copious amounts of a rice spirit. Salt provisions from India were bad, and little fresh food could be found. Within a short time more than one-third of the soldiers were rendered unfit for duty. After a month twelve or more coffins a day were needed to cope with the death toll. By the end of the year 450 men were dead, out of the 3,000-strong garrison. The heaviest casualties were suffered by the Cameronians, who had relied almost entirely on food supplies from India; packed in old bags or insanitary boxes, these quickly proved inadequate. That regiment started with 930 officers and men. They lost 240 dead through sickness, while only 110 men were fit enough for active duty.

The British had expected the capture of Chusan to shock the Chinese into surrender. The Chinese believed, however, that the British could not fight on dry land and since Chusan had been taken by naval bombardment, its fall did not destroy that belief. Their confidence was shaken when the fleet moved up towards the Peiho and imperial advisors warned that the invaders were planning to take Peking itself. As the British prepared to battle their way past the Taku forts guarding the mouth of the river, a court envoy was sent to negotiate with them.

A letter from Palmerston was dispatched to the imperial court, which mistakenly gained the impression that the British would be satisfied if Lin Zexu, the architect of opium suppression, was removed from office. Lin had his enemies at court and they prevailed – he was stripped of his rank and exiled to Ili near the border with

Russia. Quishan, the Governor-General of the Zhili territory, off which the British fleet lay, conveyed the news to Elliot and persuaded him to pull back the fleet so that the Canton difficulty could be sorted out without further violence. Quishan's ploy, endorsed by the emperor, was to exhaust and weaken the enemy by protracted negotiation. While the English talked to Quishan, sufficient forces were being assembled to annihilate the invaders. Elliot fell for it, withdrew his increasingly sick forces south, and negotiated for five weeks off Canton.

Even his patience eventually snapped and he authorised a salutary attack on the outer Bogue forts guarding the Pearl River. On 7 January 1841 *Nemesis*, the navy's first iron steamer, used its shallow five-feet draught to float towards the shore, under the angle of the Chinese battery's embrasures, spreading carnage and panic. Some 1,500 troops outflanked the forts after an amphibious landing commanded by Major J.L. Pratt of the 26th Foot and launched a direct attack. Pratt reported in dispatches:

> After advancing a mile and a half, on reaching the ridge of hill, we came in sight of the upper fort, and of a very strong intrenchment, having a deep ditch outside, and a breastwork round it which was prolonged upwards, connecting it with the upper fort; it was also flanked by field batteries. . . . The whole was strongly lined with Chinese soldiers, who immediately on seeing us cheered, waved their flags in defiance, and opened a fire from their batteries; our guns were promptly placed on the crest of the ridge, and commenced firing; this was duly returned by the Chinese for about 20 minutes, and indeed in this, as well as our other encounters with them, it is but justice to say they behaved with courage.

The British troops, made up of men from the 26th and 49th Regiments, the Royal Marines, the 37th Madras Infantry and the Bengal volunteers, forced back 'considerable numbers' of the enemy from neighbouring hills and woods to the front of the fort. Pratt took a detachment 'into the intrenchment and proceeded up inside the breastwork to the upper fort, in which there were still a number of men; these were speedily dislodged by the two marines who first reached it; the fort was entered, and the British ensign hoisted by a Royal Marine'. Pratt continued:

> The lower fort, which had sixteen guns facing the sea, and was surrounded by a high wall, and a small battery between [were now] completely exposed, but the fire of these had been silenced by the ships attacking on the sea face. They were still in considerable numbers in the lower part of the fort, and had locked the gate; a fire was therefore kept up from the hill, and the advance coming round the lower side to the gate, fed it by musketry. On entering they met with considerable resistance which was speedily subdued; some men then entering an embrasure on the flank, the fort was taken and our flag hoisted.

Such laconic dispatches do little but suggest the carnage inflicted on the defenders by naval and field artillery, musket fire and the bayonet. The defenders fought bravely and almost all were killed. Pratt reckoned that between 300 and 400 were slain. The British suffered thirty-eight men wounded but not a single man killed. Up to 200 more Chinese died when *Nemesis* and boatloads of marines from other vessels attacked eleven large war-junks anchored in shoal water to the east of the forts. They were all set on fire and blown up; one exploded with the loss of her entire crew when a lucky rocket found the magazine. The magazines in the forts were also blown up and the surrounding barracks and houses were levelled by fire. About 100 prisoners were taken but released at nightfall.

Elliot, anxious to prevent further slaughter, withdrew to let his lesson sink in. Again, this gave the Chinese the chance to present the action as a victory for them. Elliot then ordered an attack on the inner Bogue forts. Captain Sir H. Fleming Senhouse of *Blenheim* led a small naval force, including four rocket boats, and opened fire on Anunghoy fort. Its batteries were destroyed after less than an hour's bombardment. Other ships flattened the shore batteries at Wantong. Senhouse and a detachment of marines went ashore and drove the surviving gunners and their soldier escorts from battery to battery until the whole chain was taken at a cost of five men slightly wounded. Again the Chinese suffered heavy losses including Admiral Kwan and several other high-ranking mandarins.

On the 27th a light squadron went further up-river under the command of *Calliope*'s Captain Herbert. They found the enemy strongly fortified on the left bank of the river, with over forty war-junks and a former East Indiaman. Several vessels had been scuttled to block the passage. The Chinese opened fire but their cannon were no match for the British salvoes. Marines and small-arms men stormed adjacent batteries, driving out over 2,000 Chinese troops and killing nearly 300.

Again Elliot withdrew and awaited a positive response. None came, so he reluctantly ordered the fleet up-river to Canton itself. A Chinese fleet of thirteen war-junks proved little obstacle. Ten were captured and the admiral's flagship was destroyed by a rocket fired from HMS *Calliope*. *Nemesis* found a passage for the warships through the mudbanks and the force anchored 5 miles from the city. The Chinese launched a useless fire-raft attack, provoking the British into moving on to the Canton factories, over which the British flag once again flew.

The commander of the British troops, Major-General Sir Hugh Gough, took the heights around Canton itself and confronted four strong forts and the city walls. Gough reported that his rocket battery, with two mortars, two 12-pounder howitzers and two 9-pounder guns, kept up well-directed fire on the two western forts 'which had much annoyed us with heavy fire'. His mainly Indian troops cut off the two eastern forts. He recorded: 'At about half-past nine o'clock the advance was sounded, and it has seldom fallen to my lot to witness a more soldier-like and steady advance or a more animated attack. Every individual, native as well as European, steadily and gallantly did his duty.' The first two forts were captured with 'comparatively small loss' and a little over thirty minutes after the advance was sounded British troops were within 100 paces of Canton's walls.

Gough was about to attack the last obstacle, the Hill of the Five-Storeyed Pagoda, when Elliot ordered a halt. Gough obeyed, but his inaction was interpreted by the Chinese as a sign of weakness. They organised a militia and, in a typhoon downpour, 700 British and

Indian troops were attacked by up to 10,000 irregulars. The rain-soaked British muskets were initially useless. An officer of the 37th Madras Native Infantry later wrote:

> At this time not a musket would go off, and little resistance could be offered against the enemy's long spears. The men, after remaining in this position for a short time, were enabled to advance to a more defensible one, where they were soon surrounded by thousands of the enemy, who, had they possessed the slightest determination, could have at once annihilated them. The rain ceasing to fall for a time, enabled a few of the men to discharge their muskets. The enemy was not removed above fifteen yards and every shot told as a matter of course.

The British forces retreated in good order with no losses and a few flesh wounds.

The next morning Gough warned that if the Chinese militia was not recalled they would be devastated by firepower. The Canton authorities obeyed and pulled back their men. At about the same time Elliot informed Gough that a peace deal had been reached and he should return to the main force. The sight of Gough's forces heading back down-river created another myth – that the British could be defeated by irregular troops. The bigger myth, that the foreigners were not much good on land, was reinforced. From then on any official who tried to reach terms with the British was denounced as a coward.

British losses that day were 15 dead and 112 wounded. To that toll was later added the gallant Senhouse who fell ill with a fever 'brought on by his great exertions and exposure to the sun during the operations against Canton' and died aboard HMS *Blenheim*. The *Annual Register* also reported with some astonishment: 'The soldiers of the 49th, finding a quantity of a spirit called sham-shu in the village they had taken, without order or previous knowledge of their officers, brought the jars containing this pernicious liquor and broke them in front of their corps, without the occurrence of a single case of intoxication.'

* * *

The peace deal which Elliot and Quishan signed at Chumpi on 20 January reflected both men's desire to avoid further massacre. Its terms called for the secession of Hong Kong, a $6 million indemnity paid by the Chinese, official communications on an equal basis, and the widening of Canton trade on terms beneficial to the British. In return the British agreed to lift the siege of Canton and hand back Chusan and the Bogue forts. Both governments, in Peking and London, rejected it.

The emperor, who now felt that the English were 'outrageous and not amenable to reason', would not countenance the surrender of Hong Kong. To put Chinese citizens, even the scattering of fishermen and farmers on the island, under such barbarian jurisdiction was repugnant to him. Even before the Chumpi Convention was signed he had ordered 4,000 reinforcements to march to Canton from neighbouring provinces. By the end of January he had appointed his cousin, I-shan, to lead an 'Army of Extermination' to destroy the foreigners. Rumours circulated in Canton that Quishan had accepted a huge bribe in return for Hong Kong. The emperor was thrown into a fury. He wrote: 'In governing the country as the Emperor I look upon every inch of our territory and every subject as belonging to the empire.' The treaty was disavowed and Quishan, his vast properties confiscated, was led out of Canton in chains on 13 March.

The reaction of Lord Palmerston when he received the Convention was equally scathing. In a savage dispatch he castigated Elliot for giving up the important naval base of Chusan for the inhospitable rocks of Hong Kong. He said that the indemnity was not only too small but had been agreed in terms which allowed even that to be recouped in taxes on British trade. The young Victoria wrote to a relative: 'The Chinese business vexes us much, and Palmerston is deeply mortified of it. All we wanted might have been got, if it had not been for the unaccountably strange conduct of Charles Elliot . . who completely disobeyed his instructions and tried to get the lowest terms he could.' Elliot was to be recalled home.

Unaware of his impending disgrace, Elliot was kept busy facing the build-up of imperial forces at Canton. I-shan was now in command alongside the Manchu noble Lung-wen and the seventy-year-old general Yang Fang, a stone-deaf veteran of Jehangir. During

February they strengthened their forces, recruited a local patriotic militia, rebuilt redoubts and dammed waterways. All this activity convinced Elliot, unaware of developments in the two capitals, that the Convention was about to be breached. He moved his fleet back up-river, blowing up several forts as he went, and again threatened Canton with naval guns. Yang Fang, well aware that the city was in no fit state to withstand a bombardment – new, 5-ton cannon fresh from local foundries as yet had no mountings – agreed to a truce. This was quickly over-ruled by I-shan.

On 21 May flaming rafts were sent down-river to engulf the British fleet anchored at Whampoa. As before, the attack failed dismally and in the following battle seventy-one war-junks were destroyed and sixty shore batteries seized. Bremer described one part of the action in dispatches: 'On arriving at Whampoa, I found . . . that the enemy were in considerable force at the end of "Junk Reach", having as usual sunk several large junks in the river, and further protected themselves by a strong double line of stakes across it, and large bamboos and branches of trees between them.' He ordered the ship *Sulphur* up-river to reconnoitre, towed behind three boats commanded by Lieutenant Symonds, an officer of *Wellesley*. Bremer continued:

> On rounding a point on the right bank, they came in front of a low battery of twenty-five guns, masked by thick branches of trees, which opened a heavy fire on them. Lieutenant Symonds instantly cut the tow-rope, and gallantly dashed into the battery, driving the enemy before him, and killing several of their number. The *Sulphur* anchored and some shot from her completely drove them from the thick underwood in the vicinity of which they had taken shelter. The guns were destroyed, and the magazines and other combustible material set on fire. The number of troops was probably 250, and they were the chosen Tartars; their loss was about fifteen or twenty killed; ours was one seaman of the *Wellesley* mortally wounded (since dead), and the boats were repeatedly struck by grapeshot.

Troopships protected by *Nemesis* landed forces which occupied the northern heights above the city's crumbling walls. Gough urged a pulverising onslaught but Elliot held back once more, not wishing to inflict slaughter on the 'unoffending populace'. Instead another truce was agreed under which the three Chinese commanders were required to pay a ransom of six million dollars and to leave the city, taking with them all troops from outside the province. Their departure was followed by looting and civil disorder as local pirates and robbers went on the rampage.

The ransom of Canton was seen in Peking as weakness. The emperor wrote: 'The English barbarians . . . are like dogs and sheep in their disposition – a dog in forehead, but in heart a deer – they are not worth an argument. Moreover they had already been chastised and repressed, and the terrific majesty of my soldiers has already been manifested.' He added:

> It is impossible to fathom the disposition of the barbarians; and it is right to prepare secret means of defence, nor should there be the least degree of negligence or remissness. Wait until after the barbarian ships have retired, then quickly resume possession of the forts, and guard and maintain the important passes and such-like places. Build new and strong forts and put the old in the best possible state of defence. If the English barbarians evince any disposition to be proud or domineering, then the troops should be led on to exterminate them.

Elliot's replacement, Sir Henry Pottinger, was appointed in May 1841 but did not reach Hong Kong until August. He was a workmanlike, 52-year-old Irishman with long experience as a political agent in Sind. His instructions from Palmerston were simple: to retake Chusan and force the Chinese into humiliating terms. These included the retention of Hong Kong, the opening up of four more ports and compensation of almost $12 million covering the cost of the destroyed opium, Hong debts and the expenses of the expeditionary force itself. Palmerston also wanted the abolition of the Hong monopoly and the legalisation of opium 'for the interest of the Chinese government itself'.

Pottinger arrived in Hong Kong just as his new expeditionary force was gathering from ports across the Indian Ocean and Singapore. Eventually it would consist of 25 warships, 14 steamers, numerous support vessels and 10,000 infantry in troopships. Its commander-in-chief was 59-year-old Admiral Sir William Parker, a former captain of *Volage*. As a young officer he had sailed and fought in the West Indies, off Cuba and Mexico. He was highly commended for his part in the action which led to the capture of the French warship *Belle Poule*. After the war with the French he lived the life of a country gentleman near Lichfield before returning to the navy where, after commanding the royal yacht *Prince Regent*, he became an Admiralty Lord. He was regarded as a skilful campaigner and tactful negotiator but is largely remembered as a naval disciplinarian who pursued his duty with religious zeal. He had a hatred of tobacco and no officer who smoked remained long aboard his flagship. He drilled his crews relentlessly and it was later reckoned that no subsequent commander ever achieved such drill perfection. He required all around him to wear a sloping peaked cap, a type that was later adopted as part of the regulation uniform.

Gough remained troop commander and Parker was well aware of his fine reputation. Aged sixty-two then, by the end of his career Gough had taken part in more general engagements than any other officer in that century. He was popular with men and officers because of his proven personal courage, his racy language, delivered with a Limerick accent, and his sense of chivalry. Sir Charles Napier wrote: 'Every one who knows Gough must love the brave old warrior, who is all honour and nobleness of heart.' Others were not too sure of his military judgement, and Lord Ellenborough wrote later that Gough 'despite his many excellent qualities, had not the grasp of mind and the prudence essential to conduct great military operations'. A descendent of a Bishop of Limerick, Gough had fought with the 78th Highlanders at the recapture of the Cape of Good Hope, and with the Prince of Wales's Irish in St Lucia, Trinidad, Puerto Rico and Surinam. He was severely wounded at the battle of Talavera in Portugal and became the first British officer ever to receive brevet promotion for battle service at the head of a regiment. At the battle of Barossa he led a famous charge against the French 8th Light Infantry at which the first French 'eagle' was captured. At Tarifa the dying French commander, Laval, surrendered his sword to Gough through the bars of a portcullis. Gough suffered another disabling wound at the battle of Nivelle and spent several years on his Tipperary estate. In 1837 he was appointed to command the Mysore division of the Madras Army, and it was from there that he had sailed to China.

The first task facing Parker and Gough was the capture of the important port of Amoy in the north. Some 2,000 British troops, the first to arrive, faced 9,000 Chinese infantry, over fifty junks and three recently improved forts which were deemed 'impregnable'. A long battery of seventy-six cannon stretched for a distance of over half a mile. The fleet anchored offshore on 26 August and engaged in a duel with the shore gunners at point-blank range. The granite ramparts of the defences deflected the British shellfire with little damage but the Chinese gunners were unable to concentrate their fire on the landing parties of the Royal Irish who overran their artillery emplacements. One mandarin, who was second-in-command, ran into the sea and drowned himself. Another was seen to cut his own throat and fall in front of the advancing soldiers. The Chinese commander, Yen, had been so sure of his outer defences that he had not bothered to fortify the narrow pass between them and the city. The British marched through and took the city of 70,000 inhabitants at a cost of just 2 dead and 15 wounded.

The city's citadel was found to contain five arsenals holding 'a large quantity of powder, gingals, war-pieces, matchlocks, and a variety of fire-arms of singular construction . . . military clothing, swords of all descriptions, shields, bows and arrows, and spears'. Within the sea defences there was also a foundry with moulds and materials for casting heavy ordnance.

Amoy was garrisoned and the fleet moved on through bad weather to Chusan, which had been re-fortified after the Chinese reoccupation. The town of Tinghai proved hard to crack, and the Chinese defenders held out for three days. Gough was shot in the shoulder during the attack but finally the island fell. There were only two British fatalities. One was Ensign Richard Duel of the Westmorlands, a veteran of thirty-two years' service, who was killed while carrying the regimental colour into action. Only the day before he had been promoted from sergeant-major. Marines dodged the fire from Chinese howitzers but the defenders broke and ran after suffering the heavy offshore barrage from ships and steam vessels covering the landing party. Several Chinese, including one who was waving a banner, were hit by a single cannon-shot fired from 700 yards. Admiral Parker wrote:

> We had the gratification of seeing the British colours planted by the troops in one of the batteries on the opposite shore; and in a few minutes the others on that side were all carried, and the Chinese [were] observed flying in all directions before our gallant soldiers on the heights . . . the wall of the citadel was breached by the fire from the ships, and the defences being reduced to a ruinous state, the Chinese abandoned their guns.

The next target was the nearby port of Ningpo, the fall of which would allow the British to control much of the Chekiang coast. The river-mouth fort of Chen-hai was swiftly overrun. On 13 October the main city's troops ran away after their cannon overheated. Gough reported:

> No enemy appeared, and it was evident that no ambuscade was intended, as the inhabitants densely thronged the bridge of boats, and collected in clusters along both banks. The troops landed on and near the bridge and advanced to the city gate, which was found barricaded; but the walls were soon escaladed and the Chinese assisted in removing the obstructions and opening the gate. The little force of soldiers, seamen and marines drew up on the ramparts, the band of the 18th playing God Save the Queen. The second city of the province of Che-keang, the walls of which are nearly five miles in circumference, with a population of 300,000 souls, has thus fallen into our hands. The people all appear desirous of throwing themselves under British protection, saying publicly that their mandarins had deserted them, and their own soldiers are unable to protect them.

Ningpo served as the expeditionary force's rest and refitting base over the winter. Pottinger's forces were now largely spread among the occupied cities and reinforcements would take some time to arrive. He decided to wait until the late spring or early summer before embarking on the next phase of his plan – to sail up the great Yangtse, effectively cutting China in two, and prevent grain moving up the Grand Canal, thus blockading Peking itself. The delay, however, allowed the Chinese to prepare a spring counter-offensive.

The preparations were entrusted to the emperor's cousin I-ching, director of the Imperial Gardens and Hunting Parks and commander of the Forbidden City's police force. An excellent planner, he agreed with the emperor that the foreigners were now committed to land warfare and could thus be swallowed up by China's teeming population. At Soochow he organised 12,000 regular troops and 33,000 militia. They made an impressive spectacle, with their bright uniforms and fluttering pennants. A month before they clashed with the British, a noted artist painted their victory in traditional style. Tea parties, feasts and poetry readings entertained the commanders, and I-ching held a contest for scribes to come up with the best-written proclamation for the coming victory. Such confidence was misplaced. The army was officered largely by young scholars who had read about the glory of combat but had no experience of it. Regular units refused to take orders from other provincial officers, and there was no clear chain of command. Supply lines broke down. The troops reached Ningpo exhausted and starving, having had no food for several rain-sodden days.

I-ching's overall plan involved his main force seizing Ningpo, with 15,000 more men taking Chen-hai and 10,000 marines snatching back Chusan. In reality only a fraction of these numbers would be in the vanguard of any attack. I-ching kept his own personal guard of 3,000 men close to his headquarters in the wine-producing town of Shaohsing and 60 per cent of the whole army actually served as bodyguards for the general staff. Only around 4,000 men attacked each British garrison. An oracle told I-ching the best time to attack – between 3 a.m. and 5 a.m. on 10 March 1842: a tiger-hour on a tiger-day in a tiger-month during a tiger-year.

The frontal assault on Ningpo was launched by 700 Szechwan

aborigines. It was a disaster. Their commanders had mistranslated a Mandarin order to hold fire until close to the enemy, thinking it directed them to leave their muskets behind. Armed only with long knives the soldiers were slaughtered by British howitzers and mines. Other inexperienced Chinese troops were pushed forward on to the piles of bodies, only to be cut down in turn. So many corpses were piled up outside the city's West Gate that blood flowed down the gutter channels. Some of the attackers were allowed to climb over the city walls and were lured by the British into the central market-place. There they were massacred by disciplined volleys. Those who retreated in confusion were pulverised by field guns drawn by ponies, which discharged grape and canister into the dense, panic-stricken mass at a range of less than 100 yards. Around 250 bodies were counted within the city walls. Veterans said they had not seen so many dead in the street since the siege of Badajoz during the Peninsular War. About twenty Chinese wounded were treated in a British hospital station but some died on the crude operating tables.

The Chinese forces besieging Chen-hai were better disciplined and the coordinated attack might have succeeded if their reserves had backed them up. But the reserve commander lay in a litter at Camel Bridge, puffing opium until he fell into a stupor. It was the ultimate irony of the war.

It was during the Chinese attack on Chen-hai that the British first encountered a form of booby-trap which claimed several lives. Boats were floated down-river carrying large red boxes of the sort Chinese women used to contain their furs and silks. If an unwary British sailor opened the lid of a box it immediately exploded. A mine of another sort exploded in a nearby river battery, killing one sailor. Rear-Admiral Parker reported: 'Considering the number of our men which were assembled at this time, it is most providential that the consequences were not more disastrous.'

I'ching had intended that the marines attacking Chusan should be ferried to the island on war-junks and fishing boats. Most had never been to sea and on leaving port they were horribly seasick. Their cowardly commander sailed up and down the coast for twenty days, sending in false reports of doing splendid battle with the English.

The Chinese forces were reduced to harrying British supply lines and Gough decided to attack a camp of around 4,000 soldiers at Tse-kee, 11 miles to the west of Ningpo. A force of 1,100 men in transports was towed up-river behind the steamers *Nemesis* and *Phlegethon*, and scaled the walls of the town without any resistance. When the British went out to attack the troop encampments, however, the Chinese fought back strongly with gingalls and matchlocks. The Chinese included 500 elite members of the imperial bodyguard and Kansich troops from the Turkestan frontier whom Gough described as 'a strong and muscular race' and whom the Chinese regarded as invincible in battle. But a three-pronged attack by the better-armed British forced them into retreat and the troops 'then did execution on the flying mass'. Estimates of the Chinese dead varied from 400 to 900 compared to British losses of 3 dead and 20 wounded. The British burnt the camp and several suburban houses before returning to Ningpo.

For several months the war degenerated into a sordid affair of small-scale atrocities and reprisals which did not reflect well on either side. The Chinese picked up stragglers on marches, and British and Indian troops were captured drunk in ale-houses and brothels. They were taken away for execution. A British sea captain, Stead, wandered into the wrong harbour and was tied to a post and publicly flayed alive. When the British forces left Ningpo the town was burnt behind them in retaliation. That did not prevent Gough reporting to London that the evacuation of the city left among the Chinese inhabitants of Chekiang province 'a deep feeling of respect and gratitude for the orderly and forbearing conduct of the British soldiers'. It proved, he said, that 'while pressing on the [Peking] Government, and overthrowing every opposing display of military force, it has been our object to protect the Chinese population of every class and grade as much as lay in our power.'

Pottinger launched his Yangtse campaign on 7 May 1842. The first city to fall to the river-borne troops was Chapu, despite stiff resistance put up by its 1,700 Manchu bannermen. About 300 Tartar troops, finding escape impossible, mounted a desperate last stand in a joss-house which they defended with 'wonderful obstinacy'. Rockets and powderbags were hurled at them by the Royal Irish, whose Colonel Tomlinson was killed making a frontal charge at the door. The Chinese continued fighting until the blazing building fell in on them. Only 53 were taken alive and those were almost all wounded. An elderly Chinese officer, skewered by British bayonets, refused to surrender, despite promises of good treatment. He said he could neither give nor accept mercy, but added, 'If you wish to gain my gratitude and can be generous, write to my reverend sovereign and say I fell in the front fighting to the last.' Total Chinese losses were estimated at over 1,200 for just 9 British dead and 55 wounded.

At Chapu and elsewhere the British were shocked by the ferocity of the defenders and their actions once reconciled to defeat: they killed their own wives and children, slitting their throats to save them from rape and shame, before hanging themselves from rafters. After capturing a temple the 18th Royal Irish found a 'butcher's shop' inside. An English officer explained in a letter home that it was impossible to report accurately Chinese battle losses, 'for when they found they could stand no longer against us, they cut the throats of their wives and children, or drove them into wells or ponds, and then destroyed themselves'. The officer added: 'In many houses there were from eight to twelve dead bodies, and I myself saw a dozen women and children drowning themselves in a small pond, the day after the fight.' Gough wrote: 'I am sick at heart of war.'

The British forces certainly did rape and loot their way across China, despite the harsh punishments, erratically enforced, for such offences. Gough admitted that there had been misconduct but claimed instances were few 'when it is considered that they were in the midst of temptation, many of the houses being open, with valuable property strewed about, and many shops in every street deserted, but full of sham-shu'. Worse were the Chinese camp-followers, described as 'hoodlums of the delta', who plundered homes in captured towns and villages. Many Chinese townspeople fled before the barbarian advance, leaving the defending garrisons with no provisions.

Another factor accounting for the collapse of Chinese resistance in some areas was the widespread belief that the British were employing nei-ying, 'inner allies', or traitors. Local commanders spent more time searching out supposed fifth columnists from among the Han minorities, salt smugglers and market hooligans than on preparing their defences. Manchu soldiers murdered suspects, and civilians feared local commanders more than the invaders. Rumour and suspicion spread to further undermine morale.

British forces marched unopposed into an abandoned Shanghai. But at Jinjiang bannermen disputed every alley, house and street of the city. Those not killed by the British died by their own hands. Lieutenant Alexander Murray of the Royal Irish was appalled when he saved a Chinese soldier from being killed out of hand and 'the ungrateful fellow, instead of being pleased at his escape, deliberately began to cut his throat with a short sword'. However, Murray was not one to mock the tremendous casualties the Chinese suffered against massively one-sided firepower. He wrote: 'Far from their great losses being proof of the cowardice of the Chinese, I take it to be a strong proof of their courage; for if cowards they would have taken very good care that we should never have got within reach of them.'

The British squadron moved into the Yangtse, much to the alarm of the Chinese generals, and engaged in a running duel with shore batteries. In all 364 guns, 76 of them brass, were captured. Some of the brass cannon were very new and were inscribed with Chinese characters signifying 'the tamer and subduer of the barbarians'. Most of them were of heavy calibre, over 11 feet long, and mounted on pivot carriages 'of new and efficient construction'. They were fitted with bamboo sights. This naval expedition cost 2 dead and 25 wounded; it is astonishing casualties were not higher. All the warships engaged were hit by cannon fire: the frigate *Blonde* took fourteen cannonballs through her hull, and the steamer *Sesostris* eleven.

The hardest fight of the war was the taking of the garrison town of Chinkiang, the chief military depot of the province, on 21 July. The main body of British troops charged the walled city's south gate which they blew open with powder bags. The men rushed through but found themselves in a labyrinth of alleys leading to outworks. A smaller party had meantime clambered over the north walls and taken the inner gateway after vicious hand-to-hand combat. Gough recorded:

I have seldom witnessed a more animated combined attack: the Chinese cheering until we got close to them, now poured in a very heavy but ill-directed fire, and displayed in various instances acts of individual bravery that merited a better fate; but nothing could withstand the steady but rapid advance of the gallant little force that assailed them; field-work after field-work was cleared, and the colours of the 49th were displayed on the principal redoubt above the sea and river batteries.

At the same time the 18th Foot charged up a steep gorge into the central military encampment. Gough added: 'From 1,200 to 1,500 of the enemy, that had stood longest, were driven down the heights into the river, their retreat being cut off by the flank movement of the 55th; many were drowned in attempting to swim across; others sought concealment on a rock in the stream, and were afterwards picked up by the boats of the Queen.' Parker reported: 'A body of Tartars was driven into one division of the western outwork, without a possibility of retreat; and as they would not surrender, most of them were either shot or destroyed in the burning houses, several of which had been set on fire by the Tartar troops themselves, or by our guns.' Another report said:

> The Tartars fought desperately, and the heat of the sun was so overpowering that several of our soldiers dropped down dead from its effects. This prevented the advance of the troops into the town until about 6 o'clock in the evening, when they pushed forward into the streets. Dead bodies of Tartars were found in every house that was entered, principally women and children, thrown into wells or otherwise murdered by their own people. A vast number of Tartars who escaped the fires of our soldiers committed suicide after destroying their families. The city was nearly deserted before we had fully taken possession of it . . .

The Chinese commander, Hai-lin, realising that defeat was certain, returned to his sumptuous home, sat down in his favourite chair and ordered his servants to torch the building around him. British troops shot dead one Tartar soldier as he cut his wife's throat with a rusty sword. They bound up her wound and pulled her children, alive, from the garden well into which they had been thrown, but the newly made widow cursed them all the same. Parker said: 'A great number of those who escaped our fire committed suicide, after destroying their families; the loss of life has been, therefore, appalling, as it may be said that the Mantchoo race in this city is extinct.' Gough described it as a 'frightening scene of destruction' and kept his troops away from the human abattoirs. British casualties totalled 34 dead (16 from sunstroke), 107 wounded and three missing.

The following morning the British destroyed all arms and ammunition found in the city and confiscated 60,000 dollars worth of Syce silver. However, Gough claimed in his dispatches that the city was looted not by the British but by plunderers who flocked in from the surrounding countryside. 'Such is their systematic mode of proceeding,' Gough wrote, 'that in one instance which came to my knowledge they set fire to both ends of the street in the western suburb, where there was a large pawnbroker's shop (uniformly the first object of pillage) in order to check all interruption while they carried off their booty by the side lanes.' He was anxious to stop such 'scenes of devastation' but decided that it was not practicable to deploy his troops in the maze of streets and alleys during the hottest season of the year, especially given the number of Tartar corpses. He said: 'From the decomposed and scattered state of these bodies, it would have been impractical to bury them without much risk to the health of the troops employed.' Cholera also appeared and the first to die was Ensign Weir of the 49th Regiment.

The capture of Chinkiang achieved Pottinger's main aim of blocking the Grand Canal. Nanking, the former southern capital of the Ming Empire, was exposed and vulnerable to the remorseless British advance. The city of a million people was guarded by a Tartar garrison of 6,000, swelled by several thousand fugitives from Chinkiang who, Gough reported, 'are all trained to arms, and perhaps the most formidable opponents, as they fight for their families and their homes'. The city walls varied from 28 to 70 feet high. *Cornwallis*, *Blonde* and the heavy steamers were brought into position 100 yards from a main gate, ready to start the bombardment. Gough deployed 4,500 'effective fighting men', most of whom had fought with him through the entire campaign. Sappers and engineers prepared to destroy outworks.

In the event, they were not needed. The Governor-General of Nanking reported to the Emperor that the city simply could not be defended. The Celestial Son was forced to accept the inevitability of defeat. He appointed two princes, Yilibu and Qiying, to negotiate the best terms possible. They first sent a domestic slave, Zhang Xi, dressed as a mandarin, to spy on the foreigners. He convinced them that the British were more interested in trade than in war. The two princes boarded Pottinger's flagship, HMS *Cornwallis*, where they bowed to a portrait of Queen Victoria as an indication that they were prepared to negotiate with the British on equal terms.

This simple gesture sliced through the tangle of courtly etiquette and diplomatic posturing which might otherwise have tripped up the peace process. The Treaty of Nanking was speedily concluded and with it the war came to an end.

The opium ships had followed Pottinger's fleet up the Yangtse. As soon as the treaty was signed notices were nailed up in occupied territories proclaiming: 'Opium is on sale very cheap – an opportunity not to be missed.'

*   *   *

The treaty was signed aboard *Cornwallis* on 29 August 1842. Given the scale of the Chinese defeat the terms could have been much sterner. The main British objectives were achieved: compensation of $21 million to be paid in instalments; the opening up of the trade ports of Canton, Amoy, Foochow, Ningpo and Shanghai, with British consuls at each port; diplomatic relations on equal terms; the abolition of the Hong monopoly; uniform tariffs on both imports and exports; and the secession of Hong Kong island as a British territory. The Chinese negotiators played down or omitted until later details of the biggest concessions in their dispatches to the emperor. The strict interpretation of the draft treaty kept negotiators and diplomats busy for a long time. It was a decade before Foochow began foreign trade and rights of foreign entry to Canton were not secured until 1858. The British could have demanded a much greater degree of free trade and annexed far richer territories. Instead they insisted only on the bare minimum to guarantee reasonable conditions for trade. The British Government had serious qualms about developing Hong Kong as a British territory, but as traders and builders poured in they were left with no other option.

Opium was not even mentioned in the Treaty of Nanking. The new Hong Kong administration briefly outlawed the drug and consuls were instructed to help stamp out smuggling, in the expectation that the Chinese trade ports would do the same. Instead the Chinese authorities at first did nothing and then actively encouraged the trade in order to obtain tax revenues from it.

Such official duplicity did not, however, stem world-wide dismay over a war in which the might of the British Empire was harnessed on behalf of drug-dealers. The Dutch ambassador to London told an English MP 'that Palmerston had contrived to alienate all nations from us by his insolence and violence, so that we had not now a friend in the world, while from the vast complication of our interests and affairs we were now exposed to perpetual danger'. That was an exaggeration but the humbling of a mighty empire by a small seaborne force brought little glory. The *United Service Journal* reported: 'The poor Chinese – with their painted pasteboard boats – must submit to be poisoned, or must be massacred by the thousand, for supporting their own laws in their own land.'

Not all overseas judgements were so harsh. Some people then, and revisionist historians now, blamed the Chinese for their refusal to embark on trade as equals and their insistence on such degrading practices as the kow-tow, whereby visiting dignitaries were obliged to display their supposed inferiority. The US President John Quincy Adams wrote that the seizure of chests of opium had no more caused this war than the throwing overboard of chests of tea in Boston harbour had caused the American War of Independence. He went on: 'The cause of the war was the kow-tow! – the arrogant and insupportable pretensions of China, that she will hold commercial intercourse with mankind not upon terms of equal reciprocity, but upon insulting and degrading forms of relation between lord and vassal.'

The morality of the war may have been in doubt from beginning to end, but the courage of the participants was not. General Gough wrote in dispatches: 'It is now my pleasing duty to bring to your Lordships' notice those gallant officers and troops who, throughout the active operations in China, in a warfare new to the British arms, exposed in various instances to temptations of no ordinary kind, assailed by sickness which in some cases left but few effective men in strong corps, and often subjected to great fatigue, under a burning sun, have never in any instance met a check.' This, he said, 'was not because their foes were few in number, devoid of courage, or slow to hazard life in personal contact, but because their own science, discipline, and devotion, made them irresistible'.

Elliot's career continued despite the circumstances in which he had been recalled home. He was appointed chargé d'affaires in Texas as the Opium War ended and from 1846 held governorships of Bermuda, Trinidad and St Helena, one of the empire's most remote outposts. He was knighted in 1856 and held honorary rank in the navy's retired list, becoming a paper admiral in 1865. He died ten years later at Witteycombe, Exeter. His cousin, Admiral Sir George Elliot, continued to be prone to ill-health and died in London in 1863 after a protracted sickness.

Sir Gordon Bremer received the thanks of Parliament and was later appointed commodore-superintendent of Woolwich Dockyard before his death in 1850. Admiral Parker was awarded a baronetcy and an annual good service pension of £3,000. He commanded the Channel Fleet and later the Mediterranean Squadron. He chaired a committee which recommended far-reaching reforms in naval manning. He died of a bronchial attack a few weeks short of his 85th birthday and a monument to his memory still stands in Lichfield Cathedral.

Gough was also made a baronet and continued his remarkable military career as Commander-in-Chief in India. He led the forces that routed the Maharatta army and defeated Sikh invaders at the battles of Mudki, Ferozshah and Sobraon. In the Second Sikh War he again beat them at Ramnuggar and Chillianwallah, although the second battle was not decisive. He re-established his reputation with the crushing defeat of the Sikh armies at Gujerat. He was made a viscount, was granted a pension of £2,000 a year for himself and the next two heirs to his title, was voted the thanks of Parliament and the East India Company, and was awarded the freedom of the city of London. In 1862 he became a field marshal and died peacefully at home near Booterstown in 1869, aged almost ninety.

The East India Company enjoyed a boom time with the legalisation of the opium trade, while Jardine & Matheson flourished in Hong Kong. But opium damaged other British merchants because of the squeeze it put on the market for manufactured goods. Two hundred merchants, in a petition to the British Government, had warned that it would 'operate for evil . . . by enervating and impoverishing the consumers of the drug' and prevent them buying British goods. They were proved right.

Emperor Daoguang died in 1850, by which time further western incursions had undermined China's wall of isolation. In Britain public attention switched elsewhere but for years a popular exhibit at Madame Tussaud's waxworks was entitled: 'Commissioner Lin and his Favourite Consort, Modelled from life, by the Celebrated Lamb-Qua, of Canton, with Magnificent Dresses actually worn by them.'

FOURTEEN

The Persian War, 1856–7

'They drew their swords in triumph . . . all smeared with blood.'

To the Victorian public, not yet weary of imperial glories, the short war on Persian soil had everything. There was an epic march in foul conditions, a tremendous cavalry charge and a swift victory; best of all, few British sons were left buried under foreign soil. In addition, this British success helped to wipe away the awful memories of the muddy trenches of the Crimea and restore the reputation of British generalship. It also helped to maintain the delicate balance of interests which in turn kept the Russians out of India. British force of arms again seemed irresistible. Yet the gunfire had barely faded when British soldiers and civilians were caught up in the horrors of the Indian Mutiny, and the Persian expedition became just another forgotten war.

*   *   *

During the first half of the nineteenth century Britain, France and Russia, each intent on dominating the crumbling empires of the Middle East, competed for influence over the ancient land of Persia. Its strategic importance at the crossroads of East and West was obvious. British officers aided the Persians in their war against Russia in 1812 and many stayed on as private soldiers of fortune and advisors. After a series of Persian defeats and the 1828 Treaty of Turkmanchai which ended hostilities, Russian influence over Persian policy increased. Russian, rather than British, officers organised and disciplined the Persian army along European lines. Anglo-Persian relations became increasingly strained, and the flashpoint came on a dusty city-state road to India.

When Tamerlane conquered Khorassan in the fourteenth century, the city of Herat within the Douranee empire of Afghanistan, fell under the dominion of Persia. On the death of Nadir Shah it ousted its Persian rulers and took as its sovereign General Ahmet Khan, who assumed the crown at Khandahar. In 1829 Herat was governed as an independent state by the Afghan Prince Khamran-Mirza; in order to gain protection from his neighbour, the king of Kabul, the prince acknowledged the sovereignty of Persia and agreed to pay an annual tribute to the Shah. That tribute was not paid and in 1836 Mohammed Shah, using the capture and enslavement of a number of Persians as a convenient excuse, marched against Herat. A long and obstinate siege followed, with the Shah deploying a battalion of Russian mercenaries led by the Polish General Berowski. The city held out, helped by Lieutenant Eldred Pottinger, and Berowski was killed. After more than nine months the Persians withdrew when Britain threatened military intervention.

Britain had good reason to demand Herat's continued independence. It had huge strategic importance, being described as the 'Gate of India', and its security was vital to prevent Russian encroachments on the Raj. Within the limits of the city-state's territory converged all the main roads leading to India. The contemporary historian J. Kaye wrote:

> At other points, between Herat and Cabul, a body of troops unencumbered with guns, or having only a light field artillery, might make good its passage, if not actively opposed, across the stupendous mountain ranges of the Hindoo-Koosh; but it is only by the Herat route that a really formidable, well-equipped army could make its way upon the Indian frontier from the regions of the north-west. Both the nature and the resources of the country are such as to favour the success of the invader.

Mohammed Shah died in 1848 after ruling for just fourteen years. His son, Nasir ud-Din succeeded him and was faced with an empire crippled by internal strife. He took two years to suppress an insurrection in Mashhad, during which time three Babi revolts broke out. In 1852 an assassination attempt by Babis led to savage reprisals. Russian influence on the Shah continued to increase, although a

British mission in Tehran also convinced him of the need not to antagonise Queen Victoria.

Meanwhile Herat's new ruler, Sa'id Mahommed, allowed Persian troops into the city to help quell discontent. Britain protested and in January 1853 a convention was agreed between the Persian Government and the British envoy. Under its terms the Shah undertook not to send troops to Herat, unless that territory was invaded by a foreign army. In that case, if troops were sent, they must be withdrawn as soon as the foreigners were expelled. The Shah pledged not to interfere in the internal affairs of Herat, while the British promised to use their influence to induce foreign powers to leave Herat alone. The convention was never formally ratified by the British Government.

Diplomatic relations froze late in 1854 when the new British envoy to Tehran, Mr Murray, took offence at some alleged insult and withdrew his mission beyond Persia's borders. Russian diplomats happily filled the void.

In September 1855 Mahommed Yusuf Sadozai, a member of the old, deposed royal family, led a revolt in Herat, executed Sa'id Mahommed and seized power. At the same time Afghanistan was in uproar, with Dost Mahomed, the king of Kabul, capturing Kandahar. The Shah used both events to annexe Herat formally and a Persian force again besieged the city. Following the failure of diplomatic efforts, war was declared on 1 November 1856. The proclamation, issued by the Governor-General of India, said in part:

> The siege of Herat has now been carried out by the Persian army for many months. Before its commencement, and during its progress, the unfriendly sentiments of Persia towards the British Government have been scarcely veiled; and recently the movement of troops in different parts of Persia have indicated a determination to persist in an aggression which is as unprovoked as it is contrary to good faith.

* * *

The British fleet and transport ships rendezvoused at the port of Bunda Abbas at the mouth of the Persian Gulf, under the command of Rear-Admiral Sir Henry Leeke, the 67-year-old commander-in-chief of the Indian Navy. As a young midshipman Leeke had served during the later years of the Napoleonic War and once, waving a cutlass, had single-handedly halted a rush of escaping French prisoners. But his reputation was built mainly on patrolling the west coast of Africa, 'reducing the native kings to order and obedience'. He and his fleet came together on 23 November. They sailed on three days later and on the 29th the first four vessels of the fleet, the corvette *Falkland* and the steam-frigate *Feroze*, towing two merchant ships, appeared off Bushire. The governor of that town sent a message to the British Resident of the Gulf, Commander Felix Jones, 'begging to be apprised of the object of their visit'. Jones, who had left Bushire to join the squadron, responded by enclosing the proclamation of war.

The squadron took, unhindered, Karrak Island to the north of Bushire for use as a military depot. More ships arrived and Leeke decided to land his force in Hallila Bay, 12 miles south of the town. The operation began on 7 December. Persian troops posted themselves in a date grove 200 yards from the beach and fired a few ineffectual shots at the approaching boats. They were soon driven out by fire from the ships and well-directed shot from the steam-frigate *Ajdaha*. Over two days the troops were landed without any casualties, although there were difficulties in bringing ashore the horses and cannon owing to a lack of available native boats.

On 9 December the army, commanded by Major-General Stalker, advanced on the village and old Dutch fort of Reshire, about 4 miles south of Bushire. This time the enemy were strongly entrenched among the ruins of old houses, garden walls and steep ravines. Shells fired from the fleet burst among the defenders, causing considerable losses. The remainder were driven out after a short but savage skirmish in which the British and Indian troops made extensive use of the bayonet. The defenders, members of the Dashti and Tungestoon tribes, were regarded as among the bravest and most skilful irregulars on the Persian side. In the confused hand-to-hand fighting Brigadier Stopford of the 64th Regiment and the popular Lieutenant-Colonel Malet of the 3rd Bombay Light Cavalry were killed. The army camped outside the ruins for the night but Leeke pushed on with the fleet and the following morning took position off Bushire.

Commander Jones, aboard the small steamer *Assyria* which was carrying a flag of truce, proceeded to summon the garrison to surrender on honourable terms. As the craft passed through the narrow channel two shore batteries opened fire. Jones reported: 'Deeming it might be a mistake, I caused the vessel to stop, but a second and third shot passing close to us, I was compelled to retrace my steps, and even then two more guns were discharged. I could scarcely account for this conduct, having taken some pains to explain the meaning of a flag of truce before quitting the town.' Shortly afterwards a Persian vessel bearing its own flag of truce approached the fleet, bearing a written apology from the governor. He explained that he had been outside the town walls inspecting its defences, and blamed the unfortunate incident on the ignorance of his artillerymen. Leeke and Fox accepted the apology for themselves but added that 'the act itself, in whatever way originating, must stigmatize the Persian Government and its officers in the eyes of all civilized States'.

Stalker was poised to attack the town from land while Leeke disposed his fleet in order of battle, aiming first to dismantle the newly erected outworks and then to breach the south wall. The following morning a second flag of truce was waved out as the governor asked for a 24-hour delay but this was refused. At 8 a.m. the signal was hoisted to engage. Shot and shell were aimed at the redoubts thrown up to the south of Bushire. The bombardment at first appeared to have little effect, owing to the great range, but eventually the Persian troops manning the redoubts had had enough and retreated with their guns to the town.

The ships moved closer but captains and crew were over-eager to close in and every vessel ran aground at the turn of high water. For almost four hours they continued to cannonade the defences while stuck fast. The Persians fired back. Most of their guns were not large enough to reach the stranded flotilla but Jones recalled 'the perseverance of the Persian gunners in firing from the more heavy pieces was admired by every one'. Shot repeatedly hit the hulls of *Victoria*, *Falkland*, *Semiramis* and *Feroze*. Jones said: 'Although the hulls, masts and rigging of the ships were frequently struck by the enemy's shot, not a single casualty to life or limb occurred.' Finally the Persian batteries were silenced both by the fleet's stationary cannon and by Stalker's vanguard, now approaching the town. The Persian flag was cut down in token of submission.

After the surrender the governor and garrison, some 2,000 men, hesitated to come out of the town. The British commanders sent them a reassuring note, coupled with the threat of a resumed attack within half an hour. This created panic among some of the garrison. Many escaped by back routes while others drowned as they tried to scramble down the cliffs to the sea. When the remaining Persians finally agreed to the terms, the town gates were opened and the garrison laid down their arms. They were later escorted inland by British cavalry and ordered to disband. The British colours were hoisted at 4.30 p.m. on the Residency flagstaff by Lieutenant Clarkson of the Indian Navy. The troops ordered to take control of the town moved in at sunset. The *Annual Register* said:

Nothing could have exceeded the vigour and efficiency of all the arrangements, both by land and sea, which led to the success of the expedition, and both services vied with each other in the gallantry and skill with which they carried out the separate duties which each had to perform.

The town of Bushire was declared a military post under British rule, and subject to martial law. Among other regulations it was proclaimed that the traffic in slaves was abolished, and that newly imported Negroes of every age and sex would be seized and set free. Stocks of coal were stored and arrangements were made to obtain cattle and grain from the surrounding area. The damaged ships were patched up and all floated free on the next tide. The expeditionary force settled down to await orders and reinforcements, but it was no cosy billet, despite the lack of any apparent threat from the Persian army. The Paymaster, Major Barr, wrote to a friend:

Such a coast along which we have been sailing, and that which surrounds us, I never saw before – barren and burnt up is no term for it. Except in the vicinity of Aden and of Suez, I never remember to have seen such a wild scene as the hills around us present. The nearest approach both in structure and character are the hills on the Cosseer Desert. The town of Bushire is dirty and filthy in every direction; and to look at the streets one would imagine the place was uninhabited, as the houses are built with a courtyard to the centre, and all the windows open on this court; so that, except the door that leads from the street into the court, there are nothing but long rows of blank walls visible. The streets are rarely more than five or six feet wide. A few miles from the town flocks of gazelles and rock partridges are seen.

A book newly published by a jaded traveller was equally disparaging:

Bushire looks a miserable place . . . it can never look otherwise than a poor apology for a great commercial seaport town. Ships of any large size are obliged to lie off in a roadstead, three miles from the town, in consequence of the sandbanks which prevent any but small craft from entering the harbour. It stands on the end of a peninsula ten miles or more in length and three in breadth. The extremity on which the town is built consists of a crumbling, stony formation; and the further portion, joining with the mainland, is low and swampy, being often over-flowed by the sea. The town possesses no claim to antiquity. It was originally a small fishing village and rose to importance during the last two centuries. With the exception of the Residency there is not really a good or comfortable building in Bushire. Most of the dwellings are built of a soft, friable mud full of shells, like indurated marl; and some of brick plastered with mud, or imperfectly whitewashed. The habitations of the poorer classes consist of *kappars*, or mere hovels, covered with mats made by the date-leaf, called *peezur*, which grows in swampy soil. The largest is so low that one cannot stand upright in it, except in the centre.

Another contemporary account described the unhealthiness of the region:

> It is a peninsula surrounded on the land side by marshy swamps, from which deadly exhalations arise in the heat of summer. And the access to the interior is so blocked up by a chain of lofty mountains as to be almost impracticable for an army. The paths which lead across these mountains wind through defiles where a single false step precipitates the traveller into an abyss, and where a few marksmen could easily arrest the advance of an invading force. And if an attempt were made to turn the barrier which nature has imposed by marching either to Darabgherd, on the east, or to Bebahan, on the west, difficulties of the same kind must be encountered, for the rocky chain extends in both directions.

*　　*　　*

A stronger force was needed to impress on the Persians the seriousness of Britain's intentions. The man picked to lead it was 54-year-old General Sir James Outram, a renowned big-game hunter.

Outram, the son of a Derbyshire engineer, secured an East India cadetship when he was sixteen. His legendary hunting exploits won him the affection of his Indian troops. During the ten years from 1825 he shot and killed 191 tigers, 25 bears, 12 buffalo and 15 leopards. His military adventures were also bloody. He seized the hill-fort of Malair from rebels in 1825 with much slaughter. He suppressed insurrection in the Yawal and Sauda districts. He captured a standard in the First Afghan War and was made major in 1839. After his defence of the Residency at Hyderabad he was nicknamed 'The Bayard of India'. As a political agent he exposed corruption within the Bombay Government and in 1854 was appointed Resident at Lucknow. He carried out the annexation of Oudh and became chief commissioner of that province. He chain-smoked cigars and was generous in sharing his supplies. He was small and had rather a hesitant manner but seems to have been universally liked by officers and men.

He sailed from Bombay on 15 January 1857 and landed at Bushire on the 27th. His force comprised two divisions, one commanded by Stalker, the other by the renowned Christian soldier Sir Henry Havelock, a veteran of campaigns against the Afghans and the Sikhs. On his arrival Outram sent officers to reconnoitre the town of Mohammerah to investigate reports that Persian troops were erecting new fortifications there. They discovered a large Persian force assembling at the village of Burazjoon, 46 miles inland from Bushire. Outram decided to strike first rather than await attack. A garrison of 1,800 infantry and 14 guns were left at Bushire. His strike force consisted of over 4,650 infantry and cavalry, a company of European artillery and 18 guns. Units included the Poonah Horse, 2nd Europeans, 3rd Cavalry, 64th Foot, 78th Highlanders, 20th and 26th Native Infantry, 4th Rifles and 3rd Troop Horse Artillery.

It was acknowledged that the enemy was much more than a disorganised rabble. The veterans in the Persian infantry and cavalry had, after all, been trained in modern warfare by both the British and the Russians. The army facing Outram included a 900-strong battalion of the Kashkai Regiment – the Shah's guard, who wore British-style uniforms of red jackets and white trousers – four Sabriz regiments, two from Karragoozloo and one from Shiraz, an Arab regiment, and 500 regular cavalry. In all, these totalled 4,200 fully trained and experienced soldiers. Units of irregular cavalry, mobilized only in wartime, brought the strength up to almost 7,000. By common consent the Persian artillery was the most efficient in their army, although the gunners were hampered by the wide variety of ordnance and ammunition.

The British set out from Bushire on the evening of 3 February. Each man carried his great-coat, blanket and two days' provisions. No tents were taken nor any other equipment. Ahead of them lay a 41-hour forced march in deluging storms of rain and bitterly cold nights. The drenched troops reached the enemy's entrenched positions on the afternoon of the 5th but the Persians had abandoned their positions on hearing the army's approach, leaving behind their camp equipment and large quantities of stores and ammunition. Local plunderers were attempting to carry off stores, but fled when the British column arrived.

Outram said in his dispatch:

The enemy having succeeded in withdrawing their guns to the strong passes, where I did not deem it prudent to follow them, and being satisfied with the moral effect of our occupying their position . . . I decided upon moving the troops. The return march was accordingly commenced on the night of the 7th, first destroying their magazines, found to contain about 40,000 lbs of powder, with small-arm ammunition and a vast quantity of shot and shell, and carrying away large stores of flour, rice and grain, which the Persian Government had been collecting for a long time past for their army, thereby effectively crippling their future operations. Some of their guns were supposed to have been cast into wells, and as their wheels and axles fell into our hands, it will be impossible that they can be used again for the present

The destruction of the magazine almost ended in tragedy. An infantryman and an artilleryman fired two rifle shells into the stacked ammunition from a range of only 70 yards. The concussion sent them and their rifles 'flying in the air' but they landed unharmed, if first dazed and then deeply embarrassed.

Meanwhile the Persian Commander, General Soojah-ool-Moolk, had only retired to the Shiraz road and now planned to attack the British in the camp with up to 7,000 men, including the Eilkhanee cavalry. The explosive destruction of the powder and ammunition gave him notice of the British departure and he hurriedly gave chase. At midnight advance cavalry units of the Persian army attacked the British rearguard and threatened the line of march on all sides. The troops halted and formed a protective ring around the baggage train. Four enemy guns opened up on the column unhindered, as the darkness prevented any bid to capture them. The British and Indian soldiers kept the Persian Horse in check until daybreak.

At dawn the entire Persian army was drawn up ready for action to the rear left of the British column, near a place called Khoosh-ab. Outram's artillery and cavalry moved rapidly to the attack, supported by two lines of infantry. (The third line was left protecting the baggage.) The cannon slashed bloody gaps in the enemy's massed ranks and the cavalry brigade charged twice 'with great gallantry and success'. The Poonah Horse captured a standard of the Kashkai regular infantry regiment. The pole was topped by a 900-year-old silver hand, engraved with the inscription 'The Hand of God is above all things'. But it was the charge of the 3rd Bombay Light Cavalry against a disciplined Persian square which won the greatest glory.

An anonymous officer writing in the *Bombay Telegraph* gave a first-hand account of the action:

When Forbes, who commanded this regiment, gave the order to charge, he and his Adjutant, young Moore, placed themselves in the front of the 6th troop, which was the one directly opposite the nearest face of the square. The other Moore, Malcolmson and Spens came the least thing behind, riding knee to knee, with spurs in their horses' flanks, as if racing after a hog. In the rear of them rushed the dark troopers of the 3rd, mad to avenge the death of poor Malet at Bushire. In spite of steel, fire and bullets, they tore down upon the nearest face of the devoted square. As they approached Forbes was shot through the thigh and Spens' horse was wounded; but, unheeding, they swept onward. Daunted by the flashes and the fire and the noise and crackle of the musketry, the younger Moore's horse swerved as they came up. Dropping his sword from his hand and letting it hang by the knot at his wrist, he caught up the rein in both hands, screwed his horse's head straight, and then coolly, as if riding at a fence, leaped him at the square. If, therefore, any man can be said to have been first, the younger Moore is the man. Of course the horse fell stone dead upon the bayonets; as did his brother's, ridden with equal courage and determination. The elder Moore – 18 stone in weight and 6 ft 7 in, or thereabouts, in height – cut his way out on foot. Malcolmson took one foot out of his stirrups when he saw his brother officer down and unarmed (for his sword had been broken to pieces in the fall) and, holding on to [the empty stirrup], the younger Moore escaped. The barrier once broken, and the entrance once made, in and through it poured the avenging troopers. On and over everything they rode, till getting clear out, they re-formed on the other side, wheeled and swept back – a second wave of ruin. Out of 500 Persian soldiers of the 1st Regular Regiment of Fars, who composed that fatal square, only twenty escaped to tell the tale of its destruction. Thus the 3rd Light Cavalry, to use their own phrase, gave our enemies a *jewab* (answer) for the death of Malet Sahib Bahadur.

An artilleryman, whose account was published in the same newspaper, wrote:

All say that the cavalry charge was one of the most splendid ever witnessed . . . Next morning I went out to meet the force coming in, the rearguard of the army; and as the cavalry came in by two and threes, and salaamed to us, they drew their swords in triumph, crying out 'Dekho Sahib', and there they were, sure enough, blades and hilts, all smeared with blood, and their white belts bespattered all over; they must have made a glorious charge. Poor Frankland, of the 2nd Europeans, was made Brigade-Major of Cavalry, to go out with them, only the day before they started, and in the charge he cut down three men, but the fourth shot him dead, right in the bridge of the nose, the ball penetrating into the head.

The artillery and cavalry bore the whole brunt of the battle as the Persians moved away too rapidly for the British infantry to overtake them. By 10 a.m. the Persian defeat was complete. Two 9-pounder brass cannon were captured, along with gun ammunition loaded on mules, and at least 700 men lay dead. Outram said: 'The number of wounded could not be ascertained, but it must have been very large. The remainder fled in a disorganised state, generally throwing away their arms, which strewed the field in vast numbers, and nothing but the paucity of our cavalry prevented their total destruction and the capture of the remaining guns.' British and Indian losses were 16 men killed, including Lieutenant Frankland, and 16 wounded. Outram said: 'The loss on our side is, I am happy to say, comparatively small, attributable, I am inclined to believe, to the rapid advance of our artillery and cavalry, and the well-directed fire of the former, which almost paralysed the Persians from the commencement.'

Outram was himself out of action for most of the battle. He took a nasty fall from his horse at the first cannonades, and lay insensible in his tent for two hours, as he acknowledged in his dispatch: 'I myself had very little to do with the action, being stunned by my horse falling with me at the commencement of the contest, and recovering only in time to resume my place at the head of the army shortly before the close of this action.'

The anonymous artilleryman wrote:

> They spoke very well on the whole of the Persian troops, and especially of their artillery. Certainly, the two guns that were captured were as good as any of ours – horses, harness, limbers, and all in very fine order. They have got 25 prisoners, two of whom they say are Russians. The Sukh-el-Mulk, who commanded the Persian army, narrowly escaped being taken himself, escaping without his hat. And going back with a bare head in this country, I suppose you are well aware, is disgrace.

The troops bivouacked close to the battlefield and the day was marked by further alarms as stragglers and wounded from both sides came into camp. The artilleryman and two others went out, armed, to find more stragglers:

> One wounded man was bundled out of his *dhooly*, the bearers running away, leaving the poor fellow on the ground with the calf of his leg shot off by a round-shot. I returned and took him back in a *dhooly*, but he died just after he came in. We were out until two in the morning, having picked up ten unfortunate devils who would not move, some of them asking us to let them die.

That night the troops marched 20 miles over countryside made almost impassable by the incessant heavy rain. After a six-hour rest most of the infantry continued their march to Bushire which they reached before midnight, thus completing 44 miles, including rest and fighting a battle, in fifty hours. Some had passed through a notorious swamp and were 'masses of mud, dropping with fatigue'. The cavalry and artillery followed on. In his dispatch, Outram wrote:

> The greatest praise is due to the troops of all arms for their steadiness and gallantry in the field, their extraordinary exertions on the march, and their cheerful endurance of fatigue and privation under circumstances rendered doubly severe by the inclemency of the weather, to which they were exposed without shelter of any kind; and I cannot too strongly express the obligation I feel to all under my command for the almost incredible exertions they have undergone and the gallantry they have displayed on this occasion.

Two senior officers did not share his sense of glory. On 14 March, in the rain-sodden camp at Bushire, General Stalker committed suicide. Commander Ethersay followed suit three days later. No explanation was given in dispatches for what were then considered shameful acts, other than they were both 'labouring under aberration of mind'.

The Persians had for several months been fortifying their position at Mohammerah. Batteries were erected of solid earth, 20 feet and 18 feet high, with casement embrasures, on the northern and southern points of the Karoon and Shat-ool-Arab, where the two rivers join. They and other earthworks armed with heavy guns were so skilfully and scientifically placed as to command an immense sweep of the river approaching the town. An intelligence report said:

> Everything that science could suggest and labour accomplish in the time appeared to have been done by the enemy to effectively prevent any vessel passing up the river above their position; the banks, for many miles, were covered by dense date groves, affording the most perfect cover for riflemen; and the opposite shore, being neutral territory [Turkish], was not available for the erection of counter batteries.

The Persian army of 13,000 men, with 30 guns, was commanded in person by the Shahzada, Prince Khauler Mirza. Outram decided to attack, sailing up the Euphrates delta with 4,886 men in steamers and transports and assisted by sloops of war. His expedition was delayed by the non-arrival of reinforcements owing to 'tempestuous' weather in the Gulf and he was not able to leave Bushire until 18 March.

The flotilla began to move up-river a week later and at daybreak on the 26th the warships opened fire on the shore batteries. Outram also positioned four mortars under the command of Captain Rennie on a raft towed by the steamer *Comet*. The combined fire was swiftly effective, 'bursting immediately over the inside of the enemy's works, while, from the position of the raft, but few of the Persian guns could be brought to bear upon the mortars'. Within two hours of constant bombardment from ships and raft the northern and southern batteries were silenced, with an estimated 200 defenders dead, including a well-respected enemy officer, Brigadier Agha Jan Khan.

At 9 a.m. the infantry was able to land above the ruins of the northern battery without any casualties among the troops, although they had to run the gauntlet of musket fire from the shores on both sides. An officer noted in passing: 'Two or three native followers only were killed in consequence of their unnecessarily exposing themselves.' The troops formed into ranks and advanced relentlessly through the date groves and across a plain to the enemy's entrenched camp. The Persians, after blowing up their largest magazine, turned and fled without waiting to be attacked, leaving behind seventeen guns and all their camp equipment. The abandoned artillery included five brass 12-pounders, one of them Russian, three 9-pounders and two whose calibre was unknown because they were buried in mud. Only five guns and the Shahzada's personal property were carried away in the panicked retreat. The town itself was taken without any opposition.

Outram said:

With the exception of the artillery, with the mortar battery, no portion of the military force was actively engaged with the enemy, beyond some European riflemen sent on their war vessels; but I am not the less indebted to all for their exertions and zeal, and especially for the greater order and despatch with which the landing of the troops was effected under Brigadier-General Havelock.

Lack of cavalry prevented Outram pursuing the foe but he sent a party of Scind irregular horsemen under Captain Malcolm Green to follow for some distance. He reported that he came upon the Persian rearguard retiring in good order but that the road was in many places strewn with property and equipment. Outram next sent an armed flotilla of three small steamers, with a hundred European infantrymen in each, on a reconnaissance under Captain Rennie of the Indian Navy up the Karoon River to Ahwaz. Rennie's mission was to ascertain the movements of the Persian army and, if possible, destroy the magazines in the town. The expedition set off on 29 March.

Near Ahwaz a Persian force of around 7,000 men with cavalry and some artillery was spotted occupying a low range of hills at right angles to the river on the right bank. Rennie decided to attack the town, having reason to believe it was either abandoned or weakly guarded. He landed his 300 troops, deploying them in formations which gave the appearance of many more men than he actually had, while the gunboats took up a position within range of the enemy's camp and opened fire. As the tiny British force advanced to occupy the town the Persians were seen in full retreat towards Dizful. After buying supplies from the townspeople, who were grateful for the business, Rennie's force returned to Mohammerah.

This was the last action, if it can be called that, of the war. Soon after Rennie's return the news arrived that peace had been concluded between Great Britain and Persia.

*   *   *

The Treaty of Peace between Her Majesty the Queen and the Shah of Persia was signed at Paris on 4 March, and the ratifications were exchanged at Baghdad on 2 May. It provided for 'perpetual peace and friendship' between the two nations. The Shah agreed to withdraw his forces from the territory and city of Herat and from every other part of Afghanistan within three months. Persia agreed to relinquish all claims to sovereignty over those territories and never to demand any tribute from them, or interfere with the independence of those states. It added: 'In case of differences arising between the Government of Persia and the countries of Herat and Afghanistan, the Persian Government must engage to refer them for adjustment to the friendly offices of the British Government, and not to take up arms unless those friendly offices fail of effect.' The Persians also agreed to allow the thin-skinned Mr Murray back into Tehran and that he 'on approaching the capital, shall be received by persons of high rank deputed to escort him to his residence'.

The British Government, for its part, agreed to remove its troops from Persian lands within three months and free all prisoners of war. Persia would be allowed to take action against Afghan tribes who crossed her border but any military incursions must be recalled as soon as the culprits were caught and punished. 'The British Government engage at all times to exert their influence with the States of Afghanistan to prevent any causes of umbrage being given by them, or by any of them, to the Persian Government; and the British Government, in the event of difficulties arising, will use their best endeavours to compose such differences in a manner just and honourable to Persia.'

Britain was by now much more concerned with India. The Great Mutiny, which started on 24 April 1857 when eighty-five men of the 3rd Bengal Cavalry refused to accept new cartridges rumoured to be greased with cow and pig fat, sent shock waves across the Empire, especially when Sepoy mutineers began to massacre Europeans. The Bombay Cavalry's heroic charge at Khoosh-ab was quickly forgotten.

Outram was recalled to India along with Havelock. He was given command of two divisions and the commissionership of Oudh. He joined his force with Havelock's and unselfishly conceded command to his brother-officer, saying he wished only to serve as a volunteer. Together they achieved the relief of Lucknow after first defeating a large enemy force at Fatehpur without the loss of a single soldier. Havelock said that the victory was due to 'the blessing of Almighty God on a most righteous cause, the cause of justice, humanity, truth and good government'. He conceded, however, that the British artillery, the Enfield rifle and British 'pluck' had also played their part. Aged sixty-two and worn out by the march, Havelock died in the besieged town on 27 November. Outram commanded the Lucknow garrison until the second relief. He was created a baronet in November 1858 and remained as commissioner of Oudh, where he advocated leniency in the vicious aftermath of the Mutiny. He returned to Europe in 1860, his health broken by hard campaigning, and he died at Pau in March 1863. He is buried in Westminster Abbey. Leeke missed the Mutiny, returning to Britain at the end of five years' service heading the Indian Navy. He was made an admiral in 1860 but died less than four years later.

Both sides honoured the Treaty of Paris. The British army was withdrawn, apart from a small force under General John Jacob, which was left at Bushire for three months. Anglo-Persian relations became cordial and in 1862 an agreement was concluded for a telegraph line to connect India with England via Persia. Shah Nasir ud-Din visited Britain amid great pomp in 1873 and 1899 and was received by Queen Victoria herself. The Shah also kept up his ties with Russia and in 1882 the Persian Cossack Brigade was formed, officered by Russians but subject to the Persian minister of war. In 1888 the Karoon (Karun) River was opened to international navigation, while European sciences began to be taught in Persian schools. A naturalised Briton was involved in setting up the first Persian state bank while in 1889 the Russians were granted concessions covering Persian railways. In 1891 a tobacco concession was granted to a British subject but it was withdrawn after strikes and riots broke out.

Throughout these years Nasur ud-Din served Persian interests by balancing those of Britain and Russia. The wily Shah sat on the Peacock Throne for forty-eight years but during his latter years poverty, corruption and misgovernment increased. In 1896 he was assassinated by a follower of the revolutionary and anarchist

Kemalu'd-Din. The Shah's son, Muzaffar ud-Din, succeeded him and in 1903 he was invested with Britain's highest award of chivalry, the Order of the Garter.

Anglo-Russian rivalry over Persia continued but British interests became dominant after the Russian Revolution, to the enrichment of her oil companies. With supreme irony, a joint British-Soviet force invaded Persia during the Second World War to protect the oil supply lines to Russia.

FIFTEEN

The Arrow or Second China War, 1856–60

'This mode of warfare is hard to deal with . . .'

Present at the signing of the Treaty of Nanking, which ended the Opium War, was fourteen-year-old Harry Parkes. A year earlier Harry, an orphan from a Staffordshire iron-making family, sailed to China to join his two sisters who were already settled with the family of the explorer and clergyman Charles Gutzlaff. In Macao Harry learnt Chinese and made himself useful as an interpreter to Sir Henry Pottinger, then still Governor of Hong Kong. In the last months of the war he impressed military men and diplomats alike with his 'manner and energy of character'. Two years later, barely sixteen, he took delivery of three million dollars of Chinese war indemnity.

Subsequent years saw him prosper as a diplomatic agent, and in 1845 he was transferred as interpreter to the consul of Foochow, where a Tartar garrison was established. He suffered insults and stoning from drunken Tartar soldiers. Later, while he was serving in Shanghai, the husband of his elder sister was among three missionaries beaten and almost murdered by a gang of junkmen. Parkes was heavily involved in encouraging a blockade by a single British gunboat until the attackers were caught and punished.

Duties followed in Amoy, Formosa and the interior at Hinghwa which helped him better understand and exploit the intricacies of Chinese diplomacy. A successful mission with Sir John Bowring to help negotiate the first European treaty with Siam resulted in Parkes being received by Queen Victoria. In June 1856, aged only twenty-eight, he was appointed acting consul at Canton.

Parkes was short and slight, with a fair complexion and bright, alert blue eyes. He was earnest, religious and zealously devoted to his country. His absorbing passion was how best to serve the interests of the British Empire, and he had a short fuse when anything or anyone tried to block those interests. He was not an evil man, but his youthful stubbornness and first-hand experience of barbarity led directly to a war which claimed thousands of lives and was perhaps the greatest piece of vandalism ever inflicted by the West on the Orient.

*   *   *

The Treaty of Nanking had created little more than a troubled truce. Other western powers, notably France and America, scrambled to take advantage of the emperor's humiliation in order to win trade concessions of their own. The deals struck by all satisfied no one. The Chinese believed that, as the terms had been imposed by brutish force by the 'barbarians', they had no moral worth and should not be adhered to in any great detail. The foreigners discovered that they still could not trade in the interior, nor settle and trade anywhere except the five open ports which included Hong Kong. A supplementary treaty was signed in 1844 guaranteeing protection to British seafarers from arrest while conducting legitimate trade. But clashes continued along a thousand miles of coast, infested with smugglers, pirates and adventurers on all sides. On the mainland the new emperor, Hien-feng, who succeeded to the imperial throne in 1850, was at first preoccupied with fighting Tai-ping rebels in genocidal clashes which saw whole cities destroyed. But another major confrontation with Britain was inevitable, and it was a relatively minor incident that lit the fuse.

In October 1856 Chinese police seized a *lorcha*, or merchant vessel, near the Dutch Folly Fort off Canton, after hearing claims that a crew member was a pirate. *Arrow* had been trading for two years in Chinese waters under a British flag. Owned by a Chinese Hong merchant in Canton, it was Chinese-built and Chinese-crewed. But it had been registered in Hong Kong and therefore, by the British interpretation of the 1844 treaty, it came under Crown protection, even though the annual registration had technically expired. All but two of the fourteen-man crew were arrested and taken on board a Chinese war-boat which anchored close to *Arrow*.

Consul Harry Parkes was outraged on hearing reports that the British flag had been disregarded. He was rowed out to the war-boat, where he demanded that the arrested men should be taken to his Consulate where the charges against them might be investigated. The Chinese officers refused on the grounds that as they had already reported the matter to their own superiors they must await orders. To break the deadlock, Parkes appealed to the Governor of Canton, Commissioner Yeh Ming-ch'en, demanding both the release of the crew and an apology to the British Crown. He must have known that his appeal would be rejected. Commissioner Yeh was an 'arrogant' official with a well-known hatred of foreigners, who had used every bureaucratic trick to block the interests of European merchants.

His rejection, however, was couched in reasonable terms. He stated that *Arrow* was not the property of a British firm, that the British flag was not flying at the time of the seizure and that no foreigner had been on board. He added: 'Hereafter Chinese officers will on no account without reason seize and take into custody the people belonging to foreign *lorcha*s, but when Chinese subjects build for themselves vessels, foreigners should not sell registers to them, for if this be done it will occasion confusion between native and foreign ships, and render it difficult to distinguish between them.'

Parkes would not back down. Even before receiving Yeh's reply he sent a message to the Governor of Hong Kong, Sir John Bowring, calling for support. Bowring gave it gladly, despite admitting in his return message that the British case was fundamentally flawed: 'It appears, on examination, that the *Arrow* had no right to hoist the British flag; the licence to do so expired on the 27th of September.' Bowring believed, however, that the Chinese had broken the spirit of the treaty because they 'had no knowledge of the expiry of the licence'. The Chinese were therefore guilty of an act of provocation. He told Parkes: 'You will inform the Imperial Commissioner that I require an apology for what has taken place, and an assurance that the British flag shall in future be respected; that forty-eight hours are allowed for this communication, which being passed, you are instructed to call on the naval authorities to assist you in forcing redress.'

Parkes now had the authorisation he needed to bring Yeh, who had previously obstructed his work as Consul and whom he personally detested, to heel. He told Yeh that he had 'clear and satisfactory' proof that *Arrow* had been flying the British ensign and that a hired English master had been on board – neither was true – at the time of the seizure. Threatened with British naval might, Yeh signalled he might relent and release the prisoners. This was not enough for Parkes, as no formal apology was forthcoming. He thus called on Rear-Admiral Sir Michael Seymour, commander-in-chief of the British fleet on the China station, to restore the honour of the flag.

A Chinese junk was seized by the tender *Coromandel* and brought down to Whampoa. This action produced no further reply and on 23 October Seymour, with a fleet of gun-boats, bombarded and captured the forts guarding the Pearl River approaches to Canton. After burning several buildings Seymour's force captured the Dutch Folly, a fort of fifty guns on an island opposite Canton. The British blockade of the Canton River had begun. Both sides paused to allow further negotiations before they resorted to further hostilities.

Yeh offered to surrender ten of the twelve prisoners. When this was rejected he sent all of them to Parkes, with a demand that two be sent back to face trial for piracy in the Chinese courts. There was still no apology, so Parkes refused to accept the prisoners and the men were once more taken away by the Chinese. Bowring, meantime, wrote to Yeh saying: 'There is no doubt that the lorcha Arrow lawfully bore the British flag under a register granted by me.' That was a flat contradiction of the earlier statement sent by the Governor to Parkes. He must have known it was a lie but by then British resentment at being treated as second-class by an Oriental was so acute that honesty seemed no longer relevant.

Bowring's behaviour, to modern eyes, makes him appear a dishonest, pompous and racist example of the British colonial administrator. But that is too simple. He was one of the most extraordinary men of his age. Born in 1792 to an ancient

Devonshire family, he had become a Radical; still in his twenties, he was imprisoned by the French Bourbons, accused of spying and conspiring to free men sentenced to death for singing revolutionary songs. He helped to found, and then ran, the *Westminster Review* to offer a philosophical platform to Radicals. As an MP for the Clyde burghs, and later Bolton, he helped to found the Anti-Corn Law League and championed the causes of hand-loom weavers, Irish students and the arts. He successfully pushed through legislation to free the Manxmen from feudal tyranny, and advocated the abolition of flogging in the army. During extensive travels he became fluent in Spanish, Portuguese, German and Dutch, translated Swedish, Danish, Russian, Serbian, Polish and Bohemian, studied Magyar and Arabic, and later made good progress with Chinese languages. In the 1840s he invested most of his fortune in ironworks in Glamorganshire which failed owing to a general depression in prices. He won the job of Consul at Canton thanks to his friendship with Lord Palmerston, and immediately clashed with the mandarins over their refusal to allow any foreign dignitary access to the city. He got on well, however, with the Chinese merchants and ordinary people of the area, with whom he mixed a great deal. He saw parallels with the Manxmen and other modern victims of feudal rule. From 1852 he was acting governor of Hong Kong, and that appointment was made permanent in 1854. As well as governor, he was also commander-in-chief and vice-admiral of Hong Kong, Britain's plenipotentiary to China and chief superintendent of trade. He had been Parkes's superior on the mission to Siam, and their success there had helped to forge a close friendship.

Bowring decided to make still further demands on the Chinese while British guns threatened Canton. He instructed Parkes to write to Yeh, demanding that he allow all foreign representatives the same free access to Canton as applied to the other four free ports. The legality of this demand was dubious. When no reply was received, on the 27th Seymour opened fire on government buildings in Canton, including Yeh's own residence; a body of Chinese troops who had taken up positions on high ground behind the city was also shelled. Yeh's response was to issue a proclamation offering a reward of 30 dollars for the head of every Englishman.

The bombardment continued and the city walls were breached. On the 29th a force of seamen and Marines landed, climbed the broken parapet and blew the city gate to pieces. Three Britons were killed and eleven wounded as the attacking force entered the city and took possession of Yeh's house. Chinese troops regrouped, keeping up a steady sniper fire, and at sunset the British were recalled to their vessels.

After a further exchange of correspondence with Yeh the attack was resumed on 3 November but the cannon fire was concentrated to destroy Chinese government buildings and property. A large group of war-junks at anchor below the Dutch Folly came under attack by British steamers and gunboats. After a spirited firefight which lasted thirty minutes the Chinese were driven off the stationary junks and the vessels were burnt. At the same time the nearby French Folly fort was taken in a 'smart fight' by Marines with the loss of one dead and four wounded.

A week later Admiral Seymour sent a summons to the commander of the Bogue Forts, scene of much bloodshed in the previous war, demanding that they be surrendered, on the understanding that they would be kept intact and given back if there was a satisfactory conclusion to the dispute which had already claimed numerous lives. The commander replied that if he agreed to such terms he would lose his head. Seymour's squadron first attacked two of the forts on Wantung Island, which the Marines took in an hour in the face of 'considerable, though ill-directed resistance'. Seymour added:

These forts were fully manned, had upwards of 200 guns mounted, and were found stronger than when captured in 1841. The Chinese troops stood to their guns up to the moment our men entered the embrasures. The Mandarins had boats in readiness to facilitate their own escape, leaving their unfortunate followers, who rushed into the water until they were assured of their safety by the efforts made to save them.

British boatmen ferried many to shore and let them go. The attackers lost one boy killed and four men wounded from *Nankin*. The following day the Annunghoy Forts, on the opposite side of the Bogue entrance, were taken without casualty after only token resistance from their 210 guns.

Chinese gunners in another fort mistakenly fired at an American warship which was keeping an eye on proceedings. The American captain fired a few salvoes in retaliation but 'as what had happened was evidently an accident, and no outrage upon the United States flag was intended, the Americans took no further part in the action'.

Admiral Seymour was by now as determined as Bowring to humble Yeh and force him to allow British authorities free access to the city. Parkes made this clear to a delegation of Canton merchants, telling them that if 'simple reparation for outrage in the *Arrow* case had been all we required, the Admiral would doubtless have been long ago satisfied with what had been done; but a principle was at stake which could not be abandoned'. Seymour had the firepower necessary to level outlying forts but not the manpower to take the city. He was obliged to wait for reinforcements while a rioting mob, encouraged by Yeh, ransacked foreign factories on the outskirts of Canton and burnt them down.

As 1856 drew to a close the small steamer *Thistle*, used to carry mail from the Canton factories to Hong Kong, took on board a party of Chinese soldiers disguised as passengers. As the ship steamed down-river they killed all eleven Europeans on board, ran the vessel aground and set it on fire before making their escape. Two weeks later, on 12 January 1857, Seymour landed raiding parties of troops in Canton's western suburbs carrying fire-balls and lighted torches. The raid left the suburb blazing for two days. But Seymour's forces were too spread out for comfort and he abandoned several forts, including the Dutch Folly. His steamers were withdrawn from the upper part of the river and his troops took up new positions in the Teatotum fort near the Macao passage. Another full-blown war was now inevitable.

*   *   *

Commissioner Yeh issued another proclamation promising a set tariff of rewards for anyone who succeeded in killing or capturing any of the 'red-haired foreign dogs'. Capture of an English or French 'rebel chief' was worth 5,000 dollars, the head of a barbarian 50 dollars, exposure of a traitor 20 dollars, destruction or seizure of a shallow-water steamer 2,000 dollars, and the burning or capture of a large war steamer 10,000 dollars. In addition all those Chinese employed by the English or French were given a month to return to their home villages – or suffer beheading.

The proclamation had an immediate effect, which almost wiped out the European population of Hong Kong. The large bakeries on the island supplied all the bread to the foreigners. On the morning of 15 January large quantities of arsenic were mixed in with the dough and delivered to breakfast tables in the new-baked loaves. Several hundred Europeans were poisoned and became violently ill, including Sir John Bowring and his family. Fortunately the arsenic had been mixed in such heavy proportions that it acted as an emetic and was vomited too quickly to be absorbed through the stomach in any great quantity. Analysis of samples later sent to Berlin laboratories found that each pound of bread contained between 38 and 42 grains of arsenic, spread so evenly that it must have been kneaded with the dough. No one died, although the arsenic affected Lady Bowrigg's lungs. For several days she, her husband, daughters, guests and servants suffered racking headaches, bowel pains and other complaints. Bowring wrote home: 'This mode of warfare is hard to deal with, and will, I am sure, excite a general sympathy and indignation.' Lady Bowrigg, his wife of forty years, was never well after the attack. The following year, for health reasons, she returned to England where she died shortly after her landing.

The bakery owner, a Chinese speculator called A-lum and several of his employees escaped from Hong Kong aboard a steamer but were pursued and arrested. They were put on trial before the colony's Supreme Court. The prosecution provided evidence that A-lum had been present when the poisoned dough was kneaded and baked. Commissioner Yeh's reward scheme was cited as his motive. His defence claimed that he too had eaten the bread and had been ill. His flight from Hong Kong was explained by an official requirement to present himself at Canton. No witnesses could prove conclusively that he or his men had added the arsenic to the dough. All were acquitted.

Bowring appealed to London for an expeditionary force to take and hold Canton for Britain. Lord Palmerston, the Prime Minister, was eager to oblige. He told an election rally at Tiverton: 'An insolent barbarian, wielding authority at Canton, has violated the British flag, broken the engagements of treaties, offered rewards for the heads of British subjects in that part of China, and planned their destruction by murder, assassination and poison.'

The opposition, recalling the international contempt piled on Britain during and after the Opium War, did not agree. Votes of censure against Bowring's actions and the government's support of him, were moved in both Houses of Parliament. The Earl of Derby moved the hostile resolution in the Upper Chamber but after a long and loud debate his motion was rejected by a majority of thirty-six. In the Commons Cobden led the attack, claiming that Bowrigg had violated international law and acted against his orders in the matter of the unregistered *Arrow*. Cobden's motion was carried by a majority of sixteen. Palmerston appealed to the country and in the subsequent election many of Cobden's supporters lost their seats while Palmerston's administration was strengthened.

The Earl of Elgin, a former Governor-General of Canada, was sent to China as envoy to the emperor. He had full powers to negotiate a peace treaty or, if satisfactory terms were not available, to 'prosecute the contest with vigour'. An expeditionary force was prepared, supported by the French who had become involved to avenge the murder of a missionary.

Regardless of the political debates raging at home, Admiral Seymour was not idle. Born in 1802 to the son of an admiral, he was eleven when he first went to sea. His naval career saw him shipwrecked on the desolate shores of Chile, court-martialled for the wreck that put him there (he was acquitted), and a flag-captain on the North America and West Indies station. During service in the Baltic a small sea-mine he was inspecting blew up in his face, destroying the sight of one eye. Despite such narrow scrapes he had generally been a peacetime commander and was eager to see real action in China before he was pensioned off. His target now was the fleet of war-junks in the Canton waters.

On 25 May 1857 he sent Commodore Charles Elliot with a

squadron of gunboats steaming up Escape Creek, the most northerly of four inlets which ran eastwards up the Canton river. Elliot soon reached a large number of heavily armed junks moored across the stream. The two sides exchanged vigorous gunfire which saw sixteen junks taken and destroyed. The shallow-draught junks retreated into waters where the British vessels could not follow. The next day Elliot pursued them via a deeper channel. When shallow water again denied further progress bluejackets and Marines took to the ships' boats and rowed 12 miles upstream. On rounding a point they were suddenly faced with the enemy fleet anchored under the protection of shore batteries in front of the large town of Tang-koon. The Chinese, startled by the arrival of the British in river waters, abandoned their junks and took refuge in a nearby fort. From there they opened a heavy fire with *jingals* (matchlocks) on bluejackets who had boarded the junks and were busy destroying them. Under constant fire the British succeeded in blowing up twelve junks before returning down-river.

Meanwhile Seymour led a flotilla comprising the steamer *Coromandel* and four gunships to Fatshan Creek where he found seventy-two junks moored under the protection of nineteen large guns on the ramparts of a hilltop fort on Hyacinth Island and a six-gun battery on the opposite shore. A correspondent wrote: 'The Chinese believe they are here impregnable. They know you cannot get at the junks without first taking the fort, and they believe no man can go up that hill in the face of their guns. Several vessels have from time to time gone in and exchanged shots with the fort and come back again. This confirms their confidence.' *Coromandel* ran aground, exposed to fire both from shore and the nearest junks. Again, ships' boats manned by sailors and marines won the day. They landed on the island and charged up the hill, and the Chinese defenders, after only brief resistance, abandoned the fort. The marines then stormed the stationary junks, destroying almost all of them with powder and shot.

At the same time a small squadron of ships' boats under Commodore Keppel took the shore battery and pressed on up the creek until they were halted by 'tremendous fire' at an island shaped like a leg of mutton. The channels on either side were narrow and exposed to the concentrated fire of twenty junks lying moored or aground alongside. Three British boats became stuck while two more dashed for the nearest channel. The correspondent reported: 'No sooner did the boats appear in the narrow passage, than 20 32-pounders sent 20 round shot, and a hundred smaller guns sent their full charges of grape and canister at a range of 500 yards right among them. The effect was terrible.'

Keppel retired but resumed the chase when the tide flowed to his advantage. The Chinese junks fled towards the town of Fatshan through narrow channels but one by one they became stuck and were deserted. During the 6 mile pursuit all but three of the junks were taken and destroyed. The ships' boats reached the walls of the town. A volley from the Marines drove back a body of Chinese soldiers but the British, their task completed, returned to join Seymour.

The general stalemate continued and was extended by other events in another part of the East. Elgin, stopping off at Singapore, was met by letters from Lord Canning telling him of the spread of the Indian Mutiny. The crisis on the sub-continent was more pressing than events in China, and Elgin's force was diverted to Calcutta. Elgin continued to Hong Kong, expecting that the revolt in India would quickly be suppressed and that his force would speedily follow on. He reached Hong Kong at the beginning of July but quickly realised his error and set sail westward for Calcutta with a force of Hong Kong troops on board HMS *Shannon*. He and his men were deployed to protect that city from the insurgents. The China War would have to wait.

*   *   *

James Bruce, 8th Earl of Elgin and 12th Earl of Kincardine, was a product of the aristocracy, Eton and Oxford. Now aged forty-six, he had been an able governor of Jamaica, but his later governorship of Canada was soured by rebellion and disturbances. During one riot his coach was stoned and he was accused of timidity in dealing with the rioters. Others praised 'the thoroughly practical manner in which he habitually dealt with public questions, his readiness to assume responsibility, and the strong sense of duty which enabled him to suppress personal considerations whenever they appeared to conflict with the public interest'.

It was not until late autumn that Elgin, his Indian duties done, arrived at Hong Kong. He was joined by a French squadron and that nation's envoy, Baron Gros. At the beginning of December they sent a letter to Commissioner Yeh stating that the English and French governments were united in their determination to seek 'by vigorous and decisive action' reparation for past misdeeds, including the *Arrow* incident and attacks on French missionaries. War would be prosecuted unless British subjects were given free access to Canton and compensation was paid for loss of property during the 'disturbances'. If these demands were met within ten days the blockade of the Canton River would be raised, although any captured forts would be kept until any peace treaty was ratified.

French public opinion had turned in favour of war after the 'judicial murder' two years before of the Roman Catholic priest Auguste Chapdelaine. Despite imperial edicts to tolerate Christian missionaries, a local magistrate embarked on a virulent purge of Christians in which twenty-five Chinese converts were imprisoned and tortured, two of them dying. Chapdelaine himself was arrested and put on trial, charged with preaching the Christian gospel. He was flogged and put in a *cangue* – a heavy wooden cage clamped around the neck like a portable pillory. When he unexpectedly failed to die of this mistreatment his head was chopped off and thrown to the dogs. The French Government demanded reparations.

Yeh conceded nothing to Britain or France but sent Elgin an evasive reply: 'Our two nations regard themselves as on friendly terms with each other. This being the case, there can be nothing which makes it impossible for us to consult together . . .'. Yeh's letter was dated Christmas Day 1857. By then active operations had already commenced, with the British forces under the command of Major-General Charles von Straubenzee and the French naval brigade under Rear-Admiral Rigault de Genouilly. A squadron of war steamers advanced up the Canton River and troops were landed to construct batteries on Dutch Folly island and the peninsula known as French Folly. The crews of the Chinese shore batteries watched them avidly but did not fire a shot. Groups of British and French troops made reconnaissance sorties closer to Canton. The city was given forty-eight hours to surrender before the attack began.

On the morning of 28 December the fleet opened up a heavy bombardment, while joint Anglo-French forces stormed the outlying Linn fort. The cannonade continued all day and throughout the following night until Canton 'was engirdled on the south and east sides with a wall of fire'. The next morning the battered walls were scaled and the Chinese defenders were driven from the parapets. The British troops under Colonels Holloway and Graham, with their French allies, raced along the walls, pouring fire down into the enemy as they fled into the city streets. A battery on Magazine Hill at the wall's northern extremity was soon captured, and its guns turned against the enemy, while a courageous sortie by Tartar troops who threatened to outflank the attackers was beaten back. Gough Fort, further to the north, was also taken and blown up with gunpowder. Casualties were 13 British dead and 83 wounded, 2 French dead and 30 wounded. Canton was effectively taken and the firing stopped, but the allied forces remained on the parapets while a strange calm hung over the city streets below. For several days the city inhabitants appeared to go about their normal business, studiously ignoring the foreign devils above them.

On 5 January several parties descended into the labyrinth of streets. The troops captured Canton's governor, Peh-kwei, in his residence within a walled enclosure. The Tartar General Tseang-keun was also taken without a struggle. It took a few hours more to snatch the real prize. Commissioner Yeh, dressed as a coolie, was found hiding in the small mansion (or *yamun*) of a senior official and was captured by a party under Captain (later Sir) Astley Cooper Key with Parkes as interpreter. A correspondent wrote a gloating account of the capture in *The Times*:

The place was full of hastily-packed baggage. Mandarins were running about, yes, *running* about; and at last one came forward and delivered himself up as Yeh. But he was not fat enough. Parkes pushed him aside, and, hurrying on, they at last spied a very fat man contemplating the achievement of getting over the wall at the extreme rear of the *yamun*. Captain

Key and Commodore Elliot's coxswain rushed forward. Key took the fat gentleman around the waist and the coxswain twisted the august tail of the Imperial Commissioner round his fist. Instinctively the bluejackets felt it must be Yeh, and they tossed up their hats and gave three rousing cheers.

The writer described Yeh as around 5 feet 11 inches tall, very stout, with a remarkably receding forehead, a large protruding mouth, rotten teeth and eyes which 'glared with terror and with fury'. He added: 'No habit of looking at Yeh deadens the feeling of repulsion which the expression of his huge face inspires.'

Yeh and the other captives were marched under guard to a joss-house on Magazine Hill, which had become the British headquarters. Lord Elgin decided that Yeh should be put on board HMS *Inflexible* and sent to Calcutta as a state prisoner. However, Tseang-keun was allowed to return to the city on condition that he disband his troops. Peh-kwei was reinstated as a governor, but his real powers were usurped by a European tribunal under Parkes. The puppet governor was told by Elgin that any attempt, 'whether by force or fraud, by treachery or violence', to harm the occupying force would be met with severe punishment. Elgin in turn promised that when the current dispute was settled the foreign troops would withdraw from the city and restore it to the Chinese authorities.

The emperor immediately degraded the prisoner Yeh from his office as commissioner, accusing him of reckless obstinacy in his dealings with the barbarians. Elgin and Baron Gros determined to go to Peking for an audience with the emperor to conclude a peace treaty. Their envoys were at first courteously received but the negotiations, unsurprisingly, soon became bogged down. The two western commanders quickly lost patience and the allied squadron sailed from Canton waters; heading towards Peking, the fleet reached the mouth of the Peiho River on 19 May. The Chinese had lost no time in rebuilding and strengthening the Taku forts guarding the approaches. Earthworks, sandbag batteries and parapets stretched for almost a mile on both sides of the river. The muzzles of eighty-seven big guns were visible, while forty-nine more poked out from strong mud batteries further up-river. Entrenched camps behind the batteries showed that troop reinforcements had been sent from Peking.

The forts were summoned to surrender but instead the Chinese batteries fired on the advancing gunboats. The artillery duel lasted ninety minutes and left the shore batteries silent and ruined and the forts abandoned. Further up the Peiho a barrier of fire-ships was also deserted and the Chinese troops were nowhere to be seen. The squadron continued up to the city of Tien-tsin at the entrance to the Grand Canal and on 29 May landed under a flag of truce. Dispatches noted: 'Not the slightest hostility was displayed by the Chinese either there or during the passage up the river after the capture of the forts at the mouth.' A telegram to the Foreign Office said: 'The Chinese continue to consider the proceeding as something between peace and war, but not exactly one or the other.'

High-ranking Chinese commissioners were sent by the emperor and, after several weeks of often frustrating diplomatic negotiations and ruffled feathers on both sides, the Treaty of Tien-tsin was signed on 26 June 1858. The terms included Chinese reparations for the recent war, the opening of ten more ports to European trade in future, freedom of movement for European merchants and missionaries, the right to trial under British law for any British subjects caught committing a crime in Chinese territory, the legalisation of the opium trade, consuls to be allowed to live in any open port, and foreign diplomatic missions to be opened in Peking. British and French honour was satisfied but it is difficult to see how, as was reported at the time, the dignity of the emperor was not damaged by such an unequal treaty.

Elgin and Admiral Seymour now set off for another adventure – delivering a steam-yacht to Japan as a gift from Queen Victoria to that nation's emperor. Their real agenda, however, was to negotiate another treaty to throw open Japan's closed ports to British commerce and break the monopoly then jealously guarded by the Dutch. British priorities switched elsewhere while public attention was still on the horrors of the Indian Mutiny. Peace with China, however, did not last long.

*   *   *

The Earl of Elgin's brother Frederick Bruce was appointed Her Majesty's Envoy Extraordinary to China and the Celestial Court. He reached Hong Kong in May 1859 and superseded Sir John Bowring as governor of that colony. Born in 1814, Bruce was the youngest of three siblings and had held senior diplomatic posts in Hong Kong, Newfoundland and Bolivia. His orders demonstrate clearly that the British Government expected the Chinese to prevaricate further, despite the Treaty of Tien-tsin, over Bruce's access to Peking and the establishment of a permanent mission there. They said: 'All the arts at which the Chinese are such adepts will be put in practice to dissuade you from repairing to the capital, even for the purpose of exchanging the ratifications of the Treaty; but it will be your duty firmly, but temperately, to resist any propositions to that effect, and to admit of no excuses . . .' A naval force was placed at his disposal to see that the Treaty was enforced.

Accompanied by the French ambassador M. de Bourboulon, Bruce sailed on to Shanghai. British and French suspicions were quickly proven well-founded. Chinese officials proposed that the Treaty should be ratified there rather than in Peking. The two envoys refused and headed for the Peiho River with a squadron of gunboats and other vessels under the overall command of Rear-Admiral Sir James Hope, who had succeeded Seymour as commander-in-chief on the China station. The 51-year-old Hope came from a distinguished naval family and had served in North America, the West Indies and the Baltic, but had seen comparatively little action.

At the mouth of the Peiho the squadron found their way barred. The Taku forts had again been rebuilt after the hammering they had taken the previous year. Their earthworks had been improved and strengthened with additional ditches and *abattis*. Furthermore, the river was blocked with several large booms, a series of bulky timber rafts, chains and rows of stakes and iron piles. Chinese officials at first promised to clear the obstructions, but after several days nothing had been done, so the British gave notice that they would do it themselves, using force if necessary. On 24 June several parties cut the cables of one boom, and blew two others away with gunpowder, but the following day the British saw that two had been repaired during the night. Bruce told Hope he must force a passage through.

The morning of the 25th was occupied in putting the gunboats into position. At 2 p.m., during high water, *Opossum*, under Captain Willes, was ordered to push her way through the first barrier. The ship succeeded in bursting through a line of iron stakes lashed together and proceeded towards the second obstruction followed by Hope's flagship *Plover* and other gunboats. At that moment a 'tremendous fire' was opened from the Taku forts, where large-calibre guns were concealed behind matting. This time the Chinese gunners' fire was accurate and the results were devastating. *Plover* quickly sank, and Rear-Admiral Hope was severely wounded in the right leg. Refusing to be taken out of the action, Hope and his flag were carried aboard *Cormorant*, but it too was quickly disabled. *Kestrel* fell victim next, and *Lee* was forced aground. Despite his country's declared neutrality, the American commodore Josiah Tattnall came to Hope's aid in his steamship, crying 'Blood is thicker than water'. It was almost certainly the first time that British and American servicemen saw action side by side, albeit only on a rescue mission. As a young midshipman Tattnall had fought the British in the 1812 War but felt that he could not stand by as a neutral observer. His launch rescued Hope and other British wounded. At the end of their efforts his crew were black with powder smoke. The battered remnants of the British squadron fell back to slightly safer positions and began pounding the forts in return. The British fire was effective and by 6.30 all but one gun in the North and South forts were silenced.

Admiral Hope later justified his subsequent decision to attack, taken while his wounds were tended. 'In these circumstances,' he wrote, 'it was clear that no other mode of attack was open to me, except that on the front of the works . . .'. Another commentator put it differently: 'Unfortunately our contempt for our cowardly enemy was carried too far, and the Admiral thought that the forts might be taken by a *coup de main* if a body of men were landed from the vessels.' It was to be a costly mistake.

The landing force selected for the assault included a detachment of sappers and miners, a brigade of Marines, and a division of

British and French seamen. The British were commanded by Captain C.F.A. Shadwell of the gunboat *Highflyer* and the sixty Frenchmen by Captain Tricault. In all around a thousand men set off in landing boats at 7 p.m. An eye-witness recorded the disaster:

Just as the first boat touched the shore, bang went a gun again from the fort, immediately followed by a perfect hurricane of shot, shell, gingal balls and rockets, from all the southern batteries, which mowed down our men by tens as they landed. Nevertheless, out of the boats they all leaped with undiminished ardour (many into water so deep that they had to swim to the shore), and dashed forward through the mud, while the ships threw in as heavy a covering fire as they possibly could.

The enemy's fire, however, continued to be deadly, and the mud proved so deep – in most places up to the men's knees at least, often up to their waists – that out of the men who landed, barely 100 reached the first of the three deep and wide ditches, which, after some 500 yards of wading through the mud, presented themselves before the gallant few who got so far, and out of that small number scarcely 20 had been able to keep their rifles or their ammunition dry. Nevertheless, they boldly faced these new difficulties, and some 50 of them, with a crowd of officers, succeeded in getting as far as the furthest bank of the third ditch, from which they would certainly have made a good attempt to scale the walls had ladders been forthcoming; but, out of the number that were landed, all but one had either been broken by shot or had stuck in the mud. With the remaining one, however, ten devoted men sprung forward, three of whom were immediately shot dead, and five wounded severely.

A vertical fire of arrows, as well as a constant fusillade, was kept up on the select band, who now crouched in the ditch, waiting, but in vain, for reinforcements; and that any of them afterwards escaped alive is miraculous. Seeing what insurmountable difficulties presented themselves, the order was at last given to retire . . .

Midshipman John Fisher, later Admiral of the Fleet Lord Fisher of Kilverstone, wrote to his mother: 'We had a hard fight for it, but what could we do against such a fearful number of guns, and us poor little gunboats enclosed in such a small place, not much broader across than the length of our ship?' He described wading back through the mud:

> I had to fling all my arms away coming back from the forts, and was nearly smothered once, only one of our bluejackets was kind enough to heave me out. You sank up to your knees at least every step, and just fancy the slaughter going 500 yards in the face of about thirty pieces of artillery right in front of you and on each flank. It was dreadful, horrible work, but thank God I came out all right.

Captain Shadwell had been shot in the foot shortly after the landing but had struggled forward to the last ditch. Captain Vansittart of *Magicienne* had a leg shot off, while Colonel Thomas Lemon of the Royal Marines was also wounded as he took what little shelter he could find. Hundreds more officers and men huddled behind banks and inside the outer ditches. Dragging the wounded, the survivors used darkness to cloak their mud-drenched retreat. The Chinese used blue lights and rockets to pinpoint the exhausted men, and more died in the mud. On arriving at the water's edge the survivors were horrified to find that so many boats had been smashed by roundshot that there were simply not enough to take off all of them. Several men were drowned trying to reach the overburdened craft which remained. Others remained up to their necks in water for up to an hour before they could get a place on a boat. Even then their nightmare was not over. Several boats full of wounded men were hit by continuing fire from the forts and were swamped on the return trip to the ships. The last survivors were brought off at 1.30 the following morning. *Coromandel* was turned into a temporary hospital ship and 'the scene on her upper deck was truly horrible'.

In all, the British force lost 89 men killed, including 4 officers, with 252 wounded. A further 25 men were killed and 93 wounded on the stricken gunboats. Two men, one English, the other claiming to be an American, were taken prisoner. The tiny French force lost 4 dead and 10 wounded. Hope reported on the fighting of his forces ashore: 'Had the opposition they experienced been that usual in Chinese warfare, there is little doubt that the place would have been successfully carried at the point of the bayonet.' The *Annual Register* reported:

> Our losses were out of all proportion to the numbers engaged, and we sustained a mortifying repulse from a people with whom our only chance of ultimate success is the conviction forced upon their minds that we are invincible. Such a defeat is likely to do away with the effect of previous victories, and to involve us in another war with the barbarian empire of China.

A Chinese description of the battle, by General San-ko-lin-son, proved such fears correct. In his dispatch he claimed that the British had fired first on the forts and shore batteries. He wrote:

> Our soldiers, pent in as their fury had been for a long time, could no longer be restrained; the guns of every division, large and small, opened upon all sides, and at evening the firing had not ceased . . .
>
> More than 20 boats now came alongside the bank of the southern Fort, and the barbarians, having landed in a body, formed outside the trench; our gingal and matchlock divisions were then brought up to oppose them, and fired several volleys. The barbarians did not venture to cross the ditch, but threw themselves down among the rushes, and fired on us from their ambush. Such murderous ferocity was, indeed, calculated to make one's hair stand up with rage; and to vindicate the honour of the State, and fulfil at the same time the expectations of the Government, your slaves were obliged to bring forward their troops to oppose them with their utmost strength . . .
>
> As we could not tell how far these were off, our soldiers kept them back by projecting fireballs through bamboo tubes; and, as these blazed up, our guns and cannon . . . fired into them at point-blank range; till, their skill and strength alike exhausted,

1. The last stand at Adowa, 1896 (*Illustrated London News*)

2. A typical hill fort, this one at Badulla

3. Hone Heke Pokai, the Maori chief, and his wife, by J.J. Merrett.
(Alexander Turnbull Library, Wellington, NZ)

4. Edward John Eyre, Governor of Jamaica. (*Illustrated London News*)

5. Assistant-Surgeon Campbell Mellis Douglas VC leading the rescue in the surf of the Andaman Islands. (*RAMC Historical Museum*)

6. The Emperor Theodorus of Abyssinia by Baudran from *Theodore II Le Nouvel Empire d'Abyssinie*, by C. Lejean. (Paris, 1865)

7. General Sir Robert Cornelis Napier, later Baron Napier of Magdala. (*Illustrated London News*)

8. Naval Rocket Brigade firing at Senafe. (*Illustrated London News*)

9. The burning of Magdala. (*Illustrated London News*)

10. Kientpoos, better known as Captain Jack, 1873. *(US National Archives)*

11. Louis Riel, *c.* 1880. *(Public Archives of Canada)*

12. Sir Frederick Hodgson directing the defences in the Kumasi fort.
(*Illustrated London News*)

13. The relief force is ambushed at Bali. (*Illustrated London News*)

14. The storming of Montevideo. *(National Army Museum)*

15. The storming of the stockade outside Rangoon.
(National Army Museum)

16. Chinese 'rebels'. *(Illustrated London News)*

17. Capture of Tinghai, Chusan, from a sketch by Lieutenant White, Royal Marines.

18. Punjab battery preparing to enter the Durwanzal Pass.
(Illustrated London News)

19. The charge of the 3rd Bombay Light Cavalry against Persian squares at Khoosh-ab. *(Illustrated London News)*

20. Harry Smith Parkes, British Commissioner at Canton.
(Illustrated London News)

21. The French attacking the bridge at Pa-le-chiao, 6 miles from Peking.
(Illustrated London News)

22. Rear-Admiral Sir Harry Holdsworth Rawson by C.W. Walton. *(National Maritime Museum, Greenwich)*

23. Rear-Admiral Rawson's 7,700-ton flagship *St George* with the *Philomel* in the background. *(Illustrated London News)*

24. The first fight at Ologbo, as depicted by H.C. Seppings Wright.
(Illustrated London News)

25. The King's Own Scottish Borderers storming Afridi positions above Datoi.
(Illustrated London News)

26. A sketch by Melton Prior showing the bodies of dead officers being taken
down country for burial, escorted by Bengal Lancers.
(Illustrated London News)

27. 'The Aftermath at Omdurman', by H.C.S. Eppings Wright.
(*Illustrated London News*)

28. Bulbudder Singh, commander of the Gurkha defences at Kalunga. *(Gurkha Museum)*

29. James Brooke as a young man, by Grant. *(National Portrait Gallery)*

30. The British attack on the pirates near Maluda Bay.
(*Illustrated London News*)

31. The fort at Tamatave, sketched from the mast-head of HMS *Conway*.
(*Illustrated London News*)

32. Sikh lancers. (*Illustrated London News*)

33. The death of Major Broadfoot at the battle of Mudki. (*Illustrated London News*)

34. The death of General Cureton at Ramnuggar. (*Illustrated London News*)

35. British light dragoons engaging the enemy at Chillianwalla.
(*Victoria & Albert Museum*)

36. The King's Own Light Dragoons charging the Sikh cavalry at Chillianwala.
(National Army Museum)

37. 'The battle of the Eureka Stockade', by Thaddeus Welch and Izett Watson. *(Engraving from the La Trobe Collection, State Library of Victoria)*

38. Major-General Sir William Fenwick Williams, the commander of Kars, from a photograph by John Watkins. (*Illustrated London News*)

39. The battle of Kars. (*Illustrated London News*)

40. General Thomas Francis Meagher at the battle of Fair Oaks.
(New York Public Library)

41. The West India Regiment with a seven-pounder in action on the Meli
river. *(Illustrated London News)*

they dared no longer to continue the engagement, but slunk back to their ships. The barbarian dead lay piled in heaps . . .

Bloodied and dispirited, the British squadron limped back to Shanghai, having first managed to refloat the grounded *Kestrel*. British firepower had, for the first time, been defeated by the Chinese and further warfare was indeed certain.

*   *   *

As Hope nursed his wounds at Ningpo, reaction in Britain was intense. Military rivals criticised his tactics, questioning the wisdom of attacking the Chinese in the same manner and in the same place as Seymour had successfully done a year earlier. The Chinese were bound to have strengthened their defences in the meantime. Such comments were, however, overshadowed by the gallantry of Hope and his men. The enormity of the setback gave rise to several myths, including the totally unsubstantiated claim that the shore guns were manned by Russians or Americans. The 'treachery' of the Chinese in opening fire was also underlined, even though Hope had attacked first by trying to force a passage through the river barrier. The Chinese had openly manned the forts and barricades. Several officers under Hope's command repudiated the idea of any treachery, saying that they had known for days that the forts would resist any British attempt to force a way up-river. A later commentator said:

> A man who, when he sees you approaching his hall-door, closes and bars it against you, and holds a rifle pointed at your head while he parleys with you from an upper window, may be a very inhospitable and discourteous person; but if when you attempt to dash in his door he fires at you with his rifle, you can hardly call him treacherous, or say that you had no expectation of what was going to happen.

At the time such views were in a minority, and war fever gripped both Britain and France. During an acrimonious debate in Parliament, Hope and Bruce were heavily criticised. Lord Elgin staunchly defended his brother and urged further diplomacy. He said that negotiations with Peking were necessary 'if we intend to maintain permanent pacific relations with some 400,000,000 of the human race, scattered over a country 1,500 miles long by as many broad'. Karl Marx, in a dispatch to the *New York Daily Tribune*, reported: 'The whole debate in both Houses on the Chinese war evaporated in grotesque compliments showered by both factions on the head of Admiral Hope for having so gloriously buried the British forces in the mud.'

The following year Britain and France fitted out an expeditionary force to avenge the defeat, win reparations and enforce the Treaty of Tien-tsin. The British forces consisted of around 11,000 men, including several Sikh regiments who had volunteered for the task, under Lieutenant-General Sir James Hope Grant. This 52-year-old Scot had served in the Opium War and had built a fearsome military reputation. He took part in the hard-fought battle of Sobraon, commanded the 9th Lancers in the Punjab War and saw the most ferocious action during the Indian Mutiny. His experience of hand-to-hand fighting was legendary among the rank and file, while senior officers relished his performances on the violoncello. Wolseley described him as 'a tall man of muscle and bone and no unnecessary flesh about him. He had all the best instincts of a soldier, and was a brave daring man that no amount of work could tire. He was liked by every good man who knew him.' Despite his excellent reputation for soldiering, Grant was no text-book soldier. He was ill-educated, read nothing but the Bible, could not sketch maps, never learnt to read anyone else's maps, and was so prone to issuing confusing, badly expressed orders that some of his officers called him 'puzzle-headed'. His courage, however, was never doubted. He once explained: 'To die is nothing; it's only going from one room to another.' Grant divided his command into two brigades under Major-Generals Sir Robert Napier and Sir John Michel. The fleet amounted to around 200 frigates, gunboats and transport ships. The French had 6,000 men under General Charles Montauban.

Lord Elgin and Baron Gros, again appointed plenipotentiaries in China for the two western powers, set sail in the English frigate *Malabar*. Stopping on the way at Point de Galle in Ceylon, their vessel was totally wrecked on a rocky reef in the harbour. The two ambassadors had a lucky escape and emerged unscathed, but were chagrined to lose many important papers. They were delayed in Ceylon until another ship, aptly named *Pekin*, arrived to collect them.

Meanwhile, on 8 March 1860, an ultimatum was sent by Bruce from Shanghai to the Chinese Government requiring an 'ample and satisfactory apology . . . for the act of troops who fired on the ships of Her Britannic Majesty from the forts of Taku in June last, and that all guns and material, as well as the ships abandoned on that occasion, be restored'. Bruce also demanded that the river by Taku should be cleared, Britain's envoys should be admitted to Peking with due honour, and the Chinese Government pay war indemnity of four million taels. The French made similar demands.

Peking's Great Council replied that the ultimatum caused them great astonishment, while the demand for restitution was 'yet more against decorum', especially as China's own war expenses had been enormous. The demand for a British Residence in Peking was rejected outright. The reply concluded that the ultimatum was couched in 'insubordinate and extravagant' language and warned that if Bruce continued on his obstinate course 'he will give cause to much trouble hereafter'.

Harry Parkes, meantime, was temporarily recalled from his service in Canton, where he had been busy rebuilding the destroyed British settlement and organising an emigration house for the despised Chinese coolies. Parkes's first suggestion was to lease the peninsula of Kowloon, opposite Hong Kong, as a convenient camping ground for the allied army. Astonishingly, in return for hard cash, the Chinese Governor-General agreed to lease a portion of the Celestial Empire to be used as a depot for hostile troops.

Lord Elgin and Baron Gros arrived in Hong Kong on 21 June and proceeded to Shanghai to meet up with General Grant and Admiral Hope, who remained in command of the British fleet. The British and French forces moved towards Taku, the British anchoring in the Bay of Tah-lieu-hwan, the French at Chefow on the north side of the promontory of Shantung. The troops disembarked at Pehtang, 12 miles north of the Peiho River, where they made camp. A soldier described the area as 'a wilderness of mud and water, destitute of tree, plant, shrub or grass, amidst a scene of utter misery and desolation'. Heavy rain kept them in that grim spot until the allied forces were able to march out on 12 August.

With the troops was the special correspondent for *The Times*, 43-year-old Thomas William Bowlby. The son of an artillery officer raised in Sunderland, he was a not-too-successful lawyer before turning to journalism in Berlin. He married the sister of his father's second wife and through her inherited a sizeable fortune which he spent. His debts forced him abroad and he was involved in building a railway to Smyrna when he got the call from *The Times* to accompany Elgin to China. He left behind his wife and five small children.

Napier's column of infantry, the Madras Sappers, the Cavalry Brigade, a rocket battery and three six-pounders struck off to the right of the road leading from Pehtang to Sinho, intending to turn the left flank of the Chinese defendants, but got bogged down in heavy ground. This delayed the departure of Michel's main column and the following French force. Tartar cavalry moved rapidly to attack Napier's smaller force but luckily Michel's artillery managed to bring their guns and rockets to bear in time to avert a possible massacre. So heavy was the fire that the enemy cavalry, about 4,000 strong, was forced into retreat and two lines of Chinese entrenchments were abandoned. Chinese losses were estimated at around 100, mainly horsemen who had been 'cut up' by Sikh cavalry.

The following day Grant ordered the bridging of creeks and ditches intersecting the ground between the allies and Chinese defences at Tangku. On the 14th the allies moved up-river to within a mile of the town. Two Armstrong guns and two nine-pounders swiftly silenced a Chinese battery, while a party of sailors slipped across the river and burnt a number of junks. The whole of the artillery was moved to within 600 yards of the enemy earthworks and opened a heavy fire on the walls, supported by two French batteries. The Chinese replied with twelve guns and a brisk fire of gingals and matchlocks. Grant reported:

The artillery gradually advanced to within 350 yards, and, the enemy's guns being silenced, a breach was commenced . . .

by the 60th Rifles and an entrance was effected, the Chinese retiring with great precipitancy. At the same time the French advanced with great gallantry, and entered by the main gate, which had been partially broken in by artillery fire. I am happy to say that our losses in these two engagements were very slight, owing to the enemy being completely paralysed by the superior fire of our artillery.

The Chinese garrison retreated, leaving behind forty-five cannon. The Chinese had been commanded by General San-ko-lin-son. A mishearing of his name sparked the widespread rumour that he was a maverick Irishman called Sam Collinson.

The allies then moved on to attack the Taku Forts by land and river. The land force, predominantly British, hauled cannon along hastily improved tracks to within 800 yards of the inner North Fort on the left bank of the Peiho. At night batteries were built for the heavy guns, mortars and field pieces. Gunboats steamed to engage the outer North and South Forts. The Chinese forts were all constructed on the same plan: massive redoubts with thick ramparts strongly defended with heavy cannon. They were protected by two unfordable wet ditches, between which and the parapet sharp bamboo stakes were thickly planted, forming two belts, each about 15 feet wide. Any advance could be made only on a narrow front. The French commander, Montauban, believed the forts to be impregnable and, in a formal written protest, refused to commit his forces to what he believed would be almost certain slaughter. At the last minute he partially relented and dispatched 400 infantry and two batteries to 'put in an appearance'. At 5 a.m. on 21 August the Chinese opened up with every gun that could be ranged upon the attackers, forcing the allies to begin their onslaught an hour earlier than planned.

A British storming party formed up while the French contingent pushed on through wet ditches to assault the salient of the inner fort. They failed to scale the walls owing to the vigorous resistance of the defenders. The Chinese fire was so effective that fifteen Sappers carrying a pontoon bridge were knocked down by a single discharge. Fifteen-year-old Hospital Apprentice Arthur Fitzgibbon of the Indian Medical Establishment broke cover to bind the wounds of a dhoolie-bearer, and then ran further under intense fire to tend other injured men before he too was severely wounded.

Napier ordered two howitzers to within 50 yards of the fort's main gate. A small breach, big enough only for one man at a time, was made and the storming party headed for it, some of them swimming across water-filled ditches. Bowlby recorded the action:

> All this time the fire of the enemy continued incessant. Cold shot, hand grenades, stinkpots, and vases of lime were showered on the crowd of besiegers . . . The ladders placed against the wall were pulled into the fort, or thrown over, and in vain did man after man attempt to swarm through the embrasures. If the defence was desperate, nothing could exceed the gallantry of the assailants. Between English and French there was nothing to choose. A Frenchman climbed to the top of the parapet, where for some time he stood alone. One rifle after another was handed up to him, which he fired against the enemy. But his courage was unavailing, and he fell back, speared through the eye. Another, pickaxe in hand, attempted to cut away the top of the wall. He was shot, and Lieutenant Burslem, of the 67th, caught hold of his pick and continued the work. Lieutenant Rogers attempted to force his way through an embrasure, but was driven back. He ran to another, but it was too high for him. Lieutenant Lenon came to his assistance, forced the point of his sword into the wall, and placing one foot on the sword, Lieutenant Rogers leaped through the embrasure . . .

Rogers was the first Briton into the fort, followed by Private John McDougall of the 44th. They were seconds behind the first Frenchman, Drummer Jean Fanchard of the 102nd who had scaled an angle wall. Ensign John Worthy Chaplin of the 67th planted the Queen's colours in the breach before being badly wounded. He was assisted by Private Thomas Lane, who had also helped Lieutenant Burslem to widen the hole in the wall. Both men were also wounded. The troops plunged through the breach and embrasures, forcing the

Chinese back step by step until the defenders fled over the fort's opposite walls.

For their outstanding courage in this action Apprentice Fitzgibbon, Lieutenant Robert Montresor Rogers, Private McDougall, Lieutenant Edmund Henry Lenon, Lieutenant Nathaniel Burslem, Private Lane and Ensign John Chaplin were all awarded the Victoria Cross – Britain's foremost honour for valour – the highest number to be awarded in a single action, a record only later surpassed at Rorke's Drift. At fifteen years and three months old, Fitzgibbon was the youngest person to wear the Victoria Cross, before or since.

The outer North Fort was then attacked but its commander offered no resistance. The allied infantry scaled the walls without a shot being fired and took 2,000 prisoners. That evening the garrison of the South Forts were abandoning them, and the allies took possession of empty buildings. The Chinese army melted away. In all 400 Chinese guns were captured. The allies lost 17 men killed in the attack on the first position, and 183 wounded. It had been no pushover.

The emperor appointed Kweiliang, who had negotiated the 1858 treaty, and Hang Fuh, Governor-General of Chi Li province, as imperial commissioners charged with reaching a peace with the foreign invaders. Admiral Hope was sent up the Peiho in *Coromandel*, accompanied by Consul Parkes, to meet them at Tien-tsin. With them went a division of five gunboats. On being told that Sang-ko-lin-son had passed the previous day, Hope decided to occupy the treaty city with his small force. The British and French flags were hoisted over the east gate. The local people met the foreigners with smiles, having been told by proclamation that the barbarians had been defeated and there was nothing to fear from them. Negotiations with the imperial commissioners proved inconclusive, however, and the rest of the allied force pushed up-river to join Hope.

Elgin swiftly became frustrated with imperial prevarication and gave notice that he would push onwards to Tang-chow, 65 miles closer to Peking. Some 5 miles short of his target, it was agreed that a convention would be signed at Chang-tsin-wan. The allies' agreed campsite was found to be occupied by a large force of Chinese cavalry and infantry. On 18 September Consul Parkes was sent to

Tang-chow to negotiate with Prince I, a nephew of the emperor, to arrange for Elgin's reception and to protest at the proximity of the Chinese force. With him went an escort of Fane's Horse, under Lieutenant Anderson, Elgin's private secretary, Henry Loch, and several others including Bowlby of *The Times*. The party set off under a flag of truce.

Meanwhile the Chinese cavalry advanced on both flanks of the allied force. Within two hours the British and French were almost entirely surrounded. Grant was anxious not to engage the energy while Parkes and the others were behind Chinese lines, but the decision was taken out of his hands when the guns and matchlocks in the centre of the Chinese emplacements opened fire on a small party under Lieutenant-Colonel Walker as they galloped through their lines. Grant recalled:

> Colonel Walker reported that, while waiting for Mr Parkes, a French officer joined him, who was suddenly set upon and cut down by a Chinese soldier and, on his riding up to prevent him being murdered, his own sword was snatched from his scabbard and some men tried to throw him off his horse. Seeing that it was a deliberate attempt to assassinate the whole of them, Colonel Walker set spurs to his horse and galloped out with his party, under fire of the Chinese line.

One of his men was wounded and one horse had a spear thrust into its back, but they all returned safely to the British positions.

Parkes and his companions were not so lucky. The consul, Loch and a sowar carrying the flag of truce were taken to San-ko-lin-son who received them with 'rudeness and insult' and ordered them to be bound. The three foreigners and two French prisoners were paraded in an open cart 'of the roughest sort' through Tang-chow and, bound to the same vehicle, transported onwards to Peking. The remainder were also captured and bound tightly – Lieutenant Anderson, Captain Brabazon, Mr de Norman of the British Legation, the journalist Bowlby, an English dragoon and eighteen sowars. They were carried off into the interior where all the Europeans and several sowars died of mistreatment. Their hands and feet were bound so tightly with cords that the flesh burst and mortification ensued. Captain Brabazon was beheaded near Peking, on the orders of a mandarin who had twice been wounded with shell-splinters. Private Moyes of the Buffs suffered the same fate when he refused to kow-tow, although Chinese authorities later claimed that the Scots veteran, a well-known hell-raiser, had died of drink. Moyes was immortalised in a poem by Sir Francis Doyle:

> Last night among his fellow roughs,
> He jested, quaffed and swore;
> A drunken private of the Buffs,
> Who never looked before.
> Today, beneath his foeman's frown,
> He stands in Elgin's place,
> Ambassador from Britain's crown,
> And type of all his race.

Brabazon had volunteered to go with Parkes in place of Colonel Garnet Wolseley, the future viscount and commander-in-chief of the British Army, who had lagged behind the column to do some sketching. Elgin and Grant were unaware of the imprisonment of the delegation but knew that treachery was involved and, immediately following Walker's report, formed their men into a line of attack. Despite the large numbers of Chinese cavalry, the battle was little more than a rout. The Tartars advanced to within 200 yards of the British line, a 'whole cloud of horse'. The 99th fired a volley too early and the Chinese cavalry wheeled around. The dragoons gave chase. One Marine, Captain Carrington, wrote: 'The Tartars waited until our men had neared them within fifty yards, and then they fired a volley, wounding a Captain rather badly and killing a trooper. They then turned about and moved smartly on.' The Chinese were on the other side of a broad ditch which the first line of dragoons leapt easily, but in doing so they raised a cloud of dust which prevented the second line seeing enough to follow them. There were enough dragoons, however, to lay into the enemy. With the British on the left and General Montauban's men on the right, they dispersed a Chinese army reckoned to be 20,000 strong. British and French guns blasted great holes in the massed Chinese ranks at short range and San-ko-lin-son's army fled. Several hundred bodies were left on the field. The British lost one man dead, seventeen wounded and one missing.

The allied forces cleared out and burnt four military camps. After taking a nearby village with no casualties the men were allowed to fill their empty water-bottles. Carrington later recalled: 'I assure you it is very hard and thirsty work charging cavalry about such a dry and unsupportable country. The millet is but lately cut, and you have a plain of stalks, standing about a foot and a half high, with sharp tops that pierce like spikes. Several of the horses have been lamed by these points.'

Elgin blamed the Tartar general both for the treachery and for the ensuing carnage. He said that San-ko-lin-son believed the imperial commissioners had compromised his military position by allowing the allies so close to his lines.

> He sought to counteract the evil effect of this by making a great swagger of parade and preparation to resist when the allied armies approached the camping ground allotted to them. . . . I cannot believe that after the experience which San-ko-lin-son had already had of our superiority in the field, either he or his civil colleagues could have intended to bring on a conflict in which, as the event has proved, he was sure to be worsted.

The allies marched on towards Peking. Six miles from the imperial city they met another Tartar army at Pal-le-chiao. While the French infantry stormed across a narrow bridge to destroy the main Chinese emplacement which guarded the imperial high road, the King's Dragoon Guards charged the Tartar cavalry, inflicting heavy losses. Large bodies of the enemy advanced to within 200 yards of Grant's hastily unlimbered cannon before salvoes of cannister drove them off. On the left flank Fane's Horse, thirsting for revenge after the capture of their comrades, attacked another body of horsemen, supported by the 1st Sikh Cavalry. The charges were across fields where crops of maize and millet had recently been cut, leaving sharp-pointed stubble which gouged the legs and bellies of the horses and made rapid movement very difficult. Despite these handicaps the charges were 'most effective'. Grant reported:

> The enemy, though defeated on the spot, yet still remained in front, in clouds of horsemen who, though constantly retiring from the advance of any party of our cavalry, however small, never allowed more than 1,000 yards between us, and showed a steady and threatening front. At this time I had with me the cavalry, the 4th Infantry Brigade, and three Armstrong guns; the rest of the artillery, with the 2nd Brigade, having been left in the centre . . . With the three Armstrong guns under Captain Rowley, we fired occasional single shots on their thickest masses. Those shots, fired singly at slow intervals, served admirably to illustrate the good quality of the Armstrong guns; not one failed to strike the thick masses of the enemy, at once dispersing them from the spot.

The 99th Regiment took and burnt the headquarters camp of the imperial princes; seeing the flames and losing heart, the Chinese army retreated to Peking. Forty-three guns were taken in the action. In the centre of the field small piles of dead showed the effect of Grant's measured artillery fire. Allied losses were 2 dead and 29 wounded, most of them only slightly.

Meanwhile, in Peking Harry Parkes was separated from his companions and brought before a board of examiners who ruled that he be placed in a prison for common criminals. Parkes wrote in his memoir:

> I found myself in a throng of 70 or 80 wild-looking prisoners, most of them offensive in the extreme, as is usual in Chinese gaols, from disease and dirt. I was again carefully examined and searched by the gaolers, who also saw that my chains were properly secured, and bound my arms with fresh cords, not so tightly as to prevent circulation or to occasion serious inconvenience. At the same time they removed, to my intense relief, the cords from my wrists which, being very tightly tied, had caused my hands to swell to twice their proper size, and

were now giving me great pain. They then laid me on the raised boarding on which the prisoners sleep, and made me fast by another large chain to a beam overhead. The chains consisted of one long and heavy one, stretching from the neck to the feet, to which the hands were fastened by two cross chains and handcuffs, and the feet in a similar manner.

Parkes was repeatedly interrogated because of his knowledge of the language but refused to give useful information on Elgin's intentions. His gaolers may have been rough but he was well treated by his fellow prisoners.

It was only from the prisoners that I obtained sympathy or a hearing . . . Many of these unfortunate men were glad, when so permitted, to come round me to listen to my story, or any description that I would give them of foreign countries and usages. Instead of following the example set them by their authorities, and treating me with abuse or ridicule, they were seldom disrespectful, addressed me by my title, and often avoided putting me to inconvenience when it was in their power to do so. Most of them were men of the lowest class, and the gravest order of offenders, as murderers, burglars, etcetera. Those who had no means of their own were reduced by prison filth and prison diet to a shocking state of emaciation and disease; but those who could afford to fee the gaolers, and purchase such things as they wanted, lived in comparative fullness and comfort.

After only a few days in such primitive conditions Parkes was removed from the common prison to a separate cell which measured 8 feet square, with four gaolers appointed to watch him. He was frequently visited by Hang-ki, a Mandarin he had known in Hong Kong, who was sent by Prince Kung, the emperor's brother, to extract information and make use of him to obtain the most favourable terms from the British. He told Parkes he was to be taken out of prison, but Parkes bravely refused to leave unless Loch was released also. After a short stand-off, and after eleven days in captivity, both men were taken to a temple where quarters were provided and they were treated well. On 5 October, however, they were told they were to be executed that evening, but the order was countermanded by Prince Kung after the defeat at Pal-le-chiao.

Elgin and Gros refused to negotiate with the Chinese authorities until all the British and French prisoners had been released. They were still unaware of the deaths of most of the hostages. On 25 September Elgin gave Prince Kung notice that Peking would be bombarded and taken by force unless, within three days, the prisoners were surrendered, the convention signed at Tang-chow and the ratifications exchanged in Peking. Kung used his diplomatic wiles to delay and evade the ultimatum, and on 6 October the allies closed on the city.

The French column lagged behind, claiming later they had lost their way, and made straight for the Yueng-min-yeun, or Summer Palace of the emperor. Around twenty poorly armed eunuchs offered brave but hopeless resistance and were cut down by the rifles of the French. They began looting its treasures on a massive scale. One observer described the scene shortly afterwards:

> The public reception-hall, the state and private bedrooms, anterooms, boudoirs, and every other apartment has been ransacked; articles of vertu, of native and foreign workmanship, taken or broken if too large to be carried away; ornamental lattice-work, screens, jade stone ornaments, jars, clocks, watches and other pieces of mechanism, curtains and furniture – none have escaped from destruction. There were extensive wardrobes of every article of dress; coats richly embroidered in silk and gold thread in the Imperial Dragon pattern; boots, headdresses, fans, in fact, rooms all but filled with them . . .

Montauban, the commander-in-chief, obtained a magnificent diamond necklace. General Grant later succeeded in getting a small share of the booty for his own army. In the subsequent auction he gave his own share to be distributed among his men, for which he was rebuked by the Russell Government. Queen Victoria signalled her approval of his action. In total every British private received around a £4 share of the Summer Palace loot.

Two days later Parkes, Loch and the other surviving prisoners were released. Parkes wrote:

> We were placed in covered carts, without being able to see each other, and were escorted by a large party of soldiers and mandarins through streets which wore a deserted appearance to the Se-che, or north-western gate of the city. We soon saw, with grateful hearts, as those great portals opened and then immediately closed behind us, that we were already free men, for our guard, not daring to follow us out of the city, had left to ourselves the pleasant task of finding our own way to the allied camp.

What they did not know then was that fifteen minutes after the gates shut behind them, an express message was received from the emperor ordering their instant execution.

The British and French guns were lined up to bombard the imperial city and the Chinese authorities were told that the cannonade would begin at noon the following day unless Peking was surrendered and one of its gates placed in allied hands. The emperor, just twenty-nine years old but already dying of dropsy and debauchery, had abandoned the city and fled to Manchuria on the pretext of a hunting expedition, and it was left to Prince Kung to capitulate unconditionally. A gate was opened and for the first time in history the British and French flags flew above Peking's walls.

As part of the surrender terms it was agreed that the city be spared. Elgin did not know the fate of all the hostages: he had been told that they were all safe and comfortably lodged. When the truth emerged Elgin was understandably furious. He wrote to Kung, upbraided him for deception and added:

> Of the total number of twenty-six British subjects seized in defiance of honour and of the law of nations, thirteen only have been restored alive, all of whom carry on their persons evidence more or less distinctly marked of the indignities and

ill treatment from which they have suffered, and thirteen have been barbarously murdered . . . Until this foul deed shall have been expiated, peace between Great Britain and the existing dynasty of China is impossible.

Some advised Elgin to burn down the Imperial Palace but he felt that such action would only drive Kung and the rest of the Chinese Government to evacuate the city and threaten the allied forces from the countryside. Elgin learnt that several prisoners had been tortured in the Summer Palace, now largely gutted by both French and Chinese looters. He proposed to Baron Gros that it should be burnt down in retribution for a 'great crime'. The French ambassador refused to take part, even though his own forces had plundered the place, and Elgin resolved to carry it through on his responsibility alone. Although Parkes negotiated the surrender of Peking, he played no part in this decision, although he later said it was just punishment for the cruelty shown towards the prisoners.

It took a detachment of British soldiers to burn every building to the ground, as the Summer Palace occupied a large area of ground and consisted of some two hundred separate structures laid out in the style of the Trianon at Versailles. Wolseley compared it to 'a city composed only of museums and Wardour Streets'. The buildings themselves were set among gardens, temples, small lodges and pagodas, groves, grottos, lakes, bridges, terraces and artificial hills. Charles George Gordon, a 27-year-old captain in the Royal Engineers (and later to meet lasting fame and death at Khartoum), helped organise the destruction. He wrote to his mother:

We went out, and, after pillaging it, burned the whole place, destroying in a Vandal-like manner most valuable property which would not be replaced for four millions. We got upward of £48 apiece prize money before we went out here, and although I have not as much as many, I have done well. The people are civil, but I think the grandees hate us, as they must after what we did to the Palace. You can scarcely imagine the beauty and magnificence of the places we burnt. It made one's heart sore to burn them; in fact, these places were so large, and we were so pressed for time, that we could not plunder them carefully. Quantities of gold ornaments were burnt, considered as brass. It was wretchedly demoralizing work for an army. Everybody was wild for plunder.

The only consolation for the Chinese was that British and French looters preferred porcelain – much of which still graces English country houses whose present owners do not normally admit to handling stolen goods – and neglected the bronze vessels locally prized for cooking and for burial in tombs. Many such treasures dated back to the Shang, Zhou and Han dynasties and were up to 3,600 years old.

Once the Summer Palace was reduced to a charred desert a sign was raised on the site with an inscription in Chinese, reading that this was the reward of perfidy and cruelty. It was the last act of a bloody war.

*   *   *

General Sir Robert Napier, with Parkes at his side, marched into Peking on 13 October 1860. The Summer Palace was still burning. Eleven days later Elgin made his official entry into the city as a conqueror, not as an emissary. His escort consisted of 600 soldiers and 100 officers led by a cavalry detachment. Elgin was seated in a chair of state carried by sixteen Chinese in crimson robes. As he was carried into the Hall of Ceremonies a band played 'God Save the Queen'. His Lordship treated Prince Kung with a haughty politeness. The prince was alarmed when the lens of Signor Beato's camera was pointed at him, until reassured it was not a weapon. The photography intended to mark the historic occasion, however, was bungled.

The Treaty of Tien-tsin was ratified and further humiliations were heaped on the Quing Dynasty with the signing of the Convention of Peking. The war indemnity to be paid by the Chinese was increased by eight million taels. Tien-tsin itself was opened up to foreign trade, Kowloon was ceded to the British and foreign ambassadors were allowed to reside in Peking. The emperor was forced to apologise for the 'treachery' of the Taku garrison in firing upon Hope's squadron. The Allied forces stayed until reparations were paid and finally retired on 5 November.

Lord Elgin returned to England the following April, having stopped at Java on the voyage home. There was much criticism of his burning of the Summer Palace which many saw as an act of 'unintelligible and unpardonable' vandalism. The need to avenge the murder and ill-treatment of British subjects was not under question, merely the manner of that vengeance. 'Would any act of treachery committed by a Spanish sovereign justify the destruction of the Alhambra?' one critic asked. Elgin argued, with some force, that to demand the punishment of the actual murderers would have been absurd. The Chinese would simply have handed over as many victims as he asked for, or executed as many as he demanded should pay the price. But there would have been no guarantee that they were the actual perpetrators. That argument was accepted by at least one commentator who added: 'It is somewhat singular that so many persons should have been roused to indignation by the destruction of a building who took with perfect composure the unjust invasion of a country.'

Elgin and Grant may have delivered a victory, but political feelings in Britain were divided over both the cause and the conduct of the war. Earl Grey called a House of Lords debate in which he accused Elgin of abusing the various treaties with China, of promoting the opium trade instead of stifling it, and of allowing an even more pernicious trade – the export of coolies – which, he said, was a slave trade in disguise. Lord Ellenborough asked whether 'Sir John Bowring's war' was really over and said that the Chinese had suffered great injustices. For the government, however, Lord Wodehouse claimed they had done everything to discourage both the opium and coolie trades. On the need for military action he added: 'If the Chinese once entertained the idea that we would depart from the words of the treaty, they would circumvent us by their tricky diplomacy, and oblige us at last to cut the matter with the sword.'

Barely a month after landing in England Elgin was appointed viceroy and governor-general of India. He arrived there in March

1862 and for twenty months threw himself into the task with his customary energy, despite frequent bouts of heat sickness. While travelling in the Himalayas he crossed a twig bridge over the River Chandra, a structure so battered by the rainy season that he over-exerted himself in getting across and suffered a heart attack. He died, aged fifty-two, at Dharmsala on 20 November 1863 with his wife and youngest daughter beside him. One obituary complained:

> In China and in India, where he was brought into contact with Englishmen and other Europeans settled among Asiatic populations, he seems to have formed a strong, and some persons thought an exaggerated, impression of the tendency of Europeans to ill-use the inferior races, his letters, both public and private, containing frequent and indignant allusions to this subject.

Thomas Bowlby's body was given up by the Chinese and buried in the Russian cemetery outside Peking's An-tin gate on 17 October. *The Times* took responsibility for the education of his eldest son.

General Grant returned to Britain a hero, having conducted what many regarded as a textbook campaign. After serving briefly as commander-in-chief of the Madras army he was made quartermaster-general at the Horse Guards and camp commander at Aldershot. He reformed army manoeuvres, introduced war games and military lectures, and greatly influenced his successor. Lord Wolseley said in 1872: 'If I have attained any measure of military prosperity, my gratitude is due to one man, and that man is Sir Hope Grant.' The subject of his admiration died, aged sixty-seven, in 1875 of an internal malady aggravated by active service in tropical climates.

Admiral Hope stayed on in China to help his erstwhile enemies fight off Taiping rebels. In the spring of 1862 he cooperated with the Chinese imperial troops under the American General Ward to clear the insurgents from the neighbourhood of Shanghai and Ningpo. In one attack, which he led in person, Hope was again wounded by a musket-shot. He then served in the West Indies but his retirement in Linlithgow was plagued by ill-health and pain from his numerous wounds. He died, aged seventy-three, in 1881.

Of the VC heroes of the Taku forts, Robert Rogers rose the highest. The Dublin-born lieutenant commanded the 90th Cameronians in the Zulu War and became a major-general before dying at Maidenhead, aged sixty, in 1895. Private John McDougall was just twenty-nine when he died in his home city of Edinburgh in 1869. Lieutenant Edmund Henry Lenon had a long military career, reaching the rank of lieutenant-colonel; he died at Lambeth in 1893, aged sixty-two. Lieutenant Nathaniel Burslem was promoted captain in the 67th, which later became the Hampshire Regiment, but he died just five years later, aged twenty-seven, drowned in New Zealand's Thames River. Private Thomas Lane, a Cork man, died in Kimberley, South Africa, in 1889 at the age of fifty-two. Ensign John Chaplin rose to the rank of colonel and died, a heavily whiskered eighty-year-old, at Market Harborough in 1920. Apprentice Andrew Fitzgibbon became an apothecary and died in Delhi in 1883, a few weeks short of his 38th birthday.

Sir Frederick Bruce did not stay long in China, despite the efforts and lives expended to get him to Peking. In 1865 he was made Britain's representative in Washington. He died in Boston two years later. His remains were embalmed and sent to Scotland, where they were interred in Dunfermline Abbey.

Sir Michael Seymour received much praise for his naval leadership during the earlier stages of the China War. One biographer said: 'The invariable success which attended his operations in the war in China was entirely due to his calm foresight and careful attention to the minutest of details.' China merchants presented him with a handsome service of plate. For three years, from 1859 to 1862, he was MP for Devonport. He died, a full admiral on the retired list, in 1887.

Sir John Bowring's passage home aboard *Alma* was not an easy one. The ship struck a rock in the Red Sea and sank; Bowring, the crew and his fellow passengers were marooned for three days on a coral reef where they suffered greatly before being rescued. The rest of his life was relatively quiet. He was sent on a trade mission to Italy but in Rome was struck by illness aggravated by the effects of the arsenic poisoning he had suffered in Hong Kong three years before. After a long convalescence he concentrated on translating, lecturing and writing poems and hymns, including the classic 'In the cross of Christ I glory'. Aged almost eighty he addressed a crowd of 3,000 at Plymouth in 1872. Weeks later, after a brief illness, he died at Exeter, just yards from the house where he was born.

General Charles Montauban was awarded the title Comte de Palikao in recognition of his services in China. He was best known by that title when he became prime minister of France at the start of the Franco-Prussian war.

The career of Sir Harry Smith Parkes and the opening up of China and the Orient continued to be inextricably linked. After acting as interpreter when Bruce was formally introduced as the first British minister to the court of Peking, Parkes returned to his duties as commissioner at Canton. Later he established consulates at Chinkiang, Kiukiang and Hankow, and orchestrated the opening up of the Yangtse to foreign trade, a move which added 3.5 million dollars a year to Britain's export trade. Admiral Hope ascribed the success of the dangerous and delicate operation to Parkes's 'unwearied zeal and thorough knowledge of the Chinese people and language'. In 1864 he was consul at Shanghai and then diverted his attention and energies to Japan. There he used his diplomatic skills to maintain British interests through years of turmoil and civil war, persuaded the Mikado to embrace western technology – such as a Mint, railways and lighthouses – and mediated in disputes with other nations. During his years in Japan he was attacked by a two-sworded warrior, assaulted by several swordsmen who wounded twelve members of his escort, and was waylaid by two fanatics who cut at him with blades. Parkes, unscathed throughout, captured one of the latter assailants.

In 1883 Parkes was appointed minister to China. After negotiating a successful Anglo-Korean treaty, he returned to Peking in time to encounter a new wave of anti-foreign feeling caused by the French attack on Tonking. The Chinese made no distinction between Britons and French in the ensuing riots, but Parkes kept a cool head and forced the Chinese to withdraw their proclamation to the Chinese population to poison the French where and when they found them. Worn out by overwork, he died in 1885. His death was ascribed to Peking fever.

Emperor Hien-feng died a year after his defeat and the entry of foreigners into Peking. He was succeeded by his five-year-old son T'ung-chi; during the child's minority the regency was held jointly by his mother, the former concubine Tsz'e Hsi, and the Empress Tsz'e An. The end of the war with the barbarians gave them the chance, with British, French and American help, to crush the Taiping rebels. But the power of the emperors never fully recovered, and the 'Unequal Treaties' were a constant reminder of their humiliation. The jealously guarded isolation of the emperors was shattered. Marx wrote: 'Isolation having come to a violent end by the medium of England, dissolution must follow as surely as that of any mummy carefully preserved in a hermetically sealed coffin, whenever it is brought into contact with the open air.'

China was condemned to a century of further revolts, disastrous wars, famine and then permanent revolution. Shanghai and Hong Kong became boom ports. And the fruit of the poppy spread across the globe.

SIXTEEN

The Shortest War – Zanzibar, 1896

'The suspense was intense . . . as the hands of the clock crept on.'

The bombardment of Zanzibar by British warships was probably the shortest war on record, and arguably the most one-sided. Within 40 minutes hundreds of people died under the impact of high explosives. It was little more than mass murder using the latest military technology. Like most such 'policing' actions it was intended to crush any opposition to Britain's imperial might and to protect lucrative trading and political interests. Yet it cannot be dismissed simply as just another cynical massacre, another stain on the reputation of the British Empire. One factor in the events which led to the slaughter was Britain's ultimately high-minded determination to stamp out, by the end of the nineteenth century, the institution of slavery. That does not, however, excuse the actions of one of Britain's most brutal and ruthless commanders.

*   *   *

The island of Zanzibar, like the nearby coastal areas of East Africa, was first settled by Persians and Arabs who intermingled with the native population. It was fertile and well-cultivated land, producing cloves and other tropical spices, using slave labour. It quickly became the hub of the flourishing eastwards slave trade. Other exports from the 'Great Land' – ivory, copal, skins, grain, local cloves and coconut – were sold through the ideally positioned island port, but it was the market in human beings that flourished and allowed the island to prosper. Those slaves snatched from the vast hinterland were dispersed across the Musselman territories bordering the Indian Ocean. Caravans penetrated deep into the mainland bearing both Oriental and European goods – glass, copper wire, cotton, pickaxes and guns – to be exchanged for human cargo.

Through a network of trade routes and local pacts the Sultanate of Zanzibar wielded massive influence across large parts of the African continent – areas that became increasingly coveted by the European powers.

Vasco da Gama took possession of Zanzibar and the neighbouring island of Pemba for Portugal in 1499 and founded an Augustinian convent there. The Portuguese were expelled in 1698 by the Arabs of Muskat and Oman but missionaries, traders and explorers continued to foster foreign interest in the region. Zanzibar and Pemba were under the nominal control of Oman and in the early part of the nineteenth century became the region's trade capital, through which up to sixty thousand slaves were sold annually.

Britain's interests were largely due to Zanzibar's position on the world trade routes. It was roughly equidistant, around 2,400 miles, from the Cape and Bombay (and later the Suez Canal) and was the 'key to the ocean front door' of East Central Africa. Together with Mombasa and the proposed Uganda Railway, it allowed access to the vast, rich interior of the Dark Continent. Zanzibar town contained many British and European residents, as well as Arab and Indian Quarters, a variety of mosques and an English Universities Mission cathedral. There were several fine buildings, towers and libraries and a busy waterfront. The most important houses featured massive brass-studded doors with lintels and doorposts elaborately carved with Arabic and Indian motifs. The central streets were narrow and winding. The harbour was on an open roadstead on the western shore.

In 1858 Seiyd Madjid, Sultan of Zanzibar, declared himself independent of Oman, with the agreement of Britain. In 1873 and 1875 his successor, his brother Barghash, signed treaties with Britain declaring illegal the sea traffic in slaves. In 1886 the Sultan's sovereignty over Zanzibar island, Pemba and a substantial strip of the mainland coastline was recognised by Britain, France and Germany. In return Barghash's successor Khalifa granted to the German East African Company a lease, later bought by the German Government, of the coastline of what later became Tanganyika. A similar lease granted to Britain covered land to the north of the German concession. The transfers antagonised some sections of the local population, especially those rich Arab traders whose family fortunes were built on slaves.

The Germans, somewhat arrogantly, refused to fly the Sultan's flag in their territory. Twice German troops were landed from men-of-war to tear down such flags raised by the outraged populace, while German seamen in landing parties were fired upon. A commentator remarked at the time: 'The actions of the Germans had for some time past been rough and high-handed, showing an utter want of tact in their dealings with the natives, and betraying their ignorance of the Arab nature.' After one clash a German gunboat shelled the town of Tanga, landed an armed force and drove Arab troops into the jungle, killing twenty of them.

The Sultan sent in troops under General Sir Lloyd Mathews, a Briton who had won the trust of coastal natives over fifteen years and who now commanded Zanzibar's military forces, to restore order. This was done but anti-German feeling sparked more conflict at Bagamoyo in which German forces cut down 150 natives. At the same time, at Ketwa, several German officials and their servants were attacked; after killing some of their assailants, they were themselves murdered. Local tribesmen seized the town and re-hoisted the Sultan's flag. British missionaries in the area were left unharmed, confirming that the uprisings were not directed against foreigners or Christians in general, only against the Germans.

In 1888, at the height of the troubles, the Sultan granted the British East African Company exclusive trade rights over a territory of 50,000 square miles. The territory comprised a strip of mainland coastline 10 miles broad and 150 miles long, including the valuable harbour of Mombasa. The Company was required by its Charter to 'discourage and, so far as may be practicable with existing treaties, to abolish any system of slave trade or domestic servitudes within its territories'.

The British and German governments, with the concurrence of the ailing Sultan, agreed to a joint naval blockade against the slave ships and others carrying war contraband. Over 1,400 runaway slaves were discovered in hiding at three English mission stations near Mombasa and set free. France was reluctantly forced to take action against slavers flying their tricolour and to allow British and German warships to search suspect French vessels.

Meanwhile Khalifa was growing increasingly sick in mind as well as in body. He ordered the street executions of four untried murder suspects – the first instances of capital punishment in Zanzibar for twenty-five years. The brutality with which the sentences were carried out aroused much public anger. The Sultan ordered that the spectacle be repeated every day for a week, with the executions of twenty-four men and one woman previously sentenced to life imprisonment. British officials protested against such 'barbarous proceedings' and the prisoners were reprieved.

Khalifa died suddenly in 1890 and his brother Seyyid Ali was elected unanimously by the leading Arabs to succeed him. The new Sultan ordered the release of untried prisoners and suppressed insurgents with the help of British officers. In June he declared Zanzibar a British Protectorate and abolished all slave trading within his dominions, although that did not prohibit slave ownership. The following year a regular government was formed in which a British representative would serve as first minister. The British also had a veto on the succession and appointment of future Sultans. Britain's grip on Zanzibar continued after the death of Seyyid Ali in 1893 and the succession of Hamid-bin-Thwain. But dissent was growing within the Sultan's court, members of which saw their powers taken by British-run government institutions, and their wealth undermined by the suppression of the slave trade. The Sultan was permitted to raise a body of soldiers as a personal bodyguard, which was distinct from the British-controlled Zanzibar army. Numerous complaints were made about their swaggering behaviour.

At 11.40 a.m. on 25 August 1896 Hamid died suddenly and in very suspicious circumstances. He was almost certainly poisoned. His cousin Sayid Khalid, a 'rash and wilful' young man of twenty-five, was ready to act swiftly. It can never be proved conclusively that Khalid murdered his kinsman, but he very quickly took command of 1,200 of the late Sultan's troops and seized the Palace with the obvious intention of proclaiming himself the new Sultan.

General Mathews and Basil Cave, the British diplomatic agent to Zanzibar, had arrived at the palace within ten minutes of the old

Sultan's death and were greeted by Khalid and his retainers a few minutes later. The British were brushed aside in their attempts to persuade Khalid to think carefully about his actions, and the two men retired to the New Custom House as Khalid's supporters, all heavily armed and well prepared, streamed into the Palace Square. Shortly after noon there were 900 men, under the command of the former Sultan's Captain Saleh, lined up in the square behind field guns that had been presented to Zanzibar by the German Emperor. Within a few hours their numbers had swelled to 2,500, with several Maxim guns ready for action. One Zanzibari machine-gunner sat in a chair behind his weapon, which was sighted steadily on the English Club. Their artillery also included a Gatling gun and a seventeenth-century bronze cannon. In the harbour Khalid's men took over the entire Zanzibar Navy − which consisted of the former British frigate *Glasgow*, a creaking, out-dated wooden hulk which had been presented to Zanzibar in 1878.

Mathews and Cave were joined by Zanzibar *askaris*, troops loyal to the government, and 150 naval men from Her Majesty's ships *Philomel* and *Thrush*, providentially anchored in the harbour. The *London Gazette* reported that officers and crew reacted 'with a promptness characteristic of the British Navy'. The shore parties 'landed, ready armed and equipped within 15 minues of the first signs of the disturbance'. The naval contingent was commanded by Captain O'Callaghan, while the askaris were under their own General Raike. All the British women and children were sent to the consulate which was guarded by bluejackets under Lieutenant Watson of *Thrush*. Another British ship, *Sparrow*, entered the harbour and was ordered to anchor alongside *Thrush* at moorings opposite the palace, their guns aimed at its frontage.

During this time many messages were sent from Cave to Khalid warning him against any defiance of the 'protecting power' − Britain − and calling on him to leave the palace, disperse his troops and return to his own house. Khalid replied by giving notice that at precisely 3 p.m. he would proclaim himself Sultan. He was told in turn that such a move would be regarded as an open act of rebellion.

At 2.30 the Arabs in the palace buried the old Sultan and thirty minutes later Khalid, true to his threat, proclaimed himself the new

Sultan and ordered a royal salute from his guns. Cave informed all the other foreign consuls that there was no new sultan and all flags remained at half-mast, save for a large red flag flying from the Palace Square. The news was also telegraphed to the London administration of Lord Salisbury; nothing further could be done until an answer was received.

The night of the 25th passed in uneasy peace. The majority of the womenfolk remained in the consulate building, although several moved to a British steamship and the German consulate. At 10 a.m. another British warship, *Racoon*, arrived and berthed in line with *Thrush* and *Sparrow*, threatening the palace. The day dragged on with no reply from London and both sides remained warily watching each other but doing nothing to provoke bloodshed. At 2 p.m. a steamer signal went up on the clock tower and to British surprise and delight the flagship *St George* joined the armoured armada in the harbour. On board were enough men to protect the town, under the command of Rear-Admiral Harry Rawson, commander-in-chief of the Cape and East Africa station.

Sir Harry Holdsworth Rawson was well known as the successful commander of a punitive expedition against the Arab chief Mourah a year earlier. The son of a Surrey JP, he was born in Lancashire in 1843, educated at Marlborough College, and joined the Navy in 1857. As a midshipman he served with distinction in the Chinese War of 1858–60, commanding 1,300 Chinese troops at the defence of Ningpo and being commended for jumping overboard at night to save the life of a drowning Marine. As a lieutenant he was one of the officers who took the gunboat *Empress* to Japan, after it had been presented by Queen Victoria to the Mikado in 1863 to form the nucleus of his navy. As a captain he was principal transport officer in the 1882 Egyptian Campaign. He proudly wore the silver medal of the Royal Humane Society, awarded for saving life, but when it came to suppressing impudent challenges to the British Crown and its representatives across the globe he was utterly ruthless.

As Rawson was rowed to shore the eagerly awaited reply from London arrived. Broadly, it gave the British authorities on the spot permission to act as they saw fit. Further brief negotiations were held through emissaries but Khalid still refused to leave the palace.

Rawson sent him an ultimatum – haul down the royal flag and leave the palace by nine the following morning, or be blasted out.

During the afternoon all merchant vessels steamed around to the south harbour so that the British frigates would have a clear line of fire. All foreign consuls were informed of the ultimatum and British subjects were instructed to put themselves in places of safety. Most European residents barricaded themselves in their homes to protect their property from looting. Thirty ladies were taken on board *St George* while girls of the Universities' Mission took refuge on the British India Steam Navigation Company's steamship where 'everything was done for their comfort' by Captain J. Stone. The night passed quietly and very slowly.

At 8.00 on the morning of the 27th there was no sign of capitulation from the palace and the signal was hoisted from the flagship to prepare for action. At 8.30 Khalid sent an envoy to Cave to ask what the British intended to do, and the ultimatum was sternly repeated. A Reuters correspondent present wired home: 'The suspense was intense during the last quarter of an hour, as the hands of the clock on the tower gradually crept on towards 9 o'clock.'

Two minutes after the hour *Racoon*, *Thrush* and *Sparrow* opened fire simultaneously. *Thrush* dismounted one of the Arabs' 12-pounders at the first shot. The palace was raked with shellfire, buildings were pounded into dust, and people were buried under falling debris. The palace, together with its adjoining harem, were just yards from the waterfront. It was no great stone citadel, but a flimsy wooden structure made up of spindly balconies and verandahs. The impact of high explosive and shell splinters on up to 3,000 defendants and servants packed inside the palace's narrow alleys and courtyards, and behind hastily erected barricades of baled goods, crates and bags of rubber, is all too easy to imagine. The Reuters man wrote: 'Khalid, in spite of his saying that he would rather die in the Palace than leave it, fled at the first shot with all the leading Arabs, who left their slaves and followers to carry on the fighting. This they did most pluckily, fighting to the last, probably from fear of being cut to pieces by their masters afterwards if they ran away.'

The *Illustrated London News* reported:

Some fighting on land took place at the barriers of the approaches to the palace, the enemy firing on local Askaris from behind the stockades; but the greatest loss of life was in the palace, when it was knocked to pieces and set on fire by the guns of our ships. The palace and harem buildings, with their lofty wooden balconies and open upper floors, would seem likely to be consumed by a conflagration with frightful quickness; and if it be a fact, as it now said, that nearly five hundred men perished in the burning of that flimsy edifice, crowded together without a chance of escape, we can understand how that happened.

In the harbour the rickety, wooden *Glasgow* was sunk at its moorings, having had the effrontery to fire one of her little brass cannon at *St George*. She hoisted the British flag in token of surrender, and British launches were sent to pick up her crew, all of whom survived. Two small steam launches were also swiftly sunk after their Arab occupants aimed ineffectual rifle and musket shots at *Thrush*.

The bombardment ceased at about 9.40 a.m. when the older portion of the palace caught fire, the enemy artillery was silenced and the usurper's flag had been cut down by a stray shot. One British seaman, a petty officer on *Thrush*, was severely wounded in the pathetically unequal artillery duel but later recovered. The casualties on the opposing side topped 500, of whom most died in the scorched wreckage of the old palace, which was totally gutted.

The Times correspondent wrote:

No-one believed for a moment that Said Khalid would be so foolish as to defy us, and the only regret over the occurrence is that he should have escaped . . . and that more of the leading Arabs were not killed instead of their unfortunate slaves. It is acknowledged by everyone that the bombardment was unavoidable owing to Khalid's open defiance, and it is trusted that the Arabs who supported him with their advice, and whose names are believed to be known, will be made to bear the expense of the bombardment and pay claims for loot, which already amounts to three lakhs of rupees.

Khalid and his leading followers took refuge in the German consulate. The German consul refused to hand him over because an extradition treaty with Britain stipulated that a fugitive should not be given up for a political offence. On 2 October Khalid was smuggled on board a war vessel and taken to German territory. Cave protested but Khalid was granted asylum in German East Africa. He was finally apprehended by British forces in 1917. He suffered exile in the Seychelles and on St Helena for his challenge to the might of the British Empire. After several years he was permitted to return to East Africa but never posed a threat again.

Zanzibar's townspeople had largely stayed loyal to the British but there was a great deal of looting in the Indian Quarter. The steamer *Kilwa* brought 150 Sikhs from Mombasa to help restore and maintain law and order. Rawson sailed off to colonial glory, as we shall see.

On the afternoon of the 27th the new Sultan, 45-year-old Hamud-bin-Mahomed, was proclaimed with British support and much reduced power. The *Illustrated London News* described him as 'an elderly gentleman, respected for his prudent and peaceable conduct, acceptable to the better class of the Musselman townsfolk and trusted as a ruler likely to preserve the traditional policy of the realm'.

The British could have abolished the Sultanate and created a Crown Colony but did not want the expense of running a direct administration. They chose instead to keep the Sultan as a figurehead while tightening their own control on all military, financial and executive affairs.

Within months the legal status of slavery was finally abolished in Zanzibar. But this was no consolation to the dead, many of them slaves, buried after the ironclad firepower of the British Empire was turned against the balconies of a ramshackle Muslim palace.

SEVENTEEN

The Benin Massacre, 1897

'Now this is white man's country.'

In 1884 the American Hiram Maxim set up a company to manufacture a battlefield weapon of mass destruction. The machine-gun that bore his name was able to discharge 600 bullets a minute, using energy captured from each successive detonation. The British Army enthusiastically adopted the weapon for use not against massed ranks of troops but to police the Empire's most unruly lands. Its firepower, properly used, showed natives the industrial might that could and would be used against anyone who dared challenge the authority of Queen Victoria.

A punitive expedition against bloodthirsty 'savages' who had murdered white men offered an excellent opportunity to demonstrate the superiority of civilised technology over pagan superstition. The outcome was inevitable because, in the words of a contemporary ditty:

> Whatever happens, we have got
> The Maxim gun, and they have not.

*   *   *

Benin was already well established as an important kingdom when the Portuguese first reached the Nigerian coast in the fourteenth century. A small city-state to the east of Lagos, it dominated the Yoruba country and the land that forms the south-west region of present-day Nigeria. The terrain inland from the coast was flat, criss-crossed by numerous creeks, and covered by dense forest. One European visitor recorded: 'Lagoons traversing the country connect Benin with Lagos, but the waterways are only fit for the passage of native canoes.' Another wrote: 'The climate appeared much healthier than at the coast, as there were numbers of bullocks and goats grazing on the common, and all were fat, well-conditioned, and therefore very different from the poor skinny creatures to be seen in the coast towns.' The subordinate people of Benin were of the Sobo, Mahin and Jekri tribes, the latter being regarded by Europeans as 'the most active and warlike'.

Trade, mainly in slaves, flourished between the Portuguese and the Beni people, adding to the wealth of the nation. The region was fertile and agriculture provided abundant crops of banana, yam and palm oil. Benin City became a true capital of commerce and tribal power, with fine buildings that rivalled any in West Africa. The most coveted western goods bartered for slaves and palm oil were gin, rum, tobacco, cotton goods, silk handkerchiefs and, most prized of all, guns and gunpowder.

The religion was fetishism, or ju-ju, based on the worship of the spirits of ancestors. One missionary publication said it involved 'ridiculous and cruel practices often admitting of human sacrifice'. But enlightened missionaries conceded that 'purer religious elements are found beneath all these superstitions', in particular a firm belief in God, the survival of the soul and the distinction between good and evil. Human sacrifice undoubtedly took place but some visitors confused fetish practices with simple Benin justice. On one occasion, a witness reported, 'Twelve men were taken with 12 cows, goats, sheep and chickens. The animals were killed near the altar, and the blood from them sprinkled on big ivories and brasswork.' The human prisoners, gagged and each held by four men, were led to a well and beheaded. But the human victims turned out to be convicted criminals, and at least some of the ju-ju practices relied on victims who were already condemned.

For two centuries European explorers were drawn to the River Niger and the surrounding lands, most famously Mungo Park's expeditions between 1795 and 1805. By then the power of the Beni Oba, or king, had been undermined by a loose theocracy of fetish priests who increased the practice of wholesale human sacrifice and discouraged contact with Europeans. As tales of barbarity – many of them doubtless exaggerated – spread, trade dwindled and Benin lost much of its influence over the region.

In contrast British influence grew immeasurably during the first half of the nineteenth century, curbing the slave trade in the Niger delta and on the Oil rivers. Britain encouraged the export of palm oil to replace the lost business. John Beecroft was appointed British consul for the Bights of Biafra and Benin in 1849 to further encourage legitimate trade. He used force to halt the slave trade through Lagos and imposed a treaty on the people which included abolition of human sacrifice. The authority of the consul was gradually widened, by negotiation and diktat, to cover most of the nations abutting the Niger. The region was declared a British Protectorate.

Fetish rules, however, continued to interfere with trade. The Oba exacted stiff taxes from Benin merchants trading with the outside world and the fetish priests ruled that certain valuable products should never be touched, including gum copal and palm kernels. Trading licenses were withdrawn with no warning and no explanation. One European complained: 'Of ivory the king claims one half of all that is obtained in his dominions, and declines to trade with the Europeans, keeping all that he receives for the purpose of purchasing slaves. When the supplies are less plentiful than he desires he raids the caravans and seizes their produce.'

In 1886 the Royal Niger Company was authorised by charter to administer the delta and the countryside through which flowed the rivers Niger and Benue. The company set up courts of justice and raised an armed constabulary. It was kept busy. In 1894 the constabulary aided a naval force in capturing the town of Brohemie on the Benin River, the headquarters of the Jekri chief Nana, who traded in slaves in defiance of British orders. Nana fled to Lagos where he gave himself up, claiming that five hundred of his followers had been killed in the operation. Spoils taken from his headquarters included 7,000 cases of Rotterdam gin and 600 cases of tobacco. Nana was tried and deported, and a British military post was established at Sabele.

At Akassa natives objecting to anti-smuggling measures and the high duties imposed on spirits attacked the Company's factory and killed several black employees. According to British reports they celebrated their 'victory' with a cannibal feast on Sacrifice Island. Constabulary and Marines attacked and burned the town of King Koko in retaliation.

This left Benin as the one nation adjoining the Protectorate not to submit to British commercial rule. An article in *The Times* said: 'In other parts of the back country the policy of controlling the more turbulent chiefs and developing direct trade with the interior has been successful, but in the Benin district advance has been rendered impossible by the attitude of the king of Benin and the savage system of pagan theocracy of which he is the representative.'

Benin's virgin forests were especially attractive to the Company, which was deeply involved in the booming rubber trade. They had a champion in the Protectorate's governor, Ralph Moor, a former inspector in the Royal Irish Constabulary. He argued long and eloquently that Benin should be opened up to trade, by force if necessary. Stories of cannibalism and other horrors helped in the propaganda, although it is undisputed that Benin was by then the centre of the illicit slave trade. The *Annual Register* for 1896 noted tersely: 'The tyrant of Benin, on the border of the protectorate, was causing obstructions to British trade, and repelled all friendly negotiations. Great cruelties were practised by this King, including human sacrifices.'

The 'tyrant' was forty-year-old Oba Overami, a pragmatist caught between the competing demands of the British and his fetish priests, and a patriot determined to keep his kingdom independent. The long-time trader D.P. Bleasby described him: 'As to the appearance of the King, he is, for a negro, a very pleasant-faced man. His eyes, though rather small, have a laughing expression. He has a short, curly beard, and altogether his face shows remarkable intelligence.' Bleasby said that he believed Overami would not authorise the execution of white prisoners but added that as the king was confined to his royal compound he did not always know what his chiefs were doing. He continued: 'There is in Benin no regular army. The inhabitants are natural huntsmen and every man, when he can raise the money, buys a flintlock gun. That is about the first thing he does. It is understood that every man in the country is the king's slave and under his orders, so that they would have to come to his aid when he commanded.'

British merchants who claimed to have visited Benin fed the public appetite for horror stories about the 'cannibal kingdom'. James Pinnock, who traded mainly from Sierra Leone, described a visit in which he saw 'a large number of men all handcuffed and chained to a longitudinal pole running around the building, standing about three feet from the ground, all with their ears cut off with a razor'. Another traveller, T.B. Auchterlonie, said that when he and his party approached the city they walked through a lane of large trees with between thirty and forty dead bodies on each side in all stages of decomposition, 'the idea being to impress those approaching the town with the power of the King'. He added: 'After passing the lane of horrors the approach to the city is across common, covered with good grass, and practically free of all trees or brush, but thickly strewn with the skulls and bones of sacrificed human beings.'

In 1892 Overami had signed a treaty agreeing to the abolition of both the slave trade and human sacrifice, but it was clear that he could not implement it even if he wished to. Negotiations with an increasingly exasperated Moor dragged on inconclusively, until in 1896 Moor returned to Britain on home leave. The matter was left in the hands of his eager subordinate Lieutenant James Phillips, who became Acting Consul General.

Phillips was a young man in a hurry. He was educated at Uppingham and Trinity College, Cambridge, where he graduated in 1886. He was appointed Sheriff of the Gold Coast and in charge of prisons in 1891, and an Acting Queen's advocate in 1892. Phillips apparently hoped to make his mark while his superior was away and opened his own 'goodwill' negotiations with the Oba through emissaries. Privately he wired the Foreign Office asking for permission, which was not forthcoming, to 'depose and remove the King of Benin'. He sent a message to the Oba announcing an impending visit to his kingdom. It would be an unarmed, he said, and peaceful mission, to discuss trade, not war.

Without waiting for a reply, Phillips left the coast for Benin City via Sapele on 2 January 1897. With him went Deputy Commissioner

Major P.W.G. Copeland-Crawford, Captain Alan Boisragon, commandant of the Niger Coast Protectorate Constabulary, Captain A.J. Malings, wing officer of the same force, Robert Locke and Kenneth Campbell of the Consular staff, medical officer Dr R.H. Elliott, two civilian trading agents, Powis and Gordon, and around 250 native porters, servants and guides, all accompanied by a drum and pipe band.

Confusion still surrounds the purpose of Phillips' mission and the reason why he chose to take such large numbers with him. A column of that size suggested military intent, even though its European members were armed only with revolvers – a standard item of bush traveller's attire. The *Daily News* later commented: 'One of the strangest circumstances surrounding this unlucky enterprise, and one which will have to be fully explained, is why the march was made in the Consul-General's absence on leave.' If the expedition was meant to convey the impression of peace, then the fewer people the better – on previous occasions small numbers of British officers had been allowed to enter Benin City without any difficulty or danger. If it was meant to demonstrate the potential power of the British Empire, it should have been armed to the teeth. Instead it was strong in numbers but almost defenceless in arms. The newspaper said: 'The most mysterious part of the whole story is that, whereas the number of Mr Phillips' band was large enough to excite the suspicions and arouse the hostility of the natives, they were not prepared to resist anything like an organised attack. Nine or ten official whites and two or three hundred native followers provoked assault without inspiring alarm.'

Phillips' timing was bad, too, as his arrival in Beni territory coincided with a religious festival. The Oba, faced by what he took to be an invasion force, called a national emergency which brought tribesmen from all corners of his kingdom. The outcome was, to modern eyes, horribly predictable. It was, however, an enormous shock to a generation weaned on the notion of imperial invincibility.

On 12 January *The Times* reported: 'The Press Association states that alarming news reached the Foreign Office yesterday from the West Coast of Africa, to the effect that a party of British officials had been captured and possibly murdered in Benin City.' It proved to be a laconic understatement.

* * *

Phillips and his column were ferried by steamer 25 miles up-river, then took boats up the Gwato Creek. Men and supplies were landed on the riverbank and set off on foot towards Benin City, about 25 miles away, on 4 January. By the next day they had travelled half the distance and, according to later reports, 'were received in every town and village which they passed on their way to Benin with friendly greetings from the people and kindly messages from the King himself'. They marched through swampy forest in blistering heat. After stopping to confer with envoys from the Oba the party pushed on. Most of the revolvers were locked up in boxes carried by native porters. Commissioner Locke later told reporters:

> As soon as we had passed a fallen tree the natives, who were in ambush, fell upon us. Some were armed with long Danish guns and others with hatchets. A place had been cleared in the bush, and the men with guns were lying down with the muzzles of their long flintlocks nearly touching the path. They fired upon the white men indiscriminately.

Major Copeland-Crawford, being carried in a chair, was the first to be hit and wounded. Phillips, Dr Elliott and Captain Maling fell dead on the spot. Locke was luckier – he had been in the leading party with them but had fallen behind when he stopped to tie a bootlace. Copeland-Crawford was picked up by Locke and Captain Boisragon amid a shower of musket balls fired by mostly unseen attackers. The major was wounded again, this time fatally. Before he died he urged his comrades to leave him and save themselves. Powis, who spoke the Benin language, called out to the hidden warriors, trying to pacify them, but before he could say more than a few words he and Gordon were shot dead. Locke and Boisragon, both wounded, crawled into the bush and hid themselves. The bodies of the white men that they left behind were all decapitated in the ensuing blood frenzy.

A vanguard of natives had already been butchered, unknown to the main party, and the Beni attackers continued to slaughter the rest of the native porters. All but seven of them died. One of the survivors was a servant of Mr Powis, who found his master's headless body on the track before escaping to take the news back to the coast. Campbell was captured and taken to the city. The Oba refused to allow him to be brought within its boundary and he was taken to an adjacent village where he was beheaded. Phillips' finger rings were sent back to Overami, an act taken to indicate defiance of the British Crown.

Locke and Boisragon, a tough veteran of the Royal Irish Regiment who had seen action on the Nile and the Gold Coast, wandered for five days in the swamp-ridden bush, aided by Copeland-Crawford's dropped compass. They survived by eating cassava leaves. The only water they could drink was dew. Locke was still armed with a revolver and shot several natives during their odyssey. Boisragon was again wounded while beating off a band of natives with a stick. Eventually, half delirious and dressed in bloody rags, they reached a Beni village whose inhabitants treated them kindly. They were ferried down the creek in a covered canoe and delivered safely to the consulate, which was installed on a floating hulk at Sapelle.

Locke had four wounds, two in his right arm, one in the forearm and one in the abdomen. Despite their deprivations both men were reported to be in 'fairly good health'. Locke was sent home aboard the steamer *Volta* to recover fully. Boisragon sent his wife a telegram with just one word: 'SAVED.'

In Britain public opinion was inflamed. Reuter's Special Service reported: 'The King of Benin was carrying out an annual butchery of slaves, and did not want to see the white men, who had been received at Gwato with a friendly welcome, and who, under the impression that matters were all right, had proceeded on their journey. They simply intended to remonstrate with the King against these fearful butcheries.' The MP and historian Justin McCarthy wrote:

The greatest devotee of peace could hardly expect that the English Government would take no steps to avenge the deeds of the King of Benin. It seems impossible to believe that there was not deliberate treachery on his part; for no company of sane Europeans experienced in the ways of that region of Africa would have ventured on an unarmed movement to the city of Benin without some assurance of peaceful welcome from the sovereign. The bravest men do not go out to die for no purpose whatever, and these men who died so bravely must have set out with some assurance that their peaceful offers were to be met in a peaceful way. [It was] absolutely essential that the Imperial Government should take the quickest and the sternest measures to punish the King of Benin for a course of treachery and murder which apparently had not all the sympathy of even his own subjects.

The Times thundered:

The power of the fetish customs is so great that until it has been abolished it is believed that trade with Benin cannot materially be advanced. The rule of the king is one of terror. The most barbarous customs prevail, and the people are brutalized by the habits of human sacrifice, torture and cannibalism . . . These conditions, apart from the cruelty and savagery of his rule, naturally dispose the surrounding tribes to view without displeasure any measures which may tend to control his power and to enable them to pursue their profitable avocations of peace. His country is the most barbarous spot of the whole Protectorate, and the outrage which he has not feared to commit upon the British expedition renders inevitable the speedy end of a system which has been allowed to endure too long. The King of Benin must now share the fate of Nana, Ja-Ja, and other savage potentates who have mistaken the patience of the British Government for weakness which could with impunity be defied, and when his stronghold of brutality has been destroyed British authority will most effectively be vindicated by the opening of an important district to civilised intercourse.

Lord Salisbury, after meeting with Moor, immediately authorised a punitive expedition against the Oba. Nine men-of-war were summoned by telegraph from their African and Mediterranean stations. West Indian troops were brought by yacht from their quarters in Sierra Leone. The cruisers *Theseus* and *Forte* were ordered to the region. The former carried 12 guns with a complement of 544 officers and men under Captain Charles Campbell. The latter carried 10 guns and a complement of 318 under Captain R.F.O. Foote. At a press conference before embarking for the Niger, Moor said that the King of Benin was certainly a barbarian who knew little, if anything, of Britain. It was within the bounds of possibility that he would, when in a frenzy worked up by the priests, encourage his people to any act of massacre. He said he was confident that the forthcoming expedition would achieve its objects and 'lead to the completion of the administration in the Niger Protectorate'.

At Lagos, Moor was joined by Rear-Admiral Sir Harry Rawson, the commander-in-chief of the Good Hope station, who took charge of the expedition. Just a few months earlier Rawson, as we have seen, supervised the bombardment of Zanzibar. He reckoned on another pushover. His 500-strong naval brigade, comprising Marines and landing parties from the warships, was backed by 500 men of the Niger Coast Constabulary under Lieutenant-Colonel Bruce Hamilton of the East Yorkshire Regiment. A detachment of Hausa troops and local levies brought the entire force to be landed to 1,400 men. They were to be supported by 1,700 native bearers brought from Sierra Leone, Bonny and other places along the Gold Coast. The warships included Rawson's flagship *St George* and the cruiser *Philomel*, which had also taken part in the pounding of Zanzibar. A Liverpool company lent the expeditionary force the twin-screw, light-draught steel steamer *Kwarra*, which was ideal for navigating the intricate and shallow creeks up to Gwato.

Rawson had no shortage of advice. Sir Alfred Jephson, a veteran of the Nana expedition who had toured Benin lands, said:

Owing to the massacre the King will know that an expedition will be sent against him and he will strain every nerve to put his place into a state of defence. I do not anticipate that there will be any great difficulty in getting at him. The principal difficulty will be the want of roads and the large amount of bush fighting involved. It has always been recognized that eventually Benin City must be taken and trade allowed to flow towards the sea, but it was clearly understood that the King could not be smashed without the employment of a properly prepared force. There can be no doubt that he has plenty of weapons of various sorts. We found that Nana had a quick-firing gun, and no doubt the King of Benin has plenty of arms, good, bad or indifferent.

A correspondent signing himself 'Old Calabar' warned:

The natives of the Bight of Benin have been in trading communications with Europeans for a number of years, and a large number of, comparatively speaking, modern weapons have been sold to them – ten years ago Sniders were quite common articles of commerce – so that our troops must not expect to have only the Birmingham-made flintlock gun to fight against.

The ill-fated Phillips expedition had taken a circuitous route from Sapele, but this time local traders advised a forced march overland to Benin City, a route only 18 miles long as the crow flies. What roads there were consisted entirely of forest tracks leading over a soil of red clay. The thick brush interspersed with jungle and swampland made it ideal territory for ambush.

Rawson's force sailed up the Benin River in hired steamers on 10 February and travelled in relative comfort along 55 miles of winding creeks and tributaries. A correspondent aboard one of the steamships wrote:

The river was at places very narrow and, as the ships steamed along, the trees on either side could almost be touched. The luxuriant vegetation, the huge trees, the thick foliage, and the sharp bends of the river, all combined to make one of the most entrancing scenes that the eyes of man have ever beheld. Animal life was not wanting, the birds were singing on every branch, the alligators and crocodiles were basking in the sun on the low river banks, hundreds of flies darted about, and lastly, on board the steamer lived a pet monkey, which kept up a continued squirming and squeaking in his pleasure or his disgust at his home being invaded by so many human beings.

They landed at Warrigi on the following morning and marched directly to Siri, about 7 miles away, to make camp. The writer continued: 'For some time after our start the journey seemed exactly like a stroll in the early morning along an English country lane, but affairs were soon to wear a different aspect; the sun came up and temperatures quickly reached 130 degrees in the shade, and all began to gasp for breath, many men falling out.'

On the 12th a naval unit and Hausa troops under Lieutenant-Colonel Hamilton attacked and occupied Ologbo, a riverside village which Rawson intended to use as a base-camp, after a short skirmish in which one officer and three native troops were wounded. A Reuters correspondent reported that Maxims on board the launch *Primrose* swept the bush before the troops landed and 'the enemy fought stubbornly, firing repeated volleys, which were effectively returned'. The enemy occupied the perimeter of a clearing 'firing, shouting and playing tomtoms'. Skirmishers lay down and fired volley after volley for over an hour until the tribesmen pulled back. The attacking force followed closely behind and the enemy were driven on to the village, which was then shelled remorselessly, rushed and captured. Thirty enemy bodies were found next day, which must have been only a portion of their casualties.

Two smaller naval units attacked and took Gwato and Sapoba with heavier British losses. At Sapoba the commander, Lieutenant C.E. Pritchard, was shot dead and Private Colin Mill of Plymouth died of sunstroke. These early skirmishes showed that the battle for Benin was not going to be a pushover. The Oba's generals were adopting classic African tactics against a European force – allow them to move deeper and deeper into the disputed territory before trying to cut off supply lines. The population of Benin was hostile to the invaders and so was the blisteringly hot and humid terrain. The greatest difficulty faced by Rawson was the provision and transport of water for such large numbers of men. Anything that could hold water was requisitioned, including large, basket-covered glass demi-johns. Hundreds of benzine oilcans, each holding four gallons, had been supplied. But Rawson still found it necessary to ration officers and men to two quarts per day on the march.

The Reuters man wired home: 'At Abou, which was reached about 11 a.m., a party of black troops, with two Maxims, one seven-pounder, and one rocket tube, supported by a party of bluejackets, rushed the enemy, after firing volleys into the bush for nearly an hour. The first village on the road to Benin was shelled and taken.'

The British troops placed great reliance on their new machine-guns. Naval surgeon Felix Roth described one action: 'We shelled the village, and cleared it of the natives. As the launch and surf-boats grounded, we jumped into the water . . . at once placed our Maxims and guns in position, firing so as to clear the bush where the natives might be hiding.' He noted 'no white men were wounded, we all got off scot-free,' adding: 'Our black troops, with the scouts in front and a few Maxims, do all the fighting.'

Rawson decided to keep garrisons at the captured towns and split his attack force in two. The native Scouts and Protectorate troops were to spearhead the advance on Benin City. The naval brigade columns would follow later. The black troops would again bear the brunt of the casualties and test the enemy's defences. In fact both columns were to face a gruelling march along narrow tracks, in sweltering heat, and under almost constant sniping and regular ambush.

British and Hausa troops in West Africa were well aware of the perils of bush-fighting, following early campaigns against the Ashanti and other impressive foes. Military historian Lawrence James explained the tactics that had been developed by the time of the march on Benin City:

The officers in command relied on the drill and training of their men. As it moved through the bush, the column was in three sections . . . The first was the advance guard which was followed by one and a half companies (150 men) with a Maxim gun and seven-pounder, both dismantled and carried in pieces on the heads of porters. The rearguard comprised fifty men, who protected the remaining porters with their loads of ammunition, food and medical supplies. When the trackway was narrow, the whole column proceeded in single file and was at its most vulnerable. To meet ambush in these conditions, a special drill had been devised by which the front rank halted, turned right and fired volleys into the bush at the commands of an officer, and the second rank turned leftwards and did likewise. Where the bush was less dense, it was possible to send out flanking parties which fanned out ahead to draw fire or give warning of an ambush.

Rawson's columns faced additional horrors. Their path was marked by hundreds of corpses, men and women disembowelled on the orders of the fetish priests to appease the Beni gods and encourage them to drive back the invaders. Captain Boisragon, who accompanied the expedition but was too ill to fight, recorded: 'Everywhere sacrificial trees on which were corpses of the latest victims.' Grisly remains were spread-eagled on lattices tied to the tree-tops and dangled by their ankles from plaited ropes. Another witness said: 'We came to a human sacrifice, lying in the path, a poor native female slave who had a piece of stick tied across her mouth, and her entrails cut out. As we proceeded these sights became quite common, so I shall forbear from remarking on them.'

The correspondent for the *Illustrated London News* described the column's tense progress through thick bush and jungle:

The path now got much narrower, and on account of the trunks of trees which barred the way our progress was necessarily very slow. Every now and then a halt had to be made, and rounds of Maxims and volleys to be fired, to prevent the enemy, who were hovering all around, closing on us, and thus doing damage with their rain of bullets and slugs . . .

The advance party fired all the way, to clear the enemy out of the bush, and drive them on. At every clearing, evidences of their proximity were found in the fires which had hardly burnt out and the gourds and other things left behind in their haste . . . The camp was lined and volleys were fired at the enemy, who could be seen running from tree to tree all around. More shots were fired, but the natives, warned to keep out of the way of our volleys, did not take aim, so the slugs that reached us were nearly all spent, and only inflicted trivial wounds.

The march was punctuated by both tragedy and lucky escapes. Sydney Ansell, the torpedo-instructor on the *St George*, who was in charge of the demolition parties clearing obstructions, was shot three times in the chest and died. He was buried in a clearing by his crew-mates. A consular official was surprised by a native who jumped out from behind a tree and fired at him, the muzzle of his gun just inches from his face. According to an observer, 'The rush of air bowled him completely over, but he suffered no damage, his helmet only being blown to atoms.'

Rawson's ninth telegram of the expedition said simply: 'Advanced from Ologbo 14th in two columns, joining up on 16th. Benin city taken afternoon 18th. Distant 24 miles. Running fight entire route. Great difficulty with carriers getting up water. Considerable resistance taking city. Entire force brought up numbers 540 men.'

The 18th saw an epic eight-hour running battle which was described in greater detail by Reuters:

We left Awakon with our whole force at 6 o'clock in the morning of the 18th inst. and came to a clearing in the bush near Benin city at 1 in the afternoon. All the way volleys were fired at us from right and left. At one place a stockade containing a large gun was blown up with guncotton.

When we reached the clearing the enemy gave considerable trouble, but after firing rockets and seven-pounders in the direction of the city and again advancing we suddenly emerged from the bush into the main thoroughfare. Here we met with a most determined resistance from the enemy, who were massed in the thoroughfare in front and also fired upon us from the thick bush on the opposite side and from behind the trees. There is no doubt they used repeating rifles. They then charged the road, which was flanked on each side by dense bush.

Our division opened out into skirmishing order. The

Maxims soon disposed of the enemy in front, but a harassing fire was kept up on the right flank in spite of the volleys we discharged in that direction. Two hundred yards from the King's compound, or clearing, the enemy fired a big gun, after which our troops charged with a cheer and we met with no further opposition.

Another reporter described the same action: 'About two hundred of the enemy were seen, and many were shot down, but the wounded and the bodies of the killed were in nearly every case dragged into the bush and carried off. The war-rockets and the Maxims did their work well, and the force rushing on, headed by the Admiral, captured the principal compounds.'

Four whites were killed in that action, including naval surgeon C.J. Fyfe of *St George*, who was shot while tending the wounded. Sixteen were injured. A black sergeant, one scout and one carrier were also killed. Three protectorate soldiers, a messenger, three carriers and a guide, all black, were wounded. No estimate is given for enemy casualties. Reuters continued: 'All the troops, both white and black, behaved splendidly. They had to keep up a continual running fight for eight hours in the tropical heat and to undergo what is one of the most demoralizing forms of warfare – namely bush-fighting.'

The Oba, his chiefs and the fetish priests fled the city, leaving behind much grisly evidence which helped to feed the British propaganda machine and to justify the terrible revenge inflicted by machine-guns on the people of Benin. On the principal sacrificial tree facing the main gate of the king's compound were two crucified bodies. Rawson's telegram reported: 'City now deserted. Neither King nor Ju-ju men captured. A few natives from Phillips' party have come in from the bush. Dreadfully mutilated human sacrifices met en route and in city, crucifixions and mutilations. Ju-ju houses, compounds surrounding them, reek with human blood. Several deep holes in compounds filled with corpses.' Another witness recorded that the city was 'full of dead men's bones and all uncleanness'. The Reuters report said: 'The whole town reeks of human blood, and the bodies of many sacrificed and crucified human beings have been found about the place. This afternoon the forces have been occupied in the destruction of 'crucifixion trees' and Ju-ju houses, thereby breaking the power of the fetish priests.' The *Illustrated London News* report said: 'Benin is indeed a city of blood, each compound having its pit full of dead and dying; human sacrifices were strewn about on every hand, hardly a thing was without a red stain . . .' In the king's palaver house troops found possessions taken from the whites in Phillips' party – their sporting guns, helmet cases and cameras, together with merchandise brought by traders.

On the morning of the 19th a large party was sent out to procure water. They found a stream with good, fresh drinking water. About 3 miles from the city walls, they heard moaning; drawn to investigate they found a servant boy from Phillips' party still alive in a well piled high with dead.

Benin city was laid out in a uniform pattern in the shape of a cross with two principal roads, each 100 feet wide, crossing each other. Many of the mud-brick houses had been built by the Portuguese, although some were derelict. The king's compound was enclosed by strong mud walls 7 feet high and the royal throne was carved from red clay. Almost every house in the city had a more modest compound, at one end of which was a raised platform for fetish worship, decked out with carved figures of ivory, brass and bronze. Outside the city walls was a large clearing carpeted in human bones. This was where the dead were routinely brought and left on the ground to decompose in the sun, 'tainting the air for miles around, and making one of the most horrible sights that has ever been seen'.

The first task of the troops was to dismantle the palace and loot its treasures. The booty included 900 bronzes depicting important events in the history of the Benin people and quantities of carved ivory. Ju-ju houses were torched and on the third day of occupation the fires got out of control and began to engulf the entire city and the billets of the troops. *The Times* reported:

No-one was injured, this being chiefly due to the energetic action which was promptly taken by both officers and men, but a considerable quantity of personal effects, as well as provisions, was lost. The wounded in the hospital had a narrow escape. There were barely five minutes available in which to secure their safety, but the rescuers worked with a will and all were successfully removed from the hospital before it was seized by the flames.

The fire raged for two hours before it was brought under control. The arms and ammunition were saved, but large numbers of valuable ivory tusks and other curios stored in the palaver house were destroyed. So too were most of the troops' personal possessions and any clothing they were not actually wearing.

Rawson, his staff and the naval brigade returned to their ships. Messengers came in from the fugitive Oba to 'beg the white man' for clemency. On 25 February seven chiefs arrived to ask that a palaver with Moor be put off for a week. The consul-general released four of the chiefs to convey his agreement to the Oba, the remainder being detained as hostages.

British and Protectorate troops spent six months scouring the countryside for the Oba, burning villages as they went, but it was not until August that the king was cornered and brought back to his ruined city. Overami suffered ritual humiliation in front of an immense throng of his people. He was forced to kneel in front of the British Military Resident and eat dirt. With two other chiefs he had to make obeisance three times, grinding his forehead into the dust, and was told he had been deposed. Several weeks later he and his chiefs faced a show trial orchestrated by Moor. The consul-general told him: 'Now this is white man's country. There is only one king in this country, and that is the white man.'

*   *   *

Queen Victoria sent a telegram congratulating the victors. The newspapers echoed her praise. One said: 'The blood of our countrymen has been avenged, and a system of barbarism rendered hideous by the most savage, horrible and bloodthirsty customs that even Africa can show has been effectively broken up.' Overami's life was spared and he was exiled to Calabar, but six of his chiefs were condemned to death. Sentence was swiftly carried out on five of them. The sixth, Ologbosheri, remained at large and for two years waged a guerrilla war against the British until he too was captured and hanged.

Overami was replaced as Oba by a British puppet, Oba Seki, who controlled villages in rubber-producing areas. Much of that forest land was quickly sold to European firms supplying rubber to the empire. A council of chiefs was established under the direction of a British Resident to administer the territory. After a further minor expedition in 1899 Benin was completely pacified and added to the Niger Protectorate. The trade in indiarubber multiplied many times over and by the turn of the century the land was so civilised to the white man's taste that several golf links were created.

Rawson went home to a hero's welcome and an extra clasp for his KCB. He had pacified a bloody kingdom for the loss of just 11 men killed in the naval brigade, 5 dead from sunstroke, and 45 wounded. Other casualties in the ranks of the black Protectorate troops were not reported. A remarkable feature of this short expedition was that no troops in the field died from malaria and other fevers endemic in the region, although scores began to show the wasting symptoms during the march. On the voyage home 7 officers and 70 men did contract the fever, and Sergeant M'Kettrick died, while Sergeant Bruce died of 'heat apoplexy'.

The number of Benin casualties can only be guessed at. In the fighting along the road to Benin machine-guns constantly raked villages and forest and those hit would generally lie undiscovered where they fell or crawled deeper into the bush to die. A much smaller policing operation in 1898 left 150 natives dead. It would be a fair guess to suggest that Rawson's men and machine-guns accounted for ten times that number or more.

Rawson commanded the Channel Squadron from 1898 to 1901 and was Governor of New South Wales from 1902 to 1909, his term being lengthened by a year owing to his popularity. He returned to London to preside over the Interview Committee for Naval Cadets, a role model for young men. In November 1910 he died, aged sixty-seven, after an operation. Moor committed suicide in Barnes in September 1909. He drank potassium cyanide bought to kill wasps in his garden.

The Protectorate saw several further wars before it was truly colonialised. At the same time as the Benin expedition the Royal Niger Company also invaded the Islamic state of Nupe in the north. Just 30 officers and 50 Hausa troops of the Royal Niger Constabulary defeated a force of 3,000 at Bida using artillery and the murderous Maxim guns. They went on to subdue the neighbouring land of Borin. Troops were sent to wipe out slave-traders at Kano in 1903 and Sokoto later the same year. In 1906 a small force of the Northern Nigerian Regiment was defeated at Satiru by rebels whose leader claimed to be the Mahdi. The rebels were wiped out by artillery and machine-guns in an action in which the British suffered no losses – but as many as 2,000 rebels were killed.

The 900 looted Benin bronzes, some caked with dried animal and human blood, were auctioned by the Admiralty to offset some of the costs of the expedition. Most were bought by German museums, but around fifty went to the British Museum where they are still displayed on the hall-landing of the main staircase. Numerous attempts by successive Nigerian governments to recover them for their nation have been rejected.

Overami died, still a prisoner in Calabar, in January 1914. Over the next four years at least some of the men who had so successfully deployed machine-guns against his followers would see their own sons cut down in the same way in the muddy fields of another continent.

EIGHTEEN

The Tirah Campaign, 1897–8

'Stiff climb, eh, Mackie?'

The north-west frontier held a particular glamour for armchair generals and schoolboys fed on a regular diet of Boy's Own stories of adventure in the rugged mountains, of gallantry against a cruel foe, of songs sung round campfires and medals won by the chestful. But for the real veterans the strips of coloured ribbon did not ease the loss of comrades who never came home, nor remove the stain of barbarous warfare in which the British Empire, at the height of its power, behaved like brigands and arsonists in a land which was not their own.

* * *

Afghanistan is a cruel, inhospitable country of savage mountains and arid plains where hardly a tree grows. Its people were hard, proud and independent, quick to avenge the mildest slight with a blood feud. The great beauty of the high country was matched by the terror of travellers lost inside its vastness. But to the Victorian Raj the value of Afghanistan was immense. Its mountains provided a natural battlement protecting India from an avaricious Russia. Invaders from the north and west could only negotiate a few narrow passes through the ice-covered barrier of the Hindu Kush.

British attempts to dominate and occupy the land were met with ferocious resistance and fanatical uprisings. The almost continual military and diplomatic skirmishing which spanned most of the nineteenth century was known as the 'Great Game', and Britain twice invaded Afghanistan with bloody consequences on both sides. The north-west frontier inspired Kipling and generations of adventurers, and the battle honours won there adorn most old regimental museums.

The British referred to the tribesmen who lived on the Indian side of the Afghan border as 'Pathans' but there was little ethnic distinction on either side of it. Herodotus referred to them as subjects of Darius the Great, men who wore 'cloaks of skin and carried the bows of their country and the dagger'. In the fourteenth century the Arab traveller Ibn Batuta wrote: 'They hold mountains and defiles and possess considerable strength and are mostly highwaymen.' The British observer Mountstuart Elphinstone described them as a people 'whose vices are revenge, envy, avarice, rapacity and obstinacy; on the other hand they are fond of liberty, faithful to their friends, kind to their dependents, hospitable, brave, hardy, frugal, laborious and prudent'. Dr Hugh Luard said of some Afridi elders: 'They were grim, earnest serious men, in dirty clothes, but with piercing blue eyes, firm strong mouths, strength of character firmly marked on their weather-beaten faces. It is absurd to call them savages.' More ominously Lady Sale wrote in 1842: 'Here every man is born a soldier, every child has his knife, every Afghan is armed complete with some three or four of these knives of different sizes, pistols and a jesail.' The latter, she said, was a flintlock rifle much superior to the British muskets, having a longer range.

Although friendships and alliances were formed with the British, most Afghans regarded the foreigners as infidels and any period of peace was uneasy and short-lived. A major problem was defining the southern boundary of Afghanistan with India. Much of the territory was barely explored, and was occupied by warlike tribes who laughed at the idea of owing allegiance either to the rulers in Afghanistan or to those in British India. In 1893 Sir Mortimer Durand and the Amir of Afghanistan agreed a line on the notional map which passed through areas that were completely unmapped. Sir Ambrose Dundas said: 'It is a vague sort of line, sometimes following watershed, and sometimes not. There is the same mountainous tangle of country on both sides of it, and nowhere is there anything artificial or natural to tell you when you have reached it.' Another man who knew the country better said maps were no use anyway and when shown one said: 'It is all wrong. I know, I have been in those places. Your maps are guesswork.'

Bordering Khyber, on the British side of the invisible line, was Tirah, the land of the Afridis. The tribesmen levied tolls on the Khyber Pass and Elphinstone described them as 'the greatest robbers among the Afghans'. Their homeland was almost completely unknown to foreigners, being within what the Afridis themselves called the 'Purdah nashin' – 'concealed behind the curtain'. The 'curtain' was the range of high mountains which ringed it on all sides. Tirah was closed to all foreigners and the Afridis maintained an isolation which was jealously guarded. One tribesman told a later traveller that foreigners were only admitted as prisoners. Colonel Sir Robert Wharburton, who made friends with many Afridis during eighteen years on the frontier, wrote:

> The Afridi lad from his earliest childhood is taught by the circumstances of his existence and life to distrust all mankind: and very often his near relations, heirs to his small plot of land by right of inheritance, are his deadliest enemies. Distrust of all mankind and readiness to strike the first blow for the safety of his own life have therefore become the maxims of the Afridi. If you can overcome this distrust, be kind in words to him, he will put up with any punishment you like to give him except abuse.

Winston Churchill, then the correspondent for the *Daily Telegraph*, described the Afridis as 'amongst the most miserable and brutal creatures of the earth . . . Their intelligence only enables them to be more cruel, more dangerous, more destructive than wild beasts.' Generally the Indian Government left the Afridis alone and the furthest any expedition went was the Samana Range, which guarded the southern side of the Afridis' summer home, the Tirah Maiden. A valley covering some 900 square miles, this was the only part of the land fertile enough to sustain the tribesmen's flocks.

The demarcation of the Durand Line caused unrest all along the Afghan border. In 1897 tribes from Malakand to Tirah answered a call from the mullahs to revolt in a *jihad* or holy war against the British. Foremost among them was Saidullah of Swat, known to the British as the 'Mad Mullah'. Churchill compared him to the medieval monk who preached the First Crusade: 'Civilisation is face to face with militant Mohammedanism. What Peter the Hermit was to the regular bishops and cardinals of the Church, the Mad Mullah has been to the ordinary priesthood of the Afghan border.'

It is likely that the Amir of Afghanistan, Abdurrahman Khan, encouraged the unrest because he regretted the extra influence granted to the British by the Durand Line. Lieutenant T.P. Dowdall wrote:

> Three months ago the Amir sent agents all over Afghanistan telling all to be ready for the *jihad*. This was all in the papers but of course it never occurred to anyone that it could be directed against us, though there is absolutely no-one else against whom he could possibly proclaim a *jihad*. He then sold 80,000 rifles (made in Cabul under English supervision) to the frontier tribes at 2/6 each . . . he could afford this as we give him a large subsidy yearly to insure his friendship.

Whether such widespread suspicions were well founded or not, the Amir gave no further help to the rebel tribes.

Open warfare broke out in the Tochi valley in June 1897 when the commander of a small party escorting a British agent was killed in an ambush. A field force under Major-General G. Corrie Bird occupied the valley, meeting little resistance. Much more serious was an attack later that month on forts in the Swat valley. In a counter-action at Chakdara 60 Bengal Lancers and 180 Sikhs of the 45th killed over 2,000 tribesmen for the loss of five dead. The tribesmen from then on avoided committing large numbers in conventional battles. A punitive expedition under Brigadier-General Sir Binden Blood inflicted more bloodshed on the Swat tribes. In August Shabkadr Fort was attacked by the Mohmands but the police garrison held out until a relief column arrived a month later.

In Kohat district on the borders of Tirah the Afridis and their neighbours the Orakzais joined forces and closed the crucial Khyber Pass. Then, in September, they attacked the much-resented British strongholds built earlier in the decade along the Samana Ridge. The small Saragarhi fort, held by just twenty-one men of the 36th Sikhs, was wiped out. The cleric Dr Theodore Pennell, who was camped on the range and who had read the Sunday service before the attack, watched from far away: 'The Sikhs knew that the Pathans would give them no quarter, so they prepared to sell their lives dearly. The Afridis worked nearer and nearer, and many of the brave defenders fell . . . So the noble garrison fell at their posts to a man.' The Afridis admiringly told of one Sikh who, refusing to run or surrender, killed twenty of them while defending the guardhouse and only perished when the building was burnt down around him. The dying hero, whose name was never known, had his throat cut. Two other forts, Lockhart and Gulistan, held out until relieved. *The Times* roared:

> With minds inflamed by the preachings of their mullahs, the Afridis recklessly broke a faith they had kept for 16 years, and, throwing prudence to the winds, put to the sword their own kinsmen – levies in our pay who gallantly resisted their assaults – and declared war to the knife against a Government which has ever treated them in the past with forbearance and with generosity.

A correspondent wrote that the most worrying aspect of the attack on the forts was that the Afridis, despite a war-like past which had made them 'notoriously vain', had for sixteen years stayed aloof from the revolts of their neighbouring tribes. The Afridi chiefs and their allies demanded the withdrawal of all British forces from the Samana Range and the Swat region, together with the release of all Pathan prisoners and hostages. These terms were unacceptable to the British, while the attacks on the forts were considered outrages that must not go unpunished. Now it was Tirah's turn to face an expeditionary force.

Colonel Warburton wrote: 'My mind is very heavy over this hideous disaster, which I feel could have been staved off even up to the day of mischief. It makes me quite sad to think how easily the labour of years – of a lifetime – can be ruined and destroyed in a few days.

*   *   *

Two well-equipped divisions left Kohat on 11 October 1897 to punish and subdue the Afridis and the neighbouring Orakzais in the Tirah heartlands. The majority of the troops were Indian and Gurkhas but there were also four British battalions, with each man carrying the new bolt-action Lee-Metford rifles. The columns were completed by two squadrons of cavalry, four mountain batteries, a machine-gun detachment and Pioneers. The mobile field hospital possessed an X-ray camera. Another brigade was mustered to keep open lines of communications while the Rawalpindi Brigade was kept in reserve. In total the Tirah Field Force numbered 35,000 combatants and around 20,000 followers, making it the largest single force ever to be committed to the frontier. For baggage all mounted officers were allowed one mule each, while in native regiments the allowance was one mule to two officers. To aid mobility no bakeries were allowed in the vanguard and troops were rationed to biscuits.

The force was commanded by General Sir William Stephen Alexander Lockhart, an experienced soldier and veteran of the Indian Mutiny, who was regarded as a disciplinarian. He had previously led similar punitive missions against the Orakzais. Born in 1841, the son of a clergyman, he joined the Bengal Native Infantry as an ensign when barely eighteen. Promotion followed swiftly through the Indian Mutiny and the Bhutan campaign where he distinguished himself in reconnaissance. His skill at scouting and outpost duty was noted in dispatches along with his 'keen eye for ground' which was particularly useful in hill warfare. He was again commended during the Abyssinian campaign which culminated in the capture of the Magdala mountain fortress in terrain just as rugged, if rather warmer, than the Himalayas. More campaign ribbons were pinned to his tunic after further service in India but he was especially proud of the bronze medal of the Royal Humane Society, won for rescuing two women from drowning in a Gwalior lake. Lockhart's service as quartermaster-general in Bengal was interrupted by a bout of malaria which almost killed him. During the earlier 1878 Afghan campaign he commanded British forces at the Khyber Pass who successfully kept the Afridis in check. During the early 1880s he was an effective intelligence officer and envoy and during the 1890s he commanded the Punjab Frontier Force. Most of his time was occupied in hill warfare, including the Waziristan expedition. He was a grizzled old soldier who had earned the respect of his men. His deputy commander, leading the Second Brigade, was General A.J. Yeatman-Biggs, who did not always enjoy the same esteem among the rank and file. Yeatman-Biggs had served in China (where he was slightly wounded during the storming of the Taku forts), South Africa and Egypt before his Indian Army service.

The combined active manpower facing them in the two tribes was estimated at 50,000. The mullahs circulated a story intended to stiffen the resolve and religious ardour of the warriors. They said that hundreds of years before a venerable prophet called Sheikh Mali Doba blessed and buried a red and green flag enclosed within an earthenware pot. His prayer was that in any time of great tribulation the flag would show the Afridis whether or not they would emerge safely from their troubles. The pot was dug up as the British army approached and at a great public ceremony presided over by their religious leader, Said Akbar, nine cows were slaughtered and their blood sprinkled over the vessel, which promptly burst open to reveal the flag. When it was hoisted on a pole, all the standards of the clans bowed down to it of their own accord. This was interpreted as an omen that the Afridis would be victorious.

The first difficulty the British encountered was the lack of accurate information about the terrain, or even the direction of their target. The available maps were almost blank and the little information they did contain was inaccurate. One private complained: 'As no white man has ever been in the country, so there is nothing definitely known.'

The British forces set off from Kohat to Shinwara on the southern edge of Tirah in October 1897. Gunner subaltern George MacMunn described the spectacle:

The roads in every direction were full with gathering troops. Highland regiments, Gurkhas, Sikh corps, long lines of Indian cavalry, their lances standing high above the acrid dust that they stirred. By the side of the roads strings of laden camels padded on beside the troops, the jinkety-jink of the mountain guns, the skirling of the pipes, all contributed to the wild excitement and romance of the scene.

After a week's march into increasingly hostile country the first clash of arms occurred when the 3rd Gurkhas cleared out a small village at Dargai at a cost of 2 dead and 13 wounded. The King's Own Scottish Borderers and the Gurkhas then took the commanding Dargai Heights, which dominated the left flank of any force descending the Chagra valley, with minimal casualties. But no supply arrangements had been made to allow them to consolidate their position and they were forced to withdraw owing to inadequate stocks of food, fuel and ammunition. It took a further two days for pack mules to bring the necessary supplies up from the main army and by then the Heights had been reoccupied by Afridi tribesmen. It was to prove a costly mistake.

Nineteen standards were counted on the ridge top, representing the principal Afridi clans, as well as their Orakzai allies, with a total of 8,000 men defending what looked like an impregnable position. The British officers pinned their hopes on the eighteen guns of the mountain batteries and the toughness of the gun-crews.

On the morning of the 20th the British nine-pounders began to shell the enemy positions from 1,800 yards. The bursting shrapnel did little damage among Afridis shouting defiance from behind rocky parapets. They waved their standards and kept up a hot fire on the slowly advancing Second Division. After three hours the bombardment succeeded in forcing the tribesmen's heads down, allowing some Gurkha scouts to cross the open ground and form up in new positions sheltered from Afridi sniper fire. Their colleagues were too slow to follow, however, and the main Gurkha force was badly cut up by tribesmen armed with breech-loading Sniders and Martini-Henry rifles. The survivors were pinned down behind what little cover they could find below a sheer cliff. Several companies of the Dorset and Devonshire regiments tried to support them but also came under withering fire. The situation looked desperate as the well-positioned tribesmen threatened to halt the Field Force at its first major obstacle.

Lieutenant-Colonel Mathias of the Gordons was told that the ridge must be cleared 'at all costs'. He told his men, to ringing cheers, 'The Gordon Highlanders will take it!' He ordered his officers and pipers to the front and the ensuing charge across bullet-swept open ground became one of the most famous military exploits of the late Victorian age. The pipers played 'Cock of the North' as the kilted Highlanders roared up the exposed neck of rock under heavy and accurate fire which left sprawling heaps of bloody tartan. Piper Milne was shot through the lung and fell unconscious. Piper George 'Jock' Findlater was shot in both ankles but calmly sat himself down on a boulder and, after catching his breath, carried on playing. His coolness won him the Victoria Cross. Colonel Mathias was in the thick of his men and told his colour-sergeant: 'Stiff climb, eh, Mackie? Not quite so young as I was.' Mackie gave him a resounding clap on the back and said: 'Ye're gaun verra strong for an auld man.' The battalion lost thirty-two men dead but crossed the open ground as ordered and bounded up the rocky heights, quickly followed by the Gurkhas, Sikhs and the Dorset and Devonshires. The combined forces, better sheltered from the Afghan marksmen, then scaled a precipitous goat path weaving through outcrops and crevices. During the mêlée Private Edward Lawson of the Gordons, Private Samuel Vickery of the Dorsets and Captain Henry Singleton Pennell of the Sherwood Foresters also won VCs. The Gordons reached the ridge crest first, their bayonets fixed, but the enemy had already melted away. Total casualties among the attacking force topped 200, most of them wounded. Colonel Mathias was grazed but other men had even narrower escapes. A bullet passed through one major's helmet without injuring him, while Lieutenant Dingwall was hit four times without suffering more than scratches – one bullet struck his revolver, and another his cartridge case, exploding the ammunition within.

Reuters reported: 'It is impossible to speak too highly of the gallantry of the Gordon Highlanders . . . As they were led down the slopes back to camp after their splendid and successful charge, they were spontaneously cheered by all the other regiments.' Special mention was also made of the Gurkhas and their commander, Captain Robinson: 'He led his men across the exposed ground to cover and, finding that the force there was insufficient, he returned alone over the fire-swept space and was wounded leading a second rush in support of the first contingent.' The reporter added: 'Individual instances of conspicuous bravery among the troops were numerous, and many men lost their lives in heroic attempts to save their wounded comrades.'

In that action, like many on the Afghan border, many casualties were incurred while carrying off the wounded. The reason was simple enough: the tribesmen had a fearsome reputation for torturing and mutilating their injured foes, and burial parties had often seen the sickening results. The rule was that no one still breathing should be left behind. Rudyard Kipling wrote:

> When you're wounded and left on Afghanistan's plains
> And the women come out to cut up what remains,
> Just roll to your rifle and blow out your brains
> And go to your Gawd like a soldier.

Queen Victoria telegraphed from Balmoral: 'Please express my congratulations to all ranks, British and Native troops, on their gallant conduct in actions. Deeply deplore loss of precious lives among officers and men in my army. Pray report condition of wounded, and assure them of my true sympathy.'

The victory was achieved by late afternoon, but once again it was marred by the incompetence of staff officers who failed to make proper provision for supplies. In failing light the men were ordered to bivouac on the crest without greatcoats, blankets or fuel for fires in temperatures which swiftly fell below zero. Their only food and water was what they carried into battle on their belts and in their haversacks. Six miles away officers neglected to look after several hundred mules. They were left without food and water, and their full loads were not removed as they were tethered for the night. The following morning most of the mules died as they climbed towards the base camp up the Khanki valley. The whole expedition was halted for a week as patrols were sent out to gather the 3,000 camels needed to bring up 600 tons of stores.

At last, on 29 October, the army began to move against the 6,700-foot Sampagha Pass. This gorge was quickly taken with only token resistance, and the Arhanga Pass also fell before the Pathans had recovered from their surprise. A correspondent wrote:

> When from their eyries in the rocks they note the General's skilful dispositions, the quiet businesslike way in which they were carried out, the steady unwavering advance of the men, the numbers launched against them, the menace to their flanks, the searching fire of the guns, and the deadly precision of our artillery fire, their hearts fail them, and they go.
>
> The strength of the enemy on this occasion or their losses it is impossible to estimate. It was expected they would muster in thousands for the defence of this particular pass, and that here if anywhere they would make a great and gallant stand. But it may be doubted if more than 1,000 of them were actually in line when attacked. The remainder were probably more concerned in removing their families and flocks and herds to places of safety and refuge than in meeting us in fair fight. It may be supposed that as they have had weeks of warning they might have done this sooner . . . possibly they could not bring themselves to believe, until literally the eleventh hour, that after centuries of inviolate seclusion we should dare, or should be able, to lift the purdah and penetrate into their sacred valley. Blood splashes were found in many places along their line of defence, and some of them were killed and others wounded, chiefly by artillery fire.

The Field Force could now look down on the Tirah Maiden, the first foreigners ever to have seen it. Colonel Hutchinson wrote to *The Times*:

> We have all been very much struck by the appearance of this valley. It is wide, well-watered land even here at its head, fairly timbered with apricot and walnut trees about the houses, which are very numerous and well built. A great deal is under cultivation, the fields are carefully terraced and signs of plenty and comfort are abundant . . . the Autumn tints remind me of England.

The contrast with the arid, treeless country around this huge hidden valley was dramatic. Hutchinson reported two-storey stone houses and barns stocked with Indian corn, barley, potatoes, beans, walnuts and onions. The colonel gloated: 'It has been the proud boast of the Afridis from time immemorial that no enemy of whatever race or creed has ever attempted to cross the mountain barriers which shut them in. Well, we have changed all that.' Another correspondent wrote: 'Here we are in the promised land at last. A land not exactly flowing with milk and honey, but extensive, fertile, highly cultivated and capable of much development under a settled Government.' The Field Force descended into that green lushness and began to plunder the abandoned food stores.

The main camp was established about 3 miles from Arhanga, in the centre of the Tirah Maiden, close to the hamlet of Nureddin. *The Times* correspondent wrote:

> There are no villages but there are innumerable houses dotted all over the country. They occur every quarter mile or so, and are large, strong, substantial buildings, generally including a tower or keep, and capable of mounting a strong defence so long as artillery is not brought against them. In each of these houses lives a family, or a group of blood relations; in one, for example, several brothers, with their wives and children, and fathers and mothers; in another, a petty chief with his immediate followers, his sisters, cousins and aunts, and so on. But, needless to say, they are all empty now. With one accord the people have fled before our approach, and we have the valley to ourselves.

The tribesmen had not deserted their valley, however, merely vanished into the surrounding hills and ravines, from which they emerged to ambush supply columns and pick off unwary patrols. They cut telegraph wires and at night crept close to the British camps to snipe at figures marked out by the firelight. Hutchinson said: 'It is extremely unpleasant, this whizz and spatter of bullets while you are at dinner or trying to enjoy a pipe round a camp fire before turning in.' Private Walter Ware wrote to his parents after counter-measures were taken:

Afridis used to come down on the low hills in the night. Thousands of them, and fire in our camps, in fact we had to sleep in our trenches all night long. I say sleep, but it was very little of that. . . We are being fired on every night now but they can't hurt us much as we have built fortifications all round the camp and they won't come too near us so we don't take any notice of them.

Dispatches reflected the growing frustration of the British:

During the last two nights the firing into camp by prowling marauders has been very bad, but no casualties have been incurred. Last night the 5th Gurkha scouts stalked a firing party, and a *mêlée* ensued, with the result that eight Afridis and one Gurkha [were] killed. It was a very plucky and creditable performance of the Scouts who, under Lieutenants Lucas, Bruce and Tillard have done excellent service since the expedition started. The nights are extremely cold now, with hard frosts, but the sun is hot in the day time. The health of the troops is good, and the wounded are doing well. . .

General Kempster's Brigade destroyed the home of the Mullah Said Akbar, a prominent leader of the revolt. Incriminating correspondence was found there, which has been taken charge of by the Political Officer for examination. Our foraging parties were today fired on and more or less seriously engaged in several directions. There were a few casualties among the men, but none among the officers . . .

A party, while engaged in fixing a site for a new camp and signalling station, were treacherously fired on at short range by Afridis. Nobody was touched, but the party had a miraculous escape . . . Major O'Sullivan, of Sir William Lockhart's staff, and three other officers narrowly escaped being cut off. Some of the enemy, concealing their rifles, sauntered up with apparently friendly intentions. Major O'Sullivan, however, suspected treachery and whistled to the other officers as a signal to them to return. The enemy immediately opened fire but the officers, who escaped unhurt, took shelter in a neighbouring house. Luckily a company of the 3rd Gurkhas were close at hand and were able to rescue them. It is expected that the object of the enemy was to capture them alive. A similar attempt was made in the case of some of the infantry, but owing to the careful precautions taken it proved futile.

Among the papers discovered in the Mullah's house were letters written by the 'Mad Mullah' stating that the Turks had beaten the Greeks and seized the approaches to India, and that, with the British army isolated, now was the time to strike a blow for Islam.

A steady stream of supplies flowed through the Arhanga Pass and the baggage trains were in constant danger of ambush. The Afridis knew to attack when both men and animals were exhausted. In one raid the Queen's Royal West Surrey Regiment lost 3 men killed and 4 wounded, 10 boxes of Lee-Metford ammunition – a total of 11,000 rounds – 3 rifles, 350 kits and 71 baggage ponies which stampeded away into the darkness as soon as the firing started. On another night nine drivers were killed or wounded and 188 kits belonging to the 15th Sikhs were carried off. The Afridis had a well-deserved reputation as craftsmen and they became adept at making booby-traps from captured supplies. In Mastura an armoury was found containing anvils, mechanical appliances, 150 Nobel dynamite cartridges, Lee-Metford bullets with the lead withdrawn from their nickel cases, and dozens of Curtis and Harvey red powder tins.

The artist Melton Prior, attached to the Field Force, described a 'spirited affair' when a body of King's Own Scottish Borderers stormed an enemy position above the camp at Datoi: 'Our men had to climb almost precipitous rocks and then rush the enemy's position under a fire so close that not more than five yards' distance lay between the English officer in command and the foremost Afridie. After a brief stand the tribesmen retreated down a wooded ravine.' This action was untypical in that the Afridis allowed the British to get so close.

One of the most frustrating aspects of this sort of warfare was that many of the tribesmen were either former sepoys themselves or had been trained by sepoys. They also used modern rifles, in many cases stolen from the British, which used smokeless powder, making it almost impossible to pinpoint snipers in the rugged hills. Surgeon-Captain Pollock observed: 'They never show and don't stand up to be killed.'

Lockhart decided that if he could not beat his invisible enemy in pitched battle he would force them to negotiate by destroying their own Eden. He ordered the systematic burning of farms and homes across the Maiden. Entire hamlets were dynamited and the wreckage torched until nothing was left but ashes and rubble. Orchards were cut down and wells filled with sand. Grainfields were trampled by horses' hooves and the ground laced with salt. The troops were given free rein to loot anything from food and firewood to tribal keepsakes and the few personal possessions left by the fleeing tribesmen. It was a scorched-earth policy exacerbated by vengeance for the innumerable pinprick ambushes on the British forces. The Reuters correspondent Lionel James reported: 'One of the most magnificent sights one could wish to see was the destruction of the valley by fire and sword as the evening waned into night. The camp was ringed by a wall of fire – byres, outhouses, homesteads and fortresses one mass of rolling flame, until the very camp was almost as light as day.' Hutchinson, writing in *The Times*, said: 'Whether these measures will have the effect of making them yield their submission, or whether it will exasperate them into making a big attack on our camp, time alone can show.'

Lockhart was convinced that stern measures were necessary to bring in chieftains willing to negotiate. 'Seeing us in possession, occupying their land, devouring their stores, and noting our determination and our power to punish, with the winter, too, coming on while they are wanderers on the bleak mountain sides, they must see the hopelessness of prolonged resistance.'

Lockhart's scorched-earth policy was heavily criticised by some fellow officers and politicians. After the campaign Lord Roberts said in a parliamentary debate: 'Burning houses and destroying crops, necessary and justifiable as such measures may be, unless followed up by some form of authority or jurisdiction, means starvation for many of the women and children . . . and for us a rich harvest of hatred and revenge.' But Sir Neville Chamberlain wrote in favour: 'To have to carry destruction, if not desolation, into the homes of some hundreds of families is the great drawback to border warfare; but with savage tribes to whom there is no right but might, and no law to govern them in their intercourses with the rest of mankind, save that which appeals to their own interests, the only course as regards humanity as well as policy is to make all suffer, and thereby, for their own interests, enlist the great majority on the side of peace and safety.'

The stripping of the land continued, and with it the officially sanctioned looting. *The Times* correspondent noted:

> Strings of mules go out every day, with sufficient escorts, and return in the evening laden up with forage, which abounds, and with sacks of potatoes, wheat, Indian corn, pumpkins, walnuts . . . The foragers not infrequently find odds and ends of booty, which they annex for themselves, old *jezails*, swords, daggers and Korans. These are retained by the finders as mementoes of the campaign. Of Korans there are two kinds – one printed in Peshwar or Lahore, and of no particular interest or value, the other hand-written and generally illustrated and illuminated. These are rare and are very precious finds indeed. A few have been taken.

The mosques, as religious establishments, were spared the torch. But one at Bagh, reputed to be where the Mullahs had hatched the revolt, was the target of a punitive column. The building itself was untouched, but the stately trees surrounding it were 'ringed', the bark sliced round by Gurkha kukris so that they would die in a year. This petty act was to leave a permanent reminder of British wrath and to reduce the site's religious importance and sanctity.

With no towns to occupy and no formal army to beat, the campaign became a war of attrition with columns spiralling out in different directions. Repeatedly the enemy melted away before them, only to re-form and harry the soldiers as they returned to their scattered camps. One reconnaissance sortie on 9 November by General Westmacott and the Dorsetshire and Northamptonshire regiments and the 36th and 18th Sikhs is typical. Their target was the Saran Sar ridge in the west range of the valley, where enemy positions had been spotted. Sharp-shooters peppered the column as it approached but when the soldiers scaled the ridge they found it deserted. Reuters reported:

The retirement was slow and difficult. When it had been proceeding about an hour, the enemy, who had meanwhile had time to collect and choose points favourable for an attack, were again in great force and opened fire upon the troops.

It was seen that the five companies of Northamptons on the summit of the cliff were making no progress. In reply to inquiries which were heliographed they signalled back, 'Several wounded; cannot carry them down; need support.' General Westmacott then ordered up the 36th Sikhs to the support of the Northamptonshire men. They went up like greyhounds as soon as they understood that the rearguard was in difficulties, and all were withdrawn without further loss to the foot of the hill under cover of the guns.

But the necessity of transporting the wounded still greatly retarded the retirement of the force. Between the hill and the camp lies a stretch of quite the worst country over which a general could be called upon to withdraw his force in the face of a strong enemy skirmishing on over-hanging crags, consisting as it does of deep and broken *nullahs* intersecting the line of march every hundred yards or so. It was here that the enemy concentrated their attack. Their knowledge of the country enabled them to creep up the ravines to within short range of the retiring British force. The Northamptons fought with great bravery, and most of their casualties occurred while they were engaged in saving their wounded. Owing to the nature of the country and the broken formation in which they arrived at the foot of the hill, they were obliged to retire in groups. All the wounded were brought into camp as darkness was setting in, but an officer, Lieutenant Macintire, and 12 men, appear to have been cut off. It is hoped that they may yet come in.

The enemy followed their usual tactics, and during the fighting in the ravines displayed wonderful audacity. Considering the force in which they gathered, it was only the dispositions made by General Westmacott which saved the rearguard from annihilation. General Westmacott personally held his men together and saw all the wounded sent on before him on the road to the camp, himself coming in with the rearmost party.

The day's operations cost the general 7 dead, 13 missing and 45 wounded. More severe casualties were suffered by General Francis Kempster's Brigade when their flanks were attacked as they crossed the Teeri Kandao Pass. The rearguard, comprising Gordon Highlanders, Sikhs, Gurkha Scouts, two companies of Dorsetshires and a mountain battery, left the Waran valley long after the main body had set out. They reached the summit of the pass in mid-afternoon, exhausted and constantly harried by enemy snipers. A young lieutenant was killed, shot through the head. His death marked the start of a serious attack by a large body of Afridis who swarmed down the mountainside. Hand to hand fighting was hardest in thick woods abutting the trail. In one bayonet charge the Sikhs killed up to sixty of the tribesmen, whose marksmen were hampered by the trees and foliage. The Sikhs were in a precarious position, however, and their commander, Colonel Abbott, was painfully wounded in the neck and face. Another officer was shot through the heart. Other Sikh units and the Dorsetshires came to their support and all were able to retire down the pass. One report of the engagement said:

It was now nearly dark and the enemy, getting round the flank, were found to be holding a cluster of houses directly in the path of the retreating column. Colonel Haughton at once formed up the whole force with fixed bayonets and, with loud shouts and cheers, the Afridis were driven out, many being shot and bayoneted.

Darkness had now fully set in, so Colonel Haughton decided to stay during the night in the position gained. Half a company of the Dorsetshire Regiment here joined his party. The remaining company and a half seem to have missed the direction and, getting separated, were attacked by the Afridis in the gathering gloom and suffered the disastrous loss of two officers and 13 men killed and 11 wounded. Several rifles were also lost. The enemy in this action have lost very heavily.

Meanwhile one company of the 36th Sikhs rushed another village in the dark and took possession of two blockhouses from which they steadily repulsed an Afridi attack. The enemy were so close that they could be heard abusing the defenders and in particular Gul Badshah, the Orakzai orderly of an officer.

The following day, as the dead were buried, General Lockhart commended all units for their heroism and stamina. He went on:

We must remember that we are opposed to perhaps the best skirmishers and best natural rifle shots in the world, and the country they inhabit is the most difficult on the face of the globe. Their strength lies principally in their intimate knowledge of the ground, which enables them to watch our movements unperceived and to take advantage of every height and every ravine. Our strength lies in our discipline, controlled fire and mutual support, and our weakness in our ignorance of the ground and the consequent tendency of small parties to straggle and get detached. The moral, therefore, is that careful touch must be maintained; and if small bodies do from any cause get separated from their regiment they should, as far as possible, stick to the open and not enter ravines or broken ground where, with such an enemy, they at once place themselves at a terrible disadvantage.

I hope that before long we may obtain an opportunity to meet the enemy on such terms as will enable us to wipe out old scores, and I am confident that when the time comes you will all conduct yourselves with steady courage worthy of our best traditions. In the meantime there is no occasion for depression because some of us have been surprised, outnumbered and overwhelmed on bad ground.

Later, addressing the Sikh and Gurkha regiments he praised their endurance, courage and resolution and said that he was proud to have such battalions under his command. He told them that the Queen-Empress was personally watching their performance.

The Tirah Maiden was healthier than most of the frontier region, but as winter set in the army of occupation regularly sent back sixty or seventy men a day, some wounded in action but most suffering from pneumonia, frostbite or dysentery. While the British and Indian soldiers shivered in their billets, however, the approach of the winter snows also affected those tribesmen who had watched their means of winter survival destroyed. The first tribal leaders to come down from the hills to talk peace were the *maliks* of the Orakzais. These 'venerable old greybeards' listened with quiet dignity as Lockhart spelled out tough terms. All captured British arms were to be returned along with 300 of their own breech-loading rifles plus a fine of 50,000 rials. The Orakzai chiefs agreed these terms on hearing that the British would not occupy their lands permanently. Churchill watched the arms handover, writing: 'These tribes have nothing to surrender but their arms. To extort these few had taken a month, had cost many lives, and thousands of pounds. It had been as bad a bargain as ever was made.'

The Afridis, freezing in the snow-laden hills, refused to follow the Orakzai surrender. Their hit-and-run guerrilla tactics increased the toll of casualties. Hutchinson told his readers:

They have absolutely nothing to learn from us, these Afridis. Contrariwise, their dashing and bold attack, the skill with which they take advantage of ground, the patience with which they watch for a favourable moment, and their perfect marksmanship – all these qualities have again and again won our admiration.

It was now December and the British, unequipped to suffer the deepest winter, left the fire-blackened valley. In icy sleet, biting winds and dense mist they began to march down the 40-mile Bazar valley. Lockhart's aim was to use the withdrawal to reopen the Khyber Pass and thus achieve his military objectives. That involved crossing the Bazar River, a boiling stream with steep banks and dangerous overhangs. Men's moustaches and horse's tails froze solid. The fields along the banks were ice-encrusted bogs which swallowed up mules and their packs. Most of the army's tents were lost and the men spent the nights huddled around spluttering camp fires, risking the light which made them targets for Afridi snipers in return for meagre warmth.

The tribesmen launched sporadic night attacks on isolated parties and occasional daylight attacks on the rearguard of the main column. The most determined of these was on 13 January while the 4th Brigade was packing up the remaining camp equipment. The Afridis' target was the baggage train and their heavy fire swiftly killed ten pack animals. The native drivers panicked and ran between the lines. Many fell during the confused firefight while the British and Indian troops fought back as they carried their wounded to cover. A stand was made near a ford in the river and the defenders were only saved by a mountain-gun battery and Peshawar pickets who turned back to hammer the attackers. By then the Afridis had cut down many men and beasts. Casualties among the British soldiers topped 40 but the main carnage was inflicted upon the baggage train. The official history recorded that 'upwards of 100 followers and about 150 animals seem to have been lost that night'.

Churchill wrote:

> People talk of moving columns hither and thither as if they were mobile groups of men who had only to march about the country and fight the enemy wherever found; and a very few understand that an army is a ponderous mass which drags painfully after it a long chain of advanced depots, rest camps and communications . . . In these valleys, where wheeled traffic is impossible, the difficulties and cost of moving supplies are enormous.

It took Lockhart five days and nights to fight through the Bazar valley and his army suffered 164 casualties, but he was now on more familiar ground and could concentrate on the Khyber Pass. His men began to systematically locate and capture or destroy the tribal flocks of sheep and goats. The Afridis continued to put up stout resistance and there was a tough fight at the Shinkamar Pass in January. In a repeat of the earlier Dargai blunder, British troops first held, and then abandoned, rocky heights above the main column. Several companies were ordered to retake the position. One, led by Lieutenant Thomas Dowdall, succeeded but in the very 'moment of triumph' he and several others were killed by snipers. His commanding officer told the young man's mother: 'There was nothing of the drawing room or carpet soldier about him, only a plucky desire to be in the thick of the fight and share the danger with his men by whom his loss will be deeply regretted.' In all, 6 officers and 20 men were killed and 31 wounded in the last major action of the war. Also among the dead were Lieutenant-Colonel John Haughton, who had so bravely commanded at the Saran Ridge engagement, and Lieutenant Arthur Turing whose obituary recalled his youth at Bedford School 'where he distinguished himself both as a scholar and as an oarsman'.

The loss of their flocks finally persuaded the Afridis to abandon the struggle. As the snows began to melt in the weak spring sunshine, the fighting petered to an end. One Afridi chief pledged that British forts on the borders of their lands would be safe from attack. 'Leave us alone,' he said. 'We will fight the Russians or any other European armies that come against India.'

*   *   *

Sporadic fighting continued in some areas but gradually all the tribal *maliks* tendered their submission. Lockhart issued an ultimatum that all fines must be paid by 23 February but an extension was granted because of snow clogging the passes. In March the Afridis gave up seventy hostages, and the final surrender of arms was completed on 1 April. The Afridi chieftains were surprised that Lockhart did not take more vindictive action and when the general left Peshawar on 5 April their entire *jirgah* assembled at the station to bid him farewell.

Lockhart returned a conquering hero. He received the thanks of the government, was showered with further honours and quickly succeeded Sir George White as commander-in-chief of India. He died suddenly in Calcutta two years later. One obituary referred to his command in Tirah: 'He showed exceptional skills in handling his force of regulars in an almost impracticable country, in a guerrilla warfare, against native levies of sharpshooters, who were always trying to elude him, but he outmanoeuvred them and beat them at their own tactics.' Another said that he had brought the Tirah campaign to a 'rapid and successful conclusion'. The price had been heavy. The Tirah Field Force took five months to subdue an elusive enemy at a total cost of 287 dead, 853 wounded and 10 missing. Among the dead was 67-year-old Sir Henry Havelock-Allen, who had won the Victoria Cross at Cawnpore and was once described as the bravest man in the British Army. He had accompanied the expedition as a newspaper correspondent, but ignored repeated advice to stay close to the column and his butchered body and that of his horse were eventually found by a search party.

General Yeatman-Biggs came in for particular criticism for the logistical blunders and delays, and for failing to adequately support the other columns. He was swiftly beyond such criticism, however, as he died of dysentery at Peshawar, his body weakened by exposure and fatigue. Lockhart, in his final set of dispatches, said that his fellow-officer had been in poor health from the start of the campaign. Gossip sent back to Britain by Churchill suggested that General Kempster had been reported as 'no longer possessing the confidence of his troops'.

Winston Spencer Churchill, a young officer heartily despised for his vaunting ambition, missed most of the action in Tirah but that did not stop him offering a critical opinion. 'I am afraid the Tirah campaign has ended disastrously,' he wrote to his 'Mamma'. 'The troops have done what they were ordered – but they were disastrously led. The last retirement to Peshawar has been a most terrible blunder. Whatever the inconvenience of wintering in Tirah, it was preferable to the chance of the Afridis thinking they had driven us out. All the officers who have come down here sick and wounded show a most unsoldierlike spirit, declaring that it is not good enough and they are glad they are out of it.'

In another letter he wrote:

> The troops have done all that was asked of them. They have marched freely into all parts of Tirah and have burned and destroyed everything that came to hand. The tribesmen have been powerless to stop them but have been able to make them pay heavily in men and officers.
>
> The whole expedition was a mistake because its success depended on the tribesmen giving in when their country was invaded and their property destroyed. This they have not done. We have done them all the harm possible and many of them are still defiant. Had they cannons we could have captured them. Had they towns we could have destroyed them. Had they any points of strategical or political importance we could have occupied them. But regular troops cannot catch or kill an impalpable cloud of skirmishers. It is because we have no real means – except by prolonged occupation – of putting the screw on these tribesmen and making them give in – that it is a great mistake to make the attempt.

In public, however, Churchill could not risk such forthright views and in a letter to *The Times* he toadied to his superiors and, with no hint of self-irony, condemned the grumblings of armchair generals:

> I daresay you meet many in England . . . who imagine that the Field Force is sulking in its tents, quivering with anger, and quaking with fear. To such a visit to the scene would be an education. They would observe in the Khyber Pass or along the Bara river, the camps of five brigades of men, hardened by war, proud of their experience, confident in their strength, ready and eager to advance against the enemy. They would see at Jamrud that enemy, begging only for time to collect their fine, fighting amongst themselves to gather the *tale* of rifles, anxiously offering hostages, and abjectly imploring that whatever may happen, the soldiers shall not come back.
>
> I suppose that on all military operations there must be a proportion of cases of cowardice and incompetency and a much

larger proportion of errors of judgement. Outpost affairs may be disastrous, troops may be exposed to unnecessary hardships, supplies and commissariat will at times go wrong, many tempers must be tried. When civilised forces collide one side or the other wins the battle, and a victory covers everything. The peculiar difficulty which attends mountain warfare is that there are no general actions on a great scale, no brilliant successes, no important surrenders, no chance for *coups de theatre*. It is just a rough hard job, which must be carried through. The war is one of small incidents.

Churchill's praise of the Tirah Field Force and its commanders may have been faint, but the force had beaten, for the first time, frontier guerrillas fighting in their own homeland, and, by example, curbed the warlike tendencies of other tribes. General Sir George White said that no campaign had ever been conducted in India in more arduous and trying circumstances: 'The country was physically most difficult, and the enemy were well-armed and expert in guerrilla warfare. Severe punishment was, however, inflicted on them. The officers and men conducted themselves in a manner thoroughly befitting the traditions of the Queen's Army.'

The campaign also added to the battle honours of the regiments which took part. Around 200 officers and men were mentioned in dispatches and no fewer than seven Victoria Crosses were won, four of them on the Dargai Heights. Piper Jock Findlater and Private Vickery received theirs personally from Queen Victoria while recovering in Netley Hospital. Findlater tried to hobble to his feet but was waved down by the monarch. As she left the hospital corridor he played 'Haughs of Cromdale'. Findlater was promoted to Pipe-Major and fêted across Britain. He died in Turriff, near his birthplace, in 1942. Vickery, from Somerset, was made up to sergeant and died in Cardiff in 1952. Private Lawson, a Geordie, also witnessed two world wars before his death in Northumberland in 1955. Captain Pennell, from Dawlish in Devon, did not enjoy a similarly long life. He died in St Moritz early in 1907, aged thirty-two. These men, and many others, felt that equal honours should have gone also to Sikhs and Gurkhas who had borne the brunt of the initial assault on the ridge. But it was not until 1911 that Indian Army officers and men were made eligible for Britain's foremost award for valour.

Three more VCs were awarded for bravery during the early part of the uprising: Brevet Lieutenant-Colonel Robert Bellow Adams, a staff officer and Indian Army Guide, led two officers and five men under heavy and close fire to rescue a lieutenant of the Lancashire Fusiliers lying disabled by a bullet wound and surrounded by enemy swordsmen at Nawa Kili. While he was being brought to cover, the lieutenant was shot again and killed. Four horses, including the colonel's, were shot. Adams was later knighted and promoted to major-general. Punjab-born, he died in Inverness in 1928 and his body was cremated in Glasgow. Lieutenant Hector Lachlan Stewart MacLean's VC was posthumous. He died of wounds suffered during the action at Nawa Kili, not too many miles from the place of his birth twenty-eight years earlier. His Kent family erected a memorial in St Alban's Church, Marden. The third officer involved, Lieutenant Alexander Edward Murray Fincastle of the Queen's Lancers, received his medal from Queen Victoria at Buckingham Palace. He later became a major and the Earl of Dunmore. He served in the early part of the Boer War and the first half of the First World War. He died in London in 1962, aged ninety.

Churchill, who had not reached the Tirah army until the hard fighting was finished, wanted a medal to further his military, literary and, above all, political career. In a letter to a more senior officer whom he had befriended he said: 'I am entitled to a medal and two clasps for my gallantry, for the hardships and dangers I encountered. I am possessed with a keen desire to mount the ribbon on my breast.' In another letter to his mother he boasted that as a result of the campaign he had made 'a great many friends in high places – as far as soldiering is concerned'. He also reckoned that he was entitled to three months' leave on full pay. His subsequent career does not need to be recounted here.

The mixed victory in Tirah committed ever more numerous troops to garrison the forward positions along the frontier and this was questioned in both India and Britain. Secretary of State Lord Hamilton wrote: 'If we can conciliate and attach to us these tribes, then from a military point of view we are greatly the gainers. If we only make them more hostile, whatever benefit we gain theoretically in strategy, by occupying their country, we lose tactically by the forces locked up in maintaining our communications.'

Such sentiments were echoed strongly by Lord Curzon, who in 1899 became the new Viceroy of India. The 39-year-old statesman hit upon a political solution – to remove the frontier from within the jurisdiction of the Punjab and turn it into a province in its own right which would act as a buffer between the Raj and the unruly regions to the north. The frontier was to be defended by the tribes themselves, formed in local militias trained by British officers and, ironically, given the terms of the Tirah capitulation, armed by the British. Minor tribal uprisings, banditry and kidnapping continued to flare up but the strategy largely succeeded into the following century in holding firm the boundaries of British India. Typically, the Afridis continued to behave independently and at the turn of the century carried on a gun-running trade, while the 1923 kidnapping of a seventeen-year-old English girl, Molly Ellis, caused outrage. There was great relief when she was freed unharmed.

Across the border there was cooperation from Abdurrahman Khan and relative peace continued after his death in 1901. Unrest in India and calls for a new holy war sparked the third major Anglo-Afghan conflict in 1919 and sixty years later Soviet tanks opened another chapter in Afghanistan's bloody history. The blood shed since then dwarfed Britain's earlier invasion of a paradise valley hidden high in the mountain fastness.

Appendix

The War Correspondents

A substantial number of the first-hand accounts of the distant wars included in this book have been gleaned, in the safety and warmth of my home, from the contemporary accounts of war correspondents who generally shared the discomfort and danger suffered by nineteenth-century soldiers and sailors. Their courage and tenacity has too often been neglected. They were a motley crowd: full-time professional reporters and enthusiastic amateurs; tradesmen, adventurers and failed businessmen; commissioned soldiers, with a talent for words which could supplement their army pay; scholars and missionaries; distinguished writers and hacks; glory-hunters, charlatans and heroes.

At first they were generally despised, and regarded as dangerous meddlers at worst and lickspittle propagandists at best. Wellington's view dripped contempt: 'every man who can write, and who has a friend who can read, sits down to write his account of what he does not know, and his comments on what he does not understand'. Much later Kitchener referred to a posse of professional reporters as 'drunken swabs', while Wolseley referred to 'those newly invented curses to modern armies'. But with the dramatic rise in literacy as the century progressed – between 1841 and 1900 the rate rose from 63 to 92 per cent – and the reduction and then abolition of newspaper tax, generals and politicians began to appreciate the power of a mass circulation press.

Its power to wreck reputations and reform absurdly redundant practices was proven by the reports from the Crimea of William Howard Russell (1821–1907) of *The Times*. His reputation is so firmly set that it does not need to be enhanced here, other than to quote one general's verdict: 'An honest truth-telling man.' Russell may be the 'father' of war correspondents, but many others followed him to feed the public's appetite for news and sensation with equal integrity and zeal. Some of them were driven by self-aggrandisement and bravado; most by the desire to earn an honest crust by informing, enthusing and entertaining the public.

The best of them, then as now, were always found as close to the action as possible, sharing the privations of the front-line troops rather than the fine wines of a general's table far from the sound of gunfire. They too suffered dysentery, rotten food, seasickness, malaria and the range of other tortures which often proved more dangerous than an enemy's bullet or spear-thrust. Robert Furneaux wrote of Russell's successors:

> Without a continental war, or even one of great historical significance, for them to chronicle, they galloped their horses and rode the trains, through many campaigns in the mountains and valleys of the Balkans, the frontiers of India, the plateaux of Central Asia, the veldt of Zululand and Natal, the sands and deserts of Egypt and the Sudan, in fever-ridden Cuba and the Philippines, while a new and eager newspaper-reading public clamoured for their stories.

Their reports often had important consequences. When the American reporter J.A. MacGahan was engaged by the *Daily News* in the Balkans he exposed the mass murder of Bulgarian Christians by the Turks. The global outcry that ensued led to Bulgarian independence.

Sometimes the way news was brought out of war zones was as heroic as the military actions themselves. MacGahan's colleague on the *News*, Archibald Forbes rode 140 miles in thirty hours on a succession of post horses over the Carpathian mountains to bring news of the Russians' failed assault on Plevna. After further reportage in the Balkans and India, Forbes was sent to cover the war with the Zulus. Having witnessed Cetewayo's defeat at Ulundi he rode all night through enemy-infested and unknown territory to the nearest telegraph station and, having wired his story, rode on a further 175 miles to Durban to mail war artist Melton Prior's sketch of the battle.

At least one correspondent became the story. When the *Morning Post*'s Winston Churchill was captured by Boers he remarked: 'This will be good for my paper.' His escape and evasion of his pursuers became an epic avidly lapped up by the British public. He returned a national hero and his accounts, in both newsprint and book form, netted him £10,000, earnings which laid the foundation of his political career.

Most correspondents were listed as non-combatant observers but that did not stop them carrying arms and, on occasions, using them. The *Daily Telegraph* reporter Bennet Burleigh, a Glaswegian by birth who fought on the Confederate side in the American Civil War, was mentioned in dispatches for helping to steady the line at Abu Klea. During that action he was hit in the neck by a spent bullet but calmly asked a colleague to pluck it out as he continued firing. His scoops included the first reports of Gordon's death at Khartoum, the safety of the relief column and the victory at Omdurman.

Men such as Burleigh escaped death many times during long, illustrious careers. Others weren't so lucky, as we have seen with the grisly fate of Thomas Bowlby, *The Times* correspondent in the China War. They never came home or filed their final report. The death toll included many veteran correspondents.

John Cameron of *The Standard* and St Leger Herbert of the *Morning Post* were shot dead at the battle of Abu Kru, the latter as he was opening a tin of sardines.

The Times correspondent Frank Power was captured and killed by the Mahdi's men as he tried to reach a telegraph station to appeal for help for the besieged garrison at Khartoum.

Another *Times* correspondent, the Honourable Hubert Howard, who also wrote for the *New York Herald*, was killed by a stray British shell at Omdurman, while Henry Cross of the *Manchester Guardian* died after the battle from a fever.

Reporters Edmond O'Donovan and Frank Vizetelly were killed at Tel-el-Kebir, sharing with the soldiers the hardships and hazards of desert warfare.

George Warrington Steevens covered colonial campaigns for the *Daily Mail* with an accuracy and eloquence which impressed even hostile old generals, but died of fever during the siege of Ladysmith.

Steevens drank a hoarded bottle of champagne on his deathbed, surrounded by fellow correspondents. One colleague described his special talents: 'In a scientific age, his style may be described as cinematographic. He was able to put before his readers, in a series of smooth-running little pictures, events exactly as he saw them with his own intense eyes.' Another said: 'What Kipling did for fiction, [Steevens] did for fact.'

The names of these journalistic dead, and those of many others, are not recorded on regimental war memorials. But they, too, must not be forgotten.

Bibliography

General

Briggs, Asa, *The Age of Improvement 1783–1867* (Longman, London, 1959)
Brooks, Richard, *Naval Brigades from the Crimea to the Boxer Rebellion* (Constable, London, 1999)
Callwell, Colonel C.E., *Small Wars* (London, 1906)
Dictionary of National Biography (Oxford University Press, 1921–2)
Farwell, Byron, *Queen Victoria's Little Wars* (Allen Lane, London, 1973)
Featherstone, D., *Colonial Small Wars 1837–1901* (Newton Abbot, 1973)
Haythornthwaite, Philip J., *The Colonial Wars Source Book* (Arms & Armour Press, London, 1995)
James, Lawrence, *The Savage Wars – British Campaigns in Africa, 1870–1920* (Robert Hale, London)
Judd, Denis, *Empire – The British Imperial Experience from 1765 to the Present* (HarperCollins, 1996)
Lucas, T.J., *Camp Life and Sport in South Africa* (London, 1878)
Morris, James, *The Pax Britannica Trilogy* (Faber & Faber, London, 1968)
Mostert, Noel, *Frontiers – The Epic of South Africa's Creation and the Tragedy of the Xhosa People* (Jonathan Cape, London, 1992)
Pakenham, Thomas, *The Scramble for Africa* (Weidenfeld & Nicolson, 1991)
Spiers, Edward M., *The Late Victorian Army* (Manchester University Press, 1992)
Strawson, John, *Beggars in Red – The British Army 1789–1889* (Hutchinson, London 1991)
——, *Gentlemen in Khaki – The British Army 1890–1990* (Secker & Warburg, London, 1989)

Buenos Aires

Annual Registers, 1806–7
Auchmuty, General Sir Samuel, *Dispatches*
Backhouse, Lieutenant-Colonel J.T., *Dispatches*
Beresford, Major-General William Carr, *Dispatches*
Court-Martial of General Whitelocke (Official Papers, 1808)

Ferns, H.S., *Britain and Argentina in the Nineteenth Century* (Oxford University Press, 1960)

Graham-Yooll, Andrew, *Small Wars You May Have Missed* (Junction Books, London, 1983)

Marley, David F., *Wars of the Americas – A Chronicle of Armed Conflict in the New World* (ABC-Clio, California, 1998)

Murray, Admiral George, *Dispatches*

Pendle, George, *A History of Latin America* (Penguin, London, 1981)

Popham, Commodore Sir Hugh, *Dispatches*

Rock, David, *Argentina 1516–1982 – From Spanish Colonization to the Falklands War* (Taurus, London, 1986)

Scobie, J., *Argentina: A City and a Nation* (New York, 1964)

The Times

Whitelocke, General John, *Dispatches*

The First Burma War

Annual Registers, 1824–6

Sheppard, Eric, *A Short History of the British Army* (Constable, London, 1926)

Stewart, A.T.Q., *The Pagoda War* (Faber & Faber, London, 1972)

Tarling, Nicholas (ed.), *The Cambridge History of Southeast Asia, Volume Two* (Cambridge University Press, 1992)

The Times

Vincent, Frank, *The Land of the White Elephant* (Harper, New York, 1874)

The Black War

Bonwick, James, *The Daily Life of the Tasmanians* (London, 1970)

Calder, J.E., *Some Accounts of the Wars and Habits etc., of the Tribes of Tasmania* (Hobart, 1873)

Davies, David, *The Last of the Tasmanians* (Harper & Row, USA, 1973)

Dodd, Agnes F., *A Short History of the English Colonies* (J.M. Dent & Co., London, 1901)

Fenton, James, *A History of Tasmania from its Discovery in 1642 to the Present Time* (Hobart and London, 1884)

Robson, Lloyd, *A Short History of Tasmania* (Oxford University Press, Melbourne, 1985)

Younger, R.M., *A Concise History of Australia and the Australians* (Hutchinson, 1969)

The Opium War

Annual Registers, 1840–43
Bremer, Commodore Sir James Gordon, *Dispatches*
Burrell, Major-General George, *Dispatches*
Cotterell, Arthur, *China – A History* (Random House, London, 1988)
Ebrey, Patricia Buckley, *China – Cambridge Illustrated History* (Cambridge University Press, 1996)
Elliot, Charles, *Dispatches*
Fairbank, John *King, China – A New History* (Harvard University Press, 1992)
Gough, Major-General Sir Hugh, *Dispatches*
Gray, Jack, *Rebellions and Revolutions – China from the 1880s to the 1980s* (Oxford University Press, 1990)
Inglis, Brian, *The Opium War* (Hodder & Stoughton, 1976)
Low, Sidney, and Sanders, Lloyd C., *The History of England During the Reign of Victoria* (Longmans, London, 1913)
Martineau, Harriet, *A History of the Thirty Years' Peace* (George Bell, London, 1878)
Morton, W. Scott, *China – Its History and Culture* (Lippincott & Cromwell, New York, 1980)
Peyrefitte, Alain, *The Collision of Two Civilisations – The British Expedition to China 1792–4* (HarperCollins, London, 1989)
Pottinger, Sir Henry, *Dispatches*
Pratt, Major J.L., *Dispatches*
Roberts, J.A.G., *Modern China – An Illustrated History* (Sutton Publishing, 1998)
Twitchett, Denis and Fairbank, John K. (eds), *The Cambridge History of China, Volume 10, Late Ch'Ing 1800–1911* (Cambridge, 19??)
Webb, Frank, *A History of Hong Kong* (HarperCollins, 1993)
Wood, Frances, *No Dogs and Not Many Chinese – Trading Port Life in China* (John Murray, London, 1988)
Yong Yap and Cotterell, Arthur, *Chinese Civilisation – From the Ming Revival to Chairman Mao* (Weidenfeld & Nicolson, London, 1977)

The Persian War

Annual Registers, 1856–7
Illustrated London News
Jones, Felix, *Report to Secretary to Government in Bombay* (1856)
Outram, Sir James, *Dispatches to C-in-C, Bombay* (1857)

The Arrow War

Annual Registers, 1856–60
Bowring, Sir John, *Dispatches; Autobiographical Recollections* (1877)
Cotterell, Arthur, *China – A History* (Random House, London, 1988)
Ebrey, Patricia Buckley, *China – Cambridge Illustrated History* (Cambridge, 1996)
Elgin, James Bruce, Earl of, *Dispatches*
Fairbank, John King, *China – A New History* (Harvard University Press, 1992)
Grant, Sir James Hope, *Dispatches; Incidents in the China War* (with Major Knollys, 1860)
Gray, Jack, *Rebellions and Revolutions* (Oxford University Press, 1990)
Holt, Edgar, *The Opium Wars in China* (Putnam, London, 1964)
Hope, Admiral Sir James, *Dispatches*
Lane-Poole, S. and Dickins, F.V., *The Life of Sir Harry Parkes* (1894)
McCarthy, Justin, *A History of Our Own Times* (Caxton, London, 1908)
Osborn, Sherard, *Fight on the Peiho* (Blackwoods Magazine, 1859)
San-Ko-Lin-Son, *Memorial to the Emperor* (1859)
Seymour, Admiral Sir Michael, *Dispatches*
Spence, Jonathan D., *The Search for Modern China* (Hutchinson, London, 1990)
The Times
Yong Yap and Cotterell, Arthur, *Chinese Civilisation* (Weidenfeld & Nicolson, London, 1977)

The Shortest War

Annual Registers, 1880, 1890, 1896
Brooks, Richard, *Naval Brigades from the Crimea to the Boxer Rebellion* (Constable, London, 1999)
Illustrated London News
Reuters, *Reports from Correspondent* (1896)
The Times

The Benin Massacre

Annual Registers, 1888–9, 1894–8
Gott, Richard, Article in the *Independent*, 1997
Illustrated News, Special Supplement (1897)

James, Lawrence, *The Savage Wars – British Campaigns in Africa, 1870–1920* (Robert Hale, London)
Jephson, Sir Alfred, *Correspondence* (1897)
Keegan, John, *A History of Warfare* (Hutchinson, London, 1993)
McCarthy, Justin, *A History of Our Own Times* (Caxton, London, 1908)
Reuters, *Special Service* (1897)
The Times

The Tirah Campaign

Churchill, Randolph S., *Winston S. Churchill, Volume 1* (Heinemann, London, 1966)
——, *Volume 1 Companion, Part 2* (1967)
Churchill, Sir Winston, *Story of the Malakand Field Force* (London, 1898)
Hutchinson, Colonel H., *The Campaign in Tirah* (London, 1898)
Illustrated London News
Keay, John, *The Gilgit Game* (Murray, London, 1979)
Richards, D.S., *The Savage Frontier – A History of the Anglo-Afghan Wars* (Macmillan, London, 1990)
Schofield, Victoria, *Every Rock, Every Hill – The Plain Tale of the North-West Frontier and Afghanistan* (Buchan & Enright, London, 1984)
Shadwell, Captain L.J., *Lockhart's Advance Through Tirah* (Calcutta, 1898)
The Times

Part Three
Blood in the Sand

Introduction

The common soldier was rarely honoured in Britain in the first half of the nineteenth century. The accolades, medals and fame went mainly to aristocratic officers and generals who planted the flag in the far corners of the world. Ordinary men were not eligible for most medals of valour and battlefield promotions were rare. The vast majority of heroes went unrecognised. The best they could hope for was a decent pension – the worst was a beggar's bowl.

The Crimean War changed all that, and not just with the introduction of the Victoria Cross, the highest honour of all and open to all ranks. The British administration, faced with undeniable evidence of poor generalship and official incompetence, needed heroes from all strata of society. An early example was Private John Penn of the 17th Lancers.

Penn was born into the 14th Regiment of Light Dragoons around 1820, and spent his childhood moving between barracks and stables where his father was a farrier-major. He was orphaned at the age of eight and later was taken as a servant into the household of Lady John Bethell. Discontented with that form of service, he joined the cavalry as soon as he had grown to the required standard height.

He saw much action in the Afghanistan campaign under General Pollock and in the First Sikh War under Lord Gough. He was severely wounded at the bloody battle of Mudki, having been struck on the head by a Sikh artilleryman's sponge-staff during hand-to-hand fighting. Despite his injury he slew the gunner and captured his cannon before wandering dazed into the night. He was found the following day, cold, confused and close to death. His wounds were dressed and just a few weeks later he was in action again at the battle of Sobraon, where the great Sikh army was wiped out.

In the Second Sikh War he saw more action with the 3rd Light Dragoons, taking part in the shambles at Ramnuggar, the crossing of the Chenab, the attack on Soodoolapore, the bloodbath of

Chillianwalla and the final battle of Gujerat. His regiment arrived back in England in July 1853. Within days Penn heard that the 17th Lancers were ordered for Turkey and he immediately volunteered to join them. His detachment, including fifty-seven horses, arrived in Varna in July 1854 under the command of Captain the Honourable Hercules Rowley, shortly to become Lord Langford. They arrived in the Crimea on 1 September.

Penn fought at the battle of Alma and at Mackenzie's Farm where a quantity of Russian baggage and stores was captured. By now he had an array of campaign medals but his first for distinguished conduct in the field was won in the famous Charge of the Light Brigade at Balaclava. His actions were witnessed by several officers who also survived that tragic waste of courageous lives. A contemporary account said:

> He speaks very highly of the lance, a weapon of which the Russians are very much in dread. Unfortunately for many of the brave fellows of his regiment, they had their poles shattered by the enemy's shower of grapeshot. On their coming up to the Russian guns, they were ordered to charge, when he made a point at a gunner, which took effect – the lance going through his body. He could not extricate it, as he was at a gallop.
>
> Passing through the enemy's guns, the 13th Light Dragoons and 17th Lancers were obliged to open out, when our hero came into contact with a Russian officer (a Hussar); he made for him, and the officer wheeled his horse around for the purpose of making a bolt; he, therefore, took a favourable distance on the officer's left (both at the time being at a gallop), when he delivered cut six, which instantly dismounted the officer, whose head was nearly severed from his body.
>
> At the same time his horse halted, and on dismounting, to his grief, he found that his horse had received a ball in the near shoulder. He then took a view of the Russian officer; he must have died in an instant, as the body never moved after falling to the ground; he cut his pouch-belt off, and took his sword, and a clasp knife, which he wore in a belt around his waist.

Penn rejoined his comrades, who were now surrounded by Russians. He used the captured sword to cut his way through but it broke as he slashed at a seventh enemy soldier. Penn and the bloodied, tattered remnants of the Light Brigade made it back and he and his wounded horse cantered into legend. (The horse, happily, recovered after the ball was speedily removed.)

Penn saw further action at Inkerman. His superiors noted: 'He was never ill during the whole of the season, although much exposed. He was always employed on general duty.' However, he suffered sunstroke when on outpost duty at Baldar in July 1855. His condition was exacerbated by old injuries suffered when at field-drill in India three years earlier: his right collar-bone had been fractured and his lower jaw broken when a horse fell on him. He was invalided home with no fewer than eleven decorations, and joined a much-needed gallery of popular heroes. The *Illustrated London News* said that 'his honours for military services are equal to any in the British Army' and that his eventful career 'presents a noteworthy instance of devotion to a noble object'. His portrait shows a grizzled, battle-hardened veteran – hardly the sort of man you would wish to tangle with. After his fifteen minutes of fame he stepped back into the shadows of obscurity.

Not so those heroes who came from a higher and therefore more acceptable class. Those aristocrats and officers who survived their battlefield exploits went on to become fêted generals, admirals, diplomats and politicians. They received peerages, knighthoods, medals, baubles and generous life-time pensions, and won membership of an exclusive elite: their portraits hung in the National Gallery, and they enjoyed favoured places at Court, the lion's share of the spoils, public acclamation, rich wives and glamour. There is no point in railing against such gross inequalities. This was a time, after all, when just 710 people owned a quarter of England and Wales. But such disparities disguised the heroism shared by all ranks. Courage was not the exclusive preserve of the officer class. Nor were all the other traits and instincts found in war: cruelty, compassion, comradeship, betrayal, cowardice, greed, fortitude, intelligence and stupidity. The silver spoon-fed, lisping fop, his rank bought for him by money and influence, was certainly present in most Empire campaigns. But there were also talented and competent upper-class officers who shared the privations and dangers of their men.

Take the career of General Sir Redvers Henry Buller, for example. Born into the family of the Dukes of Norfolk in 1829, Buller's wealthy and privileged upbringing had nothing in common with Penn's rough childhood. He served with the 60th in China, where his massive physical strength proved a boon in negotiating the rapids during the Red River campaign of 1870. He was General Wolseley's intelligence chief during the Ashanti expedition and the subsequent Egyptian conflict, becoming Chief of Staff in the Sudan in 1884.

He commanded the Irregular Light Horse during the Zulu War in South Africa and won the Victoria Cross for rescuing Captain D'Arcy and two men at Hlobane in 1879. He served in the Transvaal War and commanded a brigade in the Sudan where he was made a major-general, later being commemorated in song by Gilbert and Sullivan. Back in the Sudan he received a KCB for achieving victory against astounding odds at Abu Klea during the abortive bid to rescue General Gordon.

He was popular with his men and C.N. Robinson wrote: 'There is no stronger character in the British Army than the resolute, almost grimly resolute, absolutely independent, utterly fearless, steadfast and always vigorous commander. This big-boned, square jawed, strong-headed man was born a soldier . . .' Here there were echoes of Private Penn.

Buller was one of the greatest popular heroes of his day, but his fame was forever tarnished when he led the South African Field Force in the 1899. Much of the blame for the early shambles of the Boer War was put on his shoulders, including the disaster at Spion Kop. He was indecisive when boldness was required, foolhardy when he should have been cautious. He was a fighter rather than a strategist. Buller was subsequently recalled to duties at Aldershot and he too withdrew into obscurity — but his was a far more comfortable and well-rewarded obscurity than Private Penn's.

But both men's lives were packed with excitement and adventure in foreign lands. And the lives of such Victorians seem to have been so much more eventful than those of today's popular heroes. Those individuals who survived gruelling sea voyages, deadly diseases, starvation, exhaustion and savage foes could indeed carve out fortunes for themselves. Some, like James Brooke, could even win their own empires.

But all of this came at a fearful cost. The casualties in those forgotten wars, comrades and foes alike, were uncountable. The bleakest picture to come from those *Boy's Own* adventures is of vultures hovering over the dead and dying at Omdurman. The real tragedy is that this picture could have been painted at any one of a thousand places across the globe dominated by the red of Empire in the nineteenth century.

NINETEEN

The Gurkha War, 1814–16

'. . . few things look so formidable'.

In May 2000 Agansing Rai died, aged eighty, at his home, some three days' walk from Khatmandu. His death reduced to twenty-six the number of living holders of the Victoria Cross, Britain's highest military honour for valour.

Fifty-six years earlier, already a battle-hardened veteran of the Royal Gurkha Rifles, he and his comrades had faced a desperate Japanese counter-attack in Burma. Pinned down on Mortar Bluff near Imphal, Agansing Rai led his section in a charge on a machine-gun post, firing as he ran. He killed three of the four-man gun-crew. They then came under fire from a 37mm gun in the jungle. He again led a charge; this time all but three of his men were killed or wounded before they had covered half the distance. Rai's Thompson sub-machine-gun jammed and he snatched up the section's Bren; continuing the charge alone he wiped out the enemy gun-crew. He and his men, both standing and wounded, then came under intense machine-gun fire and grenades from a hidden bunker. After ordering his Bren gunner to cover him, Agansing Rai again advanced alone. Making his way along a shallow communication trench he stormed into the bunker and dispatched all four occupants with a single burst. He received his decoration from the Viceroy of India, Field Marshal Lord Wavell, in 1945.

Agansing Rai's astonishing courage typified both the reality and the legend of the Gurkha soldiers who have fought in British ranks since the second decade of the nineteenth century. For the best part of two hundred years they have been regarded as among the world's best soldiers. The mere mention of their *kukris*, the distinctive curved knife which, according to myth, must drink blood every time it is unsheathed, has sent some opponents running. Gurkhas have fought under the flags of other countries, but it is to Britain that they have traditionally owed the greatest allegiance outside their own mountain terrain. They have won admiration and respect from the officers and men who have served alongside them in Britain's colonial wars and global conflicts. They have also been held in the greatest regard in Britain, although that regard has rarely been matched in terms of pay, pensions and conditions. The respect is, by and large, mutual.

Yet it is often forgotten that before a single Gurkha served alongside a British soldier the Gurkhas fought a brief but bloody war against British military might in the foothills of the Himalayas. Like all such wars in savage places during that blood-soaked age the fighting was ferocious. Unusually, it was also marked by the honourable behaviour of both sides. It was a war with many casualties, but honour was not one of them. That was truly remarkable.

The ancient history of Nepal, a vast isolated country on the southern slopes of the Himalayas, is one of myths and legends. According to the folk tales, its central valley began as a lake which was drained by a single sword-cut wielded by the saint Manjushri. Successive dynasties traded and fought with China and the Indian moguls. Its people were always a rich ethnic mix. The Rajputs and the Aryans arrived during the wars with the Mongols, bringing with them the Hindu faith. Those tribes with Mongolian roots are generally Buddhists. In the central hills were the Brahmans and the Chetris, belonging to an ancient warrior caste. Higher in the mountains were the Magars and the Gurungs, both of fighting stock. Elsewhere were people from Tibet, including the Sherpas and the Bhutias. They were more peaceable, but tough, like all mountain dwellers.

The backbone of Nepal is the range of the Himalayas which includes Everest and many of the world's other highest mountains. Below them the central hills enjoy pleasant summers but severe winters with heavy snows above 8,000 feet, and valleys which endure torrential rain during the monsoon season. There was no wheeled traffic in the hills. The low-lying Terai region bordering India has a subtropical climate, hot in summer and extremely humid during the monsoons. The vegetation and wildlife varies dramatically according to altitude. In the valley of Khatmandu every square inch of suitable land was terraced for rice-growing during the monsoons and for wheat and vegetables during the drier months. There were, and still are, dense pine forests scattered with magnolias and wild cherry. In the uncultivated parts of the Terai were vast, impenetrable jungles teeming with deer, buffalo and wild ox, as well as elephants, tigers and leopards. In summer the hills blazed with dwarf rhododendrons, primulas and the blue poppy but the riotous colour was whited out when the winter snows came and temperatures dropped below zero. Nepal could be paradise or hell.

The Gurkhas took their name from the old city-state of Gorkha in the hills of the north-west. Its ruling family was descended from the Rajput princes of Udaipur who had been driven out of their own lands by the Muslims. The Gurkhas were both feared and admired by their neighbours. They seemed to enjoy warfare, not just for loot but also for a chance to test their own honour. A favourite proverb was 'It is better to die than to be a coward.'

They were devout Hindus who respected their kings, generals and elders. The caste system was sacrosanct. They were farmers and family men as well as fighters. Few took more than two wives and they were extremely fond of children. The birth of a son was the cause of much feasting. Divorces were permitted but a widow was not allowed to remarry. The men were square-built and sturdy, fond of sports and unafraid of hard work. Their average height was 5 foot 3 inches, although some tribes, such as the Chetri, were taller and darker. Their vices were gambling and some overenthusiasm for a grain beer called *janr*. They discouraged visitors, but Britons who managed to penetrate their borders spoke warmly of their good humour and generosity. Many saw their potential. One British officer said: 'Gurkhas are bold, enduring, frank, very independent and self-reliant; in their own country they are jealous of foreigners and self-asserting . . . though hot-tempered and easily roused, they are in general quiet, well-behaved men, and extremely amenable to discipline – from the warlike qualities of his forefathers, and the traditions handed down to him of their military prowess, he is imbued with, and cherishes, the true military spirit.' Another observer wrote: 'Their fighting qualities, whether for sturdy, unflinching courage or enduring elan, are *nulli secondus*.' A later minister, Brian Hodgson, wrote: 'In my humble opinion they are, by far, the best soldiers in India; and if they were made participators of our renown in arms, I conceive that their gallant spirit, emphatic contempt of *madherias* (plain-dwellers) and unadulterated military habit, might be relied on for fidelity . . .'

In 1742 the land-hungry Prithvi Narayan Shah reached the throne of Gorkha and fought a series of wars against the neighbouring Malla kingdoms of Khatmandu, Bhadgaon and Patan. He adopted European standards of discipline for his small but effective army which soundly defeated his strongest opponent, the Nabob of Moorshedabad. By 1768 he had subjugated the entire Valley of Nepal and declared himself king, with his capital at Khatmandu. His armies then turned east and west, conquering further principalities and defeating an ill-conceived and British-led expedition ordered by the government of Bengal. After Shah's death in 1775 his successors continued his ferocious policy of expansion, advancing as far west as the Kangra Valley in the Punjab where they were halted by the great Sikh leader Runjeet Singh. The Gurkhas then occupied Sikkim and invaded Tibet but were driven back by a Chinese counter-invasion. Such warfare and the mountainous terrain bred a nation of tough, adaptable soldiers. Their vast kingdom, skirting the northern frontier of Hindustan, was ideally placed for raids from their high strongholds into the plain regions below.

During this turbulent period relations were repeatedly strained with the East India Company, who complained of incursions into the territories under their control and protection. The Company tried to develop friendlier relations but the Nepalese kings resolutely refused to allow a British Resident in Khatmandu. They had seen for themselves how the Company used such means to extend its influence and power. The Gurkhas also pointed out, not unreasonably, that the remorseless territorial expansion of the British robbed them of the moral high ground. By the end of the eighteenth century Nepal shared an 800-mile border with the territories of John Company and the Nawab of Oudh, who was under its protection.

Numerous border disputes were resolved without bloodshed, but it was Oudh that proved to be the flashpoint.

At this time Nepal's nominal king was a beardless boy and the real power lay in the hands of the Thappa family, who held the most important positions. Bheim Sein was prime minister, while his brother-in-law Umur Sing, a renowned general, commanded the army. They had long coveted the rich kingdom of Oudh to their south and in 1801 Nepal occupied its northern districts of Gorakhpur and Saran. The British protested and the Governor-General, Lord Minto, opened up protracted negotiations with Khatmandu. Bheim Sein did not believe the British were serious and in 1813 a Gurkha army swept deeper into Oudh, garrisoning the Bhutwal region. Bheim Sein told the Khatmandu court: 'The Chinese once made war on us but were reduced to seek peace. How then will the English be able to penetrate into our hills? Our hills and fastness are joined by the hand of God and are impregnable.'

The Bengal administration, now led by Lord Moira, who had succeeded Minto as Governor-General, recalled the negotiators and dispatched a strong force of troops to the disputed area. The Gurkhas, for once, meekly withdrew from the occupied lands in the face of such a show of armed might. But the British blundered. Under-estimating their opponents, and with the onset of the unhealthy rainy season almost upon them, the expedition was withdrawn. The Gurkhas immediately returned. In Bhutwal three police stations were stormed and among the dead was a British officer. Moira, later better known as Lord Hastings, sent a letter to Khatmandu accusing the young Raja of Nepal of 'wantonly' making war on the British government. A formal declaration of war was made in November 1814.

*   *   *

Francis Rawdon-Hastings, the first Marquis of Hastings and second Earl of Moira, had only arrived at Calcutta in October, but he was determined to tackle the Nepalese head on and to punish their 'arrogance'. Aged fifty-nine, the product of Harrow and Oxford, he was a veteran of the American War of Independence and had won a signal victory against a larger body of rebels at Hobkirk's Hill. He was known as a martinet and was publicly rebuked for the execution of the American colonel Isaac Hayne. He served as an MP for Irish seats in County Antrim and acted as the Duke of York's second in a duel. He was appointed Governor-General as an antidote to Minto's more faint-hearted administration.

Many British officials and politicians believed that the proposed campaign would be a walkover. Lord Metcalfe called it 'a mere affair with a troublesome Raja of the frontier'. Advisers to the new governor consistently under-rated the Gurkha's military prowess, concentrating on their relatively small numbers. Others were not so sure. Company civil servants could not understand the need to wage war across inhospitable lands for no obvious reasons of profit. Colonel Sir David Ochterlony, the military commander in the north, described the planned expedition as 'the most impolitic measure we have ever attempted'.

Hastings had available an army of 22,000 men. He and Ochterlony agreed that this force should be divided into four columns for the invasion of Nepal: Ochterlony himself was to lead 6,000 men and 16 guns to the western frontier, Generals Wood and Marley were to command the two central columns, while General Gillespie, the hero of Java, was to lead an eastern column of 3,500 men; a garrison of 2,700 men was left for the defence of the border region east of the Coosy River. Hastings was to direct overall operations from Lucknow. The Gurkhas, meanwhile, had retreated to their mountain kingdom, preferring to fight on home territory which they believed to be impregnable.

The omens for the British were poor from the start. One observer noted: 'The British troops had to advance through a rugged, unknown and almost impracticable region, full of defensive defiles. They had no experience of mountain warfare, while the Gurkhas were a very warlike people who understood the value of the mountain passes, and had occupied and fortified them.' Hastings hoped to recruit men from local tribes threatened by the Gurkhas but the advice of the political agent in Kumaon was not encouraging: '. . . for the dread entertained of the Goorkha [sic] soldiery is such, their activity, enterprise, hardiness, patience and abstinence so remarkable, that even harassing his troops cannot be relied upon.' The comforts normally enjoyed by the gentlemanly officers of the Company's army were also not conducive to the sort of rapid-marching mountain campaign which Hastings envisaged. His adjutant-general ruled: 'Two mules and two asses will be sufficient to carry a captain's baggage, with the addition of two hillmen who carry loads. Servants must be reduced; subalterns can have three, captains five. The officers must have small, light tents with low poles, eight feet high.' The baggage and the lack of porters proved to be crucial handicaps in the following campaign in one of the world's most gruelling regions. Gillespie's column faced the toughest terrain as they sweated and froze and stumbled up rocky paths towards the small fort of Kalunga a few miles north of Dehra Dun.

Major-General Sir Robert Rollo Gillespie had for forty-eight years enjoyed a life that could have come straight from *Boy's Own*. He was a free-spirited adventurer with an Irish brogue, the product of a rumbustious background. The son of a Scots-Irish family who settled in County Down, he was educated at private schools in Kensington and Newmarket but refused to go to Cambridge. Instead he joined the 3rd Irish Horse as a cornet. Three years later he contracted a 'clandestine' marriage with Annabell, a pretty Dublin girl. Soon afterwards he acted as the second to an officer friend in a duel with the brother of Sir Jonah Barrington. Both men fired twice without hitting the other, and it was proposed that the matter should end there. But an argument erupted between the two seconds and Gillespie challenged Barrington to fire across his handkerchief. Gillespie fired back and Barrington fell dead. Gillespie fled and was hidden by some of his in-laws before he and his wife escaped to Scotland. He later returned voluntarily and stood trial for wilful murder at the summer assize of 1788. The judge was hostile but the jury, which included several half-pay officers, was not and they reached a verdict of 'justifiable homicide'.

Gillespie, desperate to see active service, escaped the scandal at home by accepting a lieutenancy in the newly raised Jamaica Light Dragoons. On the way out he was shipwrecked at Madeira and suffered yellow fever when he arrived. He saw action against the French at Tiburon and was fired on while swimming ashore at

Port-au-Prince with a white flag to demand the surrender of the town. His gallantry was evident at the capture of Fort Bizotten and he was wounded several times during the attack on For de l'Hopital. He was appointed adjutant-general of St Domingo to put down an insurrection there. A gang of eight men broke into his quarters, murdered his slave-boy and attacked Gillespie. He fought back with his sword, killing six, and the two survivors fled. A faulty report that the assassination attempt had succeeded reached Europe and hastened his mother's death.

After the Peace of Amiens Gillespie returned from Jamaica in command of his regiment but now faced accusations of fiddling the funds. His accuser had himself been arrested by Gillespie for sedition. The affair dragged on for two years until Gillespie was finally acquitted at a court martial in 1804. By then the cost of the proceedings, together with his 'open-handedness and misplaced trust', had left him financially ruined. The answer was to sign up for service in the 19th Light Dragoons in India. He travelled overland, disguising himself in Hamburg to escape French agents, via Greece and Baghdad. On arrival in India he was appointed commandant at Arcot. In 1806, after sepoy troops mutinied and massacred Europeans at Vellore, he rode to a fort where the British survivors were making a last stand against the mutineeers. He was hauled up the battlements by a rope and commanded the defence until heavier reinforcements arrived. The following years saw him commanding the Mysore division of the Madras Army. Astonishingly, his greatest adventures were still ahead of him.

In 1811 Gillespie, now a brigadier-general, commanded the advance expedition against Dutch Java and swiftly took the city of Batavia. Although wracked with fever he continued to direct operations against the Dutch forces. The overall commander, Sir Samuel Auchmuty, said that the success of the whole enterprise was due to Gillespie's 'gallantry, energy and prompt judgement'. Gillespie was left as military commander of the island, with Stamford Raffles as the civil governor. The following year the Sultan of Palembang on Sumatra murdered the Europeans within his domain. Gillespie took a small force, deposed the sultan 'in a most summary manner' and extended British influence. On his return to Java he found that a confederation of anti-British chiefs had gathered with 100 guns and 30,000 men at a stockaded fortress at Yodhyakarta, threatening the lives of all European settlers. Gillespie promptly attacked the fort with 1,500 men and broke up the rebellion. His victory, however, was tarnished by a dispute with Stamford Raffles about the scale of military occupation. He laid charges against Raffles over the sale of lands. The issue was unresolved when Gillespie returned to India to take command of the Meerut division. His men admired both his confidence and his abilities as a sportsman. One one occasion he killed a tiger in the open on Bangalore racecourse.

*   *   *

Gillespie's men toiling towards Kalunga knew of his colourful past and, above all, his track record of victory. Intelligence had already revealed that the Gurkha garrison numbered barely 600 men. The battle, they felt, would be a pushover despite the cruelty of the terrain. But when they reach the approaches to the fort victory did not appear so certain. Kalunga was perched in an almost inaccessible position, surrounded by deep crevices, the snowy Himalayas providing an impressive backcloth. The attack was fixed for 31 October 1814.

Gillespie divided his force into four small columns, one to assault each face. Three of the columns would have to make long detours over difficult ground and a prearranged signal for the attack was agreed. As the four columns were getting into position the Gurkhas launched a sortie. They were repulsed but Gillespie, thinking he could follow them back into the fort, attempted to rush the defences with a dismounted party of the 8th Dragoons. The manoeuvre failed. Gillespie impatiently renewed the attack with several companies of the 53rd Foot – without waiting for the other two columns. During his desperate gamble some units appeared to panic. Gillespie, leading from the front, a sword in one hand and a pistol in the other, attempted to rally his men just 30 metres from the fort's gate. A Gurkha sharpshooter aimed at the distinctive figure, and shot him through the heart. As his body was being taken back down to Meerut, the attack collapsed.

Another attempt on 27 November met with similar failure when troops refused to storm a wide breach in the stockade. The men had been told to unload their muskets and charge with the bayonet only; they were understandably reluctant to advance, given the fearsome reputation of the Gurkhas and their *kukris* in hand-to-hand combat. The two assaults cost the British 740 casualties. The British were unused to meeting powerful opposition in such strong positions. The defeats taught them caution and the column besieging Kalunga, now commanded by Colonel Sebright Mawby, turned to their cannon and an intense bombardment was opened up. After three days the Gurkha commander Balbahadur, known to the British as Bulbudder Singh, slipped away unnoticed with the survivors of his garrison, leaving behind over 500 dead and wounded, mainly dead, piled high. Mawby said that the sight 'presented so much misery that the most obdurate heart must have bled'.

A dispatch to Calcutta said: 'The garrison is now known to have suffered most severely from the fire of the British artillery, and particularly from the shells thrown by the mortars. The place was found crowded with dead and wounded, whom the enemy was unable to carry off in his precipitous flight . . . The arduous and difficult nature of the service, the fatigues and the privations the troops had for some time undergone, and the strength of the enemy's position, demanded exemplary exertions of activity, zeal and personal bravery from the European officers . . .' The Gurkhas found alive in the rubble of Kalunga included several small children whose parents had died in the bombardment. The British took care of them and the adult wounded. Not all the Gurkhas appreciated such humanity. Mawby reported:

To show the determined conduct of these people, the orderly Jemada to Bulbudder Sing, in attempting to escape with his Chief, was wounded and taken prisoner – finding that the wound would not put him to death, he abused both Officers and Men in the grossest terms in hopes that they would by that means shoot him – but finding that this would have no effect on their feelings – he beat his head against the Stones in the hope of putting an end to his existence – which all failing, he requested fire to warm himself, and when left by the Sepoys, he took an opportunity of throwing the whole of it on his breast – which was no sooner discovered than it was removed – he has, however, since died.

The British admired such single-mindedness. The courage of the Gurkha defenders, most of whom now lay dead, was also recognised. James Fraser, the brother of Gillespie's political agent, wrote:

The determined resolution of the small party which held this small post for more than a month, against so comparatively large a force, must surely wring admiration from every voice, especially when the horrors of the latter portion of this time are considered: the dismal spectacle of their slaughtered comrades, the sufferings of their women and children thus immured with themselves, and the hopelessness of relief, which destroyed any other motive for the obstinate defence they made, than that resulting from a high sense of duty, supported by unsubdued courage. This, a generous spirit of courtesy towards their enemy, certainly marked the character of the garrison at Kalunga, during the period of its siege.

Whatever the nature of the Ghoorkhas may have been found in other quarters, there was here no cruelty to wounded or to prisoners; no poisoned arrows were used; no wells or waters were poisoned; no rancorous spirit of revenge seemed to animate them.

The British raised a small obelisk outside the fort to honour their enemy. Its inscription read: 'They fought in their conflict like men and, in the intervals of actual conflict, showed a liberal courtesy.'

A month later another attack on a fort at Jaithak failed. British troops were halted at the first stockade, and they turned and ran as the Gurkhas counter-attacked, their *kukris* glistening. Sepoys coming up as reserves panicked when they saw the European troops in retreat and they did not stop running until they reached their base at Nahan. Gillespie's original force had by now been cut by a third and further offensive operations were halted.

The lesson of caution had perhaps been too well taken by the commanders of the two central columns. Major-General John Sullivan Wood's 4,000-strong force operating from Gorakhpur made slow progress owing to sickness and a lack of hill-porters. His intelligence and scout units were also poor and on one occasion he and his staff officers blundered to within 50 metres of an enemy stockade without realising it. After a January attack on a stockade at Jeetgarh failed, Wood wrote in dispatches about his initial success in taking a hill on the right of the redoubt: 'This party was led by a brave and cool officer, Captain Croker, who drove the enemy before them up the hill, killing a chief Sooraj Tappah; still the fire from the enemy, concealed by the trees, was kept up with great obstinacy, and the hill which rose immediately behind the work, was filled with troops, rendering the post, if it had been carried, wholly untenable; I therefore determined to stop the fruitless waste of lives, by sounding retreat.' Wood decided his force was not strong enough to advance deeper into Nepal's hill country. He reported: 'Some confusion occurred in consequence of the majority of the bearers having thrown down their loads, but the soldiers, both European and native, brought away most of the boxes of ammunition.' Wood, who appears to have exaggerated the numbers of Gurkhas facing him, also believed exaggerated reports of a Gurkha army poised to sweep down on to the plains and ordered his men on to the defensive. Or rather, as one contemporary noted, 'he did nothing'.

Meanwhile the largest column of 8,000 men under Major-General Bonnett Marley failed in its main thrust against Khatmandu. Marley crossed the Nepal border in December but, in defiance of his orders, halted the column to await further supplies. He established two outposts many miles from the main body. Unsurprisingly the Gurkhas surrounded and captured both, inflicting heavy casualties. The British lost 125 killed, 73 missing and 187 wounded. Marley tried to dodge the blame. Writing to his superiors he said that the two posts had only been taken 'after a considerable but ineffectual resistance on the part of our troops against the overwhelming numbers and superior means opposed to them'.

Dispatches from junior officers under Marley's command told their own dispiriting story. Lieutenant E. Strettell reported:

It is with the deepest regret that I have to acquaint you with the information that the left wing, 2nd battalion, 22nd regiment native infantry, was this morning attacked and compelled to retire. The enemy advanced about five-o'clock and immediately opened a very severe and well-directed fire from about twenty pieces of cannon. Captain Blackney and all the officers of the wing did their utmost endeavours to bring on our sepoys to the charge, which failed in every attempt, from the very destructive fire which opposed them.

Blackney and Lieutenant Duncan were killed.

On the fall of these two gallant officers, the sepoys became quite dispirited, and began to retire with some confusion, upon which the enemy advanced upon and destroyed our tents by fire. The village of Summunpore, in which was the commissariat, was burnt at the commencement of the action by the enemy. Finding that the detachment had suffered most severely, added to the great numbers and strength of the enemy, it was judged most prudent to retire; and as the enemy had taken possession of the road to Barra Ghurrie, we directed our course to this place. I am unable to state the exact loss of the detachment, as stragglers are coming in every moment.

Major J. Greenstreet wrote:

I am sorry to acquaint you that the post of Persa Ghurrie was this morning attacked by an overwhelming force of Goorkhas, who, I regret to say, carried their point after an hour's hard fighting which ended in the repulse of our troops there, the loss of the gun, and every kind of baggage. At break of day, when I was about to march for that post, we heard a heavy firing in that direction when I pushed on with all speed; but within three miles of the place I met a vast number of wounded, and immediately afterwards some officers, who informed me that any attempt by me to recover the fortune of the day must be unavailing . . .

Sepoys in the main camp now began to desert although reinforcements swelled Marley's force to 12,000. But the general was unnerved by wild estimates of the enemy strength. He convinced himself that he was facing some 18,000 of the best Gurkha fighters – in fact there were 8,000 at most, many of them poorly armed militia. Marley retreated to the border and sat there for a month, also doing nothing. On 10 February he appears to have broken down emotionally or mentally. Before dawn he rode out of camp without handing over command to anyone. It was a rare case of a general deserting his own army.

Three months of campaigning in some of the world's toughest territories had left three British columns more or less where they had started. Only Ochterlony's own column in the easier countryside to the west was making slow but steady progress, aided by local tribes who had little love for the Nepalese regime. He crossed the plains from Ludiana, entered the hill country and on 1 November reached the fort of Nalagur which surrendered after thirty hours of continuous bombardment.

His limited successes, however, could not disguise the overall failure. The initial defeat at Kalunga, the death of a renowned general and hero, and the further humiliations inflicted on the Empire by mountain tribesmen caused a scandal at home. The official history of the Bengal Army said that the campaign contained 'a greater number of disastrous failures and of ill-arranged and worse-carried-out enterprises, due generally to an entire want of appreciation of the necessities of hill warfare than had ever before, or ever since, befallen the arms of the British in India'. Hastings admitted that the Gurkhas had 'intimidated our troops and our generals'. British defeats sent out the wrong message to other tribal nations bordering the Raj and the would-be rebels within them. The Sikhs of the Punjab, the Afghans and the Maratha chiefs all posed a real threat. Some alarmists forecast that Britain would lose the entire sub-continent. Lord Metcalfe, the Resident at Delhi, wrote: 'Our power in India rests upon our military superiority. It has no foundation in the affections of our subjects. It cannot derive support from the good will or the good faith of our neighbours.' He said that before the war the power of the Gurkhas was ridiculed, their forts described as contemptible, their weapons as useless. 'Yet we find that with these useless weapons in their contemptible forts they can deal out death among their assailants, and stand to their defences.' He went on:

> We have met with an enemy who shows decidedly greater bravery and greater steadiness than our troops possess; and it is impossible to say what may be the end of such a reverse of the order of things. In some instances our troops, European and Native, have been repulsed by inferior numbers with sticks and stones. In others our troops have been charged by the enemy sword in hand, and driven for miles like a flock of sheep. In this war, dreadful to say, we have had numbers on our side, and skill and bravery on the side of our enemy.

Hastings, who largely agreed with Metcalfe's analysis, pledged to throw everything he could at the Gurkhas, even if that meant leaving British India's other borders dangerously exposed and their forces under-strength. By the end of January 1815 there were almost 40,000 troops facing no more than 12,000 Gurkha regular soldiers and an unknown number of militia.

*   *   *

As spring approached General Ochterlony provided a much-needed boost to British morale. Sir David, fifty-six and Boston-born, was the son of a gentleman who had settled in America. His service stretched back to 1777 when he had enlisted as a cadet in the Bengal army of the Company. He fought against Haider Ali, the French and the Marathas. In 1804 he commanded the successful defence of Delhi, despite weak ramparts and a shortage of ammunition. One plaudit said: 'No action of the war . . . deserves greater commendation than this brave and skilful defence of an almost untenable position.' He was known to his sepoy troops as 'Lonely-ackty'.

Ochterlony was determined not to suffer a repeat of the Kalunga disaster. He made it a rule never to directly assault Gurkha stockades, choosing instead, whenever possible, to blow them to smithereens with artillery. This involved building rough roads and bridges across the broken terrain and jagged ravines. Hundreds of coolies and porters were employed. Ochterlony wrote: 'Manual labour, strength and perseverance are our main dependencies in these Alpine regions.' He shared with his men the hardships of the campaign.

By the end of March Ochterlony, in his slow and steady fashion, had reduced and occupied all the Gurkhas forts along the route of his advance to Bilaspur. He then began a long and arduous chase of the Gurkha general Umur Sing. A fine tactician, Sing was operating a long way from his real homeland, and some of the hill tribes were hostile to his army. His main strength lay in the ability of his soldiers, fighting in a homeland of which they knew every inch, to move swiftly and with apparent ease. It was a quality envied by the British, laden as they were with heavy baggage. One officer wrote: 'These highland soldiers, who despatch their meal in half an hour, laugh at the rigour of the sepoys who cannot be in marching trim again in less than three hours.'

Ochterlony slowly advanced against a strongly fortified position near Simla, 5,000 feet up in the Himalayas, during the worst of the winter. His engineers blasted rocks and opened roads for his two 18-pounders which were hauled up by men and elephants. On 14 April he attacked Umur Singh at night and carried two strongpoints. The Gurkhas retreated to the Maloun Heights, a string of fortified hilltops, with drops of 2,000 feet on two sides. Although his position was strong, Umur Sing was effectively bottled up.

Ryla Peak was the first to fall, with little opposition. The second peak, Deothul, proved a tougher nut to crack. It was taken on 15 April only after a costly action. The British set about strengthening the captured position with further earthworks. A determined Gurkha attack of 2,000 men under Bhagtee Thapa came within a whisker of driving them out again, breaking through the British defences at several points. The Gurkhas recognised, from bitter experience, the power of the British artillery and concentrated their fire on the gun positions. After several brutally effective volleys only one artillery officer and three men were left standing. One soldier recalled: 'The Gurkhas came on with furious intrepidity, so much so that several were bayoneted or cut to pieces within our works.

Umur Sing stood all the while just within musquet [sic] range, with the Goorkha Colours planted beside him; while Bhagtee was everywhere inciting the men to further efforts.' The position was saved by reinforcements from Ryla Peak. The British suffered 213 casualties, the Gurkhas more than twice that. Each side's respect for the courage and fighting ability of the other increased enormously.

Meanwhile Hastings ordered two columns of irregular troops under Colonel Gardner and Captain Hearsay to march on Kumaon, a poorly organised province in the centre of the Nepalese front. The local tribes regarded the British as saviours rather than invaders and were ready to help overturn Gurkha rule. Hearsay blundered by attacking a superior force, but Gardner scored a signal success. He outmanoeuvred the Gurkhas and soon penetrated deep into their territory, threatening the province capital, Almora. He was reinforced by 2,000 regular native troops with some cannon under Colonel Jasper Nicolls, who promptly took command. After several skirmishing successes his force prepared to take the town. The Gurkha garrison was by now disheartened and, after some initial fighting, hauled up a flag of truce on 28 April. They agreed to British terms to evacuate both Almora and the entire province, and to withdraw beyond the Kali river.

The loss of Kumaon had a profound effect on Umur Sing's men, corralled along the Maloun Heights. As the news filtered through they began to desert in large numbers, some of them defecting to the British. By 10 May just 200 men were left to make a last stand in the fort of Maloun. Initially Umur Sing rebuked all those, mainly members of the royal house, who talked of appeasement. But Ochterlony's tactics of steady attrition impressed him greatly and said that the British general was the only opponent who had robbed him of the chance to give battle at the time and place of his choosing. Umur Sing was left with no choice but surrender. The British acknowledged a gallant foe and on 15 May he was allowed to march out unharmed, with his personal possessions and all the honours of war, provided he withdrew to the east of the Kali river. The British fired a royal salute at the army's principal stations. The *Annual Register* noted: 'It seems evident that the contest has been with a bold and adventurous foe, with whom the establishment of a lasting pacification is perhaps more to be desired than expected.' As a reward for his victory Ochterlony was created a baronet, and the East India Company granted him a pension of £1,000 per annum from the date of the Gurkha capitulation. The British now controlled all the mountainous country between the Kali and Sutlej rivers. Ochterlony formed the Gurkha deserters into battalions of the Company's regular army.

The proud Gurkha leaders were forced to sue for peace and an armistice was agreed. Hastings set tough terms. All the conquered territory west of the Kali should be ceded permanently to the British, along with much of the Terai region – the swampy jungle in the foothills of the Himalayas. A British Resident must also be allowed to dwell in Khatmandu. Negotiations dragged on for several months. The Gurkhas were realists and understood that the British conquests had been won fair and square. In their turn the British understood that the Gurkhas had not been subjugated, and some concessions were made on the extent of ceded territory. The main obstacle was the question of a British Resident but in November even this was agreed and a treaty was signed on 29 November and ratified by the supreme government at Calcutta on 19 December 1815.

To the astonishment of the British, the Nepal durbar refused to accept the treaty. The war was back on.

* * *

During the protracted negotiations Ochterlony was given charge of the Eastern Command. When the war resumed he was ready with an army of 20,000 men to advance on Khatmandu. He split his force into four columns. One on the right was directed towards Hariharpur, another on the left towards Ramnagar, while the two in the centre, which Ochterlony commanded personally, was to strike at the Nepalese capital. All four columns were to act cohesively and in support of each other. It seemed the British had learned some lessons from the previous campaign – as had the Gurkhas. During the lull the Gurkha commanders had fortified virtually the entire length of the Dun hills to prevent another invasion from the south.

Ochterlony began his advance at the beginning of February 1816. On the 10th he and his main force reached the entrance of the Chuviaghati Pass, having crossed the formidable Sal forest without losing a man. The enemy were entrenched behind three lines of defences, which Ochterlong decided were too strong for a frontal assault; instead he determined to turn its flank. Under cover of darkness he stripped one brigade of all their usual baggage, and during the night of the 14th led them in single file up an unguarded path. A correspondent wrote: 'They moved laboriously through deep and rocky defiles, across sombre and tangled forests, and by rugged and precipitous ascents, until the next day he reached and occupied a position in rear of the enemy's defences.' Lieutenant John Shipp of the Royal Irish Fusiliers recalled: 'Our gallant general walked every yard of this critical approach with his men, encouraging them as he went, and that sort of thing works wonders.' The Gurkhas were taken wholly by surprise by the sudden appearance of the British to their rear, complete with two elephants and guns. Uncharacteristically they panicked and hurriedly evacuated their positions, fleeing northwards without firing a shot. Ochterlony and his brigade spent four miserable days huddled on the bleak and exposed mountainside waiting for their tents and baggage trains to catch up.

The war now became a question of pursuing and wearing down the remnants of the Gurkha army. With desperation came cruelty. Lieutenant Shipp described the treatment of a prisoner taken by the Gurkhas as a spy:

This poor creature was seized and literally cut to pieces; and it was supposed by the medical people, that he must have died a death of extreme agony, for the ground under him was dug up with his struggling under the torture which had been inflicted on him. His arms had been cut off, about halfway up from the elbow to the shoulder, after which it appeared that two deep incisions had been cut in his body just above the hips, into which the two arms had been thrust. His features were distorted in a most frightful manner . . .

The two brigades of Ochterlony's main column formed a junction on the banks of the Rapti Rover and built a strongly stockaded depot. They caught up with the enemy at Magwampur, roughly 20 miles from Khatmandu, and seized a small village to the right of the Gurkha positions. A ferocious counter-attack by 2,000 Gurkhas before the village could be fully occupied came close to giving Ochterlony his first defeat. Repeated attacks on the British positions were beaten off but the Gurkha onslaught was only crushed by a spirited charge from the 2nd Battalion of the 8th Native Infantry. Lieutenant Shipp found himself in desperate single combat with the Gurkha commander Kishnabahadur Rana, and killed him with a sabre cut to the neck, almost severing his head. Shipp recognised a noble enemy and wrote in his memoirs:

> They maintained their ground and fought manfully. I hate a runaway foe; you have no credit for beating them. Those we were dealing with were no flinchers; on the contrary, I never saw more bravery or steadiness exhibited in my life. Run they would not, and of death they seemed to have no fear, though their comrades were falling thick about them, for we were so near that every shot told . . .

The British six-pounders pulverised the Gurkhas. 'The havoc was dreadful, for they still scorned to fly,' Shipp continued. Eventually there was little left but carnage on the field.

> As long as it was light we could plainly see the last struggles of the dying. Some poor fellows could be seen raising their knees up to their chins, and then flinging them down again with all their might. Some attempted to rise, but failed in the attempt. One poor fellow I saw got on his legs, put his hand to his bleeding head, then fell, and rolled down the hill, to rise no more. This was the scene that the evening now closed upon. Believe me when I assure you that these results of war were no sights of exultation or triumph to the soldiers who witnessed them. Willingly would we one and all have extended the hand of aid to them, and dressed their gaping wounds.

The battle could not have been more decisive. The Gurkhas lost up to 800 men and all their heavy guns. Ochterlony's force lost 45 killed and 175 wounded. One report noted that the British, as on former occasions, had to contend with 'antagonists defective neither in courage nor discipline'. Ochterlony prepared to attack Magwampur itself. The following day he was joined by the left brigade which had advanced by Ramnagar with little determined opposition.

The right brigade, meantime, had been delayed by rough ground in its advance upon Hariharpur. But on 1 March the enemy positions there were successfully turned and a Gurkha attack repulsed with great loss of life. Officers once again recorded that the Gurkhas had behaved with 'desperate bravery'. Hariharpur was converted into a depot. The British were now within striking distance of Khatmandu itself. The column was about to march to join Ochterlony when envoys arrived from Khatmandu. The durbar had realised that further resistance was futile and ratified the peace treaty previously rejected. The war was over.

*   *   *

The Treaty of Saguili reimposed Hastings' conditions, stripped Nepal of the Terai and imposed a British Resident in Khatmandu. It was honoured by both sides. Ochterlony's biographer wrote: 'The Gurkhas, who were not only the most valiant but the most humane foes the British had encountered in India, proved also to be the most faithful to their engagement.'

Ochterlony was rewarded with a GCB, a parliamentary vote of thanks for his 'skill, valour and perseverance', and a piece of plate from the officers who had served under him. During the following year he fought successfully, and often without serious bloodshed, to suppress the Pindari tribes who had been looting and despoiling British territory. His diplomatic skills were rated as highly as his generalship and by 1822 he effectively supervised the affairs of Central India. But in 1824 he became embroiled in a succession crisis when the Raja of Jaipur died and his son, heir to the throne, was imprisoned by his nephew. Ochterlony, acting on his own responsibility, issued a proclamation urging the Jats to rally around their rightful ruler and ordered 16,000 men into the field to support the rights of the young Raja. His order was countermanded by the Governor-General, Lord Amhurst, who feared a costly campaign while the British were also fighting a war with Burma. Ochterlony resigned. He was deeply hurt, feeling that his honour was tarnished. He told friends that after nearly fifty years of active and conscientious service he felt his actions should have merited confidence from his senior. He retired to Delhi where he suffered 'agonies of the mind'. He died there just a few months later. Sixty-eight guns were fired in his honour, corresponding to his age. Shortly afterwards Ochterlony was vindicated. It later took an army of 20,000 men several months to restore the ruler of Jaipur. Senior officers reckoned that if Ochterlony's original plan had been supported it would have taken just a fortnight – and a fraction of the eventual cost.

Lord Hastings, having initiated and won the Third Mahratta War, of which the actions against the Pindari were a part, now settled down to his duties of civil administration. Despite numerous squabbles with the board of the East India Company, he supported the education of the native population, the freedom of the Press and the removal of oppressive laws. His feud with the directors continued, however, and they finally won after he blundered over a land deal. Charges of corrupt transactions, for which the evidence was profoundly suspect, were considered. Embittered at his treatment, Hastings resigned in 1821 and treated as arrant hypocrisy a vote of thanks from the Company for his zeal and ability. He was appointed Governor of Malta. There his health, already weakened both physically and mentally by service in India, began to fail and he was further injured in a fall from a horse. He died on board HMS *Revenge* in 1826, aged seventy-one.

Astonishingly, no disciplinary action was taken against Major-General Marley, the man who had deserted his own troops when he believed he was facing superior numbers. He was not even dismissed from the service but continued to hold further commands, eventually reaching the rank of full general. He died in 1842.

Sir Penderel Moon wrote: 'An unnecessary war was followed by a lasting peace. The British and the Gurkhas never fought again. Nepal remained an independent kingdom, an ally but not a vassal of the British.' For the next forty years relations between the British administration of India and Nepal amounted to frosty friendship, diplomatic indifference and occasional tensions. Those tensions were eased when the British handed back parts of the Terai to Nepal. The Khatmandu court was too busy with internal intrigue to consider further conquests to the south. Bheeim Sein Thappa, who ruled in the name of the young king, himself fell victim to lethal plotting. Chaos followed, reaching its bloody peak in the 1846 massacre of the Kot, or royal court of assembly, in which many of the most noble families were slain. Bheeim Sein's grandson, a young soldier called Jung Bahadur, seized power, became prime minister and banished the royal family. He visited England in 1850 and became a firm friend of the British.

Until Bahadur, the rulers of Nepal during this period of turmoil may have stayed aloof from the Raj, but not so the common man and soldier. The seeds of lasting friendships between fighting peoples had been sown during the bloody days of war when both sides forged a deep respect for the other. (Ochterlony privately told Lord Hastings that the Company's sepoys 'could never be brought to resist the shock of these energetic mountaineers on their own grounds'.) Part of the credit for their mutual respect must go Lieutenant Frederick Young, the thirty-year-old officer of the 13th Native Infantry who had held Gillespie as he died at Kalunga. After that siege Young was leading a party of native irregulars in the hills when they were surrounded by Gurkhas. The sepoys fled, leaving the British officers to face the enemy. The Gurkhas were amazed that the Britons did not also run and laughingly asked why they had not done so. Young replied: 'I have not come so far in order to run away. I came to stay.' According to contemporary reports, maybe romanticised, a Gurkha commander told him: 'We could serve under men like you'. Young was allowed to live and was held as an honoured prisoner. He was treated well and made friends with his captors, who taught him their language.

Young never forgot their honourable conduct or their fighting skills. During the 1815 armistice he proposed that a corps of Gurkhas should be raised to serve in John Company's army.

Permission was granted and men flocked to the British colours from the surrounding hills. Some were paroled prisoners, others deserters, but most had been valiant opponents who had been astonished by the perseverance and technology of the British forces. Young said: 'I went there one man and came out three thousand.' The Khatmandu government was not happy about the defection of some of their best soldiers but there was little they could do. As the peace treaty clearly stated: 'All the troops in the service of Nepal, with the exception of those granted to the personal honour of Kagjees Ummersing and Rangor Sing, will be at liberty to enter into the services of the British Government if agreeable to themselves and the British Government choose to accept their services.'

Four local battalions of Gurkhas were raised: the 1st and 2nd Basiri, the Sirmoor and the Kumaon. The British were impressed from the start with the enthusiasm with which they trained. Within six months of its formation, Young, who commanded the Sirmoor battalion for twenty-eight years, was able to report it ready for battle. His battalion was the first to see service, in the 1817 Mahratta War. They proved their worth at the battle of Sambhar and Ochterlony expressed his satisfaction by granting the Gurkhas the honour of escorting to Delhi the 300 enemy guns captured during the campaign.

In 1824 Young led 200 of his troops against Goojar rebels and decisively beat a force four times their number at Koonja. The surviving rebels retreated into a fort which the Gurkhas took by using a felled tree as a battering ram. Over 150 rebels died in ferocious hand-to-hand fighting within the mud walls. Since that day Gurkha battalions have worn a ram's head on their regimental badges. Many more battle honours followed. After the 1825 siege of Bhurtpore the Gurkhas were praised by officers of the East Lancashire Regiment. A Gurkha soldier almost returned the compliment: 'The English are as brave as lions; they are splendid sepoys, and are very nearly equal to us.'

Over the years the original battalions were reformed into the Gurkha Rifles. More heroic service was performed in the Burma wars, against the usurper Durjan Sal and in the brutal battles with the Sikhs in the Punjab. After the bloodbath at Sobraon, which shattered Sikh power, the British commander, General Sir Hugh Gough, wrote: 'I must pause in this narrative especially to notice the determined hardihood and bravery with which our two battalions of Ghoorkas, Sirmoor and Nusserree, met the Sikhs wherever they were opposed to them. Soldiers of small stature but indomitable spirit, they vied in ardent courage in the charge with the Grenadiers of our own nation and, armed with the short weapon of their mountains, were a terror to the Sikhs throughout this great action.' Jung Bahadar sent his Gurkha armies to help the British during the Indian Mutiny. During that tragic conflict the mutineers' leader Bahadur Shah offered 10 rupees for the head of every Gurkha brought to him. The Sirmoor Battalion distinguished itself during the final assault on Delhi. On the North West Frontier Gurkhas were engaged for over fifty years in almost constant campaigning to protect the Raj from border encroachments and warring tribes. In the battle of Kandahar in 1880 the Gurkhas and the 92nd Gordon Highlanders conducted a classic bayonet charge which cemented their relationship as partners in the brigade. The Scots and Nepalese stormed a hilltop and a Gurkha stuffed his cap into one of two captured guns, signifying it was their prize. During the 1891 Manipur campaign 200 Gurkhas, whose British officers had been killed by treachery, held out in the British Residency until their ammunition ran out. Then they fixed bayonets and drew their *kukris* for a final charge, which few survived. In 1897 Gurkhas again charged alongside the Gordon Highlanders up the Dargai Heights during the Tirah campaign.

Gurkha troops continued to serve as an integral part of the Indian Army until Indian Independence in 1947. Twenty-four years earlier Britain had acknowledged Nepal's complete independence. During the First World War Gurkhas fought in Flanders, Mesopotamia and Palestine. A sizeable detachment joined the Arabs fighting the Turks under Lawrence of Arabia. At Loos the 2nd Battalion suffered so many casualties that it ceased to exist as a fighting force; General Sir James Willcocks said that the battalion had 'found its Valhalla'. At Gallipoli the 6th Gurkhas captured a key bluff, topped by a nest of machine-guns, which had previously repulsed the Royal Marines and the Royal Dublin Fusiliers.

Gurkha service during the Second World War was second to none. They were found in the thick of the fighting at Tobruk, El Alamein, Wadi Akarit, Monte Cassino and in Greece. They fought the Japanese in Malaya and Burma. Field Marshal the Lord Hardinge wrote: 'I have had experience of their skill and prowess, their courage and endurance on many a different battlefield, and I know for a fact that they are the finest comrades in arms – happy warriors indeed.' Field-Marshal Sir William Slim said: 'Nothing looks so uniform as a Gurkha battalion, nothing looks more workmanlike and few things look so formidable.' On another occasion Slim referred to the regiment's 'magnificent reputation' for discipline and battle-worthiness. In total, the Gurkhas won twenty-six VCs, an astonishing total given their small numbers.

After Partition, some Gurkha forces were transferred to the new Indian Army and served with the United Nations in the Congo and other hotspots. Others chose to stay with the British Army as licensed mercenaries. Brigadier A.E.C. Bredin wrote:

> The Gurkha is, of course, an enthusiastic soldier, second to none in smartness and turnout, both in uniform and in mufti. For generations he has been a soldier and tends to look down on non-military people or individuals. His bravery in action has won him great renown and much esteem where the British Army has fought for the past one hundred and forty years. Though often a yeoman of some substance, he joins the Army because of tradition and for the standing it gives him.

Their meagre pay, less than a third of that of their British compatriots, fed and clothed their families in the high mountains. Bredin, who commanded the 6th Gurkha Rifles in Malaya, wrote:

> Virtually the highest pre-war standards exist in the Brigade of Gurkhas and it is a joy as well as an honour to command, or to serve with, such men; men who love being soldiers, are intensely proud of their military record and rightly regard soldiering as the most honourable and manly profession. Like their predecessors in the old British Indian Army, they

are capable of fighting anywhere in the world and against any enemies.

The presence of Gurkhas in the Falkland Islands in 1982 wrecked Argentinian morale – even though they never took their *kukris* from their scabbards.

Agansing Rai's citation in 1944 concluded that 'his magnificent display of initiative, outstanding bravery and gallant leadership so inspired the rest of the company that, in spite of heavy casualties, the result of this important action was never in doubt'. These words could easily have applied to many of his comrades over the previous century.

TWENTY

The Defeat of the Borneo Pirates, 1840–9

'The miserable creatures were crushed under the paddle . . .'

A young British officer forced himself to look at the handiwork of Borneo's notorious pirates. Women captives had been slain and their bodies, abused in life, were horribly mutilated in death. Heads festooned hundreds of poles. The long-houses were stuffed with booty from across the globe.

The defeat of such a scourge was a factor in making the British adventurer Sir James Brooke the White Rajah of Sarawak. But the slaughter his campaigns entailed led to heated debates in Westminster. It was alleged that once again British military might was being used against primitive foes who were chopped up by canister shell and the paddles of the new war steamers. The question was: who were the real pirates?

*   *   *

Piracy was a way of life in the crowded, narrow straits of Malaysia and among the coastal tribes of Borneo. Small-scale barter in sixth-century Borneo had grown into large-scale traffic with both China and Siam by the thirteenth century. Later the South China Sea was to act as a funnel for the rich trading fleets that sailed between East and West. Peaceful and weak tribes along the coastline were easy targets for more warlike neighbours. All provided rich pickings and as powerful princedoms grew wealthy on plunder it became an almost legitimate arm of business. The island of Borneo traded in gold, diamonds, spices, pearls and rattan.

The early Hindu-Javanese people were overrun by the Malays from Singapore, and in the fifteenth century the Muslim states seized power. Sarawak, on the north coast of Borneo, became the southern province of the sultanate of Brunei. Magellan's fleet visited Brunei, whose city contained 25,000 houses. 'The King was a Mahomedan of great power,' wrote an observer, 'keeping a magnificent court, and was always attended by a numerous guard. He has ten secretaries of state, who write everything concerning his affairs on the bark of trees.' The Spanish and other early visitors from Europe agreed that the native Dyak people were peaceable and generous, while the Malay overlords were treacherous and 'piratical'.

The Portuguese tried to move in, and, according to many contemporaries, their actions created conditions for a more organised form of piracy. They disrupted the old trade routes, created their own colonies and discouraged Chinese junks from visiting the archipelago. The Dutch and the British did much the same in Indonesia and Malacca, distorting local economies and throttling established trade. By the start of the nineteenth century the islands from the South China Sea to Australia had been cut off from trade with China for a century. As a result North Borneo saw its riches disappear and its people were forced to put piracy on a much more organised footing. The historian Owen Rutter wrote:

> The Malay potentates were driven to replenish their depleted coffers; their people sought new outlets for their frustrated energies. They were accustomed to the sea, and under the leadership of their princes they turned their ways to piracy and plunder. In course of time this guerrilla warfare by sea developed for many into a habitual mode of life, more lucrative and certainly more exciting than their former ways of peace. Piracy became looked upon as an honourable occupation . . .

The Malay and Dyak people, pirates or peaceful fishermen and traders, were skilled in river and coastal warfare. They excelled in building boats for speed and ambush. Most impressive were their *prahus* – low-slung vessels up to 70 feet long. They ranged from 'spy-*prahus*', light and sleek with a handful of paddlers and used for reconnaissance and testing defences, to war-*prahus* heavily armed with cannon and capable of carrying hundreds of fighting men. Pirate fleets could number several hundred vessels and voyages could last up to three years.

The main centres of piracy were Brunei and Sulu, a Philippine island east of Borneo with a renowned slave-market. The sultans of both either condoned piracy or turned a blind eye to it in return for their share of the loot. The chief pirate tribes were the Balagnini, the Maluku, the Sea Dyaks of the Seribas and, most feared of all, the Lanun or Illanun, known as 'the pirates of the lagoons'. They spent much of their time attacking and pillaging one another's possessions, but the mayhem also, inevitably, touched other nations. In 1838 the East India Company steamer *Diana* captured a fleet of six pirate *prahus* from Sulu after they attacked a Chinese junk and the British sloop *Wolf*. The pirates numbered 360 men, including some galley slaves wearing collars around their necks.

By then Sarawak, a country measuring about 60 by 50 miles, had for several years been embroiled in an ineffectual rebellion against the Sultan of Brunei, the nominal head of almost the entire island of Borneo. The main grievance was a system of forced trade imposed by the Sultan, Omar Ali Suffedin, on the Dyak tribesmen, who had to pay fixed and exorbitant prices for goods sold to them by their Malay overlords. The governor, a royal kinsman called Pangeran Makota, exacerbated the problem by sweating his labourers, forcing men into the mines and greedily snatching most of the profits. Unlike those in other provinces, the Sarawak tribes were forced to pay the fixed tariffs all year round. When the wretched Dyaks and the poorer classes of Malays fell into debt they were seized as slaves. Any tribes who objected were threatened with attacks from the sea pirates of Seribas and Sakarang who were in the Sultan's pay. The Sultan sent his uncle, Rajah Muda Hassim, to suppress the long-drawn-out revolt and restore order. Muda Hassim was reckoned by foreign traders to be generous and humane and, more importantly, pro-British. But he was no great general and the revolt dragged on in a desultory way. Into this volatile, if relatively bloodless, civil war sailed James Brooke, a young man who was soon to prove himself one of the greatest adventurers of the Victorian age.

* * *

The son of Thomas Brooke, a judge in the East India Company's Bengal Civil Service, James was born in 1803 in Benares and spent the first twelve years of his life in India, enjoying all the privileges and pampering attendant on the youngest son of a powerful administrator. He was expected to become a Company officer, and was sent to England to get a proper education at Norwich grammar school. He was popular, industrious and brave, and saved a fellow pupil from drowning in the River Wensum. After two years his best friend ran away to sea as a midshipman. The young James decided on a similar adventure but was caught. The school would not have him back so he was privately tutored until he returned to Bengal in 1819 and was commissioned as an ensign in the 6th Native Infantry, where he established a fine reputation for pig-sticking and big-game shooting.

He saw his first action during the First Burma War in January 1825, where he drilled a volunteer body of native cavalry. He was mentioned in dispatches for leading a daring and successful frontal charge on enemy positions. A few days later his courageous, if foolhardy, tactics saw him shot during the battle of Rangpur in Assam and left for dead on the field. He was later rescued, barely alive, and was sent to Calcutta where surgeons operated and declared he must have a long convalescence in England. He was awarded a wound pension of £70 a year for life. Officially Brooke was shot in the lung but rumours persisted during and after his life that he had in fact suffered a musket ball in the genitals. According to the evidence of a serving girl in the household where Brooke was laid up and where, a year later, the wound broke out again: 'The slug, which had been allowed to remain in the wound, was now extracted from his back near the spine, and afterwards kept by his mother as a relic, under a glass case.' On the other hand, Brooke carried out a long, passionate but platonic love affair with

Angela Georgina Burdett-Coutts, one of the richest society beauties of the day. There is a widespread belief that she proposed to him but he politely rejected the offer 'for the best of reasons'. Indeed, he never married.

After four years he set sail back to India. His ship was delayed by storms and numerous stop-overs and Brooke, fearing that he would not reach Bengal within the Company's maximum five-year leave of absence, resigned his commission. He wrote: 'I toss my cap into the air, my commission into the sea, and bid farewell to John Company and all his evil ways. I am like a horse who has got a heavy clog off his neck.' On the voyage back to England he visited the Straits settlements of Penang, Malacca and Singapore, China and Sumatra. His taste for the East was well aroused by the time he returned to his family in Bath. He conceived a vague plan to ply a schooner around the islands of the South China Sea, seeking trade, profit and, above all, adventure.

He remained at home until 1834 when, aided by his doting mother, he persuaded his ailing father to buy him the brig *Findlay* and fit out a trading expedition to the Indian archipelago. The voyage was a financial disaster, due at least in part to clashes with the ship's captain, and Brooke soon discovered that he was a commercial incompetent. He was not deterred, however. The following year Brooke's father died and he spent much of his £30,000 inheritance on buying and fitting out a 142-ton schooner, the *Royalist*. Brooke wrote in the prospectus that she was entitled to carry the white ensign, sailed fast, was armed with six 6-pounders and a number of swivel guns. Already aged thirty-three, Brooke knew he could not squander his life on chasing adventures which neither turned a profit nor made his name. He began to focus on Borneo and the opportunities it could offer. In 1838 he set off for Maluda Bay, where the British already had a toehold in Borneo. His stated purpose was to survey the coast and to observe and collect botanical specimens. After a halt at Singapore he and his crew arrived at Kuching, the chief town of Sarawak, on 15 August 1839.

Brooke was graciously received by Rajah Muda Hassim who was 'a little man, mid-aged with a plain but intelligent face'. Hassim assumed Brooke was a spy and treated him with the greatest respect. Brooke also met Governor Makota, whom he regarded as 'the cleverest man here'. Brooke set off on an expedition 100 miles upriver and fell in love with Sarawak. He wrote:

> The glorious moon rose upon our progress as we toiled slowly but cheerfully on. It was such a situation as an excitable mind might envy. The reflection that we were proceeding up a Borneon river hitherto unexplored, sailing where no European had ever sailed before; the deep solitude, the brilliant night, the dark fringe of retired jungle, the lighter foliage of the river bank, with here and there a tree flashing and shining with fireflies, nature's tiny lamps glancing and flitting in countless numbers and incredible brilliancy.

He visited huge long-houses, admired graceful women and was appalled by the grisly spectacle of captured heads dangling from the rafters. He was persuaded that the heads were mere trophies of war taken from 'bad people who deserved to die'. Brooke spent ten days living in a Dyak long-house and spent his time surveying 150 miles of coast and river shore. During another voyage to the mouth of the Morotabas river a party of Hassim's men, acting as guides, were attacked by Saribas Dyaks as they slept in their *prahu* near the shore. One of the twelve men on hoard was speared in the breast but survived. Brooke wrote: 'I would have given the fellows a lesson, but they came in darkness, under the shadow of the hill, and in darkness departed on our firing a gun and showing a blue light.'

After several weeks Brooke left Kuching, firing a 21-shot salute for the Rajah and receiving 42 in return. Muda Hassim said: 'Tuan Brooke, do not forget me.' It was probably a mere term of courtesy, but it lodged in Brooke's mind.

Brooke sailed on to Celebes, where he impressed the inhabitants with his riding and shooting skills. He was not well received by their rulers, however, as he had strayed into an area of Dutch influence. Brooke began to suffer badly from bouts of fever and decided to return to his more hospitable hosts in Borneo. He arrived back at Kuching in October 1840.

He discovered that the Sarawak revolt was still dragging on. Muda

Hassim, impressed by the firepower on the *Royalist*, asked Brooke to help in the suppression. At first he refused, but his curiosity soon led him to the field of action. He found that Makota's army had the rebels surrounded at Sarambo. Brooke thought that the war was as good as won, but he was astounded to find that Makota's troops, a mixture of Malays, Chinese and Dyak turncoats, were reluctant to attack. It was not their way. For six days the besiegers inched forward, demolishing and rebuilding stockaded forts as they went, but consistently refused to rush the Dyak positions. Brooke surveyed the enemy through a telescope and saw barely 300 men behind simple bamboo structures. Makota had 650 men in his force, although some were poorly armed and hardly raring for a fight. Brooke wrote:

> With 300 men who would fight, nothing would have been easier than to take the detached defences of the enemy. But our allies seemed to have little idea of fighting except behind a wall; and my proposal to attack the adversary was immediately treated as an extreme of rashness amounting to insanity.

In disgust Brooke returned to Kuching and prepared to sail away. Muda Hassim begged him to stay, offering him the country of Sarawak and its government and trade if he didn't desert him. Brooke, his head reeling with ambition, returned to the front not as a friendly observer but as commander-in-chief of the Rajah's army. Makota was furious but powerless to object. Brooke selected as his second-in-command Pangeran Budruddin, one of the Rajah's brothers, who had shown signs of bravery. Brooke ordered an attack, but Makota persuaded the troops that such action was hopeless.

In frustration Brooke decided to lead his crewmen from the *Royalist* in a frontal assault. The little band was joined by just one native, Si Tundo from Mindanao. Brooke described his enthusiasm for battle: 'He danced or galloped across the field close to me, and, mixing with the enemy, was about to despatch a Hadji or priest who was prostrate before him, when one of our own people interposed and saved him by stating that he was a companion of our own.' The defenders had become accustomed to the Malay method of battle, which amounted merely to loose firing and shouted insults.

The sight of a compact body of Europeans advancing on them – and the wild bloodlust of Si Tundo – threw them into a panic. The rebel line broke and they ran away. Brooke boasted: 'Our victory was complete and bloodless.'

It was the end of a four-year war. A few days later the rebel leaders sued for peace. Brooke brokered the deal and insisted that all rebel prisoners be spared. Muda Hassim began to doubt the wisdom of his promise to give Brooke the governance of Sarawak, and his doubts were exploited by Makota who had no wish to see such power handed to a foreigner. Eventually Brooke, losing patience, trained the guns of the *Royalist* on Hassim's audience chamber, and then took an armed party ashore to negotiate. Muda Hassim prudently put aside his qualms and on 24 September 1841 Brooke became Governor of Sarawak. The episode convinced Brooke that the Malay princes were untrustworthy schemers who quickly responded to force when diplomacy failed. Muda Hassim and other lords recognised a tough operator.

In the meantime a pirate fleet of eighteen *prahu*s swept up the river at Kuching, 'one following the other, decorated with flags and streamers, and firing both cannon and musketry'. Their stated purpose was to pay their respects to Muda Hassim. Brooke mused: 'The sight was curious, and its interest heightened by the conviction that these friends of the moment may be enemies the next.' The rumour spread that their real purpose was to sack the *Royalist*, but they thought again after seeing her firepower. Brooke went aboard several of the large *prahu*s as a guest. He quizzed the pirate chiefs about their methods of slave-trading and learnt a lot about their tactics.

The following July Brooke went to Brunei and was, again after much negotiation and delay, confirmed as the Rajah of Sarawak. He was formally installed back at Kuching on 18 August 1842. Not yet forty, Brooke now had a kingdom of his own to administer.

*　　*　　*

James Brooke, the 'white Rajah', took his work seriously. His aim was to restore a country 'beset with difficulties, ravaged by war, torn by dissension and ruined by duplicity, weakness and intrigue'. He regarded the natives as a father would unruly children, and although he believed the white race was superior he also believed that brown-skinned people should be treated as equals. His reforms were designed to bring justice and prosperity to the people, to generate a fair income for the Sultan, and ultimately to forge trading links with Britain to the benefit of all. Cynics have portrayed him as an imperialist exploiter, but Brooke himself expected only modest personal benefits. He was a dreamer who had been given the opportunity to make those dreams come true.

The first item on his agenda was to end Makota's cruel system of forced trade and exorbitant tariffs, which he replaced with a simple form of taxation in kind. He ended the enslavement of defaulters and their families. He released prisoners, women and children first, captured during raids and the rebellion. And, as Rajah, he dispensed justice from a long-room built into his house at Kuching. His zeal and fairness greatly impressed his new subjects, particularly those who had been impoverished by his predecessors. The saying − 'The son of Europe is the friend of the Dyak' − became common. His friend Spenser St John described how Brooke heard petitions even during dinner:

> Often a very poor man would creep in, take up his position in the most obscure corner and there remain silent but attentive to all that passed. There he would sit till every other native had left, neither addressing Mr Brooke nor being addressed by him, but when the coast was clear the Governor would call him to his side and gently worm his story from him. Generally it was some tale of oppression, some request for aid. None of these stories were forgotten . . .

Brooke set about educating the people of his new domain. He wrote to his mother and sisters asking for such articles as 'an electrifying machine of good power', a magic lantern, bell-ropes and old carpets. The latter the Dyaks found especially useful for making war-jackets. Brooke tried, without much initial success, to get the country's finances in order but he was hopeless at accounting. He estimated

Sarawak's entire revenue as between £5,000 and £6,000, but the true figure was anyone's guess. With the crew of the *Royalist* frequently away on voyages, Brooke had only a handful of Europeans around him. He wrote in his journal: 'The time here passes monotonously, but not unpleasantly. Writing, reading, chart-making, employ my time between meals.'

During this period piracy was low on his list of priorities. More important to him were his constantly frustrated attempts to get the British government interested in the opportunities offered by a friendly land in Borneo. London, however, did not want to become embroiled in any costly enterprise which could have disastrous diplomatic consequences. Brooke seethed with frustration, dangling the carrot of supposed coal deposits in front of disinterested British eyes. Brooke was a patriot and wanted both Britain and Sarawak to gain, but he also considered making overtures to Holland and France.

Ironically, piracy on the frontiers of his land offered him a chance to involve Britain directly in his enterprise. The English Navy was charged with hunting down slavers and stamping out the slave trade around the globe. The pirates were notorious slavers: human traffic was as much the point of raids as more conventional plunder. Brooke's journals report many instances. In one village alone, on the Sanpro, twenty-two women and children were dragged away as slaves. Another common practice guaranteed to raise Christian hackles was head-hunting. Matari, a Sakarran chief seeking a treaty with Brooke, was astonished to hear him stipulate that he was not to engage in piracy by land or sea. The chief asked what he would do if any tribe entered his territory to hunt heads. Brooke replied: 'To enter their country and lay it waste.' Matari asked him again: 'You will give me, your friend, leave to steal a few heads occasionally?' 'No,' Brooke replied, according to his journal, 'you cannot take a single head; you cannot enter the country; and if you or your countrymen do, I will have a hundred Sakarran heads for every one you take here.' Brooke sent letters to the Malay sheriffs, the chiefs of tribes who practised such piracy, warning them that British seapower would be called in to take reprisals if they made further raids on territory under his control.

In fact, Brooke had no such authority but he soon found a willing ally among the Royal Navy captains who crisscrossed the seas protecting trade routes and chasing slavers. Brooke first met Captain the Honorable Henry Keppel, commander of HMS *Dido*, during a visit to Singapore. Then aged thirty-one, Keppel was the son of the 4th Earl of Albemarle and a born adventurer. The two men instantly became friends. When it was reported that a large pirate fleet was approaching north Borneo, Brooke asked his friend for help.

Keppel was eager to intervene, and so were other captains in the area. Their motives were not entirely humanitarian: an 1825 Act offered a bounty of £20 for each pirate killed or captured. The main intention of the legislation was to halt the trans-Atlantic slave trade and the law-makers had not envisaged Far Eastern slavers whose crews might number hundreds. But the law was the law and there were enough British officers ready to exploit it. Keppel, the youngest son of an aristocratic family, needed cash. His wife was an invalid and he had left England to escape the expensive temptations of racecourses and gambling dens. He was also high-spirited and energetic, and shared Brooke's love of excitement. Without any official authorisation, Keppel agreed to take his ship to Borneo and Brooke returned to Sarawak aboard the *Dido*.

The ship was immediately attacked by three marauding *prahu*s, which were easily repulsed. Brooke, who had taken to a smaller craft, fought a battle with a larger *prahu* and scattered its crew of thirty-six men. It was only a small skirmish but made a timely impression on the British officer. The pirates were a real menace, that much was clear. Keppel, like almost every other first-time visitor, was also dazzled by Sarawak. He wrote:

The scene was both novel and exciting; presented to us, just anchored in a large fresh-water river and surrounded by a densely wooded jungle, the whole surface of the water covered with canoes and boats decked out with their various-coloured silken flags, filled with natives beating their tom-toms, and playing on their wild and not unpleasant-sounding wind instruments, with the occasional discharge of firearms.

The natives were equally impressed with *Dido*: 'her mast-heads towering above the highest trees of their jungle; the loud report of her heavy two-and-thirty pounder guns, and the running aloft to furl sails, of 150 seamen in their clean white dresses and with the band playing . . .', he wrote.

Worried that pirates might attack the mail-boat due to arrive from Singapore, Keppel sent on patrol the locally built *Jolly Bachelor*, armed with a brass six-pounder, under the command of one of his lieutenants. Three *prahus* were spotted but each escaped as night fell. The British slept on board. In the small hours the lieutenant was awoken by a 'savage brandishing a *kris* and performing his war-dance on the deck in an ecstasy of delight'. The pirate believed he had single-handedly taken possession of a fine trading-boat; when he realised his mistake, he dived overboard. When dawn broke two large war-*prahus* were pressing the *Jolly Bachelor* on both sides, while another, larger, vessel waited around a point of rocks. After a 'sharp battle' one of the pirate vessels was sunk by the brass cannon and the other two were driven off. One of these was crippled and its galley-slaves quickly rebelled; they killed the remaining pirates on board and escaped upriver.

Keppel was now fully convinced of the piracy problem. Urged on by Brooke, the Rajah Muda Hassim made a formal request that the *Dido* be employed in clearing out the pirates, and Keppel readily agreed. Keppel's plan was to root out two bands of local pirates, operating from the Sarebas and Sakarran rivers, before tackling larger fleets on the high seas. Under his command were about 110 officers and men from *Dido* and about 1,000 Borneo men happy to serve under Brooke. Their transport was *Dido*'s pinnacle, two cutters and a brig, plus *Jolly Bachelor* and numerous native craft. Keppel wrote:

The whole formed a novel, picturesque and exciting scene . . . The odd mixture of Europeans, Malays and Dyaks; the different religions, and the eager and anxious manner in which all pressed forward. The novelty of the thing was quite enough for our Jacks, after having been cooped up so long board ship, to say nothing of the chance of a broken head.

The force made slow progress, hampered by a tidal bore, and the force was slimmed down to 500 men in the fastest vessels, the rest being left to guard supplies. Around 70 miles upriver the force camped and Keppel contemplated his position: 'about to carry all the horrors of war amongst a race of savage pirates, whose country no force had ever yet dared to invade, and who for more than a century had been inflicting, with impunity, every sort of cruelty on all whom they encountered'. The force advanced with the flood-tide to Padi, the furthest inland Sarebas town, with Keppel and Brooke in the lead boat. From the crest of the bore they got their first glimpse of the enemy performing 'a most awe-inspiring war-dance' in the first fort. The river was partly blocked by a boom but Keppel steered his gig through the opening while native allies cut loose the boom's lashings, allowing the British seamen to dash ashore. They attacked the nearest fort, making no attempt at concealment in their headlong rush. The defenders panicked and fled. This pattern was repeated in all the area's stockades.

The next task was to root out the Sakarrans but before the second expedition could be launched Keppel received orders to sail to China. The captain could only obey, but promised Brooke he would return to complete the job as soon as he could.

Shortly after his departure Brooke was gratified to see another Royal Navy ship, the surveying vessel HMS *Samarang*, arrive in harbour. But her captain, the gruff Sir Edward Belcher, was not so easily captivated by the 'white Rajah'. The son of Nova Scotia colonisers, Belcher had spent thirty years at sea and had previously surveyed the coasts of west and north Africa, North and South America and the Pacific. He was able and experienced, but taciturn, bad-tempered and certainly no romantic. He was unimpressed by Brooke's assertion that Borneo was a fertile sphere of influence for British interests. Brooke offered enticements: the small island of Labuan, commanding the approaches to Brunei harbour, was, he claimed, rich in coal and would make an excellent coaling-station for the Royal Navy's new steamships. He argued that the Sultan would willingly cede it to the British in return for protection against piracy. Belcher was sceptical but agreed to go with Brooke to Brunei to see for himself. The start to their voyage was inauspicious:

Belcher managed to run *Samarang* aground twice on the same reef. Eventually an impressive flotilla of seven vessels reached Brunei. Belcher refused to enter the town because of an outbreak of smallpox there and Omar Ali agreed only to a hurried conference aboard *Samarang*. The Sultan was impressed by the show of naval might, not realising that most of the ships were to follow Belcher to China, where he had been summoned in the aftermath of the Opium War. The Sultan agreed to the exchange, although somewhat warily, with Brooke's assurance that the Brunei Court wanted to see their ports open to trade and piracy suppressed. Belcher merely made notes. He glanced at two small coal outcrops on Labuan and declared them unworkable. Then he set sail for China.

Hugely disappointed, Brooke decided to approach Admiral Sir William Parker in Penang. Parker, who had heard fine things from Keppel about the 'white Rajah', pledged support for further action against the Borneo pirates. But first, Parker said, he had to deal with a similar problem in Sumatra and he invited Brooke to join him. Brooke eagerly agreed, if only to win credit with the region's foremost naval commander. The offensive against the Sumatrans was a short campaign, but bloodier than the onslaughts in which Brooke had made his name. The first town, Batu, was easily taken and burnt. But the Murdu Malays, who saw piracy as a legitimate enterprise and who were contemptuous of foreign trading rights, proved tougher. They were well armed and had recently sacked a merchant ship and massacred its crew. The fighting lasted five hours. Two Englishmen and many native allies were killed and Brooke himself was twice wounded in reckless charges. He was cheered for his bravery when he returned to his ship. Among most officers and men of the Royal Navy he had already become a hero. It was the beginning of a legend.

Travelling home via Penang Brooke met his old friend Keppel, who later recalled: 'I took the liberty of giving him a lecture on his rashness, he having quite sufficient ground for fighting over in his newly adopted country.' Keppel was more than willing to return with him to complete their earlier task, but naval business took him first to Singapore and China. In May 1844 Brooke returned alone, hitching a lift on *Harlequin*, to find Sarawak again in turmoil.

Serif Sahib of neighbouring Sadong, who had opposed Brooke's reforms and whose power base lay among the supposed pirates on the Sakarran river, had taken advantage of Brooke's absence to rally opposition to the 'white Rajah'. In this he was egged on by Makota, the disgruntled former governor who had moved to his princedom. Serif Sahib had built up a large flotilla of vessels with which to raid Brooke's territory. Keppel provided Brooke's salvation from this latest threat. Late in July he arrived with *Dido* and the Company steamer *Phlegethon*. Also on board was Brooke's young nephew, Charles Johnson, a callow midshipman.

Keppel and Brooke embarked on an expedition to punish Serif Sahib and the pirates on the Sakarran. This campaign was to prove tougher than their previous adventure. Patusen, Serif Sahib's riverside stronghold, was attacked and taken, with heavy losses on both sides. The battle featured a determined and brutal charge by RN blue-jackets armed with cutlasses. Three British officers and gentlemen were killed. One of them, John Ellis, was cut in half by a cannon shot as he loaded *Jolly Batchelor*'s bow gun, just a few yards from the young Charles Johnson who was drenched in blood but unscathed. Serif Sahib, whose forces suffered much higher casualties, escaped. Brooke's Dyak allies reaped a crop of heads from their fallen enemies. Keppel recorded the celebrations: 'The whole of the late expedition was fought over again and a war-dance with the newly acquired heads of the Sakarran pirates was performed for our edification.'

The expedition moved up the Batang Lupa river. The lead spy-*prahu*, captained by Patinga Ali, was ambushed by 600 pirates in six war-boats who cut off their retreat with a fallen tree-trunk. All aboard were slaughtered, including Patinga Ali, one of Brooke's best and most loyal fighting men. That sacrifice, however, alerted the main British and Sarawakan fleet who pounded the pirate craft into blood-soaked matchwood. The fighting was the most vicious of the whole campaign. The enemy dead numbered hundreds, while Brooke's force lost 30 killed and 56 wounded. The cost was high, but in two weeks Brooke and Keppel, with their native allies, had destroyed the main pirate power base in the region.

The chase continued upriver and Makota was captured. Typically, and despite the protestations of his more war-like friends, Brooke refused to execute Sarawak's former governor. Instead he gave him a lecture and let him go. Similar treatment was given to other captured princes who agreed to keep the peace and stop attacking Sarawak. Brooke's mercy was much appreciated and it was a wise move. The 'white Rajah', by forcing pledges from other chiefs, effectively extended his own domain.

*   *   *

During this period Brooke's main concern was to create a pro-British regime in Brunei. His chief allies at court were Muda Hassim and his brother Budruddin. His main enemy was Pangeran Usop, who had been prime minister before being supplanted by Muda Hassim. Inevitably Brooke regarded all those who opposed him as the 'piratical faction', Usop included. The historian Graham Saunders wrote: 'In this there was some truth, in that their policies were inimical to those of Brooke and they included under the category of trade the exchange of goods acquired by piratical means; but their main fault in Brooke's eyes was to oppose his interests. Brooke had in fact intervened in a Brunei dynastic quarrel which had little to do with piracy.' In brief, Muda Hussim was aiming to strengthen his claim to eventually succeed the Sultan, while Usop was determined to stop him, citing his reliance on the foreigner Brooke.

Brooke, increasingly prone to fever and constantly frustrated by London's lack of interest, grew daily more irascible. He claimed the moral high ground and would not tolerate any dissent from his divisive and, some would later say, hypocritical tactics. He expressed a wish to 'change the native character'. If the British government did not support him he would halt all further negotiations and 'trust to God and my own wits'. However, Brooke's growing reputation in England was beginning to work in his favour and in February 1845 he was finally given official recognition. He was appointed Confidential Agent in Borneo to Her Majesty, with the power to act as a government agent.

Brooke interpreted this to mean he could negotiate British trade terms with Borneo and he rushed back to Brunei. The Sultan was by now 'dizzy and confused' and did not appear to understand the significance of the developments, but Muda Hassim, keen to succeed his nephew, grasped it immediately. He informed Brooke that his rival, Usop, was now in league with Serif Osman, a notorious slave trader and pirate at Maluda Bay. Brooke agreed to help flush out the 'traitors' and in August he found a new ally to help in the task.

Admiral Sir Thomas Cochrane arrived at Brunei in August with a squadron of eight ships to obtain the release of two Lascar seamen captured and sold into slavery, allegedly to Usop by Osman. Cochrane was a 69-year-old veteran of the Napoleonic Wars and a passionate advocate of steam power in warfare. He had already met Brooke, agreed with him on the private threat, and had a mandate from the Admiralty to take whatever action he saw fit. Budruddin accused Usop of holding the captured sailors and of slave dealing. Usop refused to attend a meeting with Cochrane and the admiral ordered a shot to be fired by the steamer *Vixen* through the roof of his house. Usop briefly returned fire with a heavy calibre weapon which sent a shot through *Vixen's* rigging. The British warships bombarded the compound for 50 minutes before the 'rebels' fled. Twenty-one cannon were found in Usop's compound, which the Sultan declared were British spoils of war. Also found were European-manufactured goods, indicating the receipt of pirate booty. Brooke and Cochrane now had the excuse they needed to attack Serif Osman at Maluda Bay. This was done with the full authority of the Sultan, although he probably had little choice, given the encouragement of Muda Hassim and the presence of a powerful British armada in his harbour. Brooke, now a government official and a civilian who could not be placed in the front line, travelled with the squadron in *Vixen* but was honour-bound to stay well away from danger.

Cochrane commanded twenty vessels, including *Vixen*, *Agincourt*, *Vestal*, *Daedalus*, *Cruiser* and *Wolverine*, plus two smaller Company steamships, the battle-hardened *Nemesis* and *Pluto*, with a total force of around 500 men. Serif Osman was believed to command up to 1,000 fighting men and enjoyed the support of the local populace. One correspondent wrote that he would oppose any British settlement in Borneo Proper: 'It was the utmost importance that he should be expelled the island and the horde dispersed.' Another writer, justifying the attack on Serif Osman's own territory, wrote: 'This man, a half-bred Arab, had succeeded in obtaining over the poorer classes an immense influence, having employed a large capital in the most nefarious manner by investing it in boats, arms and ammunition for the purpose of the less powerful and influential tribes carrying on their only trade – a diabolical piracy.' In other words, he was a popular leader.

The fleet proceeded to Maluda Bay 'into which from many mouths debouches the water of a shallow river, the navigation of which is difficult even for boats. Upon the banks of this river the Arab chief had his settlement, and from thence his fleet could prey upon vessels in the China, the Celebes or the Sooloo seas.' Osman's settlement was well protected by a stockade with a battery of eight cannon commanding the shallow river and another of eight mounted gingalls facing inland. There were a further two batteries, one of them on a raft. The writer continued:

> The defences were protected by a double boom thrown across the river, formed of enormous trees, bolted together by large iron plates on the lower part, and bound round and round by the iron cable of a vessel of considerable size, the ends of which were secured on each bank by numerous turns round many stumps of trees. It was as formidably and ingeniously contrived a boom as ever savage put together.

The intricacy and shallowness of the river prevented even the small steam vessels approaching the boom. Cochrane sent a flotilla of 25 small boats and 450 men under the command of captains Talbot and Lyster. The first day was spent trying to find the river mouth in the maze of channels and the men spent an uncomfortable night offshore until finding the right access on the morning of 19 August 1845. After pulling on the oars for 10 miles they came within sight of the town and its defences. The officers saw that a determined resistance would be made and that they were in great peril from the enemy cannon mounted just 150 yards away. 'The crew stood perfectly cool at the guns, with which eight boats were armed, ready for the commencement of hostilities.' Osman sent out an envoy under a flag of truce and invited Talbot and a small number of his men to a parley inside the fort. The captain said he would accept, provided the boom was opened but Osman insisted that he could allow only two small boats to enter. The messenger was told to say that Osman was required on board the admiral's ship and when his boat returned to the fort a 'murderous' cannonade immediately opened up. The British boats were caught in the cross-fire from the fort, a shore battery, the floating battery and the guns of pirate vessels. The very first shot killed two men and wounded three others. Leonard Gibbard, *Wolverine's* first mate, took grapeshot in the chest and quickly died. The seamen returned fire for 50 hot minutes while *Agincourt's* gunner lieutenant set up a rocket battery on the beach. Its missiles were then thrown into the fort with 'perfect accuracy'. A small gap was forced in the boom and the British boats passed through in single file 'under a terrifically galling fire from a 12-gun battery in the flank and a stockade of three guns in front'. As the first disciplined waves of troops landed on the shore the fort was abandoned and the shore battery was overrun. The correspondent for the *Illustrated London News* reported:

> A landing being at length obtained, the slaughter commenced, and the absurdity of an irregular body of men attempting to make a stand against a corps of regular disciplined troops was here very perceptible. The infatuated beings fell like grass, their chief standing to the last on a wing of one of the principal embrasures, amid the fire of about 300 Marines, with an apparent degree of physical bravery worthy of a better cause; he received a shot at last through the neck, and was borne from his comrades from the scene of action.

The British lost 10 killed and 15 wounded. The correspondent continued:

> It would be no easy task to compute the loss on the part of the enemy, but from the statements of two prisoners it was understood to have been immense, for it appeared they, who

were slaves, had been employed for upward of five hours throwing dead bodies in the river. [That was the custom, to prevent the corpses falling into the hands of their enemies.] The great loss the enemy had suffered – their leaders, five of whom were dead or desperately wounded, and the remainder having fled – convinced them that victory was hopeless, and they deserted in all directions. A few of the most daring, in bringing off the last of their wounded and dead, were shot down by the marines and seamen. Spoils of every description were found; and in one hour the villages and forts for a mile up were wrapped in flames. Thirty proas [sic] were burnt and two very fine ones on the stocks, two magazines of powder, and houses filled with camphor, china ware, English manufactured goods, French prints and splendid timber were found and fired.

The chain cable on the boom was found to be from a vessel of 400 tons. In and around the stockades were found more chains, a European long-boat and two ship's bells, one of which was ornamented with grapes and vine leaves and inscribed 'Wilhelm Ludwig, Bremen.' Another observer wrote: 'Bales and boxes of European and Chinese goods, with crates of earthenware, anchors, chains, spars, etc., etc., gave abundant proof of the nature of the pursuits of the inhabitants of Maluda Bay.' Throughout the action Brooke stayed on board ship with the admiral, well out of danger and hating it. He was sick with worry for his nephew, midshipman Charles Johnston, who was with the landing parties. Again the lad emerged unscathed but plastered with the blood of comrades.

Next day boats were again sent upriver to burn the main town. A woman and her infant child were found in the smoking ruins of Osman's home. The mother had been one of his slaves and was severely wounded with a British musket ball through her elbow. Her arm was amputated by a naval surgeon, and mother and child returned with Brooke.

The magazine *Friends of China* reported:

It is to be hoped that the severe lesson they have received will for a time intimidate the pirates of Borneo; but nothing short of a European settlement, with a garrison and one or two small steam-vessels of war permanently on the coast, will effectually drive the pirates from their present haunts. Many a ship that has been reported missing has met her fate on the coast of Borneo, and the crew murdered or sold as slaves.

*   *   *

Meanwhile the struggle for supremacy continued in the Sultanate of Brunei. Usop tried to reassert his lost authority by force. Defeated by Budruddin, he retreated back to his own estates at Kimanis, where he was arrested and executed on the orders of Mudam Hassim and, nominally at least, the Sultan. The pro-British faction appeared to have won. The suppression of piracy, however, and the interference by foreigners only increased resentment at court. Sultan Omar Ali declared that his son, married to one of Usop's daughters, should eventually take power. Various factions intrigued and gossiped and convinced the Sultan that Muda Hassim, previously nominated as successor, was about to launch a coup. As 1845 closed the Sultan ordered the assassination of Muda Hassim and Budruddin and their families. Budruddin was surrounded but blew himself up, along with his sister and one of his wives, rather than surrender. Muda Hassim was wounded but escaped across a river; then, all hope gone, he shot himself with a pistol. Two of Brooke's greatest allies were dead.

Brooke, hearing of the slaughter from an escaped slave, organised an expedition to avenge the deaths of his friends and to bring the Sultan to heel. In July Admiral Cochrane sailed directly to Brunei. Faced with prevarication and excuses, an armada of longboats from the warships, together with the steamer *Phlegethon*, moved threateningly upriver. Shots were fired at them at every bend and the steamship was slightly damaged. By the time they reached the city itself the Sultan was gone. So too was the entire populace, fearful of retribution. But they did find one of Muda Hassim's brothers, who was badly wounded but had escaped the massacre. The British fired the forts but sent out messengers to persuade the people to return. Most did, although the Sultan remained in hiding and an expedition into the interior failed to find him. Cochrane and the main British force then sailed away, leaving Brooke in Brunei with the steamship *Iris* and HMS *Hazard*. Eventually he persuaded the Sultan to come out of hiding, but forced him to pay penance at the graves of his murdered uncles, and to write a humiliating letter of apology to Queen Victoria. Brooke also bullied him into signing over all mining rights on the island of Labuan.

This time London took notice and agreed to accept the offer. On 18 December Captain G. Rodney Mundy of *Iris*, whose guns had maintained well-aimed diplomatic pressure on the Sultan, signed a treaty under which the island became part of the British Crown. It was followed the next year by another treaty, negotiated by Brooke, which increased the stranglehold of British trade on all the Sultan's lands. It forbade 'any cessation of an island or of any settlement on the mainland in any part of [the Sultan's] dominion to any other nation, or to the subjects or citizens thereof, without the consent of Her Britannic Majesty'. Sarawak was also freed from paying tribute to Brunei. Brooke had got all he wanted and more, partly by dealing with all his opponents as if they were common pirates. Sir Spenser St John wrote:

> The tables have been strangely turned in the Eastern Archipelago. Weak, and few in number, we were (once) too happy to receive the protection and countenance of the Sultan of Borneo, of whom the buccaneers of the Sulu group seemed to have stood in awe. Now the Sultan is our humble ally and dependant, and, but for the British flag which waves in his neighbourhood, and the treaty he has concluded with us, might any hour in the twenty-four be seized in his capital by the Sulus, or any other piratical tribe, and sold like the humblest individual into slavery.

Brooke returned to England to a hero's welcome. Queen Victoria invited him to tea at Windsor Castle. She asked him how he managed to rule so many of the wild Borneans with so little force. He replied: 'I find it easier to govern thirty thousand Malays and Dyaks than to manage a dozen of Your Majesty's subjects.' It was exactly what she wanted to hear in her early imperial age – and so too did a

British leadership avid for exotic tales of adventure and the inherent superiority of their island race. Brooke was knighted, given the Freedom of the City of London and awarded an honorary degree by Oxford. He returned to Borneo as British commissioner and consul-general to the entire island, and as governor of Labuan, while retaining his own title over Sarawak.

Brooke's methods, and his rewards, had their critics, particularly among the Radicals and the Liberal Opposition at Westminster. They were backed by such bodies as the Peace Society and the Aborigines' Protection Society. Brooke's overwhelming popularity thwarted their attempts to block the colonisation of Labuan. They bided their time until another expedition by the increasingly fever-ridden 'white Rajah' gave them the ammunition they needed.

*   *   *

The Albatross expedition, as it became known, was sparked by further outbreaks of piracy from bases on the Sarebas and Sakarran rivers, the scene of Brooke's earlier campaigns in north-west Borneo. The marauders captured two trading boats in the Rejang delta and launched an abortive assault on Serikei, which proved too well defended. Thwarted, the fleet headed for targets skirting Brooke's territory. Brooke's subsequent action was justified by Sir Spenser St John. He wrote:

> During the first six months of 1849 these pirates attacked Sadong twice, as well as Susang on the Kaluka, and Serikei, Palo, Mato, Bruit and Igan. Almost all intercourse by sea ceased, as few who attempted to pass the mouths of the pirate rivers escaped unhurt. I calculated at the time that above 500 of the Sultan's subjects had been killed or taken captive between January and July 1849; and we know that one large fleet had passed the mouths of the Sarawak river to attack the subjects of the Sultan of Sambas.

St John, then a young and inexperienced officer, witnessed at first hand the aftermath of the raids. He saw piles of corpses, their heads removed. He saw the pathetic evidence of mass rape and infanticide. He was horrified.

Brooke reckoned, correctly, that the pirate forces would hug the coastline as they paddled towards undefended villages. He marshalled his own forces, with the sanction of the Sultan, to exact retribution. They were joined by a naval force under Captain Farquhar, consisting of his warship HMS *Albatross*, *Nemesis* and the steam tender *Ranee*. Their combined strength was about 3,000 men, of whom 120 were European. The pirate force was later estimated at 4,000 in 120 *prahus*. The two forces collided at Batang Marau, a sandy spit at the entrance to the Sarebas river.

On the evening of 30 July the British ships were in position to halt pirates heading for home after a raid on Palo, where they had threatened the area with destruction unless supplied with salt. Brooke and his men moved up the Kaluka river to block off one exit, while the naval men assembled at the entrance of the Sarebas. The steamer *Nemesis* took up position slightly offshore, from where she could swiftly move to wherever she was most needed. The trap was set.

As the pirate fleet approached, the British ships opened fire. The result was carnage. The British and their Malay allies had attacked at night, and the enemy boats were far away from familiar waters. The guns of *Nemesis* alone destroyed seventeen *prahus*, and in all ninety enemy boats foundered. The smaller boats, both British and native, cut in and out of the pirate flotilla as they tried, desperately and unsuccessfully, to escape out to sea. Each time their way was blocked by the warships; they were trapped by the sandy spit and the tangled coastline.

An anonymous British correspondent wrote:

It was now dark and the great danger was that of firing into each other or into our native allies. The password selected was *Rajah* and the Malays screamed this out at the top of their voices when they thought any of the Europeans were near them. Commander Farquhar, who directed the operations, was in the midst of the mêlée, giving orders and exhorting the crews of the various boats to be careful, and not to fire into each other.

Two large *prahus* were seen by the Commander escaping seaward, and the steam-tender was ordered to give chase; the nearest one, having barely escaped one of her six-pounder rockets, made for the river and met a pirate's doom – the *Nemesis*, which had been dealing death and destruction to all around her, ran her down, and the scene which took place as her crew, above sixty in number, came in contact with the paddle-wheels, beggars all description. A large Congreve-rocket from the little steamer entered the *prahu* that had continued out to sea, and rendered her destruction complete.

The master of *Nemesis* described the whole action:

On coming abreast of them I fired the starboard broadside with canister shot along the whole line, the nearest *prahu* being about 20 or 30 yards distant, the small-arm men at the same time keeping up a constant and important fire upon them. We then wore [sic], breaking the line and driving many *prahus* ashore in a very crippled state, where they fell an easy prey to a division of native boats under Mr Steele of Sarawak, who did good service, without interfering with our fire.

We now followed five *prahus* which still pressed on for the Batang Lupar, and on coming up with them passed round each successfully, and destroyed them in detail, by keeping up a constant fire of grape shot and musketry, until they drifted past us helpless as logs, without a living being onboard, with the hope of swimming on shore, which few could possibly accomplish.

The pirates had hitherto preserved good order, but now finding themselves surrounded and cut off wherever they turned, they fled indiscriminately, running their *prahus* aground in all directions, abandoning them, and taking refuge in the jungle . . .

From the first exchange of shots it was obvious that the British and their allies had won, but a rapid running fire was kept up until shortly after midnight. Farquhar then sent dispatches to Brooke, who was in the Kaluka river with his Sarawaks, away from the main action. It was dawn before the full extent of their handiwork became evident. The correspondent quoted above said it took everyone by surprise: 'At daylight the bay was one mass of wrecks – shields, spears and portions of destroyed *prahu*s extended as far as the eye could reach; whilst on the sandy spit were upwards of seventy *prahu*s which the natives were busy clearing of all valuables and destroying them.'

Around 400 pirates were slain for the loss of only 13 native allies killed or wounded. Captain Wallage of *Nemesis* reported gleefully:

> The pirates, having landed in a hostile country, without food or arms, will probably lose 800 or 1,000 men more before they reach their home . . . Thus, notwithstanding the smallness of the European force, and under all the disadvantages of a night attack, was fought the most decisive engagement that has ever taken place on this coast, and which (without severe loss on our side) has resulted in the annihilation of one of the most desperate piratical tribes.

A more critical writer, the Radical Richard Cobden, saw the battle of Batang Marau in a different light:

> The attacking party, without calling upon them to surrender, or in any way communicating with them, with the view of ascertaining what they wanted, fired a broadside into them of shot, balls and rockets, and the unfortunate wretches were unable to make the slightest attempt at resistance or defence. The English steam vessels of war were then driven among the boats, and the miserable creatures were crushed under the paddle wheels and annihilated by the hundreds in the most inhumane manner.

The controversy sparked a heated debate, especially when the naval officers claimed bounties on the men slain under the old system of hunting down pirates and slavers. Given the numbers of dead the total claim could exceed £30,000. Cobden claimed there was no proof that the destroyed flotilla were pirates. He described the battle as closer to the massacre of sheep or rabbits than honourable warfare: 'After this mighty feat of valour had been performed, they came to a Christian assembly and demanded twenty pounds a head for slaughtering the unhappy wretches.'

The Peace Society focused on the 'blood-money,' suggesting that thousands of innocents had been slain to claim a bogus bounty; it was no more justified, said the Society, than collecting heads. Brooke was the villain of this scenario, despite the fact that the 'white Rajah' and his staff were, as civilians, not eligible for a penny of the bounty. The payments due were later agreed by the Admiralty Court in Singapore to be £20,700, a staggering sum for the time.

A joint submission by the Peace Society and the Aborigines' Protection Society claimed there was no evidence that the attacked *prahus* were manned by pirates. It was, rather, 'a fleet waylaid on its return from a predatory excursion against some neighbouring tribes'. Brooke's allies pointed out that this was a rather strange defence. But their submission did make some pertinent points which Brooke's supporters had difficulty refuting:

According to Sir James Brooke's own shewing, four-fifths of the hands on board piratical fleets in the Eastern Seas are slaves, generally unarmed and employed at the oars, prohibited from fighting and in no case free-agents. Granting, then, the act of piracy on the part of the tribes in question, the laws of this country would treat with leniency men in this position, who could prove that they were acting under compulsion. But in the present instance a *very few* prisoners were made, whilst the slaughter was pitiless to extreme degree, the Dyaks having no firearms, but only spears and shields.

Brooke, now in Singapore, was unable to respond to such attacks in person, but he did so prodigiously by letter in tones of increasing hurt and indignation. In one he said of Batang Marau:

I was ill of the ague when the fight commenced, and during the whole night information was brought to me that a desperate struggle had taken place between the pirates and our people, and rumours were rife that we had been defeated. The morning assured us of victory. Now, will anyone state at what time the action should have been discontinued? Should all the pirates have been allowed to escape, or a half of them, or a quarter, and by what patient means is an action to be stopped at any given moment? We had one *prahu* from Sadong manned by Malays, every one of whom had lost a near relative, killed by the Sarebas during the year.

Under further attack Brooke said that there was a difference between the 30 or 40 Malay and Dyak tribes who lived in peace with each other and those of the Sarebas and Sakarran who 'constantly go to sea on piratical cruises and devastate the other countries'.

He was supported by the British officers present. One wrote:

The observer was compelled to ask himself, could destruction so great, success so complete, at least a third of this ruthless horde sent to their account, be effected in a space so brief, and with a European force so small? Had success attended the pirates our fate was certain. No more convincing instances of their inhuman disposition need be cited than the fact that the bodies of women were found on the beach on whom they had wreaked their vengeance. They were all decapitated, and the bodies gashed from shoulder to foot. These are supposed to have been captives taken by the pirates in the expedition from which they were returning.

The debates continued and Cobden, supported by Gladstone, called for an inquiry into charges that the destruction of the enemy fleet had been 'promiscuous and, to some degree, illegal'. The motion was rejected by a large majority. Lord Palmerston declared that Brooke 'retired from the investigation with untarnished character and unblemished character'. Later, with the Liberals refusing to let the matter lie, the new government of Lord Aberdeen granted a commission of inquiry. It met finally at Singapore but failed to find any evidence of inhumanity or illegality on Brooke's part. Rajah Brooke was too proud to call any witnesses in his own defence, but the Commissioners summoned twenty-four of their own. All testified that the Saribas were pirates and murderers. Brooke subsequently received a letter from Palmerston, fully approving 'the course which you have pursued for the suppression of the system of wholesale piracy in the seas adjoining to Borneo'.

Brooke's long war against the Borneo pirates was over and he was vindicated, at least in the eyes of the British government.

* * *

It had taken Brooke three years to clear his name. In the meantime he had established a series of forts and out-stations which, even more than the final battle, broke the power of the Sea-Dyaks and extended Brooke's Peace far up the rivers of Borneo and along the coastline.

But the 'white Rajah' was physically and emotionally drained by the time he returned to Sarawak from his 'trial'. Although vindicated he felt occasional bitterness at the aspersions levelled against him. St John wrote: 'Sir James was of a very excitable and nervous temperament. The savage attacks to which he was subjected roused his anger, and did him permanent injury. He never was again the even-tempered gay companion of former days.' He also suffered a severe bout of smallpox which left him permanently disfigured, while numerous attacks of malaria left him tired. He lost some of his fire and all personal ambition, saying that 'titles, fine clothes, penny trumpets and turtle soup' were all the same to him. He was content to administer his state, which prospered through years of peace, and to enjoy his rose garden, his library and the company of his friends. His greatest consolation was that his 'own people' remained loyal to him. Sarawak had come to peace and so too, after a while, did Brooke. St John wrote:

This was perhaps the happiest time he ever spent. He could live in the capital or in his country cottage as he felt inclined, and he returned to a course of chess and pleasant reading. We had at this time in Sarawak the famous naturalist, traveller and philosopher Mr Alfred Wallace, who was then elaborating in his mind the theory which was simultaneously worked out by Darwin – the theory of the origin of the species; and if he could not convince us that our ugly neighbours, the orang-utans, were our ancestors, he pleased, delighted and instructed us by his clever and inexhaustible flow of talk – really good talk. The Rajah was pleased to have so clever a man with him, as it excited his mind, and brought out his brilliant ideas.

But in 1857 Chinese gold-workers from the interior launched a surprise night attack on Kuching with the intention of killing Brooke and his European entourage. Brooke's servant, Penty, wrote: 'I hurried out of my bed and met the Rajah in the passage in the dark, who at the moment took me for one of the rebels, grappled me by the throat, and was about to shoot me when he fortunately discovered it was me.' Brooke managed to escape by jumping into the river in darkness and swimming under the bows of a Chinese barge. Eighteen-year-old Harry Nicholette, recently arrived to join the Rajah's civil service, was less lucky. He was cut down as he ran towards the house. The Chinese, thinking he was Brooke, cut off his head and carried it about in triumph on the end of a pike. The attackers occupied Kuching for several days, destroying the Rajah's house and his precious library. Loyal Malays and Dyaks eventually drove them off, with heavy losses.

Brooke continued to expand Sarawak's borders by playing rival chiefs off one against another, by exploiting weaknesses in the Brunei regime, and by reaching uneasy alliances. Naturally those who opposed him were, as in earlier diplomatic exchanges, branded 'piratical'. Robert Pringle summed up Brooke's tactics: 'He used this word partly because he deeply and sincerely believed that his enemies were the wilful, lawless adversaries of free trade and good government, and partly because he hoped that public support in maritime England would be disposed to support an anti-piracy campaign.'

Brooke finally returned to England in 1863 and persuaded the British government to recognise Sarawak as an independent state.

This was his lasting legacy. He died in Burrator in Devonshire in June 1868 after a series of strokes which had left him speechless and unable to move. He was sixty-five.

Sir Henry Keppel, his old friend and comrade in arms, lived much longer. He destroyed Chinese junks at Fat-shan Bay in 1857 during the Arrow War and commanded the naval brigade before Sebastopol. He became Admiral of the Fleet in 1875 and died in 1904 aged ninety-five. Admiral Cochrane took command of the West Indies and North American naval stations, and died in 1860. Sir Edward Belcher, who had failed to support Brooke's efforts, was put in command of an ill-starred expedition to the Arctic in search of Sir John Franklin. His appointment was described by his obituarist as 'unfortunate', owing to his lack of good temper or tact. The writer concluded: 'Perhaps no officer of equal ability has ever succeeded in inspiring so much personal dislike . . .' Through the rules of seniority alone he became a non-serving admiral. He died in 1857.

Sultan Omar Ali died in 1852 and was succeeded by Pengiran Mumim. The Brunei court was still riven by factions and the new Sultan was forced to remain on friendly terms with the British as he needed their naval firepower. The battle of Batang Marau had crushed the independent pirate chiefdoms and sea-borne larceny now became a tool of the state. Brunei prospered.

Brooke was succeeded as Rajah of Sarawak by his nephew Charles Johnson. He took the name Charles Brooke and tried, with some success, to emulate his uncle's rule. The *Annual Register* reported: 'Under his firm but benevolent government, based upon the principles introduced by his illustrious relative, Sarawak, now comprising of 28,000 square miles and a population of a quarter of a million, is a flourishing settlement. Trade has expanded and agriculture is advancing . . .' He died in 1917 and was succeeded by his son Charles, who in 1941 scrapped the Rajah's absolute powers and enacted a new democratic constitution. This was halted by the three-year Japanese occupation, and liberation saw the ruined country become a British colony. It moved steadily towards self-government and in 1963 joined the formation of Malaysia.

The 'white Rajah' remains a potent symbol in the lands he controlled. Through sheer force of will and personality he created a dynasty which lasted a hundred years in an alien land. Sarawak expanded and became a nation, and, as one contemporary wrote, 'piracy and head-hunting have been rooted out'.

A new type of a pirate, equipped with a speedboat and a machine-pistol, now roams the shipping lanes of the South China Sea. Unlike their forefathers, their loot is not cinnamon, porcelain and gold, but jet fuel, computer software and aluminium ingots.

TWENTY-ONE

The Storming of Madagascar, 1845

'The queen has been amusing herself . . .'

Not all of Britain's military expeditions ended in slaughter or glory. Some ended in farce – and one such was also one of the shortest conflicts in the Empire's history. It was a joint Anglo-French operation and it concluded with the two allies brawling over a captured standard. The official foe was one of the most feared despots in history, a woman who ruled a vast island almost completely unknown to the outside world.

*   *   *

Queen Ranavalona loved Paris fashion and on state occasions wore elaborate dresses in the style of Marie Antoinette. She commanded well-drilled, well-armed troops and employed the latest technology to build massive palaces and fortresses. Her own quarters tinkled with the sound of tiny silver bells.

She was also a cruel despot who held on to power through terror. Her armies wiped out entire peoples in the hinterland of Madagascar and her executioners slew thousands more. She killed Christians, drove out missionaries, enslaved shipwrecked sailors and banned all foreigners apart from a favoured few whose technological skills or western goods she craved. She favoured the traditional method of interrogation that used *tanguena* poison. The Irishman James Hastie, in favour before Ranavalona took ultimate power, described the torment suffered by servants suspected of causing the illness of a princess: 'They had to prove their innocence by this ordeal, which consisted of having to swallow the poison, also bits of the skin of a black fowl, and drink many bowls of lukewarm rice water. They were considered guilty if, when vomiting, the head did not fall to the south. Only one escaped with her life, the others, after having had ears, noses, legs and arms cut off, were cast down a steep rock.' To Hastie's disgust, royal schoolchildren laughed at their suffering and threw stones at the pitiful corpses.

*   *   *

Madagascar is one of the world's largest islands, measuring almost 1,000 miles by 360 miles at its widest point. Its isolation, well off the south-east of Africa, resulted in a unique wildlife, with many of its species not found anywhere else in the world. There are lemurs, aye-ayes, and peculiar types of bats, tortoises, chameleons, geckos, civet cats and rodents. The people are a mixture of Africans and Indonesians who arrived by sea during several millennia. Their religion was ancestor worship, with a heavy accent on fetish symbols.

Madagascar was first spotted in 1500 by the Spanish seafarer Diego Dias, who had been blown off course. In the early 1600s Portuguese missionaries made unsuccessful attempts to convert the native tribes, and in 1642 the French won a foothold on the island's south-west tip. After little more than thirty years their garrison was massacred. For some fifty years the island's few ports were the haunt of pirates such as William Kidd and John Avery. From the 1760s the French again established settlements and in 1805 set up an agency in the main port of Tamatave. During the war with Napoleon the island was occupied by the British. A Victorian visitor noted:

Madagascar is not only immensely extensive and in parts very thickly peopled, but is also a most fertile island, offering a great variety of temperature, with some of the finest harbours and timber in the world, and the interior is remarkably healthy. It is, however, chiefly surrounded by a narrow border of swamp, owing to the sea and the mouths of the rivers being frequently on the same level, as is the case on the west coast of Africa. This swamp is most deadly, and at one season of the year Madagascar, in those parts, is almost certain death to a European.

During all that period trade in slaves and arms led to the creation of various Malagassy kingdoms. They were unified, through conquest and treaty, by the great king Andrianampoinimerina by the end of the eighteenth century. His aim, he told his son and heir, was simple: 'The sea will be the boundary of my ricefield.' That son, Radama, ruled shrewdly from 1810 to 1828. He was aided by the British Governor of Mauritius, Sir Robert Farquhar, who wanted to replace French influence on Madagascar. Radama launched a programme of education for his subjects, encouraged trade and agreed to abolish the export of slaves. In return he received an annual subsidy of arms, ammunition and uniforms along with British military instructors. Christian teaching was introduced in the capital, Antananarivo, by the London Missionary Society. Schools were established to teach the scriptures, and printing was introduced for the first time. After ten years the missionary schools had taught some 15,000 people to read; thousands of apprentices were taught the skills of ironmongery, masonry and leather-working. The capital's single printing press produced thousands of primers and copies of the New Testament. Foundries were set up to produce the necessities of both civilian and military life. The island was at last coming out of the shadows.

All that changed when Radama died, aged just thirty-six, and the crown was seized by his first wife, Ranavalona. The new queen was all-powerful, and regarded education and Christianity as threats to her supreme authority. She hated all foreigners and her declared intention was to destroy the men of all but her own Hova tribe so that her position was truly unassailable. The women of other tribes were to be the property of her Hova soldiers. From the day of her coronation the purges began. Surrounded by Hova soldiers dressed in the uniform of the British Grenadiers, Ranavalona swore to return to the worship of idols. At the ceremony she spoke to her own sacred idols, a cornelian as big as a pigeon's egg and a green stone attached to the top of a staff, 'My predecessors have given you to me. I put my trust in you; therefore, support me.' Her anti-Christian fury was aroused when a diviner was converted and publicly destroyed his idols and charms. Schools were closed and Christian worship on the Sabbath was banned. European advisers at the court, ambassadors and artisans were assassinated. Passing a chapel and hearing the sound of hymn singing inside, the queen muttered: 'These people will not leave off until some of their heads are taken off.' All Malagassy citizens, high and low, who had been baptised were ordered to declare themselves on pain of death. Some came out, trusting the queen's justice. Others worshipped in secret. Most died anyway.

The dreaded *tanguena* poison was increasingly employed, but so were other methods which the queen herself enjoyed watching, such as flogging, spearing, boiling and sawing of spines. Common 'criminals' were simply thrown off high cliffs. Ranavalona proclaimed:

> With respect to these people who pray and read the books of the foreigners, I have admonished them several times, yet they persevere in opposing my will. Some have been put to death, others have been reduced to perpetual slavery, others fined and reduced in rank for praying and worshipping the god of the white people. But they contrive to pray in spite of all I do.

Within a month of her coronation one missionary wrote:

> The idols and diviners govern all things, as they did twenty years ago. Every superstition is renewed; the schools and divine service on the Sabbath in the native language are stopped, and I do not know when things will wear a more pleasing aspect.

In 1835, after many had died or taken prudent exile, the Christian religion was officially declared illegal. As most of the surviving missionaries had already fled, the tag of covert Christianity was a convenient way of getting rid of anyone, either individuals or whole communities, deemed to be disloyal. Then the terror really began.

People who fled Ranavalona's oppressive regime and took to the hinterland became outlaws. Every tribe or region which in any way aided them became the queen's enemies and savage retribution was exacted. In one expedition alone her Hova guards slaughtered 5,000 civilians. Furthermore her soldiers were themselves unpaid, often forced, labour, expected to live off the land. Everywhere they went they left burning, pillaged towns in their wake. Expeditions returned with anything up to 10,000 slaves, mainly widows and orphans. All shipwrecked sailors of any nation immediately became the property of the queen and were condemned to life-long slavery, although few survived long after landing on that terrible shore. Various outrages were committed against British subjects: a naval officer and seven of his men were killed, another was sold as a slave, others were falsely imprisoned. Not all these acts were ordered by the queen but the perpetrators certainly had her tacit approval. The Admiralty in London told the fleet in the region to 'watch over proceedings in Madagascar and to give prompt and effectual protection to British subjects'.

One Western observer wrote: 'The queen is constantly drunk – a clever woman, about 50. She has three or four lovers and they are said to be very desirous to keep all civilisation away.' Foreigners, especially the British whom she hated, were banned as the queen raged against the rest of the world. There were some exceptions. Ranavalona may have been brutalised by her lust for both power and blood, but she was never stupid and she understood that some alien artefacts and knowledge were worth having. Such an asset was the Frenchman Jean Laborde, the son of a blacksmith who gained special influence in the queen's court. In 1831 he took part in a bizarre and ultimately unsuccessful project to salvage treasure ships lost off Madagascar's west coast. He was himself shipwrecked and ended up on the island. When it was realised that he was a master mechanic skilled in armaments and the use of steam, he was put to work manufacturing muskets and powder for the queen's army. Ranavalona excluded him and several other Frenchmen from the general pogrom, realising that her expulsion of the British had left a technological hole in her resources. Laborde constructed an armaments factory at Mantasoa with 20,000 forced labourers supplied by the queen. It manufactured huge quantities of cannon, muskets, swords and bayonets. Connected workshops also produced porcelain, bricks, tiles, glass, cement, sealing wax, ink, dyes, rum, sulphuric acid and lightning conductors for the palaces and fine houses of Antananarivo. Laborde also constructed the queen's great wooden palace, as big as most stone cathedrals, with the central support of a single tree trunk 130 feet high. Five thousand slaves were needed to bring that trunk from the eastern forest. Over time the industrial complex at Mantasoa, with its foundries and mills, sugar refineries and silkworm nurseries, became virtually a second capital. An artificial lake was dug, gardens planted and vast stone buildings erected, with columns of pink granite. The queen and her top officials had summer houses there, and Laborde entertained them with fireworks and rockets of his own manufacture. He wrote to his brother about Ranavalona:

> I'm convinced that in spite of all the crimes of which she is, so to say, the cause, she is not as wicked as is said. She is a good mother and has still other good qualities, which would astonish those who hear only of the crimes committed in her name. Unfortunately, fanaticism has made her undeniably barbarous.

Laborde's industries reduced Madagascar's reliance on foreign imports and enabled the queen to crack down on foreign traders who had used Tanatave and other ports on the east coast for generations. Most trading ships lay offshore while local agents ferried their goods ashore. For the agents it was a dangerous game, evading Malagassy embargoes and relying on the tolerance bought for them by economic necessity. Some were expelled on the queen's orders.

In May 1845 the European traders at Tanatave, of whom twelve were British and eleven French, were told that Malagassy law would in future apply to them. This included ordeal by *tanguena*, the imposition of forced labour at the queen's whim, and the penalty of life-long slavery for many transgressions. When news of their predicament filtered out, the British and French authorities were appalled. They had repeatedly objected, fruitlessly, to the treatment of their nationals who had the misfortune to be washed ashore on Madagascar. Despite such behaviour, both European nations had failed to take action, bogged down as they were by often competing diplomatic intrigue. This time something had to be done to save both British and Gallic pride.

A *Times* correspondent wrote from Port Louis: 'The Queen

has been amusing herself by burning or cutting the heads off all the native Christians she had been able to lay hands on – many thousands.' The *Illustrated London News* reported that the foreign traders, mostly from Mauritius and Bourbon, were victims of the queen's edict. They were 'subject to a law which amongst other things makes them slaves, under certain contingencies'.

The Governor of Mauritius, Sir William Gomm, sent off Captain Kelly in the corvette HMS *Conway* to threaten repercussions and also to demand the release of a British shipmaster, Jacob Heppick, who had been enslaved after his barque *Marie Laure* was wrecked. The Governor of Bourbon, Admiral Bazoche, sent the men-of-war *Berceau* and *Zelee* under Commander Romain Desfosses to join the Anglo-French venture. An ultimatum produced no response. Kelly landed and met the Governor of Tamatave, Razakafidy, and other Malagassy lords. They behaved 'insolently' and told him plainly that they had imperative orders from the queen to enforce the orders against the traders. If the foreigners interfered they would be driven into the sea. Meanwhile the traders were locked up in the port's Customs House, suffering considerable intimidation. Two Frenchmen, a Spaniard, some Manila traders and a handful of Creoles from Mauritius agreed to be 'slaves of the queen'. The others, however, steadfastly refused. They were told by the Tamatave governor: 'To-morrow you must all be off or you will take your chances of losing your life during the looting.' The following day British and French longboats took off the frightened traders, who were obliged to leave behind all their possessions. M. Rautoney, for example, had to abandon 3,000 head of cattle and 16,000lb of rice. As soon as they left, their houses and warehouses were looted and torched.

Once the traders were safely aboard the warships and the French merchantman *Cosmopolite*, the two commanders held a shipboard conference and agreed, without approaching any higher authority, to bombard the town as punishment and to attack the Malagassy fort guarding its approaches the following morning. During the day the Malagassy were busy evacuating the town and carrying off the spoils. The garrison was reckoned to be 400 seasoned Hova soldiers with 600 auxiliaries.

On Sunday 15 June 1845 the three warships, lying 660 yards offshore, opened fire and their big guns wreaked much destruction in a town built largely of wood. The Customs House was completely gutted, along with 'a considerable part of the town'. That afternoon 350 men, of whom 100 were French soldiers and the rest crew members of the three vessels, crowded into fourteen boats, landed on the beach and headed for the fort 200 yards across a small plain. The landing was screened by a dense plantation. Desfosses said in his report:

> In less than 10 minutes our combatants were drawn up in battle array, with two howitzers of the *Berceau* placed on mountain carriages, in the centre of the column. The enemy confined himself, during the landing, to a few grapeshots which produced little or no effect. Captain Fiereck soon after gave the signal for the charge, and the small band rushed with incredible ardour towards the enemy, who was afraid to quit his entrenchments. The men of the *Zelee*, joined by 20 sailors and an ensign of the *Berceau*, immediately entered the low battery to the south, spiked three pieces of cannon and dismounted two others, and drove the Hova cannoneers into the principal fort, which they vainly tried to enter.

Five Frenchmen were killed storming the battery, and Ensign Berthe was run through the chest and fell on the fort's threshold. Sub-lieutenant Monod of the French Marines also fell to a spear just yards away.

The joint force soon came under sharp fire from another direction. The *Conway*'s guns soon silenced those of that battery, which was then quickly overrun and its guns spiked. Massive outworks were then stormed but the attackers soon realised that their commanders had made an enormous error in assuming that the earthen ramparts were the fort itself. Instead, they formed a screen which hid the real citadel, a solid circular structure, 30 feet high, mounted with 30 cannon and surrounded by a dry moat 30 feet wide. An observer wrote: 'It may appear incredible, but it is positively asserted that the existence of the interior fort, the keep, was not known even to the traders and people of Tamatave.'

The French were joined by the British contingents for the main assault. Desfosses wrote: 'In the fosse which separated the two enclosures, a desperate close combat ensued in which the English and French vied with each other in ardour and courage.' The Hova defenders, 'having bravely disputed every inch of ground,' retired into their casements. The attacking force held the rim of the earth screen for 40 minutes, but the fort's guns began to take their toll.

The warships poured shot into the fort – a total of 1,500 rounds during the entire engagement – but the only damage appeared to be to the flagstaff on the upper rampart. *The Times* correspondent reported: 'It was shot through and it fell inside the circular fort; it was then put on a lance, or something of that sort, and stuck again on the wall, in a crevice of the stones. It was shot away again, and this time it fell outward, hanging down within a few feet of the bottom of the ditch, between the inner fort and the screen.' It was swiftly ripped down by Ensign Granville, and a handful of British and French sailors. There then ensued an extraordinary dispute: the British and French, under heavy fire, conducted an unseemly brawl over who should take away the enemy standard. Musket balls whistled overhead and men dropped as the brawl turned into a tug of war between uneasy allies. One correspondent wrote: 'They were about to come to cutlass-blows with one another, in the very hottest of the Malagash fire, when Lieutenant Kennedy of the *Conway*, to prevent mischief, rushed down and with his sword cut it, giving half to each party.' The French carried off that portion of the pure white standard bearing the word 'Ranavalona', while the British took the half inscribed 'Manjaka', the second part of the queen's favoured title. Moments later Kennedy attacked a gun embrasure just as the Malagassy cannon was fired. Several men were killed and he was wounded, with a large splinter through both thighs.

The Malagassy cannon thundered in a land–sea artillery duel with the foreign vessels, tearing topmasts off the *Berceau* and *Zelee*. Desfosses reported: 'The firing of the Hovas had a precision which would have surprised us, had we not been informed that their artillery was directed by a renegade Spaniard who makes a most improper use of his talents.' Most of the Malagassy balls sailed harmlessly overhead, cutting only a few ropes aboard *Conway*.

By now the attackers on the rim were increasingly exposed to fire from within the fort and to the danger of Malagassy reinforcements arriving. The howitzers were able to fire only one shot because their quick matches had become wet during the shore landing. Captain Fiereck was disabled by a wound, the men were exhausted and running low on ammunition. Desfosses reported: 'Although the complete destruction of the enemy artillery, the great object of our enterprise, was not entirely attained, the lesson we had given those barbarous spoilaters of our merchants was of a nature not to be forgotten by them.' He duly gave the order to retreat and the men scrambled back down to the beach, carrying their wounded and the captured flag with them.

The disembarkation was carried off without a hitch by early evening. Priority was given to taking off all the wounded, 43 French and 12 British. That was achieved, but the dead were left behind – 17 Frenchmen and 4 Britons. One of the latter was a captured sailor who was tortured to death and mutilated. The heads of the dead men were cut off and impaled on stakes set at intervals along the beach. The grisly sight greeted visitors for the next eight years.

A Malagassy deserter who boarded *Berceau* told Desfosses that around 200 defenders had died on the batteries and inside the fort. They included the Deputy Governor, the queen's Standard Bearer, the Director of Customs and six other chiefs. On 17 June, two days after the assault, the allies went their separate ways, and the farcical brawl over the Malagassy standard was forgotten, at least in the official dispatches. Desfosses reported:

I have just received and returned the farewell salute of the English frigate *Conway*; at the moment of parting, as during their presence here, the officers, sailors and soldiers of both nations did not cease to give each other the most hearty proofs of high esteem and cordial sympathy.

The following day Kelly wrote to Queen Ranavalona to justify his action, referring to 'the insolence and brutal injustice of the

Tamatave authorities, which demanded punishment'. His response 'would be justified by all civilised Powers, especially as all proposals to arrange amicably the questions of dispute between us have been refused. We have not declared war on the Hovas, we have merely chastised your insolent offices.' The queen replied that all the blame lay at Kelly's door as his ship had fired first. She boasted that she had defeated 'the united forces of England and France'. Her officials demanded Kelly's surrender, 'dead or alive'.

The heads on the beach enraged public opinion in Britain and France, but the queen would not countenance their removal. In a letter to Kelly she said it was 'very strange and highly impertinent' that the European powers should seek to deny she was mistress in her own country, like Queen Victoria, and to deny her the right of fixing the heads of her prisoners on lances according to the custom of her country. She said that future correspondence to her must come from Victoria alone. The Mauritian newspaper *Le Cercen* stormed: 'This is what is called talking, or rather writing, like a Queen? It remains to be seen whether the two great heads of the two greatest nations in the world will approve, or at least excuse, the logical ultra-arrogance of Her Majesty of Madagascar.'

A few months after the bombardment a young Hova official, who had been educated in Paris, ordered the heads to be taken down and buried. His reward for this humane act was that the heads were exhumed and put back on the beach – along with his own.

Ranavalona ordered the expulsion of all remaining foreign traders and halted the export of beef and rice to Mauritius and Reunion. Huge military preparations were made in anticipation of another foreign attack, including a mad scheme to encase the whole vast island behind a sea-wall, but the expected invasion never came. The French government did indeed propose a punitive expedition. It was estimated that an invasion of Madagascar would need a minimum of 30,000 men, an army three times bigger than any ever sent to sea in the Indian Ocean. It would take three months to arrive and would require 300 men-of-war, store ships and transports. The *Examiner* reported:

The first object of a judicious enterprise will be to make for the interior, so as to avoid the pestiferous marshes of the coast, and strike a blow at the capital and power of the Hovas. That capital is in the centre of the broadest part of the island, and consequently at least 200 miles from the coast, laying in a country without roads, where the thermometer is seldom under 80 degrees, and where some resistance must be expected, at least 20 marches, and the establishment of at least 20 posts to maintain the communications with the fleet. If, instead of this, the army remains on the coast, the malaria and the Hovas will do the business – decimate it in a month, and cut off nine parts out of 10 within a twelve-month.

Not surprisingly, the Chamber of Deputies vetoed the expedition. Desfosses proposed that they should send arms and ammunition to rebel chiefs in the Madagascar hinterland, both to topple the queen and to extend French control. The minister responsible wrote in the margin of his report: 'Nothing of the sort must be done.'

Likewise, the British government had no stomach or political will for an expensive military undertaking. However, pressure from beef-strapped Mauritius led to diplomatic overtures to the queen to resume trade. She said she would consider it provided the British and French paid reparations for the bombardment of Tamatave. Lord Palmerston's government had no stomach for that either, and Madagascar remained closed to British and French goods. The Americans took advantage of the situation and for years enjoyed a virtual monopoly of foreign trade there.

The chief victim of Kelly's punitive action was Mauritius, which lost more than £22,000 in commerce annually. More seriously, the embargo caused serious food shortages as the small island colony suffered from the lack of beef and rice. After several years the merchants of Mauritius clubbed together and sent Ranavalona 1,500 dollars in reparations for Tamatave, stating that 'all the people regretted the attack' and entreating the queen 'to accept it for the injury done by Captain Kelly'. She accepted, considering it payment of a fine, and the ports were opened to the smaller islands. The heads on the beach were finally taken down and buried.

The queen's domestic reign of terror continued, and in 1849 there was another purge of native Christians. Noble converts were heavily fined and reduced to the rank of a common soldier. Over a hundred were flogged and sentenced to a lifetime's hard labour in chains. Fourteen were thrown over a 200-foot precipice below the queen's palace, known as 'the place of the hurling'. Another four nobles, including a husband and his heavily pregnant wife, were granted the privilege of being burnt alive. The wife went into labour when she was tied to the stake and the infant was consumed with her in the flames. A rare European visitor, Ida Pfeiffer, wrote in her diary: 'Terror . . . The streets are resounding with cries and howling; every one is fleeing from the town as though an enemy is threatening it.'

Generally the queen's vengeance now turned inwards against her own people – suspected plotters and displaced farmers she branded as 'brigands'. When even her most loyal subjects grew weary of the spectacle of mass public executions, they were carried out at night. Britain's role in arming and training the Hova army before the queen's coronation caused much heart-searching. A former missionary, the Revd J.J. Freeman, wrote:

Great Britain, having supplied a handful of men with weapons of destruction and taught them how to wield them more effectually, by sending a few men to drill the natives, lent herself ungraciously to the task of abetting the ruin of independence, liberty, property, homes and lives of many tens of thousands of the peaceful inhabitants of the island, who had never raised a finger against the British throne, nor against the Hovas, but who now, furnished with British weapons, could desolate whole regions of inoffensive agriculturists and glory in schemes of conquest and rapine.

Laborde eventually fell from the queen's favour and was exiled, along with several other Europeans who faced a trumped-up charge of 'having wished to establish a republic, to liberate all slaves, and to establish equality without distinction of nobles'. Laborde sailed for the Île de Bourbon, and his workmen at Mantasoa reacted with frenzy, smashing factories, workshops and machinery. He later returned and after his death was buried under a large monument at Mantasoa.

Ranavalona died, aged eighty-one, in 1861, after a reign of thirty-three blood-soaked years. Freeman estimated that one million deaths were due directly or indirectly to wars during her reign; another 100,000 people were executed or massacred, and 20,000 women and children were taken as sex-slaves for the Hova troops.

Her beloved son and heir Radama II was sickened by her excesses and proved a benign ruler. He had been born twelve months after the death of his regal father – wise courtiers ignored the discrepancy – and had been raised by French tutors under the doting eye of his mother. He reopened his kingdom to Europeans and proposed a treaty with the French. He also released those chiefs and their families who had been prisoners for all his mother's reign, allowing them to take home the bones of those who had died in captivity. He abolished trial by *tanguena* and other barbaric punishments. He even, unheard-of in royal circles, paid wages to the workmen who built new palaces and civic structures. Two years later he was murdered in his palace and his wife Rasoherina took the throne. She continued his work and treaties were signed with Britain, France and America.

French influence grew, along with trade interests which the Republic needed to protect. In 1894 the French invaded and Madagascar became a colony. There were revolts and suppression, a British occupation in 1942, after the island had declared for the Vichy regime, and Madagascar eventually achieved independence in 1960. For most of the world, however, the island's history remains largely an untold story.

TWENTY-TWO

The First Sikh War, 1845–6

'. . . A brutal bulldog fight.'

In the rose-red dusk of 21 September 1845 at Lahore, capital of the Punjab, the four widows of Jawahir Singh walked serenely through throngs of people towards a funeral pyre. Their husband, the late Wazir, had been chopped to bits by his own army the previous day and, as was the custom of *suttee*, his wives were to join the pieces of his body to be consumed by the flames. Each was young and beautiful; they were dressed in their best finery, gold embroidered in their silk trousers, jewels studding their ears and noses. They carried silver coins to toss to the multitude.

The dignity of the occasion did not last long. Several Sikh soldiers, members of the dreaded Khalsa army, grabbed the girls and brutally ripped the gold and jewellery from their flesh, tearing nostrils, ears and cheeks, and snatched the silver from their hands. It was a despicable act, inspired not just by greed but intended to dishonour the young widows and prevent them from making their final holy offerings. The girls mounted the pyre with their faces streaming blood.

The Maharani Jindan, the dead man's sister and mother of the Punjab's eight-year-old ruler, lay prostrate before them and asked for their blessing. The four about to die gave it willingly to her, but not to the men of the Khalsa. These they cursed robustly, forecasting that their military sect would be conquered, that their wives would be made widows, and the country made desolate. *Suttees* were held to be sacred with the power of the prophecy. Shaken and enraged soldiers swung at the girls with rifle butts as the flames crackled around their robes. The women died without making another sound.

Within a few short months, their prophecy was proved correct as the Khalsa were slaughtered by the thousand in the swollen

Sutlej river, at what later became known as the 'Indian Waterloo'. It marked the end of the bloodiest war the British ever fought in India and decided the history of the sub-continent for a century.

* * *

In ancient times the Punjab, the Land of the Five Rivers, was inhabited by three races, the Jats, Rajputs and Afghans. Bounded by the Himalayas and the Indus and Sutlej rivers, it straddled the main access route to India for northern invaders and thus suffered from ceaseless warfare and conquest. Its people learnt to wear their swords while ploughing their land. It was ruled successively by Afghan invaders, Mongols, Turks, the Timur dynasty and the Mughal Empire. The intermingling of blood, languages and customs created a new people with their own tongue, the Punjabi. They in turn created a new faith which was to challenge and overturn the power of traditional rulers.

The founder of the Sikh religion, Baba Nanak, was born in 1469. His creed, an amalgam of Hindu and Sufi Islamic mysticisms, was based on the unity of God and the brotherhood of all men. Over successive generations the Sikh faith became transformed into a military order represented by the Khalsa, or the Pure, a religious army united against the Mughal Empire which ruled from Delhi. In the late seventeenth century the guru Gobind Raj decreed that all Sikhs should take the name Singh, meaning warrior. They must leave their hair and beards uncut, wear knee-length military trousers and a steel bangle on their right wrists, and always carry a sword. Honour could be gained in war alone. They were forbidden to molest women, drink alcohol, smoke tobacco or eat meat unless the animal was killed with a single blow. Their military prowess flourished as they beat the Mughals and the orthodox Hindus and Moslems who surrounded them. A foreigner who lived among them wrote:

All that a Sikh chief asked in these days from a follower was a horse and a matchlock. All that a follower sought was protection and permission to plunder in the name of God and the Guru under the banner of the chief. All Sikhs were theoretically equal, and he who could pierce a tree through with an arrow, or who could kill a tiger with a blow of his sword, might soon ride with followers behind him and call himself a *sirdar*. No man could consider his land, his horse or his wife secure unless he was strong enough to defend them.

James Browne, an officer in the East India Company, wrote more sympathetically: 'The Sikhs from necessity confederated together, and finding that their peaceable deportment did not secure them from oppression, they took up arms to defend themselves against a tyrannical government.'

From the turmoil that followed the defeat of the Mughals emerged one man strong enough to unite the Sikhs and turn the Punjab into a nation, Runjeet Singh. Born in 1780, in his teens he led the resistance to Afghan invaders, beating two armies from the north and driving them from the capital city of Lahore. In 1801 he proclaimed himself Maharajah of the Punjab and ruled his country firmly until his death in 1837.

He was a one-eyed despot with an insatiable thirst for women and wine, and his court orgies were notorious and unashamed. He was cruel and greedy, and had little formal education. But he was a natural leader of men and no fool. He watched closely the expansion of British power to the south of his domain and the victories won by John Company's armies against all-comers. For a while he allied himself with the Marathas against the British, who were then mostly concerned with consolidating their possessions in India so they could focus on defeating the armies of Napoleon.

In 1802 Runjeet took the city of Amritsar, underlining his supreme authority. In 1803 he visited a British encampment disguised as an ordinary soldier. He observed the skill of the redcoats and sepoys as they drilled and were trained in weaponry. After concluding a humiliating treaty with the British he resolved to match them in modern firepower, ready for the day, which he knew must come, when the British Empire came knocking on his door.

He built the Khalsa into a superbly armed and drilled army of 29,000 regular infantry with 192 guns, staffed with French, Italian,

British, German, American and Russian instructors. British muskets were bought in their thousands and copied in Lahore's belching foundries. Runjeet's favourites were the Ghorcharas, his own irregular cavalry, which received the best arms, equipment and training. British observers were especially impressed by the Sikh Lancers, who trained by riding full pelt at tent pegs stuck in the ground, more often than not striking them with their long weapons. The heavy dragoons, clad in chainmail, were also formidable. Captain William Osborne regarded the Sikh soldiers as 'the finest material in the world for forming an army'. He, like other British visitors, was especially impressed by their drill and appearance. He recalled:

> I never saw so straight or beautiful a line with any troops. They were all dressed in white with black cross belts and either a red or yellow silk turban; armed with muskets and bayonets of excellent manufacture . . . The commanding officer beats and abuses the major, the major the captains, the captains the subalterns, and so on till there is nothing left for the private to beat but the drummer boys, who catch it accordingly.

Such discipline, however, could not destroy the individualism inherent in the Sikh nature, or their lust for booty. In successive wars they grew rich on the spoils won by beating the Gurkhas, the Kashmiris and the last Afghan contingents in the Punjab. And they expected to get richer fighting the British. That meant that their discipline disintegrated under their desire for battlefield looting. Runjeet understood the defect and conceded: 'The system of the British is [so] good that even if the enemy threw gold coins in the course of their flight, the soldiers would not even look at them. On the other hand, if the Khalsa soldiers saw mere corn, they would break their ranks, dash towards that and spoil the whole plan of operations.'

Runjeet prized his artillery above all and employed many foreigners in order to raise its standards to the European level. Foremost among these was Colonel Alexander Gardner. An American soldier of fortune who dressed in tartan, he became a powerful figure both in the Khalsa and the Lahore court. Two

British 24-pound howitzers that had been presented to Runjeet were swiftly copied in the local foundries. Osborne witnessed a practice by the Khalsa gunners, firing at a curtain hung 200 yards away, and said their skills would have been a credit to any artillery in the world. 'At the first round of grape, the curtain was clean cut away, and their shells at eight and twelve hundred yards were thrown with a precision that is extraordinary, when the short period of time since they have known even of the existence of such a thing is taken into consideration.'

The first real test of Runjeet Singh's new army was against Kashmir, and it passed the test easily, routing its enemies and rescuing Shah Sujah, the captured former ruler of Afghanistan. The ex-captive had no choice but to award to Runjeet the fabulous Koh-i-noor, then the largest diamond in the world, as a mark of gratitude. This 105-carat gem, known as 'the mountain of light', was mined in the twelfth century in southern India and was the figurehead of the throne of the Moghul emperors. Legend said it was a gift from the sun god Surya. Each successive ruler fought to gain and retain possession of it, and it was said to be worth the value of one day's food for all the people in the world. Runjeet Singh wore it proudly on his bracelet.

In 1818 Runjeet captured Multan and the neighbouring districts and a year later annexed the whole of Kashmir. By 1823 the Khalsa had destroyed the Afghan and Pathan forces in the north-west frontier province. Runjeet controlled all the land as far as the Khyber Pass. This was the peak of Sikh power. For some years Runjeet's court at Lahore rivalled any of the royal courts of Europe. Sikh art flourished and weapons became both functional and illustrative of the artisans' finest skills. Captain Osborne described the sumptuousness of one chief, Raja Suchet Singh:

His dress was magnificent; a helmet or skull cap of bright polished steel inlaid with gold, and a deep fringe of chainmail, of the same material, reaching to his shoulders, three plumes of black heron's feathers waving on his chest, and three shawls of lilac, white and scarlet, twisted very round and tight, interlaced with one another and gathered round the edge of the helmet, a chelenk of rubies and diamonds on his forehead. Back, breastplates, and gauntlets of steel, richly embossed with gold and precious stones, worn over a rich, thick-quilted jacket of bright yellow silk, with magnificent armlets of rubies and diamonds on each arm, a shield of the polished hide of the rhinoceros, embossed and ornamented with gold, a jewelled sabre and matchlock, with his long and glossy black beard and moustaches he looked the very beau ideal of a Sikh chief.

As the Khalsa secured victory and wealth for the fledgling state, its power increased. The soldiers were commanded by the Akalis, also known as the Crocodiles, a strict sect devoted to 'misrule and plunder'. They demanded their share of political power and played a full part in court intrigue. They were hostile to the British and other faithless men, and they watched suspiciously as the British took other strategic lands in an attempt to keep their neighbour under control. The Khalsa, in their turn, cast covetous eyes across the Sutlej at the rich lands of the Raj. As long as Runjeet lived their power could be checked and channelled in useful directions, but when he died in June 1837 there was no one strong enough to replace him. He was placed on a pyre of sandalwood along with four of his eighteen wives and seven of his slave girls. Henry Princep, a Briton who admired the Sikh nation, wrote: 'Ranjit Singh has, in the formation especially of his military force, evinced the same enquiring activity, the same attention to minutiae, which characterised the first Peter of Russia.'

After his death there followed six years of turmoil and murder. Runjeet's only legitimate son, Kharak Singh, was a degenerate opium-eater. He was swiftly poisoned by his son, the eighteen-year-old Nau Nihal Singh. That young man fell from power even more quickly, and in suspicious circumstances – he was killed by a falling archway as he returned from his father's cremation. He was replaced by Shere Singh, the eldest of Runjeet's illegitimate sons, who lasted a full two years. During that time Kharak's widow, Chaund Cour, conspired against the new ruler, but was crushed to death by her own slave girls, who dropped a great stone on her while she bathed. Shere Singh could not honour his promises of greater wealth, despite his lavish expenditure on his own decadent court, and the Khalsa ran amok, sacking bazaars and killing unpopular officers. In 1843 Shere Singh was reviewing his troops when an officer shot him with a double-barrelled shotgun and stuck his head on the point of a spear. Runjeet's youngest son, the six-year-old Duleep Singh, became Maharajah of a country divided between warring factions and dominated by an uncontrollable army. When Duleep's Wazir, Hira Singh, tried to impose his authority he too was cut down by the mutinous Khalsa.

Within the Lahore Palace the power was divided between Maharani Jindan, the young mother of the nominal ruler, her lover Lal Singh, and her brother, the drunken Jawahir Singh. Together they tried to control the Khalsa in the traditional way, by bribery, by increasing its manpower to almost 80,000, and by promising them that the day would soon come when they could sweep down on the British and plunder the rich cities of the Raj.

Jindan was a former concubine with a colossal appetite for sex and drink. She was regarded as a great beauty grown a little flabby through indulgence. She was determined to seize real power and keep it in trust for her son. She used her physical charms to woo supporters and divide opponents. Reports which reached the British described her as 'a handsome, debauched woman of thirty-three, very indiscriminate in her affections, an eater of opium'. Lord Ellenborough saw her as a 'woman of determined courage, the only person at Lahore apparently who has courage'. Major George Broadfoot, Britain's political agent on the north-west frontier, thought differently. He reported that she had become deranged by excess and claimed that four young fellows took turns to service her each night. Jawahir Singh, who was made Wazir, was simply a drunkard. 'I sometimes feel as if I were a sort of parish constable at the door of a brothel rather than the representative of one government to another,' Broadfoot complained.

The British administration was appalled by such reports and by the succession of royal murders. The new Governor-General in British India, Sir Henry Hardinge, had initially believed that a strong, stable Sikh state could be re-established in the Punjab and would act as a solid buffer zone to protect Britain's interests. He soon realised his error, and began to build up forces at the border. This was noted by the Khalsa leaders, who also knew of Hardinge's reputation as an aggressive soldier. Sikh agents were sent to sow the seeds of mutiny among the sepoys, offering better pay and the prospect of loot to the poorly paid Company men. Few responded but the attempt caused great concern among the British officers.

Back across the Sutlej, the Khalsa grew increasingly impatient. Jawahir, terrified that he would 'die a dog's death' like his predecessor Hira Singh, offered them ever larger bribes of gold and silver, but his promises could not be kept as the treasury emptied. He promised war with the British, but the Khalsa said they would not be led by a fool. The *panchayats*, or military councils, decided to seize power themselves. On 21 September 1845 they ordered the Maharani, with her son and all the government officials, to attend the Khalsa parade outside Lahore. She agreed, telling her trembling brother that the Khalsa would not dare challenge their authority. Jawahir Singh, despite his fears, rode out with the party on an elephant, nestling the young Maharajah on his lap.

Gardner described what followed:

An ominous salute ran along the immense line of the army – one hundred and eighty guns were fired. After the salute had died away, not a sound was heard but the trampling of the feet of the royal cavalcade. As soon as the procession reached the centre of the line one man came forward and shouted 'Stop,' and at his voice the whole procession paused. A tremor ran through the host . . .

Maharani Jindan was dragged screaming to a sumptuous tent. Her royal son was pulled from her brother's grip and handed to her. 'Meanwhile,' Gardner wrote, 'the bloody work had been done . . . A soldier had gone up the ladder placed by Jawahir Singh's elephant, stabbed him with his bayonet and flung him upon the ground, where he was despatched in a moment with fifty wounds.' The Maharani, mad with grief, was allowed to crouch by his dismembered body where she screamed lamentations and pledged that every man in the Khalsa would meet a similar end.

The Khalsa leaders, shaken by her words and by those of the *suttees* at the funeral pyre, realised that they had gone too far. Two days later, when the Maharani took over the government of the country, they acknowledged her as Regent. She charmed them by appearing dressed as a near-naked dancing girl. But behind the scanty veil she embarked on a dangerous double game. The Khalsa believed that the legendary invincibility of the British Army had been dealt an irrevocable blow by the massacre by Afghans of a column retreating from Kabul, and they wanted to capitalise on that disaster. The Maharani urged caution and for a time they complied. But privately Jindan still wanted both to avenge her brother and to break the power of the Khalsa for the sake of her son's future rule. She was determined to see her own army destroyed. She delayed every military order, to give the British a chance to mass their forces, while sending Broadfoot's agents secret intelligence on the Khalsa's intentions and strength.

Hardinge responded by strengthening the British frontier defence forces to 25,000 men. They were, however, dangerously dispersed between brick barracks at Ludhiana, Ferozepore, Ambala and Meerut, 130 sweltering miles from the border. Sir Henry refused to believe intelligence reports that six Khalsa divisions totalling perhaps 60,000 men under the command of the cowardly and treacherous Tej Singh were poised to cross the Sutlej. Many British factions actively encouraged war, believing it would give them the excuse to expand British territory. Sir Henry reported:

> I do not expect that the [Khalsa] troops will come as far as the banks of the Sutlej, or that any positive acts of aggression will be committed; but it is evident that the Rani and the Chiefs are for their own preservation, endeavouring to raise a storm which, when raised, they will be powerless either to direct or allay . . .

His doubts that the Sikhs meant business were proved wrong on 10 December 1845 when Sikh cavalry and skirmishers crossed the broad, muddy Sutlej at Hariki, near Ferozepore. The news provoked a shout of defiance from men of the 8th Foot, and wails from local women. The Sikh war had begun while the British were muddled and confused, and the Sikhs themselves were weakened by treachery and betrayal among their leaders.

*   *   *

Sir Henry Hardinge may have dithered in the run-up to the war, but there was no doubting he was a man of action. Now aged sixty, he was a veteran of the Napoleonic Wars, and had lost his left hand at Quatre Bras, two days before Waterloo. He became MP for Durham in 1820 and, under the patronage of his former commander Wellington, was Secretary of War until his appointment as Governor-General of India, where he replaced his brother-in-law Lord Ellenborough. At the War Office he was popular as a 'just, upright and considerate chief'. He was already in Umbullah when the Sikh invasion began and his first priority was to bring together his forces to face the threat.

The man in charge of those forces was Sir Hugh Gough. An old soldier born in Limerick, Gough attracted controversy throughout his career, and at sixty-six was an old warhorse whom his own soldiers affectionately called 'Tipperary Joe'. Slightly older than Hardinge, he had seen more action: he was at the surrender of the Dutch fleet at Saldanha Bay, at the capture of both Trinidad and Surinam, at the battle of Talavera, where he was severely wounded and had the first of many horses shot from under him, and at the battle of Barossa, where he led a famous charge to capture a French eagle standard. He was severely wounded at the battle of Nivelle in 1813 and spent most of his middle years on half pay, being given his first big command when he was sixty. After heroic service in the Opium War he was created a baronet and transferred to India. His command of forces in the Gwalior War was not universally praised. His critics regarded him as vainglorious to the point of incompetence. Lord Ellenborough, then Governor-General, wrote to Wellington: 'Despite his many excellent qualities, he had not the grasp of mind and the prudence essential to conduct great military operations.' That view was never shared by the men under his command who, in a brutal military age, appreciated his concern for their welfare. Private George Tookey of the 14th Light Dragoons proudly told his mother that when Gough visited him and others in hospital he treated them as if they were officers. He always led from the front, sharing the same dangers as his men. A sergeant in the Bengal Artillery wrote: 'When he was present the men looked upon success as certain, and it was not as a commander alone that he was respected, but as a kind-feeling and good-hearted old man . . .' What confounded Gough's critics the most, as will be seen, was that he won battles, despite his perceived failings.

The plan agreed between the Governor-General and the army commander was to join up General Sir John Littler's 7,000-strong garrison at Ferozepore with the main British force at Ludhiana. Gough led the main column of 11,000 men with 42 guns while Littler waited for several days, expecting his light defences to be overrun at any moment by Sikh cavalry. But Tej Singh, the Khalsa commander, and Lal Singh, the prime minister, who held joint command, were in league with the Maharani. In a secret dispatch to Littler Lal Singh reaffirmed their friendship with the British. Major Carmichael Smyth of the Bengal Light Cavalry wrote with disgust that Tej Singh and Lal Singh, 'instead of watching for opportunities to employ the force to the best advantage, were intent only on placing their troops in such a position as might render them an easy and complete conquest to their foes'. They held back from attack and split their forces, Tej Singh investing Littler's garrison while Lal Singh went out to meet Gough's column.

Gough, the ultimate fighting general, drove his parched men by rapid marches through choking dust clouds. Incredibly, given the awful conditions and lack of both food and water, the column marched 114 miles in just five days. They reached the small village of Mudki, 18 miles south-east of Ferozepore, on 18 December, having marched 20 miles that day alone. Village shops were ordered to open to sell grain to the British, who had their first proper meal for days during the mid-afternoon. But the food had to be bolted down as the Sikhs, drawn by the smoke from the soldiers' fires, began to advance. Lal Singh commanded some 8,000 cavalry, 2,000 infantry and 22 guns. The first salvo from the Sikh guns shot a horse from under Major Henry Havelock, who was later to win glory defending

Lucknow during the Indian Mutiny. Gough pushed forward his own horse artillery and cavalry across the flat terrain, dotted with sandy hillocks and thick patches of jungle. The Sikhs took advantage of whatever cover was at hand, while the British advanced in the same rigid formations that had been deployed against the French Emperor thirty years before.

The five troops of horse artillery under Brigadier Brooke galloped forward in a line towards the Sikh guns and the first part of the battle became an artillery duel at 300 yards' range. Gough reported: 'The enemy opened a very severe cannonade upon our advancing troops, which was vigorously replied to.' A young gunner tasting action for the first time recalled seeing a ventsman 'running about disembowelled,' a corporal whose hand was shattered by round-shot as he was firing his own gun, a fallen comrade shot through the eye, and another friend sitting upright in his saddle with a great hole punched through his chest. 'These sights were not pleasant,' he wrote home.

The Sikh cavalry advanced through the thick dust and smoke as the day's light began to fade, aiming to encircle both flanks. Gough saw the danger and ordered the 3rd Light Dragoons and units of the 4th Light Cavalry to stop them. The British horsemen charged with their long lances and drove into the lighter Sikh cavalry. The dragoons turned the enemy's left flank and swept down the entire line of Sikh gunners and infantry. Lieutenant John Cumming wrote: 'Oh, how I wish for a thousand more good British horse to join that whirlwind charge.' The British casualties mounted, however, as Sikh infantry hidden behind the scrub shot down horses and butchered fallen men with their swords. Sikh snipers picked off the British officers.

It was now the turn of the British infantry. With less than an hour of daylight left, twelve battalions of redcoats, mainly sepoys, marched forward. The Sikh fired disciplined volleys into their ranks while the enemy guns blasted away with grapeshot. Some sepoys began firing indiscriminately, hitting British units in the back, while others broke and ran. Lieutenant Robertson of the 31st Foot described that action as 'a regular mob, and nearly as many shots coming from behind us as in front'. Havelock, newly rehorsed, rode around them shouting 'The enemy are in front of you, not behind you.' Order was restored but the battle became a confused mêlée as darkness fell.

The Sikh gunners kept their guns 'vomiting forth at a fine rate showers of grape' while British and sepoy units lost their sense of direction in the choking, dusty gloom. Two officers carrying the colours of the 31st Foot fell and Sergeant Jones won an immediate battlefield commission by rescuing the flag. Brigadier Wheeler fell badly wounded but the divisional commander, Sir Harry Smith, led a charge into 'the very teeth of a Sikh column'. The British momentum failed again in the confusion, while Gough rode up and down yelling 'We must take those guns.' No one knew precisely where they were. Men of the 31st stumbled on one Sikh battery and took it in a rush. Others followed as the British army's five-to-one superiority in foot soldiers began to tell. But it was no easy matter as the Sikhs fought on with brave determination even when their big guns fell silent. Lieutenant Herbert Edwardes wrote: 'The last two hours of the battle were a series of dogged stands, and skirmishing retreats on the part of the Sikh troops, of sharp struggles, gun captures and recaptures, and a British pursuit over five miles of the worst ground that armies ever fought for.' Gough reported that the Sikhs,

> were driven from position after position with great slaughter and the loss of seventeen pieces of artillery; our infantry using the never-failing weapon, the bayonet, whenever the enemy stood. Night only saved them from worse disaster, for this stout conflict was maintained during an hour and a half of dim starlight, amid a cloud of dust from the sandy plain, which yet more obscured every object.

Among British soldiers unused to fighting at night, the battle became known as the 'Midnight Mudki'.

The Sikhs were driven back to their camp at Ferozeshah but were far from decisively beaten. Gough's losses were surprisingly heavy, particularly as he faced a weaker foe. Among his ranks 215 were killed and 657 wounded, many of who would not survive. Senior officers were in the thick of the fighting and their high casualty rate reflected that. Generals Sir John McCaskill and Sir Robert 'Fighting Bob' Sale, the hero of Jellalabad, were among the dead, as were Brigadiers Bolton and Wheeler. Sale's left thigh was shattered by grapeshot and McCaskill was shot through the chest. Major Broadfoot was hacked to pieces with spear and sword. Hardinge was highly critical of Gough's actions and reported that at Mudki 'the confusion of the attack had created a feeling that the army was not well in hand'. From then on Hardinge lost no opportunity to criticise his army commander, even though it was largely his own earlier refusal to allow Gough to deploy forces closer to the border which had made Gough's mad dash necessary.

The British forces, half-dead with fatigue after a long march and a gruelling battle, reached their camp shortly after midnight to snatch a few hours of sleep. The bugles woke them at dawn, and they rose ready to fight another battle.

*   *   *

The exhausted British troops had some respite while their commanders considered tactics. They were joined by reinforcements, 3,200 men made up of the 29th Foot, the 1st European Light Infantry, and two sepoy regiments. Hardinge, the Governor-General, was eager to taste battle himself after a lapse of thirty years. Although they had been appointed lieutenant-generals on the same day, Hardinge came below Gough on the army list and he accordingly placed himself under Gough's command on the battlefield. Gough had no option but to accept him as his second-in-command, writing in dispatches 'I need hardly say with how much pleasure the offer was accepted.' Diplomacy or sarcasm? Gough must have known that to have his political superior as his military second could only cause complications at best and, at worse, confusion in the chain of command.

At 4 a.m. on 21 December, after a day's rest which enabled the Sikhs a day to strengthen their entrenchments, the British marched towards the enemy positions surrounding the small fortified village of Ferozeshah. By 11 a.m. they were ready to attack the Sikh defences which were around a mile in length and half a mile deep. Gough wanted to push on at once, while there was plenty of daylight left. Hardinge insisted on waiting until they were joined by Littler's column of 7,000 men which was marching in a sweep from Ferozepore, 13 miles distant. In a tense confrontation Gough snarled that to wait was to risk another night battle, while to move towards Littler's force would mean abandoning his wounded at Mudki. He also pointed out that the day before Hardinge had put himself under his, Gough's, command. Hardinge, who had not been impressed by Gough's pell-mell tactics at Mudki, replied: 'Then, Sir Hugh, I must exercise my civil powers as Governor-General and forbid the attack until Littler's force has come up.' Gough had no option but to comply and for several hours the general fumed as his army waited, equally impatiently.

Eventually a cloud of dust was seen and Littler's division at last took its place in the centre of the British line. Gough took personal charge of the left wing while Hardinge, who now reverted to second-in-command, took the left. Sir Harry Smith's division and a small cavalry force formed a second line. Forming up took more time and it was 3.30 p.m. before everything was in place. Already the shadows were getting longer. The bulk of the 18,000 men were to attack the Sikhs' western and southern positions, under the gaping jaws of every enemy gun.

At 4 p.m. the British moved forward as an artillery duel whistled overhead. It was an uneven fight: unaccountably, the British 18-pounders had been left behind at Mudki, while the Sikh artillery was much heavier. Captain John Cumming wrote home: 'Long before our artillery was in range, their cannon were making fearful havoc of us.' Littler, believing that only speed could save his men from the butcher's block, advanced without giving neighbouring units time to deploy. The 62nd Foot rushed towards the Sikh guns, yelling savagely. Within three minutes 17 of the 23 officers and 250 men had been cut down. Three regiments of sepoys held back; parched by the heat and dust, they went to drink from a nearby well. Gough, seeing Littler's plight, ordered a general attack to support him. Cummings recalled:

We advanced against a hailstorm of roundshot, shells, grape and musketry. The slaughter was terrible. Yet our fellows pressed nobly on with the charge, and with the bayonet alone rushed over the entrenchments and captured the guns in front of us. The Sikhs flinched not an inch, but fought till they died to a man at their guns.

A sepoy veteran, Sita Ram, said: 'This was fighting indeed. I had never seen anything like it before.' But exploding mines and ammunition boxes forced the British back and most of the survivors of Littler's division played little further part in the brutal battle, now reckoned to have been the most savage in Anglo-Indian history.

The Sikh guns kept up a continuous barrage as the British charged into the setting sun. The light infantry overran one Sikh battery, slaying every defender, but were then caught in a murderous cross-fire. All along the lines the battle degenerated into hand-to-hand combat around the Sikh guns. As one battery was taken, the British came under volley fire from the enemy infantry. A young ensign said: 'The air was so filled with fire and smoke that it seemed to be dark as night.' Sir Walter Gilbert's division was threatened by a mass of Sikh cavalry and the battle hung on a knife-edge. A ferocious charge by the 31st Light Dragoons led by Brigadier Michael White put them to flight, but at heavy cost.

As real darkness fell, units, brigades and even divisions became intermingled in the confusion, but still the attack pressed on. To the left the red-coated lines faltered but were stiffened by General Smith's advance. Smith reported:

I saw there was nothing for it but a charge of bayonets to restore the waning fight. I, Colonel Petit and Colonel Ryan put ourselves at the head of the 50th and most gallantly did we charge into the enemy's trenches, where such a hand-to-hand conflict followed as I have ever witnessed. The enemy was repulsed at this point, his works and cannon carried and he precipitately retreated.

Similar success was won on the right flank, as men poured over the outer breastworks and clambered over corpse-filled ditches. But the Sikhs would not accept defeat.

The battle now raged within the camp itself, along the lines of tents, outside the mud and stone defences of Ferozeshah village, every inch fiercely contested. Combatants on both sides were hit by a 'frightful roar' as a Sikh powder magazine exploded. Eighteen-year-old Ensign Percy Innes wrote later:

> The ground heaved and the men in the vicinity were blown away amongst the tents, the air being filled with fire, and a dense smoke arising, which, as it cleared away, exposed to view a horrible and appalling scene, numbers of our men having fallen frightfully burnt and mutilated, and in some instances their [ammunition] pouches ignited, causing terrible wounds, agony and loss of life.

The fire spread, casting a ruddy light on Smith's brigade as it threw itself against the heavily defended village at the camp's centre. The British line ran through the encampment and overwhelmed the Sikhs, who were hampered behind their mud walls by large numbers of richly clad horses and camels, maddened by fright. Smith pushed on past the village but his force was then encircled by Sikhs mounting a counter-attack. He formed a defensive half-circle, but his men were exhausted. Some were killed as they fell asleep, and Smith was forced to retire back into the main encampment.

Pitch darkness and fatigue forced both sides to call an uneasy halt. The British pulled back from positions hard won and settled down for a hellish night. Gough's forces held some parts of the camp while the Sikhs slipped back into others. The nights was punctuated by the crack of exploding ammunition, the screams of the wounded and dying, the sudden crackle of musketry as both sides stumbled into each other. For the British the chief priority was water. The Sikhs had laced the wells with gunpowder and corpses. Horses turned away from them with disgust but many officers and men did not, later suffering the consequences with crippling stomach cramps and vomiting. Lieutenant Robert Bellers wrote:

> No one can imagine the dreadful uncertainty. A burning camp on one side of the village, mines and ammunition wagons

exploding in every direction, the loud orders to extinguish the fires as the Sepoys lighted them, the volleys given should the Sikhs venture too close, the booming of the monster gun, the incessant firing of the smaller one, the continual whistling noise of the shell, grape and round shot, the bugles sounding, the drums beating, and the yelling of the enemy, together with the intense thirst, fatigue and cold, and no knowing whether the rest of the army were the conquerors or the conquered – all contributed to make this night awful in the extreme.

Hardinge spent most of the night moving among the men, trying to raise morale with heavy-handed humour, while Gough tried to bring some order into the regiments and units mixed up together. Neither man knew whether the battle was won or lost. Hardinge, despite his attempts to reassure the troops, obviously feared the worst. He sent a messenger back to Mudki with orders to destroy his private papers if they were indeed defeated. But dawn showed that they had captured most of the battlefield, along with seventy-one Sikh artillery pieces. But the enemy remained close by and the early sun reflected off thousands of bayonets. Gough immediately gave the order to attack.

Three troops of horse artillery advanced at the gallop, unlimbered and another artillery duel began, with the Sikhs answering effectively. But Gough sensed a faltering in the Sikh morale. He led the right wing and Hardinge the left in an infantry charge as a flight of rockets streaked overhead. During three hours of fighting the remaining Sikh trenches were taken, lost and re-taken. Gough wrote in dispatches:

Our infantry formed line, supported on both flanks by horse artillery, whilst a fire was opened from our centre by such of our heavy guns as remained effective. A masked battery played with great effect upon this point, dismounting our pieces and blowing up our tumbrels. Our line advanced and, unchecked by the enemy's fire, drove them rapidly out of the village and their encampment.

Lieutenant Robertson described one encounter:

> We advanced very quietly upon a strong battery; they did not see us till we were right upon them, and they had only time to fire one or two rounds when we gave them a volley and charged right into them. We bayoneted a great many artillerymen and infantry who stood to the last, we also took a standard, and then charged on through the camp, polishing off all we could get at.

By lunchtime the enemy had been completely driven out of the camp and the victors were saluted by their commanders. Hardinge wrote: 'The brave men drew up in an excellent line, and cheered Gough and myself as we rode up the line, the regimental colours lowering to me as on parade.' However, the euphoria of victory did not last long. Scouts swiftly reported that another Sikh army, that of Tej Singh, was rapidly advancing on them, their fresh troops anxious to avenge their beaten comrades. For some moments even Gough's spirits fell. His men were exhausted, thirsty, hungry and almost out of ammunition. Their position seemed hopeless. As his men groaned and looked in horror at the advancing multitude, the old soldier pulled himself and his men together and prepared for another fight.

The British formed themselves into squares around Ferozeshah while the horse artillery limbered up. Troop after troop trotted out to challenge the Sikh guns. Each was either beaten back or retired when their ammunition ran out. The opposing lines of infantry, the British in red jackets, the Sikhs in blue, moved steadily towards each other. Forty Sikh guns cut bloody holes in the British ranks but the heavy guns fell silent as the Sikh cavalry skirted the plain ready to charge and sweep away their tired foe. It was 2 p.m. and the devout among the British prayed for a miracle.

The 3rd Dragoons, supported by two regiments of native cavalry, tried gamely to provide it. Led by Colonel White, they managed to lash their exhausted horses into a gallop and drove straight into the Sikh cavalry. The enemy fell back, momentarily stunned. They soon recovered from the shock, however, and their artillery again pounded the British lines. Gough spurred his horse and rode out in front of his men, aiming to draw a portion of the enemy fire. 'We, thank God, succeeded,' he later wrote, 'my gallant horse being a conspicuous mark – unheeding the thunder of a shot ploughing up the earth around him.' Such a gallant gesture momentarily put new heart in his men.

The uplift of morale was short-lived as all the surviving British and Bengal cavalry and the horse artillery suddenly wheeled around and began to canter off the battlefield towards Ferozepore, leaving the generals and the infantry alone to face the Khalsa. The cause of their abandonment, although they did not know it at the time, was an officer driven crazy by the battle. Captain Lumley, the acting Adjutant-General, had used his authority to order the artillery to retire to Ferozepore to refill their ammunition boxes and had instructed the cavalry to escort them. (Lumley, the son of a general, was later allowed to resign rather than face a court-martial.) There was nothing Gough could do, and he and his infantry stood firm, apparently facing certain massacre. The infantry's ammunition was almost exhausted and Gough told his troops to 'trust to the bayonet'.

Tej Singh's infantry began to advance to loud drum beats. Suddenly the noise of the drums was pierced by Sikh bugles sounding the retreat. In full sight of the astonished British, they turned on their heels and began to march back towards the Sutlej. Once again the Khalsa had been betrayed by their commanders when victory was within reach. Tej Singh, who always had to disguise his treachery from his army commanders, convinced them that the cavalry and artillery withdrawal was a feint and that they would attack them from the rear. The action of a madman and the response of a traitor had rescued a British army from a certain annihilation. Havelock said with awe: 'India has been saved by a miracle.'

The Sikhs did not stop until they reached the Sutlej and crossed its muddy waters. Gough had won another victory, but it was a costly one. The British suffered 2,415 casualties, of whom 694 were dead; many more would later succumb to their wounds. Gough had lost one-seventh of his entire force. A sergeant of the 16th Lancers, who arrived too late for the battle, wrote:

On our arrival at the camp ground the stench was horrible. A great many were buried within a few yards of our tents. As soon as we had pitched our camp we walked out on the field of battle to view the place and for miles around we could see the dead lying in all directions.

Hardinge said tartly: 'Another such victory and we are undone.' Once again the casualty rate among officers was especially high and Gough took the unprecedented step of giving commissions to five sergeant-majors. He later defended his move against staff disapproval by saying: 'I scarcely had an alternative; my losses in officers were so great that it was absolutely necessary.'

Hardinge did his best to get Gough dismissed. He wrote secretly after the battle to his close friend Sir Robert Peel, the British prime minister:

It is my duty to Her Majesty, and to you as head of the Government, to state, confidentially, that we have been in the greatest peril, and we are likely hereafter to be in great peril, if these very extensive operations are to be conducted by the Commander-in-Chief. Gough is a brave and fearless officer, an honourable man, and a fine-tempered gentleman, and an excellent leader of a brigade or a division. However, he is not the officer who ought to be entrusted with the conduct of the war in the Punjab. I cannot risk the safety of India by concealing my opinion from you. Sir Hugh Gough has no capacity for order or administration. His staff is very bad, and the state of the army is loose, disorderly and unsatisfactory.

Hardinge did not, of course, report his interference and his role in the delays which had come so close to causing a disaster. He further proposed that Sir Charles Napier should take over command of the field army. But his damning report could not overcome the fact that Gough had, again, won a victory, albeit an expensive one. The government could not justify the sacking of an officer who had won a battle. They did, however, agree in London that Hardinge should himself take overall military command. That authorisation, luckily for Gough, took a long time arriving, and by then it was too late to implement.

Gough and his men camped in a fortified position north of Ferozeshah while Hardinge went with Littler to Ferozepore. Both awaited much-needed reinforcements while the Khalsa snarled defiance on the other side of the Sutlej. The war was far from over.

*   *   *

The Khalsa generals did not regard themselves as defeated. They suspected betrayal and demanded reinforcements from Lahore. The Maharani, who was still in secret communication with the British, agreed to meet a deputation of 500 Khalsa leaders. She whipped them up into a frenzy, throwing one of her petticoats in their faces crying: 'Wear that, you cowards! I'll go in trousers and fight myself.' The warriors did not know it, but she was still determined to see the Khalsa, murderers of her brother, completely destroyed.

The reinforcements were provided, however, and the Khalsa established a bridgehead on the south side of the Sutlej near the ford of Sobraon, protected by their biggest guns on the far bank. A pontoon bridge was lashed into place to connect the advance force to their supply lines. The Khalsa generals also sent a force of 7,000 men and 70 guns under Runjur Singh upstream to cross the river near Ludhiana, aiming to break the British supply lines. They crossed the river and laid siege to the weakly garrisoned town, setting fire to part of the cantonment. A force under the 58-year-old General Smith was sent from Ferozepore to relieve it and deal with the menace to supplies.

Sir Harry Smith was another brave veteran of the Peninsular War who rarely dodged any opportunity for glory. The son of an Ely surgeon, he was the fifth of thirteen children. As a young officer he saw action in the disastrous expedition to Buenos Aires and the battle of Corunna and was seriously wounded near Almeida. As a major in the Light Brigade he fought at Sabugal, in the battle of Fuentes d'Onoro and the storming of Badajoz. After the latter he gave protection to a fourteen-year-old Spanish girl who had been ill-treated by the French. They married and she accompanied him for the rest of that war. More battles followed, including Vittoria, the Heights of Vera and Toulouse. Smith fought against the Americans during the 1812 war and was present at the burning of Washington and the battle of New Orleans. He witnessed Napoleon's final downfall at Waterloo. Peacetime saw him serving in Gosport, Glasgow, Belfast, Nova Scotia and Jamaica. In 1828 he was appointed army quartermaster-general in South Africa, where he and his wife gave their names respectively to the towns of Harrysmith and Ladysmith. African campaigning followed against warlike natives before Smith was sent to India. He was knighted for his distinguished service during the 1843 Gwalior campaign. One biographer wrote:

> Smith was not devoid of the self-assertion characteristic of men who fight their own way in the world and owe their successes solely to their own energies and ability; but he was popular with his colleagues and subordinates who were fascinated by his daring, energy and originality, and admired his rough and ready wit.

His men fondly recalled how he wandered through camp at night, and upon meeting a group of soldiers, would call out: 'Trumpeter, order a round of grog, and not too much water.'

On 16 January 1846 Smith set off two hours before dawn and led his brigade on a march of 26 miles to capture Dharamakot, a Sikh outpost largely garrisoned by mercenaries. A few shots from a British howitzer encouraged the defenders to hoist a white flat and Smith captured large supplies of grain. He marched on towards Ludhiana, his baggage train of mules and elephants struggling to keep up. Parts of his force were attacked near Badowal on 21 January. Private John Pearman was in the thick of the minor but brutal skirmish as hidden Sikh guns opened up on the column. He later described how a ball hitting a comrade's head sounded like 'a band-box full of feathers flying all over us', adding, 'He was my front-rank man and his brains nearly covered me. I had to scrape it off my face, and out of my eyes, and Taf Roberts, my left-hand man, was nearly as bad.' Sikh cavalry picked off stragglers, but the column marched on.

They camped outside Ludhiana, skirmishing with the enemy and exchanging artillery fire until they were joined by Brigadier Wheeler and his brigade, who had marched at a more leisurely pace from Delhi. Smith's force was now 12,000 men with 28 field guns and 2 howitzers. They faced Runjur Singh, whose army had swelled to around 20,000 men − not the 60,000 later claimed by the British. Runjur Singh was preparing to storm Ludhiana and Smith decided to intercept him on a level, grassy plain near the small village of Aliwal. The position favoured Smith because the Sikhs, drawn up along a ridge with their backs to the river, had little room for manoeuvre.

Corporal Cowtan of the 16th wrote:

> All this moment the view of the two armies was beautiful indeed − a fine, open, grassy plain, and the enemy in line out of their entrenchments ready to commence; the river in their rear, and in the distance the snowy range of the Himalayas with the sun rising over their tops.

On the bright, clear morning of 28 January Smith deployed his infantry, cavalry and artillery with textbook precision and ordered the attack.

Brigadier Godfrey's mixed brigade of sepoys, Gurkhas and the 31st Foot launched a rapid onslaught against Aliwal itself, which Smith judged to be the enemy's weakest spot and which was successfully taken. The two armies met in a general mêlée, the crystal air soon becoming befogged by the black smoke of the cannon. The British infantry charged 40 yards at a time, lying flat as the balls from disciplined Sikh volleys flew over them. The horse artillery galloped to within 200 yards of the Sikh batteries. The 16th Lancers charged past the Sikh guns, killing the gunners as they passed them, and found themselves in the centre of a large square of Khalsa soldiers. Sergeant William Gould wrote:

> At them we went, the bullets flying around like hailstorm. Right in front of us was a big sergeant, Harry Newsome. He

was mounted on a grey charger, and with a shout of 'Hullo boys, here goes death or commission,' forced his horse right over the front rank of kneeling men, bristling with bayonets. As Newsome dashed forward he leant over and grasped one of the enemy's standards, but fell from his horse, pierced by nineteen bayonet wounds. Into the gap made by Newsome we dashed, but they made fearful havoc among us. When we got to the other side of the square our troop had lost both lieutenants, the cornet, troop sergeant-major, and two sergeants. I was the only sergeant left.

Another lancer wrote:

Our brave fellows fell very thickly here, and every man whose horse was killed was to a certainty slain also, for the moment those savages saw any one on the ground they rushed at him and never ceased hacking at them, till they had literally severed them to pieces with their *tulwars*, which were like razors. All of us that escaped owed our lives, under God, to our horses, for no one escaped which once came to the ground.

Corporal Cowtan was in the thick of the same action:

Sergeant Brown was riding next to me and cleaving everyone down with his sword when his horse was shot under him, and before he reached the ground he received no less than a dozen sabre cuts which, of course, killed him. The killed and wounded in my squadron alone was 42, and after the first charge self-preservation was the great thing, and the love of life made us look sharp, and their great numbers required our vigilance. Our lances seemed to paralyse them altogether, and you may be sure we did not give them time to recover themselves.

General Smith asked where the officers of C Troop were. 'All down,' was the reply. The 16th Lancers lost more than a third of its strength in the action, suffering 'most severely, much more so than in any battle in the Peninsula or at Waterloo', one officer told his wife.

The 53rd Regiment came under deadly fire from a strong Sikh force hidden below the lip of a ravine, but a flanking charge by the 30th Native Infantry saved the Britons from destruction. The Sikhs, hemmed in and blasted at close range by the British horse artillery, began to stampede towards the river ford beyond their camp. The battle became a rout as the Sikhs scrambled for the boats or splashed through water churned into mud by the British howitzers. Sikh gunners deployed to cover the fleeing Khalsa were cut down before they could fire twice.

General Smith vividly described the scene in his dispatch:

The battle was won, our troops advancing with the most perfect order. The enemy, completely hemmed in, were flying from our fire, and precipitating themselves in disordered masses into the ford and boats, in the utmost confusion and consternation. Our eight-inch howitzers soon began to play upon their votes, when the debris of the Sikh army appeared upon the opposite and high bank of the river, flying in every direction, although a sort of line was attempted to countenance their retreat, until all our guns commenced a furious cannonade, when they quickly receded.

The Sikhs left behind 2,000 dead, 60 guns, and all their baggage and ammunition trains and stores of grain. It was the first complete victory of the war and Smith made sure his superiors knew it. He wrote:

I have gained one of the most glorious battles ever fought in India. A stand-up gentlemanlike battle, a mixing of all arms and laying-on, carrying everything before us by weight of attack and combinations, all hands at work from one end of the field to the other. Never was victory more complete, and never was one fought under more happy circumstances, literally with the pomp of a field day; and right well did all behave.

Thackery later wrote of Smith's dispatch: 'A noble deed was never told in nobler language.' The Duke of Wellington, in a House of

Lords debate, said: 'I never read an account of any affair in which an officer has shown himself more capable than this officer did of commanding troops in the field.' When news of Smith's victory reached Gough he became 'frantic with joy', leapt from his horse and gave three cheers for the 'gallant gentlemen' of Aliwal.

The Sikhs saw the bloated bodies of their comrades floating downstream to the entrenched positions at Sobraon. Tej Singh was all for reaching terms with the British, but his generals were not. They strengthened their defences, believing that the enemy would be destroyed in the inevitable assault on their earthworks. Tej Singh concentrated less on orchestrating the defences than on supervising the construction of his own private shelter. Shaped like a beehive, it was built to the peculiar specifications of Brahmin astrologer: the inner circumference was thirteen-and-a-half times Tej Singh's waist measurement, while the walls were the thickness of 333 long grains of rice laid end to end. Tej Singh spent much of the time before the battle praying inside it. Characteristically, Gough wanted to make an immediate assault on the heavily defended Sikh position in a bend of the river. Again Hardinge over-ruled him and the British waited for reinforcements and, most crucially, for the arrival of heavier guns. (In Gough's defence, the heavy artillery had been delayed because Hardinge had earlier decreed that they were not necessary.) Eventually, the artillery train arrived and Gough's army, now grown to 20,000 men, prepared to face the Sikh army of around 30,000 men with 70 guns, some of them on the other side of the Sutlej. Henry Lawrence, the new political agent, received from the treacherous Lal Singh a rough sketch of the Sikh trenches at Sobraon. The fortifications had been designed by Colonel Hurbon, a Spanish officer who served with the Khalsa. The date for the attack was set for 10 February. Three days of heavy rainfall before that turned the normally sluggish Sutlej into a boiling torrent, straining the tethers of the pontoon bridge that offered the bulk of the Khalsa an escape route.

Dawn was obscured by a dense fog, but when the sun finally broke through, the entire line of British artillery – thirty heavy howitzers and five 18-pounders – opened up a bombardment on the three lines of Sikh defences forming a semi-circle. An observer said it raised such a noise ' no thunder was ever equal to'. Trooper Bancroft of the Bengal Horse Artillery saw a body of Sikh cavalry charge his battery:

> We immediately gave them a salvo of rockets, followed by single doses; the hissing noise of the long destructive shafts and the shells bursting unerringly among them suddenly threw their ranks into the utmost confusion and they were driven back in a whirlwind of defeat, leaving hundreds slain upon the field.

The Sikh batteries returned the fire and the combined detonations of over a hundred guns were the heaviest combination yet heard in India. After two hours British ammunition began to run low. Gough was told that only four rounds per gun were left and famously replied: 'Thank God, then I'll be at them with the bayonet.'

In his dispatch Gough recorded how the infantry and horse artillery moved forward, each supporting the other, until they were within 300 yards of the heaviest Sikh batteries. 'Notwithstanding the regularity and coolness, and scientific character of this assault,' he wrote, 'so hot was the fire of the cannon, musketry and *zumboorucks* kept up by the Khalsa troops, that it seemed for some moments impossible that the entrenchments could be won under it. . . .'

The 10th Foot led the advance on the Sikh right, and went forward into terrible Sikh fire of musket-ball and grapeshot. They pressed on despite heavy casualties and took the first line of Sikh trenches with the bayonet. The divisional commander, Sir Robert Dick, was slain in fierce close-quarter combat. But attempts by Generals Gilbert and Smith to draw the enemy's fire by a feint attack on the left failed, and the Sikh infantry counter-attacked. Firing steady volleys they forced the 10th backwards, step by step, from the hard-won trenches. Meanwhile, on the Sikhs' extreme left the British tried desperately to scramble up steep ramparts, only to be repulsed by muskets and slashing *tulwars*. At one point, Gough, seeing his men throw themselves at the defences, exclaimed: 'Good God, they'll be annihilated.' As the tide of battle ebbed and flowed the British were enraged to see the Sikhs, in intervals in the mayhem, hacking to pieces their wounded comrades left lying below the earthworks.

The British attacked again with renewed frenzy, while the Gurkhas 'used their *kukris* with unaccountable zeal among the Sikhs'. In some areas the British scaled the defences by climbing on one another's shoulders. Sergeant Bernard McCabe planted his regimental colours high on the ramparts as a rallying point. Smith, as always leading from the front and not shy of recalling the fact, wrote:

> I carried the works by dint of English pluck, although the natives corps stuck close to me, and when I got in, such hand-to-hand work I never witnessed. For twenty-five minutes I could barely hold my own. Mixed together, swords and targets against bayonets, and fire on both sides. We are at it against four times our numbers, sometimes receding, sometimes advancing. The old 31st and 50th laid on like devils . . . a brutal bulldog fight.

Gough wrote:

> The battle raged with inconceivable fury from left to right. The Sikhs, even when at particular points their entrenchments were mastered with the bayonet, strove to regain them by the fiercest conflict, sword in hand.

A Sikh gunner, Hookhum Singh, later wrote of the eerie silence with which the British attacked, without shouting or firing, but appearing 'as evil spirits bent on our destruction'. The British paused to take breath and then,

> with a shout such as only angry demons could give and which is still ringing in my ears, they made a rush for our guns, led by their colonel. They leapt into the deep ditch or moat in our front, soon filling it, and then swarmed up the opposite side on the shoulders of their comrades, dashed for the guns, which were still bravely defended by a strong body of our infantry. But who could withstand such fierce demons, with those awful bayonets, which they preferred to their guns – for not a shot did

they fire the whole time – and then, with a ringing cheer, which was heard for miles, they announced their victory.

All across the front line the British broke through but the Sikhs, with their backs to the river, fought on and the battle was far from won. Engineers blew a small gap in the ramparts on the enemy right, where they were lowest, and Gough ordered in the cavalry under General Sir Joseph Thackwell. The 3rd Light Dragoons trotted through the gap in single file but were halted by a surviving Sikh battery. The blue-jacketed dragoons, helped by the Bengal Light Cavalry, soon rallied and cut down the gunners.

Still the Khalsa fought on, contesting every inch of ground within their encampment. Their treacherous commander, Tej Singh, had fled the field early in the battle, but there were other generals determined to die with their men. Thackwell commented: 'They never ran.' The veteran general Sham Singh Attariwala, who had spent forty years fighting in the Khalsa, was the centre of one last-ditch resistance. A British officer wrote:

He repeatedly rallied his shattered ranks, and at last fell a martyr on a heap of his slain countrymen. Others might be seen on their ramparts amid a shower of balls, waving defiance with their swords . . . The parapets were sprinkled with blood from end to end; the trenches were filled with the dead or the dying.

Horse artillery was drawn up to fire at point-blank range. At last, their leaders dead or fled, the Sikh resistance crumbled into a rout. Thousands rushed for the head of the pontoon bridge. The press of men, jumbled together in a bottleneck, made an easy target. Those who could crowded on to the 400-yard bridge, already weakened by the floodwaters and by the accidental unmooring of a boat at its centre. Rumours later abounded that Tej Singh deliberately sabotaged the bridge to ensure the complete destruction of the Khalsa, but that does not square with eyewitness accounts of its collapse under sheer weight of numbers. The Governor-General's son, Arthur Hardinge, described the outcome:

I saw the bridge at that moment overcrowded with guns, horses and soldiers of all arms, swaying to and fro, till at last with a crash it disappeared in the running waters, carrying with it all those who had vainly hoped to reach the opposite shore. The river seemed alive with a struggling mass of men. The artillery, now brought down to the water's edge, completed the slaughter. Few escaped; none, it may be said, surrendered.

Gough later wrote:

Policy precluded me publicly recording my sentiments on the splendid gallantry or the acts of heroism displayed by the Sikh army. I could have wept to have witnessed the fearful slaughter of so devoted a body of men.

These fine Christian sentiments, expressed much later, did not mean he called a halt to the fearful slaughter. Heavy guns and muskets continued firing into the river until was a red stew. A civilian observer, Robert Cust, said: 'The stream was choked with the dead and the dying – the sandbanks were covered with bodies floating leisurely down. It was an awful scene, a fearful carnage.' A sepoy, Sita Ram, described watching men choking the river, their long black hair streaming in the white water, scrabbling hold of each other in their panic, until the teeming mass sank, 'to rise no more alive'. No mercy was shown. The men were prompted by the fresh memories of wounded comrades butchered below the Sikh parapets. Gough later said of the Sikhs:

Their awful slaughter, confusion and dismay were such as would have excited compassion in the hearts of their generous conquerors, if the Khalsa troops had not, in the early part of the action, sullied their gallantry by slaughtering and barbarously mangling every wounded soldier whom, in the vicissitudes of attack, the fortune of war left at their mercy.

Gough also knew that only the complete annihilation of the Khalsa would bring the war to an end. And the battle – later dubbed the Indian Waterloo – had been costly. By noon the British forces had lost 320 dead and 2,063 wounded, many of whom would not survive. The Khalsa losses were estimated at 10,000 dead, perhaps most of them killed in the last doomed attempt to cross the river. The Maharani's revenge was complete.

* * *

The bloodbath at Sobraon crushed Khalsa resistance. It was perhaps the most decisive battle fought by the British in India, and it ended any real threat to the Raj for a century. The war, one of the shortest on record, lasted just fifty-four days, in which time four major battles were fought to bloody effect. The Duke of Wellington wrote to Gough:

> Great operations have been planned and undertaken and successfully carried into execution under your command, glorious battles have been fought and victories gained, and the war has been brought to a termination by the destruction of the army of the enemy . . . and peace has been dictated to the enemy upon terms equally honourable to the Army and to the Nation.

Gough lost no time in crossing the Sutlej to pursue the beaten foe. The first units crossed by the early evening of the day of the battle. Most of his forces followed within two days and occupied Kasur, 30 miles from Lahore. On 15 February Hardinge there met Rajah Gulab Singh who had been authorised by the Lahore Durbar to negotiate the peace. Gulab Singh was an acceptable envoy because he and his Dogra Hindu troops had remained broadly neutral during the conflict. He was a canny operator and persuaded Hardinge not to annexe the Punjab. Although the Khalsa had been beaten, there were still as many as 35,000 Sikh soldiers between Lahore and Amritsar, with others at Peshawar and Multan. The Sikhs agreed that the British should control both banks of the Sutlej and take the rich and fertile Jullundar Doab lands between the river and the seas. British territory effectively advanced 100 miles. In addition, the Sikhs were to pay a war indemnity of £1,500,000, to allow Sir Henry Lawrence to be stationed in their capital as Resident, and to reduce their army to a maximum of 20,000 infantry and 12,000 cavalry. These may have been the best terms a defeated side could hope to gain from the victors, but the main winner proved to be Gulab Singh. Faced with a shortage of riches in Lahore to cover the war indemnity, the Sikh administration handed over instead the hill territories which included Kashmir and Hazara. These the wily Gulab bought from the British for the knock-down price of £750,000.

Hardinge and Gough, with their staff and escorted by four cavalry regiments, entered Lahore on elephants as a band played 'See the Conquering Hero Comes'. Sikh salutes were fired and the beasts threatened to stampede but were quickly calmed down. They were greeted by Maharajah Duleep Singh, described by one officer as 'a child of an intelligent and not unpleasing appearance', his still glamorous mother and Gulab. Hardinge agreed that the treacherous Lal Singh should be appointed vizier or chief minister, while the equally treasonable Tej Singh should be commander-in-chief of the much-reduced Khalsa. They were to be protected at home from their ungrateful followers by a British force which would remain in Lahore until the end of the year. British officers and officials would effectively administer the outlying regions. Lieutenant Herbert Edwardes told Bannu tribesmen:

> You shall have the best laws that an enlightened people can frame for you; but they will be administered by a Sikh governor. He cannot oppress you, for the English will be over him. You shall be justly ruled, but you shall be free no more.

The treaty of Lahore was ratified on 9 March. Included in the small print was the gift of the Kho-i-noor diamond, the 'mountain of light', to Queen Victoria.

Gough was raised to the peerage by his grateful queen, while the Governor-General became Viscount Hardinge of Lahore and Durham, with a lifetime's pension of £3,000 from the British government and a further pension of £5,000 from the East India Company. Hardinge assured Victoria that there was no native power left anywhere in India capable of again taking on the British Army. The contemporary historian W.L. McGregor wrote: 'The battle of Sobraon may be justly termed the Waterloo of India; it was the last, and one of the most hardest contested; like that great and ever memorable engagement, it completely broke the power of the foe.' But Joseph Cunningham countered that the Sikhs' strength 'is not to be estimated by their tens of thousands, but by the unity and energy of religious fervour and warlike temperament. They will care much, and they will endure much . . .'

Certainly many in the remaining Khalsa were convinced they had only been defeated by treachery. They were probably right, and Hardinge's assurances to the queen were all too soon to be proved disastrously wrong.

TWENTY-THREE

The Second Sikh War, 1848–9

'Every gun was turned on them . . .'

In the grounds of the Royal Chelsea Hospital stands a stone obelisk that bears the names of 238 officers and men of the 24th Foot, a regiment that later knew greater fame as the South Wales Borderers. These men fell at an unremembered battle in the Punjab, charging massed cannon head on, cold steel against heavy artillery.

Unlike the Charge of the Light Brigade little more than five years later, there was no Lord Tennyson to immortalise the 24th Foot in verse. Unlike the mad charge at Balaclava, in which 113 died, they did not enjoy the glamour associated with dashing cavalrymen. Their's was a bloodier affair – almost half the regiment were casualties – but their exploits barely registered in the public consciousness then, and are entirely forgotten now.

What the two incidents have in common, apart from breathtaking courage, is that both were the result of a monumental blunder. The 24th at Chilianwalla were ordered to take the Sikh cannon by the bayonet, without a shot being fired. It was, as their own general later admitted, 'an act of madness'.

*   *   *

For some time after the slaughter of the Khalsa at Sobraon the British and Sikhs cohabited uneasily, and their forces cooperated in suppressing minor frontier uprisings. British officers and officials accompanied an expedition led by General Shere Singh to deal with the Sikh Governor of Kashmir, who had refused to surrender his authority to Gulab Singh. The recalcitrant governor gave up without a fight and Gulab entered Kashmir city as its ruler in November 1846. Such military alliances were frequently strained, however, not least by the intrigues of the Maharani Jindan and her allies in Lahore. The Sikh generals knew they had been betrayed by their leaders in the first war. Their pride was hurt and they did not believe in the notion, accepted elsewhere, of British invincibility. Thousands of discharged and unpaid Khalsa soldiers roamed the countryside, spoiling for a fight and looking for plunder.

In addition, Sikh sensibilities were gravely upset when the British took guardianship of the young Maharajah Duleep Singh. The queen-mother was furious at being sidelined. Always a libertine, she began to approach British officers with offers of marriage, convinced that such a union would advance her cause. She was wrong and Sir Henry Lawrence, the British Resident in Lahore, ruled that she was a malign influence on her son. A plot to kill Lawrence, in which the Maharani was said to be involved, offered an ideal pretext to get rid of her. To the delight of some Sikh generals and courtiers, but to the consternation of many others, she was banished to a distant fortress at Sheikapur. She wrote to Lawrence:

> You have been very cruel to me. You have snatched my son from me. For ten months I kept him in my womb. Then I brought him up with great difficulty. Without my fault you have separated my son from me. You could have kept me in prison. You could have dismissed my men. You could have turned out my maidservants. You could have treated me in any other way you liked. But you should not have separated my son from me. In the name of the God you worship, and in the name of the king whose salt you eat, restore my son to me. I cannot bear the pain of this separation. Instead of this you put me to death.

The Punjab was simmering like a cooking pot, but Lord Hardinge appears to have been oblivious to the unrest. The Afghan and Sikh wars had left British India with massive debts. Determined to balance the books, Hardinge decided to reduce the Indian Army by 50,000 men. He was convinced that peace was secure and when he returned home in 1847 he forecast that 'it would not be necessary to fire a gun in India for seven years to come'. He was replaced by 35-year-old Lord Dalhousie as Governor-General of India. Dalhousie was a product of the aristocracy, Harrow and Oxford. He was a natural politician and attracted the attention of Wellington and Peel when he entered the Lords after his father's death. He was an active member of the General Assembly of the Church of Scotland, and in 1845 succeeded Gladstone as vice-President of the Board of Trade. He was known as a tireless worker, the first in and last out of his office daily. Although a Tory, he owed his new job to the new Whig administration of Lord John Russell. When he reached Calcutta a leading Anglo-Indian newspaper declared that the new governor had 'arrived at a time when the last obstacle to the final pacification of India has been removed, when the only remaining army which could have caused alarm has been dissolved and the peace of the country rests upon the firmest and most permanent basis'. Events quickly persuaded Dalhousie to ignore such rosy sentiments.

The flashpoint came in the province of Multan, lying between the left bank of the Indus and the right bank of the Sutlej. Multan had been conquered by Runjeet Singh only after many ferocious battles. In April 1848 the governor, a Hindu called Diwan Mulraj, resigned after expressing dissatisfaction with the new regime and the presence of the British. After negotiations with the Lahore Durbar it was agreed that Sirdar Khan Singh should replace him. The new man travelled to Multan city with a small escort. He was accompanied by two British representatives, 26-year-old Patrick Alexander Vans Agnew, a Bengal civil servant and assistant to Lawrence, and Lieutenant W.A. Anderson of the Bombay Fusiliers. They entered the city without incident and officiated at the formal transfer of power to Khan Singh. But on the following day, 18 April, Mulraj's supporters revolted and attacked the two Britons. Desperately wounded, they were carried with Khan Singh to a small fort outside the city which swiftly came under fire from Multan's parapets. Three days later Mulraj's troops attacked the fort and its Sikh defenders, members of the initial escort, immediately opened the gates and let in the assailants. Lieutenant Anderson could not move from his cot but Agnew tried to fight. A battle-scarred veteran, Goodhur Singh, cut off his head with three blows. Anderson was hacked to death where he lay. Both bodies were dragged outside, mutilated and left in the courtyard. Mulraj always claimed that the fort had not been attacked on his authority, but the murders left him no option but to declare open revolt. A Sikh commander fastened on to him one of his own war bracelets. Mulraj sent the fiery cross of revolt around the countryside, the signal to rise up against the British who 'are treating the Maharajah and our proper rulers as prisoners'. All across the land disenchanted Sikhs and Muslims answered the call.

Sir Frederick Currie, standing in for Dalhousie, then on leave in Europe, ordered a Sikh army under Shere Singh to suppress the rebellion. He wrote: 'The fort at Multan is very strong and full of heavy cannon of large calibre. This cannot be taken possession of by direct attack. Except the Multan garrison, Mulraj has not many troops, and only five or six field guns. He is very unpopular both with the army and the people.' But before Shere Singh's force could march, more independent action was already being taken. The main instigator was an extraordinary young officer and poet, Lieutenant Herbert Edwardes of the Bengal Native Infantry. Aged twenty-nine, from Shropshire, slender and multi-lingual, Edwardes did not look like a fighting soldier. When he arrived at Calcutta in 1841 an observer described him as 'slight and delicate-looking, with fully formed features and an expression of bright intelligence; not given to the active amusements by which most young men of his class and nation are wont to speed the hours, but abounding in mental accomplishments and resource'. His language skills in Urdu, Hindi and Persian made him a natural interpreter and he served on Gough's staff at the battles of Mudki and Sobraon. Before the revolt erupted, Lawrence, who had spotted his talents early on, put him in charge of a small force engaged, ironically, in collecting land taxes for Mulraj in outlying districts. On hearing of the murders and the rebellion, Edwardes began putting together a native army. He occupied the trading city of Leia, where he enlisted mercenaries, both to strengthen his own tiny force and to prevent them going over to the enemy. Without funds and no outside aid, this remarkable young man raised a levy of 3,000 Pathan fighters with the promise of a mere 15 rupees a week and all the plunder they could carry. He said: 'War is their trade and also their pastime.' He also persuaded the Nawab of neighbouring Bahawalpur to send him troops. On 18 May a contingent of his men left at Leia were charged by 400 Multan horsemen. The attackers were beaten off, leaving behind them ten light field guns.

As Edwardes set off for Multan his force was swelled by 4,000 men under Colonel Van Courtlandt, the commander of the British garrison at Dhera Ismael Khan; this new force included three mixed Sikh regiments, 1,500 irregular horse, 8 guns and 20 swivel pieces. Together they easily beat off a determined attack by Sikh rebels. The native levies, Edwardes noted, 'fought bravely and showed no disposition to fraternise with the rebels'.

Mulraj moved out of Multan to prevent the British gaining further reinforcements. His men attacked Edwardes when his force was split by the Indus river near Soojabad. Edwardes, who had barely seen any action in his short life, was confident of success. He later wrote: I doubted only for a moment – one of those long moments to which some angel seems to hold a microscope and show millions of things within it. It came and went between the stirrup and the saddle.' After several grim hours' fighting on a baking-hot, waterless plain, the outcome was still in the balance until two of Van Courtlandt's troops of horse artillery were able to ride to the rescue. Edwardes wrote:

Oh, the thankfulness of that moment! The relief, the weight removed, the elastic bound of the heart's main-spring into its place after being pressed down for seven protracted hours of waiting for a reinforcement that might never come! Now all is clear. Our chance is nearly as good as theirs, and who asks more?

Van Courtlandt's gun-crews unlimbered and opened up a close-quarter duel with the Sikh cannon. The range was so close that both sides fired grapeshot rather than shot at each other's crews. Edwardes wrote:

For the first time and the last in my short experience of war, did I see hostile artillery firing grape into each other . . . General Courtlandt's artillery were well trained and steady, and their aim was true. Two guns were quickly silenced and the rest seemed slackening and firing wide. A happy charge might carry all. I gave the order to Soobhan Khan's regiment to attack, and away they went, Soobhan Khan himself, a stout, heavy soldier, leading them on, and leaping over bushes like a boy. Before they could reach the battery . . . a cluster of half a dozen horsemen dashed out from the trees behind me, and passing the regiment threw themselves on the enemy's guns. Their leader received a ball full in his face, and fell over the cannon's mouth . . . The regiment followed, and carried at the point of the bayonet the only gun which awaited their assault. Another gun lay dismounted on the ground.

Dispatches reported: 'After an obstinate conflict the enemy gave way and fled, leaving behind them six guns and all their baggage and stores.' The Sikhs lost around 500 men dead or mortally wounded on the field. British casualties were some 300 killed and wounded.

Mulraj fell back on Multan and Edwardes pursued him there. But the lieutenant's force, even with Van Courtlandt's reinforcements, was not strong enough to mount a proper siege. Mulraj, after some savage skirmishing, withdrew his whole force behind the city walls. Edwardes remained outside, however, waiting for Lahore to send a proper army under Major-General William Whish to complete the job. Edwardes was a hero and Sir Henry Lawrence, now back from his European travels, said, 'since the days of Clive no man has done as him'. Another accolade said: 'Young, alone, untrained in military science and unversed in active war, he had organised victory and rolled back rebellion.' Now, however, it was the turn of a veteran.

Whish was, at sixty-one, relatively old but he was an experienced artilleryman. The Essex-born son of a vicar, he had served in India since 1804 and later commanded the rocket troop of horse artillery in the Pindari and Maratha campaigns. He was mentioned in dispatches for his part in the 1826 capture of Bhartpur and was promoted for distinguished service in the field. Early in 1848, after a long furlough in England, he took command of the Punjab Division at Lahore. Whish arrived at Multan with an 8,000-strong field force made up of the 10th Regiment, a troop of horse artillery, the 7th Irregular Horse and other troops. They were swiftly joined by a column from

Ferozepore, including a train of heavy guns, bringing the total army assembled outside Multan's thick walls to about 28,000, of whom 6,000 were British. The Sikh troops in the army were commanded by Shere Singh.

After several days of skirmishing and sharp firing, Whish decided to launch a general attack on the city's outworks on 12 September. At daybreak around 2,500 troops under Brigadier Harvey marched against a group of defenders deeply dug in around a garden and hamlet near the city walls. The British took one trench but were forced out of a second by a shower of shot, bullets and arrows. They took their revenge on the defenders of a small, enclosed courtyard. One eyewitness told the *Dehli Gazette*: 'The men, both European and native, mounted the walls, determined that not a soul should escape. Certainly the massacre that took place within – enclosed on all sides by loop-holed walls and entrenched all round – was something awful to one who had never been in service before.'

The correspondent, an unnamed officer, went on to give a graphic account of the close-quarter fighting and the losses it entailed:

At this entrenchment Lieutenant Cubitt of the 49th Regiment Native Infantry, was shot by a wounded man. After being sent up to camp he survived only about seven hours. Poor fellow! He will be a sad loss to his regiment, for a better soldier never breathed . . . After setting fire to this entrenchment in several places we returned to the one we had first taken, and this we were obliged to get scaling ladders to take, as it was so strong. No sooner were the scaling ladders up than Colonel Pattoun was the first to ascend, and down he jumped, right amongst the enemy within, when, as a matter of course, he was instantly cut to pieces; for these fellows, immediately you attempt to close with them, draw their *tulwars*, and they know how to use them too . . . Here too fell Lieutenant Taylor, Quartermaster of Her Majesty's 32nd Foot, and Major Montizambert of Her Majesty's 10th Foot . . . But not a man [of the Sikh defenders] escaped, for the doors were burst open, and an attack from above and below made; every man within these walls fell a victim to the bayonet . . .

The following day the Multanese troops launched a desperate sally against Lieutenant Edwardes' camp but they were repelled. Edwardes counter-attacked and captured an important breastwork. It looked as if Whish could swiftly wear down the defences, but any such hopes were shattered by the next dawn.

Shere Singh, who had never been a lusty campaigner against the rebels, defected to Mulraj with 5,000 men and 10 cannon. The British should have seen it coming as his father, Chuttar Singh, Governor of Hazarch, had joined another 'mutiny' in north-west Punjab. Newspapers in Delhi stormed that such treachery 'proved the folly of placing any reliance upon the fidelity of the Sikhs'.

Shere Singh's defection, forced on him by the changing allegiances of both his family and his men, meant that Mulraj's force now totalled 15,000 men and up to 80 guns. Whish had 20,000 men and 44 guns – nowhere near enough to sustain a siege against strong defences. He had no choice but to lift the siege of Multan and retire his army to a defendable position a few miles away at Tibi to await reinforcements.

Shere Singh, in the meantime, issued a statement accusing the British of tyranny and violence against the Maharani and the Sikh people. He called on all the people of the region, Sikh, Muslim and Hindu, to join together in a holy crusade against the oppressors. Fearful that many more sepoys and native mercenaries would answer that call, Edwardes promised his own men that if they stayed loyal and fought against the rebels they would be taken on as regular soldiers for the lifetime of the Indian government. They agreed, but Shere Singh's call to arms spread elsewhere across the Punjab. At Peshawar and Lahore government troops mutinied and attacked the Residency with shot and grape. Troops in the Bunnoo district, near the Afghan border, also rose and killed both the Muslim governor and Colonel John Holmes, a British soldier of fortune. Several thousand Khalsa troops, pensioned off under the Treaty of Lahore, retrieved their arms and swarmed to Shere Singh's banner.

The *Annual Register* reported:

What had at first been considered as an isolated act of contumacy on the part of Mulraj assumed now a more serious aspect, and it became evident that we should have to engage in another struggle with the whole of the fierce soldiery of the Sikhs, whose spirit was no-ways disheartened by their former collision with British troops.

A minor revolt had now escalated into the Second Sikh War.

*   *   *

For several weeks there was little skirmishing as the two opposing armies gathered strength. Early in October Shere Singh left Multan with his force and headed north-west along the line of the Chenab, the central of the Punjab's Five Rivers. His father, Chuttar Singh, marched south to join him. They met near Ramnuggar, and there Shere Singh took overall command of a Sikh army numbering no fewer than 30,000 men.

Meanwhile Dalhousie announced: 'Unwarned by precedent, uninfluenced by example, the Sikh nation have called for war, and on my word, sirs, they shall have it.' A large force was to gather at Ferozepore under the commander-in-chief, Lord Gough. More troops were sent from Bombay until the numbers had swelled to one cavalry and three infantry divisions. Any attempts at a diplomatic solution were thwarted by British outrage at what they considered Sikh treachery and desertion. Dalhousie gave Gough full discretion to punish the offenders but financial considerations were always at the forefront of his mind. He wrote at the end of July: 'Where I am to find the money to pay for this, God above only knows.' By then, however, Dalhousie had decided that the only satisfactory outcome would be the complete annexation of the Punjab. That he later confirmed in a letter to Sir John Hobhouse, President of the Board of Control: 'There no longer remains any alternative for the British Government. The die is cast.' He brushed aside complaints at home that the war was a cynical attempt to steal the kingdom of the boy Maharajah. He described the lad as 'a brag begotten of a Bhistie – and no more the child of old Runjeet than Queen Victoria'. And he told the directors of the East India Company that a successful outcome would greatly increase revenue because 'the defection of so many chiefs will be followed by extensive confiscation'.

Gough took command of his army on 21 November. His arrival was not welcomed by all, as men remembered the massive casualties he suffered during the First Sikh War. Engineering officer Richard Baird Smith warned that 'our success will be gained by the blood of the officers and men and will owe nought to the genius of the Chief'.

Gough immediately set off for Shere Singh's positions at Ramnuggar on the east bank of the Chenab. At 2 a.m. on the 22nd orders were issued for a strong force of cavalry and infantry to parade silently and in marching order in front of the British camp. They moved forward in darkness and assembled at the river. The strength of Shere Singh's forces, both on the opposite bank and on an island in midstream, quickly became apparent. Some Sikh troops left on the west bank were quickly driven across the river fords by the 3rd Dragoons and the 8th Light Cavalry. An officer in the Bengal Horse Artillery wrote home:

The Sikhs had placed their guns in masked batteries; and, as you might suppose, the sudden discharge took our people by surprise; nevertheless they went on, seeing a great number of the enemy beyond the nullah. The ground was very heavy and sandy: a large portion of our cavalry got into a quicksand, and the horses, being somewhat exhausted by the march over heavy ground, were not able to extricate themselves as soon as they might have done. The enemy's infantry were, in the meantime, behind large sand hillocks, and steadily firing into our men, as well as from the large Sikh guns on the other side of the river.

The Horse Artillery pushed on slowly and painfully, and opened up a duel with enemy batteries on the far bank. They soon found that their 6-pounders were ill-matched against the heavier guns facing them, and they were forced to pull back. Seeing that, Shere Singh ordered more than 3,000 of his cavalry across the stream, which had shrunk during the dry season, under cover of his guns. Gough now made a serious blunder. He seems to have been unaware of the poor nature of the terrain − or perhaps he let his impetuous nature get the better of him. He ordered the 14th Dragoons, under Lieutenant-Colonel William Havelock, and the 5th Light Cavalry to attack the larger Sikh body. The British troopers managed to drive the Sikhs back and then charged down the sandy river bank after them. Here, however, they were exposed to a murderous fire from the Sikh batteries. Men and horses were scythed down by the well-trained and experienced Sikh gunners. The 5th had charged blindly into a trap laid by the cunning Shere Singh. The Sikh cavalry now turned and wreaked more havoc. Colonel Alexander tried to rally the troopers but his sword arm was shattered by a cannon ball, which then careered on its way, killing a quartermaster-sergeant and striking a lieutenant on the foot. Alexander fell, and the Sikh swordsmen who rushed to hack at him were beaten off by Sergeant-Major Mallet. Alexander survived but the arm was later 'removed from the socket'. Captain Scudamore took a sabre cut across the face, Lieutenant Macmahon was shot in the head, and Lieutenant Chetwynd was punched in the side by a spent cannon ball. Sergeant Todd's head was cleanly taken off by a round-shot. The *aide-de-camp*, Lieutenant Hardinge, was shot through the shoulder.

Colonel William Havelock, a Peninsular War veteran and the brother of the more renowned Henry, fell dead during a second charge on the Sikh positions. An observer said that Havelock was last seen in the thick of the enemy, 'his left arm half severed from his body, and dealing frantic blows with his sword'. His second-in-command, Colonel King, reformed the line for a third charge. After that proved unsuccessful the British cavalry commander, General C.R. Cureton galloped up with orders from Gough that they should retire. Within moments of uttering the words two matchlock balls hit him in the throat and head and he too fell dead. The squadron was withdrawn. Gough had succeeded in clearing the west bank of the river but the main Sikh positions were untouched. And, as one report put it, 'we had to mourn the loss of many brave soldiers, whose lives were lost in a useless and unmeaning combat'.

Twenty-one officers and men were first posted as dead, although the eventual death toll must have been higher given that there were 55 wounded and 9 listed as missing. Over a hundred horses were lost. The high casualty rate among his senior officers shocked Gough.

For a week the two armies sat facing each other across the muddy waters. At the end of November Gough ordered Major-General Sir

John Thackwell to march a strong body of troops upriver so that he might cross and attack the Sikhs from the rear while Gough himself led a frontal assault. Shere Singh was too canny a tactician to be outmanoeuvred. Instead of sitting still, he moved forward to meet Thackwell's force. The British troops crossed the river in pitch darkness on the night of 1 December. Captain Lawrence Archer recalled:

> In the mazes of small channels and pools of water, which chequered the loose sands, many a regiment lost its way, while the increasing darkness added to the general confusion, and the knowledge of abounding quicksands produced a sense of insecurity. It is hard to say what might have befallen the force, had the enemy only taken the trouble to guard this ford, or form an ambuscade.

The following morning Thackwell's force came under heavy bombardment at Sadullapur. Gough ordered an answering fire on the Sikh batteries facing him but a mix-up over orders delayed Thackwell's gunners from following suit. In addition, unknown to Gough, his gunners were pounding largely empty entrenchments. Heartened by this the Sikhs threw themselves on Thackwell's detached column. The Sikh attack was further encouraged when Thackwell made a tactical retreat to better positions 200 yards back. The Sikhs cried: 'The English are running.' The position was extremely hazardous until the British gunners under Lieutenant-Colonel C. Grant at last began pouring shot and grape into the enemy. After two hours of heavy shelling the Sikh guns were silenced and the Sikhs withdrew to their original positions after suffering heavy losses. But by then the British combatants were so exhausted that Gough decided to postpone the general attack until the next day.

During the night Shere Singh withdrew his entire army. Sikh sources point to a tactical and highly disciplined retreat; the British claimed they left 'in great disorder'. Either way, Shere Singh had not been defeated. Senior British officers, however, believed that the war was virtually over. Lancers and dragoons immediately crossed the

Chenab, and were followed over in the next few weeks by Gough and the rest of the British forces.

*   *   *

While Gough was engaged around the Chenab, General Whish, reinforced by Bombay troops, was resuming his siege of Multan 230 miles to the south-west. The city was home to 80,000 people and it was a rich centre of trade. The *Bombay Times* wrote of it:

> Never perhaps in India have such depots existed of merchandise and arms. Her opium, indigo, salt, sulphur, every known drug are heaped in endless profusion – ancient granaries in the bowels of the earth disclose huge hoards of wheat and rice; here bale on bale of silks and shawls; there some mammoth chest discovering glittering scabbards and gold gems, there tiers of copper canisters crammed with gold coin . . .

Such riches were not going to save it. But the citadel's strong walls, through which eighty cannon poked their black barrels, might.

Whish's force now consisted of 32,000 men, of whom 15,000 were British; the remainder consisted of loyal native units and Indian allies. Whish could also deploy 150 cannon and mortars. On 27 December Whish ordered a general attack in four columns and the defenders were forced to abandon the suburbs, allowing the British artillery to close within 500 yards of the main fortress walls. On the 28th a general cannonade and bombardment opened up and on the 29th the British heavy guns were pulverising the walls at a range of just 80 yards. Corporal John Ryder wrote in his diary:

> Salvo after salvo went thundering into the town, both shot and shell, and must have committed awful destruction . . . killing men, women and children. We got more guns into play during the night, and approached much nearer the walls. Two breaches were commenced in them, one at the Delhi Gate and the other more to the left. A great many prisoners were taken in trying to make their escape from the town; but numbers were women and children. They were treated well.

An officer noted with the callous humour of the time: 'Great damage was caused in the town by our shot and shell practice.' In the fort a granary and several small magazines were set on fire. There was a bigger bang to come on the morning of the 30th. Another eyewitness wrote home:

> Yesterday I saw one of the most awful and grand sights I am ever likely to witness; the whole of Mulraj's principal magazine, which he has been five years collecting, was blown up by one of our shells. The shock two miles off knocked bottles off the tables, and the report was terrific . . . At first we felt a slight shock, like that of an earthquake, and then, a second or two afterwards, such a tremendous and prolonged report, that it was like an awful clap of thunder. I hardly know what to liken it to – it was so inconceivably grand; then a mass of dust rose to the very clouds, yet so perfectly distinct was its outline, and it was so dense and thick, that nobody at first could tell what it was. It looked like an immense solid brown tree, suddenly grown up to the skies, and then it gradually expanded and slowly sailed away.

Sikh prisoners told the besiegers that the fort's magazine had contained 16,000lb of powder, and as many as 800 men blew up with it. But although the fort's main buildings, barrack houses and temples were destroyed, its battlements were untouched because of the upward thrust of the explosion. The city, where most of the Sikh defenders were, was also largely undamaged. For several minutes after the explosion there was silence, which was broken by Sikh gunners in the citadel who, once they had recovered from the shock, redoubled their fire with furious disdain. Mulraj sent word to Whish the next day that he still had enough powder and shot to hold out for a year. He urged the British to 'do their worst' and said that he would never surrender as long as there was a single Sikh standing.

The cannonade continued for two more days, and more breaches were made in the Delhi and Bohur gates. On the last day of 1848 the Sikhs made a sortie from the south-west gate and attacked the division commanded by Edwardes, who had been promoted major for his earlier gallantry. The Sikhs were driven back with heavy losses and Whish ordered a two-pronged attack on the city, by-passing the fort, two days later. The first storming parties were repulsed in the narrow breaches by defenders hurling not just gunfire but also boulders, broken furniture and wooden beams. Three companies of the 1st Bombay Fusiliers under Captain Leith, a giant of a man, followed. An officer noted:

> Up we charged and the moment we arrived at the top we were saluted with a volley of Sikh matchlock balls, which, wonderful to relate, all went clear over our heads, except one which struck poor Leith in the shoulder. The enemy had made a large stockade, which we scrambled over somehow (I am sure I cannot recollect how, for it looked a horrible place afterwards), and there stood about a thousand of the enemy with their swords drawn. We gave a volley and a thundering cheer, and charged them with the bayonet. Poor Leith had his left hand cut off through the wrist by a sword. The enemy could not stand a charge with British steel, and fell back; we followed them closely.

The Bombay column fought its way through the outer defences and the first colours were planted in Multan by a sergeant-major of the Company's Fusiliers.

More troops poured into the narrow streets, to be met with fire from the windows and house-tops, and the siege became a house-to-house battle with no quarter given. Corporal Ryder, in his famously graphic diary, wrote:

> We broke open the doors with the butt ends of our muskets, and blew off the locks, when not one of those within was left alive: everyone being killed on the spot. They were despatched wholesale. One place was fought very hard for by the enemy. This was a Hindu mosque [sic], occupied by a brave officer and a number of determined men. They had a colour, a very handsome one. They were attacked by a party of our men, who took the colour and killed nearly all the men. We were confined

for room: our muskets with bayonets fixed we found rather awkward, as we had not room to turn them about. A man by the name of McGuire, a corporal, was attacked by the officer bearing the colour: he came sword in hand, and the corporal not being loaded at the time (for he had just fired) had quite as much as he could do to defend himself. However, he parried off the cuts of the swords until he had a chance, when he made a thrust and gave the officer the bayonet, and at the same time, received a cut from the sword upon his left arm. They closed upon each other, and grappled each other by the throat; when the corporal gave him the foot and threw him upon the floor. The corporal then took his opponent's sword and cut off his head, and brought the colour away as his prize.

The murderous fighting did not spare women and children who were fatally intermingled with their menfolk in the narrow streets. Ryder was haunted by their 'wild terrified screams . . . the cries of the affrighted children as they clung around their mothers'.

Before sunset on 2 January 1849 the city was in British hands but the slaughter continued. Whish ordered his British and sepoy troops to herd the city's inhabitants into the main squares. Ryder wrote:

some of this work was attended with horrible brutality by our men. In several instances, on breaking into the retreats of these unfortunate creatures, a volley of shots was fired amongst them as they were huddled together in a corner. All shared the same fate. One of my fellow-corporals, who never was worthy of the jacket he wore, was guilty of cold-blooded murder. He shot a poor, grey-headed old man while he was begging that he would spare and not hurt his wife and daughters; nor take away the little property they possessed, consisting of a few paltry rings upon their fingers and in their ears. This fellow pulled the rings off in a most brutal manner. I learned that several of our men were guilty of murder. Our native soldiers were much worse, and more brutish; but they were more to be excused, as they were natives.

Ryder also reported several cases of rape, including that of a young girl in front of her mother by a man of the 3rd company of his own regiment. 'Had I been upon the spot at that time,' Ryder wrote, 'I would have shot him dead.' Ryder's frank account contradicted the official reports. Dr John Dunlop, surgeon of the 32nd Foot, said: 'The soldiery were glad to extract from the town whatever enjoyment it afforded. Few excesses were, however, committed.'

The citadel still held out. Within its scorched but strong walls Mulraj surrounded himself with his finest soldiers. For two full weeks the fort was constantly bombarded while engineers dug trenches ever closer. Sappers, too, had been busy and on the 18th three mines were exploded, hurling masonry into the ditch. A further shaft was driven under the walls, while 24-pounders and 8-inch howitzers battered at close range against the defences. Live shells buried themselves in the mud and brickwork of the main citadel and 'exploded like mines, tearing vast masses away with them'.

Mulraj sent out several messages saying he would concede provided his life was guaranteed. Whish insisted on unconditional surrender and on the morning of the 22nd, as British columns were preparing for the final assault, Mulraj gave in. A contemporary account said:

> First appeared about 200 miserable wretches who seemed broken and dispirited; then followed about 350 hard, trained, stern, and stalwart-looking men; they had defended the fort to the last, and only abandoned it when it was untenable. They looked as if they would have fought to death in the breaches, if such had been the will of their chief. They brought camels, and horses, and large bundles of things along with them. These, together with their arms, were placed in charge of the prize agents as they passed. At last came Mulraj, and his brethen and chiefs . . . He was gorgeously attired in silks and splendid arms, and rode a magnificent Arab steed, with a rich saddle-cloth of scarlet, which bore no marks of suffering or privation. No small curiosity was experienced to discover the appearance of one who had maintained a defence obstinate and protracted beyond

any related in the annals of modern warfare. He but little exceeds the middle size; is powerfully but elegantly formed; his keen, dark, piercing, restless eyes surveyed at a glance everything around. He neither wore the face of defiance or dejection, but moved along under the general gaze as one conscious of having barely done his duty, and aware of being the object of universal regard.

Ryder's account of the fall of Multan was less flowery and much more direct:

Heaven only can tell what were the sufferings of those poor creatures after the siege commenced. And no-one can tell how many were killed. No respect was paid to nobility of blood, innocence of youth or to the tears of beauty. Mountains of dead lay in every part of the town, and heaps of human ashes in every square, where the bodies had been burnt as they were killed. Some were only half consumed. Many had been gnawed and pulled to pieces by dogs; and arms, legs, heads and other parts lay in every place. The town swarmed with millions of flies.

Soldiers broke into Mulraj's treasury and found a hoard of gold and silver coins and bars; the quantity was so vast that it took three days to weigh and count it and pack it into ammunition wagons. The prize agents reckoned its worth at nearly £3 million sterling. Not all the treasure was officially counted. Soldiers who got there first filled their pockets to spend in the grog shops. Ryder reported: 'The money was so plentiful that the men would not carry copper; and some of the men who had got the most would not carry silver!'

Mulraj was sent a prisoner to be put on trial for his life and the revolt in his region was extinguished. But the real war had still to be won. Leaving a strong garrison at Multan, Whish ordered an immediate march northwards to join Gough's grand army facing Shere Singh.

*   *   *

While Whish was on the march, Gough was already in hot pursuit of his Sikh enemy. The proud old general was clearly stung by Dalhousie's jibes about his lack of success so far. He noted in his diary: 'Heard from Governor-General that he would be glad if I gained a victory.' His determination to counter such snide remarks, coupled with his own instincts for frontal assaults, contributed to the near-disaster that followed.

At noon on 13 January 1849 Gough's army approached Chillianwalla, a small village on the left bank of the River Jhelum roughly 85 miles from Lahore. His 12,000 men had been on the march for three days. Spies told him that Shere Singh's army of between 32,000 and 40,000 men, with 62 guns, were encamped around nearby settlements and along a low range of hills intersected with ravines. They were hidden from the British view by thick jungle and the broken terrain. Gough reported that the nature of the country was 'excessively difficult and ill-adapted to the advance of a regular army'. Gough's scouts cautiously probed the area, and the following morning his army advanced in equally tentative fashion. Gough detoured to the right, partly to distract the enemy's attention but mainly to get as clear as he could of the embracing jungle 'on which it would appear that the enemy mainly relied'. A strong picket of Sikh cavalry and infantry was driven off a mound just outside the village. From this vantage point Gough was shocked to see the entire Sikh army drawn up in battle order. The enemy, having moved from their positions either overnight or earlier that morning, occupied the ground in front of him which 'though not a dense, was still a very difficult jungle'. By now it was past noon and Gough sensibly held back while scouts tested the enemy flanks. He intended to make camp for the night and leave the fight to the following day.

However, just as engineers and the quartermaster were preparing the camp, a troop of Sikh horse artillery advanced and blasted the skirmish line in front of the village. The heavier British guns were unlimbered and opened up an artillery duel. Their fire was instantly returned by the whole of the enemy's field artillery. The British commander decided to attack at once. Defending his actions later, Gough said that the cannonade had exposed the positions of the

Sikh guns, which until then had been well hidden. He added: 'It was now evident that the enemy intended to fight, and would probably advance his guns so as to reach the encampment during the night.' Other officers, however, believed that Gough had been stung into foolhardy action by the Sikh horse artillery attack.

While the guns blasted each other for more than an hour, Gough drew up his battle lines. Sir Walter Gilbert's division was on the right, flanked by Brigadier Pope's brigade of cavalry, strengthened by the 14th Light Dragoons. Brigadier-General Colin Campbell's division formed the left, flanked by Brigadier White's cavalry brigade and three troops of horse artillery. The 24th Foot, flanked by the 25th and 45th Native Infantry, were in the centre, under orders to take the Sikh guns directly in front of them.

To the footsore and weary infantry it seemed madness from the start. The *Annual Register* later commented:

> Such was the order of the attack; but the question now arises, was it prudent under the circumstances to make the attack at all? The troops were wearied with their march, the day was almost spent, and there was no time to make proper arrangements so as to avoid unnecessary loss of life. The truth seems to be that Lord Gough was irritated by the fire from the horse artillery of the Sikhs, and suddenly changing his plan of waiting, he resolved to chastise their presumption on the spot. If such be the fact, the Commander-in-Chief was certainly, in this instance, more brave than discreet, and his indiscretion cost us dear. No sufficient reconnaissance was made of the ground that lay between our troops and the enemy, and it was not known in what part of his line his chief strength lay.

The 24th Foot, a regiment that had been battle-hardened in the Napoleonic Wars forty or more years before, had taken no part in the First Sikh War and had arrived in India only six months earlier. The regiment was nearly at full strength, with 31 officers and 1,065 men. It had a reputation for both courage and ill-luck.

At around 3 p.m. they began their advance, under Brigadier Mountain, through thick scrub and jungle, picking up speed as the foliage cleared. In front of them was a wide open space commanded by twenty Sikh guns. The enemy gunners barely needed to take aim before opening up. Round shot and grapeshot mowed down officers and men in their dozens, the cannon being no respecters of rank. They moved steadily forward, but the order to charge was given when they were still too far from the Sikh positions. Gough reported: 'This unhappy mistake led to the Europeans outstripping the native corps, which could not keep pace, and arriving completely blown at a belt of thicker jungle, where they got into some confusion.' Astonishingly, the 24th were given orders that muskets should not be fired and only the bayonet used against the enemy. The blame for the disaster later fell on Brigadier Pennicuick, who had given an over-literal interpretation of Gough's orders that the guns should be taken by the bayonet point.

A young officer noted that his men, with their colours unfurled, made a 'good target' for the Sikh gunners. The 24th rushed blindly forward. Captain Thackwell wrote: 'It fell to the lot of this gallant regiment to experience an atmosphere solely compounded of fire, grape and roundshot.' They were mown down, gaping holes appearing in the advancing redcoat ranks as the Sikh gunners in their yellow turbans battled to maintain their ceaseless barrage. Lieutenant Andrew Macpherson recalled:

One charge of grapeshot took away an entire section and for a moment I was alone and unhurt. On we went, the goal is almost won, the ground clears, the pace quickens . . . the bayonets come down for the charge. My men's pieces were loaded but not a shot was fired, with a wild, choking hurrah we stormed the guns and the battery is won.

The fight which began when the bloodied remnants of the 24th reached the Sikh guns was close-quarter and savage, with the blade the main weapon used. Half-blinded by smoke, deafened by blast and pumped up with adrenaline, men grappled in a stabbing, slashing, cursing mêlée. Major Paynter was shot through the lungs; his horse carried him to safety but he later died. Lieutenant Lloyd Williams suffered twenty-three sword and lance wounds and a fractured skull, and his left hand was severed. Astonishingly, he survived. Pennicuick did not, nor did his seventeen-year-old son, an ensign who fell across his father's body during his first taste of action. The queen's colours were lost in the confusion, but not the regimental colours. The Sikh batteries were taken and several guns spiked. General Campbell reported in dispatches: 'This single regiment actually broke the enemy's line and took large numbers of the enemy's guns to their front without a shot being fired or a musket being taken from the shoulder.'

As soon as the central Sikh guns were silenced the 24th came under flanking fire from other cannon, with musket fire from almost all sides. They were forced to retreat 'in good order and with determined bravery' over the bodies of their fallen comrades. One report of the action said:

> The Sikhs no sooner saw they were deprived of the use of their guns than they renewed such a fire with musketry, not only on the flank, but in the rear of the brigade, that common prudence dictated a retreat, and it was effected with the same determination that had distinguished the three brigades throughout.

Virtually every correspondent described the charge, unsupported by artillery or cavalry, and caught in a vicious cross-fire, as 'magnificent'. Charles Napier wrote: 'Their conduct has never been surpassed by British soldiers on a field of battle.'

It was a victory of sorts, as some enemy guns were spiked, but it was a costly one. By the end of the day the regiment had lost nearly half its men, with 515 casualties, including 238 dead. Of its 29 officers, 13 were killed and 10 wounded. The dead officers were laid out on their polished mess table later that night.

Elsewhere other men were either distinguishing or disgracing themselves. Gilbert's brigade marched through thick jungle to confront a large body of Sikh infantry, which easily outflanked them. Two companies of the 2nd European Regiment wheeled up and charged, but found themselves quickly surrounded. They immediately faced right-about, fired and charged, the rear rank to the front. Horse artillery was effectively deployed to help them beat off the enemy. Lieutenant D.A. Sandford of the 2nd Bengal Europeans described another infantry charge on the British right:

> The men bounded forwards like angry bulldogs, pouring in a murderous fire. The enemy's bullets whizzed above our heads; the very air seemed teeming with them; man after man was struck down, and rolled in the dust. But a passing glance was all that we could give them. And onward he went, bearing on their line with a steadiness which nothing could resist. They fired a last volley, and then turned and fled, leaving the ground covered with dead and wounded. Pursuit in a jungle like that was useless, where we could not see twenty yards before us . . .

Later, when Sandford's unit was itself surrounded, the horse artillery blasted them an escape route in the enemy's ranks. He recalled:

> Every gun was turned on them, the men working as coolly as on parade; and a salvo was poured in that sent horse and man head over heels, in heaps. The fire was fearful; the atmosphere seemed alive with balls. I can only compare it to a storm of hail. They sang above my head and ears so thick that I felt that if I put out my hand it would be taken off.

On the extreme left a dashing cavalry charge led by Brigadier White was successful. And the 61st Foot captured several guns, much ammunition and an elephant. Their officer said that his men 'saw game ahead and I couldn't hold them in'. Such successes were almost thrown away by the performance of the cavalry under Brigadier Pope.

Pope was a distinguished veteran of the East India Company army but he was now old, infirm and almost blind. He was a known ditherer and had only a shaky grasp of command. Gough, who rarely had a bad word to say about any officers under his command, said that Pope was unfit for the responsibilities to which his seniority entitled him. Pope's men had little confidence in him and their doubts were swiftly confirmed. Pope's cavalry division was made up of the 14th Light Dragoons, the 9th Lancers and two regiments of native cavalry. They were ordered to move against a large body of enemy horsemen, variously estimated at between 1,000 and 5,000 men. Pope had difficulty in getting his men faced in the right direction and his orders were confused and conflicting. Finally he halted them to give himself time to think. Suddenly, some Sikh cavalry appeared in front of them and Pope, by now thoroughly confused, ordered 'Threes about' instead of giving the signal to charge. The troopers obediently wheeled about and galloped away. Only a body of the 9th Lancers were rallied by screaming officers. The rest rode straight through the British artillery lines in a compact mass, upsetting four cannon and several wagons. Leaving a trail of wreckage, they continued to a field hospital and were only halted by the Revd W. Whiting, who was attending the wounded. The panicky troopers told him that the battle was lost. Whiting said that he was a man of God but he would shoot any trooper who continued to retreat. Gough, tongue in cheek, later proposed that Whiting be made a brevet-bishop.

The Sikh cavalry, meantime, took advantage of the mayhem and followed the troopers into the now-chaotic British artillery lines, a mass of thrashing horses and upturned limbers. They cut down seventy-three gunners who had, by the flight of their own cavalry through their ranks, been deprived of the means of defending themselves. A cannonade of grapeshot halted the Sikh advance but they carried off four guns, two of which were later recovered.

The battle dragged on inconclusively until eight that night. Under cover of darkness the Sikhs withdrew, taking most of their guns (including several previously captured by the British), five stands of regimental colours, and several British guns. According to British reports the Sikhs 'in their night excursions to recover their guns, killed many of our wounded, and stripped and plundered all the bodies within their reach'.

After possibly the hardest battle the British ever fought in India, Gough rode along the lines, bareheaded in the pouring rain, and was cheered everywhere by his bloody and exhausted men. But there was precious little cheering when news of the 'victory' reached London.

The British had remained masters of the battlefield and Gough naturally claimed a resounding success, which was 'complete as to the total overthrow of the enemy', estimating Sikh casualties at up to 8,000. But the cost shocked his masters at home. The losses, including those incurred by the ill-advised charge of the 24th, were 26 European officers and 731 men killed, 104 missing, 66 officers and 1,585 men wounded. Nearly 1,000 of the losses were British rather than native troops and the public at home were unused to such slaughter of their own boys during Indian campaigns. Gough, previously seen as a hero for his 'up and at 'em' tactics was now roundly condemned by all, from Queen Victoria to the tavern tactician. Dalhousie regarded Gough as a relic who was overly fond of the bayonet and ignorant of the sciences of modern warfare. The Governor-General wrote: 'If he again fights an incomplete action with terrible carnage as before, you must expect to hear of my taking a strong step: he shall not remain in command of that army in the field.' Such threats were soon exceeded by the outcry in London. The *Illustrated London News* stormed: 'Though masters of the field, our laurels are drenched with blood, and it is the universal opinion that two more such victories would be virtual ruin.' The post mortem focused on Gough's initial decision to attack without a proper reconnaissance. The same periodical published an explanation which was widely accepted:

The old chief had merely given an order to change ground, and it was not his intention to have attacked the Sikhs until the next day, but they seem to have enticed him on; they allowed their advanced posts to be driven in, and then opened a heavy fire, which put him into a passion, and he swore that he would drive them from the face of the earth. Several people advised him not to fight them until the next day, but he would listen to no one, and even said he would put any officer under arrest who presumed to suggest anything to him.

The *Annual Register* reported:

The news was received in England with a burst of sorrow and, we must add, indignation. Want of due caution on the part of the General was patent on the face of the accounts of the engagement, and it was felt that it ought not to have been hazarded, nor so great a waste of life so wantonly incurred. There was no need to test the courage of the soldiers who had been engaged in this campaign against the Sikhs, and the duty of the Commander-in-Chief was to effect the overthrow of the enemy by superior strategic skill, rather than by dashing exploits of personal valour and hand-to-hand conflicts with the sabre and the bayonet. The consequence was an almost unanimous demand for the recall of Lord Gough and the appointment of a general who would carry on the war in a more scientific and less desperate fashion.

Within 48 hours of the dispatches being received the government agreed to replace Gough with Sir Charles Napier, the conqueror of Sind, who was then in England. The queen wrote: 'The news from India is very distressing, and makes one very anxious, but Sir Charles Napier is instantly to be sent out to supersede Lord Gough, and he is so well versed in Indian tactics that we may look with safety to the future *after* his arrival.'

Napier was appointed Commander-in-Chief of the Forces and Member Extraordinary of the Council of India, and set sail from England towards the end of March to take charge of the campaign. By the time he arrived events had turned Gough back into a hero and the war was over.

* * *

After the bloody 'victory' of Chillianwalla, Gough sensibly decided to wait until he was reinforced by General Whish's army. Dalhousie, the severest critic of Gough's previous foolhardiness, now rebuked him for the delay. In a letter to Sir John Hobhouse he wrote:

I regret to say that every man in the army – generals of divisions – officers, Europeans and sepoys – have totally lost confidence in their leader – loudly proclaim it themselves, and report it in their letters to their friends. It is with pain that I state my opinion that I can no longer feel any confidence that the army is safe from disaster in the hands of the present C-in-C, and add that there is not a man in India who does not share that feeling with me.

On 12 February Shere Singh and his father Chuttar Singh deployed a cavalry screen while their army struck their tents and retreated to Gujerat near the Chenab river. Their force, strengthened by 1,500 Afghan cavalry sent by Dost Mohammed, now numbered up to 60,000, with 59 guns. When Whish joined him, after securing several fords across the Chenab, Gough had 24,000 men under his command, and set off to pursue the enemy. Gough's scouts reported on the Sikh position:

It was found to be immensely strong, and consisted of a double line of entrenchments, in front of which they had planted large bushes in every direction, so as to mask themselves, and to prevent the movement of cavalry. Their camp had been pitched upon the slope of a hill, with a battery in the midst of broken ground. Close to this battery was a deep and rugged ravine with a narrow bridge. To the rear of this natural fortress was a perpendicular wall of rock.

The camp encircled the small town and the Sikh army was drawn up between it and the dry bed of a small river. Despite the strength of the enemy positions and their numerical supremacy, Gough, knowing his career was finished unless he could win a quick victory, decided to attack. On 21 February 1849 he fought his 'last and best battle'.

A half-hearted Sikh cavalry attack was repelled on the flanks and at 7.30 a.m. Gough ordered his army to advance against the Sikh centre. The enemy artillery opened fire at long range, thereby exposing their positions in the scrub. Gough halted his infantry and brought forward his own cannon. The general wrote in his dispatches:

The cannonade now opened upon the enemy was the most magnificent I ever witnessed, and as terrible in its effects.

The Sikh guns were served with their accustomed rapidity, and the enemy well and resolutely maintained his position; but the terrific force of our fire obliged them, after an obstinate resistance, to fall back.

Gough then ordered a general advance under cover of his cannon. A large body of Sikh infantry concealed in the small village of Burra Kalra was taken 'with great slaughter' by the 3rd Brigade under Brigadier Penny, a mixed force of the 2nd Europeans and the 31st and 70th regiments of native infantry. Lieutenant Sandford wrote:

The round-shot flew about us, and ploughed up the ground in all directions. Five or six men were knocked down in as many seconds . . . A company from each regiment in the brigade was sent up to the front to support the troop of horse-artillery attached to us; and, poor fellows, they suffered dreadfully, being brought in one after another wounded – some with legs shot off, some cut in half, some torn with grape – scarcely half of our rifle company was left. All this time, the fire was very hot on us, carrying off three men at a time, shells bursting over us, or burying themselves in front, scattering the earth in our faces.

At the same time a 'very spirited and successful' move was made against troops in another hamlet, Chota Kalra, by the 10th Foot under Lieutenant-Colonel Franks. This proved to be the toughest engagement of the battle. The Sikhs fired through loopholes in the village walls and in 30 minutes killed or wounded ninety-four attackers. Light artillery blasted the defences from yards away and an infantry charge reached the walls, but the Sikhs fought on with fanatical stubbornness. Once again the rifle butt and bayonet were used against sword and spear in house-to-house fighting which left the flagstones slippery with blood. Gough reported:

The heavy artillery continued to advance with extraordinary celerity, taking up successive forward positions, driving the enemy from those they had retired to, whilst the rapid advance and beautiful fire of the Horse Artillery and light field-batteries, which I strengthened by bringing to the front the two reserve troops . . . broke the ranks of the enemy at all points. The whole Infantry line now rapidly advanced and drove the enemy before it; the *nulla* was cleared, several villages stormed, the guns that were in position carried, the camp captured and the enemy routed in every direction.

Campbell's division pursued them on the east flank, and the Bombay column on the west. Gough's report continued:

The retreat of the Sikh army thus hotly pressed, soon became a perfect flight, all arms dispersing over the country, rapidly pursued by our troops for a distance of 12 miles, their track strewn with the wounded, their arms and military equipment, which they threw away to conceal that they were soldiers.

His victory was genuine and complete, as Gough underlined in his gleeful report to Dalhousie: 'A result, my lord, glorious indeed for the ever-victorious army of India.' The Sikh army had been routed with heavy losses, leaving behind fifty-seven guns. It was the end of the Khalsa. Given the scale of the battle Gough's casualties were astonishingly light: 96 killed and 682 wounded, of whom many were saved by the use of anaesthetics for the first time on a British battlefield. One commentator sniffed, however, 'The success of the operation at Gujerat renders it more painful to contemplate the sacrifice of life at Chillianwalla.'

The following morning Major-General Sir Walter Gilbert, with 15,000 men, set off in pursuit of the demoralised remnants of Shere Singh's army. It became a simple chase through rain-drenched ravines and across swollen rivers. The revolt had effectively been crushed. On the 24th Major Lawrence crossed the Jhelum river and opened communications with Shere Singh. Four days later Gilbert's main force crossed the torrent with extreme difficulty. Shere Singh retreated further, his army now reduced to 10,000 men and 10 guns. But on 6 March Major and Mrs Lawrence, who had been held captive by the Sikhs, arrived in Gilbert's camp and announced that Shere Singh was ready to lay down his arms. Two days later the Rajah himself arrived and was told that only unconditional surrender was acceptable. He returned to consult with his father and other chiefs while the British advanced steadily. At Rawalpindi on the 11th he again crossed the British line, this time with his Sirdars and the guns captured at Chillianwalla. An observer noted:

> Shere Singh then returned again to the remnant of his army, to prepare it for the surrender that was to take place the following day. This humiliating act occupied some time, and it was not until the 14th that the whole of the Sikh officers and soldiers had delivered up their arms. Each man as he passed received one rupee to provide him with the means of subsistence until he reached his home, and they were all allowed to retain their horses.

General Campbell was impressed by the dignity of one old Khalsa soldier who put down his musket, saluted and cried out: 'Today Runjeet Singh is dead.' The British campaign medal later struck showed Sikhs laying down their arms in front of a mounted general in a cocked hat.

After witnessing the surrender, Dalhousie gloated in a letter to Queen Victoria: 'Your Majesty may well imagine the pride with which British officers looked on such a scene, and witnessed this absolute subjection and humiliation of so powerful an enemy.'

Gilbert then set off after the fleeing Afghan cavalry, under Akram Khan, hoping to cut them off before the crossed the Indus. He just failed, reaching the river just as the Afghans were destroying the bridge of boats they had used to cross. A few desultory shots from light Afghan cannon marked the end of the Second Sikh War.

*　　*　　*

The revolt and subsequent war offered the excuse to annexe the Punjab to British India, which is precisely what the Governor-General had intended all along. A proclamation issued by Dalhousie on 29 March referred to the first war and the clemency then shown by the British government. It went on:

The Sikh people and their chiefs have grossly and faithlessly violated the promises by which they were bound. Of their annual tribute no portion whatever has at any time been paid, and large loans advanced to them by the Government of India have never been repaid. The control of the British government, to which they voluntarily submitted themselves, has been resisted by arms. Peace has been cast aside. British officers have been murdered when acting for the State; others engaged in the like employment have been treacherously thrown into captivity. Finally, the army of the state and the whole Sikh people, joined by many of the Sirdars in the Punjab who signed the treaties, and led by a member of the Regency itself, have risen in arms against us, and have waged a fierce and bloody war for the proclaimed purpose of destroying the British and their power.

On 2 April the Punjab officially became a British province under a three-man administrative board, which was replaced by a commissioner four years later. The process of conquest which Clive had begun was now complete: Britain possessed the whole of India. Gough told his men: 'That which Alexander attempted, the British army have accomplished.'

British troops were stationed within the Punjab's borders. Former Khalsa soldiers were recruited into the new Punjab Frontier Force and from then on Sikhs provided some of the finest fighters in the British Army. They proved invaluably loyal during the Indian Mutiny. All sirdars and chiefs who had waged war on Britain saw their property confiscated. All strongholds and forts not occupied by British troops were destroyed. Those few chiefs who had not joined the revolt retained both property and rank. The young Majarajah Duleep Singh and his mother the Maharani Jindan were to be exiled. Freedom of religion was guaranteed and the British government forbade 'any man to intervene with others in the observance of such forms and customs as their respective religions may either enjoin or permit'.

Mulraj was put on trial before a special military commission consisting of four British and two native officers and a colonel of the Sikh army. He was charged with the murder of Vans Agnew and Anderson; he was an accessory before the fact in that he had instigated the attack, and an accessory after the fact in that he had rewarded the actual killers. He asked Edwardes to speak for him but the gallant major refused, saying afterwards: 'I believed him guilty, and would not defend him; I had hunted him with an army in the field and had no wish to follow him into the dock.' Instead a British advocate, Captain Hamilton, spoke for him with 'great zeal and ability' and the trial lasted fourteen days. Mulraj was found guilty and sentenced to death, although the sentence was later commuted to life imprisonment after the tribunal judged him 'the victim of circumstances'. He was banished. No mention was made of his looted fortune.

His citadel at Multan, which had resisted so much British artillery pounding, was almost entirely washed away the following August when the Chenab and Jhelum rivers breached their banks. The waters of the swollen rivers entered the ditches of the fort and ate away at its walls of sun-baked brick. Within hours the walls of the scarp and counterscarp slipped down 'like shaken sand' as the brickwork melted into slime. Over the next few days the enormous dome of the Bahwul Huk fell with a tremendous crash and other large buildings followed. Eventually the whole citadel resembled 'a mere island of mud amidst the expanse of water'. A British observer wrote in a private letter: 'Mooltan [sic] seems this season to be the victim alternately of fire and water – of the British Artillery and the Naiads. What Whish was so long in effecting, and then performed but imperfectly, the waters of the Chenab have accomplished noiselessly and without difficulty.'

Lord Gough, who had come so close to disgrace, returned home a hero. He had fought in more battles than any other living soldier and Gujerat had, thankfully, topped the lot. During a House of Lords debate no less a general than the Duke of Wellington praised him. Skimming over earlier 'untoward accidents which it was impossible to avoid', the duke described the overall campaign as 'brilliant in the extreme'. Sir Robert Peel said that he had never doubted that the campaign would 'rebound to the honour of Lord Gough'. Sir J.W. Hogg said that a more complete victory than Gujerat had never been fought. Gough was created a viscount and given a pension of £2,000 for his own lifetime and for that of his next two heirs. *Punch*, which had previously labelled him an 'incompetent octogenarian' now lauded him as a 'gallant veteran'. Gough, despite the accolades, resented the criticism of his generalship at Chillianwalla and other battles in the earlier war. He wrote: 'Thanks to a gracious God for not only covering my head in the day of battle, but for granting me a victory, not only over my Enemies, but over my country.' The East India Company voted him thanks and a further pension, and the City of London gave him its freedom. He saw no more active service but became a full general in 1854 when he was appointed colonel-in-chief of the 60th Royal Rifles. The following year he became colonel of the Royal Horse Guards after the death of Lord Raglan. In 1862 he became a field marshal. Sir Charles Napier, on taking up his Indian appointment, wrote of him: 'Everyone who knows Lord Gough must love the brave old warrior, who is all honour and nobleness of heart. Were his military genius as great as his heart, the Duke [of Wellington] would be nowhere by comparison.' His wife Frances, by whom he had a son and four daughters, died in 1863. He followed her at St Helens, his County Dublin seat, in 1869, aged eighty-nine.

Whish received the thanks of the court of directors of the East India Company and both Houses of Parliament. He was promoted a knight commander of the Order of the Bath and took command of the army's Bengal Division as a lieutenant-general. He died at London's Claridge's Hotel in 1853, aged sixty-five, leaving two sons, both soldiers.

Edwardes returned to England in 1850 and found himself lionised. He was knighted, showered with further honours and publicly entertained in London and Liverpool. The East India Company struck for him a unique gold medal, the mould of which was afterwards destroyed. This was the high water mark of his career. Long and worthy political service followed in frontier stations, where he deftly used his diplomatic skills to avert crisis after crisis. During a long trip back to England he was invited to stand as MP for Glasgow but declined. He died following a serious attack of pleurisy late in 1868. His mural tablet is in Westminster Abbey and his first district posting in the Punjab was named, by the Sikhs themselves, Edwardesabad.

Dalhousie ruled India for eight years and extended its boundaries even more after the annexation of the Punjab. His real legacy to India derived from his role as a reformer and moderniser – his projects included a railway, telegraph networks, a postal service and the development of irrigation and roadworks. He died in 1860 at Dalhousie Castle. His predecessor as Governor-General, Lord Hardinge, was blamed for many of the logistical failures of the Crimean War but that did not prevent him being raised to the rank of field marshal in 1855. He was stricken with paralysis while attending the queen and died, aged seventy-one, in 1856.

The conquest and annexation of the Punjab brought riches to many men of differing ranks. Sergeant John Pearman received a bounty of £3 16s after Gujerat. Private Perry, who had saved his regimental colours at Chillianwalla, was promoted to corporal and received a Good Conduct Medal. General Campbell, the son of a Glasgow carpenter, was knighted. After a distinguished career he ended his life as a field marshal, the Lord Clyde and a hero of the Indian Mutiny.

But the biggest prize went to Queen Victoria herself. Dalhousie was at last able to present her with the fabled 'mountain of light'. The Koh-i-noor diamond was a token of submission from the defeated Sikhs. Dalhousie reasoned that its removal from India would snuff out any lingering Sikh hopes of resistance. A British officer described the scene when it was taken from its imported Chubb safe in the grand palace at Lahore: 'I wish you could have seen the vast quantities of gold and silver, the jewels yet to be valued – and the Koh-i-noor, far beyond what I had imagined.' Shah Shuja, whose wife had included it among her jewels, said that whoever owned it would enjoy good fortune and victory over all enemies. However, the stone's history had been bloody, and those who took it wrongfully were cursed. Nadir Shah, who seized it after the 1739 sacking of Delhi, was murdered as he slept in his tent. Runjeet Singh may have escaped the curse but his successors did not (see Chapter 22). The curse appears to have stayed with the diamond: the ship which transported it to Britain barely survived a storm and its crew were ravaged by cholera. Within a month of Queen Victoria receiving it she was attacked twice, first by a deranged would-be assassin who fired a pistol at her, and then by a retired junior officer who swung at her with a walking stick. She never again wore the diamond. In 1854 it was poorly cut down by an incompetent artisan to 106 carats, little more than half its original size. It graced several royal crowns after Victoria and was last worn by the Queen Elizabeth the Queen Mother at her coronation in 1937. Some would even claim that the curse has continued down the House of Windsor line. It is currently on display among the other crown jewels in the Tower of London. In May 2000 the Indian government asked for it back. Kuldip Nayar, the MP who tabled the relevant motion said: 'The Koh-i-noor is so much part of India – so much part of our history, our psyche, our honour. It is one of the symbols of India. When you talk to any Indian about the Koh-i-noor, it stirs up a lot of emotion.'

The strangest story of all to come out of the Sikh wars concerns the fate of the child Maharajah, Duleep Singh. The ten-year-old signed away his kingdom under pressure from Dalhousie. He abdicated, gave up all his rights, titles and claims to sovereignty and was placed in the care of his guardian, a Bengal Army surgeon called Dr John Login. All his wealth was sold off as indemnity. In return he was to receive a life-time pension of £50,000 a year, which was admittedly a massive fortune. He was also obliged to leave his homeland, but could choose his destination. Under advice from Login he chose England. His long Sikh hair was cut, and the boy and the doctor took first-class cabins on the next available P&O steamer. Duleep travelled in his fine clothes, taking with him a casket of jewels and a favourite hawk.

He was warmly welcomed by Queen Victoria, who insisted that everything should be done 'to render the position of this interesting and peculiarly good and amiable Prince as agreeable as possible'. Victoria praised his 'pretty, graceful and dignified manner'. She was, however, clearly embarrassed about wearing the Koh-i-noor, and sensitive to any charge of receiving stolen goods. The boy tried to put her mind at rest, saying that it gave him great pleasure to hand over such a magnificent gift.

Duleep settled on the Elveden estate near Thetford, purchased with money from the British government, and under Login's tutelage grew to like his new country. He became a Christian and practised with Purdey shotguns until he was reckoned the fourth-best shot in England. His mansion was conventional on the outside, but its interior was transformed into a Mughal palace filled with parrots. Apes played in the kitchen garden and kangaroos hopped across the manicured lawns. Duleep built up his 17,000-acre estate into one of the most sought-after venues in the country among the shooting gentry. Hunting parties would slaughter up to 3,000 birds in a single day. He kept a string of mistresses and was a frequent guest in London's most fashionable salons. As a thoroughly Anglicised young gentleman he was granted permission by the government to meet his mother and, after thirteen years apart, their reunion took place in Calcutta early in 1861. Jindan wept with emotion and vowed that she would never be separated from her son again. She was allowed to return to England with him, a betel-chewing curiosity, an old lady dressed in crinoline and dripping pearls. She told him all the tales of his ancestors and the way his inheritance had been stolen. In 1863 she died, followed two months later by Login, who had become Duleep's much-loved surrogate father. He married the seventeen-year-old daughter of a German missionary and sired three sons and three daughters, several of whom became Queen Victoria's godchildren. The names he chose for his children speaks volumes about the royal connection: Victor Albert, Frederick Victor, Bamba Sofia, Catherine, Sophia Alexandra and Albert Edward. He was a local magistrate, squire, Conservative, gentleman of leisure, a portly figure of the Establishment.

But a mixture of Jindan's words and growing money concerns set his mind into turmoil. Elveden was hugely expensive to run and Duleep also incurred heavy gambling debts. His bank, Coutts, sent him warning letters. These he simply sent on to the India Office, with copies to the queen. Ministers, fearful of a scandal if the bank foreclosed, reached an agreement whereby his debts were cleared provided that on his death Elveden would be sold to repay the loan and to provide pensions for his family. Despite such generous terms, Duleep grew ever more resentful and fired off numerous letters to the queen complaining of the lost power and wealth of his dynasty. When that did not work he turned to intrigue. He fantasised about winning back his lost kingdom, influenced by the words of the guru Gobind Singh who prophesied that a man with his name would 'drive his elephant throughout the world'.

Such fantasies made him easy prey for con-men and spies. He embarked on convoluted plans involving the agents of Irish nationalists, Bismarck and the Tsar. Duleep was kept under constant surveillance and some officials feared that he could become an active participant in the Great Game then being played out on north-west frontier between Britain and Russia. Queen Victoria was so concerned that she wrote to him about,

> extraordinary reports of your intending to transfer your allegiance to Russia! I cannot believe this of you who have always professed such loyalty and devotion towards me, who you know have always been your true friend and who I may say took a maternal interest in you from the time when, now 32 years ago, you came to England as a beautiful and charming Boy!

She need not have worried. Hardened schemers regarded him as a comic figure and all his intrigue came to nothing.

The flames of Sikh nationalism were fanned, however, in 1886 when Duleep became a Sikh again in a ceremony conducted in the Punjab. The British government was by then so relaxed about him that they allowed him to go. By now he was regarded as more of an embarrassment than a threat to the British Empire. He travelled to Paris, where he became involved with notorious anti-British factions. He made his way to Russia in 1887, taking a train across Europe with his teenage mistress and a number of dogs wearing embroidered jackets, and announced that he could 'guarantee an easy conquest of India'. The Tsar was initially impressed but the scheme foundered when it emerged that Duleep's chief of staff was a Foreign Office spy, and when his main political backer died. The plot quickly fell apart and he returned to France after less than a year. His first wife died and in 1889 he married Ada Wetherill, the twenty-year-old daughter of a London gas-fitter. They had two daughters, named

Pauline and Ada. From France Duleep wrote to Queen Victoria, demanding the return of the Koh-i-noor which he intend to sell to fund an Indian revolt. His letter, like many others written during his middle age, was signed 'Implacable Foe of the British Government'. Soon afterwards, his dreams shattered by more experience of the cruel world outside his pampered normality, he wrote again, this time begging Victoria's forgiveness. He said: 'I feel that in fighting against your country I have been fighting against God. I would return to England were I assured of your free pardon.'

In 1893 Duleep Singh, the last Maharajah of the Punjab, died of a seizure in Paris. He was just fifty-five. By the end he had returned to the Christian faith. His body was taken by his son Frederick in an oak coffin from France to a funeral in St Andrew's church next to his Elveden estate. A wreath sent from Balmoral said simply: 'From Queen Victoria.' His grave in the churchyard remains a place of pilgrimage for Sikhs.

In 1947 India gained independence and the Punjab was divided as part of a tragic ethnic carve-up. Lahore, the Sikh capital, was included in the new Pakistan, while the Sikh holy city of Amritsar was part of the new India. Millions of Sikhs became displaced and homeless refugees.

In July 1999 Victoria's descendant, Charles, the Prince of Wales, unveiled an equestrian statute of Duleep at Thetford. Commissioned by a Sikh Trust, its inscription reads, in part, 'Even today the Sikh nation aspires to regain its sovereignty.'

TWENTY-FOUR

Eureka Stockade, Australia, 1854

'A riot becoming a revolution.'

James Scobie, a Scots gold-digger who was going through an unlucky patch on his claim, spent the afternoon and evening drinking and jawing with his countryman Jimmy Martin in the Star Hotel in the mining township of Ballarat. Apart from bawdy jokes at the expense of the 'gold lace' gentlemen who presumed to exercise their authority in the Victoria goldfields, their behaviour was good-natured, if loud. Eventually the landlord grew tired of their singing 'Fanny, My Queen from Top to Toe' and threw them out. They found someone to sell them another bottle of grog and sat under a tree until midnight, talking weepily about the mists and mountains of home. Their drink gone, they stumbled towards their claims but stopped at the only light showing, the Eureka Hotel.

Behind the barred doors, enjoying some late-night drinking of their own, were hotel-keeper James Bentley, an ex-Norfolk Island convict notorious for cheating miners, for running a rough house and for bribing officials, his young wife Catherine, several guests and one of the recipients of Bentley's backhanders, the police magistrate John D'Ewes. The two Scots diggers banged loudly on the door, demanding service, and a lamp was somehow broken. Bentley called them 'drunken scum' but did nothing more. The magistrate urged him to do something about the disturbance, threatening him with the loss of his licence. What followed remains unclear.

The two diggers, thwarted, apparently set off home. Martin later recalled only the sound of several pairs of running feet in the moments before he was attacked; beaten senseless in the dark, he was left all night in a ditch. His mate was less fortunate. James Scobie was kicked to death by heavy boots. It was a grubby, senseless death, but one that was far from unique on the rough edges of the civilised world. It was, however, to have enormous and tragic consequences, fanning the flames of rebellious republicanism and creating a legend which still remains sharp and pertinent in modern-day Australia.

*   *   *

On 12 February 1851 Edward Hargraves, sifting gravel in Lewes Pond Creek near Bathhurst, found the fleck of yellow he was looking for. He told his companion: 'There it is . . . I shall be a baronet, you shall be knighted, and my old horse will be stuffed and put in a glass case and sent to the British Museum.'

His luck swiftly ran out but gold fever swept southern Australia. Extensive goldfields were found in New South Wales and Victoria. The goldfields changed the social structure of a continent still being colonised and better known as a dumping-ground for convicts than as a land of fabulous wealth. Men flocked to the fields where, it was said, nuggets could be had for the simple energy it took to bend down and pick them up. They came from all across the continent – stockmen, bushrangers, farmers and merchants; refined gentlemen sifted dirt alongside Irish, Scots and German immigrants; ex-convicts rubbed shoulders with their former gaolers. As word spread, they came from further afield: miners from the Californian goldfields, revolutionaries from strife-torn Europe, Sikhs and Chinese, the already wealthy, greedy for more, and the dispossessed. The population of Victoria swelled from 75,000 in 1850 to almost 290,000 four years later. A sparsely populated but prosperous land of sheep ranchers changed almost overnight to a boom zone where money was swiftly earned – and just as speedily spent. With the diggers came the profiteers, exploiters, entrepreneurs, grogshop owners, suppliers and criminals. Many indeed got rich quick, but all too often saw their new wealth taken from them; others squandered it at the Melbourne races, in ornate city saloons and on equally painted ladies. No matter, there was always more where that came from.

The boom time was heady indeed. Manning Clark wrote:

The diggers lived in a constant state of excitement which found outlets in all kinds of emotional extravaganzas. In their professions of loyalty to Her Majesty they were profuse; in their account of their feeling for each other they were excessive; in their account of their feelings for their enemies they were bloody, murderous and extreme. When a strike was made the fields rang with enthusiastic huzzas. The eager cry went up, 'There's a speck.' A gleam of wild delight shone in the eyes of the successful; a terrible despair darkened the eyes of the men who had missed out.

Gold there was in abundance, but little was found on the surface. It had to be dug for with spade and pickaxe, often in vertical shafts 160 feet deep. By 1854, when Victoria overtook New South Wales in population, the number of miners in the Victorian goldfields was almost three times that of two years earlier – but the amount of gold taken had fallen to half the 1852 total of £12 million. Big business could afford heavy machinery to pulverise rock and rape the ground, and thus took an ever-bigger share. Increasingly, the ordinary diggers lived a subsistence life, scrabbling for gold dust under mountains of grit. It was too hard for most of the 'gentlemen', who left the fields to the desperate and dispossessed from Ireland and Scotland and other places which had exiled their 'trouble-makers'. There were Chartists and Reformers, Fenians and Republicans, even the occasional anarchist. Most were simply men desperate to build a new life for themselves and their families.

As the population of largely landless men grew, so did the avarice of corrupt officials and police officers. The government saw a need to raise more revenue to build roads, schools, sanitation works and public buildings. In the last three months of 1851 the Victoria diggers brought in £374,000, yet none of that money went into government coffers. The government's answer was 'that bloody licence fee', the hated poll tax.

Victoria had become a colony in July 1851, and a digger's licence of £1 a month was imposed. It was a crippling amount for those struggling diggers who had sunk all their savings into their shafts with little return. Furthermore, such men had no representation on the fledgling Legislative Council, no vote, no say in how their money was spent. Unrest spread through the goldfields, fanned by the arrogance of the gold lace and the brutish tactics of the police – the hated 'traps' – sent to collect the tax. Public meetings were held, licences burnt, threats of civil insurrection issued. At Bendigo and Ballarat placards bore the slogan 'No chains for free Englishmen'. At View Point 12,000 diggers protested with red ribbons tied to their hats. Pistols were discharged. There was the occasional riot and crazy rumours spread of a German – or American, or French – brigade formed to rush to assist the diggers. The government saw the hand of agitators everywhere.

The man presiding over this powderkeg was simply not up to the job. Governor Charles Joseph La Trobe, a scholarly clergyman's son, briefly suspended the licence fee and was accused of giving in to ruffians and malcontents. Newspapers branded him an 'imbecile'. During his tenure Victoria's deficit approached £2 million and the capital, Melbourne, remained a foul-smelling sink. His announcement of impending retirement, following the early death of his wife, was widely greeted with relief.

His replacement, who arrived in June 1854, was charged with raising revenue and crushing discontent. A Royal Navy veteran from Suffolk, Captain Sir Charles Hotham was expected to instill quarterdeck discipline and make the new colony solvent. He did not want the job – he would have preferred to sail with his naval comrades to glory in the Crimean War – but accepted it out of his strongly defined sense of duty. After the usual civic receptions he embarked on a tour of the goldfields. He appeared initially sympathetic and the diggers cheered him as their champion. He soon disillusioned them. He was appalled by the threats of insurrection and was uncomfortable with the hearty familiarity of diggers he regarded as his inferiors. He prepared to exercise the firm hand of authority. He was encouraged to do so by the Resident Gold Commissioner, Robert Rede, another well-educated, impeccably dressed gentleman from an old Suffolk family. Rede was convinced that the goldfield unrest had nothing to do with the licence fee, but was stirred up by European revolutionaries who wanted nothing less than the overthrow of the established order. He regarded the

Irish as the worst, a 'drunken, shiftless, violent race'. He believed they needed to be taught a harsh lesson and he hoped that the troublemakers would go one step too far so that the lesson could be vigorously enforced at the point of a bayonet.

One outcome was the notorious 'digger-hunts'. 'Traps' were empowered to demand production of the licence at any time, anywhere. Failure to provide it resulted in a £5 fine – half of which the arresting officer could pocket himself – and a stay in a stinking blockhouse or chained to a log. No excuse was permitted, even if the licence had simply been left in a tent or with another official. Hotham, to Rede's delight, ordered sweeps at least twice a week to catch tax-dodgers. The operations were conducted like fox hunts. Armed 'traps' rode down diggers for sport. Men toiling 160 feet underground were expected to haul themselves back up to produce their licences for the entertainment of a smirking policeman. Even when the licences were produced the men could be left broiling in the sun for several hours until the paper was scrutinised. Independently minded, proud and hard-working men seethed as much over the indignity of the digger-hunts as over the fee itself. Others believed that only those with the hearts of slaves paid up.

A select committee inquiry found plenty of evidence that the diggers were being treated badly. Doctor Owens reported: 'The main objection of the diggers is to the mode of collecting the licence fee, since this is managed with so much offensiveness as to make the diggers appear like a criminal class, and digging like a crime.' George Purchase told the inquiry: 'The police are unpopular because of the power they have, and which they exercise frequently, of going into a man's tent and rifling and turning over his property to find grog, just whenever they please.'

Resentment was running highest in the Ballarat Basin, where Rede's writ was most enthusiastically enforced. It only needed one spark to trigger turmoil. The murder of James Scobie provided it.

* * *

The inquest into Scobie's death convened the next Monday and, to the astonishment of the onlookers, returned an open verdict. Bentley and his murderous friends were to escape justice. The resentment of the diggers boiled over. Here was proof positive that they were treated like vermin, liable to be killed at will by cronies of the ruling class. When nine of the jurors at the inquest had a change of heart, claiming they had been misdirected by the coroner, a court of inquiry was set up. John D'Ewes, a witness to the incident – possibly even its instigator – and well-known as a taker of bribes, sat on the board which decided by two to one that no charges should be laid against Bentley and his associates. It was a blatant fix, and fury spread through Ballarat and its outlying diggings.

On 17 October a meeting was convened outside the Eureka Hotel to discuss the 'unholy compact' between magistrates and crooked publicans. The mood was ugly as 5,000 diggers milled around outside while a terrified Bentley hid inside, drinking brandy. Rede dispatched a file of troopers under Sergeant-Major Robert Milne, a well-known bully, to ride through the crowd to support a line of policemen guarding the hotel. There were fiery speeches but order was kept, despite the provocation, by Peter Lalor, a quiet Irishman who was rapidly emerging as a leader of the diggers. His brother James was a hot-headed journalist who had been killed during an attack on a Tipperary police station during the 1849 Young Ireland uprisings. A trained engineer, who had worked on the Melbourne–Geelong railway before heading for the goldfields, Lalor was the son of a Home Rule supporter and landowner. But Lalor was no revolutionary and wanted little more than to work his claim to raise the cash he needed to buy a farm for himself and his planned bride. He believed that the rule of law would eventually redress wrongs. Lalor proposed that the meeting should pledge to 'use all lawful means to have the case brought before other, and more competent, authorities'. That proposal was carried, along with demands for a reward for the prosecution of Scobie's killers, and the meeting was then formally closed.

And that could have been it. But a hot wind was blowing, nerves were frayed, emotions aroused, and flasks of grog passed around. No one knows who started the violence. Some claimed that it was a trooper who sneered that the subscriptions would be used for drink, others that a drunken digger, Henry Westerby, called on his mates to pull Bentley out of his refuge. The cry went up: 'We'll smoke the bugger out.' Either way, the wood and tar paper hotel was soon blazing and Bentley, having been bundled out of the back door by a policeman, was soon riding for his life towards the army camp on the edge of the township.

Commissioner Rede watched the mob go wild, smashing everything which the flames did not consume. He was powerless to intervene as the official who had come ready to read a copy of the Riot Act dropped the document in panic. Troopers and police also stood impotently by. Rede, though horrified by the display of mob rule, later said that he was pleased that the diggers had now 'gone too far'. Rede reported the outrage in person to the governor in Melbourne the following day. Newspaper editorials expressed horror, and the capital's good burghers and property-owners demanded firm action. It was music to Rede's ears. Two diggers, Thomas Fletcher and Andrew McIntyre, were arrested virtually at random and were held at the Ballarat Camp. Later a hung-over Henry Westerby, who could barely remember the torching of the Eureka Hotel, was also picked up. They were to stand trial as an example to the rest.

Things did not go all Rede's way, however. Police Commissioner Charles McMahon said openly that the whole affair was Bentley's fault. It also began to dawn on the Melbourne administration that an open trial would involve evidence from the magistrate D'Ewes which might expose the level of official corruption. And then Attorney-General William Foster Stawell examined the evidence and concluded that Bentley and his associates should themselves stand trial. Sir Charles Hotham reluctantly agreed to hold an inquiry into the series of events but stipulated that the inquiry report would be for his eyes only. The results smelled so strongly of official corruption that Hotham was forced to conclude that some appeasement was necessary. D'Ewes was sacked as a magistrate and Sergeant-Major Milne was arrested for taking bribes. The governor agreed that Bentley and two associates should stand trial for manslaughter and cheers rang out across the goldfields when they were convicted and sentenced to three years' hard labour on the roads.

Again, the crisis could have been settled at this point. But the diggers had challenged authority and won a partial victory. They had become better organised under the committee elected to fight Scobie's case. Three of their comrades were also facing trial for riot and tumult at the Eureka Hotel. And the 'damned licence' was still there, despite Hotham's promise of a wider-ranging commission of inquiry into goldfield grievances. On the other side, the governor, Rede, the gold lace and the military were seething that crimes of insubordination to proper authority had gone unpunished. The downhill slide towards tragedy picked up pace again.

Feelings were inflamed when the rumour spread that the authorities were about to introduce 'Government by artillery' in the goldfields, enforcing the tax with cannon as well as bayonet, truncheon and chain. Another mass meeting at Ballarat on 11 November declared that taxation without representation was tyranny. That meeting passed off peaceably as diggers gathered with their wives and families in their Sunday best and voted for the Ballarat Reform League. But fury reasserted itself when the diggers learned that their three comrades had been sentenced to terms in Melbourne gaol – six months for Westerby, four for Fletcher and three for McIntyre.

By now several leaders had emerged among the unkempt diggers and they formed the backbone of the new Ballarat Reform League. Lalor, a civilising influence at every meeting, still believed there could be a peaceful resolution. He remembered the terrible injustices he had witnessed as a boy in Ireland and regarded himself as a true democrat rather than a republican or communist. 'If a democrat means opposition to a tyrannical press, a tyrannical people, or a tyrannical government,' he said, 'then I have been, I am still, and will ever remain a democrat.' George Black, the editor of the *Gold Diggers Advocate*, also wanted justice without further bloodshed and believed it was just possible. So, too, did John Basson Humffray, a curly-haired Chapel man with a fine tenor voice from Newton in Montgomeryshire, who hated the thought of taking another's life. Humffray, who articled as a solicitor, before succumbing to the lure of gold, was a Chartist with a lawyer's faith in legal channels.

More hot-headed were the balding Scots Radical Thomas Kennedy, a friend of the murdered Scobie, and Rafaello Carboni, a red-bearded Italian from Ursino who once trained for the priesthood.

Instead, he had become a clerk, then a soldier, being wounded three times in the service of the Young Italy movement, and later a language teacher in London. After emigration to Australia he had been a shepherd and lived for a time among the aborigines. He regarded British rule as akin to the Austrian oppression of his own home country. He was an exotic character and popular among the diggers. The same could not be said of Friedrich Vern, a bombastic Prussian who bought his way into the diggers' committee by promising a £100 loan, and then tried to dominate meetings with his boasts of unlikely military exploits in the service of red republicanism. Carboni, whose martial record was proven, detested him.

The men of the Ballarat Reform League shared common aims but had different agendas. All of them alarmed the Melbourne administration. Henry Seekamp, editor of the *Ballarat Times*, fed their paranoia when he wrote that the League was,

> not more or less than the germ of Australian independence. The die is cast, and fate has cast upon the movement its indelible signature. No power on earth can restrain the united might and headlong strides for freedom of the people in this country.

Black, Humffray and Kennedy comprised a delegation sent to see Governor Hotham in Melbourne on 27 November in one last attempt at conciliation. He greeted them stiffly and without offering any concessions beyond his earlier promise of a long-term Commission into goldfield conditions. The three jailed diggers would remain inside, the licence would be enforced, the digger hunts would continue. Hotham treated them 'with disdain' but by then it was probably too late anyway.

While they were still negotiating, a detachment of the 40th Regiment marched from Geelong to Ballarat to reinforce Rede's garrison. The miners greeted them first with foul oaths and ridicule, then with sticks and stones. Several soldiers were hurt in a vicious brawl around the baggage cart, and a drummer boy was shot in the leg during the confusion, most probably by a digger. A squadron of mounted police was also attacked with cudgels. The diggers, convinced that the iron might of the British Empire had been sent to crush them, fired weapons into the air all night. The soldiers and policemen, nursing their bruises and lost dignity, vowed bloody vengeance.

On 29 November another monster meeting was held on Bakery Hill, just outside the town. Here, the diggers unveiled their new, home-made standard, the Southern Cross, the work of Charles Ross. Friedrich Vern urged all those present to burn their hated licences. The next time the 'traps' came they would stand or fall together. One man set fire to his licence and threw it on the ground. One by one others followed suit until there was a bonfire blazing in the hot still air. A grog seller did good business with his black bottle. The chairman of the meeting, the normally placid Irishman Timothy Hayes, asked the company: 'Are you ready to die?' They replied with loud cries of affirmation and pistol shots.

All this was reported back to Commissioner Rede, who had a network of informers. He called a council of war with the senior army officers in Ballarat Camp and convinced them that only a show of force would prevent an armed rebellion. It was announced that the following morning there would be another licence hunt. At 10 a.m. Rede, backed by mounted police with swords drawn and foot soldiers with bayonets fixed, set out for the diggings. There was immediate trouble. A maddened crowd of about 70 diggers hurled stones and broken bottles.

Dozens of individual brawls broke out and above the bedlam Rede could be heard reading the Riot Act. Eight miners were surrounded and taken prisoner. Shots were fired by both sides, but not yet at each other. Some order was restored on both sides too, but by now it was too late. The die was truly cast. Diggers fell into line two abreast, and marched together towards that part of the diggings known as Eureka. Rumours spread that diggers had been butchered and that cannon were on the way. The call 'To arms' rang through the Ballarat Basin. 'This is madness,' Peter Lalor thought, and later recorded the same sentiment in his diary.

*　　*　　*

By 5 that afternoon 500 diggers had gathered on Bakery Hill below the Southern Cross, fluttering from a makeshift flagstaff. They were light-headed with excitement, pride, drink or fear, or any combination of the above. Each recorded his name and knelt below the flag to swear 'to stand truly by each other, and fight to defend our rights and liberties'. They elected Lalor their commander-in-chief, much to Vern's chagrin; he petulantly refused the Irishman's offer of second in command. Lalor, who abhorred violence, knew that they must prepare for the inevitable military onslaught. He said: 'I tell you, gentlemen, if once I pledge my hand to the diggers, I will neither defile it with treachery, nor render it contemptible with cowardice.'

The night passed in confused preparations for the oncoming storm. One last attempt was made at conciliation. George Black and Carboni went to the government camp under a flag of truce to submit their demands one last time to Rede. The commissioner would offer them nothing and objected strongly to the word 'demand'. The two-man delegation returned by starlight to Eureka.

Rede decided to play a waiting game. The diggers, he contemptuously reckoned, would disperse in the morning when their hangovers cleared. If not, reinforcements were on their way from Melbourne, armed, he had been assured, with field guns and howitzers. In the meantime the perimeter fence of the camp was strengthened with logs and bales. The 12th and 40th Foot were on stand-to, their pouches bulging with extra ammunition for their modern Minie rifles. Spies were sent into the enemy camp and Rede surmised that order would be swiftly imposed and the ring-leaders quickly and suitably dealt with. The morning light proved Rede wrong. Dawn showed that the number of diggers had swelled from 500 to 800, as mates came from across the goldfields. Throughout the first two days of December the diggers built their own stockade on high ground above the Eureka claim. Moreover, Rede soon received word that the promised heavy artillery had not left Melbourne.

The Eureka Stockade was poorly constructed from wooden pit-props known as slabs, branches and logs. It enclosed an acre of ground, and included John Diamond's store, Lalor's own hut and a smithy run by the German John Hafele. Shallow diggings outside the barricade were transformed into useful rifle pits. The stockade commanded the main road to Melbourne, but it could not have withstood cannon fire for a minute. Inside, Vern, wearing a long and cumbersome sword on his belt, drilled hobnail-booted diggers in Prussian style. The blacksmith produced a steady supply of pike-heads to be attached to shafts. The hill resembled a disturbed ants' nest.

On the first afternoon Thomas Kennedy, who had missed the previous day's mayhem, arrived with almost 300 new recruits from Creswick. Lalor's pleasant surprise turned to dismay when he realised the new men were armed only with pitchforks, and expected to be supplied with guns, beef stew and copious amounts of whiskey. Lalor could offer them only water after their long hot march. The commander-in-chief gloomily surveyed the crowded stockade and its outlying huts and realised that he could barely feed and house his own men, never mind the newcomers. He need not have worried. By the following morning most of the Creswick mob, realising there was no free grog, had drifted away, muttering that they would not fight with empty stomachs and clear heads.

That same Friday afternoon Governor Hotham, sweating in his airless Melbourne office, finally received the news that Major-General Sir Robert Nickle was on the march for Ballarat. His force consisted of the rest of the 12th and 40th Foot, naval detachments from HMS *Electra* and HMS *Fantome*, and heavy artillery which would shatter the Eureka stockade and all those within it. The governor had already sent Rede ambiguous orders to 'act with temper, caution and judgement, but to enforce the law'. He added that 'a Riot was rapidly growing into a Revolution'. Rede decided to wait for Nickle.

Early on Saturday morning the church made a half-hearted bid to stop a bloodbath. Ballarat's idealistic young priest, Father Smythe, was abandoned by his bishop and walked into the stockade alone to address his congregation. He told them:

I know you are preparing to do battle in what you believe to be a just cause, but I implore you to count the cost. There are seven or eight hundred men under arms within the Camp.

I know for a fact that more are on their way. You are not well-armed or well-trained. Although your hearts may be pure, you cannot fight cannon with pikes.

Looking individual diggers in the eye he went on: 'I ask you to give thought to your womenfolk and children. Don't deprive them of husbands and fathers. Don't reap a harvest of tears, my sons. Bring them instead to Mass tomorrow and let us all pray together for salvation.' At that, a man in the front rank threw down his pike and walked away. The ranks disintegrated as others followed him, to the catcalls of former comrades and the curses of Vern. Most, however, stayed.

That afternoon, tired of meaningless drill, many of the defenders drifted between stockade and home. As night approached it became clear that more of them, nagged by wives or tempted by the normal Saturday night pub session, were not coming back. However, at 4 p.m. the tide was turned when James McGill arrived with 200 men of his Independent Californian Rangers Revolver Brigade, marching stoutly uphill in riding breeches and slouch-hats, wearing pistols and long knives on their belts. McGill was a mysterious figure who recruited fellow Americans to spread the Republican movement across the goldfields. Some suspected he was an *agent provocateur* or a double-agent. The diggers cheered their new comrades from across the ocean and clapped them on the back. Their reputation for deadly pistol-fighting matched the drill and discipline of the redcoats. McGill also brought Lalor the long-feared news that General Nickle was on his way with two field guns and two howitzers. The confident American offered to intercept Nickle's column and destroy the artillery in a guerrilla strike. Lalor gave the enterprise his blessing and all but twenty of the Americans marched off again. Later it was said that McGill had been warned by American envoys that he and his men would pay dearly if their intervention sparked a diplomatic crisis with Britain. Whatever the truth, McGill never found Nickle's column and never returned to the stockade.

More diggers, convinced that the British would not attack on the Sabbath, set off for the hotels and their other usual Saturday night drinking haunts. There they spouted whiskey breath and fine words about how they would slay the oppressors. Lalor sent seventy men away on some ill-conceived errand. By midnight there were barely 150 diggers left within the stockade, although many more intended to return the following day once they had slept off the effects of their binge.

Intelligence to that effect was passed to Commissioner Rede by an American spy, Doctor Charles Kenworthy, who had visited the stockade on the pretext of offering medical help. He reported:

> A more disorganised gang I never did see. Some of them presenting broomsticks to a Prussian who keeps falling over his sword. Others out looting. Lalor is more like a schoolmaster whose pupils like and respect him for his honesty and high purpose but who also like to get up to mischief behind his back. And that stockade of theirs – why, it wouldn't keep out a prairie dog.

Kenworthy also boasted to Rede that it was he who had persuaded McGill and his men to leave.

The soldiers and policemen in the camp were eager to take revenge for their earlier humiliations. To the delight of their senior officers, Captains Pasley, Thomas and Wise, Rede decided on a gamble. He would not wait for Nickle but would strike before dawn while the rebels were depleted, at their weakest and asleep, possibly intoxicated. He argued that it would mean a swift end to the deadlock and would reduce the heavy casualties which were certain to be incurred once Nickle's artillery arrived. The officers also would win greater credit for themselves if the rebellion was crushed before their commander-in-chief arrived.

A plan of action was devised by lamplight, and the force of 276 men was given an hour's notice early on Sunday 3 December. The storming party was to be led by Captain Henry Wise, with forty picked men of the 12th and 40th, and twenty-four foot police. They were to be flanked by 70 mounted police on the right and 30 mounted infantry on the left. The remainder of the attacking force would be held to the south as a reserve. Their route was not along the main road, as the rebels expected, because the noise of marching boots would be sure to give them away. Instead it was to be a circuitous slog through heavy bush, converging on the stockade at first light. Captain Thomas, the most senior officer, said: 'A dawn assault, sir, should be highly effective, catching most of the beggars fast asleep but giving us enough light to see by.' Rede replied: 'Then let us take a glass together, gentlemen, and drink to your success.'

The approach went as planned. Captain Wise, twenty-six years old, popular with his men, and raring for his first real taste of action, was sure that the enemy would hear the snap and crack of dry leaves and twigs as they neared the stockades. He was right, but the noise was twice regarded as a false alarm by those digger watchmen who remained awake. More splashings and whinnies were heard and ignored as the mounted police and soldiers crossed a small creek.

Dawn's red light shone on the buckles and blades of the government force as the men lined up to attack. Captain Thomas gave the order: 'Pass the word. Advance.' A line of redcoats, bayonets fixed, walked steadily towards the stockade, with Captain Wise and Lieutenant Paul out in front. Inside the defences Lalor was woken by a sudden crackle of fire and the shout: 'Stand to. Stand to. Redcoats.' On the west side of the stockade the diggers and some of the remaining Americans opened up a ragged but well-directed fire. Mounted redcoats were seen pouring out of the bush on one side, while a solid mass of blue-coated troopers emerged from the other. Carboni, who had been sleeping in his tent outside the stockade, heard an English voice cry: 'Steady men. A volley when you hear the bugle.'

At 200 yards Wise's infantry dressed into two lines, one kneeling, the other standing, and let rip the volley as the boy bugler sounded his horn. The Minie rifle was accurate up to 300 yards and the infantry were well-practised. The effect on those diggers who, bleary-eyed, had reached the stockade's parapet was devastating. Carboni later described how every head that was showing when the volley crashed was gone an instant later. The bullets tore through the spindly defences into the muscle, bone and guts of men. Lalor, who had stood on the parapet to urge on his men, fell with wounds in his shoulder, arm and sides. A high proportion of the overall casualties were suffered in that first, terrible blast. Vern, the Prussian braggart, was among the first to run. Others followed but many more stood firm while the remaining Americans kept a cool fire with their Colts from the rifle-pits. Patrick Curtain, who had tried to shoot Vern when he saw him run, rallied his band of pike-men, their blades newly gleaming from the forge.

Captain Wise ran full-pelt up the hill, roaring his head off as his men struggled to keep up with him. On each flank the cavalry and mounted police reached their ends of the stockade. But, 100 yards short of his target, Wise was hit in the knee. He struggled to rise but was shot again in the other leg. The official dispatch noted: 'Wounded in two places at the head of his men, as he lay on his back he cheered them on to the attack.' The stricken officer told Sergeant Hagerty: 'Keep going! At 'em, the 40th!'

His men did just that, their bloodlust high. Several soldiers fell in that last charge, but they were swiftly avenged by their comrades as infantry and horsemen swept over the flimsy defences. The long, unwieldy shafts of Curtain's pike-men were hopeless against disciplined bayonet-thrusts and sabre-cuts. The result was, inevitably, a bloodbath. A pike-man shot in both legs swept his weapon around like the hands of a clock until he was shot in the head. An American, shot in one leg, was seen hopping on the other, firing his Colt until the chambers were empty and he was cut down. John Hafele, the blacksmith and pike-maker, suffered a sabre slash which took off the top of his skull. Another German, the talented chess-player and lemonade-seller Edward Thonen, was shot full in the mouth. Some diggers who tried to escape into the bush were in turn run down. Police and military men stabbed and shot indiscriminately, and set fire to everything that might burn. Several wounded diggers took refuge in John Diamond's store but it was set ablaze. Carboni wrote: 'The howling and yelling was horrible. The wounded are now burnt to death; those who had laid down their arms, and taken refuge within the tents, were kicked like brutes and made prisoners.' Diamond was shot down as he tried to escape the flames. Two diggers, who had slept unawares in a drunken coma throughout the mayhem, were consumed by fire when their tent was torched.

Charles Ross was cut to pieces as he tried to defend the Southern Cross, the flag which he had so lovingly designed himself. Trooper

John King from County Mayo climbed the flagstaff and hauled down the standard. Cheering soldiers stabbed it with bayonets, and trampled it into the dirt. The soldiers threatened to murder every prisoner but Captain Pasley ordered that any man who did so should be shot. Captain Thomas ordered the firing to cease. The blood-lust ebbed away and his men obeyed. The entire battle had taken just 15 minutes. A contemporary report said:

> After burning all the tents within the enclosure, and in the immediate vicinity, the troops returned to camp, and carts were sent out for the dead and wounded. The latter thus obtained immediate medical aid. They were covered in blood and mostly shot in the breast. Among the arms taken in the fight were pikes of a rude construction, made on the spot and furnished with a sort of hooked knife to cut the bridles of the cavalry.

Throughout the engagement Peter Lalor lay semi-conscious under a pile of slabs and cut turf outside the stockade. His arm shattered, he was hidden by a digger called Ashburner. Carboni, who had taken no part in the fighting, tried to rescue some papers from a burning tent, but was stopped by a trooper who shot his cabbage-tree hat off his head. He became a meek captive, shocked by the speed with which his dreams had been destroyed.

Twenty-four insurgents died in the brief battle. At least ten were from Ireland, with two each from England, Scotland, Germany and Canada. Several names went unrecorded, including the real name of a man known on the goldfields as Happy Jack. The death toll may have been much higher, if subsequent reports of diggers dying in the bush or being hunted down by vengeful troopers are to be believed. Around 20 more were wounded and 114 taken prisoner. Father Smythe read the last rites over smouldering corpses while Doctor Carr did his best for the wounded, before being arrested as a rebel sympathiser. Inevitably, in such a confused and bitter engagement, there were conflicting reports, particularly over the performance of both sides and the behaviour of the police units. One correspondent to the *Argus*, who described himself as a 'military man', wrote:

The Camp Officer says the police were first to enter the Stockade. He is wrong. There was not a single policeman killed or wounded during the whole affair. When Captain Wise fell the men cleared, and were over in the Stockade in a second, and then bayonet and pike went to work. The diggers fought well and fierce, not a word spoken on either side until all was over. The blacksmith who made the pikes was killed by Lieutenant Richards of the 40th. Honour to his name: he fought well and died gloriously.

It was rumoured that the police were cruel to the wounded and prisoners. No such thing. The police did nothing but their duty, and they did it well for men that were not accustomed to scenes of blood or violence. To my knowledge there was only one wounded man despatched, and he kept swinging his pike around his head as he sat on the ground. He was shot in the legs and had a ball in his breast. He could not live and it was best to despatch him. His name was O'Neill, a native of Kilkenny, Ireland. I heard this statement from a sergeant of police and I know it was correct.

Another correspondent recorded the aftermath:

The dead was buried the same day in the cemetery. The bodies of the insurgents, placed in rough coffins made hurriedly, were laid in a separate grave, the burial service being performed by the clergyman to whose congregation they belonged. At night we were again under arms, as constant rumours of an intended attack kept us on the alert. This is exhausting work, and a severe trial, especially for the military, as the men have had no real rest for several nights. Indeed, no-one within the lines has undressed for the last four nights at the very least.

Government men buried that first day were Privates Michael Roney and Joseph Wall of the 40th. The wounded wagons took away thirteen men, including Privates William Webb, Felix Boyle and John Hall, all of the 12th, who would subsequently die of their injuries. Captain Wise joked with his men that his dancing days were over. Gangrene infected his legs, and the *Argus* reported: 'Amputation is considered necessary. This is but the beginning of the end.' He died four days before Christmas. The governor praised the 'gallant and valuable officer'.

Around the wreckage of the Eureka stockade the dust settled to the cries of newly made widows and orphans, but the business of the day soon reasserted itself. The great chronicler Manning Clark wrote:

> The shopkeepers were wondering when buying and selling would start again; the tipplers were wondering how long they must wait before they could get a drink. No-one on the field or in the camp detected any majesty in the moment or prophesied that the diggers would one day be heroes of the people and hailed as the founders of democracy in Australia. Law and order had been restored. The shutters of the shops could now be removed and the flaps on the sly-grog tent tied back.

*　　*　　*

Peter Lalor, buried under a pile of wood, slipped in and out of consciousness. He was found by Father Smythe and a manservant who took him to a trusted digger and his wife near Mount Warrenhelp. More dead than alive, he was treated by a Kilkenny man, Doctor Timothy Doyle, who decided that his arm was beyond repair – shattered fragments of bone protruded from the flesh. The following day the arm was amputated.

The digger prisoners were meanwhile squashed into the government camp lock-up alongside more common criminals, riddled with lice and fleas. Carboni wrote: 'This vermin, and the heat of the season, and the stench of the place, and the horror of my situation, had rendered life intolerable to me.' The authorities, fearful that some rebels would die before they could stand trial, eventually moved the Eureka men to the better-ventilated camp storeroom.

Major-General Sir Robert Nickle finally arrived at the Ballarat diggings with his field guns and howitzers. But instead of menacing the truculent diggers he visited their encampments, unescorted, and found 'not the slightest expression of feeling' against the Crown.

Embarrassed by his report, Governor Hotham lifted Martial Law three days later.

Hotham, as ever egged on by Rede, was still convinced that the goldfields were about to explode in revolutionary fury. Posters were tacked up offering a £500 reward for Friedrich Vern, still supposed to be the ringleader – due to his own boasting, and £200 apiece for Lalor and George Black. He thanked the queen's faithful subjects for ending the anarchy created by 'strangers in their midst'. And he ordered that every one of the 114 prisoners should be charged with insurrection, a capital offence. Henry Seekamp, the editor of the *Ballarat Times*, responded with an editorial calling for vengeance for the 'foul massacre' inflicted on the Eureka diggers. Hotham had him thrown into a gaol on charges of sedition. The governor's tough reaction split the population. In Melbourne, which had been thrown into panic by the first reports of insurrection, people were divided into those who demanded the restoration of law and order, and those who condemned the government as a 'set of wholesale butchers'.

Gradually tempers cooled on both sides. On 6 December 6,000 people gathered next to the city's St Paul's Church and vowed that in future reform must be sought by peaceful, constitutional and moral force alone. It soon became clear, also, that Govenor Hotham had over-reacted. It was simply not feasible to feed and house over 100 prisoners and mount a full and fair trial of them all. The numbers had already been whittled down by pragmatic officers and by the intervention of Doctor Kenworthy, who negotiated the release of all captured Americans in order to avoid a diplomatic row with his country. The only exception was John Josephs, the blacksmith's assistant who had helped to make rebel pikes. He was black, and therefore his execution was hardly likely to provoke a storm at home.

On 8 December just thirteen of the Eureka prisoners were committed for trial at the Supreme Court in Melbourne on the charge of high treason. They appeared to have been chosen more or less at random. Carboni, who protested that he had never fired a shot or raised a pike, was shackled to Josephs. Timothy Hayes, Michael Tuehey and John Manning were designated as ringleaders. The remainder appear to have played only small roles in the Eureka drama. The following Tuesday they were chained into three carts which set off for Melbourne under the command of Captain Thomas. He told them that if they so much as turned their heads they would be shot. They were guarded by over thirty troopers until they were safely locked up in the city gaol.

A campaign immediately began to win them amnesty. John Basson Humffray, who had taken no part in the fighting, presented a petition signed by 4,500 Ballarat miners. The document claimed that the Eureka men 'did not take up arms, properly speaking, against the government, but to defend themselves against the bayonets, bullets and swords of the insolent officials in their unconstitutional attack . . .'. The delegation argued that clemency would prevent further dissent from turning into a movement for separation from the Mother Country. Hotham remained, however, a stiff-backed Royal Navy officer, and to his mind there was to be no shirking the due process of law. That process, from his point of view, quickly became a shambles.

The state trials of the Eureka men began on 22 February. The first to stand trial for their lives were John Josephs and John Manning. After an impassioned speech by Butler Cole Aspinall, a brilliant young lawyer from Liverpool, the jury found them not guilty. They were carried out shoulder-high by a cheering crowd. Hotham and his Attorney-General, William Foster Stawell, delayed the subsequent trials in the hope that the public mood would swing against the diggers. The next were held on 19 March before Justice Redmond Barry, a graduate of King's College, Dublin. Timothy Hayes spoke in his own defence, saying: 'I did everything in my power to bring about a peaceful resolution of our grievances. But that final licence-hunt was the last straw and, from then on, we were overtaken by events beyond the control of mere mortals.' He walked from the dock a free man. So too, a little later, did Rafaello Carboni. Evidence from soldiers and policemen that he had picked up a pike in the stockade was contradictory, and the assertion that he was one of those who had burnt his digger's licence was refuted when the Italian flourished the intact, and correctly dated, document in the courtroom. Another bout of 'spirited, cutting and withering' defence from Aspinall ensured that the jury took only 20 minutes to clear him.

The governor and his law officers were lampooned in the Press and *The Age* reviewed the proceedings as it would 'an exceedingly successful farce'. A Dutchman, Jan Vennik, was cleared next, and then James Beattie, Michael Tuehey and Thomas Dignam from Sydney. On 27 March the remaining accused – Henry Reid, James MacFie Campbell, William Molloy, Jacob Sorenson and John Phelan – also walked free. The *Argus* reported that the men were 'escorted from the Court by a large company who frequently raised loud plaudits on their way down Stephen Street'.

This legal fiasco was a bitter blow to Hotham's pride and authority. It was followed, on the same day, by the report of the Gold Fields Commission which Hotham himself had set up as a delaying tactic, and which he was committed to implement. With one stroke the Ballarat Reform League won virtually all the reforms they had demanded before the bloodshed. The hated licence tax was abolished in favour of a Miner's Right, costing just £1 a year, which would act as the title deed to his claim and thereby give him the right to vote. Diggers were to be elected to local courts and the power of the 'gold lace' was over. The diggers, as part of a burgeoning democracy, would have the right to manage their own affairs. The loss of revenue to the government was to be made up from an export duty on gold bullion.

Further humiliated, Sir Charles Hotham continued to do what he regarded as his duty and thus became ever more unpopular. After a clash with the Legislative Council in 1855, he offered to resign, but before it took effect, he went to open the new Melbourne gasworks in December. Sadly for him, he caught a chill and died on New Year's Eve. The wily Commissioner Robert Rede fared better. He married the daughter of a renowned explorer, became Sheriff of Melbourne in 1877 and lived in the city until his death from pneumonia in 1904.

The collapse of the Eureka prosecutions and the commission's report allowed the fugitive rebels to come out of hiding. George Black and Thomas Kennedy had fled to Geelong, changing their clothes and cutting their hair as a disguise. Frederick Vern, who sent boastful letters to the Press claiming he had escaped tyranny by boat, had in fact tramped to his hiding-place in Melbourne dressed as a woman.

Peter Lalor, recovered from his amputation, emerged as a hero. He married his fiancée Alicia and bought a farm with a cheque for £1,000 from a fund raised by grateful diggers. He was the first digger to be elected to the Legislative Council in 1855. He was later appointed Postmaster-General and Commissioner for Trade and Customs. In 1880 he became Speaker of the House of Assembly. He died in Melbourne in February 1889.

Rafaello Carboni published a popular account of the events at the Eureka stockade from the diggers' point of view a year after the tragedy. He served on the new Local Court at Ballarat but left Australia for further adventures early in 1856. He travelled to India, China and the Middle East, promoting the cause of Italian freedom. He became an unsuccessful dramatist in Naples and died in Rome during the 1870s.

The two men whose villainy led directly to the tragedy of Eureka did not enjoy the peace. The crooked magistrate John D'Ewes emigrated to British Columbia, where he was arrested for embezzlement. He later committed suicide in Paris. James Bentley, his drinking companion on that fateful night in the Eureka Hotel, served only part of his sentence for the killing of James Scobie. After his release in 1856 he turned to the brandy bottle and the medicine cabinet. In April 1873 he deliberately took a huge overdose of laudanum at his house in Ballarat Street, Melbourne. He left a wife and five children.

A monument in the Old Cemetery, Ballarat, carries the inscription: 'Sacred to the memory of those who fell on the memorable 3rd December, 1854 in resisting the Unconstitutional Proceedings of the Victorian Government.' And schoolchildren are still taught the stirring words of Peter Lalor, the reluctant leader of the Eureka uprising, who wrote:

I looked around me; I saw brave and honest men who had come thousands of miles to labour for independence. The grievances under which we had long suffered, and the brutal attack of that day, flashed across my mind; and with the burning feelings of the injured man, I mounted the stump and proclaimed Liberty.

However, Governor Hotham was right in one sense at least. After the shock of Eureka, moderates took over on both sides. The only call to revolution ever made on Australian soil was quickly snuffed out and the diggers became good, true capitalists. Their earnings increased and they spent their wealth freely, creating a new market for goods and a boom time for the young colony. It was a new colonial phenomenon and it was exploited to the hilt. Thus the real victors of Eureka Stockade were bankers, merchants and gold-buyers. In London Karl Marx mourned another lost opportunity.

TWENTY-FIVE

The Defence of Kars, Turkey, 1855

'Firm as a rock on duty . . .'

A correspondent for the *Illustrated London News* reported:

> In a few minutes the whole force of the Russians charged up the
> hill with loud cries; they were received with a terrible fire of
> grape and musketry which mowed them down whole ranks at
> every volley. The position was attacked by eight battalions of
> the enemy; they advanced very gallantly to within five paces of
> the work, when so heavy a fire was opened at the head of the
> column that the whole corps wavered, halted, then turned and
> fled in the greatest confusion . . .

This account, though written in 1855, did not describe an action
at Balaclava or any of the other well-remembered battles of the
Crimean War. Instead, it concerned a generally forgotten sideshow
to the main event, peopled by a handful of remarkable British
adventurers and one of the most unjustly neglected generals of the
Victorian era.

*   *   *

In 1854 a 21-year-old artillery lieutenant, Christopher Charles
Teesdale, met up with a handful of British officers in the wilds of
eastern Turkey. With the Crimean War raging on the other side of
the Black Sea, it was a strange appointment for ambitious young
soldiers eager for battle and advancement. Teesdale, the son of
General Henry Teesdale of South Bersted in Sussex, had entered
the Royal Military Academy at Woolwich at the age of fourteen and
received a commission at eighteen. A conventional Victorian army
career seemed inevitable. His first posting was to Corfu, but he then

embarked on an unconventional adventure which was to win him glory and a favoured position by Queen Victoria's side . . .

Teesdale was appointed *aide-de-camp* to Colonel William Fenwick Williams, a 53-year-old fellow misfit with fourteen years' service in Turkey, who had just been appointed British commissioner to the Turkish army in Anatolia. It was not reckoned to be a very difficult task, hence the appointment of such junior staff. In fact, Williams and Teesdale were to play leading roles in one of the epic sieges of the nineteenth century.

Their role in what in London was called the 'War in the East' was the result of the complex power struggles between an ever-expanding imperial Russia and its neighbouring empires. The Ottoman Empire had been in decline for 200 years and Russia had been the main beneficiary. The early Russo-Turkish wars – and there were ten after 1676 – were generally sparked by Russia's attempts to secure a warm-water port on the Black Sea, then an Ottoman lake. In the war of 1768–74 the Russians captured the Crimea, Azov and Bessarabia and defeated several Turkish armies. The treaty which concluded that war gave Russia the right to maintain a fleet on the Black Sea, advanced her territory in the south and gave her vague rights of protection over the Ottoman Sultan's Christian citizens. Further wars saw Russia take control of much of the Balkans and the Ukrainian Black Sea coast, and her victory in the 1828–9 conflict threatened Turkish sovereignty over the straits which flowed into the Mediterranean. Britain and France viewed the Russian expansion as a threat to their own interests in the Middle East. The Treaty of Edirne gave Russia most of the eastern shore of the Black Sea, and Turkey recognised Russia's claim over Georgia and parts of present-day Armenia. Russian influence was creeping ever closer towards India.

The Crimean War was detonated by a row between Russian Orthodox monks and French Catholics over who had precedence at the holy shrines of Jerusalem and Nazareth. After some bloodshed, Tsar Nicholas I demanded the right to protect all the Holy Land's Christian shrines. To back up his demands he moved troops into the Ottomon provinces of Wallachia and Moldavia. His fleet sank a Turkish flotilla off Sinope in the Black Sea and again threatened the straits of Constantinople. British newspapers carried reports that the Russians had slaughtered Turkish wounded in the water. Propaganda or not, it prepared the populace for a 'just' war. Britain, deeply suspicious of Russian intentions in Central Asia, sided with the Turks. The French Emperor Louis Napoleon III, anxious to recreate the military glory of his illustrious uncle, in turn allied France to Britain. Both countries dispatched expeditionary forces to the region, which arrived in March 1854. Britain's military commander was Lord Raglan, who had last seen action at Waterloo. The French commander, General St Arnaud, fell victim to cholera and was replaced by the veteran General Canrobert. The allied forces swiftly drove the Russians out of the Balkans, and the war could have been over by the summer if the Allies had not believed that the great Russian naval base at Sevastapol posed a direct threat to the future security of the region. In September they landed on the Crimean peninsula.

The catalogue of disasters which followed does not need to be repeated here. Apart from their victory at Alma, the bloodbath of Inkerman and the heroic absurdities of Balaclava, the allies became bogged down in the long siege of Sevastapol. The Russian winter, cholera and other diseases, infected and rotten supplies, appalling generalship and even greater incompetence among the quartermasters, starvation and exhaustion, all killed more than enemy cannon and musketball. Only the work of Florence Nightingale and other nurses in the British hospital at Scutari offered any relief from the dismal saga of negligence and stupidity. The war became one of attrition, spadework and artillery.

But there was another war being fought beyond the eastern shores of the Black Sea, between another Turkish army and the Russian divisions under General Mouravieff. It was well away from the main theatre of action, but a Turkish collapse there would have had a devastating impact on the wider conflict. Early in 1854 the Turks were badly beaten at Kuruk-deri and their demoralized eastern army was fast turning into a rabble. British observers blamed the 'corruption, ignorance, prejudice, want of public spirity' of the Pashas or officers and chiefs. The troops were badly treated and died in droves from disease and starvation. The names of many of the dead remained on the muster rolls to allow the senior officers to collect their salaries and allowances. The Turks were fighting a better-trained but numerically inferior Russian army. Moreover they were fighting in their own mountainous homelands and could invoke Islam to obtain help from the fierce but devout hill tribes of the region. The Russians should have been beaten back but Kurukderi showed that training and discipline could far outweigh numbers and local knowledge. *The Times* correspondent wrote:

> With a vivid impression of the whole engagement, from the first cannon shot to the last straggling discharge of musketry, I can use no language too strong to express my mis-approbation of nearly four-fifths of the Turkish officers present. In accounting for the defeat of an army numbering nearly 40,000 men of all arms by a hostile force of less than one half of that number, it is not sufficient to say that the management of the whole battle on the side of the Turks was a series of blunders from the first to last; strategical errors might have protracted the engagement, and added to the cost of a victory, but downright cowardice alone – which no generalship could have reduced – gave the day to the Russians.

The conduct of the Turks on the Crimean peninsula itself gave the British and French good cause to have mixed feelings about their compatriots. Around 3,000 Turkish troops fought at Balaclava, and 500 of them put up a stout resistance on the Fedioukine Heights against 10,000 Russians, despite being subjected to bombardment from thirty guns. Their stand cost them 170 dead and gave the Allies an extra hour to rally their forces. But later in the battle other Turkish troops took fright under bombardment and fled from a rise near Kadikoi, leaving Campbell's Highlanders exposed. The British judged them fine enough fighters, but badly led by decadent officers.

Mouravieff was busy collecting a large and well-equipped army at Gumri and was advancing towards the key towns of Kars and Erzerum; his long-term aim was the capture of the port of Trebizond, through which the Turks were supplied. Kars was the gateway to

Trebizond. At the end of July Colonel Williams was sent to represent British interests with the Turkish army in Anatolia, under the orders of Lord Raglan. He was to aid, inform and cooperate, but few initially saw him assuming effective command.

Williams was well qualified for his new role. Born in Nova Scotia late in 1800, the son of the barrack-master at Halifax, he entered the Woolwich Royal Military Academy. His early career was held up by the reduction of the army following Waterloo and he did not receive his commission as a second lieutenant in the Royal Artillery until 1825. His advancement through the officer ranks was also slow, due to the lack of action and the few opportunities available in postings to Gibraltar, Ceylon and home stations. His big break came in 1841 when, already middle-aged, he was sent to Turkey to work in the arsenal at Constantinople. As a British commissioner he was involved in the conferences which preceded various treaties, both to end conflicts with Russia and to settle border disputes with Persia. By 1852 he was highly regarded as a peacetime soldier, diplomat and expert on Turkish affairs and, made up to brevet-colonel, was the natural choice for the task.

In discussions with Lord Raglan it was agreed that the Turkish army needed both practical support and advice. Neither Raglan nor Williams then fully realised the poor state of their ally's forces facing the Russian forces in the east. In September Williams, with Teesdale, arrived at Erzerum, where they discovered to their dismay that the Turkish troops in that strategically important city could not muster 1,000 men. Those who were standing to arms were nursing a grievance: none had received any pay for at least 15 months. It was a taste of things to come.

Williams then moved on to Kars where the Turkish army numbered 28,000 men, many of whom were 22 months in arrears of pay; Williams wrote: 'Their patience under so glaring an injustice was truly praiseworthy.' The defences at Kars were in a poor state and the troops, who had suffered famine the previous winter, wore tattered uniforms and disintegrating boots. The four regiments of cavalry were in a 'wretched plight' and the horses were 'small and in a bad condition'. Only the artillery passed muster, with 162 guns all in working order. Another witness wrote that the condition of the garrison was so wretched 'as to fill us with forebodings for the ensuing campaign'.

There is evidence that such sentiments were shared by senior figures in the Turkish government. Rizza Pasha, the minister for war, quietly recommended to the new army commander that 'the frontier fortresses should be abandoned, if he thought they could not be held'.

Williams also quickly realised that the Kars garrison would be no match for the Russians who were already beginning to move towards this pivotal town. Leaving Teesdale behind to winter with the Turkish army and establish what discipline he could, Williams returned to Erzerum. He could see a disaster in the making and was determined to prevent it. He got precious little help.

Williams petitioned the British Embassy at Constantinople and the Foreign Office to send the Turkish forces the supplies, clothing, ammunition and money they so desperately needed if the Russians were to be halted as they swept around the eastern shores of the Black Sea. His most urgent demand was for 20,000 pairs of boots and 10,000 shirts and drawers. He was blocked at every turn by the ambassador to the Turkish capital, Lord Stratford de Redcliffe. Unsurprisingly, His Lordship's main preoccupation was the provisioning of the British forces outside Sevastapol, themselves facing a harsh winter. His incompetence, however, was demonstrated by his stewardship, as senior British official, of the appalling conditions at Scutari, which Florence Nightingale first encountered. A long and bitter correspondence began, with Williams complaining angrily to Lord Clarendon, the Foreign Secretary, about Stratford's neglect and delay in providing material. Stratford in turn blamed the corruption of the Turkish Pashas and officials.

Williams's first full report on conditions at Kars caused consternation in the British Embassy at Therapia. His language was so blunt that the report could not be passed on to the Turkish authorities without risking a severe breach in the alliance. Williams demanded the sacking of several Pashas and other commanders for cowardice, theft and incompetence. He claimed that the wounded had been forced to become beggars while 'drunkenness prevails to a great degree among those of higher rank'. Kars could not accommodate more than 10,000 soldiers within its walls, he wrote, because of the risk from disease. Europeans should be employed to oversee the drills and sanitation. The Turkish NCOs did not bother with rifle and musket practice. 'Men much neglected as to their comforts. The great copper cauldrons dangerous from want of tinning. Butter rancid and musty – as bad as possible – though used for pilaff.' On and on went his catalogue of complaints.

Eventually even Stratford was forced to take notice. He lodged an official complaint with the Turkish government, couched in rather more diplomatic terms than Williams would have wanted, saying that Britain would not tolerate inaction or cowardice by the Pashas. The Grand Vizier, Reshid Pasha, promised to investigate, although little was actually done. But later, bombarded with further evidence of their own failings, the Turkish government agreed that Williams should have overall command of Kars, with the Pashas being subordinate to his orders.

During this frustrating period Williams also busied himself building up Erzerum's defences and fortifying the surrounding heights. His efforts so impressed the Turkish commanders that he was made a *ferik*, or lieutenant-general, in their army. He was aided by another remarkable man, a 32-year-old army physician called Humphrey Sandwith. The son of a leading Hull doctor and surgeon, he at first followed his father and was appointed house surgeon at Hull Infirmary. Ill-health forced him to resign and he decided to seek adventure in the Near East. He made diplomatic friends in Constantinople, and spent nearly two years with archaeologists in Mesopotamia before he was incapacitated by a bout of fever. He was briefly a correspondent for *The Times* but its then editor Delane judged him too pro-Turkish. On the outbreak of the Crimean War he was engaged as staff surgeon to a British-officered corps of Bashi-Bazouks on the Danube. The corps saw no action but was devastated by sickness. Sandwith eked out his meagre medical supplies by gathering herbs in the meadows and leeches in the marshes. Joining Williams at Erzerum, he took charge of sanitation and the military hospital. He found the dispensary contained few drugs but was packed with cosmetics and scents.

Meanwhile Teesdale was doing what he could to improve the defences at Kars. A contemporary account illustrated some of the difficulties:

Kars is situated under a precipitous range of rocky hills which run east and west, and are divided by a deep gorge, through which flows the river Karachai. The western extremity of the range is called Takmash, and the eastern, Karadagh; the former is about two miles distant from the town, and the latter about a mile. To the south of Kars a wide level plain extends for several miles, until it meets the slopes of a line of low hills. The fortifications of the place consisted of a number of *tabias*, or redoubts placed in the most commanding positions.

On all four sides the outer defences were strengthened with small forts, breastworks and redoubts. The Turkish artillery commander, Tahir Pasha, was given clear fields of fire for his gunners. Some queried whether such preparations were justified to defend such an insignificant Asian town. Dr Sandwith himself had not been impressed on first sight. He wrote:

The streets are narrow and dirty, the people sordid in appearance, and the chief employment of the women appears to be the fabrication of *tezek*, or dried cow-dung for fuel, cakes of which are plastered over the walls of every home.

In fact Kars, sitting on a plateau 5,740 feet above sea level and dominated by an ancient citadel that overhung the river, had a bloody history which bore testimony to its strategic importance. The seat of an independent Armenian principality during the ninth and tenth centuries, it was captured by the Seljuqs in the eleventh, by the Mongols in the thirteenth and by Tamerlane in 1387. It was incorporated into the Ottoman Empire in 1514.

Throughout the winter Teesdale, aided by his interpreter Mr Zohrab, worked incessantly to improve moral, discipline and order among the Turkish troops. Dr Sandwith, in his memoirs, wrote that Teesdale 'exhibited such a rare combination of firmness and conciliatory tact that he won all hearts'. The grey-bearded General Kherim Pasha 'never ventured on any act of importance without first consulting this young subaltern of infantry'. The Foreign Office later lauded Teesdale's efforts in 'averting from the garrison at Kars the horrors that they suffered from famine the previous winter'. The Turkish army at Kars, under the nominal command of the Mushir, Vassif Pasha, consisted of 13,900 infantry, 1,500 cavalry, 1,500 artillerymen and 42 field guns.

The Russian army gathering for the attack consisted of 28,000 infantry, 7,500 cavalry and 64 pieces of artillery. The commander, General Mouravieff, had been a young officer at an earlier siege of Kars in 1828 and knew the lay-out of the town. Mouravieff was the son of an ancient Russian family, distinguished in literature as well as arms. Even the London Press regarded him as a hero of the old school. Fighting with Paskiewitsch in the earlier Turkish war he gained a reputation for bravery, while later campaigns confirmed his good generalship. The British knew him as a canny, courteous and utterly ruthless opponent.

Against such an adversary Vassif Pasha was grateful for all the help he could get from his British experts and advisers. In the early spring of 1855 Teesdale was joined by 26-year-old Henry Langhorne Thompson, an Old Etonian who had served with the British Army in Burma and now a volunteer major in the Turkish army, and Lieutenant-Colonel Sir Henry Atwell Lake, Williams's second-in-command. Lake had previously served with the Madras Engineers, engaged mainly in irrigation works in India. His engineering skills were to prove invaluable in strengthening the defences at Kars.

On 1 June Williams, now promoted by Britain to major-general, heard that the Russian army was advancing on Kars. He rushed to the fortified town, arriving on the 7th when he reviewed the troops and inspected the defences. Despite the minor miracles worked by Teesdale, Lake and Thompson, vital supplies had still failed to materialise. There was food for three months but enough ammunition for only three days of serious fighting. More earthworks were constructed as agents reported the Russian advance. On the 16th, the beginning of the Turkish festival of Bairam, General Mouravieff's army finally arrived and launched their first attack.

Williams reported:

Our advanced posts were driven in soon after daylight, and the Russian army appeared on the heights about half past 6 o'clock: its advance guard consisted of three regiments of regular Cossacks, supported by artillery and rockets. The main body of Infantry marched in three columns, flanked by three regiments of Dragoons and supported by six batteries of eight guns each. In the rear appeared a strong column of Reserve Infantry, then the wagons carrying, as I have since heard, three days' provisions. The whole force could not have been less than 25,000. Nothing could be more perfect than the handling of the enemy's army as it advanced upon the front of our entrenchments . . .

Mouravieff's cavalry crashed upon the Bashi-Bazouks posted on the plains to the south-east of the town, but the charge was checked and thrown into disorder by well-directed artillery fire from the Karadagh and Hafiz Pasha redoubts. The Turkish skirmishers halted a fierce Cossack attack on their camp. Teesdale, with Zohrab, was in the thick of the fighting and Williams recorded in dispatches that his 'labours were incessant'. The Russians brought up their artillery and blasted the redoubts without much effect for an hour. They then retired in good order. Williams reckoned their losses to be at least 100 men, compared to six Turkish defenders killed and eight wounded.

Williams wrote:

The spirit of the Turkish troops was excellent, evincing, as they did, as much readiness to the defence as they had shown in the construction of their epaulements. If the enemy had attempted to carry his original intention into execution he would, I confidently believe, have met with equal disaster.

But Mouravieff's plan from the start was to invest the fortress and cut all supply lines. An isolated garrison, he calculated, would be taken with only light losses. He ordered his troops to move to the west and north, encircling the defences, while his Cossacks patrolled the surrounding countryside. By the middle of July Kars was completely blockaded and it was 'almost impossible for a single horseman to pass without capture'.

Williams managed to smuggle out some messages to his superiors. One said:

> The rain has been so heavy and incessant as to prevent the enemy from any attempt to attack our lines, but he has pushed forward large bodies of Cavalry, supported by guns, burnt the surrounding villages and destroyed one of our small depots of grain at Chiplaklee, eight hours on the Erzeroom road, and probably thinking that our entrenchments are too formidable to take by *coup de main*, he has sent to Gumri for eight heavy guns belonging to that fortress, which are now on their way to his camp.
>
> The duties of our garrison have been most trying, in consequence of the torrents of rain, but the spirit of the troops is good.

The epic siege of Kars had begun in earnest. The rain continued to pour down, hampering the enemy but also washing away earthworks and flooding trenches in the defences. Teesdale shared a dug-out in the Takhsap redoubt with the renowned Hungarian soldier of fortune General Kmety, to whom he acted as chief of staff. Kmety, also known as Ismail Pasha, was the son of a Protestant clergyman, who had turned soldier when his hopes of an academic career turned sour. Now aged forty-four, Kmety and Teesdale were continually engaged in skirmishing and harassing the enemy with parties of riflemen.

The defenders constantly repaired and extended their entrenchments, while the Russians constantly probed and tested them. General Mouravieff kept a close watch for any perceived weaknesses. Williams, in a typical dispatch on 14 July, wrote:

> Yesterday the whole Russian army marched towards [the southern heights above Kars], and the force left by the enemy on

the heights in our front moved up close to Kanly Tabia to engage our attention; but we were nevertheless enabled by our central position so to reinforce the menaced heights, so that General Mouravieff, after some hours of close reconnaissance, retired to his camp. As this visit was made with his entire army, I assume he would have assailed us if he had found such a step desirable to his future operation. The enemy remains quiet today, but our new redoubts on those hills are pressed forward with vigour, and, indeed, enthusiasm by the troops.

After a third such demonstration by the Russian commander-in-chief, Williams wrote a week later:

His powerful cavalry has not been inactive, having blocked up the roads. Fortunately we have in store nearly three months' supplies of biscuits, flour and wheat; we therefore may hope to be relieved before this amount of food is consumed. Any reinforcements sent by the Turks, from whatever quarter they may be, must come with convoys of provisions; otherwise such accessories of force would amount to positive loss to the chances we now feel of holding out until the allied Governments, by wise combinations and sufficient forces, can oblige the Russian army to retire into Georgia.

There were indeed plans to relieve Kars and its beleaguered garrison, but the Allied generals could not agree on the most feasible scheme, while the Turkish sultan and his ministers could not agree on anything at all. Eventually it was decided that the Turkish general Omar Pasha could take up to 42,000 Turkish troops from the Crimean front to Redonte-Kaleh, a port on the south-east Black Sea. But, much to Omar's disgust, the Allied generals again prevaricated, not wishing to release Turkish troops from the Crimean front until Sevastapol had fallen. The French in particular regarded as sheer folly any plan that diverted troops from the main theatre of war. The emperor also suspected that Britain wished to gain postwar economic and strategic interests in Asia Minor and was prepared to risk allied lives outside Sevastapol to achieve them. Napoleon said:

We have 60,000 men at the siege, the English have 12,000. The Turks for whom we are fighting are never in the trenches . . . All this should be considered carefully. If now they still want to weaken the siege army by withdrawing Turkish troops, they will create a justified alienation in the French army. Furthermore, the great objective now is Sevastapol and not at Kars.

The wrangling continued as Omar Pasha fumed.

Lord Clarendon vehemently disagreed with the French. Early in August he wrote:

Her Majesty's Government consider the relief of the Turkish troops in Asia of such vital importance . . . It is plain that without assistance the whole Turkish force in Asia must be destroyed or captured. The force at Kars is surrounded, and even if able to defend its position against assault, which may be doubted, it must surrender when its provisions are exhausted, and that will happen in a few weeks. The immediate result would be that 13,000 Turkish troops would become prisoners of war, and a strong position be occupied by the Russians.

But, moreover, Kars taken, Erzeroom must share the like fate, and the whole of the neighbouring country would be in the hands of the Russians, while the season would be too far advanced for military operations to drive them out of it.

Clarendon recognised also that if the Allies failed to take Sevastapol before the winter, the Russians would, by occupying Asia Minor, be free to deliver a hammer blow to the heart of the Turkish Empire.

In Kars the defenders were again hard-pressed. The Russian troops destroyed vast areas of farmland. General Mouravieff continued to probe, moving 15 battalions and 40 guns to a new camp at Komansoor. Williams reported:

If we are to credit the reports brought in by our spies, General Mouravieff meditates an advance upon Erzeroom, but I believe his object to be the devastation of the country, and more especially the destruction of the growing crops, in which barbarous measures the army now in our front is daily occupied.

We steadily add to the strength of our field-works, and yesterday we seized the cattle of the surrounding villages, to prevent their falling into the hands of the enemy, and to add to the chance of our holding out till relieved by the allies.

Mouravieff led a portion of his army towards Erzerum and, during his absence on 8 August, his subordinates ordered another attack on Kars. The Official Report states that 'the enemy, losing sight of his usual precautions, advanced with large masses of Infantry, Cavalry and Artillery to within gun-shot of the Kanly Tabia, on the south-east angle of our entrenched camp, where a well-directed fire from the guns of that redoubt obliged him to retire with the loss of several officers and many men'.

General Mouravieff soon returned with Russian reinforcements, bringing his total strength up to around 50,000 men. He proclaimed his intentions to reduce Kars by starvation and take the city without another shot being fired. Mouravieff's reputation as a tough-minded veteran soldier was well known to the British officers. Lake considered him 'an officer of talent and energy who, during a long period of arduous service, had won for himself a name of which any soldier might be proud'.

Within the beleaguered garrison General Williams, given free rein by the Turkish commanders, imposed his iron will. They described him as a martinet 'with kind eyes'. But that resolve, normal and well respected at the time, meant that men died in front of firing parties or dangling from the hangman's rope. In an army of 20,000, facing such a powerful enemy, it was inevitable that some would desert – especially as they had not been paid for the best part of two years. Williams also understood that in a town located on the crossroads of Asia it was inevitable that some men would have split loyalties. His somewhat cynical response, understandable with hindsight, was to brand them criminals, cowards or spies. All who opposed him were condemned, and in that he had the enthusiastic support of the Pashas. Early in September he reported:

The execution of two spies has, in great measure, broken up the party within our camp which gave the enemy information. A dangerous amount of desertions took place on the nights of the 4th and 5th instant, but having shot an Infantry and an artillery deserter, the mischief was arrested. The town and army now know that no spy or deserter shall escape his doom if taken.

A few days later, exasperated by further desertions, he told Yassif Pasha that all the culprits came from the regiment of Redif. The regiment was duly disbanded with great shame, the officers put on half-pay, and the men distributed among the companies of other corps. Williams said: 'The sentence was executed this morning, to the astonishment of the officers and soldiers of this unworthy regiment, and I trust we have now struck at the root of the evil, for the general disposition of the garrison is admirable.'

The lesson, however, was not learnt quickly enough for the general's taste. In his next dispatch to Lord Clarendon, dated 14 September, he wrote:

In spite of the example exhibited to the troops in the disbanding of the regiment of Redif we had no less than six desertions yesterday; fortunately we recaptured two of them; they proved to be men of the corps in question. They were tried by a Council of War, and instantly shot. On their trial they denounced the parties [inhabitants of Kars] who had instigated them to this act of treason, and furnished them with peasants' clothes to enable them to effect their purpose. Three of these men were seized in a house where the musket of one of the prisoners who suffered yesterday was found, together with the clothes and appointments of seven more deserters. There can be little doubt that these wretches are in communication with the enemy, as proclamations were found on the last-captured spy, offering any deserters free passage through the Russian posts to their homes.

A council of war has tried and condemned these men who will be hanged today in the market place; and the appointments of the seven deserters who have escaped by their agency will be exhibited on the gallows, as a further proof of their guilt.

The weather grew suddenly colder and snow fell. Every supply route to Kars was now cut off. The defenders' provisions began to run out and desertions became more frequent. An outbreak of cholera increased the misery and Dr Sandwith's resources were stretched thin. The horses began to starve to death and it quickly became evident that the cavalry – which Williams in any case regarded as next to useless – under the command of the Austrian Baron de Schwartzenberg could no longer exist as a fighting force. Williams decided to give the remnants at least a chance of survival. Around a thousand horsemen were assembled with the intention of cutting their way through the Russian lines. Under cover of darkness they trotted from the town by way of a defile pointing towards Oltee. When they reached the first Russian outpost the alarm was raised. Volleys of enemy muskets poured fire into them, and there were many casualties, but most got through.

Williams sent a cryptic dispatch regarding his decision, for reasons which soon became obvious:

> The enemy's Cavalry has received a reinforcement of 2,000 men, and presses, if possible, still more closely on our picquets and advanced posts, where a daily struggle takes place for forage, which has, for several days, failed to supply our wants; a large portion, therefore, of our Cavalry horses has been sent from the camp in order to seek subsistence beyond the mountains and out of reach of the enemy Cavalry, which cannot be estimated at less than 10,000. It is with the utmost difficulty that either horse or foot messengers escape the vigilance of the enemy, and I abstain from entertaining into details which might fall into their hands. The garrison preserves its health, notwithstanding the great difference of temperature between day and night; its spirit, I am happy to add, is excellent.

As September progressed General Mouravieff appeared to be pulling back, giving every impression that he intended to abandon the siege and retire to Georgia. That impression was given greater credence on the 24th when the Kars garrison received reports that Sevastapol had been taken and the Russian fleet was destroyed. Two royal salutes were fired from the cannon – the Russian commanders answered with a sham cannonade to disguise its import from their own men – and the details of what seemed to be the final act of the war were read to all troops.

Even though the reports were later confirmed, General Williams believed that Mouravieff's tactics were no more than a ruse, intended to put the Turkish garrison off its guard. At dawn on 29 September 1855 his suspicions were proved correct.

*　　*　　*

At 4 a.m. the Russians advanced in three columns, supported by 24 guns, each targeted on a different part of the defences. They hoped to surprise the garrison as they marched through the mist in faint light. But the defenders heard their advance and quietly prepared to meet it, charging their guns with grapeshot. The Russian left flank was met with a crushing fire of artillery from all points. They answered with 'loud hurrahs' and rushed up the hill against the redoubts and breastworks, to be savaged by destructive musketry fire. They faced a battalion of 450 Chasseurs armed with Minie rifles. These muzzle-loaders could be fired twice a minute – no faster, in fact, than the muskets of the Napoleonic wars, but much more accurate and with a far greater effective range. After a desperate struggle the Russian flank broke and fled in disorder back down the hill, leaving around 850 dead on the field.

The central column stormed the Takmash and Yukseh redoubts. Teesdale, returning from his early morning rounds, rushed to the most exposed battery of the Yukseh, the key to the whole position. There, too, the Russians battered hopelessly against a firestorm of musket balls, grapeshot and shell. The *Illustrated London News* reported:

Takmash Tabia bore the brunt of the battle; about sixteen battalions, with many guns, were brought up against it, but the garrison was undaunted, and for a long time the Russians could not even get possession of the breastwork forming the left wing of the battery; but, at length, an overwhelming force obliged the Turks to retire within the redoubt. A scene of carnage now ensued perfectly terrible to behold. As the Russians came over the brow of the hill within the breastwork, to take the battery in the rear, Tchim and Tek Tabias and Fort Lake opened on them with 24-pound shot, which tore through their ranks, but they did not seem to heed this. They charged Takmash Tabia, which was one sheet of fire, over and over again, and so resolute were their assaults that many of the Russian officers were killed in the battery, but they could not succeed in carrying it.

Teesdale, General Kmety and the Turkish general Hussein Pasha won praise in dispatches for their courage in rallying their troops. Hussein Pasha was wounded in the shoulder and had two horses killed under him. For a while the fighting seemed to reach a bloody stalemate. But the Russian column, after heroic efforts and more desperate fighting, finally managed to turn the left flank of the Turkish defences at Takmash, and penetrated to the rear of the Turkish positions.

Teesdale turned some of his guns about and 'worked them vigorously'. The redoubts were enclosed so the Russians who had reached the rear had no way out and were subjected to close-range cannon fire which wreaked havoc. Nevertheless the Russians fought on ferociously, some climbing up the slippery breastworks to the gun positions. Williams reported that three were killed 'on the platform of a gun which was at that moment being worked by Teesdale, who then sprang out and led two charges with the bayonet, the Turks fighting like heroes'.

At the same time the Takmash defenders launched a sortie under Colonel Lake and attacked the wavering Russian column. An official account said that the reinforcements 'being hidden from the enemy by the rocky nature of the ground, confronted him at a most opportune moment. They deployed, and opened their fire, which stopped and soon drove back the enemy's reserves, which were then vigorously charged with the bayonet.' The two-pronged assault by Lake and Teesdale proved to be the turning point. Lake later wrote:

This horrid carnage continued until the Russians, stopped by a mound of dead bodies and dislocated by the repeated discharges of grape, were brought to a standstill. The Turks there leaping over the breastwork and led on by the gallant Kmety, finished with bayonet the utter rout of their assailants.

The Russians fled down the hill, being chopped down as they ran through relentless cannon fire. Their central column, however, overwhelmed a portion of the defences while enemy cannon fire drove many of the Turkish artillerymen from their guns. Teesdale rallied their gunners and by his own example induced them to return to their posts. Then, although hit by a piece of spent shell and suffering severe contusions, he led another bayonet charge. Williams wrote in dispatches: 'My aide-de-camp, Teesdale, had charge of the central redoubt and fought like a lion.' The young British officer was also later praised by the enemy commander, General Mouravieff, for saving 'at great personal risk' many of the Russian wounded lying outside the works from the fury of the Turks.

General Kmety, having joined up with Teesdale, saw that a battalion of Russian chasseurs were forming up behind the abandoned works of Yarem Ai and led his men in a wild charge which again sent the enemy tumbling down the hill. For that action alone, only one of many, Kmety was dubbed the 'hero of the day' by some London publications.

While the main battle was raging a Russian column of eight infantry battalions, three regiments of cavalry and 16 guns advanced from the valley of Tchakmak and assaulted the small redoubts commanding the eastern portion of the defences. The Turkish troops there were joined by townsmen and mountaineers from Lazistan who planted their clan flags on the ramparts before them. But this part of the battle was won by Turkish infantry under Captain Thompson, whose men poured down from the heights of Karadagh and Arab Tabia. Williams recorded:

This reinforcement descended the deep gully through which flows the Kars river, passed a bridge recently thrown across it, and ascended the opposite precipitous banks by a zigzag path which led into the line of works . . . These battalions, joined to those directed by Colonel Lake, gallantly attacked and drove the Russians out of the redoubts at the point of the bayonet.

A heavy cannon, moved to a key point by Thompson, was then turned on the fleeing Russians.

After the Russian infantry had been thrown back from the eastern redoubts the entire attack collapsed. They retreated along the whole line and suffered more severe losses from round-shot bearing from every battery, each of which kept up an incessant fire on the crowded columns.

General Williams, in his dispatch to Lord Clarendon, said:

During this combat, which lasted nearly seven hours, the Turkish infantry, as well as artillery, fought with the most determined courage; and when it is recollected that they had worked on their entrenchments, and guarded them by night, throughout a period extending to nearly four months, I think your Lordship will admit that they have proved themselves worthy of the admiration of Europe, and established an undoubted claim to be placed amongst the most distinguished of its troops.

With regard to the enemy, as long as there was a chance of success he persevered with undaunted courage, and the Russian officers displayed the greatest gallantry. Their loss was immense; they left on the field more than 5,000 dead, which it took the Turkish infantry four days to bury. Their wounded and prisoners in our possession amount to 160, whilst those who were carried off are said to be upwards of 7,000.

As the garrison was afflicted with cholera, and I was apprehensive of a great increase of the malady should this melancholy duty of the burial of the dead be not pushed forward with every possible vigour by our fatigued and jaded soldiers, I daily visited the scene of strife to encourage them in their almost endless task; and I can assure your Lordship that the whole battlefield presented a scene which is more easy to conceive than to describe, being literally covered with the enemy's dead and dying. The Turkish dead and wounded were removed on the night of the battle. The dead numbered 362, the wounded 631. The towns-people, who also fought with spirit, lost 101 men.

His Excellency the Mushir has reported to his government those officers who particularly distinguished themselves – a difficult task in an army which has shown such a desperate valour throughout the unusual period of seven hours of uninterrupted combat.

*   *   *

As General Williams reported, it took the Turks four days to bury the dead piled up around the town's ramparts. Each day the defenders heard distant volleys as the Russians buried, with military honours, those of their comrades killed by long-range artillery fire and those who had succumbed their wounds. Williams's original estimate of the Russian dead was later upgraded to almost 7,000 and even that may have been too modest a count as more wounded died. Mouravieff's report to the Tsar cited the loss of 6,517 men. But although the Russians had lost a costly battle, General Mouravieff had no intention of retiring. He reverted to his plan to invest Kars with 'pertinacious obstinacy', determined to starve the garrison into capitulation.

The defenders, once the heady brew of victory wore off, now faced cold, famine and disease. The heaviest burden fell on Humphrey Sandwith as Inspector General of the Kars hospitals. He had under him fifty surgeons, physicians and apothecaries, 'ignorant practitioners, surgeons, ignorant barbers, preferring to bleed, draw teeth and dress wounds'. Dr Sandwith first had to tend the large number of wounded, both Turk and Russian, in his overcrowded and poorly stocked wards. He relied mainly on horseflesh broth to bring his patients round, and he succeeded in keeping his charges free of hospital gangrene and epidemic typhus. There was, though, no defence against the cholera which swept through the lines and the town, and hit all ranks. There were 2,000 cases during the siege, and by the end of October the men were dying at the rate of 100 a day. But the biggest concern was starvation. Sandwith's diary paints a vivid picture of the sufferings endured:

October 17th – Our troops suffered fearfully from their diet of bread and water. They are no longer the stout and hardy men who fought for seven hours against overwhelming odds, and drove back a magnificent Russian army. A visible emaciation is observed throughout the ranks, and the newly-opened hospitals are filling daily with men whose only disease is exhaustion from want of nutriment. The high price of bread, too, in the town induces many poor fellows to sell half their rations; and those who yield to this temptation inevitably sink at their posts and die.

October 21st – Swarms of vultures hover round our lines, preying on the corpses that the hungry dogs, which have forsaken the city, have scratched out of their graves. These dogs gorge themselves with their foul banquet, while within the city every man, woman and child is searching for food. The grass is torn up in all the open spaces, and the roots eaten by the soldiers and the people. Crowds of women besiege the public offices for bread, which is dealt out to them with a very sparing hand.

October 28th – The wretched remains of our cavalry are inspected; and as the horses can scarcely stand, much less support the weight of their riders, their throats are cut.

November 16th – A small quantity of snow falls; the rapid mountain stream which runs through the town, the Karsachai, is already almost entirely frozen over. Old women are moaning and crying out that they are dying of starvation; the children have a gaunt and famished look . . .

In his memoirs Sandwith sometimes could not disguise a forensic fascination with the symptoms he saw all around him:

The emaciation is wonderful, yet in most no diarrhoea or other symptoms of disease is observable. Their veins are excessively feeble – a clammy cold pervades the surface of the body, and they die without a struggle. Surgeons are posted in every part of the camp with the broth of horse-flesh in the form, and under the name, of medicine. I have again and again seen men watching the batteries at midnight, some standing and leaning on their arms, but most coiled up under the breastwork during cold as intense as an Arctic winter, scarce able to respond to or challenge the visiting officer, and, in answer to a word of encouragement or consolation, the loyal words were ever on their lips, *Padishah sagh ossoum*. Long live the Sultan! It would seem that the extremity of human suffering called forth latent sparks of a loyalty and devotion not observed in seasons of prosperity.

The dispatches of General Williams over roughly the same period were more laconic, as was the Victorian soldier's way, but carried hints of the same despair:

October 12th – Notwithstanding the severe defeat experienced by the enemy, he still blockades us closely, and the erection of huts in his camp this morning shows that he intends to continue this course. He knows that all our Cavalry horses are dead of starvation, and that we cannot take the field; he is also aware that cholera inflicts severe losses on us, which are aggravated by the difficulty we have of burying the horses.

October 19th – I regret to say that desertion has again commenced, and, with it, military executions, for I am determined that no deserter who again falls into our hands shall escape the punishment due to his infamy.

October 23rd – All our horses are dead of starvation, and we have not carriage for a load of ammunition, if we are ultimately obliged to abandon Kars. The garrison has been without animal food for more than a fortnight.

November 19th – We divide our bread with the starving townspeople. No animal food for seven weeks. I kill horses in my stable secretly, and send the meat to the hospital, which is now very crowded. We can hold out . . .

Williams and the Turkish commanders were holding on in the hope of a relief. It never came. There was, indeed, a strong Turkish force in Erzerum, but the defence of that city was considered to be too important to risk. The Russians threw out bodies of troops into the neighbourhood and kept the garrison there in check. James Brant, the British Consul in Erzerum, blamed the Turkish commander Selim Pasha for not going to the aid of Kars. He wrote to Lord Clarendon: 'Selim Pasha now pretends that he fears danger to Erzeroom from the [Russian] Byazid division and talks of advancing to attack it, but this is a mere pretext to cover his cowardice. I fear there is nothing to be done to help this neglected army in Kars.' Vely Pasha made several bids to march upon Kars from Trebizond, but each time he was met by Russian detachments under General Sousloff and compelled to retire. The Turkish authorities in Constantinople and Ankara haggled about the cost of relief expeditions, quarrelled amongst themselves and prevaricated when urged into action by the British generals, although the latter could hardly boast of their own track records of indecision and incompetence. In another letter to the Foreign Secretary Brant said: 'Is the Kars army to be allowed to perish? Is nothing to be done to relieve it? I now fear it must surrender, and to confer honours on its gallant defenders, while they be left to perish is a cruel mockery, and an indelible disgrace to the Turkish Government, as well as to those of the allied Powers.'

Early in November Williams wrote: 'I have on my shoulders the management of the starving population, as well as that of the army. I take from the rich, and give to the poor, but am now obliged to issue corn from the public stores. I hope Omar Pasha is at least acting like a brave resolute man.'

Omar Pasha had landed his relief force at Redoubte-Kaleh and Chopi, and was busy creating depots to provision his men. Around 10,000 of his troops manned the depots while the main body of 20,000 pressed forward. But the expedition had been badly delayed by the indecision of the generals in Constantinople. *The Times*'s man on the spot wrote:

It is much to be regretted that this expedition was not undertaken earlier in the year. It will be impossible now before the winter to do more than advance upon Kutais. Under the most favourable circumstances the army cannot commence the march before the beginning of November; at that late season of the year the advance of a large army for more than 100 miles through a difficult and almost unknown country is, to say the least of it, a hazardous undertaking.

On 4 November the Turkish general sent several bodies of men to find passable fords across the river Ingour. One body under Major Simmonds advanced steadily under heavy fire through water up to their shoulders and took Russian entrenchments. Another body under Osman Pasha, lower down the river, marched against up to 12,000 Russian infantry who, happily for the Turks, had few cannon. A British account of the battle said:

> The Russians, who kept up a heavy fire of musketry while the troops were crossing the river, were charged at the point of a bayonet, and driven into the woods; so that soon after dark the Turkish army was in complete and undisturbed occupation of the whole of the left bank of the Ingour, so far as their line extended.

The British correspondent put the Turkish casualties at 68 dead and 242 wounded, while the Russians left over 400 dead on the field and 40 prisoners. A Russian account of the action said that their two battalion commanders, Colonels Josselian and Zvanboi, were killed in the first exchange of shots. It went on:

> Our reserve, on arriving on the ground, continued the combat for some time but, after an obstinate struggle of six hours' duration, in which the enemy had been four times driven back into the river, our troops were finally obliged to give way before the Turks, eight times their number, and, as some of the artillery horses had been killed, our detachment was under the necessity of sacrificing three guns. Accordingly, after three murderous rounds of grape fired into the dense columns of the enemy, our gunners dismounted the guns and, having rendered them unserviceable, abandoned them.

By 19 November the Russians had evacuated much of the area,

burning bridges and culverts behind them. That rendered Omar Pasha's progress steady, but slow – too slow to save Kars.

The following day Consul Brant wrote: 'I am apprehensive Omar Pasha will not advance rapidly enough, and General Mouravieff seems determined to hold out as long as possible. The season favours him signally. I am in a great state of anxiety, for bravery and skill will soon be unavailing, and they cannot stand out against famine.'

At Kars the garrison's hope of relief was fading fast. Sandwith reported how on 16 November the men heard some distant firing and 'a thrill of joy and excitement runs through the population at the idea of the near approach of a succouring army; but their hopes are doomed to disappointment'. Coded dispatches rolled up in quills were carried out each night by disguised couriers, urging the relief force to make speed 'as we cannot hold out much longer'. It was another five days before the defenders realised that the earlier reports of imminent rescue were false. Selim Pasha sent a chilling message: 'I fear you have no hope but in yourselves; you can depend on no help in this quarter.'

General Williams, in his last dispatch from Kars, wrote:

We had suffered from cold, want of sufficient clothing, and starvation, without a murmur escaping from the troops. They fell dead at their posts, in their tents and throughout the camp, as brave men should who cling to their duty through the slightest glimmering of hope of saving a place entrusted to their custody.

From the day of their glorious victory, on the 29th September, they had not tasted animal food, and their nourishment consisted of two-fifths of a ration of bread and the roots of grass, which they had scarcely strength to dig for; yet night and day they stood to their arms, their wasted frames showing the fearful effects of starvation, but their sparkling eyes telling me what they would do were the enemy again to attack them.

On 23 November Williams, ignorant of Omar Pasha's movements and hearing that Selim Pasha would not advance, called together the Turkish commanders. They told him that all hope had vanished. Soldiers were dying of famine at the rate of 100 a day. 'They were mere skeletons,' Consul James Brand reported, 'and were incapable of fighting or flying. The women brought their children to the General's house for food, and there they left them, and the city was strewed with dead and dying.' The besieging Russians were well provisioned and, with the onset of winter, were warmly housed in huts rather than tents and showed 'no inclination to retire'. Williams asked the Pashas whether they could resist longer or retreat, and they all replied that both were impossible.

The following lunchtime Williams sent Teesdale to General Mouravieff's camp to arrange an appointment to discuss terms of surrender. He also sent the gallant General Kmety to sneak through the Russian lines to report to his superiors the intended capitulation. Mouravieff immediately agreed to see Williams the following morning, the 25th. Williams was acting as Plenipotentiary with the authority to negotiate on behalf of Vassif Pasha, the nominal commander of the Kars defences and the actual commander-in-chief of the Turkish forces in Anatolia.

The meeting between the opposing generals duly took place. Mouravieff told Williams: 'You have made yourself a name in history, and posterity will stand amazed at the endurance, the courage and the discipline which the siege has called forth in the remains of an army. Let us arrange a capitulation that will satisfy the demands of war without outraging humanity.' The *Annual Register* recorded:

The conditions agreed to were highly honourable to both parties, and the conduct of General Mouravieff was marked by chivalrous courtesy towards his brave but unfortunate foes. The terms included: the surrender of the fortifications with the remaining stores, arsenals and guns intact; all the surrendering prisoners of war to be treated in accordance to the rules of civilised warfare; non-combatants and militia should be allowed to return to their homes provided they swear on oath not to take up arms against the Tsar; the occupying forces would not loot, plunder or damage the town's mosques or other public buildings.

The document further pledged: 'It being the principle of the Russian Government to respect the customs and traditions of the people subject to its Government, and especially the buildings devoted to worship, it will not allow any damage to be done to the religious monuments or historical souveniers of Kars.'

On the 28th, Williams, Vassif Pasha and the garrison discharged their muskets and marched out of Kars in full uniform, with drums beating and colours flying. Of the 20,000 men, including civilians, still drawing their meagre rations, only around half were fit to fight. The officers were allowed to keep their swords as a mark of respect. They assembled near the ruins of the nearby village of Gumbel where they were fed by the Russians. General Mouravieff wrote in his official report how he received Vassif Pasha, General Williams and the other English officers when they presented themselves to him at 2 p.m.: 'Our troops were drawn up in line of battle on both banks of Karschai. The colours of the Turkish regiments were then brought to the front of our lines by a detachment of Toula Chasseurs, and received with the bands playing and repeated cheers from our troops.'

The town was occupied that afternoon and 130 cannon, unspiked under the terms of the surrender, were taken, along with a 'great stock of arms'. Those arms included 2,000 good Minie rifles, several thousand muskets, 340,000 rounds of ball cartridge and 500 rounds for each cannon and field gun. The final victory, won by attrition and dogged determination, cancelled the shame of the earlier Russian defeat on 28 September.

In his report to the Tsar Mouravieff took full credit but also, in his chivalrous manner, shielded the reputation of his opponent. He complimented the garrison on its long defence, adding:

The besieged founded their hopes on the arrival of aid from Erzeroum. In fact Vely Pacha [sic], coming from Trezibond, had attempted to advance on Kars, but at each attempt he was met by General Souslott's detachment, which threatened his rear. Our patrols skirmished with these troops, keeping them in a state of alarm as far as the vicinity of Erzeroum. Meantime the provisions at Kars were diminishing; the cold weather was coming on; snow had fallen; cases of death, of weakness from want of nourishment occurred in the garrison;

desertion increased, and despondency became general. All these circumstances decided General Williams, who directed the defence of Kars, to surrender the fortress.

The bitterness of the defeated was not aimed at their military vanquishers. Dr Sandwith wrote: 'We lay down our arms to our conquered enemy, starved by the dishonest jobbery of rascally factions, and the bribed apathy and unworthy intrigues of modern Byzantine officials.' Mouravieff issued an Order of the Day to be read to all troops:

Companions in arms, I congratulate you! As Lieutenant of our Sovereign, I thank you. At the price of your blood and your labour, the bulwark of Asia Minor has been placed at the feet of His Majesty the Emperor. The Russian standard floats on the walls of Kars. It proclaims the victory of the Cross of the Saviour. The whole of the [Turkish] army of Anatolia, 30,000 strong, has vanished like a shadow. Its Commander-in-Chief, with all his Pashas and officers, and the English General who directed the defences, with his staff, are our prisoners. Thousands of Turkish prisoners who return to their homes will proclaim your deeds of arms . . .

Despite his triumphant tone, Mouravieff was a generous victor. Around 6,000 Turkish soldiers and militiamen, including the oldest, those most weakened by starvation and those on unlimited leave, were paroled and allowed to go home. The sick and wounded were well tended. The remainder, between 7,000 and 8,000, were fed and, where necessary, clothed and shod before being marched to prisoner-of-war camps.

But it was the British officers who were shown the most respect. Dr Sandwith was set free in recognition of his humane treatment of wounded and sick Russian prisoners during the siege. Teesdale was personally thanked by Mouravieff for saving the Russian wounded from butchery below the redoubts on 28 September. Thompson was saluted for his bravery on that same day, and General Williams was wined and dined by his admiring captor. Two days later, Williams and the other English officers were sent under guard to Tiflis where they were to sit out the remainder of the war as prisoners and honoured guests.

*   *   *

The Russian victory at Kars came too late to affect the course of the wider Crimean War. The harsh winter set in and Mouravieff had to wait until spring to strike deeper into Asia Minor. By then events had overtaken him.

Sevastapol had fallen on 6 September 1855, but it was only after Austria threatened to join the Allies that the Tsar agreed to negotiate peace terms. Lord Palmerston, fearful that Kars might become a negotiating counter over the winter, proposed sending a Turko–Egyptian force from Eupatoria to Trebizond. But he would not consider sending British troops and nothing happened. The Asia theatre of war was not reopened. The Treaty of Paris, signed on 30 March 1856, saw Russia forced to return southern Bessarabia and the mouth of the Danube to Turkey. Moldavia, Walachia and Serbia were placed under an international, rather than Russian, guarantee. The Russians were forbidden to maintain a navy on the Black Sea. The Treaty's third and fourth articles testified to the importance of Kars: the town was restored to Turkey, while Russia in exchange received back Sevastapol, Balaclava, Kamiesch, Eupatoria, Kertch, Tenikale and Kinburn.

The war marked the collapse of the arrangement under which the victors over Napoleon – Britain, Russia, Austria and Prussia – had cooperated to maintain peace in Europe for four decades. The break-up of that coalition allowed Germany and Italy to break free from Austrian dominance and to emerge as independent nations. For the Russians, the shock of defeat was a catalyst for the internal reforms introduced by Tsar Nicholas's successor, Alexander II.

In military terms the myth of Russian might and invincibility was brought crashing down, not least by the gallant defence of Kars. Few British commanders emerged from the blundering, hugely wasteful war with their reputations enhanced or even intact. The exceptions included the Britons at Kars. There was an inevitable post-mortem on the failure to relieve Kars. The *Illustrated London News* described it as

> a dismal blotch on the fair fame of a war whose results have generally been so glorious . . . Enough is known of the heroic endurance of the little garrison, during a long and dreary blockade – the culpable neglect of which rests with those who were responsible for their succour and relief – to excite at once the enthusiasm and the indignant reproaches of the world.

Lord Stratford blamed the Turkish court and Pashas for his own tardiness. The Turks blamed the British and French. The Allied commanders blamed one another. A more level-headed assessment was made the following year by Brigadier-General W.R. Mansfield, in a memorandum to the Foreign Office:

> If I may be allowed to offer an opinion on the real cause of the disastrous issue of the Turco-Asiatic campaigns, I should say that it must be found in the nature of the alliance, which absorbed all the really available means of action, whether French, British or Turkish, in the invasion of the Russian soil, to the exclusion of attention to the hostile operation on Turkish territory. The contest pursued in the former required every practicable means to ensure success, perhaps even military safety.
>
> The garrison of Kars performed a great duty in arresting the march of the Russian columns till the resources of the allies could be turned to Asia . . .
>
> Some months since I ventured to predict, in private conversation, that we should have to be satisfied with such an issue; and that, assuming the allies to be prepared to take advantage of what has been thus achieved by the devoted garrison, we should have no reason to be disappointed when viewing the two theatres of war as one comprehensive whole. I have no reason to depart from the opinion then expressed.

In other words, the real victory at Kars was in tying up an efficient and extremely dangerous Russian army for so long.

There was an unsuccessful attempt to prosecute Selim Pasha for failing to relieve Kars. Two other Pashas were held to account for not properly provisioning the garrison. They escaped blame because they were noblemen. Instead, the blame was put on the shoulders of a former Commissary, now dead. His son was thrown into prison as an accomplice.

The Sultan sent his effusive thanks to the townspeople of Kars who had shared with the troops the hardships and dangers of the siege. They were more grateful for his more practical reward – three years' exemption from taxes.

Williams and his staff were well treated during their captivity, first at Riazan and later at Tiflis in Russia. He wrote:

> We were conveyed in carriages furnished by the Russian Government, and under the charge of Captain Baschmakoff, of the Imperial Guard, whose kind and friendly care of us demands our best thanks; indeed, nothing can exceed the warm and flattering reception which we have received from the authorities, military and civil.

Williams was presented to the Tsar even before the peace was signed and by the end of March he and his officers were on their way back to England.

One of their comrades was already there. Dr Sandwith, on being released by Mouravieff, had travelled, mainly on foot, to Constantinople and crossed the Armenia mountains, undergoing great hardships and dangers on his way. He arrived in London on 9 January 1856 and became 'the lion of the season'. He related the story of the siege to Queen Victoria and her ministers, and his narrative, rushed out by the end of the month, became a bestseller. He was made a CB and Oxford gave him an honorary degree. In August that year he went with Lord Granville to Moscow for the coronation of the new Tsar, where he was presented with the Russian order of St Stanislaus for humanitarian service. The French also answered him the Legion of Honour.

Sandwith had no wish to practise medicine comfortably in England and early in 1857 he became the colonial secretary in

Mauritius. The climate there did not suit him and he returned less than two years later. He became active in politics as an ardent reformer and tried, unsuccessfully, to become MP for Marylebone. A visit to Serbia and Bulgaria reversed his previously pro-Turkish sympathies. He wrote about Turkish misrule and the threat of a massacre hanging over the region's Christians. When Serbia declared war on Turkey in 1876 he went to Belgrade and devoted himself to the relief of the wounded and the refugees. On a return visit to England he raised £7,000 for refugee relief and campaigned to prevent Britain again taking sides on behalf of Turkey and against Russia.

During his later years he agitated for improved water supplies for Londoners. His health and that of his wife Lucy deteriorated and in 1860 they were advised to winter in Davros. It was disastrous for both of them. Sandwith died in Paris the next May, aged fifty-eight. His wife and one of his five children followed him to the grave the following year. Tributes flooded in. Professor Max Muller wrote: 'I never heard him make a concession. Straight as an arrow he flew through life, a devoted lover of truth, a despiser of all quibbles.' An eminent churchman said that no other Englishman had done more to help the Christian population of European Turkey. An obituary said he had 'the one-sidedness of a strong partisan'.

Henry Thompson was honoured by the Turks and by Britain. He had no time to enjoy the accolades. He died, aged just twenty-six and unmarried, in London on 13 June 1856, just days after he returned from his captivity. He was buried in Brompton cemetery and a memorial tablet was erected to his memory in St Paul's Cathedral by public subscription.

Colonel Lake received the thanks of Parliament, the Legion of Honour from the French and a sword and silver salver from the people of Ramsgate, where his mother lived. He was made a major-general in the Turkish army. A year after his return he retired from the British army to take up his appointment as chief commissioner of police in Dublin. He retired twelve years later and died in Brighton, aged seventy-three, in 1881. He had outlived two wives. Of his five sons, one became an admiral and three were officers in either the Artillery or the Engineers.

Teesdale, although still a mere artillery lieutenant, was made a CB on his return. The queen later presented him with the Victoria Cross for his courage during the battle of Kars. For three years he continued as *aide-de-camp* to General Williams until he was promoted first to captain then to brevet major for distinguished service in the field. Further promotions steadily followed, and by 1887 he was a major-general. Always a royal favourite, he had by then also served ten years as *aide-de-camp* to the ageing queen and for longer as equerry to the Prince of Wales. He died in 1893 from a paralytic stroke, aged sixty, at his bachelor's home in Sussex after returning from a trip to Germany. He is buried in South Bersted churchyard.

General Williams deservedly returned a hero. His marathon defence, despite its ultimate failure, showed that not all senior British officers in the recent war had been nincompoops. He was created Baronet of Kars with a pension of £1,000 a year for life, was made a Knight Commander of the Order of the Bath, and received the freedom of the City of London with a sword of honour. The French gave him the Grand Cross of the Legion of Honour and the Turkish sultan followed suit with the first class of the Order of the Medjidie.

He was general-commandant of Woolwich garrison from 1856 to 1859, during which time he was also MP for Calne. In 1859 he went to Canada, where he served for six years as commander of forces, becoming governor of Nova Scotia. From 1871 to 1876 he was governor of Gibraltar and in 1881 he was appointed constable of the Tower of London. He died at eighty-two, unmarried, in Garland's Hotel, Pall Mall, on 23 July 1883. He was buried at Brompton cemetery.

His Kars comrade and devoted friend Sir Christopher Teesdale said:

He had marvellous self-reliance and perfect fearlessness of responsibility. He trusted his subordinates, but only consulted with them on points of detail. He would walk for hours alone at Kars, working out plans and ideas in his mind, and, once settled, they were never departed from. Every one knew that an order once given had to be obeyed without comment. Firm as a rock on duty, he had the kindliest gentlest heart that ever beat.

But perhaps the most fitting tribute to Williams was spoken to Dr Sandwith by an unnamed Turkish soldier and survivor of Kars: *'Veeliams Pasha chock adam dur,'* he said. Williams Pasha is no end of a man.

TWENTY-SIX

The Fenian Invasion of Canada, 1866

'And we'll go and capture Canada, for we've nothing else to do.'

On 13 December 1862 the Irish Brigade swarmed up Marye's Heights above Fredericksburg. They had already witnessed from afar other regiments of the Union Army being slashed to ribbons by the Confederate Virginian Division firing musket balls, canister and grapeshot from behind a stone wall on the summit. Their fate was to be no different. The Irishmen got further than any others had done on the corpse-strewn hillside but they were still 50 yards short of that terrible wall.

Thomas Galway, a young officer in another company, embracing the ground under the lethal hailstorm, wrote:

> Every man has a sprig of green in his cap, and a half-laughing, half-murderous look in his eyes. Poor fellows, poor, glorious fellows, shaking goodbye to us with their hats. They reach a point within a stone's throw of the stone wall. No farther. They try to go beyond, but are slaughtered.

The correspondent for the London *Times*, not noted for many Irish sympathies, wrote: 'Never at Fontenoy, Albuera or at Waterloo was more undaunted courage displayed by the sons of Erin than during those six frantic dashes which they directed against the almost impregnable position of their foe.'

An Irish officer serving on the Confederate side at Fredericksburg, one of the most savage battles of America's Civil War, wrote to his wife: 'My darling, we forgot they were fighting us, and cheer after cheer at their fearlessness went up all along our lines.' General Robert E. Lee himself, watching from above, famously remarked: 'It is well that war is so frightful. Otherwise we should become too fond of it.' An officer of the Irish Brigade saw no glory, only the bodies of his men. 'It was not a battle,' he wrote, 'it was the wholesale slaughter of human beings – sacrificed to the blind ambition and incapacity of some parties.'

That night the brigade's commander, General Thomas Francis Meagher, went ahead with a previously planned banquet in Fredericksburg town. American staff officers, unused to the Irish custom of a wake, were horrified to witness the general and others quaffing the regimental cocktail of whiskey and champagne around a cannon ball on a silver salver.

The following morning there was a roll call. Meagher wrote: 'Of the 2,200 men I led into action . . . 218 now appeared on that ground.' Three Irishmen standing alone were ordered to join their company. They replied: 'General, we are our company.'

In the minds of Meagher and many other survivors of that dreadful day a significant change of attitude towards America began to develop. Most of them were first-generation migrants who had left Ireland to escape the potato famine, with its dreadful poverty of the body and spirit. Some, including Meagher, had been the victims of political oppression and had escaped from penal colonies in Australia with the help of their American friends. All shared a great feeling of gratitude to the United States, which was one reason why they fought so heroically and enthusiastically for the Union. After Fredericksburg, they felt that they had repaid their debt in full, with interest. Some felt that America owed them help in a new enterprise which could serve all their interests and would strike at the heart of the swelling British Empire – which they had good reason to detest. That adventure was to be nothing less than the invasion of British Canada.

*   *   *

By the time the opening shots of the American Civil War were fired in the spring of 1861 the population of Ireland had fallen by two million. Half of those had died in the Great Famine, the result of potato blight, failed crops, absentee landlords, the ignorance of the people and the callous greed of the English and Anglo-Irish gentry. Most of the rest had emigrated, preferring the uncertainty of death-trap steamers and strange lands to the certainty of on-going squalor and religious persecution.

The majority crossed the Atlantic, taking advantage of the 'passenger trade' in which empty cargo vessels filled their holds with emigrants on the outward journey, before returning to Britain laden with more precious cargo, such as timber. Most landed in Quebec and New Brunswick, north of the Canadian border, but few of them wanted to settle on British sovereign territory. They had had enough of that back home. Such sentiments were not shared simply by ragged, embittered refugees. Lord Durham, High Commissioner and Governor-General of Canada, understood the attractions of the new nation being forged south of the border. In his 1839 report he said:

> On the American side all is bustle and activity . . . on the British side of the line, with the exception of a few favoured spots where some approach to American prosperity is apparent, all seems waste and desolation. The ancient city of Montreal which is naturally the commercial capital of Canada, will not bear the least comparison in any respect with Buffalo, which is the creation of yesterday.

Thousands more were transported to the penal colonies of Australia, charged by an over-zealous and often panicky British administration with sedition, riotous assembly and affray. These were the men who formed the Fenian Brotherhood, committed to freeing Ireland from British rule. One of these was Thomas Francis Meagher, born in 1823, the son of a prosperous Waterford merchant. As a law student in Dublin he became a radical, an anti-slavery campaigner and a Republican. His views were formed by the memories, still fresh among his elders, of the Irish rebellions of 1798 and 1803, put down with great harshness, and shaped by the zeal for civil and religious rights that he witnessed in the revolutionary wars of America and France. As a 'stripling' he took on the great Daniel O'Connell in debate, famously advocating Irish independence by violent rather than political means. One particularly robust speech in 1846 earned him the popular title 'Meagher of the Sword'. He said:

> I look upon the sword as a sacred weapon. And if . . . it has
> sometimes reddened the shroud of the oppressor, like the
> anointed rod of the high priest, it has, at other times, blossomed
> into flowers to deck the freeman's brow . . .

After the 1848 Young Ireland Uprising, fuelled by famine but
woefully misjudged, Meagher was sentenced to death. This was
later commuted to transportation for life to the prison colony on
Van Dieman's Land, later renamed Tasmania. In 1852 he escaped,
controversially breaking his parole, and took a ship to New York.
There he was welcomed as a hero, and lectured to crowds grown
starry-eyed about the Old Country and the boundless freedom and
opportunities of the New.

After the bombardment of Fort Sumter sparked the war between
the States, Meagher was fired with the idea of forming an Irish
Brigade to pursue the Union cause and their own. For 150 years
after the Battle of the Boyne there had been a fine tradition of Irish
exiles fighting the British in the armies of France and Spain. Now it
was time to fight for the 'land of freedom'. Moreover Britain seemed
to be siding with the Confederacy, with its strong ties of cotton
to English milltowns, and there seemed every chance that Britain
would go the whole hog and send military aid to the South. Meagher
argued for a fighting force to be recruited from the Irish communities
growing rapidly in New York, Philadelphia and Boston. He was
joined, at first reluctantly, by General James Shields, an Irishman
who had commanded a brigade in the US Army in the Mexican
war. Shields had the ear of the president. He once challenged
Abraham Lincoln, long before he entered the White House, to a
duel over an alleged libel. When asked to choose weapons, Lincoln
opted for 'broadswords at seven feet'. The two men broke down in
laughter and became firm friends. That friendship helped to win
over Washington sceptics who did not hold the Irish in high regard,
and permission was granted. Meagher was given the colonelcy of the
69th New York State Volunteers, which became the nucleus of the
Irish Brigade.

Recruiting started in earnest at the end of August in a New York
pleasure-ground known as Jones's Wood, at what was ostensibly

a picnic held to raise money for the widows and children of those killed at Bull Run. Meagher told the crowd to put aside the petty party divisions to which they were prone and unite in a great cause. The defeat of the Union, he said, would encourage European royalty and the enemies of democracy. Victory would be another blow struck for the cause of a free, independent Ireland. In 1861 the Irish made up 87 per cent of all foreign-born New Yorkers and there was no shortage of volunteers. They were labourers, navvies, railway workers, streetcar drivers, clerks, waiters, doctors, priests, schoolteachers and academics. Many were active Fenians and, like the young Meagher, had histories of violence and sedition.

By Christmas Eve 1861 the brigade, swelled by volunteers from neighbouring states, was complete, with full complements of infantry, artillery and cavalry. They camped in a downpour in North Virginia, part of the Army of the Potomac, poised to take part in General George McClellan's advance on Richmond. This huge military operation began in unassailable optimism – and ended in disaster.

At Fair Oaks, 4 miles from the Confederate capital, Meagher's Brigade broke a rebel assault designed to split the Union lines. The Irishmen charged through woods and swamp, yelling in their native tongue. Their first fatality was Private Michael Herbert, a devout Catholic and nationalist. Herbert had served in the British Army suppressing the Indian Mutiny before joining the Papal Brigade in Italy (where he served alongside Meagher's brother). He enlisted in the Irish Brigade shortly after arriving in New York.

McClellan's blundering and over-cautious approach turned the campaign in favour of the Confederates and the Irish Brigade was caught up in the battle of White Oak Swamp, as 'Stonewall' Jackson and General Robert E. Lee tried to destroy the Army of the Potomac. After seven days of intense marching and fighting Lee's hopes were shattered by heavy losses at Malvern Hill. Meagher led his men in shirtsleeves, suffering a graze from a musket ball. He reported proudly: 'Coming into contact with the enemy, the Sixty-Ninth poured in an oblique fire upon them with a rapid precision and an incessant vigour.' Afterwards he showed a fellow general the regiment's bullet-ridden colours, saying: 'That is a *holy* flag.'

Such victories boosted the reputation of the Irish Brigade in the eyes of officers who had previously considered them little more than a rabble, whose fighting prowess was confined to bar-room brawling. Meagher was a heavy drinker and often laid himself open to reports of drunkenness while campaigning, if not during actual battles, but many of his men were paid-up members of the Temperance League. In many other ways too they did not fit the stereotype forged by those hostile to their cause. One cavalry officer said: 'I preferred the Irish; they were more intelligent and resourceful as a rule.'

In September 1862 the brigade marched 50 miles to take part in the bloodiest battle to date on American soil. At Antietam Creek near Sharpsburg the brigade's three New York regiments and the 29th Massachusetts were ordered to attack. Five times they charged the strong rebel position along the infamous Sunken Road. Those who reached the lane found themselves in a brutal mêlée in which the clubbed musket was the chief weapon of necessity. Two of the New York regiments lost 60 per cent dead and wounded. Meagher's horse was shot from under him and he suffered serious concussion in the fall – although some American officers later wrongly attributed his confusion to drunkenness. The 69th alone left bodies on the field. In all, the brigade's casualties were 540 men, including 75 new recruits who had begged to be let off provost duty so they could take part in the fighting. Meagher wrote to his wife Libby:

It was an awful battle. Fancy a deafening storm of artillery and musketry ranging along a line of over two miles in length, and when at last it subsided, the glorious Stars and Stripes flying triumphantly three miles beyond where the Rebel colours had been planted in defence. The poor little Brigade was woefully cut up – I have not more than 750 in camp today – the best of my officers too, killed.

General McClellan wrote in his report:

The Irish Brigade sustained its well-earned reputation. After suffering terribly in officers and men, and strewing the ground

> with their enemies as they drove them back, their ammunition nearly expended, and their commander disabled by a fall from his horse, this Brigade was ordered to give place to General Caldwell's brigade . . . The lines were passed by the Irish Brigade breaking by company to the rear as steady as on drill.

The depleted brigade was reinforced by the 116th Pennsylvanians and was back up to strength in time to meet its greatest challenge – and heaviest losses – at Fredericksburg. The night after that battle, while Meagher was knocking back his lethal cocktails, a Cork-born Union captain, Dennis Downing, began singing the Fenian marching song 'Ireland Boys Hurrah.' The chorus spread from his campfire, voice to voice, 6 miles down the river. Irishmen in the Confederate Army on the far bank joined in.

The return of the less seriously wounded helped to rebuild the Irish Brigade but it was still a sadly reduced force which faced a further test at Chancellorsville in May. The Confederates pounded the Irish with cannon. Meagher, recovering from a leg ulcer, stayed with his men under fire. One shell burst on the spot he had vacated moments earlier, killing four men. The rest of the Union Army had been ordered to retreat northwards and the brigade's 88th regiment was the last to leave. Meagher, dispirited by the seemingly endless carnage tendered his resignation. He wrote that the Irish Brigade

> no longer exists. The assault on the enemy's works on December 13th last reduced it to something less than a minimum regiment of infantry. For several weeks it remained in this exhausted condition. Brave fellows from the convalescent camp and from sick beds at home gradually reinforced this handful of devoted men.

Such weariness grew widespread among those Irishmen mourning friends, brothers, fathers and sons. Battle-scarred veterans grew sick of fighting a war to benefit the Federal States, and recruitment dropped. The thoughts of many turned towards fighting their own unfinished, war.

Such sentiments were exacerbated by the Federal government's reluctance to recognise the heroic sacrifice of its Irish recruits. Meagher's resignation letter was cancelled after some prevarication but no new command was offered. General Winfield Scott Hancock, who would have been happy to serve alongside him, said: 'The War Department seems to regard the Irish general as a communicable disease.' Late in 1863 Meagher, now a reluctant agitator, joined the Fenian Brotherhood. He solemnly pledged 'my sacred word of honour as a truthful and honest man that I will labor [sic] with earnest zeal for the establishment of a free and independent government on Irish soil'. As the Civil War reached its final conclusion, with the crushing of the South, Meagher used his political friends and outstanding reputation to become acting governor of Montana, a state conveniently bordering Canada.

Those left in the brigade fought on, and encountered some of the fiercest fighting below Little Round Top during the war's pivotal battle at Gettysburg. Facing an enemy line barely 15 yards away they drove the Confederates from the summit, only to be surrounded. They retreated through a cornfield, loading and firing as they ran. Given their hopeless situation, the brigade suffered no dishonour.

The end of the Civil War in 1865 saw the disillusioned survivors of the Irish Brigade and their families thirsting for their own cause. The courage of the brigade in battle inspired men who shared the same blood but who had never themselves seen action to become increasingly bellicose. Many of the veterans who inspired them, however, had seen enough action to last their lifetimes. The Fenian Brotherhood was by now hopelessly split. That division, ironically, propelled thousands into backing an equally hopeless adventure.

James Stephens, who fled to France after the Young Ireland rebellion, had in 1858 formed the Irish Revolutionary Brotherhood which aimed at nothing less than the complete overthrow of British rule in Ireland. Later that year he visited America to raise funds, and left behind the nucleus of the Fenian Brotherhood under his lieutenant, John O'Mahony. A Kilkenny man, born in 1825, Stephens was a former engineer on the Limerick and Waterford railway. O'Mahony was born, in 1816, into a strongly nationalist family and both his father and uncle had fought in the 1798 Irish rebellion. As the American conflict closed, the British rulers in Ireland cracked down hard on the movement. Their numerous spies told them, correctly, that Stephens was plotting armed insurrection. In the meantime a leadership battle erupted among their American supporters. O'Mahony, Stephens' choice, wanted to continue putting all their efforts into backing, with cash, arms and men, the planned revolt on Irish soil. When the Irish revolt was postponed, O'Mahony and Stephens were prepared to wait but others, strengthened by the intake of many Irish Brigade veterans, were not. The rival faction was led by the Irish-born Colonel William Randolph Roberts, a dry goods merchant in Manhattan, backed by General Thomas W. Sweeny, who had lost an arm while serving in the US Army during the Mexican War, and who had also commanded a Union division in Sherman's campaign against Atlanta. They wanted an attack on Canada, which was closer and a poorly defended flank of the British. Such an invasion, even if the territories won could not be held, would complement any Irish uprising and see the British fighting on two fronts. Roberts and his followers argued that an Anglo-American war was imminent because of naval disputes, British support for the Confederacy and the revolutionary fund-raising activities of Americans. Whether he truly believed this himself is debatable, but the often-repeated claim helped to stiffen the sinews of his men and boosted his bid for control of the Brotherhood.

O'Mahony grew concerned at the number of brigade veterans deserting him and conceived a scheme to win them back. His aim was to restore credibility by seizing Campobello Island, which was claimed by both Britain and America. Close to the coastline of Maine and New Brunswick, this island could be used as a base for Fenian troops on their way to Ireland, and as the port of privateers who would prey on British shipping. Brigade veterans began to congregate on the north shore of Maine. Their transport was to be the small ship *Ocean Spray*, bought from the Confederates by O'Mahony's treasurer, Doran Killian.

The vessel, manned by naval veterans, was in place by April 1866. Spotting a British man-of-war on patrol, *Ocean Spray* ran for cover and some of the crew captured a British flag on nearby Indian

Island. At Calais, Maine, there was an exchange of fire across the bridge which joined the two nations. Britain complained bitterly about the incidents and the American government, which had been busily rebuilding relations with London, reacted to prevent an international crisis. Three warships were sent to the scene while Federal troops under General Meade disarmed about 200 Fenians. The disappointed Irishmen were sent away from the planned invasion point on board the steamer *New Brunswick*. The 'Border Scare' ended ingloriously. The *Tribune* newspaper reported: 'Hundreds of fine young men left their homes, threw up their situations, gave up everything to join, heart and soul, in this movement, and it was a truly melancholy sight to see them leave by the boat.'

O'Mahony was discredited and the débâcle resulted in the Fenians being held up to ridicule in the Press. It also strengthened the support for Roberts and Sweeny among members who wanted to wipe the smiles from their tormentors' faces. Ominous events began to alert the American authorities, and the British across the border, that something rather more serious was in the wind. Rumours circulated that 100,000 Union and Confederate veterans were willing to fight for Ireland's freedom. A thousand Irishmen heading for California made a detour and assembled in Buffalo. Another 500 left Boston for the same destination. And Federal marshals in St Albans, Vermont, seized a 1,000-strong stand of Fenian arms. An invasion anthem was composed:

We are the Fenian Brotherhood, skilled in the arts of war,
And we're going to fight for Ireland, the land that we adore,
Many battles we have won, along with the boys in blue,
And we'll go and capture Canada, for we've nothing else to do.

*   *   *

General Sweeny's plan of campaign was to drive four separate forces across the Canadian border early in June 1866. To the west, a small Fenian army would set off from Chicago, cross Lake Huron and draw off thousands of British regulars and Canadian militia from the main targets on the Niagara and Vermont borders. Some 5,000 more men would embark on a similar feint across Lake Erie to threaten towns on the Toronto road. The main attacks were to be from Buffalo, where Fenians were to be towed across the Niagara River to take the Niagara Peninsula and the Welland Canal, while the right wing would move through Vermont to seize Montreal and Quebec. Swift success would, Sweeny reckoned, result in the collapse of British defences and the US government's recognition of a new Fenian administration followed, possibly, by the long hoped-for Anglo-American War. He also believed that his armies would be welcomed by Catholic and French-Canadians. In an address aimed at them he said: 'We come among you as foes of British rule in Ireland. We have no issue with the people of these provinces. Our weapons are for the oppressors of Ireland, our bows shall be directed only against the power of England; her privileges alone shall we invade, not yours.' Sweeny was, however, relying on the element of surprise, and the time for that had long since passed. Only one of his four planned thrusts became reality.

This was the Buffalo assault, led by the 32-year-old, red-haired Colonel John O'Neill from Drumgallon, who had emigrated to America when he was just fourteen. Well regarded for his bravery and good humour, O'Neill had become an officer in the Federal Army after an unsuccessful career in publishing and selling books, and had campaigned with the 13th US Coloured Infantry and the 7th Michigan Cavalry. He had resigned his commission after being passed over for promotion, due, he believed, to anti-Irish bigotry. Unlike many others involved in this enterprise, he was a capable tactician and led his men with confidence.

Around 3,000 Fenians were gathered in Buffalo under his command. To confuse the American authorities and British spies, they marched up and down apparently at random. One night, however, 1,200 of them slipped away from the town and congregated on the banks of the Niagara river close to its source on Lake Erie, expecting the balance of their force to join them after daybreak on 1 June. From Black Rock they boarded canal barges and were towed across the river to land at the wharves in front of Fort Erie, an old stockade garrisoned by a handful of soldiers. When they landed the Irish sent up a wild yell and unfurled a green flag. The British were swiftly over-run in the darkness and taken prisoner. The small village nearby was also captured without casualties. Canadian propaganda and some history books depict the Fenians embarking at this point on a drunken rampage of looting. In fact, they simply employed the tactics learnt while on campaign during the Civil War – cutting telegraph lines, foraging and confiscating horses. In compensation householders were offered Irish Republic bonds printed by Roberts. There must have been some infractions, however, as O'Neill threatened to bayonet a soldier who stole a girl's shawl from an inn. The British Press reported that two houses were burnt and 60 dollars was stolen from a Customs officer. O'Neill then occupied the fort and waited for the rest of his men to catch up. They did not come.

The anti-Fenian mayor of Buffalo had ordered that the Niagara river ferry should stay on the Canadian side overnight to deny the Irish the chance to board it. Moreover, the armed steamboat USS *Michigan* had been ordered out on patrol to prevent any crossing by small vessels. It ran between Black Rock and Tonawanda, where the beginnings of the rapids above Niagara Falls make the river uncrossable. The steamer cut off all communications and O'Neill's men roared their anger as it passed back and forth in front of their own positions. O'Neill decided to march downriver, closer to the Falls, hoping that his reinforcements might somehow be able to cross over beyond *Michigan*'s reach. On the way he captured the small village of Waterloo. The steamer kept pace with him, and although crowds of Fenians and curious onlookers also marched along the opposite shore, none dared attempt the crossing. O'Neill stopped at Frenchman's Creek, where he ordered the building of a breastwork of fence rails. From behind those defences he proclaimed himself the 'Commander-in-Chief of the Army of the Irish Republic in Canada'. That night the American authorities across the river received firm orders from Washington that no Fenians should be allowed to join the invasion force. Two armed tugs were sent to reinforce *Michigan*.

In the meantime the Canadian authorities had not been idle. Canada's populace was outraged by the invasion, and Irish-Canadians had little or no sympathy for the interlopers.

The statesman Thomas D'Arcy McGee, who, like Meagher, was a veteran of the Young Ireland uprising, warned that Fenianism was not welcome in Montreal. He declared: 'This filibustering is murder, not war.' The alarm was sounded in Toronto and across the province. Thousands of militiamen were called out. The Queen's Own Rifles paraded 450 men who boarded the ferry *City of Toronto* and sailed for Port Dalhousie. From there they travelled by train to Port Culborne.

Some 25 miles to the north of the Fenian invasion force Lieutenant Colonel George Peacocke of the 16th Foot, the British commander on the Niagara front, disembarked from a train with men of the Royal Artillery and two infantry regiments. His plan was to move south-west across the peninsula to meet up with the Canadian militia regiments and the Queen's Own from Fort Colborne, drive the invaders back to Fort Erie and wipe them out. However, the militia commander, the Canadian surveyor Colonel John Dennis, left his men before dawn that day to travel in an armed tug to Fort Erie. Alfred Booker, an English merchant, was left in charge of 600 Volunteers. Booker, the recently appointed commander of the 13th Volunteer Battalion, was a military incompetent. On receiving a telegram from Peacocke directing him to move his force to meet the regular soldiers Booker decided to take 480 men by train 10 miles east to the village of Ridgeway, set in gently rolling farmland. His force was a mixture of militia, the Queen's Own Rifles, a battalion of the Royal Hamilton Light Infantry and the York and Caledonia Rifle companies. It was later claimed that by the time they left the train his men were 'well liquored'. Local farmers warned Booker that the Fenians were nearby but he dismissed their reports because his own spies told him that the enemy had been camped at Black Creek the night before. That was true, but O'Neill had decided to move up to meet Booker's weaker column before it could join with Peacocke's stronger force.

O'Neill's scouts certainly heard Booker's Volunteers laughing, shouting and blowing bugles as they formed up. The Canadians marched along a road running parallel to a long, limestone ridge about 8 miles west of Fort Erie. It was a fine, hot morning and the road was flanked by fields of tall new corn. No. 5 Company of the Queen's Own was first to come under fire and the troops returned fire with their Spencer repeating rifles. Fenian skirmishers ran down the slopes and reached a crossroads ahead of Booker's column. The Canadians did precisely as O'Neill expected and enthusiastically rushed the small band of Irishmen. The Fenians pulled back, tempting the Canadians to follow them to the next crossroads. Here the main Fenian forces were waiting in the cover of the ridge and woods. As Booker deployed the men of the Queen's Own Battalion they were suddenly met by a scattering fire from O'Neill's skirmishers concealed in a clump of low bushes. A Canadian ensign was the first fatality. He was hit in the stomach and died after 20 minutes of agony.

Both sides opened an intense fire but the Canadians soon ran short of ammunition because Booker had neglected to unload most of the munitions from their train. A *Times* correspondent wrote grudgingly: 'It appears that the Fenians fought with great desperation, taking off their coats, vests and even their shirts, and fighting half-naked with great ardour.' Booker's men also fought bravely, however, and began to put pressure on the Fenians around the intersection. The Volunteers charged three times but were repulsed each time by the Irish, who launched a counter-attack. Booker then saw some horsemen – probably either onlookers or Fenian scouts – and panicked. He formed his men into a traditional British infantry square. Canadians pressing the Fenians with some success were dragged back into the stationary, purely defensive position. When Booker realised that there were no massed ranks of Fenian horsemen threatening him, his buglers ordered the men back into a fighting line. As they attempted to do so they were blasted at close range and, in confusion, began to retreat. Booker had little option other than to order a general withdrawal but that order was delivered late to the Highland Company and the University Rifles on the far right. The Rifles were forced to retire across the Fenian front and suffered heavy casualties.

The adjutant of the Queen's Own, Captain William Otter, wrote in his official account:

The fire of the now pursuing Fenians became hotter than ever, and the Volunteers being crowded up in a narrow road, presented a fine market to their rifles, causing our poor fellows to fall on all sides. It was in vain the officers endeavoured to rally the men . . . several times as quads, and even a company, were collected, but never in sufficient force to check the pursuit, though a constant fire was kept up until the Fenians ceased following. For the first two or three hundred yards it was a regular panic, but after that the men fell into a walk, retiring in a very orderly manner, but completely crestfallen.

The Fenians chased the Canadian rearguard for a quarter of a mile beyond Ridgeway. The whole action had taken 20 minutes. The Canadians lost 23 men, and around 30 wounded, of whom at least two died a week later: Sergeant Hugh Matheson, shot in the thigh, and Corporal William Lakey, who took a bullet in the mouth. Private Charles Lugsdin was hit in the arm, chest and lung but miraculously survived. The Fenians lost 6 dead and 15 wounded. The Irish dead included at least one Irish Brigade veteran, James Geraghty. According to Otter, General O'Neill praised the performance of the Queen's Own, saying that 'we behaved splendidly and were mistaken by them for regulars, owing to our steadiness'.

By now it was about 9 a.m. and O'Neill heard reports that Peacocke's main body of Regulars was behind him, and approaching fast. He called off the pursuit of Booker's men and ordered that the wounded from both sides be quartered with local farmers and with two doctors to tend them. This was efficiently and humanely done within an hour. But reports of Peacocke's speedy advance were false; he let his men rest in a field north of Stevensville, rather than rush to the aid of the militia.

Another militia column from Suspension Bridge captured the abandoned Fenian camp at Frenchman's Creek and advanced on the Irish rear at the hamlet of Waterloo. In a skirmish in which about a hundred men fought on either side and which was later dignified by the name 'Battle of Waterloo', the Canadian Volunteers broke against the Irish muskets. But O'Neill's men gained little advantage and the main Fenian body retreated back towards Fort Erie. With a shortage of men and the whole countryside against them, it was a tactical withdrawal, not a rout, and was conducted in good military order as befitted the veterans of the brigade. Most were in exuberant mood, heartened by the victory at Ridgeway. The tracks of the Grant Truck Railway were pulled up behind them.

Meanwhile the Canadians suffered another setback. Colonel Dennis, with 70 artillerymen and sailors, landed at Fort Erie to pick up Fenian stragglers captured by local farmers. Instead of marshalling his forces, swelled by militia men after their run from Ridgeway, he left his command and travelled by road back to Fort Colborne. Dennis was later tried for cowardice but acquitted. O'Neill and his little army now marched on the Fort Erie and took it. The Canadian defenders blasted away from the cover of firewood stacks and from the house of the local postmaster. A Fenian was bayoneted to death as he tried to kick in the door of the postmaster's home. Another, Colonel O'Bailey, was shot, non-fatally, in the chest as he led his men in a mounted charge against a tug in the river shallows. Outside the fort O'Neill's force, whittled down to 800 by casualties, capture and desertion, camped rough and again waited for reinforcements.

Again, they were disappointed. When 700 Fenians tried to cross from Buffalo in a skow they were arrested by the USS *Michigan*. O'Neill sent a message across the river by a small boat, urging that the main Fenian army should join him as speedily as possible. He was told that because of the transport difficulties only one more regiment could be sent. O'Neill refused that as inadequate but said that he was prepared to sacrifice himself and his command to tie down substantial British forces on the peninsula to aid the rest of the invasion across the Canadian border. He was unaware that those forces to the west and in Vermont had not yet moved. The other invasion forces did nothing, confused by conflicting orders and dissuaded by the presence of the US generals Grant in Buffalo and Meade in Eastport. Grant issued orders to prevent anyone, Irish or American, aiding the Fenians. President Johnson issued a proclamation declaring 'the Fenian expedition an enterprise unlawful. All good citizens are warned against aiding or abetting it. The civil and military authorities are ordered to prevent, defeat and arrest all persons engaged in violating the neutrality laws.' The Fenians who had flocked to Buffalo as news of the attack spread were eager to join O'Neill but were stuck in open scows on the shore of Lake Erie, waiting for tugs that never came. General Tevis, who was supposed to be in charge of transportation, was later found guilty of cowardice by a Fenian court-martial.

All the time Colonel Peacocke's Regulars and the Canadian militia were gathering strength and moving closer to O'Neill's encampment, until they completely trapped the Irish in the toe of the peninsula. Their line extended from the bank of Lake Erie on the west to the shore of the Niagara river on the east. As well as Peacocke's men and the Volunteers, the Canadian government was mobilising the 16th and 45th Regiments and two batteries of Royal Artillery. They were descending on the Irish by road, rail and canal boat.

In a sideshow to the main action, 90 artillerymen under Captain Richard King and Captain L.M. Cullum were armed with swords, bayonets and muskets and attacked a band of Fenian stragglers. After a 'spirited action' 66 of the invaders were captured. Another group of Fenians tried to rescue their comrades and were repulsed. But in the confusion 20 Canadians became detached from their comrades and were in turn captured by the Fenians. Captain King was severely wounded and abandoned on the field; he survived but one foot had to be amputated.

O'Neill knew that as long as he was denied the promised reinforcements, his position was hopeless. One correspondent wrote: 'The Fenians had no idea of being caught this way, and imprisoned in Canadian dungeons, or hanged perhaps on Canadian gallows.' In the early hours of 3 June O'Neill ordered the destruction of their ammunition dumps. He and his men clambered into a flotilla of small tugs and canal barges and tried to escape to the American shore. In their haste they left behind 32 men on picket duty, all of whom were captured by the Canadians. Almost all the escapees were halted in mid-river by the USS *Michigan* with two armed tugs and several other smaller armed vessels. Shots were exchanged and at least five Fenians were killed. Around 700 were arrested. The remainder either drowned or escaped in the confusion. O'Neill and his staff were held aboard *Michigan*, while the men were confined in flat boats. *Michigan*'s commander telegraphed Washington to ask what he should do with the prisoners. The *New York Times* man wrote: 'From a cursory examination of these prisoners I judge them a wretched-looking lot, totally deficient in uniform, and composed of the roughest-looking specimens of humanity.' Another correspondent wrote:

> They are a woe-begone set of fellows, and they tell most mournful tales of their experience as invaders. They say that having no artillery, and finding that the Canadians had Armstrong guns and were closing around them, with no prospect of reinforcements and no supplies, they concluded not to be 'gobbled up' and perhaps hanged, as they say all those captured in Canada will be, and so they 'skeddaddled' as best they could. They were completely worn out, had been constantly on the march since they crossed over to Fort Erie, had no camp equipage or shelter, very little to eat except what they captured in Canada, and no sleep.

Other accounts, however, suggest that the captured men were still in high spirits and regarded their arrest by their former compatriots in arms as merely a temporary setback. They only grew despondent when informed that the main Fenian army, under General Spears, was not marching on Toronto. They were also shocked to discover that Roberts, the architect of the invasion, had never even left New York, while General Sweeny, the military commander, had got no nearer to the Canadian border than Albany. O'Neill said simply: 'Our people are glad they didn't fall into the hands of the Canadians.'

Across the border about 80 captured Fenians were sent to Toronto and Hamilton. Highly exaggerated reports sparked a more widespread scare, while other correspondents far from the scene painted lurid pictures of drunken Irishmen going on a spree of murder, rape and looting. Still others reported that the invaders had been massacred in their hundreds. Britain sent grateful messages to the American government which had stifled the invasion before it could be properly born. *The Times* man reported:

> The invasion was sprung upon us, but as soon as anything could be done the most vigorous measures were taken to

prevent aid of any kind being sent across the Niagara River. And thus ended the great 'Fenian War' which lasted just 48 hours from midnight on 31 May to midnight of 2 June; which resulted in the killing, wounding and drowning of about 100 persons, the capture of 800 more, and the plain development of the fact that the Fenians are utterly unable to carry on an offensive campaign. Their 'army' never got more than eight miles from Fort Erie. It is confidently believed that nine-tenths of the Irish in America denounced this invasion as a foolhardy enterprise, of no advantage whatever. Its sudden collapse, were it not for the bloodshed, would certainly provoke a smile.

The *New York World* on 4 June neatly summed up the affair:

The Fenian invasion of Canada has come to a speedy and inglorious end. After a spirited and gallant fight on Saturday, in which the Fenians did no discredit to the Irish reputation for uncalculating courage, they retreated to the Niagara River by nightfall; made themselves drunk by liquor taken on empty stomachs in the early part of the night; lost their resolution before morning; attempted to recross to the American side; and were captured in the attempt by the United States' authorities, in whose custody they remain. The first act of this drama – conceived in folly, displaying gallantry in its progress – ends in a finale, to be followed probably by a tragedy.

*　　*　　*

Despite the shambles, or perhaps because of it, Fenians continued to muster at Buffalo and other points close to the border. On 6/7 June General Spear's Fenian force finally crossed into Canada from Vermont. It was a brief incursion. They planted the green flag at Pigeon Hill and some of the Irishmen, unpaid and hungry, looted some farms. By the 8th the advance of a strong British and militia force had driven them back across the border. President Johnson deployed Federal troops to close it behind them, ending any hopes of another such adventure.

O'Neill and his captured men remained under American arrest for only a brief period. Roberts and Sweeny were also arrested and then released. Those in Canadian hands, perhaps 80 men in total, faced a much more uncertain fate. The Irish invaders were portrayed as murderers, incendiaries and drunken brigands. There was a widespread public call for their mass execution. The Canadian authorities, however, rightly feared that the creation of martyrs would only boost Fenian support in America. The *Rochester Union* commented: 'The execution of the first man now under arrest in Canada for Fenianism will be the signal for a movement here that will wrest Canada from the men who now control it, and make it part of the American Union.' That was not a universal view in the American Press, however. The *New York Times* described the attempted invasion as 'a mere conspiracy of lawless ruffians to create international disturbance and secure plunder, under the guise and pretence of a patriotic uprising'. It concluded:

The news of this untoward event will cause disappointment among us here. If there was one thing that we Americans have prayed earnestly for since these bandit gangs were first formed, it was that every ruffian that crossed the frontier might be straightaway caught and hung. The prospect of this was a sort of compensation for the intolerable nuisance of being obliged to listen to their blather day after day.

In October those Fenians held in Toronto and Sweetsburg were put on trial. An Indiana priest, John McMahon, claimed that he had been travelling to Montreal to collect a legacy from his brother when he was captured by the Fenians and press-ganged into being their chaplain. Few believed him. He and six others were sentenced to hang on 13 December. A further 26 were acquitted, given five dollars going-home money and booted across the Suspension Bridge back onto American soil. The remainder who could prove American citizenship were quietly released before the trials. There were also reports, disputed then and now, that five Fenians were shot after summary drum-head trials on the night of 2 June.

Despite the attitude of the *New York Times*, the death sentences sparked outrage in the US, especially as one of the condemned men was a priest whose only proven action was to administer the last rites to the dead on both sides. The Canadian government commuted the sentences to twenty years' hard labour, although in the event most were released after six years. Thirty more captives, including the hapless Fort Erie pickets and others taken on the Vermont border, were tried later. They were all found guilty and imprisoned. In 1872 they were pardoned and sent home, save for 23-year-old Thomas Maxwell who had died in custody on Christmas Eve, 1869.

The Canadian expedition held the Fenians up to contempt and ridicule, and destroyed the Robert–Sweeny power bid. Much was made of their decision to stay well away from danger, confining their own activities to issuing pompous and vainglorious calls to arms. At the Philadelphia conference of the Fenian Brotherhood Stephens, the Republican hero who had arrived in America too late to stop the raid, condemned such foolish actions and 'any breach of the Neutrality Laws by which this country might be compromised, and the cause of Ireland ruined beyond redemption'.

Stephens did not stop advocating an imminent rising in Ireland itself. The Canadian episode was, he believed, a damaging distraction. He realised, however, that the proposed revolt would have to be delayed yet again because of a shortage of arms and ammunition in Fenian arsenals across the Atlantic. His caution did not go down well with American Fenians eager to halt the contemptuous laughter heard after the Canadian fiasco. They deposed him as Leader of the Brotherhood and replaced him with another Civil War veteran, Colonel Thomas J. Kelly.

Kelly and his lieutenants, all experienced soldiers, decided to go to Ireland to help lead the revolt. They headed first to London, where they began preparations for an Irish rising the following February. They hatched an audacious plot to seize arms and ammunition from the English army garrison at Chester Castle, forcibly take over all the trains in the garrison town and rush the arms by rail to the Holyhead mailboat for Ireland. Unfortunately for the Fenians, there was at least one informer in their midst.

At dawn on 11 February 1867, 1,000 Fenians began to arrive

in small parties at Chester. Before any action could be taken the leaders learnt that the British authorities knew of the raid. It was immediately halted, but it was too late to stop hundreds of Irishmen being arrested in a joint police and army swoop. The chief informer was John Corydon, but there may have been others.

The disaster left 14,000 Fenians in Dublin and 20,000 in Cork desperately short of weapons. The revolt was delayed until 5 March but again they were betrayed by Corydon, who had not yet been unmasked. Several leaders were arrested but the news did not travel fast enough and there were small uprisings in Dublin, Cork, Tipperary, Drogheda, Clare and Limerick. These were easily suppressed by the Irish police force, whose diligence was rewarded by the addition of the word 'Royal' to their title. The revolt, which was meant to instigate guerrilla warfare all over Ireland, simply disintegrated. In April, far too late, the ship *Erin's Hope* left New York with Fenian officers, rifles, cannon and ammunition. Twenty-eight officers were landed at Waterford – and all were arrested almost at once.

The main participants in the disastrous Canadian invasion enjoyed different fortunes. Colonel Booker, who refused to accept blame for the Ridgeway fiasco, retired from the Volunteers in 1867 and reopened his shop in Montreal. He died four years later, aged forty-seven. John Dennis, who had abandoned his command before hearing a shot fired, faced a court-martial. The court heard evidence that he had disguised himself as a labourer, but found him not guilty. He returned to his surveying career.

In 1870 John O'Neill attempted a raid on Eccles Hill, on the border of Vermont and Quebec, with over 350 men. Forewarned, the Canadian militia force attacked them before all the Fenians were across the border. The main Fenian body returned fire from the American side. But as more Canadian reinforcements arrived, the Fenians turned and fled. The Canadian commander, Lieutenant-Colonel Osborne Smith, had to restrain his men from pursuing them on to American soil. The Canadians suffered no casualties, the Fenians mainly wounded pride. Another minor incursion was repelled two days later near Huntingdon by a combined Canadian–British force, again with no casualties. O'Neill was arrested by a US marshal, but again he was released. However, his fighting days were over and he died eight years later.

General Thomas Meagher continued as governor of Montana and tried, unsuccessfully, to become a senator. He coninued to court controversy and remained a Fenian to the end. His Irish Brigade was long held as a glorious example of what the Irish could do in arms, untarnished by the Canadian débâcle. After watching from a distance the failure of the Irish uprising, Meagher, in June 1867, set out on a gruelling 200-mile journey to Fort Benton to collect Federal muskets. He arrived on 1 July and told friends he feared assassination. His enemies later put it about that he then went on a drunken spree, a version of events still widely accepted, but he was sober enough to compose clear-headed letters to colleagues. He took a state-room on the moored steamer *G.A. Thompson*. That night several people heard a cry and a splash. A watchman said he saw a man leaning over a rail vomiting, before he fell into the water and his body sank under the keel of another boat. The body was never found. Meagher died ingloriously, though whether it was through drink, simple accident or murder remains unclear to this day.

Apart from a minor foray into Manitoba, which had no support, the Fenians' Canadian incursions were over. The Brotherhood set aside its cross-border ambitions and concentrated on rhetoric, political pressure and fund-raising. It is a process which has continued, behind different front organisations, to the present day.

A proper uprising in Ireland, followed by civil war and partial independence, would have to wait until the twentieth century.

TWENTY-SEVEN

The Battle of Orange Walk, Belize, 1872

'Our Queen has much reason to be annoyed.'

It was like a scene from a John Ford western movie. So-called 'Indians' surrounded a log cabin in the wilderness, attacked its occupants and tried to burn them out before being driven off with heavy losses. But this was neither the Wild West of America nor an invention of Hollywood. The venue was the Central American frontier of Belize. And the heroism involved cannot disguise the tragic nature of the events of which this siege was a bloody chapter.

*   *   *

Up to two million natives once lived within the borders of what is now Belize. The Maya built massive stone cities, including Caracol, Xunantunich and Lamanai, and farmed the lush but hostile land in between. The collapse of their great civilisation from the ninth and fifteenth centuries saw them retreat from the region to neighbouring Yucatan. When Hernan Cortes conquered Mexico in 1520 his lieutenants moved south and east, driving the Maya before them. The conquistadors had less success with Mayan settlements which had returned to the thick jungles and treacherous swamps of Belize. The Mayan chief of Chetumal, close to present-day Corozal Town, told the Spanish that their only tribute would be 'turkeys in the shape of spears and corn in the shape of arrows'. The Maya fought back throughout the next hundred years, retreating into the forest and tributaries when outgunned, then returning to burn the Spanish settlements and dismantle their Mission churches.

Daumier described the 'Indians' with admiration: 'They are tall, well-made, raw-boned, lusty, strong, and nimble of foot, long visaged with lank black hair, look stern, hard-favoured and of a dark, coffee-coloured complexion.' Supposedly civilised soldiers had the advantage in weaponry, but the Maya knew how to hide and strike from the countless rivers, streams and alligator-infested lagoons. The Spanish never conquered Belize with arms, but the diseases they unwittingly carried with them had a much more devastating effect. Of a population of around 400,000 when the Spanish came, only an estimated two-fifths survived.

The survivors withdrew inland and the British saw few of them when they arrived around 1638. They assumed that the disease-ridden shore was largely uninhabited. Most of the early settlers were pirates and buccaneers, who raided Spanish galleons carrying gold, silver, hardwoods and other loot from their Central American conquests. The British Settlement in the Bay of Honduras was their base and the coastal coral reefs and sandbars were their hunting grounds, offering both cover for surprise attacks and an escape route from pursuing warships and deep-hulled vessels. Sometimes they were joined by individual native warriors. Daumier wrote:

> They are esteemed and coveted by all privateers, for one or two of them on a ship will maintain 100 men . . . They do not love the French, and the Spaniards they hate mortally. When they come among privateers they get the use of guns, and prove very good marksmen. They behave themselves very boldly in fight, and never seem to flinch or hang back. They will never yield nor give back while any of their party stand.

But the 1670 Treaty of Madrid made piracy and privateering against the Spanish much more difficult. The white settlers were encouraged to cut logwood, from which was extracted a valuable dye used to colour woollen cloth for the growing domestic market. The land was treacherous for Europeans and natives alike, but rich in resources. Swamps gave way to jungle and, finally, to mountains up to 3,675 feet high. All were crisscrossed by innumerable water-courses which provided the main transport routes. A British official reported: 'I is easy to count the rivers which throw themselves into the sea, but if a line were to be drawn parallel to the coast at a distance inland of 25 miles it would cross an infinite number of Creeks or rivulets navigable for wood and boats which, after intersecting the country, lose themselves in lakes or larger rivers.'

Britain and Spain clashed repeatedly during the eighteenth century over the rights of the British to settle in Belize. The first attack, in 1717, saw Spanish soldiers marching from what is now Guatamala. Several times the British were forced to leave after strong attacks, but each time they returned. The profits from logwood, supplemented by some piracy, were too good to abandon. British warships were repeatedly sent to protect the small communities. The settlers themselves formed irregular militias, strengthened by hired Indian warriors and African slaves from Jamaica. Gradually the British trade expanded and their settlements grew more prosperous, especially around St George's Caye. When the value of logwood began to decline, they developed a new trade in mahogany. Finally, in 1763, the Treaty of Paris gave the British the right to cut the export wood, but Spain still claimed sovereignty. In 1779 the Spanish captured St George's Caye, seizing 140 prisoners with their wives and children, and 250 slaves, all of whom were shipped to the dungeons of Havana. Most died there. The settlement remained deserted for four yeras until new treaties were signed. The loggers, or Baymen, were given the right to cut logwood only between the Hondo and Belize rivers. The settlers petitioned the British government and a new agreement was reached which allowed them to cut both logwood and mahogany as far as the Sibun river. The Spanish refused to allow them to build forts, or to do any work other than woodcutting. In 1786 the Governor of Jamaica appointed Colonel Marcus Despard as superintendant of the settlement and commander-in-chief of its defence forces. Belize had begun its long journey towards self-government.

An uneasy peace held until 1798 when the Spanish again attacked the Belize settlements in force. The onslaught was fierce, with 32 vessels, 500 seamen and 2,000 troops, but the Baymen were better able to navigate the narrow channels and inlets of the coast. Helped by their African slaves, the armed sloop *Merlin* and three companies from the West India Regiment, they defeated the Spanish in the Battle of St George's Caye. The Negro slaves, most armed only with palm spears, fought bravely for their British masters from a flotilla of small craft. Many had been promised their freedom if they fought well. An English correspondent wrote:

> You will be astonished to hear that our Negromen who manned the fleets gave a hearty cheer on coming into action, and in the midst of firing of grape kept upon them by the Spanish vessels, these Negroes in an undaunted manner rowed their boats and made every exertion to board the enemy.

The Spanish retreated after two hours of hard fighting and lost all claim to Belize. The Maya watched the clash of the Europeans from afar, shunning the sounds of muskets and cannon. But they did not retreat when woodcutters' camps began to appear deep inside their inland territory. Repeated Maya attacks against the encampments were reported and in 1802 a contingent of troops was ordered upriver 'to punish the Indians who are committing depredations upon the mahogany works'. European arms, technology and numbers had pushed the Maya back into the forests around San Ignacio by 1839, but their attacks continued. Some were lethal, others not. A typical dispatch in the colony's archives, dated 17 March 1848, concerns a raid on the mahogany works in New River Lagoon and Irish Creek, a settlement of around 100 men and their families:

> The Indians crossed from Rio Hondo, armed with bows and arrows; several arrows were fired at the people at Hill Bank who were in charge of the provisions. The Indians were kept off by fire-arms in possession of the men there. No bloodshed had so far occurred, the objects of the Indians being confined to plunder.

Meanwhile Belize was transformed into the dominion of British Honduras. The slaves were freed, new laws were introduced; Belize City was founded as the administrative capital, while more towns were built with protective forts, and the whole region flourished. Spanish power in neighbouring regions waned, however, and Central America was thrown into a series of bloody revolts. In 1847 the Mayan descendants in southern Yucatan rose against their Mexican rulers and Spanish overlords in what became known as the Caste War. With bows and arrows they defeated the local garrisons, stormed Bacalar and burnt it to the ground. A small British naval force intervened and brokered a truce, which was promptly broken by Spanish soldiers. The war lasted, on and off, for twenty years.

The town of Corozal was founded just inside British territory by survivors of the Bacalar massacre, who introduced the sugar industry. The Maya in the region were barred from owning their land, being allowed only to rent property or to live on reservations. Most were small farmers, however, and they too prospered for a while, growing rice, corn and vegetables in North Belize. The borders of Belize and neighbouring Mexico and Guatamala were still either ill-defined or hotly contested. The refugees caused further strain between the British and the Mexican administration. Mexican officials complained that some of Corozal's inhabitants returned across the border to attack their former masters. The Commandant of Bacalar wrote to the British Superintendant:

> An attack was made on the 22nd instant at Juan Luis, Cayo Obispo [sic] and other places. Robberies were committed, murders committed and many other atrocities perpetrated. On the 24th instant Chac was surrounded and a poor man burnt alive. Troops sent succeeded in driving them out. Many fled back to British Territory.

He asked the Superintendant to 'endeavour to prevent a recurrence, as it might be found necessary on a future occasion to pursue them into British Territory which would affect the friendliness hitherto existing between the two Governments'. He was told in reply that the British would do their utmost to 'restrain Spanish and English alike' from crossing the Rio Hondo to join what was effectively civil war in Yucatan. But the Mexicans were warned that any cross-border incursions by Mexican forces, or by any others, would be met with 'the promptest and most decided steps to punish the offending parties'.

Back across the border Indian outrage at the harsh tactics employed by Mexican soldiers erupted again in what became known as the Yucatan Indian Mutiny in 1857. A force of Chinchenha Indians slaughtered 1,800 Spaniards at Tekax. Bacalar was again seized and its streets became a morgue. The Yucatan rebels established their own fledgling republic and the frontier was in flames as the Mexican government savagely suppressed it. An Indian raiding party killed 16 Britons south of the Rio Hondo. More raiders followed them across the border, menacing Corozal and the British settlements of Orange Walk, New River and Spanish Creek. Envoys sent to deal with them were abused at the Temple of the Speaking Cross. Parties of braves several hundred strong attacked isolated communities and melted back into the forest when confronted with troops or organised woodcutters. The sporadic fighting dragged on without conclusion, crisscrossing the deep and sluggish Rio Hondo.

The Belize administration's Blue Book for 1856 noted:

> The Hondo is interesting as being the boundary between this territory and Mexico; or more correctly – between us and the revived Maya republic which is now supreme in Southern Yucatan. The one side presents a scene of total ruin and devastation. Not a house standing, not a Spaniard left alive. The other is still happily enlivened by the industry of the English woodcutters.

In 1864 Corozal, by now a town of over 4,500 citizens, was again raided by Icaiche Indians, with three Britons murdered and 24 kidnapped. They and other European captives were ransomed. The leader of the raiders was Marcos Canul, a chief who rapidly acquired legendary status. He styled himself 'General' and claimed he had the authority of the Mexican government, which still laid claim to the frontier region of British Honduras. He demanded rent from the woodcutters, who regarded his demands as blackmail. Many, however, paid his 'protection money'. The colony's new governor, John Austin, insisted that Mexico relinquish all claims to any part of British Honduras and annul any commission, if any existed, held by Canul. Campbell Scarlett, the British Minister in Mexico City, was given such assurances – but they were then withdrawn. Months of feverish diplomatic activity followed and Scarlett came close to winning Mexico's recognition of the Rio Hondo boundary between British Honduras and Yucatan. The negotiations collapsed when the execution of the Emperor Maximillian severed diplomatic relations between Britain and Mexico.

Canul was spurred to greater activity by the wrangle over Mexico's claim to 'British' soil. He believed the land belonged to his people, although he found it convenient to wave the Mexican flag. In May 1866 he attacked the mahogany camp at Qualm Hill on the Rio Bravo with 125 of his followers. Two men were killed and 79 prisoners taken, including a number of women and children. Canul demanded 12,000 dollars ransom. The British Honduras Company demanded military protection. Governor Austin believed that the woodcutters were themselves to blame for straying outside their boundaries and failing to pay the tribes rent, which had previously been agreed. He asked a leading citizen, Mr Von Ohlafen, to act as intermediary. This former Prussian officer managed to beat down Canul's ransom to 2,000 dollars, a sum which was raised by public subscription. The prisoners were released after a month's captivity.

Later that year there was an even more serious incident. In the western part of the colony around 1,000 Indians, also refugees from Yucatan who had little wish to become British subjects, established several small towns, of which San Pedro was the largest. Its mayor, Ascension Ek, was supplied with arms by the British as defence against attacks. But a British reconnaissance patrol discovered that Ek was acting in collusion with Canul, and that the guns supplied were to be turned on the colony's forces. At the end of December an expedition under Major MacKay was sent to drive Canul and his new allies from San Pedro. The column walked straight into an ambush. The *Official Report* said:

On approaching San Pedro after 14 hours march by truck passes rendered almost impassable by heavy and continuous rain, the column, which appears to have been in no sort of fighting formation, and was marching without advance or flank guards, was suddenly and heavily attacked from the bush by Indians estimated at between 300 and 400 strong, from all sides, Major MacKay, it appears, attempted to lead his men into the bush in a counter-attack, but failed to make way. After an action lasting half an hour, having lost five men killed and sixteen wounded, Major MacKay gave the order to retire.

MacKay later claimed that his men were exhausted by the long march and that the dense bush hid the enemy. The column was forced to flee, leaving behind all their baggage. The Civil Commissioner, Mr Rhys, was also abandoned to his fate in the confusion. Governor Austin bitterly accused MacKay of cowardice, particularly for leaving Rhys behind. A court of inquiry held later in Jamaica found that MacKay, far from being a coward, had 'shewed no lack of presence of mind or courage'. But he was to blame for not providing an advance guard and displayed 'lamentable lack of firmness and judgement in sounding the retreat'. The court found that his men had 'behaved throughout in a most creditable manner'.

The defeat of a British force caused shame and panic in the colony and an armed steamer was sent to patrol the Rio Hondo, although only after much haggling over who was to pay for it. Later in January the Governor of Jamaica and overall commander of the region, Sir John Grant, arrived to assess the situation, bringing with him reinforcements from the West India Regiment, 13 white officers and 300 disciplined black men in red uniforms under the command of Lieutenant-Colonel Harley. Canul's forces seized the villages of Indian Church and Mount Hope. On 9 February Harley hit back with an all-out attack on San Pedro. His column marched for four days over swollen rivers and hard roads in continuous rain before they reached the small town. A rocket tube firing six-pound incendiary missiles was used for the first time. Canul's men, seeing the terrible effect, fled into the forest. So too did Ek, who left letters laying claim to rent for the disputed border areas. Harley left a letter condemning the murder of Mr Rhys. The column moved on, marching 32 miles in 11 hours. San Jose was taken and burnt, with three casualties. The troops found some of Rhys's personal equipment and loot from Indian Church. Mayan villages, provision stores and granaries were burnt in a bid to starve the natives into either flight or submission. Martial law was declared in the region but lifted in April when it seemed that peace was resumed.

Across the border Canul recovered from the shock of defeat and rebuilt his forces. He again launched repeated attacks on Corozal, which the British refused to garrison fully despite its increasing importance as a trade centre. In 1870 the town was captured by Canul without bloodshed, its white Yucatan and Indian inhabitants being disinclined to fight. Canul marched into the town with 116 men, shouting 'Mexico forever'. Finally a strong detachment of troops, supported by the warship *Lapwing*, was dispatched and the Indians melted back across the border. Canul still would not give in, and by 1872 the area north of the colony was a virtual no-go area, with trade at a standstill and settlements on perpetual armed stand-by. Canul then decided on one last push to drive out the white men. His target was Orange Walk, the largest settlement in the north, a logging centre 66 miles from Belize City.

*　　*　　*

Canul was a charismatic leader, a natural guerrilla fighter who knew the country and the value of swift, surprise strikes. On 31 August 1872 he led around 150 warriors across the Rio Hondo near Corosalito. His targets were the settlements at Orange Walk, August Pine Ridge and Water Bank. At the latter place they sought out and killed a Spanish woodcutter called Gonzalez before camping for the night.

At 8 a.m. the next day they advanced on Orange Walk, which contained a garrison of 38 soldiers of the 1st West India Regiment under Lieutenant Smith. As the Indians approached the outlying buildings the alarm was raised; seeing that they were heavily outnumbered, the garrison barricaded themselves within their one-roomed barracks, constructed from stout logs. The military report to the governor said:

The Indians opened a heavy fire from the buildings around and occupied piles of logwood, dumped ready for embarkation, which lay by the riverside about 75 yards from the barracks. The troops replied, using at first the 20 rounds which had fortunately been issued to every man, and later ammunition from the portable magazine which Lieutenant Smith and Sergeant Belazario very gallantly succeeded in bringing into the room.

Smith was shot and wounded after 10 minutes of the firefight but remained at his post for two hours until weakness forced him to relinquish active command to Belazario and the detachment's surgeon, Doctor Edge. The attackers crawled to within 25 yards of the barracks and kept up their heavy fire for six hours. The defenders picked off their enemies one by one. Canul, seeing that his men could not dislodge the soldiers, then tried to burn them out. The kitchen, standing just 5 yards from the barracks building, was successfully fired and burnt to ashes. The military report continued:

At about 2.30 p.m. the fire of the troops began to tell and a party of Indians commenced to retire. Sergeant Belazario led six men round to the other side and drove the Indians out of their positions [in the logwood pile], killing three and wounding many more. A general retirement of the Indians commenced and the troops followed them up as far as the outskirts of the town; they were then recalled and commenced to prepare a stockade in anticipation of a renewed attack.

Inside the garrison almost half the men had been hit: 2 soldiers died and 14 other men, apart from Smith, were wounded. Most accounts agree that the Indians lost 15 dead and many more wounded. Canul himself was seriously hurt, and lived just long enough to be dragged back across the Hondo. The so-called 'War of the Colours' was over.

Canul's place was taken by Rafael Chan, who wrote to the Lieutenant-Governor, William Wellington Cairns, asking for peace. He urged that the faults committed by his predecessor Canul be forgiven. Chan protested that he had always advocated peace with the British but had to obey his chief while he was the latter's second-in-command. He craved the pardon of 'our Queen who has much reason to be annoyed'. Cairns agreed, but there was little need. The Indians had disappeared and were no longer a threat. Cairns told his Legislative Council that 'the lesson lately taught at Orange Walk by both Civil and Military defenders of that post [were] not likely to be lost upon them.'

Just in case, however, he strengthened the garrisons in the North, improved their defences and ordered a road built from Corozal to Orange Walk to render the route fit for the quick transport of troops, light guns and stores. Corozal became the colony's main military headquarters, in place of Belize City; Orange Walk became its second garrison, with a minimum of 3 officers and 50 men housed in new barracks behind new earthworks. Fort Cairns was erected a few years later. The members of the Legislative Council, safe in their houses in Belize City, were unwilling to levy extra taxes for the provision of a permanent frontier force, but the British government insisted they should finance their own defence. Diplomatic pressure was put on Mexico to 'restore order' on their side of the Hondo. The last major Indian incursion was in 1874; this time they were unarmed, starving and begging for food.

* * *

There were a few small border raids after the Battle of Orange Walk, but these were regarded as simple banditry. A group of Icaiche Indians kidnapped several civilians but their chief, Santiago Pech, was seized and held as a hostage for their safe return. In August 1879 the governor told his council that 'the Colony has been almost free from anxiety in regard to Indian raids; no bar exists to trade and barter with the various Tribes by which we are surrounded'.

The territory, which had been subordinated to Jamaica since 1862, became a separate colony in 1884. In the preceding years its population was swelled by Chinese labourers, sepoys from India and former Confederates who arrived after the American Civil War. A proclamation declared: 'No Indians will be at liberty to reside upon or occupy or cultivate any land without previous payment or engagement to pay rent whether to the Crown or the owner of the land.'

The Indians who returned to Belize were the poor and dispossessed, and most became Catholic. Their customs intermingled with other cultures as they inter-married and became subsumed into the general Creole population, which remains the majority of Belize's people. The colony suffered civil strife rather than military attack. In 1894 mahogany workers rioted when their wages were cut as a result of currency devaluation. They were easily subdued by visiting British soldiers. In 1919 demobilised Creole soldiers, returning from service in the First World War with the British West India Regiment, rioted in protest against high prices and the lack of both jobs and homes. They proved harder to subdue and order was only achieved by the imposition of martial law.

During the 1950s Belize, like much of the remaining British Empire, saw the growth of an independence movement. Britain granted the colony internal self-government in 1964 but kept control of its defence because of Guatamala's continuing claims on its territory. Several times Guatamala threatened invasion – and was only kept at bay by the presence of 8,000 British servicemen and RAF fighters. Full independence was finally achieved on 21 September 1981, with Britain continuing to provide defence guarantees. The descendants of the proud Maya, having lost their land and their freedom, now enjoy some control over their destinies once again.

TWENTY-EIGHT

The Hut Tax War, Sierra Leone, 1898

'Here the Englishman must give the black man the lead.'

The poll-tax riots and non-payment campaigns across Britain in 1989 led, indirectly, to the downfall of premier Margaret Thatcher. As she left Downing Street, sobbing, she may have reflected that there were many precedents – not least the civil disobedience that followed the imposition of a similar tax in a British colony a little more than 90 years previously. In Sierra Leone, however, the outcome was a lot more lethal.

*   *   *

Portuguese seamen named the rocky peninsula at the mouth of West Africa's Rokel River the Serra Lyoa, or Lion Mountain, because of its resemblance to the beast. This name was gradually corrupted to Sierra Leone, covering the hinterland of dense forest and grassy plain. From the later fifteenth century European vessels traded manufactured goods for slaves and ivory from local chieftains. The two largest tribes in the following centuries were the Mendi, who gradually inhabited central and southern Sierra Leone, and the longer-established Temni who occupied the north. The Temni were subdivided into over 40 chiefdoms, each ruled by a chief and his council. They were farmers and fishermen, fighters and slavers. Both men and women belonged to secret societies which helped to maintain law and order, and settled disputes. A later British visitor claimed:

> The greater part of the natives lived in stockaded towns guarded by armed men night and day; each chief was in mutual dread of

his neighbour, and intestinal broils and organized raids for the purpose of obtaining slaves and plunder were common. Human sacrifices and cannibalism were practised, together with all the barbarous customs of the savage.

Although English trading posts were established on Bunce and York islands during the seventeenth century, the newcomers came under the protection of friendly chiefs and trading partners. Much of the country was deemed uninhabitable by white men, while the coast was the haunt of pirates and slave dealers, until it was cleared by the British Navy. Both Britons and Temni were content to trade, but otherwise left each other alone.

That began to change in 1787 when the English abolitionist Granville Sharp embarked on a scheme to found a colony for freed slaves, which he called 'The Province of Freedom'. The first group arrived that year, and the following spring a Royal Navy captain, John Taylor, bought some land from a Temni subchief called King Tom. His successor, King Jimmy, drove the former slaves away in 1789. The survivors, sponsored by William Wilberforce and the other benefactors of the Sierra Leone Company, created a new settlement at what later became Freetown in 1791. The company brought freed slaves, English-speaking and mainly literate Christians, from Nova Scotia and later from Jamaica.

At the beginning of 1808, following the British abolition of the slave trade, London took control of Freetown for use as a naval base against slavers and as a haven for slaves freed from vessels captured in mid-Atlantic. In less than sixty years the Royal Navy brought in over 50,000 such 'recaptives'. More came from all over Africa. The British government, unwilling to expand its colonial interests in West Africa, encouraged them to create a self-governing, Christian community. Schools for boys and girls were established, while the freed slaves and their children set up their own trading stores, bartering European goods for palm products from the neighbouring tribes. Treaties of friendship were exchanged with the tribes. Gradually, however, the British extended their authority along the coast, fearful that the area would be snatched by the French, who laid claim to northern Sierra Leone from across the Guinea border

Frontiers were agreed but the ever-present French threat led, in 1896, to the proclamation of a British Protectorate.

The Temni chiefs were not alarmed. They had slowly relinquished their rights to make war, take slaves and sign foreign treaties, but in their own lands they still retained absolute power. The loss of some authority was more than balanced by the boost in trade which followed the building of roads throughout the interior. They were also fearful of falling into the hands of the French, having seen what that nation was capable of elsewhere. They only became seriously concerned when the British established travelling commissioners and the Frontier Police Force, both designed to keep the peace in disputed areas. They took over from the chiefs responsibility for free passage and trade along the roads. The rights of chiefs to freely enter Freetown were also curtailed, robbing them of direct access to the governor, Sir Frederick Cardew, to voice any grievances. Such grievances were exacerbated by the arrogant behaviour of the Frontier Police, some of whom were escaped Temni slaves who used their new powers to flog, plunder and wrongly imprison their old masters. New regulations only increased the bitterness. A new court system was set up which the chiefs had earlier agreed to, only belatedly realising that it robbed them of the right to try their own domestic cases, including those concerning land titles, witchcraft, slave dealing, raiding, murder and rape. It was the beginning of the end of the chieftains' political power, and they knew it. One of them, Pa Suba, complained: 'The king of a country however small, if he cannot settle small matters, is no longer king.' The regulations also gave the government rights over mineral exploitation and what it termed 'waste lands'. The Temni chiefs, employing English lawyers, interpreted the regulations to mean the 'total dispossession of their country'.

Such objections paled into insignificance compared with the next phase of Cardew's programme. London made no financial contribution to the running of the Protectorate, and Cardew needed to raise money. His solution was a tax on all houses, from the smallest huts of the poor to the more extensive structures of the chiefs. The tax was initially fixed at 5 shillings a year for two-roomed huts and 10 shillings for larger properties, later reduced to a flat 5 shillings for all houses of two rooms or more. Cardew's ignorance of the tribes under his 'protection' could not have been better demonstrated. Having lost much of their tribal powers, the chiefs saw the tax as a means of depriving them of authority over their own homes. To them it meant having to pay the government for a place to sleep; it meant no longer owning their own property. The proposed seizure of 'waste land' also included sacred grounds and tribal meeting-places, all of which the chiefs regarded, if not as their own, then as communal property.

The chiefs initially opposed the tax through a series of legal petitions. They professed their loyalty to the queen and said they understood the expense the government had undergone to keep the country prosperous and at peace. But they complained that the tax was an unacceptable infringement of ancient rights, reducing a tribal chief and his council to the rank of peasants who could, under the new arrangement, face imprisonment or flogging for non-payment. Most blamed Cardew directly. They claimed that his administration was 'so unlike the spirit of the English people, with whom they have had to deal now over one hundred and ten years'. One later reported: 'There is a difference between the white people who come now and those before; those that come now do not respect the Chiefs.'

Cardew would not listen. He refused to believe that a land rich in rubber and gum, and with good transport to the trading centres, was too poor to sustain his tax. He was also contemptuous of the chiefs and barely bothered to hide that contempt. He believed that any isolated resistance could quickly be suppressed by the Frontier Police, which had recently been strengthened to 10 officers, 40 NCOs and 550 privates armed with Martini-Enfield rifles. He wrote to the Secretary of State: 'I do not apprehend that the chiefs will combine to forcibly resist the collection of the tax, for they lack cohesion and powers of organisation, and there are too many jealousies between them for concerted action. . . .' His district commissioners were also dismissive. One wrote:

> Great discontent has existed amongst the chiefs since the abolition of slavery. Nearly all their wealth formerly consisted of

their slaves, and the chiefs derived a large income from the sale of their surplus stock. . . . The tax is not peculiarly obnoxious or opposed to the habits and customs of the people, inasmuch as their own chiefs levy similar contributions on their subjects when they wish to raise money for any big event such as the coronation of a paramount chief, or when they consider that there is too much money amongst their people.

Such reports from Temni country convinced Cardew that there would, at most, be surly but passive resistance, which could quickly be dealt with by rounding up and jailing a few ringleaders. He was quickly proved wrong. Cardew was fifty-eight and a product of Sandhurst and the Bengal Army, where he reached the rank of colonel. No one doubted his courage: as a young officer he was mentioned in dispatches during fighting on the North West Frontier and during the Zulu War. He had served also in South Africa, China, the Transvaal and Natal. He had been Governor and Commander-in-Chief of Sierra Leone since 1894. He was a keen tactician with a good reputation for logistics and for putting first the welfare of those under his command. But he was also a classic late Victorian, ready to trample over any native sensibilities in the name of progress.

Nor was he able to grasp the objections of the Sierra Leone traders and the Freetown Press, all of whom added their voices to the clamour of discontent from the bush. Cardew – and, to be fair, most of his advisers – regarded the traders as unscrupulous crooks who exploited the natives by keeping them in ignorance of the value of the coin of the realm. One district commissioner reported that the general view was that the Hut Tax would 'ruin the traders as the natives would no longer deal to such an extent in goods when they found that they would have to pay a certain amount of coin annually to the Government, and that when the natives learned the value of coin they would send to Freetown and purchase goods for themselves'. The Press were regarded simply as trouble-makers who exaggerated the degree of opposition to the tax.

Conflict was now inevitable, partly due to the emergence of one of West Africa's most renowned warriors.

* * *

Kebalai, a veteran warrior with some Temni blood in his veins, took the title by which history knows him, Bai Bureh, meaning 'a man of importance'. He was the leader of a loose alliance of Temni chiefdoms in the northern region around the Great Scarcies River. His first battle honours were gained in 1865 when he helped to lead a holy war called by the Islamic leader Bokhari. He was prominent in intermittent tribal and religious conflicts over the next twenty years. In 1886 he became chief of Kasseh, a small chiefdom 25 miles from Port Lokko. His influence spread, leading to several diplomatic clashes with the British, who on at least two occasions tried to arrest him. In 1892 the British reluctantly recruited Bai Bureh and his warriors to take part in an expedition against the Susu leader Karimu, whom the French were encouraging to revolt to strengthen their claims to northern Sierra Leone, on the grounds that the British had lost control. Bai Bureh and his men greatly impressed British officers with their discipline and enthusiasm. Bai Bureh, for his part, closely watched the tactics of the Frontier Police and the recently deployed West India Regiment. His observations were of great value in the conflict to come.

The Times later reported that Bai Bureh was not like the other chiefs who negotiated happily with British officials, giving up some authority in return for roads, better trade and other advantages of civilisation: 'With men of the Bai Bureh type, who are constantly starting up and, by the aid of either religious fanaticism or of a warlike personality, contrive to acquire a large following, it is practically impossible to deal satisfactorily.' But the newspaper conceded: 'He is a clever and experienced fighting man, and reputed to be an adept in the native system of military organisation.'

Bureh was by then a famous war chief, while his men were experienced bush fighters. A Frontier Police officer, C. Braithwaite Wallis, wrote:

If Bureh was an unusually smart man, so did the Timini [sic] prove to be. Savages they might be, but even in their way of fighting they betrayed such admirable qualities as are not always to be found in the troops of the civilised nations. They loved their chief, and remained loyal to him to the very last, while they understand bush fighting as well as you and I do our very alphabet.

Temni boys were trained for war, serving several grades of apprenticeship with proven warriors. Warriors were recruited for specific campaigns from among allied tribes and were rewarded with a share of the plunder and domestic slaves. A correspondent wrote:

All along the West Coast the native tribes have a regular system of mobilization, and when it is completed 'war-paths' are cut through the bush and connected by communicating paths. When concentration is desired the war-drum is beaten and scattered parties of war-boys hurry by the war-paths to the rendezvous. Thousands can be collected in this manner in two or three hours.

The tribesmen were mostly armed with Birmingham trade guns, but some weapons of greater precision had been obtained. A year earlier the British had banned the importation of arms, but this royal proclamation was widely defied. It was a war-like society, held in check by the British until Bai Bureh was ready to challenge their authority.

Bai Bureh, now approaching old age, was insulted by the arrogance of the British. He saw the old order that rewarded fighting men being replaced by slavish allegiance to a foreign flag. Late in 1896 the British ordered him to the small garrison town of Karene to help build the barracks. He complied, ordering his men to complete the work, but he spent the next year coordinating resistance to the British and their hated hut tax. He sent his sub-chiefs through the chiefdoms of Sierra Leone, recruiting warriors. Other chiefs reached private agreements with him to block river traffic and barricade the roads. Spies were sent out to note the strength and numbers of British garrisons.

Meanwhile the British were already experiencing great difficulty in collecting the hut tax. Captain W.S. Sharpe, District Commissioner at Karene, even had trouble levying it from his own police contingent for their rented accommodation. Sharpe moved on to Port

Lokko, the largest town in his district and the main trading depot on a tributary of the Rokell river. The local chiefs stalled and it soon became clear they had no intention of paying. Bai Bureh was nearby ready to aid them against any British show of force. On 9 January 1898 Sharpe lost all patience. He summoned the chiefs to a meeting watched by a thousand of their resentful followers. The main chief Bokari Bamp, again refused to impose the tax on local traders who rented their homes from him. He and four sub-chiefs were arrested and convicted that same day of incitement of disobedience. They were sent as prisoners to Freetown and put to labour as felons in the town gaol. Their treatment roused bitter indignation. Bokari later eloquently expressed that bitterness:

> Since the time of our ancestors up to the present time there has never been such disgrace to one of our Chiefs as this prison dress which I wear. No Chief crowned by the Queen has been put into prison without disobeying the law, except this year. We have had to break stones. As I am telling you now, my heart is bleeding with tears. We have been brought to prison by the Hut Tax and our country is being destroyed.

A British puppet, Sorie Bunki, was installed as the new chief of a largely deserted town. The next night Bunki, clearly terrified, told Sharpe that Bai Bureh intended to attack the town and slay him as a usurper. Sharpe took the reports seriously. He wrote to Governor Cardew saying that he could not return to Karene until Port Lokko was secure. He next wrote to Bai Bureh, ordering him to levy the hut tax in Kasseh. When Bureh refused even to see the messenger Sharpe prepared to arrest him. Sensibly, he first asked Freetown to send more police reinforcements. Both sides waited uneasily until the fresh contingent arrived in the town under the command of Major Tarbet. Sharpe now determined to carry out his threat. His police column set off on the march, accompanied every step of the way by the jeers of Temni warriors lining the route. Some warriors hurled stones from slingshots. One stone, thrown by a Temni called Thambaili, hit a British officer on the head – and this blow was later credited with starting the war. Tarbet ordered his rearguard to open fire. His advance guard, hearing the shots, rushed back to help, leaving their carriers unprotected. The Temni fell on them, killed some and carried off others to be sold as slaves in French territory in return for gunpowder.

The planned arrest of Bai Bureh was put on hold as the British and their policemen were harassed all the way to the village of Kagbantama, where they were met with another British party from Karene. The entire countryside around Port Lokko and Karene was now openly in support of Bai Bureh. Almost every village between the two towns was eerily deserted, and the road itself was only passable by large and well-armed parties. A small police garrison was left in Port Lokko. The policemen, poorly commanded by an inexperienced junior officer, panicked and killed an innocent citizen, the nephew of Bokari Bamp, who refused to hand over his sword. A subsequent inquiry found that he was 'practically murdered in cold blood' by a policeman who struck the lad on the back of the neck with the butt of his rifle. The unfortunate Bunki deserted and headed for Freetown. He was overtaken by townspeople who saw him as a traitor. His body was thrown into the Rokell river, weighed down with stones.

By 19 February Bureh's forces had completely cut the British lines of communication between Karene and Port Lokko, and even threatened the route to Freetown. Three days later Tarbet led a 48-strong raiding party to burn Temni canoes at Bokupru as punishment for closing river traffic. His force was badly cut up by warriors who first retreated ahead of the British rifles, then silently circled around to hit the police as they attempted to re-cross the river. It was the first indication that the Temni were both well disciplined in guerrilla warfare and better armed than the British, with trade guns bought from the French. It was now clear that this was no simple policing action, but out-and-out warfare.

* * *

At Karene the garrison of Frontier Police was under siege, surrounded on all sides. Incorrect rumours reached Freetown that the town had been burnt. On 24 February Governor Cardew dispatched a company of regular soldiers under Major Norris with a seven-pounder, a Maxim machine-gun, camp equipment and 500 carriers. Even that number of porters was insufficient for the terrain and Norris was forced to leave some of the baggage at Robat. The column was unopposed on its four-day march to Karene, but was constantly trailed by warriors who stayed just out of range. Sharpe handed control of the Karene district to Norris, who promptly declared martial law.

After a few days Norris marched his force to Port Lokko in order to establish proper communications with Freetown. This time his column was constantly harassed, suffering 20 men wounded including 2 officers and 7 privates. The Temni suffered severely, according to the official report, because of their foolhardy tactics of rush attacks which exposed them to the rifle fire of the West Indian Regiment soldiers. However, the warriors quickly learnt their lesson and did not repeat the mistake. Once at Port Lokko Norris sent a carrier pigeon to Freetown requesting two more companies. Early the following morning an attack on the town's *laager* was repulsed by the Frontier Police with the loss of only one wounded carrier. Further attacks were discouraged by shells from the gun-launch H.M.S. *Alecto*. Later that day Major Stansfield with one company arrived on board the steamer *Countess of Derby*. Norris again sent urgent messages demanding another company at least as the entire district appeared to be in open revolt. His aim was to station one company apiece in Karene and Port Lokko, with the third acting as a flying column to keep open communications between the two. The third company, with 215 carriers and another seven-pounder, arrived on 9 March.

After further unsuccessful attacks on the two towns, the Temni concentrated on attacking the British columns employed in keeping open supply and communications routes. They fired from ambush – seemingly with an inexhaustible supply of ammunition – and rarely exposed themselves. They learnt to pick off the white officers rather than the West Indian soldiers. Bai Bureh and his war-chiefs developed bush-fighting into what would later be called guerrilla warfare. The British front-line commanders had too few fighting men and too much baggage to do anything but stay on the defensive. The only aggressive action during that March had serious repercussions.

A flying column under Major Burke was sent out from Port Lokko to destroy every village along the road which showed any sign of hostility to the British. There was no opposition on the first day, as Bai Bureh had concentrated his forces from the village of Mahera onward. As the column approached Mahera on the second day it met a ferocious fusilade from the trees. After a full day's fighting, against warriors led personally by Bai Bureh, the column's heavier firepower allowed Burke to take the village but his casualties were beginning to mount. On the third day Bai Bureh held his men back until the column approached Kagbantama. There the British found heavy stockades blocking the approach roads, from which the Temni attacked in numbers. Burke was hard pressed to resist. After several hours the Temni did retreat, but Burke's force was by now too laden with wounded to give chase. When the warriors realised they were not being followed they set fire to the grass on the windward side of the road, hoping to engulf the British. Burke's men swiftly ignited the bush to the leeward side of the path to create a firebreak. The countryside was soon swept by flames. The column, choking and smoke-blinded, sat out the inferno through a lurid night. The next day the column moved off again, meeting stiff resistance at the stockaded towns of Romaron and Katenti. Burke's men were able to deploy their machine-gun to good effect, and from then on the Temni confined their attacks to sniping.

When Cardew heard reports of the march he was alarmed, not by the risk of massacre that his men had faced, but by the systematic burning of towns and villages by the forces of the queen. He feared that such tactics would permanently alienate the civilian population. He ordered Sharpe and Norris to confine such scorched-earth methods to Bai Bureh's strongholds. The two officers closest to the action, however, were reluctant to obey. They believed such tactics to be their only option, given their own small numbers and the fact that the whole countryside was up in arms against them. Cardew got his way only because Temni resistance was now so strong that the British were forced back on the defensive. Norris reported that it would be impossible to defeat Bai Bureh with just the Frontier Police and three companies of soldiers, of whose officers more than half had been killed, wounded or incapacitated by sickness. He asked for greater use of the heavily armed West Indian Regiment. Cardew again disagreed, arguing that the Regiment was better employed manning the garrisons while the more mobile Frontier Police could be deployed in the field. Officers seethed as Cardew constantly interfered for political rather than military reasons. Moreover, he repeatedly under-estimated the strength of Bai Bureh's well-armed forces and the difficulties of a terrain which was hostile in terms of both geography and population.

Such over-confidence was seen at first-hand by Major Stansfield when he led a column charged with ferrying large numbers of sick soldiers, police and carriers from Karena. He was forced back by the sheer weight of numbers opposing him, while his own soldiers were hampered by the need to safeguard their stretcher cases. Cardew could no longer ignore or under-rate the peril. Consequently he sent Colonel Bosworth, the commander of all British troops in West Africa, to take a fourth company to Karene and assume command of operations.

Bosworth, a cautious man, decided to wait at Port Lokko for reinforcements from Captain Carr Smith, but three days later word arrived that due to a strong attack at Matiti he had been forced to retreat. Bosworth decided to press on to relieve Karene. He suffered heavy resistance from the Temni warriors at Malal, Romeni and Kagbantama, and lost 35 men dead or wounded. The column, bloody, parched and exhausted, did not reach Karene until late that night. Bosworth stumbled into the beleaguered town's British headquarters, collapsed and died of 'heat apoplexy'.

His successor was a career soldier already en route to the war zone. Colonel John Willoughby Astell Marshall was a 44-year-old veteran of operations across West Africa, including the Gambia and the Ashanti wars, during which he had served with distinction and was mentioned in dispatches three times. His colonelcy was a field promotion. On 1 April he travelled on board *Alecto* to Port Lokko. In the river port, long deserted by the civilian population, he found the troops and Frontier Police demoralized, the hospital full of sick and wounded and the officers exhausted by constant fighting and sniping. In the previous two weeks eight officers had been either killed or seriously wounded. They told Marshall that as the rainy season had already begun it would be impossible to provision Karene and that the garrison there should be withdrawn. Major H.C. Bourke reported:

> The men here at present cannot be used for anything except to garrison this place; they are nearly all suffering from fever and could not march or do any hard work; they are therefore not available for sending out as a flying column or any like duty. I am still more of the opinion from what I have learnt here that Karene should be evacuated and at as early a date as possible. The whole time of the expedition is spent in sending convoys of supplies up there, each time with the result that more and more men are killed and wounded; at present there are about 40 or 50 wounded there, which number will of course increase as long as we keep sending up supplies to that place. Out of the six companies in this district, not more than four are really available for duty, owing to the amount of casualties which have occurred in conveying supplies and communicating with Karene. Officers' and men's lives have been wasted in the most futile manner, in my opinion, in maintaining this station, with the result that the enemy appears to be more vigorous and in greater numbers than ever.

Marshall reported: 'It was evident that the course hitherto adopted, that of sending columns up from Port Lokko to Karene, could not be continued indefinitely without involving the sacrifice of the life of every officer in the battalion and those of a great number of NCOs and men.' Marshall would not, however, countenance a withdrawal from Karene which would have enhanced the power of the rebel chiefs, but he agreed that 'the delay caused in communicating between the posts gave the enemy ample time to complete new stockades, so that each force moving to the relief of Karene met with as much resistance as the force which had preceded it'. He decided to establish two intermediate posts between Port Lokko and Karene, reducing the length of marches and providing flying columns with several bases. This plan he put into effect immediately, establishing one post at Romani, 15 miles from Port Lokko, which swiftly took delivery of 18 days' supplies for 400 men and 'an equal number of carriers'. But the creation of another post at Kagbantama proved a tougher task.

On 7 April two companies of West Indian soldiers marched to Romani and camped for the night. The following morning the column split, taking two parallel paths to Kagbantama, followed three hours later by a protected convoy under Major Donovan. The column following the main road under Major Bourke, already the holder of a Distinguished Service Order, was forced to attack 13 strong stockades grouped in twos and threes on either side. In his graphic official report Marshall described the difficulties facing the British and their men throughout the war:

These stockades are composed of short logs ranging from 10 to 14 inches in diameter, or sometimes even more. The logs are imbedded in the ground to a depth of between two and three feet, leaving a length of six feet above ground, and are solidly bound together. In front of this large boulders of latterite stone are piled to a thickness of between three to four feet. Funnels made of pieces of bamboo are pushed through to form a row of loop-holes near the ground, and others are placed at different heights above them. Inside a trench of four feet is dug, which gives absolute protection to those firing below. These stockades are placed in dense bush at from 7 to 10 yards from the pathway. It is absolutely impossible for European eyes to discern them by an outward sign; occasionally an exceptionally quick-sighted native will discover the locality of a stockade by some indication, such as a dead twig or some drooping leaves overhead. The places mostly chosen are the crossing of fords and rivers, thick gullies, a sharp turn in the road, the top or bottom of a hill, so long as it commands the path, and the densest bush in the vicinity of their towns. They are often built in groups, giving mutual support. The shells of the seven-pounder break to pieces on coming in contact with these boulders, but the morale effect of the gun is good. A sheltered line of retreat down some small slope leading to a pathway cut in rear enables the defenders to retreat in comparative safety;

owing to the density of the bush it is impossible to rush them as it would take 5 to 10 minutes to cut through the bush to the stockades, during which time the assailants would be under the direct fire of the enemy at very close range. Our only plan is to engage them in front while flanking parties cut their way into the bush. It was found necessary, whenever possible, to burn the woodwork, as otherwise the enemy came back, carried off the logs and rebuilt them in another spot.

An officer with Marshall's column also described the difficulties:

The attack must be made in single file, as these stockades are always built in the narrowest part of the path. Here the Englishman must give the black man the lead. This class of bush-fighting becomes wearisome to all concerned. Almost every hour a gun goes off at someone or other in the column – sometimes in front, then again in the middle of the column, or perhaps in rear, even at night the enemy creep up to the camp and fire their guns, which are usually loaded up to the muzzle with all sorts of bits of iron, or pot-legs as we call them.

As the main column approached Rotifunk the enemy opened fire from the bush and the troops replied with sectional fire which, together with several rounds from the seven-pounder, quickly scattered them. The column arrived at Kagbantama in the early afternoon and destroyed four more stockades there. A temporary *laager* was formed in the smoking ruins of the town. During this period the garrison at Karene was ignorant of the rescue operations. A column that had set off under Major Burke now joined up with Marshall's force, and Marshall followed Burke back to the town. There he set up a regular service of convoys, using the staging posts, to keep the entire line of communications open. He had close to 700 fighting men in the field.

Marshall now embarked on the scorched-earth campaign which Cardew had earlier tried to veto. Given the lack of fit officers, he took personal charge of a flying column which set out each day. At first he confined his operations to the villages close to Kagbantama and along paths running parallel with the main Karene road, but extended the range throughout much of April. As the neighbourhood was blackened by plumes of smoke and more and more villages were destroyed, the Temni resistance increased in determination and ferocity. Skirmishing turned into fast and furious fights in densely wooded ravines and tangled shrub which shredded uniforms and flesh alike. Major Donovan was mortally wounded trying to carry his hammock-boy, who had been shot down, out of the line of fire. Casualties piled up at Rogambia, Winti and other stockaded towns. Marshall described the period from 15 April as 'the most stubborn fighting that has been experienced in West Africa'. The fighting was continuous. Every village the column reached opposed them. Up to 20 stockades were attacked and destroyed each day. As soon as they were levelled others sprang up in the rear, as if by magic. The flying column began its march at daybreak and rarely bivouacked before 5 p.m. The men were allowed 30 minutes for breakfast and a 90-minute halt was permitted during the noon-day heat. These were the only stops. 'The rest of the day was occupied in marching and fighting,' said one officer. 'It was no uncommon thing to have four or five stubborn fights during the day, while a day rarely passed without two or three.'

The surviving white officers of the West Indian Regiment began the campaign with little knowledge of the terrain or the enemy, having landed in West Africa only a few months before. A large number of their men were young, barely trained recruits. The battalion had recently given up many of their best NCOs and most experienced men to form the nucleus of another force heading for Lagos. At least some of those left were considered too raw or unfit for active service. But they learnt quickly, those that lasted long enough. Marshall later wrote:

The behaviour of the troops throughout the operations was admirable. Before the commencement of the flying column the tornado season, which precedes the rains by about three weeks, was already well advanced. The men were constantly soaked to the skin on the marches, and as they had no change of clothes, were obliged to remain in their wet garments;

nearly every night the bivouacs were deluged with rain; it was comparatively seldom that the troops were sufficiently fortunate to sleep in towns, for if the last town attacked during the day was not set on fire by the shellfire of the attacking party, it was frequently burnt by the enemy on being driven out, so as to leave no shelter for the troops. These discomforts were not only borne uncomplainingly by the men, but even cheerfully.

The precise thoughts of teenage lads from Jamaica and Trinidad, shivering in sodden camps, prone to sickness and at risk from sniper fire, is not recorded. Early on in the operation, only one blanket was carried for each man. Later, when the rains became even worse, a waterproof sheet was also carried by the porters. Marshall continued:

The conduct of the troops under fire was excellent, although they knew the enemy was sheltered behind stockades which were proof against shellfire and very nearly so against rifle fire (for occasionally a bullet would find its way through the interstices or through the bamboo loopholes of the boulders), they nevertheless fiercely faced the enemy's fire, sectional volleys being delivered with a steadiness that would have been creditable on parade. . . . The small number of casualties when compared with the intensity of the enemy's fire is partly accounted for by the celerity with which the flying column came into action, and so disconcerted the pre-arranged plans of the enemy. The men of the column were sometimes changed, but the same officers remained, and as section after section came up, a word or two from an officer was sufficient to ensure the right impulse and direction being given to it.

During the course of the campaign the columns were divided into sections of 10, the highest number one officer could eventually keep under his command because of the density of the scrub and forest. A constant source of grief was the ignorance or, it was suspected, the treachery of some of the native guides. A report said:

They were constantly leading the troops astray, and the maps supplied were too misleading to afford much assistance. The Police know the main roads, but are quite ignorant of the by-paths by which the enemy could be followed to his more remote retreats.

Another massive problem, as always in colonial wars when Europeans relied on natives to sustain them, was the casualty rate among the bearers. Their numbers were regarded as 'inadequate' from the start; even more so when over 100 were killed or wounded along the trails. This figure, though, was dwarfed by the enormous numbers who fell sick. Exasperated, Marshall blamed the lack of proper medical examinations when they were rushed to the front: 'Men with all kinds of complaints rendering them unfit for transport were enlisted.'

Smallpox broke out among the carriers, and there were daily desertions. Marshall made up the shortfall by ordering each carrier to carry two 30lb loads of biscuits, beef, ammunition and other supplies. Marshall's logic was impeccable: 'Light loads mean more carriers and more food to be carried for them.' He added: 'Everything depends on the compactness of the load – for instance the small bags of rice weighing 60lbs were eagerly sought after by the carriers, and boxes of S.G. ammunition weighing 80lbs were borne by one carrier throughout the expedition.'

The subsequent inquiry largely cleared the British forces of atrocities and there is little evidence of rape and plunder. But such a brutal form of warfare inevitably produced allegations of excess. Witnesses claimed that Captain Moore and a party of Frontier Police rampaged through several districts carrying 'fire and sword through the land, fusillading the inhabitants and burning their towns and villages'. Moore was accused of shooting one native in cold blood because he refused to drop a sword. A sick woman perished when her house in Mafouri was burnt around her. Cardew later dismissed such reports as fable or exaggeration. But Major Norris told Cardew that inhumane acts *were* committed, if not by those in uniform, then by discharged carriers who 'ravish women, steal the root crops and loot houses'.

The Temni fought with great valour and stubbornness – the hardest resistance was at the town of Mafouri on 25 April – but Marshall's tactics of attrition began to work. Most of the Kasseh district was subdued. Operations included the rescue of three white missionaries and nine black colleagues being held by one of Bai Bureh's allies at Rogberi. They were lucky; the local chief failed to carry out his threat to massacre them if the British column approached the undefended town. Bai Bureh and his men were pushed back from one stronghold to another until they became fugitives rather than an organised foe.

A vivid account of the fighting was given in dispatches by Captain E.D.H. Fairclough, who commanded a flying column sent deep into the Kwaia district:

Arriving close to the town of Mafuluma about two a.m. we found a big war-dance in progress. Whilst crossing the stream, which supplies the town with water, we were attacked but soon dispersed the rebels with a loss of six killed and several wounded. Reinforced by the natives of Maseracouli close by, the insurgents made a determined attempt to regain possession of the town about 3.30 a.m. but were driven off with the loss of seven killed. None of the Frontier Police were hurt but one of our friendlies was killed and one wounded.

After destroying Mafuluma and Maseracouli I moved towards Mayumera, meeting the war-boys gathered in force at Batipo, a village half-way. These were dispersed with a loss of several men, and we reached Maumera only to find it deserted. The insurgents having, however, collected again, attacked the town several times during the afternoon, and a night attack about nine p.m. was repulsed mainly through Fula Mansa's boys [Yonni native allies] who, walking around the bush, fell upon the rebels in the rear, killing their leader Pa Umri and several others. Hearing that the rebels had retired upon Fonde, I moved against this place on the 8th, meeting natives in ambush nearly all the way. At almost every town in the road groups of natives were posted, concealed in the bush, and fired upon us as we advanced, but as their feelings were naturally much upset by well-directed volleys from the Frontiers, their aim was very erratic, and none of our people were touched. We found the rebels collected in force at Fonde, but these were soon dispersed, the chief Pa Kuan and 14 followers being killed and several wounded. During the afternoon a village close by was destroyed and a large war-party dispersed, nine being killed, one friendly wounded. A night attack on Fonde was defeated with loss.

On the 9th I drove the rebels from Rofuta, close to Fonde, and destroyed the village but the friendlies, going too far into the bush in pursuit, lost two men killed. After destroying Fonde I proceeded to Forodugu, destroying a big gathering at Marifa en route. Here a strong mud fort and watch-tower had recently been constructed, but the fire from the loop-holes being silenced by volleys from our men, the rebels were quickly cleared out and scattered through the bush, pursued by the friendlies. Half-way to Forodugo I encountered and dispersed a large party in ambush close to Romabing which I destroyed. After driving the rebels from Rolia, and burning the town, I reached Forodugo, dispersing a war-party in this town with a loss of five killed and many more wounded.

The rebels under Suri Kamara attacked us in Forodugo during the afternoon but were repulsed and followed to Magbeni, lower down the river, Nyanba, a head warrior, and 25 men being killed. Suri Kamara and some 15 followers put off in a canoe for the Karena shore of the Rockelle [sic], but a volley from our men killing six of the crew, the canoe was upset and the Chief only escaped by swimming. . . .

And so it went on.

By the end of April Marshall decided to punish the chiefs of the neighbouring districts who had also rebelled. The territory of Alimany Amarah was the next to suffer punitive columns, burning villages at any sign of opposition. The road to Little Scarcies rivers up to 150 yards wide and swollen by the heavy rains, were forded the men struggling through water up to their chests under hot fire from stockades on the far banks.

The fighting in the territories beyond was often as rough as anything experienced so far. Ronula, the chief town of the renowned war-chief Alimany Lahai, proved a particularly hard nut to crack. Marshall wrote in dispatches:

Here was a very fierce fight. Captain Harvey was dangerously wounded. It was found necessary to shell and fire the town in rear of the enemy's position, before the enemy could be driven out. A large number of rifles were used by the enemy, but the bullets whistled harmlessly overhead. A native can seldom use a rifle at short range, for he thinks the higher the sights are put up, the more powerfully does the rifle shoot. At last the enemy were driven from their stockades and from the town with considerable loss, and as the country on the far side of the town was comparatively open, were pursued with greater loss for some considerable distance. A large quantity of powder and slugs were taken, and also Alimani Lahai's drum, which was abandoned in the bush when the pursuit became hot.

At every village officers assembled, when they could, the local people. They gave graphic and lurid accounts of what their West Indians had done in the fire-blackened townships of Kasseh. They warned that further resistance would result in the same treatment. It was another early form of the 'hearts and minds' cajoling which was later deployed by western armies on other continents. Marshall's columns swept through Kambia and headed back towards Karene. On 13 May a young officer, Lieutenant Rickets, was shot dead. He was the last Briton slain among the convoys. Marshall now controlled the whole of the northern territories of the Temni.

At Rokell Marshall, after three weeks of frustrating delays, negotiated the surrender of the Massimera chiefs. He wrote peevishly: 'Great difficulty was experienced and much time spent in the endeavour, owing to the timidity of the chiefs.'

But Bai Bureh himself remained at large, and other chiefs proved almost as troublesome. As the rainy season began to ease in September two companies of the newly formed West Africa Regiment were sent by rail into the hinterland. The Times reported:

It has been decided to patrol thoroughly the Protectorate by bodies of troops, and clearly the chief offenders in the recent troubles, whereby so many lives were sacrificed, cannot be allowed to remain at large but must be brought to justice. The weakened authority of the Government must be re-established, and not till an object lesson has been given will the country be pacified.

Sporadic fighting continued for several months as the British crisscrossed the devastated countryside. Marshall knew that until Bai Bureh was safely in custody the war could not be conclusively won and his own reputation would be that of a town-burner rather than a victorious general. A reward of £100 was offered for Bai Bureh's capture. The Temni warrior reciprocated by offering £500 for Cardew's head. The governor was not amused. The heavy rains hampered pursuit and mopping-up operations. Muslim leaders in Freetown offered to mediate and passed on correspondence from Bai Bureh offering talks. Both his offers were rejected, with Cardew insisting on unconditional surrender.

Meanwhile Bai Bureh's defiance encouraged a sympathetic uprising by the Mendi people in the south. The Mendi, like the Temni, used secret society terror tactics, or *Poro*, with 'one word' oaths which meant that any of their people who did not join them would be killed. Creole traders were slain, and the body of a frontier officer buried at Bandasuma was dug up and burnt, to rid the earth of his evil influence. Christian missions were attacked and their occupants slaughtered. In Mofwe children attending the Methodist school were burnt alive when warriors set fire to an adjoining house where frontier policemen and some traders made a last stand. Two British columns were sent against Rotifunk and Bombi, where there was fierce resistance. Further operations included the relief of a besieged garrison at Panguma and a battle at Yomundu on 6 July.

The Mendi campaign, led by Lieutenant-Colonel George Cunningham, in many ways matched the expedition against the Temni. Cunningham, a decorated veteran of six campaigns, in which he suffered three wounds, wrote:

The only means of advancing are along narrow roads bounded by thick bush. Occasionally the path widens a little and a clearing is reached in the centre of which stands a town. The Insurgents post their men armed with trade guns in a clump of thick bush by the side of the road, having cut narrow tracks behind them to retire by. As our column advanced, invariably the first notice of the enemy's presence was a discharge of guns at close quarters which almost invariably hit some of the leading rifles. It may be imagined under the circumstances how trying was the work of the advanced guard. Nevertheless the greatest keenness was always shown. . . .

After two months and the relief of Panguma, the enthusiasm of the Mendi chiefs began to flag as villages and towns went up in flames. But the British still feared further revolts as long as Bai Bureh remained at liberty.

Finally, the elusive Bai Bureh was betrayed by informers. After 23 weeks in the rain-soaked bush, he was tracked to swamplands on 11 November. A small party of the West African Regiment attacked the war chief's bodyguard. The warriors chose to fight rather than surrender but two men broke away. A local sergeant gave chase and overtook the slowest and oldest man. He was Bai Bureh. It was an anti-climatic end to a hard-fought war.

*   *   *

The British government was shocked by the outbreak of the war and by the cost in human terms. Long before Bai Bureh's capture, in July, Sir David Chalmers was charged with investigating the insurrection and its causes. A retired Scottish judge, he had served as a magistrate in the Gambia over thirty years before. He was the first Chief Justice of the Gold Coast in 1876 and later held the same post in British Guinea. Shortly before his return to Sierra Leone, where he had been a Queen's Advocate, Chalmers judged a fraud prosecution in Newfoundland. He was a roving legal eagle with a special knowledge of, and fondness for, the people of West Africa.

From the start Chalmers knew the practical difficulties he faced.

He wrote:

> Travelling in the country was practically impossible, by reason
> of the rainy season which was then in full force. During this
> season (which continues to November) roads become water-
> courses, streams are swollen into torrents, drenching rains of a
> character not known in temperate regions are almost constant.

Added to those physical impediements was the impracticality of
seeking evidence from natives in their own homes, 'nearly all of
them being scattered and taking refuge in the bush or forests'.
Nevertheless Chalmers was known to have a sympathetic ear and
many chiefs trekked to Freetown to give him their account directly.

His conclusions were devastating for Cardew and his officials on
the ground. Chalmers said bluntly that the Hut Tax and the brutal
methods used to enforce it were the main cause of the insurrection.
'The tax was obnoxious to the customs and feelings of the people,'
he said, 'There was a widespread belief that it was a means of taking
away their rights in their country and in their property.' The tax
was considered oppressive and unjust, and was higher than most of
the people could afford. Hostility to the tax was aggravated by the
actions of police, officials and, by implication, Cardew himself. 'The
inherent repugnance to the Hut Tax would by itself most probably
have led to passive resistance,' he continued. 'The sense of personal
wrong and injustice from the illegal and degrading severities made
use of in enforcing the Tax, coupled with the aversion to the Tax in
itself, produced in the Timinis [sic] a resistance enforced by arms.'
Cardew blundered by targeting Bai Bureh, a legitimate war chief
with a large personal force, who subsequently became the focus
for more widespread resistance. Chalmers wrote that it grieved him
to point out so many 'grave errors' in his report. If he could have
found that the insurrection was the result of an 'inevitable conflict
between ancient barbarism and an advancing civilisation' he would
have done so, but he could not.

He recommended that the Hut Tax, or any alternative, should
be dropped as unworkable and the British administrators should
concentrate on rebuilding both the shattered countryside and the

confidence of the native people. 'Let the Colonial Officers realise that the subjects of a Protectorate *have rights* [his italics], and that it should be a work of forbearance and patience, rather than of overpowering force, to instruct them that they also have obligations and duties towards the protecting power.'

Chalmers died in August 1899, barely a month after he presented his damning report. He did not live to see the Colonial Office reject its main recommendations. Officials and ministers accepted Cardew's assertion that the commissioner had over-stated the grievances of the natives. Furthermore, there was no more money forthcoming for the colony. The hated Hut Tax was reintroduced throughout Sierra Leone in 1900 at a minimum rate of 3 shillings a year. Much blood had been shed for the sake of a few shillings. Four more British columns marched through the back country in a show of force designed to cow the defeated natives. Paramount chiefs regarded as pro-British were appointed. And the Frontier Police were amalgamated into the West African Frontier Force, which was for military purposes only.

Cardew retired that year to his Tudor cottage in Oxfordshire. He enjoyed a long and peaceful retirement and he died in 1921. There is evidence that he was haunted by some degree of guilt. In his response to the Chalmers Report he wrote:

> I do not desire in any sense whatever to shift the burden of responsibility for all that has passed on any shoulders from my own, but at the same time I hope it will not be thought that I lightly or recklessly entered on the task before me . . . The thought of the many valuable lives which have been lost, of the gallant officers and men who have fallen, of the devoted missionaries who have been sacrificed, of the Sierra Leoneans who have been massacred, and of the many natives who have been killed, must ever remain to me a sad regret, the recollection of which can never pass away.

Given the small number of men involved, it was an expensive war. Casualties among the Karene expeditionary force totalled 277, including native carriers. Most were wounded and the fact that few died of their wounds is a tribute to the teams of medical officers and supplies of medicines given top priority by Marshall. The smaller force sent to suppress the Mendi uprising suffered 58 casualties with 6 killed in action, 5 drowned crossing swollen rivers, and more lost in the bush. The number of Temni and Mendi warriors and civilians who were killed or maimed is not recorded.

The war left a legacy of bitterness and racism which ignored Freetown's philanthropic birth. In April 1899 Freetown's mayor, Sir Samuel Lewis, a native African, boarded the first train on the newly completed Sierra Leone railway. Of the 600 people on board, 1 were white. Lewis, unaware of any restrictions, took a seat in the whites-only carriage – and he was forcibly ejected by a white NCO. The event caused much ill-feeling and the soldier was later fined 3 shillings for assault.

Marshall, who had deployed his flying columns and scorched earth policies to a successful conclusion, was well rewarded for his ruthless drive. He was made a general and put in command of British troops in Jamaica. He retired to his home overlooking Hyde Park in 1911 and died ten years later.

After his capture Bai Bureh was first held at Karene but was later moved to Freetown gaol after a Temni soldier in the West African Regiment plotted his escape. He was later transferred to more comfortable confinement in a house on the outskirts of Freetown. Crowds gathered there to see the legendary warrior who had defied British military might for so long. Commissioner Sharpe wanted to try him on a charge of treason but he was overruled by the Colonial Office because there was some doubt whether Bai Bureh could be treated as a British subject. In captivity Bai Bureh, sick of war, said that he and his people wanted only to live in peace with their 'mother', the Queen of England. Proceedings dragged on until London decreed that he owed no allegiance to the queen and therefore his actions could not be deemed treasonous. He never faced a trial but was considered too dangerous to release. The British believed that to grant his request to be allowed to return to Karene district would be regarded as a sign of weakness. Sir Matthew Nathan, standing in for Cardew, then on leave, ordered his deportation to Gambia, along with two other chiefs. All other 'insurgents' were given a general amnesty.

Bai Bureh had proved that natives could organise effective resistance to colonial rule. His defiance proved that 'savage' people could demonstrate moral superiority when faced with unjust burdens. He showed that paternalistic rule could not stifle proud and independent peoples. Full independence, however, was not granted to Sierra Leone until 1960.

Bai Bureh's companions sickened and died in exile. The old war chief, frail and crippled by disease, twice petitioned, unsuccessfully, for his own release. Finally, in 1905, he was allowed to go home, provided he accepted severe constraints on his activities and movements. He died three years later, enjoying the respectful worship of his people.

Bibliography and Sources

General

Briggs, Asa, *The Age of Improvement 1783–1867* (Longman, London, 1959)
Callwell, Colonel C.E., *Small Wars* (London, 1906)
Chandler, David (general editor), *The Oxford History of the British Army* (Oxford University Press, 1996)
Dictionary of National Biography (Oxford University Press, 1921–2)
Farwell, Byron, *Queen Victoria's Little Wars* (Allen Lane, London, 1973)
Featherstone, D., *Colonial Small Wars 1837–1901* (Newton Abbot, 1973)
Haythornthwaite, Philip J., *The Colonial Wars Source Book* (Arms & Armour Press, London, 1995)
James, Lawrence, *The Savage Wars – British Campaigns in Africa, 1870–1920* (Robert Hale, London)
Morris, James, *The Pax Britannica Trilogy* (Faber & Faber, London, 1968)
Pakenham, Thomas, *The Scramble for Africa* (Weidenfeld & Nicolson, 1991)
Spiers, Edward M., *The Late Victorian Army* (Manchester University Press 1992)
Strawson, John, *Beggars in Red – The British Army 1789–1889* (Hutchinson London, 1991)
——, *Gentlemen in Khaki – The British Army 1890–1990* (Secker & Warburg, London, 1989)

The Gurkha War

Annual Registers, 1815–16
Bredin, A.E.C., *The Happy Warriors* (Blackmore Press, Dorset, 1961)
Chant, Christopher, *Gurkha – An Illustrated History of an Elite Fighting Force* (Blandford Press, Dorset, 1985)
Gould, Tony, *Imperial Warriors – Britain and the Gurkhas* (Granta Books, London, 1999)
Hastings, Lord, *Dispatches*
Moon, Sir Penderel, *The British Conquest and Dominion of India* (Duckworth, London, 1989)
Ochterlony, Sir David, *Dispatches*
Parker, John, *The Gurkhas* (Headline, London, 1999)

Brooke and the Borneo Pirates

Annual Registers, 1846, 1851

Brooke, Sir James, *Private Letters*, edited by John C. Templer (London, 1853)

Hann, Emily, *James Brooke of Sarawak* (Arthur Barker Ltd, London, 1953)

Jacobs, Gertrude L., *Raja of Sarawak* (London, 1876)

Keppel, Captain Henry, *The Expedition to Borneo of HMS Dido* (London, 1848)

Parliamentary Reports, 1844–51

Rutter, Owen, *Rajah Brooke and Baroness Burdett Coutts* (Hutchinson, London, 1935)

Saunders, Graham, *A History of Brunei* (Oxford University Press, 1994)

St John, Spenser, *Life of Sir James Brooke* (London and Edinburgh, 1870)

Tarling, Nicholas, *The Establishment of the Colonial Regimes*, part of the Cambridge History of south-east Asia, Volume 2 (University Press, 1992)

Madagascar

Annual Register, 1845

Brown, Mervyn, *Madagascar Rediscovered – A History from Early Times to Independence* (London, 1978)

Desfosses, Commander Romain, *Dispatches*

Freeman, Revd J.J., *A Narrative of the Persecution of the Christians in Madagascar* (London, 1840)

Howe, Sonia E., *The Drama of Madagascar* (Methuen, London, 1938)

Illustrated London News, 1845

Heseltine, Nigel, *Madagascar* (Pall Mall Press, London, 1971)

Pfeiffer, Ida, *Voyage a Madagascar* (Paris, 1881)

Shaw, Revd G., *Madagascar and France* (London, 1889)

Sibree, James, *Madagascar Before the Conquest* (London, 1896)

Stratton, Arthur, *The Great Red Island* (Macmillan, London, 1965)

The Times

Villars, Captain de', *Establissment des Français dans l'Ile de Madagascar 1638–1894* (Paris)

The Sikh Wars

Annual Registers, 1845–9

Bruce, George, *Six Battles for India* (Arthur Barker, London, 1969)

Burton, R.G., *The First and Second Sikh Wars* (Simla, 1911)

Cunningham, J.D., *A History of the Sikhs* (London, 1849)

Fortesque, Sir John, *History of the British Army* (Macmillan, London, 1927)

Gough, General Sir Hugh, *Dispatches*

Hardinge, Sir Henry, *Dispatches*

James, Lawrence, *Raj – The Making and Unmaking of British India* (Little, Brown, London, 1997)

Khurana, G., *British Historiography on the Sikh Power in the Punjab* (Allied Publishers, London and New York, 1985)

Khushwant Singh, *A History of the Sikhs* (Oxford University Press and Princeton University Press, 1966)

M'Gregor, W.L., *The History of the Sikhs* (London, 1846)

Moon, Sir Penderel, *The British Conquest and Dominion of India* (Duckworth, London, 1989)

Osborne, W.G., *Ranjit Singh – The Lion of the Punjab* (London, 1846)

Ryder, John, *Four Years' Service in India* (Leicester, 1853)

Sandford, D.A., *Leaves from the Journal of a Subaltern* (Blackwood, 1852)

Smith, General Sir Harry, *Dispatches*

Thackwell, E.J., *The Second Sikh War* (London, 1851)

Eureka Stockade

Butler, Richard, *Eureka Stockade* (Angus & Robertson, Melbourne, 1983)

Carboni, Rafaello, *The Eureka Stockade – The Consequence of some Pirates wanting on Quarterdeck a Rebellion* (Ballarat, 1855)

Clark, Manning, *A History of Australia* (Random House, Australia, 1962–87)

Shaw, A.G.L., *The Story of Australia* (Faber & Faber, London, 1955)

Withers, Bramwell William, *History of Ballarat* (Queensberry Press, 1980)

Younger, R.M., *Australia and the Australians, A Concise History* (Hutchinsons, Victoria, 1969)

Kars

Annual Register, 1855

Brant, James, *Official Reports*

Cunningham, Allan, *Anglo-Ottoman Encounters in the Age of Revolution* (London, 1993)

HMSO, *The Siege of Kars – Uncovered Papers*, series edited by Tim Coates (London, 2000)

James, Lawrence, *Crimea: The War with Russia from Contemporary Photographs* (Thame, 1981)

Kinglake, A.W., *The Invasion of the Crimea* (Edinburgh, 1863–87)

Lambert, Andrew D., *The Crimean War – British Grand Strategy Against Russia 1853–56* (Manchester University Press, 1990)

Lake, Sir Henry Atwell, *Kars and Our Captivity in Russia* (London, 1856)

Royle, Trevor, *Crimea – The Great Crimean War 1854–1856* (Little Brown, London, 1999)

Sandwith, Humphrey, *A Narrative of the Siege of Kars and of the Six Months' Resistance of the Turkish garrison, under General Williams, to the Russian Army* (London, 1856)

Shepherd, John, *The Crimean Doctors – A History of the British Medical Services in the Crimean War*, Volume Two (Liverpool University Press, 1991)

Slade, Adolphus, *Turkey and the Crimean War* (London, 1867)

Strachan, H., *From Waterloo to Balaclava* (Cambridge, 1985)

The Times

Williams, General William Fenwick, *Dispatches*

Wood, H. Evelyn, *The Crimea in 1854 and 1894* (London, 1895)

The Fenian Invasion of Canada

Annual Registers, 1866–7

Comerford, R.V. (contrib.), *A New History of Ireland, Volume V: Ireland Under the Union* (Clarendon Press, Oxford, 1989)

D'Arcy, William, *The Fenian Movement in the United States* (Washington, 1947)

Jones, Paul, *The Irish Brigade* (NEL Books, London, 1989)

Keneally, Thomas, *The Great Shame – The Story of the Irish in the Old World and the New* (Chatto & Windus, London, 1998)

Litton, Helen, *Irish Rebellions 1798–1916* (Wolfhound Press, Dublin and Colorado, 1998)

The New York Times

O'Connor, Sir James, *History of Ireland 1798–1924*

The Rochester Union

Rutherford, John, *The Fenian Conspiracy* (1877)

Woodham-Smith, Cecil, *The Great Hunger* (Hamish Hamilton, London, 1962)

Belize

Burdon, Sir John Alder (ed.), *Archives of British Honduras*, Volumes II and III (London, 1935)

Caiger, Stephen L., *British Honduras – Past and Present* (Allen & Unwin, London, 1951)

Dobson, Narda, *A History of Belize* (Longman Caribbean, 1973)

Fowler, Henry, *A Narrative of a Journey Across the Unexplored Portion of British Honduras* (Belize, 1879)

Means, P.A., *History of the Spanish Conquest of Yucatan and of the Itza* (Cambridge, Mass., 1917)

Merrill, Tim (ed.), *Belize – A Country Study* (Federal Research Division, U Library of Congress, 1992)

Reed, Nelson, *The Caste War of Yucatan* (Stanford, 1964)

Sierra Leone

Alie, Joe A.D., *A New History of Sierra Leone* (Macmillan, London, 1990)

Annual Registers, 1898–9

Bourke, Major H.C., *Dispatches*

Cardew, Sir Frederick, *Response to the Chalmers Report* (London, 1899)

Chalmers, Sir David, *Report by her Majesty's Commissioner on the subject of the Insurrection in the Sierra Leone Protectorate* (Stationery Office, London, 1899)

Cunningham, Lieutenant-Colonel G., *Dispatches*

Denzer, La Ray (contrib.), *West African Resistance – The Military Response to Colonial Occupation* (Hutchinson University Library for Africa, London, 1971)

Fairclough, Captain E.D.H., *Dispatches*

Marshall, Colonel J.W., *Report – Operations in Timini Country* (London, 1898)

Norris, Major R.J., *Dispatches*

Index

Lightning Source UK Ltd.
Milton Keynes UK
UKOW04f0430131113

220985UK00001B/11/P